VICTORIAN FICTION

A Second Guide to Research

VICTORIAN FICTION

❀ ❀ ❀

A Second Guide to Research

Edited by

GEORGE H. FORD

The Modern Language Association of America

NEW YORK

1978

Copyright © 1978 by The Modern Language Association of America

Library of Congress Catalog Card No. 77-083468
ISBN 0-87352-255-9

Published by The Modern Language Association of America
62 Fifth Avenue, New York, New York 10011

Contents

Contents

TO THE MEMORY OF LIONEL STEVENSON
$$(1902-1973)$$

Preface

Some of the distinguishing features of the present volume can best be indicated by a report on how it took shape. Its predecessor, *Victorian Fiction: A Guide to Research*, edited by Lionel Stevenson, was published in 1964. Like the present volume, it was sponsored by the Victorian Literature Group (now Division) of the Modern Language Association of America. Covering some fifteen Victorian novelists, this review of the scholarship and criticism before 1963 at once established itself as an invaluable aid to scholars, and remains so today.

With each passing year since then, however, it became increasingly evident that there was a real need to provide a comparable review of the vast flood of materials that has been appearing since 1962—and the term "vast flood" is no exaggeration. In the early 1960s J. Hillis Miller spoke of a prevailing "Dickens boom." Subsequently, while the Dickens boom has itself continued, interest in other novelists has expanded comparably. To judge from the quantity and quality of publications since 1962, we could speak today of a Victorian novel boom.

In view of these developments Lionel Stevenson resolved, in 1973, that some sort of second guide ought to be published, and he began discussing the project with officers of the Victorian Literature Group. After his sudden death in December of that year, I was asked to take over the editorship of the second volume and to work out a policy that would link it to Stevenson's earlier *Guide*. One possibility open to us would have been to rewrite the previous volume—a procedure followed in the second edition of *The Victorian Poets: A Guide to Research*, edited by Frederic E. Faverty in 1968. We decided, however, that for us this would be a mistake. Some chapters in the Stevenson *Guide*, such as Ada Nisbet's widely admired discussion of Dickens, seemed not only irreplaceable but impossible to rewrite. The present volume was therefore put together, not as a replacement for its predecessor, but as a sequel. Since we have been assured that the Stevenson *Guide* will remain in print, we expect that the two volumes will be used together.

The second policy matter aired with all contributors was whether or not to enlarge the list of Victorian novelists by adding the names of several lesser figures not treated in the earlier volume, novelists such as Margaret Oliphant, Charlotte Yonge, George Alfred Lawrence, and William Carleton. It is worthy of record that our list grew to some thirty-eight names, and it could easily have been three times as long, when one considers, for example, the 121 novels to appear in the reprint series currently edited by Robert Lee Wolff, *Victorian Fiction: Novels of Faith and Doubt,* or the more than 400 novelists cited in Myron Brightfield's four-volume *Victorian England in Its Novels.* Even though relatively little has been written about most of these novelists, we realized that including them would require a separate volume and, if such a project were feasible, a different team of scholars. An additional consideration was that most of these other novelists are to be included in a projected *Guide to the Victorian Novel,* edited by Professor Pierre Coustillas of the University of Lille, a work that will feature biographies of what Coustillas calls the "second rate figures" and plot summaries of their novels.

Although we rejected most of the alternatives we had considered, there was one positive decision. It was resolved that two important figures, omitted for various reasons from the Stevenson *Guide,* should be added to the present volume: Robert Louis Stevenson and Samuel Butler. Scholarly writing on Stevenson and Butler is reviewed from the beginning to the present. In the other sixteen chapters, our aim has been to supply complete coverage from 1963 through 1974. Most chapters also feature some items published in 1975, but these have been included as chance encounters rather than as the outcome of a systematic review of research. Readers who have a special interest in some particular work appearing in 1975 may be disappointed to find no reference to it here. The easiest way to have forestalled such disappointments would have been to have rigidly enforced the cutoff date, deleting any references to publications after 1974—a simple solution but also, it seemed to me, both a silly and a timid one. We ask the indulgence of our readers in accepting the principle of nonuniformity.

Similar considerations have pertained in describing works that contributors had cited as "forthcoming." If, at the time of our going to press, such works were known to have been published, the year 1976 or 1977 has been inserted in place of "forthcoming."

In using the expression "complete coverage" through 1974, I mean, of course, the kind of coverage provided by a guide rather than by a bibliography. A guide is not a telephone book; the coverage has to be selective and, in effect, incomplete. Materials in each chapter were not amassed by a compiler but selected by a scholar-critic, who had to choose what seemed important to recommend or not to recommend. Another difference is in the style of presentation. Although a guide to research probably does not often serve as a bedside book, I believe that it should be readable and that the guidance offered in each chapter should be expressed in the author's individual voice.

Another point about coverage deserves comment. Contributors to the present guide were urged to include any significant items published earlier than 1962 that had been overlooked in the Stevenson *Guide.* For the ten new contributors, who might be expected to emphasize some interests different from those of their predecessors, this policy led to the resurrection of several pre-1962 items. But even the five contributors who had also written chapters for the Stevenson *Guide* included some earlier items that they had previously omitted.

In this connection there are two areas where we have tried to provide some fresh emphasis, areas into which the Stevenson *Guide* sometimes did not venture: the availability of manuscripts and the record of film versions of Victorian novels. The latter topic has had to be treated variously and also rather briefly, but even a short review may indicate the importance of the cinematographic qualities that have been discovered in such novelists as Hardy, Dickens, Thackeray, and Collins.

Finally, it is hoped that use of this guide may encourage research in the areas where it is most needed. The chapter on George Eliot's novels by U. C. Knoepflmacher, after its energetic review of some 367 items, concludes with a rueful question about overlappings in scholarship:

> Is it really necessary even in a fallen, publish-or-perish world to commit to print all those readings and interpretations that merely swerve a few degrees from existing discussions? And is there not also a similar superfluity in all those essays, on both sides of the Atlantic, in which the writer assumes that no one else could have noticed that Hetty Sorrel "disturbs the settled life of the entire community" or that Daniel Deronda seems "excessively idealized"?

Professor Knoepflmacher's mild complaint should not be misconstrued as aimed at discouraging responsible scholarly efforts. His object is, instead, to suggest that future studies might be most profitable to us if more consideration were given to those areas and topics, indicated in each of the following chapters, that still require further exploration—despite the extraordinarily flourishing state in which the study of Victorian fiction now finds itself.

GEORGE H. FORD

Acknowledgments

For sage counsels the editor wishes to thank David J. DeLaura and Walter S. Achtert, and, for tireless secretarial labors, Mrs. Helen Craven, whose assistance was provided by the English Department of the University of Rochester. Also deserving thanks is Andrew Ruth, who compiled the Index.

Several of the contributors also wish to express gratitude for helpful suggestions and criticisms offered to them by various scholars. These include David Leon Higdon, Sue Lonoff, K. C. Phillips, Richard Purdy, Heinz Reinhold, Edgar Rosenberg, Robert C. Schweik, Surojit Sen, and Michael Slater.

Acronyms and Abbreviations

ACer	*Anales Cervantinos*
AdUM	*Annales de l'Université de Madagascar*
AdUP	*Annales de l'Université de Paris*
AI	*American Imago*
AION-SG	*Annali Istituo Universitario Orientale, Napoli, Sezione Germanica*
AJP	*American Journal of Psychiatry*
AL	*American Literature*
ALdUB	*Annales Littéraires de l'Université de Besançon*
ALS	*Australian Literary Studies* (Univ. of Tasmania)
AN&Q	*American Notes and Queries* (New Haven, Conn.)
ArchR	*Architectural Review*
ArQ	*Arizona Quarterly*
ASch	*American Scholar*
ASR	*American-Scandinavian Review*
AUMLA	*Journal of the Australasian Universities Language and Literature Association*
B&B	*Books and Bookmen*
BallSM	Ball State Monographs
BB	*Bulletin of Bibliography*
BC	*Book Collector*
BJA	*British Journal of Aesthetics* (London)
BJRL	*Bulletin of the John Rylands Library*
BJS	*British Journal of Sociology*
BLU	*Bucurestiv Literatura Universala*
BMMLA	*Bulletin of the Midwest Modern Language Association*
BMQ	*British Museum Quarterly*
BNYPL	*Bulletin of the New York Public Library*
BRMMLA	*Bulletin of the Rocky Mountain Modern Language Association*
BSE	*Brno Studies in English*
BST	*Brontë Society Transactions*
BSTCF	*Ball State Teachers College Forum*
BStM	*British Studies Monitor*
BSUF	*Ball State University Forum*
BuR	*Bucknell Review*
BYUS	*Brigham Young University Studies*

CairoSE	*Cairo Studies in English*
CCC	*College Composition and Communication*
CdS	*Corriere della Sera*
CE	*College English*
CentR	*The Centennial Review* (Mich. State Univ.)
CH	*Clearing House*
CL	*Comparative Literature*
CLB	*Charles Lamb Bulletin*
CLife	*Country Life*
ClioW	*Clio: An Interdisciplinary Journal of Literature, History, and the Philosophy of History* (Univ. of Wisconsin)
CLQ	*Colby Library Quarterly*
CLS	*Comparative Literature Studies* (Univ. of Illinois)
ColQ	*Colorado Quarterly*
ContempR	*Contemporary Review* (London)
CorLQ	*Cornell Library Quarterly*
CQ	*The Cambridge Quarterly*
CQR	*Church Quarterly Review*
CR	*The Critical Review* (Melbourne; Sydney)
CRCL	*Canadian Review of Comparative Literature*
CRevAS	*Canadian Review of American Studies*
CritQ	*Critical Quarterly*
CS	*Critical Survey*
DHLR	*The D. H. Lawrence Review* (Univ. of Arkansas)
DiS	*Dickens Studies*
Dkn	*Dickensian*
DM	*The Dublin Magazine*
DQR	*Dutch Quarterly Review of Anglo-American Letters*
DR	*Dalhousie Review*
DRund	*Deutsche Rundshau*
DSA	*Dickens Studies Annual*
DSN	*Dickens Studies Newsletter*
DUJ	*Durham University Journal*
DVLG	*Deutsche Vierteljahrsschrift für Literaturwissenschaft und Geistesgeschichte*
DY	*Dorset Year Book*
EA	*Etudes Anglaises*
E&S	*Essays and Studies by Members of the English Association*
EDH	*Essays by Divers Hands*
EIC	*Essays in Criticism* (Oxford)
Éire	*Ireland: A Journal of Irish Studies* (St. Paul)
EJ	*English Journal*
ELH	*Journal of English Literary History*
ELN	*English Language Notes* (Univ. of Colorado)
ELT	*English Literature in Transition*
ELWIU	*Essays in Literature* (Western Illinois Univ.)

EM	*English Miscellany*
ErasmusR	*Erasmus Review: A Journal of the Humanities*
ES	*English Studies*
ESA	*English Studies in Africa* (Johannesburg)
ESIC	*English Studies in Canada*
EWN	*Evelyn Waugh Newsletter*
FK	*Filológiai Közlöny*
FMLS	*Forum for Modern Language Studies* (Univ. of St. Andrews, Scotland)
ForumH	*Forum* (Houston)
FT	*Finsk Tidskrift*
GN	*Gissing Newsletter*
GothSE	Gothenburg Studies in English
GRM	*Germanisch-romanische Monatsschrift, Neue Folge*
HES	Harvard English Studies
HJ	*Historical Journal*
HLB	*Harvard Library Bulletin*
HLQ	*Huntington Library Quarterly*
HM	*Harvard Magazine*
HMPEC	*Historical Magazine of the Protestant Episcopal Church*
HSE	*Hungarian Studies in English* (L. Kossuth Univ., Debrecen)
HSL	*Hartford Studies in Literature*
HudR	*Hudson Review*
IJES	*Indian Journal of English Studies*
IllQ	*Illinois Quarterly*
JAAC	*Journal of Aesthetics and Art Criticism*
JAMA	*Journal of American Medical Association*
JAmS	*Journal of American Studies*
JAPA	*Journal of the American Psychoanalytic Association*
JEGP	*Journal of English and Germanic Philology*
JFI	*Journal of the Folklore Institute* (Indiana Univ.)
JGE	*Journal of General Education*
JHI	*Journal of the History of Ideas*
JJQ	*James Joyce Quarterly* (Univ. of Tulsa, Oklahoma)
JML	*Journal of Modern Literature*
JNH	*Journal of Negro History*
JNT	*Journal of Narrative Technique*
JPC	*Journal of Popular Culture* (Bowling Green Univ.)
JWCI	*Journal of the Warburg and Courtauld Institute*
KE	*Kansas English*
KN	*Kwartalnik Neofilologiczny* (Warsaw)
KR	*Kenyon Review*
KSJ	*Keats-Shelley Journal*
KSMB	*Keats-Shelley Memorial Bulletin* (Rome)
L&H	*Literature and History*
L&P	*Literature and Psychology* (Fairleigh Dickinson Univ.)

LanM	*Les Langues Modernes*
LCUT	*Library Chronicle of the University of Texas*
LeL	*Langue et Littérature*
LFQ	*Literature/Film Quarterly*
LHY	*Literary Half-Yearly*
LNRCS	*Library Notes of the Royal Commonwealth Society*
LonM	*London Magazine*
LonR	*London Review*
LWU	*Literatur in Wissenschaft und Unterricht* (Kiel)
McNR	*McNeese Review* (McNeese State Coll., La.)
MDAC	*Mystery and Detection Annual* (Beverly Hills, Calif.)
MFS	*Modern Fiction Studies*
MHRev	*Malahat Review*
MLN	*Modern Language Notes*
MLQ	*Modern Language Quarterly*
MLR	*Modern Language Review*
MLS	*Modern Language Studies*
ModSp	*Moderne Sprachen: Organ des Verbandes des Österreichischen Neuphilogen für Moderne Sprachen, Litterature, und Pädagogik*
MP	*Modern Philology*
MQ	*Midwest Quarterly* (Pittsburg, Kan.)
MQR	*Michigan Quarterly Review*
MR	*Massachusetts Review* (Univ. of Massachusetts)
MSE	*Massachusetts Studies in English*
MSpr	*Moderna Språk* (Stockholm)
MT	*Musical Times*
N&Q	*Notes and Queries*
NCBEL	*New Cambridge Bibliography of English Literature*
NCF	*Nineteenth-Century Fiction*
NDQ	*North Dakota Quarterly*
NewS	*New Statesman*
NLH	*New Literary History*
NM	*Neuphilologische Mitteilungen*
NMW	*Notes on Mississippi Writers*
NRDM	*Nouvelle Revue de Deux Mondes*
NS	*Die Neueren Sprachen*
NsM	*Neusprachliche Mitteilungen aus Wissenschaft und Praxis*
NY	*New Yorker*
NYRB	*New York Review of Books*
NYTBR	*New York Times Book Review*
NZSJ	*New Zealand Slavonic Journal*
OGS	*Oxford German Studies*
OUR	*Ohio University Review*
PBSA	*Papers of the Bibliographical Society of America*
PCP	*Pacific Coast Philology*

Person	*The Personalist*
PhilP	*Philological Papers*
PLL	*Papers on Language and Literature*
PMASAL	*Papers of the Michigan Academy of Science, Art, and Letters*
PMLA	*PMLA: Publications of the Modern Language Association of America*
PMLPS	*Publications of the Manchester Literary and Philosophical Society*
PoeS	*Poe Studies*
PolR	*Polish Review* (New York)
PP	*Philologica Pragensia*
PQ	*Philological Quarterly* (Iowa City)
PrS	*Prairie Schooner*
PSE	*Prague Studies in English*
PsyQ	*The Psychoanalytical Quarterly*
PsyR	*Psychoanalytic Review*
PULC	*Princeton University Library Chronicle*
QJS	*Quarterly Journal of Speech*
QQ	*Queen's Quarterly*
QR	*Quarterly Review*
RACUTE	*Reports of the Association of Canadian University Teachers of English*
R&S	*Research and Studies*
RE	*La Revue d'Esthetique*
RecL	*Recovering Literature*
REL	*Review of English Literature*
RES	*Review of English Studies*
RLC	*Revue de Littérature Comparée*
RLMC	*Rivista di Letterature Moderne e Comparate* (Florence)
RLV	*Revue des Langues Vivantes* (Brussels)
RMS	*Renaissance & Modern Studies* (Univ. of Nottingham)
RRCU	*Research Reports: Chiba University*
RS	*Research Studies* (Washington State Univ.)
RUO	*Revue de l'Université d'Ottawa*
RUS	*Rice University Studies*
SA	*Studi Americani* (Rome)
SAB	*South Atlantic Bulletin*
SAP	*Studia Anglica Posnaniensia: An International Review of English Studies*
SAQ	*South Atlantic Quarterly*
SatireN	*Satire Newsletter*
SatR	*Saturday Review of Literature*
SB	*Studies in Bibliography: Papers of the Bibliographical Society of the University of Virginia*
SEL	*Studies in English Literature, 1500–1900*
SEM	Seijo English Monographs

SFQ	*Southern Folklore Quarterly*
ShawR	*Shaw Review*
SHR	*Southern Humanities Review*
SIE	*Studies in English*
SIR	*Studies in Romanticism* (Boston Univ.)
SlavR	*Slavic Review* (Seattle)
SLitI	*Studies in the Literary Imagination* (Georgia State Coll.)
SLN	*Sinclair Lewis Newsletter*
SNNTS	*Studies in the Novel* (North Texas State Univ.)
SoQ	*The Southern Quarterly* (Univ. of Southern Missouri)
SoR	*Southern Review* (Louisiana State Univ.)
SoRA	*Southern Review: An Australian Journal of Literary Studies* (Univ. of Adelaide)
SovL	*Soviet Literature*
SP	*Studies in Philology*
SR	*Sewanee Review*
SRAZ	*Studia Romanica et Anglica Zagraviensia*
SSF	*Studies in Short Fiction* (Newberry Coll., S.C.)
SSL	*Studies in Scottish Literature* (Univ. of South Carolina)
TCI	Twentieth Century Interpretations
TCL	*Twentieth Century Literature*
TEAS	Twayne's English Author Series
ThN	*W. M. Thackeray Newsletter*
THY	*Thomas Hardy Year Book*
TLS	(London) *Times Literary Supplement*
TQ	*Texas Quarterly*
TRSL	*Transactions of the Royal Society of Literature*
TSL	*Tennessee Studies in Literature*
TSLL	*Texas Studies in Literature and Language*
UES	*Unisa English Studies*
UKCR	*University of Kansas City Review*
UKPHS	University of Kansas Publications, Humanistic Studies
UPLC	*University of Pennsylvania Library Chronicle*
UR	*University Review*
UTQ	*University of Toronto Quarterly*
UWLM	University of Wisconsin Literary Monographs
UZMGPIL	*Učenye Zapiski Moskovski Gosudartsvennyi Pedagogicheskii Institutimeni Lenin*
VC	*Virginia Cavalcade*
VN	*Victorian Newsletter*
VPN	*Victorian Periodicals Newsletter*
VS	*Victorian Studies* (Indiana Univ.)
VSAN	*Victorian Studies Association Newsletter* (Ontario, Canada)
WBEP	*Wiener Beiträge zur Englischen Philologie*
WHR	*Western Humanities Review*
WI	*Wellesley Index*

WS	*Women's Studies*
XUS	*Xavier University Studies*
YES	*Yearbook of English Studies*
YR	*Yale Review*
YULG	*Yale University Library Gazette*
YWES	*Year's Work in English Studies*
ZAA	*Zeitschrift für Anglistik und Amerikanistik* (East Berlin)

GENERAL MATERIALS

Richard D. Altick

Introducing the review of "General Materials" in the predecessor to the present volume, the late Bradford Booth observed, correctly, that "the great bulk of significant work in Victorian fiction" had been done in the past thirty years (roughly, 1930–62), thanks to "the development of new critical approaches and the energies of modern scholarship." He concluded that although "today the study of Victorian fiction is one of the most active of scholarly fields . . . it is the consensus of leading scholars . . . that we have not yet dug very widely, and that Victorian fiction remains one of the most challenging and rewarding areas for research." In the years since Booth wrote, events have amply justified his optimism. The output of critical and scholarly writings on the Victorian novel has increased at an almost exponential rate. Critical intelligence and scholarly research have been rather unevenly applied, but there is no question that we know more about the Victorian novel than ever before and that the examination it underwent in the period covered by this volume (1963–74) has immeasurably increased our appreciation of its diversity and richness.*

---

* An excellent cross section of critical writings on Victorian fiction since the 1950s is available in Ian Watt, ed., *The Victorian Novel: Modern Essays in Criticism* (1971). Of the thirty-one selections included there, approximately one third date from 1963 or later. These will be cited, when appropriate, in the chapters by other contributors, as will the essays on individual novels and novelists that compose such collections as Elizabeth Drew, *The Novel: A Modern Guide to Fifteen English Masterpieces* (1963); U. C. Knoepflmacher, *Laughter & Despair: Readings in Ten Novels of the Victorian Era* (1971); George Goodin, ed., *The English Novel in the Nineteenth Century* (1972); Howard M. Harper, Jr., and Charles Edge, eds., *The Classic British Novel* (1972); Paul Goetsch et al., eds., *Der englische Roman im 19. Jahrhundert: Interpretationen* (Horst Oppel Festschrift, 1973); and, when feasible, Jerome H. Buckley, ed., *The Worlds of Victorian Fiction* (1975), a noteworthy collection of eighteen essays, the majority of which are devoted to Dickens and George Eliot.

Bibliography

A full record of recent work on all Victorian novelists can be compiled from the annual Victorian Bibliography in *Victorian Studies*; the fuller but slower and less convenient *MLA International Bibliography*; and the *Annual Bibliography of English Language and Literature,* published by the (British) Modern Humanities Research Association, which sometimes picks up items missed by the other two. The chief journals to be consulted for reviews of significant books are *Nineteenth-Century Fiction, Novel, Studies in the Novel, Studies in Short Fiction,* and *Victorian Studies.* The survey of recent scholarship in nineteenth-century English literature in each autumn issue of *SEL* includes brief mention of some of the more notable studies of Victorian fiction. For the last years of the Victorian era, the journal *English Literature in Transition* (before 1963 titled *English Fiction in Transition*) is useful not only for its articles but for its extensive bibliographies of the period's writers and reviews of relevant books. Lionel Stevenson's article in *Victorian Newsletter* (1973) is valuable for its review of the major works during the dozen years covered by this volume as well as for its indication of several profitable lines of inquiry that have so far been underexplored.

Students undertaking original research in the field normally begin with the third volume (1969) of the *New Cambridge Bibliography of English Literature* (except when dealing with authors for whom strong, up-to-date individual bibliographies have been compiled, as noted in the succeeding chapters of this volume). Although it is indispensable, the *NCBEL* is not infallible; there is an uncomfortable incidence of sheer error in titles and dates, to say nothing of culpable omissions, and the treatment of minor authors is notoriously uneven. The nineteenth-century volume must be used with caution and supplemented from other sources. A full bibliography of completed dissertations is Lawrence F. McNamee's *Dissertations in English and American Literature, 1865–1964* (1968), with, so far, one supplement (1969). Very recent dissertations are listed in the Victorian Bibliography in *Victorian Studies* and in the *MLA International Bibliography,* but for an exhaustive check *American Doctoral Dissertations* and *Dissertation Abstracts International* must also be consulted.

The three largest collections of Victorian novels are at the British Library, the Library of Congress, and Harvard University. All the titles that the first two hold are listed in their respective general catalogues, and for Harvard there is the *Widener Library Shelflist 35–36: English Literature* (4 vols., 1971). When it is completed in some 610 volumes, the *National Union Catalog: Pre-1956 Imprints,* now in progress, will provide a means of locating copies of all works of Victorian fiction owned by libraries in the United States and Canada. The extensive holdings of English and American fiction at the New York University Library are catalogued in the *Fales Library Checklist,* ed. Theodore Grieder (2 vols., 1970; Supp., 1974). A number of other American libraries are rich in materials, both manuscript and printed, for the study of Victorian fiction. Especially noteworthy are Yale, Princeton (the Parrish Collection), the University of Illinois, and the University of California at Los Angeles (the Sadleir Collection). Occasional notes and articles on recent acquisitions of rarities are printed in the various libraries' journals, such as the *Bulletin of the New York Public Library,* which periodically records new accessions of the Berg Collection.

The most remarkable private collection of Victorian fiction, especially of the work of minor novelists, is that of Robert Lee Wolff, who describes some of its high points in a two-part article in *Book Collector* (1965) and in the first chapter of his book *Strange Stories and Other Explorations in Victorian Fiction* (1971). A notable collection of another sort is described in *Victorian Detective Fiction: A Catalogue of the Collection Made by Dorothy Glover and Graham Greene* (1966).

Numerous Victorian novelists were frequent contributors to periodicals. For many years the record of their contributions—buried, for the most part, in the files of those magazines—was virtually lost, but now the *Wellesley Index to Victorian Periodicals* (with two volumes published of the projected four, 1966–) and the computer-produced author index (1971) to the old *Poole's Index to Periodical Literature* are of great assistance in compiling bibliographies of the fugitive writings of Victorian novelists. Anne Lohrli's *Household Words: . . . Table of Contents, List of Contributors and Their Contributions* (1973) is an encyclopedic key to the authorship of the fiction published in that popular weekly under Dickens' editorship. In this field of investigation, the specialized articles and bibliographies appearing in the *Victorian Periodicals Newsletter* are occasionally useful.

Historical Materials

Although a number of students have made profitable use of the commonplace that Victorian writers addressed themselves to a large and variegated audience with very marked tastes, it is regrettable that no work has yet appeared that examines the social milieu of the readers of Victorian fiction more specifically and intensively than was attempted in Richard D. Altick's *The English Common Reader: A Social History of the Mass Reading Public 1800–1900* (1957). The desirability of a closer examination is indicated by Lionel Stevenson in a magisterial article, "The Rationale of Victorian Fiction" (*NCF*, 1973), which rightly insists that a cardinal principle of fiction criticism is an awareness that every novel is of a certain time and place and was meant to be read by a certain audience. In *The Long Revolution* (1961), in some respects a sequel to his classic *Culture and Society 1780–1950* (1958), Raymond Williams discusses some of the sources, phenomena, and implications of the development of a mass audience for the printed word. Several books and essays that are particularly concerned with the novelist's awareness of a "participant" audience are mentioned in a later connection.

The three-way relationship among professional authors, publishers, and the reading public has been studied in a rather fragmentary fashion. Authoritative books that attempt a broad synthesis of the available information—a scholarly history of Victorian publishing, for example, to replace F. A. Mumby's unsatisfactory *Publishing and Bookselling* (updated but not improved by Ian Norrie, 1974)—are among the most pressing desiderata in the field. One of the best monographs on individual topics is Guinevere L. Griest's workmanlike *Mudie's Circulating Library and the Victorian Novel* (1970), a study of the principal way by which middle-class Victorian readers were supplied with new fiction. A pendant to this is Sara Keith's "Literary Censorship and Mudie's Library" (*ColQ*, 1973), which deals with three episodes of "censorship" in a spirit sympathetic to the perhaps unfairly maligned Mudie.

An important economic influence on Victorian publishing, the much vexed issue of discounting versus price fixing, is examined in James J. Barnes's *Free Trade in Books: A Study of the London Book Trade since 1800* (1964). The adversary relationship between Victorian authors and publishers, which made it desirable, if not requisite, for authors to be represented by an intermediary, is described in James Hepburn's *The Author's Empty Purse and the Rise of the Literary Agent* (1968). Annabel Jones's "Disraeli's *Endymion*: A Case Study" (*Essays in the History of Publishing*, ed. Asa Briggs, 1974) is, thanks to the completeness of the Longman records, the most detailed narrative yet written of the progress of a book from its best-selling author's first approach to his publisher to its reception. Studies have been made of two aspects of that perennial grievance Victorian authors had to endure, the lack of international copyright. Simon Nowell-Smith's *International Copyright Law and the Publisher in the Reign of Queen Victoria* (1968) is a well-informed examination of the general situation. Apart from the discussion of Meredith's *The Amazing Marriage* as a case study, the book is most pertinent to the history of Victorian fiction in the chapter on the Leipzig firm of Tauchnitz, in which Nowell-Smith recounts the house's dealings with a number of Victorian novelists whose work it reprinted in cheap format and, unlike American book pirates, paid for, at least in token sums. This chapter, somewhat expanded, also appears in *Book Collector* (1966). James J. Barnes explores the tangled political and commercial considerations that prevented a copyright accord between the two largest English-speaking nations in *Authors, Publishers and Politicians: The Quest for an Anglo-American Copyright Agreement 1815–1854* (1974). A rather slight article by Carol Polsgrove, "They Made It Pay: British Short-Fiction Writers, 1820–1840" (*SSF*, 1974), presents some information on the magazine outlets writers had in that early period and on how much they were paid for their stories.

Progress has been made toward the fuller utilization of such Victorian publishers' editorial and business archives as have escaped destruction. The Smith, Elder records are housed at the office of John Murray; and most of the voluminous Macmillan archives, amounting to some 500,000 pieces bound into 1,250 volumes, are now in the British Library. Philip V. Blake-

Hill has written a concise description of the latter (*BMQ*, 1973), and a longer article by William E. Fredeman (*SB*, 1970) describes the dispersal of the rest of the Macmillan records and the importance of all these documents for literary research. The office papers of four other Victorian firms that published varying amounts of fiction—Bentley, Routledge, Longman, and Kegan Paul—are now accessible (with others to come) in *The Archives of British Publishers on Microfilm* (1974), an ambitious undertaking of the English firm of Chadwyck-Healey.

Although there have been a number of studies of the relationship between Romantic and Victorian poetry, relatively little attention has been paid recently to the immediate antecedents of Victorian fiction. The most provocative work in this field, Peter Conrad's *The Victorian Treasure-House* (1973), is a facile exposition of the novel as "Victorian Gothic." The novel, Conrad maintains, was "the central form in the nineteenth century: it is, in the end, the inheritor of romanticism and it supersedes the attempts of the poets to re-create the Shakespearean drama." Conrad maintains a patronizing attitude toward Victorian fiction, as well as Victorian art, regarding "detailism" as an unfortunate artistic (and moral) obsession, but his book is full of matter for thought. It should be added that part of his thesis, that the Victorian novel inherited, by way of Romantic poetry, the Shakespearean tradition of plenitude and psychological fidelity, was anticipated in the final chapter of John Speirs's *Poetry towards Novel* (1971).

Heightened interest in the Edwardian era and its principal novelists has combined with the growing awareness of the continuity between Victorian and modern fiction to invite closer attention to developments in the final decades of the century. Donald David Stone's excellent *Novelists in a Changing World: Meredith, James, and the Transformation of English Fiction in the 1880s* (1972) begins with a panoramic account of the changes in the philosophical and literary atmosphere of the era that witnessed the passing of the major Victorian novelists and the appearance of a new, differently oriented generation, and goes on to a detailed study of Meredith and James as two leading examples of novelists who had not only new philosophical and social bearings but a radically new attitude toward their art. Another study of the same watershed decades, which deals with figures like Hardy, Wilde, Stevenson, and Gissing as principal actors in the story rather than as subordinates (as they are in Stone's design), is Paul Goetsch's *Die Romankonzeption in England 1880–1910* (1967). More specialized, and concentrating on less well known authors and titles, is Wendell V. Harris' "John Lane's Keynotes Series and the Fiction of the 1890's" (*PMLA*, 1968), which finds in the fourteen novels and the nineteen volumes of short stories included in that series evidence that "there was more going on . . . than has been examined hitherto by the historians of the period." Several of the recent books on twentieth-century developments in fiction have their springboard, naturally enough, in the last years of the Victorian era. Alan Friedman's *The Turn of the Novel* (1966) finds that the key to the transformation of the novel in the present century lies in the novelists' turning from "closed" to "open" (indeterminate) experience, with an accompanying shift in form. A somewhat related work, also emphasizing "open form" and its lack of resolution, is James Gindin's *Harvest of a Quiet Eye: The Novel of Compassion* (1971), which approaches the twentieth-century novel by way of Trollope, Meredith, and Hardy. In "The Forms of Victorian Fiction" (*VN*, 1975), James R. Kincaid argues that a mixed form "dominates the Victorian novel in its full range, from those which seem most open, say the late novels of Dickens, to those of Trollope, apparently the most closed."

The examination of the critical climate in which Victorian novelists worked, which was begun by Richard Stang's *Theory of the Novel in England, 1850–1870* (1959), is extended for thirty more years by Kenneth Graham's *English Criticism of the Novel, 1865–1900* (1966), a brisk narrative of the deepening sophistication—in some quarters, at least—of the fictional aesthetic. The materials that both Stang and Graham draw upon, contemporary discussions of novelists and, particularly, reviews of new novels, are available in quantity in the volumes of Routledge's Critical Heritage series devoted to documenting the contemporary reputations of individual novelists. A large collection of quotations from periodical reviews of 1880–1910 bearing on the crucial issue of realism in the novel can be found in Goetsch's *Die Romankonzeption in England*, mentioned above. Two specialized articles have added depth and detail to aspects of Victorian-fiction criticism that Stang and Graham necessarily studied only in relatively general terms. John O. Waller's "A Composite Anglo-Catholic Concept of the Novel, 1841–1868" (*BNYPL*, 1966) concludes, on the basis of an intensive examination of the reviews in the *Christian Remembrancer* and the *Ecclesiastic*, that the reviewers were "bent . . . upon evolving a more-or-less systematic Christian literary theory, with flexibility enough to absorb the moral benefits of secular literature, but rigidity enough to avoid its supposedly shallow or un-Christian concepts." In a highly speculative essay, "Theories of Science and Romance, 1870–1920" (*VS*, 1973), Alexander Welsh applies the history-of-ideas approach to the history of criticism, finding a significant parallel between the revolution in physics in the last third of the nineteenth century and the movement toward naturalism in the same period. In the same article Welsh boldly, and not unpersuasively, likens literary fictions to the scientific "models" that in modern systems analysis are designed to "reduce a complex system to manageable proportions or serve to crystallize our thinking and perception."

Theoretical Studies

Students proposing to read recent critical work on the Victorian novel should first acquaint themselves with the outstanding general works on the theory of fiction published since 1960. Some of these volumes draw heavily upon Victorian novels for their illustrations, some very sparingly, but as a group they capture the climate of literary opinion in which recent criticism of Victorian fiction has been written. They indicate the "givens"—the values, assumptions, and theses—that have affected, if indeed they do not directly underlie, this criticism.

The most influential of these general works has been Wayne Booth's *The Rhetoric of Fiction* (1961), which, contesting the post-Jamesian doctrine that the consciousness of a created character is necessarily a more effective medium of narration than the omniscient or participant narrator, focuses attention upon the rhetorical strategies associated with the "point of view" by which the novelist controls the reader's responses. Booth's neo-Aristotelian approach has not gone entirely unchallenged; see, for example, John Killham's "The 'Second Self' in Novel Criticism" (*BJA*, 1966), which draws most of its illustrations from Victorian fiction. On the whole, however, Booth's major premise, that all narrative strategies are legitimate and comprehensible when each is regarded as a means to a different end, has been accepted for what it has proved to be, a bracingly liberating force in the study of fiction. One aspect of his interpretation of the literary interaction we call "reading"—the creation of a fictive reader as a coparticipant with the fictive narrator—is developed further by Wolfgang Iser in *The Implied Reader* (1974). In the nineteenth century, Iser argues, the author characteristically assumed that the reader brought to his experience of the novel a subjectivity that obliged the novelist to "use a variety of cunning stratagems to nudge the reader unknowingly into making the 'right' discoveries" of the reality, however unfamiliar, that the novel purported to reflect. A brief, less complex study of "the relationships that novelists establish with their readers [and] the narrative arrangements made to elicit the responses that . . . are produced by literary fictions" is Andrew Wright's "The Novel as a Conspiracy" (*EDH*, 1972).

Dealing with the same issues is Barbara Hardy's *Tellers and Listeners* (1975). One of Hardy's chapters derives from her 1968 essay "An Approach through Narrative," a contribution to an interesting series of articles on theories of fiction appearing in *Novel* (1968–69). This series, under the title "Towards a Poetics of Fiction," includes Malcolm Bradbury on structure, David Lodge on language, Frank Kermode on history, and Robert Scholes on genre. Scholes's full-scale discussion of his topic, *The Nature of Narrative* (with Robert Kellogg, 1966), rarely deals with Victorian novels, but, like Northrop Frye's classic *Anatomy of Criticism* (1957), his book provides a useful theoretical framework for critical considerations of narratives of any period. For a capsuled version of Scholes's theories, the summary by David Lodge in *The Novel at the Crossroads* (1970) can be recommended.

"The angle of mimetic relationship between art and life" is the principal concern of W. J. Harvey's *Character and the Novel* (1965). Attempting to impose order upon the problem of how to assess the "truth to life" of a fictional narrative, Harvey isolates four universal categories of experience— time, identity, causality, and freedom—that can be used as touchstones, so that, "if a novelist convinces us that his handling of them is truthful, then there is a good chance that the particular experience he portrays as the end-product of these categories will also strike us as true to life." Barbara Hardy copes with more or less the same problem in *The Appropriate Form* (1964). The logic of life, she maintains, determines the logic of art; "the life 'given' in a novel carries with it a set of necessities (its own laws, if you will), that establish a logic of experience (the impetus to plot), a shape and potentiality of character, and an informing principle of destiny in the character-incident relation." Both Harvey and Hardy, therefore, offer mimetic theories and criteria by which students in a world of drastically revised ideas of truth can appraise the success of Victorian novelists, who wrote for readers insistent upon the experiential validity of the stories they told.

The most densely metaphysical of recent books in this field is J. Hillis Miller's controversial *The Form of Victorian Fiction* (1968). Miller's thesis is that a "novel is a structure of interpenetrating minds, the mind of the narrator as he beholds or enters into the characters, the minds of the characters as they behold or know one another. Not isolated consciousness, not consciousness at grips with natural objects, not consciousness face to face with God in meditation, but consciousness of others—this is the primary focus of fiction." In essence, in the absence of the former "transcendent origin and support," society now depends upon rules established by the individual human heart interacting with other hearts, and it is this dialectic that fiction portrays. In a related essay, "Some Implications of Form in Victorian Fiction" (*Mansions of the Spirit: Essays in Literature and Religion*, ed. George A. Panichas, 1967), Miller stresses the Cartesian dualism that, in his view, intensified the subjectivism of Victorian fiction and briefly examines the various forms of the Victorian quest for interpersonal relationships upon which to establish a purely human world.

One more of the half-dozen or so theoretical works that have most affected recent criticism of fiction is Frank Kermode's *The Sense of an Ending* (1967), which has for its premise the idea that all basic fictions in the history of culture involve an apocalypse—an end rendered tragically inescapable given the nature of the beginning—and that the novel, along with other forms of fiction, represents the plight of man, poised between beginning and end, seeking to discover a meaning that will reconcile or harmonize the two. One critic of Kermode's theory is Patrick Swinden, who in his *Unofficial Selves: Character in the Novel from Dickens to the Present Day* (1973) devotes a chapter, "Deaths and Entrances," to a study of characterization in a number of major Victorian novels.

General Criticism

In a review of Harvey's *Character and the Novel* (*NCF*, 1967), Angus Wilson observes that " 'life,' density, verisimilitude, a concern with general realities has progressively disappeared from the novel and from the concerns of the critics of the novel" since Henry James. Recent criticism of the Victorian novel has reflected this tendency, minimizing what have traditionally been taken to be the differences between Victorian and modern fiction and concentrating, instead, on the correspondences that make it possible to read Victorian novels as we read those of our own time. Assuming a perspective long enough to obscure biographical and historical circumstances and merge Victorian and modern concerns into a single entity, recent critics have dwelt most lingeringly upon philosophical, psychological, and sociocultural interpretations—the *ideas* of a novel—rather than upon the novelist's craft.

There has been no new history of the Victorian novel, nor any reasonably broad critical study, to supersede the portion of Lionel Stevenson's *The English Novel: A Panorama* (1960) that is devoted to the period. Stevenson's account is well informed and responsible; but it is too conservative to be stimulating, and a critical history that assimilates the most fruitful perceptions of the past twenty years is badly needed. Meanwhile, the most inclusive critical work, though far from comprehensive (it deals with only four of Dickens' novels, for instance), is Frederick R. Karl's *An Age of Fiction: The Nineteenth Century British Novel* (1965; paperback title, *A Reader's Guide to the Nineteenth Century British Novel*). No routine handbook with potted biographical-historical facts and dubious platitudes, this volume contains vigorous critical observations sustained by judicious enthusiasm. Although it probably is most valuable to the intelligent undergraduate, it is not to be scorned by more advanced students.

The title of William H. Marshall's *The World of the Victorian Novel* (1967) implies a breadth it does not possess. Its avowed purpose is to lay out the "philosophical orientation" of numerous novels through a procedure that combines intellectual history, theology, and, more identifiably, the modern psychological and moral concepts that cluster about such terms as "alienation," "selfhood," "value disorientation," and something called "negative absolutism." Viewing all fiction as a dramatization of abstractions (he is not the only critic to do so, of course, but his method is more single-minded and less deft than others'), Marshall tends to turn a group of commonplaces into idées fixes as he applies them to novel after novel.

In a series of Cambridge lectures gathered as *The English Novel from Dickens to Lawrence* (1970)—another deceptively titled volume, because, far from being comprehensive, it is confined to a mere handful of novels— Raymond Williams views the same shift from a God-centered universe to a man-centered one in more specifically sociological terms. The focal subject of Victorian fiction, indeed the protagonist, is not the individual human being but society, which is no longer treated as a framework but as an independent organism, an agency. The novelist's preoccupation is with his characters' attempts to explore and discover the meaning of what Williams calls "the knowable community," which, now that God is presumed dead, is "the active creator, the active destroyer, of the values of persons and relationships." Even before Williams wrote, this thesis had been implicit in one of the numerous critical approaches to Dickens, but this book attempts to show its wide applicability.

The changing relationship of the individual and society and the decline of man's tragic sense when confronted with the need for external action are the theme of James R. Kincaid's "The Novel and Social Action" (*BMMLA*, 1973). Kincaid finds that "most classic nineteenth-century novels" are characterized by a "pattern of withdrawal to a life whose moral instincts are divorced from a world of action."

Except insofar as it is at the heart of discussions of mimesis (e.g., in Hardy's *The Appropriate Form* and Harvey's *Character in the Novel*), the "realism" attributed by long custom to the Victorian novel has not come in for much detailed examination. George Levine, in "Realism, or In Praise of Lying" (*CE*, 1970), redefines the term to designate a "movement . . . toward a new romance . . . based not in the external world of action but in the internal world of sensibility, intelligence and feeling," which "assimilated and yet transcended the realistic convention." Levine extends this argument in "Realism Reconsidered" (*The Theory of the Novel: New Essays*, ed. John Halperin, 1974). "We should be ready," he says, "to see realism as anything but an unmediated record of reality (since it comes filtered through organizing perceptions, unconscious social pressures, and a language thick with conventions), and to remember that all fiction—even realistic fiction—is fiction." Ioan Williams' *The Realistic Novel in England* (1974), wholly on the nineteenth century, suffers from too unfocused a definition of the operative word and a frail theoretical underpinning. It is composed mainly of literary, historical, and critical commonplaces served up with the deceptive air of fresh discovery and profound truth that characterizes doctoral dissertations on critical subjects as much in Great Britain as in the United States.

Paradoxically, George Levine's *The Boundaries of Fiction* (1968) has substantial bearing upon the study of the Victorian novel even though it does not discuss the Victorian novel as such. Looked at from a certain angle, it is a stimulating exercise in criticizing fiction by indirection, that is, by viewing Carlyle, Macaulay, and Newman as (to put it crudely) novelists manqués. Much of their imaginative nonfiction, Levine maintains, "survives in the same way great novels survive," and, where it fails, "it fails in much the same places as the Victorian novel frequently fails." To the extent that these writers shared certain major attitudes and techniques with the novelists, the boundaries of Victorian fiction are considerably less sharp than the simplified schematism of textbook literary history recognizes.

Studies of Special Aspects

Types of Novels

The forty thousand novels that are often said to constitute the corpus of English nineteenth-century fiction are no more homogeneous than the steadily expanding audience that read them. A number of studies have dealt with particular kinds of novels, especially by way of relating Victorian literary production to the social and cultural background. One such book, Louis Cazamian's ground-breaking *Le Roman social en Angleterre 1830–1850*, was published as long ago as 1904, but its usefulness as an introduction to what has proved a profitable field of investigation has been enhanced by its reappearance in a translation by Martin Fido (1973).

Avrom Fleishman's *The English Historical Novel: Walter Scott to Virginia Woolf* (1971) is an erudite examination of a genre that, says Fleishman, "is unashamedly a hybrid: it contemplates the universal but does not depart from the rich factuality of history in order to reach that elevation." More concerned with the Victorians' ideologies of history than with the novels' literary qualities, this book provides, through its expansive and searching analysis of Scott, a valuable comparative context for such Victorian practitioners of the form as Dickens, Thackeray, Reade, George Eliot, Shorthouse, Hardy, and Pater. An interesting article on a single aspect of this relationship, considerably more illuminating than the routine reputation-and-influence report, is John Henry Raleigh's "What Scott Meant to the Victorians" (*VS*, 1963; rpt. in his *Time, Place, and Idea: Essays on the Novel*, 1968). James C. Simmons' short *The Novelist as Historian* (1973) is a superficial examination of the growing insistence upon documentable "fact," as opposed to "romancing," in the Victorian historical novel.

Several recent writers have addressed themselves to the Victorian religious novel, amplifying and in some ways extending Margaret Maison's *The Victorian Vision* (1962). In "Loss and Gain? The Theme of Conversion in Late Victorian Fiction" (*VS*, 1965), R. M. Schieder is concerned with the dynamics of the religious novel from 1868 to 1900—the way in which it responded to the post-Darwinian loss of faith by offering an assortment of substitutes for orthodox religious positions. More elaborate, yet more limited in scope (it deals only with *Marius the Epicurean, Hypatia, Loss and Gain*, and *Callista*), is David A. Downes's *The Temper of Victorian Belief* (1972), which argues that the modern relevance of Pater, Kingsley, and Newman as writers of religious novels lies in their conviction that "secular history is the major resource for rational truth for man." Downes further contends that of the three "only Newman makes any lasting claim on us today," because he alone had an intellect sufficient "to embrace the two worlds between which modern man shuffles." U. C. Knoepflmacher's *Religious Humanism and the Victorian Novel* (1965), though not a study of the religious novel as such, singles out three major figures—George Eliot, Pater, and Butler—as exemplifying different ways whereby the Victorian mind and sensibility sought replacements for the no longer comforting religious orthodoxy. The result of their quest was not a new faith erected on the ruins of the old but "a conservative clinging to [the] remains" of traditional dogma.

The novel of rural life, which until recently has had relatively little systematic study as a distinct type, is discussed in Michael Squires's *The Pastoral Novel: Studies in George Eliot, Thomas Hardy, and D. H. Lawrence* (1974). The two opening chapters on the nature and development of the type are an informative contribution to literary history. In connection with Squires's book one should read Julian Moynahan's article on pastoralism, cited below.

One of the best books on any aspect of Victorian fiction to appear in the dozen years under review is Jerome Hamilton Buckley's *Season of Youth: The Bildungsroman from Dickens to Golding* (1974), a model of lucid, quietly perceptive criticism founded on sound scholarship. Among the distinctions of this survey of the principal Victorian "novels of youth" is the ample allowance made for the element of actual autobiography each contains.

The vast and largely uncharted realm of so-called minor and subliterary fiction has begun to receive attention. In *Fiction with a Purpose: Major and Minor Nineteenth-Century Novels* (1967) Robert A. Colby develops a methodology that might well be applied in a number of similar contexts. Taking seven major nineteenth-century novels with strong didactic purpose, he examines preceding and immediately contemporary minor novels on the same theme in order to determine how far the former resemble the latter in method and content and thus, in effect, to weigh their originality against the elements derived from their literary and social milieu. In a review essay, "The Rational Amusement: 'Minor' Fiction and Victorian Studies" (*VS*, 1970), Louis James makes a series of provocative suggestions concerning the value of such minor fiction in literary and historical studies.

James's *Fiction for the Working Man, 1830–1850* (1963) is a pioneering effort, unfortunately marred by many inaccuracies in the first edition, to explore the lowest level of Victorian fictional reading matter, the neo-Gothic shockers, sentimental melodramas, and other such entertainments that attracted the pennies of the semiliterate masses. On a somewhat higher social plane, the sensation novel that was the rage for a decade in the mid-Victorian era is anatomized by Kathleen Tillotson in "The Lighter Reading of the Eighteen-Sixties," an essay that forms the introduction to her Riverside edition of *The Woman in White* (1969).

The development of short fiction in the Victorian era is traced in greatest detail by Wendell V. Harris in his monograph-length "English Short Fiction in the 19th Century" (*SSF*, 1968). The antecedents of the short story in the middle of the period are sketched by Lionel Stevenson and Harris in two adjacent articles, "The Short Story in Embryo" and "Beginnings of and for the True Short Story in England" (*ELT*, 1972). A third discussion in the same symposium, Jan B. Gordon's " 'The Wilde Child': Structure and Origin in the Fin-de-Siècle Short Story," is too opaque with jargon to be much of a contribution. Two other essays deal with the burgeoning of the short story at the end of the century, Derek Stanford's introduction to his collection of *Short Stories of the 'Nineties* (1968) and P. J. Keating's to his collection of *Working-Class Stories of the 1890s* (1971). Harris' "Fiction in the English 'Experimental' Periodicals of the 1890's" (*BB*, 1967) is a checklist of the short stories found in "the more important of the *avant-garde* periodicals." A score of characteristic short stories, mainly from the last

Victorian years, are collected by Helmut E. Gerber (*The English Short Story in Transition 1880–1920*, 1967).

Two comparative studies relate Victorian fiction to the fiction produced at the same time in France and America, respectively. In "Form and Value in the French and English Nineteenth-Century Novel" (*MLN*, 1972) Anne-Marie Dibon, adopting *Vanity Fair* and *Le Rouge et le noir* as test cases, uses the theories of Lukács, Girard, and Goldmann to refute the assumption that one difference between Victorian and French fiction is that in the former "the prevailing social order is finally accepted . . . the hero is integrated into society and bourgeois morality is more or less upheld," whereas in the latter "the hero dies or retires, having rejected the values of society or failed to realize his own ideas." The aim of Nicolaus Mills's *American and English Fiction in the Nineteenth Century: An Antigenre Critique and Comparison* (1973) is "to show that we cannot classify American fiction as romantic and English fiction as novelistic and on that basis accurately distinguish between the two traditions." Comparing George Eliot with Hawthorne, Hardy with Melville, and Dickens with Mark Twain, Mills argues that their works "have a complexity that defies easy categorization and makes it necessary to see their uniqueness in far subtler ways than their division into genres allows."

Techniques

Apart from studies inspired by Booth's taxonomy of narrative voices, relatively little has been done on particular fictional devices. Lionel Stevenson, in "The Relativity of Truth in Victorian Fiction" (*Victorian Essays: A Symposium*, ed. Warren D. Anderson and Thomas D. Clareson, Waldo H. Dunn Festschrift, 1967), explains the breakdown of the point-of-view technique as the result of the novelists' being in the midst of the transition from the old "confidence in objective fact" to the modern "unabashed solipsism." Two chapters of David Goldknopf's *The Life of the Novel* (1972) ascribe certain technical aspects of Victorian fiction to the prevailing intellectual winds. The dominance of plot as a structuring force is attributed to the "deistic" conception of the world as a machine and to the concurrent machine-centered Industrial Revolution; the changing treatment of coincidence during the period is accounted for by the rejection of God as a determining but caring providential agent and the substitution of the brutal impersonal power detected by Hardy. A somewhat similar demonstration of "the way in which a novelist's whole view of the world will depend on his metaphysical leanings and that view of the world help determine his choice of technique and formal structure" is found in Wendell V. Harris' "Fiction and Metaphysics in the Nineteenth Century" (*Mosaic*, 1971). Harris cites Harriet Martineau and Disraeli as representing, respectively, the empiricist and transcendental positions, Kingsley as combining the two, and Dickens as giving "intellectual allegiance to neither side."

Allegory is not ordinarily regarded as a common instrument in the Victorian novelist's repertory, but two essays, both on the typology of women, suggest that its importance has been underestimated. In "The Allegory of Truth in Victorian Fiction" (*VS*, 1965) Alexander Welsh shows how truth was personified in the typical heroine, whose devotion to that quality eventually earned her the reward of a happy marriage. John R. Reed in "Emblems in Victorian Literature" (*HSL*, 1970) points out that women were sometimes stylized as moral emblems in the figure of a Judith or a Griselda.

On the verbal artistry of Victorian novelists, the best recent treatment is in David Lodge's *Language of Fiction* (1966), which approaches fiction by the same route John Holloway employed earlier in his study of the language of nonfiction prose, *The Victorian Sage.* Lodge's tactful argument and his skillful demonstration of the manner in which close stylistic analysis can enrich the reading of Victorian novelists have not yet borne as much fruit as they clearly should. Apart from linguistic (including metaphorical) analysis of certain portions of the work of novelists like Dickens and the Brontës, there has been only one major response to Lodge: Karl Kroeber's *Styles in Fictional Structure: The Art of Jane Austen, Charlotte Brontë, George Eliot* (1971), an elaborate and, as the author admits, not entirely satisfactory experiment in quantification. Kroeber concludes that in any good novel there is a "consistently complex" organization whose nature can be discovered through analysis of what he calls the macroscopic and microscopic elements of structure at any given point. The statistics that form the basis of the argument are, mercifully, relegated to the last eighty pages. A more traditional method of stylistic analysis is exemplified by Norman Page's *Speech in the English Novel* (1973), which examines the various purposes, techniques, and effects of speech presentation in fiction, using Dickens, among other Victorian novelists, as a chief source of examples.

The occurrence of the other arts in fiction and the affinity of fiction to those arts are topics that have only begun to be examined with the authority they require. D. J. Smith's "Music in the Victorian Novel" (*KR*, 1963) is a pleasant, unpretentious account, ranging from Thackeray's professional pianist, Thumpenstrumpff, to various sorts of musicians in George Eliot and Hardy. In *Victorian Novelists and Their Illustrators* (1970) J. R. Harvey deals, on a broad but by no means exhaustive scale, with the close relationship between the originally published text and the illustrations in a variety of Victorian novels, emphasizing how closely, on occasion, the novelist worked with the illustrator to ensure that the pictures would be an authentic extension of the text. In the wake of Harvey's book several shorter examinations have been made of the importance of illustrations in the technique of individual Victorian novelists, notably Dickens and Thackeray, but much more remains to be done in this field. Another promising and unhackneyed field of investigation is the manifold relationships between fiction and contemporary art, some of which have been suggested by books on Victorian painting, such as Raymond Lister's *Victorian Narrative Painting* and Graham Reynolds' *Victorian Painting* (both 1966), and which have been treated more extensively by Peter Conrad in *The Victorian Treasure-House.*

Themes and Topics

Novelists, as Walter Bagehot remarked of Dickens, are special correspondents for posterity, and a substantial amount of the interest Victorian fiction has attracted has been due to its faithful and many-faceted reflection of a now vanished social scene. But, as Richard D. Altick points out in "Victorian Readers and the Sense of the Present" (*Midway*, 1970), the intense timeliness and topicality of much Victorian fiction have critical pertinence as well, because novelists, writing as they did for newspaper readers who were steeped in the details of daily living, incorporated in their novels' texture innumerable nuances and ephemeral allusions that affected readers' responses, however overlooked or inexplicable they may be today.

Access to a large body of popular Victorian fiction for its social-history content has been facilitated by Myron F. Brightfield's *Victorian England in Its Novels* (1968), a compilation of passages of social and cultural interest from 1,221 novels published between 1840 and 1870. Brightfield's four volumes incorporate primary source material on topics ranging from class structure and occupations to popular amusements and household customs. The mass of notes from which Brightfield compiled this work is available in the Bradford Booth Room at the University of California, Los Angeles.

A number of studies deal with the fictional treatment of social concerns and movements in Victorian life. Irene Bostrom's "The Novel and Catholic Emancipation" (*SIR*, 1963) is an able study that is broader than the title indicates, embracing as it does most appearances of Roman Catholic characters, dogma, and institutions in fiction from the Gothic school to the Irish one. It is a good example of the way in which a subtype of literature can be interpreted as mirroring the state of popular opinion and prejudices on an enduring subject of disagreement and fear.

The growing realization of the impact of the city upon the Victorian imagination is manifested in Alexander Welsh's "The Novel and the City: England and America in the Nineteenth Century" (*VS*, 1968), which explores the deeper social and philosophical implications of urbanization. Two other essays dealing with this theme, one by U. C. Knoepflmacher and the other by Philip Collins, are included in *The Victorian City* (ed. H. J. Dyos and Michael Woolf, 1973). This two-volume collection contains a number of other stimulating essays, more general in nature, whose findings might also be applied to the topic of how novelists bypassed or responded to the problems generated by the growth of Manchester and London and other Victorian cities. Raymond Williams' *The Country and the City* (1973) rather unsystematically places nineteenth-century literary attitudes in the wider context of the centuries-old conflict of rural and urban values. These studies should be read side by side with Julian Moynahan's "Pastoralism as Culture and Counter-Culture in English Fiction, 1800–1928" (*Novel*, 1972), which traces the decline of "a really profound culture of pastoralism . . . from a view to a death: from a rich composition of feeling and valuing centered on the destinies of people living in the country to a decomposition, or a disconnecting, as between the 'complex' life of society at large and the 'simple' fictions of private rural life." Inseparable from this encroachment of the city upon the ancient rural tradition was the rise of industrialism. In *Victorians and the Machine: The Literary Response to Technology* (1968) Herbert L. Sussman describes the attitudes of Dickens, Morris, and Butler, but a more penetrating and comprehensive study of the subject remains to be done.

Victorian politics as reflected in contemporary fiction is the topic of two studies, one on electoral practice (or malpractice), the other on ideology. In "Elections in Victorian Fiction" (*VN*, 1974) J. R. Dinwiddy discusses a dozen such contests, ranging from Eatanswill to Tankerville, but unfortunately overlooks the particularly crooked contest at Yatton, described with considerable gusto in Samuel Warren's *Ten Thousand a Year*. The several contributors to John Lucas' collection of essays, *Literature and Politics in the Nineteenth Century* (1971), take a Marxist view of the political postures of George Eliot, Meredith, Mallock, Gissing, and Morris.

The leading novelists' attitudes toward class, as expressed or implied in an even hundred novels, are reported by Richard Faber in his modest but informative *Proper Stations: Class in Victorian Fiction* (1971). One wonders whether a similar survey of a hundred distinctly third-rate novels would result in the same conclusions as Faber reasonably draws concerning the authors' personal social commitments and their novels' reliability as historical evidence. Of the several social divisions portrayed in Victorian fiction, it is the working class that has been most intensively studied. P. J. Keating's *The Working Classes in Victorian Fiction* (1971) has 1820–1900 for its nominal scope, but the novels of the pre-1880 era are disposed of in the first two chapters, and the remainder of the book is devoted to Gissing, the discovery of East End poverty, and the influence of French naturalism upon the fictional portrayal of the workers.

Patrick Brantlinger poses the question of the reliability of fictional evidence as social history in his study of "The Case against Trade Unions in Early Victorian Fiction" (*VS*, 1969), examining the classic cluster of *Hard Times, Alton Locke,* and *Mary Barton,* as well as half a dozen other novels of the forties and fifties. In another, wider juxtaposition of literary and social history, "Bluebooks, the Social Organism, and the Victorian Novel" (*Criticism*, 1972), Brantlinger demonstrates that the novelists and the social reformers shared a common concern, that of arousing general and effective sympathy for the poor. Sheila Smith's "Blue Books and Victorian Novelists" (*RES*, 1970) recapitulates material found in her earlier articles and specifically discusses the use Disraeli and Kingsley made of the 1843 *Report on the Employment of Women and Children in Agriculture*. Blue Book evidence, she concludes, was a mixed blessing to the novelists who seized upon it as graphic and authoritative raw material.

Moving up the social scale, we come to that distinctive product of nineteenth-century economics and technology, the industrial magnate, whose characterization in fifty novels of the era when he was first a commanding figure is the subject of Ivan Melada's *The Captains of Industry in English Fiction 1821–1871* (1970). A worthwhile contribution within its self-imposed limits, the book suggests how much additional profit might derive from similar work on associated subjects. The captain of finance, as personified by Merdle and Melmotte, deserves a comparable study, and both he and the tycoon Melada discusses could be closely compared with their real-life prototypes.

On the more traditional side of Victorian social life, John R. Reed deals thoroughly with "The Public Schools in Victorian Fiction" (*NCF*, 1974). (Mention also should be made here of a valuable book overlooked in the preceding volume of this guide: Mortimer R. Procter's witty *The English University Novel*, 1957.) It is regrettable that an equally broad study has not yet been made of country-house life in Victorian fiction. Richard Gill's *Happy Rural Seat: The English Country House and the Literary Imagination* (1972) gives only cursory attention to the nineteenth-century aspects of this rich topic before proceeding into the twentieth century.

The course of empire has been surveyed more attentively. Coral Lansbury's *Arcady in Australia: The Evocation of Australia in Nineteenth-Century English Literature* (1970) suggests what images and emotions were evoked in readers' minds when characters like the Micawbers set sail for a new life down under. Susanne Howe's earlier work *Novels of Empire* (1949) is supplemented by four more recent books, especially for the end-of-the-century novelists: Alan Sandison's *The Wheel of Empire: A Study of the Imperial Idea in Some Late Nineteenth and Early Twentieth-Century Fiction* (1967), Allen J. Greenberger's *The British Image of India: A Study in the Literature of Imperialism 1880–1960* (1969), Benita Parry's *Delusions and Discoveries: Studies on India in the British Imagination 1880–1930* (1972), and Jeffrey Meyers' *Fiction and the Colonial Experience* (1973). It need hardly be remarked that four books on what is essentially the same topic, published within seven years, entail a certain redundancy.

Although Steven Marcus' *The Other Victorians: A Study of Sexuality and Pornography in Mid-Nineteenth-Century England* (1966), a revisionist account of the role of sex in Victorian life, does not deal extensively with Victorian fiction (except for pornography), it has inevitably affected all subsequent critical approaches to the problem of sex in the fiction of the time. Awareness of the social realities as Marcus describes them—the flourishing under-the-counter trade in pornography and the great prevalence (and high visibility) of prostitution—forces one to reconsider the evasiveness and euphemism with which Victorian novelists handled the extremely touchy subject of sexual attitudes and behavior.

Never an especially neglected topic, the place of women, both as authors and as characters, in Victorian fiction was canvassed afresh in the early 1970s. Traditional descriptive studies, typified by Edgar F. Harden's "The American Girl in British Fiction, 1860–1880" (*HLQ*, 1963) and a decade later by A. R. Cunningham's "The 'New Woman Fiction' of the 1890's" (*VS*, 1973), were joined by more extensive ones. Two books by Vineta Colby deal responsibly and perceptively with minor women authors. The first, *The Singular Anomaly: Women Novelists of the Nineteenth Century* (1970), is composed of extended essays on mid- and late-nineteenth-century writers—Eliza Lynn Linton, Olive Schreiner, Mrs. Humphry Ward, John Oliver Hobbes, and Vernon Lee—whose work was distinguished more by ethical and didactic purposefulness than by artistic merit. The second, *Yesterday's Woman: Domestic Realism in the English Novel* (1974), calls fresh attention to the novels of such "authoresses" as Mrs. Gore, Maria Edgeworth, Susan Ferrier, Charlotte Elizabeth Tonna, Elizabeth Sewell, and Charlotte Yonge. Their stock-in-trade was quintessentially "Victorian" as the term is commonly interpreted: a novel that was at once "bourgeois-oriented, anti-romantic, un-aristocratic, home- and family-centered," laden with sentiment, decorous sexual love, and evangelical religion.

Hazel Mews's *Frail Vessels: Woman's Role in Women's Novels from Fanny Burney to George Eliot* (1969) is essentially a compilation of synopses, without reference to the historical or literary context of the various novels and revealing no acquaintance with the relevant scholarly or critical literature. It is devoid of critical value. Considerably more stimulating are two books that appeared in 1974. Patricia Beer's *Reader, I Married Him: A Study of the Women Characters of Jane Austen, Charlotte Brontë, Elizabeth Gaskell and George Eliot* is, despite the frivolous title, a solid piece of scholarship, unburdened by case making, that "reveals a network of discrepancies concerning what came to be known as the Woman Question: between what the novelists thought in real life and the views they set forth or implied in their novels; between what they accepted for themselves and what they accepted for their heroines. Sometimes the novelist was the greater rebel, sometimes the woman. Each was consistent in herself and there was little agreement among them." Thus, Beer implies, these major women novelists do not really lend themselves to any feminist (or other doctrinaire) line. That the subject is not so simple as has sometimes been urged is also the theme of Françoise Basch's *Relative Creatures: Victorian Women in Society and the Novel*, though her historical point of view is quite distinct from Beer's focus on the texts. Basch examines the fictional characters against a "triple background: first, the contemporary system of values and what it prescribes for individuals, especially women, as their function and purpose; next, a description of the conditions of life and social segmentation of the time; finally, the work of the author and his or her psychology." In a series of chapters alternating between the "real" and the "fictional" woman, Basch suggests that in the portrayal of women in the Victorian novel one sees the "tension between ideal and reality [that] is one aspect of the problem of realism."

A number of the critical volumes already mentioned rest on the premise that the Victorian age was a time of profound spiritual and psychological trauma, even deeper and more devastating than the Victorians themselves realized. A further group of studies of the Victorians' inner life as revealed in their fiction may, by their diversity if nothing else, suitably round off this survey of recent commentary.

In "The Search for Forgiveness in Some Nineteenth-Century English Novels" (*CLS*, 1966) William A. Madden traces the secularization of a theme hitherto associated with religion, a development required by "Western man's compelling need to find, in society or in nature or, latterly, in himself, some source of grace equivalent to that offered in the Christian conception of forgiveness." Despite an enthusiastic introduction by Walter Allen, John Halperin's *Egoism and Self-Discovery in the Victorian Novel* (1974) is an unsatisfactory book; much too long, it is composed of narrative explication rather than criticism. Its theme, scarcely a fresh one, is the treatment of "the moral and psychological expansion of protagonists who begin in self-absorption and move, through the course of a tortuous ordeal of education, to a more complete self-knowledge." In Elliott B. Gose, Jr.'s *Imagination Indulged: The Irrational in the Nineteenth-Century Novel* (1972) it is the novelists, rather than the fictional characters, who are in psychic difficulties. The frequency of "Fantasy, Romance, Fairy Tale, Dream, and Ritual" in the novel convinces Gose that the four authors he studies, Emily Brontë, Dickens, Hardy, and Conrad, used fiction as a therapeutic expression of their "battle for the protean self, working against materialism, impersonality, objectivity (mere realism in art); and their novels contain patterns which could lead to the symbolic process of transformation and rebirth." Heavily Jungian in commitment, this book has the modest virtue of being a counterweight to the too heavy insistence upon the realism of Victorian fiction. No such exculpation, however, can be made of Russell M. Goldfarb's *Sexual Repression and Victorian Literature* (1970), a simplistic and superficial exercise in detecting hidden and, too often, imaginary sexual allusions in, among others, the novels of Dickens, Charlotte Brontë, and Meredith.

It is almost impossible at short range to distinguish between critical systems that are destined to fade after relatively brief lives, the victims of their own modishness, and those that will retain their pertinence and vitality across the years. No doubt it is too early to decide whether the structuralist and phenomenological schools of criticism have now told us all they have to tell us about Victorian fiction. Apart from the continuing work of a few experts, the psychoanalytic approach seems to have passed the zenith of its promise, and yet Marxist criticism, which is almost as old, continues to flourish in the hands of such practitioners as Raymond Williams and John Lucas.

A few specific lines of future inquiry, set somewhat apart from those that have been most diligently pursued in recent years, have been suggested above. In general, the most promising guideposts point in two directions. On the one hand, we are reminded that a given novel, or the totality of a novelist's work, is a product of a certain moment in history, of a certain literary situation, and of a certain unique mind and temperament, and that any kind of literature is bound to be more accurately read and more richly intelligible when it is viewed against the background of its time and its authorship. In the other direction, relatively unexplored as yet by students of Victorian fiction, lies the realm revealed a generation ago by what was then called the New Criticism. The tenet that all criticism must begin with a close reading of what the author wrote is now a platitude, but it is nonetheless true on that account. First, there must be faithful texts to work with; and, in this respect, Bradford Booth's hope that "scholarly, annotated" editions of the great novels would be forthcoming has not, for the most part, been realized, among the notable exceptions being the several volumes now published of the Clarendon Dickens and the Norton Critical Edition of *Hard Times*. We still must depend on editions that a basic law of scholarship requires us to regard as suspect until proved reliable. But the establishment of an exact text is, of course, only a means to a greater end, which is the attentive study of what the words say and imply. Stylistic analysis, as demanding and rewarding as the explication of philosophical, social, and religious ideas that has preoccupied some of the best recent critics, would seem to be one of the most attractive avenues of investigation now in prospect. Between the Victorian novel as a product of a particular moment in time and the Victorian novel as a self-contained work of verbal art, there is plenty left to discover.

BENJAMIN DISRAELI

❁

Curtis Dahl

Although there have been enlightening studies of Disraeli's individual novels and good comment on his literary career, Victoria's great prime minister has continued to attract attention primarily as a vivid personality and a skillful politician rather than as a writer. Hence the most important recent book on him has been a first-rate biography, and greater emphasis has been placed on his political and social novels than on his other fiction. Like its predecessor in the Stevenson volume, this chapter deals only with those studies that throw light on Disraeli's literary achievement and passes over those that relate wholly to political and historical matters.

Bibliography, Editions, Letters

An invaluable tool for all Disraeli studies is R. W. Stewart's thorough and clear *Benjamin Disraeli: A List of Writings by Him, and Writings about Him, with Notes* (Scarecrow Author Bibliographies, No. 7, 1972). In "The Hughenden Papers: Mother Lode of Disraeliana" (*Courier*, Syracuse Univ. Library, 1972), Onesime Piette reminds us of Syracuse University's exceptional collection of microfilm copies of the Hughenden Disraeli papers.

Though no new complete edition of the novels has yet been published, a number of paperback editions of individual titles have appeared. One of the best of these is the First Novel Library edition (1968) of *Vivian Grey*, edited by Herbert Van Thal, who reprints the first edition. Stephanie Nettell's introduction is informative, balanced, and perceptive. In keeping with the current interest in Disraeli's political fiction, *Coningsby* has flowered out in three paperback editions: Capricorn (1961), with the detailed 1904 introduction and notes by Bernard Langdon-Davies; Signet (1962), with an excellent foreword by Asa Briggs, emphasizing the novel's Young England background; and Heron Books (1968), with an introduction by Malcolm Elwin. Scholars interested in *Tancred* now have a choice of text: the 1871 and the 1877 versions, both reprinted in 1970. Anthony Hern's introduction to *Henrietta Temple* (1969) emphasizes the tension between Henrietta's pure love for Ferdinand and the cynicism of the haut monde of the reign of William IV. An edition of *Lothair*, with an introduction by A. Norman Jeffares, appeared in 1965, two reprints in 1970, and in 1975 what is undoubtedly the best modern edition, that edited by Vernon Bogdanor for the Oxford English Novels series. Based on the text of the fifth revised edition (1870), this last includes a key to the characters, a chronology of Disraeli's life, a bibliography, and textual and explanatory notes. The brief *Selections from the Novels*, edited by Eric Forbes-Boyd, joined the Falcon Prose Classics in 1968. Phillip Guedalla's 1934 edition of *Popanilla, and Other Tales* was reprinted in 1970.

Though they had biographical importance, neither the five letters from Disraeli to his sister Sarah published by C. L. Cline *(LCUT,* 1967) nor those between Disraeli and R. Shelton Mackenzie edited by David W. Tutein (*VN*, 1967) throw much light on the novels.

The most exciting development in Disraeli studies is the establishment of the Disraeli Project under the general direction of J. P. Matthews and D. M. Schurman at Queens University, Kingston, Canada. All available letters from all collections—more than sixteen thousand items—are assembled there on microfilm. An inclusive, fully annotated and introduced edition of the letters, probably in thirty-two volumes, is under way, with the first volume expected to appear in 1978. A new complete, annotated variorum edition of the novels, poems, and essays in fifteen volumes is also planned. The Queens University Library is assembling a collection of printed texts that will eventually include all Disraeli's published works. The Project offers many opportunities for those interested in research on Disraeli. Starting in the spring of 1976, a semiannual *Disraeli Newsletter* will be issued containing news of the Project and brief articles on Disraeli.

Biography

Almost certainly the most important result of recent research on Disraeli is Robert Blake's *Disraeli* (1966). Appearing fifty years after the completion of Monypenny and Buckle's book, it brings that great standard biography up to date and corrects it in the light of new studies and papers earlier unavailable. The treatment of the novels, though only rarely touching on literary technique, is helpful in placing them in their political and biographical contexts and identifying the prototypes of the characters. There is good comment on the unfinished novel *Falconet*. Park Honan is probably right in calling Blake's book "the finest recent biography of a Victorian" (*VS*, 1973, p. 461), but despite its solid virtues it does not entirely supersede the immense detail, innumerable quotations, and full discussions in Monypenny and Buckle. In a few pages commenting on how and why he wrote his biography ("Disraeli: The Problems of a Biographer," *Cornhill*, 1966), Blake sharpens his view of the great prime minister.

Beside Blake's comprehensive work, other biographical studies seem pygmy. Maurice Edelman's *Disraeli in Love* (1972), obviously based on Blake, is a fictionalizing popularization of the more lurid chapters of Disraeli's life, particularly of his love affair with Lady Sykes. Edelman's sequel, *Disraeli Rising* (1975), is frankly labeled a novel. In gossipy vein it carries the tale of Disraeli's amorous and other activities up to 1852 but adds no new serious analysis. In *Disraeli's Reminiscences* (1975) Helen M. Swartz and Marvin Swartz have edited an entertaining selection of Disraeli's witty but unreliable autobiographical notes, most of them from 1863–65. Though few if any of even the literary anecdotes relate directly to the novels, some of the stories told reappear later in *Lothair* and *Endymion*. The volume includes a brief autobiography and several arresting comments on Bulwer. Similarly, in *Benjamin Disraeli in Spain and Malta* (Salzburg Studies in English Literature, 1975) Donald Sultana finds numerous details in Disraeli's letters written to his sister during his trip to Spain and Malta in 1830–31 that were later incorporated into his novels, but Sultana's presentation is pedestrian, with the result that the details remain details. Though the focus is different, Mollie Hardwick's anecdotal *Mrs. Dizzy: The Life of Mary Anne Disraeli, Viscountess Beaconsfield* (1972) also looks beyond the political facade to the man behind. It is almost as much about Disraeli as about Mary Anne. James Ogden's chapter "The Elder and the Younger Disraeli" in his *Isaac D'Israeli* (1969) adds little new information but does usefully comment on Isaac as he appears in his son's novels. Hesketh Pearson's chapter on Disraeli in *Lives of the Wits* (1962) is gracefully unimportant. Three authors have written biographies of Disraeli designed for young readers: Manuel Komroff (1963), Olga S. Phillips (1968), and Neil Grant (1969); and there have been useful reprints of the biographies by Monypenny and Buckle (1968), Brandes (1966, 1968), and Froude (1971).

General Criticism

Raymond Maitre's *Disraëli, homme de lettres* (1963) is the broadest and most thorough of the recent general surveys. Well organized, it meticulously, though sometimes too dissectingly, analyzes the personality, the thought, and the literary work of Disraeli. Despite its many useful comments, its generalizations often seem unsatisfyingly abstract and unable to set all the details into a larger context. Richard A. Levine's *Benjamin Disraeli* (TEAS, 1968) emphasizes, perhaps overemphasizes, the importance to Disraeli's fiction of his organic concept of history, spotlighting the political trilogy and those novels that lead up to it. Levine's primary interest is in Disraeli's thought; he intriguingly follows themes through the several novels. Robert Blake's survey of the novels, "Disraeli the Novelist" (*TRSL*, 1967), makes important comments on how the original texts were expurgated for the collected edition of 1853 and points out that the social problems with which the novels deal still exist. Both Disraeli's politics and his novels, Blake maintains, have gaiety and sparkle. Bernard McCabe in his chapter on Disraeli in *Minor British Novelists* (ed. Charles A. Hoyt, 1967) goes even further, arguing that Disraeli's great talent is for comedy—a comedy that rises out of an imaginative and yet at the same time rationalistic awareness of his world.

Jerome J. McGann's article "The Dandy" (*Midway*, 1969) deftly illuminates the iconographical background of Disraeli's (and Bulwer's) dandy figures in Baudelaire and in Carlyle, but much greater recent interest has been shown in the political ideas. Marius Bewley, for instance, in a delightfully polished, succinct essay, "Towards Reading Disraeli" (*Prose*, 1972), argues that Disraeli's political interests, particularly his imaginative creation of a usable past, put his novels among the most urgent, morally alive, and serious of the middle Victorian period. Far from militating against artistic cogency, the political interests lie at the center of his art. To illustrate, Bewley intriguingly expatiates on an amusing passage in *Through the Looking Glass* as it applies to Disraeli. Both Robert Blake and Bernard McCabe also address the subject: Blake in a popular but incisive article in *History Today* (1966), which maintains that Disraeli is the best political novelist to write in English; McCabe in "Disraeli and the 'Baronial Principle': Some Versions of Romantic Medievalism" (*VN*, 1968), a stimulating article that points out Disraeli's ambivalence toward the Romantic medievalizing of Young England. In "The Imperial Dreams of Disraeli" (*PsyR*, 1966) Bronson Feldman goes on, interestingly, to analyze the psychological bases for these views and for Disraeli's passionate interest in politics. He reads the novels as expressing Disraeli's neuroses in relation to his father and the Jewish race. B. R. Jerman's "The Production of Disraeli's Trilogy" (*PBSA*, 1964), with its careful dating and illuminating explanation of Colburn's publishing methods, is another sign of the particular current interest in the political and social fiction. So, too, is the publication in 1973 of an English translation by Martin Fido of Cazamian's pioneer study *The Social Novel in England, 1830–1850*. Though Brian Beyers' "Novels and Politics" (*Contrast*, 1973) presents the stimulating thesis that Disraeli's novels, particularly *Coningsby* and *Sybil*, were important in educating the new middle classes on social and political questions, the article breaks little new ground. Far more piquant will be Richard W. Davis' brief biography *Disraeli*, forthcoming in 1976 in the Library of World Biography. With refreshing irreverence it will refuse to take either Disraeli's political theories or his novels seriously, shrewdly and wittily judging both as essentially insincere and opportunistic. Davis' attitude should arouse lively controversy.

Three recent doctoral dissertations are worthy of note. Analyzing nine novels in regard to characters and social scene, physical setting, and narrative technique, Marcia R. Lieberman ("Disraeli the Novelist," Brandeis 1966) finds that there is a special, recognizable Disraelian fictional world and response to that world. Singling out the satire in the early poems and novels, Myrna M. Mosher ("Benjamin Disraeli's Early Satires," Univ. of Kansas 1970) concludes that at their best the novels are pungent commentaries on the human species. Leonard Turk ("Disraeli and the Reviewers," Univ. of Massachusetts 1973) usefully remarks that earlier reviewers did not see the innovative quality of Disraeli's experiments in the novel form. Even more helpful and full, however, is a recent published volume by Disraeli's bibliographer, R. W. Stewart. *Disraeli's Novels Reviewed, 1826–1968* (1975), an excellent supplement to Dahl's chapter in the Stevenson *Guide*, reprints with concise introductory and explanatory notes representative English, American, and European reviews, brief articles, and even personal letters difficult to find elsewhere. In the first-rate critical summary of Disraeli's fiction in his general introduction, Stewart states that he has "sought to balance contemporary and later comments and to present a representative selection of views, favorable and unfavorable, from both the 'serious' critics and more ephemeral commentators." For any student wishing to see Disraeli the novelist through the eyes of his own time this clearly edited book is essential.

Studies of Individual Novels

Of all Disraeli's novels *Sybil* currently attracts the most scholarly attention. Letters written to the Disraelis by nineteenth-century readers of *Sybil* have been compiled and edited by Sheila M. Smith in *Mr. Disraeli's Readers* (1966). They graphically illustrate how the novel struck contemporaries and why it was so exciting to them. In "Blue Books and Victorian Novelists" (*RES*, 1970) and more specifically in "Willenhall and Wodgate: Disraeli's Use of Blue Book Evidence" (*RES*, 1962) Smith points out how the novelist artistically transformed factual material from reports of the Children's Employment Commission and the 1843 *Report on the Employment of Women and Children in Agriculture*. In "Tory Radicalism and 'The Two Nations' in Disraeli's *Sybil*" (*VN*, 1972) Patrick Brantlinger cogently argues that Disraeli is unsuccessful in attempting to weld together Toryism and Radicalism, that he has no real sympathy for either the aristocracy or the poor, and that the artistic weakness of the book grows out of its political contradictions. In another useful article—"The Case against Trade Unions in Early Victorian Fiction" (*VS*, 1969)—Brantlinger points out that *Sybil* reflects Disraeli's fundamental antagonism to the trade union movement. Also concerned with Disraeli's social views, Beth R. Arnold ("Disraeli and Dickens on Young England," *Dkn*, 1967) parallels the treatment of Young England by Disraeli and Dickens and, perhaps pushing her point too far, reads *A Tale of Two Cities* as a deliberate answer to Disraeli's optimistic Young Englandism. Benny Green's "Goodbye to the Hustings" (*Spectator*, 1974) contains only a slight comment on Disraeli's treatment of elections in the novel and also compares him with Dickens; in contrast, Daniel R. Schwarz's "Art and Argument in Disraeli's *Sybil*" (*JNT*, 1974) is a major article that makes a convincing artistic defense of the novel. Schwarz thinks that it has been consistently underrated. Old critical standards, he argues, do not apply to the new panoramic political novel like *Sybil*, in which social concern and political ideas are more important than individual lives. Though specifically directed only to the one novel, Schwarz's conclusions throw light on much of Disraeli's fiction.

Though *Sybil* has attracted the lioness' share of attention, good work has been done on other novels, too. In "The Initiation Motif in Benjamin Disraeli's *Coningsby*" (*SoQ*, 1971) Paul Mitchell carefully traces the maturation of the hero in *Coningsby*, while Thomas J. Kemme's unpublished dissertation "A Study of Benjamin Disraeli's *Coningsby*" (Loyola 1971) points out how many of Isaac Disraeli's ideas surface in the book. Donald Greene's "The Wicked Marquess: Disraeli to Thackeray to Waugh" (*EWN*, 1973) sees Waugh's Marquess of Marchmain in *Brideshead Revisited* as a second-generation descendant of Disraeli's Marquess of Monmouth. A similar study in literary history is Charles C. Nickerson's "Vivian Grey and Dorian Gray" (*TLS*, 14 Aug. 1969), which suggests Disraeli's *Vivian Grey* as a major source of Wilde's *Dorian Gray*. Roland A. Duerksen's chapter "Shelley and Disraeli" in his *Shelleyan Ideas in Victorian Literature* (1966) argues that in *Venetia* Disraeli defended his own switch from radicalism to conservatism by picturing Shelley's idealistic liberalism as impractical and imagining an older Shelley turning away from it. The question of the relationship between Thackeray and the novelist St. Barbe in *Endymion* has called forth two diametrically opposed answers. Basing his conclusions on Gordon Ray's edition of Thackeray's *Letters and Private Papers*, David E. Painting in "Thackeray vs. Disraeli" (*QR*, 1964) concludes that St. Barbe is an astonishingly accurate portrait of Thackeray. Four years later James D. Merritt in "The Novelist St. Barbe in Disraeli's *Endymion*: Revenge on Whom?" (*NCF*, 1968) asserts that there is no conclusive evidence that St. Barbe is Thackeray but that he may possibly be Carlyle.

Two other able studies—they come two by two like animals to the Ark!—analyze Disraeli's religious ideas. Painting, whose article on *Endymion* is mentioned above, in a careful analysis ("Disraeli and the Roman Catholic Church," *QR*, 1966) shows that by the time of the composition of *Lothair* Disraeli's sympathy for the Roman Catholic Church had become much more ambivalent than it had been earlier. Levine, also mentioned above, in "Disraeli's *Tancred* and 'The Great Asian Mystery'" (*NCF*, 1967) convincingly demonstrates that, though much criticized, *Tancred* is actually a coherent and organic work, explicable in terms of Disraeli's belief that "Eastern" religion is needed to underpin "Western" political reform. Another brace of articles are more bibliographical. Robert Blake's "The Dating of

Endymion" (*RES*, 1966) skillfully establishes the three stages of composition of *Endymion* from Montagu Corry's notes and other evidence. In "Disraeli's *Endymion*: A Case Study" in *Essays in the History of Publishing in Celebration of the 250th Anniversary of the House of Longman, 1774–1974* (ed. Asa Briggs, 1974), Annabel Jones gives a remarkably full and detailed history of the writing, publishing, reception, and comment on the same novel, a history that clearly illuminates publishing practices of the day.

Much of the recent scholarship on Disraeli has been concerned with his political, social, and religious ideas. There is room, I think, for more studies such as McCabe's and McGann's that analyze the literary art rather than the thought of Disraeli the novelist. For he did produce a new and special kind of novel with its own rules, techniques, and comic quality. Such literary analysis will be greatly facilitated if (as proposed) the Queens University Disraeli Project publishes new, textually accurate variorum editions of the novels. The publication of a complete edition of the letters should also provide bases for deeper insights into the fiction, but one hopes that in the mass of new textual and biographical data the zest, wit, and unique comedy of Disraeli's fiction will not be forgotten.

EDWARD BULWER-LYTTON

Curtis Dahl

Often pompous and wearisomely long-winded, Edward Bulwer-Lytton in the period covered by this guide has attracted less critical attention than he may deserve. Yet several important studies of his thought and one major assessment of his total achievement have appeared. Critics have interestingly reassessed his historical fiction and paid particular attention to his occult and utopian novels.

Bibliography, Editions, Letters

A complete and accurate bibliography of Bulwer is still greatly needed. There is nowhere a truly complete list of everything he wrote and published; his contributions to periodicals, both those he edited and others, need to be fully documented. Probably many anonymous pieces, in both English and American periodicals, still remain unidentified. Nor is there a full list of extant manuscripts. Since 1962 the *Wellesley Index to Victorian Periodicals* (1962) has made a start by identifying and listing Bulwer's contributions to *Blackwood's*, and Volume III of the National Library of Scotland's *Catalogue of Manuscripts Acquired since 1925* (1968) has described letters and manuscripts among the Blackwood papers in its collection, but surveys of other periodicals and other collections need to be made. There is, for instance, no published description of the letters and manuscripts in the Hertford County Records Office or at Knebworth, nor are there printed lists of the many letters and manuscripts in the Pierpont Morgan Library (e.g., of *Alice; or, The Mysteries, Ernest Maltravers, Harold*, parts of *The Last Days of Pompeii*, and *Zanoni*). Other possible depositories have not been thoroughly investigated. Though one is in preparation at Brown University by Leo Flanagan, no full bibliography of criticism of Bulwer exists. Much remains to be done.

Two outstanding editions of novels by Bulwer have been published in the last few years. In 1967 Herbert Van Thal edited the First Novel Library *Falkland*, with an introduction by Park Honan. In 1972 appeared a first-rate reprint, edited by Jerome J. McGann, of the second (1828) edition of *Pelham*, with full textual apparatus. Rosicrucian interest in Bulwer's occult novels has resulted in paperback publications of *Zanoni* (1971) and *Vril: The Power of the Coming Race* (1972), both with brief prefaces by Paul Allen. Robert Lee Wolff's edition of the letters of the minor novelist Mary Elizabeth Braddon, "Devoted Disciple: The Letters of Mary Elizabeth Braddon to Sir Edward Bulwer-Lytton, 1862–1873" (*HLB*, 1974), includes two brief notes by Bulwer and throws light on an unusual literary relationship. Far more important are the series of letters edited by Malcolm O. Usrey in his 1964 Texas Technological College dissertation, "The Letters of Sir Edward Bulwer-Lytton to the Editors of *Blackwood's Magazine*, 1840–1873, in the National Archives of Scotland." Dealing with Bulwer's publication in *Blackwood's* of novels, poems, essays, plays, and speeches, these give real insight into his career as a working man of letters. Standish Meacham has filled an important gap by issuing a new and well-edited edition of *England and the English* (1970), with an introduction pointing out that significant book's novel-like elements. Despite this good work, a new, complete, textually authoritative, and, if possible, variorum edition of the novels and tales is much needed, as is the publication of a full collection of letters. Because of Bulwer's wide acquaintance with other literary figures and his diverse interests in theater, magazines, criticism, art, politics, and other areas, the latter would be an exceptionally important and interesting contribution to Victorian scholarship.

Biography

What little biographical notice Bulwer has received since 1962 was occasioned by the centenary, in 1973, of his death. In connection with the Centenary Exhibition at Knebworth, Sibylla Jane Flower, who is working on a full biography, published her forty-seven-page *Bulwer-Lytton: An Illustrated Life of the First Baron Lytton* (1973). Notices of the exhibition, including short comments on Bulwer's life, works, and influence, appeared in *Country Life* (in an article by Christopher McIntosh) and *Burlington Magazine* (in an article by Keith Roberts). In the same year Robert Blake wrote an anecdotal centenary essay for *Cornhill Magazine* stressing the many parallels between Bulwer and Disraeli in both literature and politics. Another centenary essay, this one by Allen C. Christensen ("Edward Bulwer-Lytton, First Baron Lytton of Knebworth, 25 May 1803–18 May 1873," *NCF*, 1973), emphasizes the importance of Bulwer's theory of fiction, his conscious craftsmanship as a novelist, and the strange vitality of the best of his work. The more workaday side of Bulwer's career comes out clearly in James J. Barnes' well-researched article "Edward Bulwer and the Publishing Firm of Harper and Brothers" (*AL*, 1936). Using letters in the Hertford County Records Office, Barnes documents both Bulwer's extraordinary popularity in America and the difficulties faced by a British author and his legitimate publisher in an age of piracy. Barnes's study admirably supplements Usrey's edition of Bulwer's letters to *Blackwood's*.

General Criticism

The best brief recent general critical summary of Bulwer as a novelist is Park Honan's admirably compressed but wide-ranging introduction to the 1967 edition of *Falkland* noticed above. Honan emphasizes Bulwer's skill in mixing seemingly incompatible appeals in a single novel, his combining of various kinds of novels in one. Honan's analysis of Bulwer's prose style is probably the best that has appeared anywhere. In contrast, Arno Schmidt's dialogue "Was wird er damit machen: Nachrichten aus dem Leben eines Lands" in *Der Triton mit dem Sonnenschirm* (1969) merely touches lightly on a number of his novels and aspects of his career. It does, however, point up his popularity in Germany. Edwin M. Eigner's "Raphael in Oxford Street: Bulwer's Accommodation to the Realists" (in *The Nineteenth Century Writer and His Audience*, ed. Harold Orel and George J. Worth, UKPHS, 1969) is far deeper. Based on wide research in printed sources and also in manuscript materials in the Hertford Record Office, it is a fascinating study of how Bulwer in *The Caxtons* and several succeeding novels, reluctantly and against his basically Romantic critical principles and theory, succumbed to the contemporary fashion for realism—and thereby, ironically, made himself a tremendous popular success. Even more exciting than Honan's and Eigner's excellent article is Allan C. Christensen's *Edward Bulwer-Lytton: The Fiction of New Regions* (forthcoming in 1977). This seems likely to prove the most inclusive and broadly based study yet written and the first to set the whole series of novels in logical groupings and rational sequence. Though all scholars will not agree with Christensen's partly mythic approach or with the details of his schematization, all will read his book with profit as the first really stimulating and inclusive full-length treatment of Bulwer's oeuvre.

Studies of Special Aspects and Film Versions

Relations to Other Authors

Bulwer's relationships with other authors continues to be a popular subject. In addition to Wolff's record of his friendship with Mary Braddon, G. R. Thompson's "Poe's Readings of *Pelham*: Another Source for 'Tintinnabulation' and Other Piquant Expressions" (*AL*, 1969) shows how important Bulwer was to Poe; B. G. Knepper's "Shaw's Debt to *The Coming Race*" (*JML*, 1971) convincingly demonstrates that Bernard Shaw adapted many Bulwerian ideas in *Back to Methuselah* and other works; and John Y. Le Bourgeois's "Swinburne, Lord Lytton, and John Forster" (*N&Q*, 1972) documents how at the time of the moral hullabaloo over *Poems and Ballads* Bulwer helped Swinburne and introduced him to Forster. In "Michael Angelo Titmarsh and the Knebworth Apollo" (*Costerus*, 1974) Anthea Trodd shows how much effect Thackeray's ten-year campaign of burlesque had both on Bulwer and on Thackeray himself: Bulwer revised his novels to remove satirized passages; Bulwer's faults led Thackeray toward the realism of *Vanity Fair*. The relationship between Bulwer and Dickens has stimulated the most interest of all. On the basis of a study of Bulwer's manuscript letters Sibylla Jane Flower has written a general account of the friendship, "Charles Dickens and Edward Bulwer-Lytton" (*Dkn*, 1973), which includes Bulwer's remarks on Dickens' novels and Dickens' on Bulwer's. Edwin M. Eigner and Joseph M. Fradin in "Bulwer-Lytton and Dickens' Jo" (*NCF*, 1969) find the source of Dickens' crossing-sweeper in *Bleak House* in Beck, a crossing-sweeper in *Lucretia*. Eigner's "Bulwer-Lytton and the Changed Ending of *Great Expectations*" (*NCF*, 1970) argues from letters that Bulwer's advice to make the ending a happy one was based much more on literary theory than on an effort to make the novel popular. All of these essays are interesting, but none is world-shaking.

Historical Novels

Over the last few years lively and productive controversy has arisen over Bulwer's historical fiction, with the various critics assessing it largely on the basis of their own political preconceptions. Moderate critics have emphasized literary and historical values, while critics further to the left have attacked Bulwer's view of history. Thus, James C. Simmons in "The Novelist as Historian: An Unexplored Tract of Victorian Historiography" (*VS*, 1971; and, in altered form, in his *The Novelist as Historian*, 1973) praises Bulwer as the innovator and foremost exponent of a new type of historical fiction stressing research and factual accuracy; John Maynard, to the contrary, harshly criticizes Bulwer's historical romances as gross examples of "dishonesty in avoiding a general view of history" and accuses the author of exploiting history almost entirely for its sensational and romantic interest ("Broad Canvas, Narrow Perspective: The Problem of the English Historical Novel in the Nineteenth Century," in Jerome Buckley, ed., *The Worlds of Victorian Fiction*, 1975). In similar manner, the Marxist critic Georg Lukács (*The Historical Novel*, 1937; trans. Hannah Mitchell and Stanley Mitchell, 1962) singles out Bulwer's historical novels as representing the worst aspects of bourgeois Romantic fiction's characteristic separation of fictional milieu from real life. Avrom Fleishman, however, in *The English Historical Novel* (1971) holds that the greatest interest of these novels lies in their close involvement with contemporary political controversy. The whole discussion is well worth study as showing the continued vitality of the Victorian historical novel and its relevance to modern artistic and political concerns.

Utopian and Occult Fiction

Current interest in utopian literature and the occult has turned a spotlight on *The Coming Race, Zanoni,* and *A Strange Story.* By far the most thorough critical treatment of the first of these is Hans Ulrich Seeber's "Gegenutopie und Roman: Bulwer-Lyttons 'The Coming Race' (1871)" (*DVLG,* 1971). In perhaps almost too orderly a fashion Seeber considers the book as philosophical statement in fiction, as satire, and as romance. A condensed English version of Seeber's excellently thorough article appeared in *Moreana* (1971). Angèle Botros Samaan's long "Bulwer Lytton and the Rise of the Utopian Novel" (Cairo Univ. *Bull. of the Faculty of Arts, Eur. Sec.,* 1964) provides many pertinent facts but does not conclusively make its point that *The Coming Race* largely caused the proliferation of utopian novels in the 1870s. G. Marc'hadour briefly notices the novel's hundredth birthday in "Lytton's *The Coming Race* (1971): A Utopian Centenary" (*Moreana,* 1971). One of the most spirited critiques is Geoffrey Wagner's "A Forgotten Satire: Bulwer-Lytton's *The Coming Race*" (*NCF,* 1964). Writing during the ferment of the 1960s, Wagner stimulatingly sees the novel as foreshadowing modern criticism of American democratic and mechanistic values and amusingly views Zee as the embodiment of the terrifyingly competent and dangerous American New Woman. Bulwer's novels both of the past and of the future, it appears, have present-day relevance.

The best study of the occult in Bulwer—and one of the best topical studies of that author to appear in the last decade—is Robert Lee Wolff's "Strange Stories: The Occult Fiction of Sir Edward Bulwer-Lytton" in his *Strange Stories and Other Explorations in Victorian Fiction* (1971). Detailing as no one has previously done Bulwer's extensive reading in philosophical, occult, and Neoplatonic literature, Wolff proceeds to the most careful, learned, and perceptive critical examination of *Zanoni* and *A Strange Story* that has been done and also shines fascinating sidelights on *Godolphin, The Last Days of Pompeii, The Coming Race,* and "The Haunted and the Haunters." His footnotes supply excellent guidance to sources and criticism. Wolff's indispensable study of the occult in Bulwer is supplemented by Richard Kelly's narrower but ingenious essay on "The Haunted and the Haunters," "The Haunted House of Bulwer-Lytton" (*SSF,* 1971). Kelly postulates that the mystery in the story involves Bulwer's electromagnetic explanation of Daniel Home's famous powers as a medium.

Other Studies of Individual Novels

Three studies of individual novels remain to be noted. The first is Thurman Brandon's solid dissertation on the impact of Bulwer's *Harold, the Last of the Saxon Kings* on the image of that monarch in literature ("The Treatment of England's King Harold II in Selected Works of Modern English Imaginative Literature," Univ. of South Carolina 1971). The second is James C. Simmons' intriguing article arguing that the immediate huge popularity of *The Last Days of Pompeii* was due in part to the chance that its publication in 1834 coincided with the most destructive eruption of Vesuvius in recent centuries ("Bulwer and Vesuvius: The Topicality of *The Last Days of Pompeii*," *NCF*, 1969). The third is Jerome J. McGann's introduction to the 1972 edition of the 1828 text of *Pelham* mentioned above. In by far the best extant analysis of the novel, McGann takes it seriously as a bildungsroman, relates it to Bulwer's theory of the novel, and shows how its literary style and form blend with its often unnoticed intellectual depth to make it what McGann considers Bulwer's finest novel. It is pleasant to end this survey of the criticism with what George Landow in his review of McGann's *Pelham* calls "the finest commentary I know on Bulwer-Lytton" (*Novel*, 1974, p. 271).

Film Versions

What of the treatment of Bulwer's works by those modern magicians, the moviemakers? Through much of the nineteenth century the drama and spectacle of *The Last Days of Pompeii* made it a favorite subject for fireworks extravaganzas, and as early as 1898 it appeared on film. The Italian version of that year was followed by seven other films based on the book, including a well-known American version in 1935. Other films derived from Bulwer's work are *Eugene Aram* (1914, 1915, 1924), *Night and Morning* (1915), *Paul Clifford* (1927), and *Night Comes Too Soon*, the film version of "The Haunted and the Haunters" (1947). None of these films has become a classic.

Future scholarship might well be devoted to collecting and publishing Bulwer's letters, to identifying his unsigned contributions to periodicals, and to studying textual changes in the novels. In addition, Bulwer needs to be taken more seriously as a literary artist. Too often he has been regarded only historically as the initiator of various trends in nineteenth-century fiction, as a Baptist preparing the way of various Lords, or as a barometer of early Victorian taste. He was not merely "the cause that wit is in other men" but "witty" in himself. Individual novels need further critical study, as do special topics such as the occult (the subject of Robert Wolff's study) and Bulwer's reading in other areas (see, for instance, Richard A. Zipser's "Edward Bulwer-Lytton and Germany," Diss. Johns Hopkins 1972). It would be useful also to know more about Bulwer as editor of the *New Monthly* and about the controversies concerning his alleged plagiarism from various authors. Bulwer did indeed, as Tennyson wrote, kill the girls and thrill the boys "with dandy pathos" when he wrote, and in his style and ideas as well as in actuality he was often "the padded man—that wears the stays." But he deserves, and is increasingly getting, a fairer hearing in a fairer court. Because of his political career Disraeli will always attract wider attention, but Bulwer, a far more serious and multifaceted author, may better reward serious critical literary inquiry.

CHARLES DICKENS

❁

Philip Collins

Ada Nisbet opened her chapter in the 1964 predecessor of this guide with a few "Gradgrindian facts" to indicate the increasing pace of Dickens studies —the number of doctoral dissertations in this field rising from seven in the 1930s to thirty-two in the 1950s, and so on. We were then but young in deed, as Macbeth put it; one mid-seventies survey listed twenty doctoral dissertations completed in the previous three months (*DSN*, March 1974). Every quarter, the invaluable checklist in the *Dickens Studies Newsletter* records another hundred or more new published items, and in a 1971 report on research in progress, for instance, it rounded up 125 academics working on Dickens—in a survey confined largely to the United States. The extra spate of publications occasioned by the centenary in 1970 merely provided further evidence that he enjoyed a status hardly conceivable even twenty years earlier. As Nisbet writes, "the mid-twentieth-century rebirth of Dickens is as much a phenomenon as his leap to fame with the publication of *Pickwick*" (*NCF*, 1970, p. 380).

Dickens has benefited from the continuing boom in Victorian studies and indeed in publishing generally (two thirds of all the books ever published have appeared since 1952), but there are special features of Dickens' genius that have lately made him seem increasingly attractive, important, and explicable, his work having chimed, for instance, both with critical developments away from mimetic assumptions about the novel and with the nature of much important recent fiction. As Jerome Beaty remarks, "No nineteenth-century novelist stands to gain more than Dickens" from such changes in critical perspective (*DSN*, 1975, p. 93). American critics, inheriting a long transcendental-symbolic tradition of thought and creative achievement, are perhaps particularly well placed to achieve rapport with this Dickens; this is the contention of a polemical essay, by an Englishman, contrasting the boldness and imaginative insight of recent American Dickens criticism with the pusillanimous thinness of the leading English Dickensians, most of whom (he observes) are, like the uptight grandees of Britain's civil service, men marred for life by Oxbridge (Robert Giddings, *DSN*, 1975). Two other remarks on the significance of Dickens today: Angus Wilson notes particularly "the horror, comedy, the black absurdity with which he tried to resolve, at once crying and laughing, the deep despair which he felt about the alienation of men and women in London, the first great industrial monster of modern times" (*Adam*, 1971, p. 12); and Nisbet contends in her 1970 essay, cited above, "The twentieth century is more like Dickens' world than the nineteenth." Dickens may indeed seem notably "relevant" to students today, and there is *some* point in seeing him, Jan Kott-like, as "Dickens Our Contemporary." But, and inevitably, Dickens is Richard D. Altick's main instance in his argument for reading Victorian fiction in its historical context ("Victorian Readers and the Sense of the Present," *Midway*, 1970).

Over a hundred book-length studies of Dickens have been published in English since 1962. I note ruefully, from George Ford's "Dickens in the 1960s" (*Dkn*, 1970)—which offers an alternative and more succinct view of much of my field—that the editor of *Bibliographies of Studies in Victorian Literature* (1967) computes that Dickens has lately been the subject of well over twice as many scholarly books and essays as any other Victorian author, and that the editor of *Nineteenth-Century Fiction* records (in 1968) that Dickens, level-pegging with Henry James (the original Dons' Delight) as his would-be contributors' favorite, is the subject of more than one in eight of the essays submitted to him. Dickens bibliography is a White Man's Grave, and I must acknowledge that I have not attempted to read everything published about my author during the years covered by this guide.

My limitations are the less injurious to the project, however, because of the recent improvement in Dickens checklists, bibliographies, etc.; these I describe in detail, and they can direct the student to items that I do not include. I do mention a few items that I have not read, usually citing some respectable authority for an opinion of their merits. I have generally omitted unpublished dissertations. To save space, voluminous Dickens commentators are referred to by surname only—names, like Fielding and Monod, that are "Familiar in our mouths as *Household Words*." Compilations are referred to by editor and date of publication: thus, "Tomlin, 1969" signifies *Charles Dickens 1812–1870: A Centenary Volume*, edited by E. W. F. Tomlin (1969). I make little attempt to cite items written in the many languages that I do not read. I would be more distressed by this limitation were it not that Ada Nisbet, with an international team of colleagues, will soon publish her *International Bibliography* (see below). Titles are often omitted if the articles can be easily located without them. Another large omission is dramatizations, radio and television versions, recordings, etc. The specialist Dickens periodicals list, or review, most of these, and Ana Laura Zambrano has compiled an international checklist of "Feature Motion Pictures Adapted from Dickens" (*DSN*, 1974–75; see also Johan Daisne, *Dictionnaire filmographique*, Vol. I, 1971, and Dilys Powell, "Dickens on Film," *Dkn*, 1970). I regret not discussing the more significant, at least, of these dramatic versions, staged or electronic, for they are a continual witness to Dickens' widespread appeal outside academia.

Dickens remains, too, one of the select band of classic novelists widely read for pleasure even by the unsophisticated. George Ford, surveying Dickens' fortunes in the 1960s, reported annual sales in the United States alone of well over a million copies. The continued worldwide existence of the Dickens Fellowship, a predominantly nonacademic though very knowledgeable body, is another instance of this unique standing, and its journal, *The Dickensian*, was edited by "amateurs" for its first sixty-four years (see *TLS* leader, 15 Feb. 1968). Nor is it irrelevant to note, as an element in Dickens' enduring "significance," that the Dickens Fellowship continues to support the Royal National Institute for the Blind (*Dkn*, 1973). Unlike his critical rebirth, Dickens' popularity is of course no "mid-twentieth-century phenomenon" but a continuation of the "love-affair with the reading-public" (Kathleen Tillotson's phrase) that began with *Pickwick* and that Philip Collins has lately reexplored (*Dkn*, 1974).

Manuscripts and Catalogues

Since publication of the 1964 *Guide*, a number of manuscripts and other research items have become more available to students. What were probably the three last great private collections of Dickensiana have lately come into institutional ownership: those assembled, respectively, by the Comte de Suzannet, J. F. Dexter, and Colonel Richard Gimbel. Selected "Treasures from the Suzannet Collection" formed the Centenary Exhibition at the Dickens House, London (catalogue by Michael Slater, 1970), and subsequently the Comtesse donated nearly half of the collection to Dickens House, the rest being auctioned at Sotheby's, 22–23 November 1971 (see *TLS*, 10 Dec. 1971). The Sotheby's catalogue, with sale particulars, is appended to Slater's *Catalogue of the Suzannet Charles Dickens Collection* (1975), which also lists the many important items Suzannet had donated during his lifetime. Exceptionally rich in autograph letters and documents (443 items) and in manuscript material relating to Dickens, this Dickens House collection also contains fragments of the *Pickwick* and *Nickleby* manuscripts, drawings and paintings, playbills and other theatrical items, and many presentation copies of special interest. Particularly valuable are six of Dickens' public-reading "prompt copies," the only examples of his work in this genre now held in Britain. The Suzannet items sold at Sotheby's included one other prompt copy, for *Mrs. Gamp*; further fragments of the *Pickwick* and *Nickleby* manuscripts (the *Nickleby* fragment went to the British Library); and over a hundred autograph letters. On other recent acquisitions by Dickens House (Carlton, Foyle, and Peyrouton collections), see the *Dickensian*, 1974–76.

The British Library acquired the Dexter Collection in 1969: see the library's *Charles Dickens: The J. F. Dexter Collection* (1974). Items include manuscripts of two essays and of the 1850 Preface to *Oliver Twist*, many letters, fragmentary corrected proofs of *The Old Curiosity Shop*, sketches for and proof copies of Cruikshank and Browne illustrations, and sets of part issues (in which the library had previously been weak). A catalogue of the Gimbel Collection, bequeathed to Yale University Library, is being prepared (see John Podeschi, *TLS*, 7 Jan. 1972); some idea of its contents may be obtained from the catalogue of an exhibition mounted by Colonel Gimbel (*YULG*, 1962), though his bequest excludes some of the items exhibited and includes some others. Manuscripts include "The Perils of Certain English Prisoners" and pages of *Pickwick* and *Oliver Twist*, and there are corrected proofs of parts of *Drood* and of the 1868 reprint of *The Battle of Life* and *The Haunted Man*. The Rosenbach Museum, Philadelphia, also possesses fragments of early manuscripts (*Pickwick* and *Nickleby*), besides other items; see the museum's *A Selection from Our Shelves* (comp. Clive E. Driver, 1973). The Dickens manuscripts—all of nonfictional works—in the Huntington Library, San Marino, are listed by H. C. Schulz (*HLQ*, 1968).

Many libraries produced catalogues relating to exhibitions held in 1970 or celebrated the centenary with some other publication; the *Dickensian* and *Dickens Studies Newsletter*, 1970–71, should be consulted for accounts of exhibitions and listings of catalogues. Outstanding among these were the Victoria and Albert Museum's *Charles Dickens* (1970) and Lola L. Szladits' *Charles Dickens 1812–1870: An Anthology Chosen from Materials in the Berg Collection* (1970). The Victoria and Albert catalogue—a model of its kind, in scholarly, conceptual, aesthetic, and typographical respects—besides presenting a documentary and visual narrative of Dickens' life and career has special sections on "Dickens at Work" (from notes and manuscript through galley proofs to first publication) and on such ancillary topics as his theatrical and editorial activities. Szladits draws felicitously on the Berg's many unpublished letters and drawings and on various manuscripts, proofs, portraits, etc. Both books are splendidly illustrated. The original Victoria and Albert catalogue of its Forster Collection has been reprinted (1971) with an introduction by K. J. Fielding. Recent acquisitions by the Berg Collection include proof sheets of the *Mrs. Gamp* reading.

The VanderPoel Dickens Collection at Austin, Texas, has lately been much augmented. It is particularly rich in part issues, in early editions (English, American, and other), and in portraits and extra illustrations, and it has notably strong *Pickwick* and *Carol* sections and a creditable number of autograph letters. Unfortunately its *Catalogue* (ed. Sr. Lucile Carr, 1968) has many bibliographical shortcomings (see *TLS*, 26 Feb. 1970, and *Dkn*, 1970, p. 251, where Timothy D'Arch Smith was moved by this occasion to generalize, disconcertingly, that "No major English author, with the exception perhaps of Milton and Thackeray, has received such universal bibliographical offhandedness as Dickens"). Another collection has lately been catalogued, but it is less rich in research materials—the Reed Collection in Dunedin Public Library (*Charles Dickens*, rev. ed., 1970, comp. Mary A. Ronnie; see also notes on some items, in A. H. Reed's *Charles Dickens: A Centenary Tribute*, 1970). The Free Library of Philadelphia, which now has over a thousand autograph letters, acquired in 1964 the manuscript of *The Life of Our Lord.* Among its Dickens parerga are some comic duologues dating from the 1860s (*NCF*, 1977).

Electronics have lately speeded the Dickens industry. The novel manuscripts and proofs at the Victoria and Albert and the manuscripts and autograph letters at Dickens House have been microfilmed by EP Microfilm Ltd., and the Wisbech manuscript of *Great Expectations* has been microfilmed by the Scolar Press. Other important microfilm/microfiche reproductions include those of *Household Words* (University Microfilms), *All the Year Round* (AMS Press), and the *Dickensian*, 1905–74 (Harvester Press). An astonishing number of out-of-print Dickens items have been republished photographically, the most active firms being Haskell House (New York), Folcroft Press (Folcroft, Pa.), and Gregg International (Farnborough, Hampshire, Eng.). Some items have been reprinted by more than one firm, and some items are so obscure that I, for one, have never heard of them; but such out-of-print essentials for the Dickens student as the Nonesuch *Letters*, Ley's edition of Forster, and Dickens' *Miscellaneous Papers* seem not to have been reprinted. Regrettably, few of the reprints contain editorial matter explaining why the book is worth reprinting or how it relates to subsequent scholarship, though some Gregg items have useful introductions. Strangely, few items by Dickens himself have been photographically reprinted in book form—only, I think, the *Carol* manuscript (1967; paperback, 1971), the two reading texts mentioned below, and a *Nickleby* in its 1838–39 part issue (1973). A facsimile of some more public-reading prompt copies is in prospect.

Bibliographies and Other Aids

This area of Dickens studies has improved enormously in recent years. Before 1964 the best guide was William Miller's erratic and inadequate *The Dickens Student and Collector* (1946). Now the field has been professionally surveyed and is kept in constant trim by the specialist periodicals discussed below. The most substantial, helpful, and critically acute survey is Ada Nisbet's, in the Stevenson *Guide*. Much the longest chapter in that book, it was immediately recognized as a paragon of its kind. Nisbet's expected *International Bibliography* of Dickens, long in preparation with the help of correspondents in many countries (see *DSN*, 1975), will certainly be the definitive work for our generation.

Fielding's British Council booklet *Charles Dickens* (1953, regularly rev.), the most helpful short survey of materials, has a select bibliography. A. O. J. Cockshut's "Dickens Criticism" (*CS*, 1964) is too brief for research purposes, but critically interesting. Slater's chapter in *The English Novel: Select Bibliographical Guides* (ed. A. E. Dyson, 1974) is judicious. Collins' Dickens entry in the *NCBEL* (1969) has been offprinted (*A Dickens Bibliography*, 1970, obtainable from Dickens House). Useful when one has mastered the curious conventions of *NCBEL*, this lists items under various aspects of

Dickens' career and under major works. Joseph Gold's *The Stature of Dickens: A Centenary Bibliography* (1971) complements it, having much fuller entries on individual novels (but none on other works except the *Carol*), and including a section on doctoral dissertations. Over half the book, unfortunately, consists of a simple chronological list of 1,948 more general items; it would be more useful if items had been grouped under topics, cross-references supplied, and an analytical index provided. There is an author index, helpful for tracing items if one remembers their authorship but forgets their location. Neither Collins nor Gold indicates the scope or merits of the items listed, but R. C. Churchill does so liberally, in his *Bibliography of Dickensian Criticism 1836–1975* (1975), and he quotes snippets to indicate critics' lines of approach. Intent on demonstrating, inter alia, the neglected merits of early twentieth-century criticism and listing items under many "Dickens and Such-and-Such" (or "So-and-So") headings, Churchill has his uses; but his compilation is disappointing, being cranky, underinformed, and self-applauding. Alan M. Cohn (see below), who promises a full new bibliography, has a great opportunity.

Studies in Dickens' Reputation

J. Don Vann's "Checklist of Dickens Criticism 1963–1967" (*SNNTS*, 1969) updates Nisbet's chapter in the Stevenson *Guide* and Lauriat Lane, Jr., offers an "overview" of Dickens Studies, 1958–68 (*SNNTS*, 1969). I have not seen John J. Fenstermaker's "Dickens Criticism 1940–1970: An Analytical Subject Index" (Diss. Ohio State Univ. 1973), but it sounds useful. Peter Gall's *Die moderne Kritik über Charles Dickens* (Wintherthur, 1970) is analytical, having sections on such topics as "Dickens ein Dadaist," "Dickens ein Marxist?" "Dickens ein Symbolist," and "Dickens ein Vorfreudianer?" Current studies are fully listed and discussed in the specialist periodicals on Dickens (see below). The centenary occasioned surveys of his critical fortunes, past and present and in many lands, and of special aspects of his life and work. In the *Dickensian* Centenary Issue, "Dickens and Fame" (1970), Sylvère Monod, Fielding, Slater, Collins, and Ford discuss his impact, both critical and popular, since 1870; this is the most substantial companion to the standard work, Ford's *Dickens and His Readers* (1955). The introduction to Collins' *Dickens: The Critical Heritage* (1971) is concerned mainly with his reputation in his own time. In centenary books (see below), one editor, E. W. F. Tomlin, reassesses Dickens' reputation, and another, Heinz Reinhold, surveys Dickens' earlier critical fortunes in Germany. Monod reflects upon the development of Dickens studies in France, of which he once held a lonely *monodpolie* (*EA*, 1970; *Adam*, 1971). He has another article in *Europe*'s Dickens number (1969), which also contains essays on Dickens in Hungary, Bulgaria, and Italy and on Dickens in films and in French television versions. Although this chapter makes no attempt to provide a comprehensive or informed survey of recent Dickensiana in all languages, some specimen roundups, mostly in English, might be mentioned. Anna Katona has surveyed Dickens' fortunes in Hungary and reported on activities there in the centenary year (*DSN*, 1971; *FK*, 1971), and Dickens' influence on Hungarian fiction is discussed by Miklos Lengyel (*Palocfold*, 1972). Nícifor Naumov's book on Dickens in Serbia and Croatia is described by Edgar Rosenberg (*Dkn*, 1970). His fortunes in the nineteenth century in Norway and Poland are discussed, in English, by J. W. Brown (*Edda*, 1970) and Maria Bachman (*KN*, 1974). Henry Gifford does the same for Russia (*FMLS*, 1968), and he reviews (*Dkn*, 1967, 1972) I. M. Katarsky's book (Moscow, 1966), evidently a distinguished one, on Dickens in mid-nineteenth-century Russia and Tamara Silman's critical study (Leningrad, 1970). The *TLS* Centenary Issue (4 June 1970) contains Alexander Anikist's "Dickens in Russia," and *Soviet Literature* (1970) reviews, under the genial title "Our Mutual Friend Charles Dickens," recent Soviet critical work on Dickens. Laurence Senelick notes how changing ideology has modified the presentation of Dickens to Russian readers (*DiS*, 1965), and Alan Burke discusses the Dickens criticism of the Formalist critic Schlovsky (*DSN*, 1973). Donald Davie reprints two Dickens items in his *Russian Literature and Modern English Fiction* (1965). In Germany, modern Dickens criticism has been surveyed by Dieter Mehl (*Archiv*, 1969) and in Werner Habicht's summary of recent German studies in English literature (*Anglia*, Supp., 1970). A collection of recent German essays appears in *Charles Dickens: Sein Werk im Lichte neuer deutscher Forschung* [*Dickens: His Work in the Light of Recent German Criticism*] (Heidelberg, 1969; English summary in Habicht, above; reviews in *Dkn*, 1971, and *DSN*, 1971). Its editor, Heinz Reinhold, recalls how he came to revere Dickens, in a Nazi Germany that neglected him (*Dkn*, 1975). There has lately been a boom in interest in Dickens in Japan and in Holland (see Michael Slater and Angus Easson in *Dkn*, 1971, 1973, 1975). The Latin countries seem to have been less caught up, but a centenary tribute was published in Mexico City (1971), *Charles Dickens 1812–1870: Homenaje en al primer centenario de su muerte*, which includes an account of his reception in Mexico (particulars in *DSN*, 1972). But for a fuller survey of Dickens outside Anglo-Saxony, see Nisbet's awaited *International Bibliography*.

Periodicals about Dickens

The *Dickensian* (founded 1905; now three issues a year) has lately been joined by other specialist periodicals, and the student needs to be aware of their respective ranges and areas of usefulness. The most substantial as well as the senior, the *Dickensian* carries both articles and reviews, and—particularly under Michael Slater, who became editor in 1968—almost everyone with a reputation in Dickens studies contributes to it. Nor should the "Dickens Fellowship News and Notes," now relegated to the rear pages, be neglected; they not only constitute a salutary reminder of what Dickens still uniquely means to unprofessional readers but also contain many remarkable assessments of Dickens, partly because the "Immortal Memory" and other such speeches presented at various annual birthday and conference dinners are delivered by distinguished authors and public figures. Their "tributes" often get close to the center of Dickens' genius besides being expressed with eloquence and elegance. Addresses on such occasions may appropriately be emotional, and readers should indeed be moved by such speeches as Dame Sybil Thorndike's and Harry Stone's (1969), Angus Wilson's (1973, 1975) and Heinz Reinhold's (1975). Nor is it unilluminating to consider the views of such unacademic speakers as a prime minister (Edward Heath, 1968) or to pick up such tidbits as the fact that Nasser had been so impressed by *A Tale of Two Cities* that he was determined to prevent bloodshed after his revolution (1975).

Articles in the *Dickensian* include important series by regular contributors such as Malcolm Morley (on dramatizations of the novels) and W. J. Carlton, whose biographical essays, mostly on the early Dickens, have been as authoritative as they are indispensable. Features particularly important to the student include the following: (1) regular information about the content and new ownership of manuscripts passing through the salesrooms; (2) reports on acquisitions of manuscripts, etc., by major collections; (3) an annual survey of Dickens studies, selective but indicating the range and quality of the items mentioned; (4) reviews not only of books about Dickens but also of studies of related figures and of such relevant topics as nineteenth-century London; (5) critiques of para-Dickensiana, such as film, radio, television, and theatrical versions, and retrospective accounts of similar phenomena, such as G. E. Miller's "Postcard Dickensiana 1900–1920" (1975); (6) reports of conferences on, or relevant to, Dickens and of exhibitions both of Dickensiana and of, for instance, Maclise (1972) and Cruikshank (1974).

The short-lived *Dickens Studies* (three issues a year, 1965–69) ended with the death of its founder and editor, Noel C. Peyrouton. It was most satisfactory in its scholarly items (Peyrouton and others contributed some particularly useful essays on Dickens in America); the critical articles were uneven in quality. The place of *Dickens Studies* as an American specialist journal was inherited by *Dickens Studies Newsletter* (begun in 1970) and *Dickens Studies Annual*, both initially edited by Robert J. Partlow, Jr. The *Annual*—irregular in its publication (1970, 1972, 1974, 1975, 1976) for financial reasons—is a weighty hardback volume, carrying articles of considerable length, latterly including groups on a particular topic (e.g., on *Great Expectations* in 1972). All these periodicals are illustrated, the *Dickensian* having always been particularly lavish in this respect, and this plenitude of plates is especially valuable in the study of an author who is as visual as Dickens and whose texts are so integrally related to their illustrations. *The Dickensian*, as its editor states in an exchange about its function (1975), has a policy of publishing "material with a historical and biographical rather than critical emphasis." The balance tilts otherwise in *Dickens Studies Annual*, which also more fully represents the nouvelles vagues in Dickens criticism.

Dickens Studies Newsletter, the organ of the newly established Dickens Society (founded in America as a more academic complement to the Dickens Fellowship), is a slim quarterly, carrying few articles but making a special feature of reviews and of its quarterly checklist. As in the *Dickensian,* the standard of reviewing is high. The checklists, compiled by Alan M. Cohn and J. E. Casel, are an invaluable complement to the *Dickensian*'s selective annual survey, for they aim at completeness and provide an up-to-date listing of books, articles, and dissertations in various countries—some three to five pages a quarter, with from twenty to thirty items per page. Though no comment or assessment is attempted, these checklists also cite reviews of books, whereas the *Dickensian* survey mentions only reviews by its own contributors. Cohn is preparing these checklists for a consolidated reprinting.

Thus, between them, the *Dickensian* and the *Newsletter* provide just about all ye need to know about current writing on Dickens. A few more items, and further information about some items, may be gleaned from the standard bibliographies such as those in *Victorian Studies* and *Victorian Newsletter.* Inevitably the two Dickens periodicals carried many special items about the glut of publications, exhibitions, performances, and such in the centenary year; q.v., for I shall not recount them all here.

Reference Books

Most of the old standbys, such as Pierce and Wheeler's *Dickens Dictionary* (1894), have been reprinted photographically, and various new compilations have appeared, though none is intended for, or will be much help to, the serious student. The only recent reference books that I have found useful are London Transport's *The London of Charles Dickens* (1970), compiled by John Greaves and Gwen Major, an alphabetical listing of places in London mentioned by Dickens, with appropriate information, references, and quotations; and Michael and Mollie Hardwick's *The Charles Dickens Encyclopedia* (1973), which covers, though imperfectly, the novels, their characters and locations, and Dickens' life and circle and has a lengthy and well-indexed section of quotations. The Hardwicks, tireless compilers of unacademic books about Dickens, have produced, among other items, *As They Saw Him: Charles Dickens: The Great Novelist as Seen through the Eyes of His Family, Friends and Contemporaries* (1970), superficial but useful on shelves that do not contain everything by Frederic G. Kitton, the arch-compiler of a former era. At an altogether more scholarly level, Dickens' journalistic circle is Who's-Who'd in Anne Lohrli's *Household Words* compilation (see below). A concordance to the novels is now being contemplated, under the direction of Joseph Gold. Currently "the biggest and best Dickens Encyclopaedia in existence" is undoubtedly the seventy-odd volumes of the *Dickensian,* as its present editor claims, and its riches have been made far more accessible by Frank T. Dunn's *Cumulative Analytical Index to the* Dickensian *1905–1974* (1975). Referring to notices of all the most important secondary works on Dickens, as well as to the many authoritative essays in this journal, this index is an indispensable reference book for the student of Dickens. See also the classified index of articles in the *Dickensian* in *Bibliotheca Dickensiana*, comp. Roger Machin (Kyoto, 1975).

Editions

When Ada Nisbet made her survey in 1962–63, the only Dickens item edited according to acceptable academic standards was the *Speeches* (ed. Fielding, 1960). Since then we have, to use the First Player's modest terms, "reform'd that indifferently"; to "reform it altogether" will take years of painful work. At least, however, the past decade or so has seen the tardy inception of a policy of publishing what Dickens actually wrote, not only in his fiction but also in his minor writings, journalism, and correspondence. To adapt G. M. Young's pretty aphorism, "By the beginning of the nineteenth century virtue was advancing on a broad invincible front": by the 1960s, Dickensian textual purity was advancing slowly and haphazardly, but certainly and definitively, on several uncoordinated fronts, and reinforcements were gathering on other fronts, though total victory over textual corruption and inadequacy seemed unlikely before 1990 or thereabouts. How necessary the struggle is may be exemplified by the now notorious nonsense word "Town" for "Tower" in the very first sentence of *Edwin Drood*—but, as Edgar Rosenberg remarks in an outstanding review article (*DSN*, 1974), this famous opening paragraph had often been critically discussed and no one had made the now obvious emendation, let alone had the sense to check the manuscript, though Henry Jackson suggested this rewording as long ago as 1911 (see *TLS*, 18 Aug. 1972). Similarly, Kathleen Tillotson lists grievous misreadings in *Dombey*, No. IV, perpetuated because an errata slip got overlooked—"But they should not all have survived an age of textual criticism and 'close reading'" (*Imagined Worlds*, ed. Maynard Mack et al., 1968).

Novels

Kathleen Tillotson is the surviving general editor of the Clarendon Dickens, John Butt having died before publication began. (One of his exploratory papers, "The Serial Publication of Dickens' Novels: *Martin Chuzzlewit* and *Little Dorrit*," has been republished in the posthumous collection *Pope, Dickens and Others*, 1969). A joint general editor, James Kinsley, has recently been appointed. Three volumes have appeared: *Oliver Twist* (ed. Tillotson, 1966), *Edwin Drood* (ed. Margaret Cardwell, 1972), and *Dombey and Son* (ed. Alan Horsman, 1974). The general editors' preface states the aims: to establish a critical text, with textual apparatus but no explanatory annotation; to provide introductions tracing the history of the novel's composition, publication, and revision, but not attempting critical appraisal; to print Dickens' surviving working notes; and to include appendixes devoted to such matters as the illustrations, public-reading texts, and descriptive headlines in the Charles Dickens Edition, etc.* Although the series has been received with general acclaim, even awe, many reviewers have regretted the decision to exclude explanatory annotation, some have questioned the policy of printing only "the more interesting first thoughts" in the manuscripts, and others have held that the appearance of the page makes this edition more suitable for reference than for reading. The one major challenge has come from Fredson Bowers, who argues against Tillotson's choice of copy-text in her *Oliver Twist*: "the root of the problem rests in the differing theories of what constitutes an 'ideal' critical, or eclectic, text. . . . The Clarendon *Oliver Twist* . . . is still something of a compromise between old-fashioned and advanced editorial ideals and methods" (*NCF*, 1968, p. 238). Rosenberg comments: "Bowers' review, a pitiless piece of precisionism, has yet . . . to be argued out of the world" (*DSN*, 1974, p. 80)—but confidence in the Clarendon edition has not been undermined by Bowers' reservations.

One other series is attempting similar textual authority, the Norton Critical Edition. Only *Hard Times* has yet appeared (ed. Ford and Monod, 1966), but the same editors' *Bleak House* and Rosenberg's *Great Expectations* are expected soon. The series includes a good sampling of textual variants (not on the page), explanatory annotation, and much appended matter, such as Dickens' letters and notes about the novel, relevant documentary material, and extracts from reviews and later critical essays. The Norton *Hard Times* is the most useful working edition among Dickens' novels.

Almost all new editions except the Clarendon have been paperbacks, but many have distinguished critical introductions and some—mostly in the Penguin English Library—have texts that, if questionable, are more authoritative than any hitherto published. Penguin editors have at least paid some attention to the substantive editions and, generally, to the manuscripts; but no common editorial policy has been imposed and some dubious textual decisions have been made. "The authority of [the Charles Dickens Edition, 1867–68, the last reprinting in his lifetime] as a text, especially for Dickens' earlier novels, is more and more frequently called into question, while Penguin editors—with a few exceptions . . . —seem to prefer it"

---

* It may be useful to list here editions, etc., that include Dickens' working notes (the "number plans"). The first known number plans (fragmentary) are for *The Old Curiosity Shop* (*Pilgrim*, II, 167, n.; Angus Easson, *DSA*, 1970). They seem not to have been published in extenso; the fullest description is in Monod's *Dickens the Novelist* (1968), pp. 203–04. Full-scale extant number plans begin with *Dombey* and are published in editions and studies as follows: *Dombey*–Clarendon; *Copperfield*–Butt and Tillotson (*Dickens at Work*, 1957); *Bleak House*–Crowell, Penguin, and Sucksmith, ed. (*RMS*, 1965); *Hard Times*–Norton; *Little Dorrit*–Odyssey Press and Herring, ed. (*MP*, 1966); *Our Mutual Friend*–Boll, ed. (*MP*, 1944); *Drood*–Penguin, Clarendon. There are (and presumably were) no number plans for *A Tale of Two Cities* or *Great Expectations*, but the "General Mems" for the latter are printed in *Dickens at Work* and in *Dkn*, 1949.

(Barry Westberg, *Dkn*, 1974, p. 134). An invaluable series of detailed assessments of paperback reprints is in progress in the *Dickens Studies Newsletter*; nearly half the novels have now been surveyed. In particular, the articles by Robert L. Patten and Anne Smith (1972 and 1973, reviewing *Pickwick* and *Hard Times* reprints) raise many issues about editorial policies. Texts generally come out badly; illustrations, annotation, and introductory material vary enormously in quality and quantity. Few reprints contain all the original illustrations and the serial cover design, the importance of which has been increasingly recognized (see below, Illustrations), and the reproduction of such plates as are included is often poor. For readers without access to the serial parts, the Oxford Illustrated Dickens (1947–58) remains the best edition for the illustrations, though it includes no cover designs and is textually and in the general quality of its introductions unsatisfactory. In the *Newsletter* surveys, no series was considered impeccable, but the Penguin—which now includes all the novels (except *Nickleby*) and some other works—proved generally the most satisfactory. More often than other recent reprints, too, the Penguins indicate the serial-installment divisions. The Signet Library reprints, textually undistinguished, have some excellent introductions or afterwords. Individual paperback reprints of special value include R. D. McMaster's of *Great Expectations* and *Little Dorrit* (Odyssey, 1965, 1969) and Duane DeVries' of *Bleak House* (Crowell, 1971). Some outstanding introductions are mentioned in the section on criticism of individual novels. The editorial matter in Monod's translations in Editions Garnier (Paris) is of great value: *David Copperfield* (1956), *Oliver Twist* (1957), *Les Grandes Espérances* (1959), and *Les Contes de Noël* (forthcoming). An elaborate exercise is in progress at the Shakespeare Institute, University of Birmingham: a number of Ph.D. candidates are each preparing, as a dissertation, a detailed annotation of a Dickens novel. The first completed, Susan Shatto's lengthy "Commentary on Dickens' *Bleak House*" (1974), will be invaluable to any future editor of the novel. Work is progressing on other texts, and those nearing completion include *Edwin Drood, Our Mutual Friend*, and *A Christmas Carol*.

The best brief introduction to the problems that editors face is Simon Nowell-Smith's "Editing Dickens: For Which Reader? From Which Text?" (*TLS*, 4 June 1970). The nature of the manuscripts and proof sheets and the reasons for variants between the substantive editions are discussed by several editors, in essays where they can be more expansive (and often more enjoyable) than in their introductions: see Monod on "Dickens [and his compositors] at Work" on *Hard Times* and *Bleak House* (*Dkn*, 1968, 1969), Angus Easson on *The Old Curiosity Shop* (a very substantial analysis, *DSA*, 1970), Slater's "Dickens (and Forster) at Work on *The Chimes*" (*DiS*, 1966), and Rosenberg's absorbing attempt to "air some of the problems which nowadays confront Dickens editors," taking *Great Expectations* as his instance (*Dkn*, 1973; *DSA*, 1972). Other items on the text include Nowell-Smith's on the cheap edition, 1847–52 (*Library*, 1967) and Patten's proposal for a superannotated edition (*DSN*, 1971). Generalizations remain perilous until more work is done, but these conclusions are emerging: that Dickens, when reading proofs, rarely checked his manuscript, so that he often made simply commonsense corrections, though the manuscript might contain an arguably preferable wording; that matter cut in proof, generally to trim installments to the right length, was never restored in the published book; and that he was rarely diligent or self-critical when correcting proofs of later reprints (hence the growing distrust of the 1867–68 edition, which has been the basis of almost all later reprints). How texts become progressively more corrupt with every reprinting is neatly illustrated by Philip Gaskell with facsimiles of successive stages of a passage from *Copperfield* (*A New Introduction to Bibliography*, 1972). One issue on which editors are divided is the status of the many interesting passages cut in proof: Should they be considered part of the text, even if Dickens had better things to do than fuss around restoring them later? Or should they appear in an appendix, or a textual apparatus, or not at all? As for the manuscript, Dickens' own account of why he sent such "foul papers" to the printer has lately come to light: if a fair copy were sent, one of the apprentices would set it up, but the manuscript "which is difficult to decipher is put into the hands of a first rate compositor whose proof will give very little trouble" (*Catalogue of the Suzannet Collection*, ed. Slater, 1975, p. 156). Hence some of the tribulations of first-rate editors today.

Minor Writings

Many uncollected (and mostly unnoticed) fragments of Dickens' journalism have been retrieved by Harry Stone in his well-illustrated two-volume *Charles Dickens' Uncollected Writings from* Household Words *1850–1859* (1968); further items appear in *Nineteenth-Century Fiction* (1970) and *Dickens Studies Annual* (1970). These items all come from collaborative essays or Christmas Numbers. Sometimes it is possible to be categorical about Dickens' authorship; where it is not, Stone makes intelligently argued guesses about which parts Dickens wrote and, in the introduction to his edition, he gives an admirable account of Dickens as editor, journalist, and collaborator. Although many of the fragments that Stone has rescued are mere workaday journalism and some are embarrassingly inferior (see reviews, *NCF*, 1969; *Dkn*, 1970), many items contain Dickensian felicities or provide useful evidence of their author's interests and attitudes. Valuable work on Dickens' journalism in the *Examiner* has been done by K. J. Fielding and Alec Bryce, sometimes in collaboration, rescuing unidentified polemical articles, mainly on the administration of justice and of the social services, written in the late 1840s (*Dkn*, 1967–70; *VS*, 1968; *DiS*, 1969). Their attribution of some of these items to Dickens is tentative. Kathleen Tillotson has discovered an important *Daily News* letter on capital punishment (*TLS*, 12 Aug. 1965) and an *Examiner* dramatic critique (*Dkn*, 1969). Further *Examiner* and *Morning Chronicle* items are identified in the Pilgrim *Letters*, Volumes 1–3, which also reprint some important journalistic items, such as Dickens' polemic against Lord Londonderry over the 1842 Mines and Collieries Bill. An article on ghosts and one on Keeley the comedian have been reprinted by Collins (*Dkn*, 1963–64). What Dickens wrote, and did not write, about *King Lear* is discussed by W. J. Carlton (*Dkn*, 1965). Some uncollected speeches have been discovered (*Dkn*, 1977).

"The *Uncommercial Traveller* (1861) may be regarded as a biographical summing up of the period of the dark novels" (Ian Watt, *DSA*, 1974, p. 170)—but no substantial study exists of Dickens the essayist, either in biographical or in literary terms, nor have the bulk of his essays been edited. The Clarendon Dickens will, however, include them. His travel books, also understudied, have lately been reprinted. The Penguin *American Notes* (1972) is the first properly edited reprint (Fielding, *Dkn*, 1972), and its introduction sees Dickens in relation to other British travelers and discusses *American Notes* as a work of art, not just as a record. David Paroissien's is the first edited reprint (1973) of *Pictures from Italy* in English; useful on the book's conception and composition, Paroissien is silent about its literary qualities and erratic in his annotation (see Alan Horsman, *Dkn*, 1974). Deborah A. Thomas' edition of his *Selected Short Fiction* (1976) includes seventeen essays besides fictional items, mainly drawn from *Christmas Stories*.

The complete *Public Readings* have been edited, for the first time, by Collins (1975). His introduction and notes describe the textual development of these twenty-one items, explaining how Dickens read them and how his performances related to other Victorian one-man shows and to the qualities of his fiction. He amplifies some of these points in several bibliographical studies (cited on p. xi of his edition). Collins has also edited a facsimile of the *Carol* reading (1971). An unedited facsimile of the "short-time" *Nickleby* reading has also appeared (Ilkley Literature Festival, 1973; see *TLS*, 22 June 1973). Dickens' plays, some of which were successfully revived during the centenary (see *Dkn*, 1970–71), have been reprinted: *Complete Plays and Selected Poems* (1970), *The Strange Gentleman and Other Plays*, introd. Jeffery Tillett (1972). Neither reprint is complete, nor is the editorial matter satisfactory. In *Under the Management of Mr. Charles Dickens: His Production of "The Frozen Deep"* (1966), Robert Louis Brannan shows that much of the text, here printed from the manuscript, is by Dickens, not Wilkie Collins. Brannan gives an admirable account of the play's composition, presentation, and reception and explains why it took such hold upon Dickens (cf. Jean Ruer, *EA*, 1970). An uncollected poem on the death of Mary Hogarth is printed in an essay by W. J. Carlton (*Dkn*, 1967). Collins has published some comic duologues written, for purposes unknown, in the 1860s (*NCF*, 1977).

Memoirs of Joseph Grimaldi has been reprinted with updated annotation and a preface by Richard Findlater (1968). Facsimiles of the first issue of the *Daily News* (Historic British Newspapers series, Brighton, 1971) and of *The Loving Ballad of Lord Bateman* (1969) have appeared; the latter wrongly attributes to Thackeray a share in the composition. *Charles Dick-*

ens 1812–1870 (comp. Ivor Brown, Jackdaw Series, No. 95, 1970) is an attractive walletful of facsimiles, reproductions of illustrations, etc., relating to Dickens and his times. Of the many Dickens anthologies lately published, Eleanor and Edgar Johnson's *The Dickens Theatrical Reader* (1964) deserves mention as admirably illustrating Dickens' perennial delight, as man and author, in the theater and other forms of popular amusements—and it includes unpublished letters. Dickens' Memorandum Book (MS. Berg Collection), inaccurately published by Forster (*Life*, Bk. ix, Ch. vii), is now being edited.

Letters

The inception of *The Pilgrim Edition of the Letters of Charles Dickens* is the most important event in Dickens studies during the period covered by this guide. "The English Scholars Get Their Teeth into Dickens," Geoffrey Tillotson headlined his account of the first Pilgrim and Clarendon volumes (*SR*, 1967), which includes personal reminiscences of their progenitors, Humphry House and John Butt. Edited by Madeline House and Graham Storey, sometimes with co- or associate editors (notably Kathleen Tillotson), *Pilgrim* has commanded universal respect: "a monumental achievement," as Nisbet says (*NCF*, 1966). Besides printing many letters for the first time, it provides true texts of many others that have appeared incompletely or inaccurately, and the annotation and other editorial matters are incomparably superior to anything offered before. While no sensational biographical discoveries have emerged in the volumes so far published—*1820–1839* (1965), *1840–1841* (1969), *1842–1843* (1974)—the texts and their annotation have added enormously to the detail, precision, and dimensions of our knowledge of Dickens' early career. A notable feature of the edition is the great amount of comment on Dickens (and his wife, family, and associates) from contemporary, and often manuscript, sources; the volume covering the 1842 visit to the States, for instance, contains many such descriptions and judgments by Americans, illustrious or obscure. Another notable feature is the substantial, and highly analytical, index to every volume—a model of usefulness to scholars. Several reviewers have compared this edition to the Hill-Powell *Boswell*, both to indicate its definitive quality and the complexity of annotation required by such allusive documents and to suggest that this edition will become as good a vantage point from which to see mid-nineteenth-century London as the annotated *Life of Johnson* is for viewing the literary and intellectual London of a century earlier. Richard D. Altick maintains this (*DSN*, 1971), but the historian Geoffrey Best denies it, partly because Dickens—or at least the early Dickens—ignored too much: "As a record of what was going on in his England, the letters . . . are as dim a source of information as they are about his day-to-day life. He was too busy living it, and transmuting it into his fiction . . . , to put more than he could help into letters" (*Dkn*, 1965, p. 73).

Sundry odd letters or groups of letters have been published, but few of these amount to much (e.g., *N&Q*, 1964; *Adam*, 1971; *MQR*, 1971; *Dkn*, 1973; *TLS*, 22 Feb. 1974). One new letter, however, deserves mention: a very David-to-Dora-like one addressed to Maria Beadnell (1831 [?]), not in *Pilgrim* (*Dkn*, 1972). Beyond that, what John Carter says of Sotheby's catalogue of the Suzannet sale of 1971 (see above) is worth noting: "devout Dickensians will find more meat in [its section about manuscript letters] than they could procure for £1 in the bookshops" (*Dkn*, 1972, p. 46).

Biography

"We might as well admit," writes Fielding, "that we sometimes find Dickens almost as fascinating a man as he was a writer" (*DiS*, 1966, p. 2). Not much substantial biographical work has been done on him lately, however, compared with the scores of critical books and (literally) thousands of critical articles—too few pennyworths of biographical bread to so heady an amount of critical sack? No biography approaching Edgar Johnson's in weight or pretensions has appeared, though reinterpretations of particular phases occur in various general studies of Dickens, the most penetrating being in E. D. H. Johnson's and Angus Wilson's (see below). The book that has added most to our biographical knowledge is certainly the *Pilgrim Letters*. The only new book-length biographical study is Christopher Hibbert's *The Making of Charles Dickens* (1967), an account of his early life and its effect on his personality and writings. This has been admired and recommended, but I find it little more than a readable rehash of familiar facts and interpretations, dodging many difficult issues and sometimes betraying substantial ignorance of Dickens (see *TLS*, 4 Jan. 1968). Hibbert's work represents a missed opportunity, for, as Angus Easson remarks, Dickens' "first twenty-five years, the most shadowy and yet so often the most interesting and most important part of his life," present the most fruitful field for establishing new facts about him (*Dkn*, 1971, pp. 35, 40). Easson has established new facts about John Dickens' financial position (he was well paid) and about his release from prison, which was *not* obtained through a legacy, as is generally stated (*Dkn*, 1974, 1971). Most of the new information about Dickens' early life, however, has been established by W. J. Carlton in a long series of meticulous articles in the *Dickensian*—not all, indeed, on his earlier years—tracing his friendships, acquaintances, homes, and activities: see Fielding's *W. J. Carlton: A Tribute with a List of His Writings on Dickens* (privately printed, 1973) or J. Don Vann's checklist (above).

Carlton has also made the one potentially significant contribution to the Ellen Ternan story, in "Dickens' Forgotten Retreat in France" (*Dkn*, 1966) —less forgotten than concealed, for this lodging near Boulogne that Dickens frequented in the 1860s was not, it would seem, a retreat for purely contemplative or literary purposes. Confirmation for Felix Aylmer's case about his "retreat" in Slough has come from New Zealand (J. C. Reid, *Dkn*, 1968). Some Ellen Ternan letters have been discovered; they are lively, but they fail to mention Dickens (*Dkn*, 1965). Further information is expected in K. L. Longley's forthcoming study of the affair. In *Dickens and the Scandal-mongers* (1965) Edward Wagenknecht again fights his rearguard action against commentators who have too easily assumed that Dickens' relations with Nelly were improperly amorous, but the name-calling evident in his title and his thwacking logic-chopping style of argument do his case a disservice; he does show, however, that many "anti-Dickensites" (as he dubs the amorous-assumption writers) have been incautious in their statements. A much revised edition of his 1929 biography has also appeared: *The Man Charles Dickens: A Victorian Portrait* (1966), a lively, well-informed, quirky, and enthusiastic picture of the man and his works, "Victorian" less in seeing Dickens in his period than in seeing him and his works in a nineteenth- rather than twentieth-century fashion—"The dark tragic complicated aspects of his personality do appear in this portrait, but the stress is upon his great-hearted, generous, optimistic and positive qualities" (*TLS*, 4 Aug. 1966). This is at least a useful corrective to the modish way of thinking about great modern and neomodern authors. Another cheerful view of Dickens appears in John Greaves's *Dickens at Doughty Street* (1975). This book, celebrating the jubilee of the Dickens Fellowship's tenure of Dickens' only surviving London residence, narrates his intoxicatingly strenuous existence there, 1837–39.

On those early years, some fascinating letters by Catherine and Mary Hogarth, and some responses to Mary's death, have been published (*Dkn*, 1967; *TLS*, 23 Dec. 1960). "Mr Dickens improves very much on acquaintance he is very gentlemanly and pleasant," his future wife decided in February 1835; and her sister Mary later reported him as being "kindness itself" to his bride, who happily praised his "kind affectionate heart." Much new information about Catherine emerges in *Pilgrim*, generally very creditable. Dickens' relations with Christina Weller, who caught his eye in 1844, and with her family are surveyed by David Paroissien (*DSA*, 1972); as interesting new material shows, all went well for some time, but acrimony ensued.

Another unsatisfying flirtation—his relationship with the United States—is recorded in accounts of his 1842 visit. Peyrouton's useful series of articles on this episode are mostly about the impression Dickens made on his hosts (*Dkn*, 1963–64; *DiS*, 1967–68). In a substantial and important survey, "Dickens and the American Press, 1842" (*DiS*, 1968), Paul B. Davis describes the shifting relationship between the two parties; an excellent account of Dickens' American "newspaper image" precedes Davis' argument that Dickens' assessment of the American press should not be taken as gospel. The Copyright Question, which he discusses, is the subject of James J. Barnes's *Authors, Publishers and Politicians* (1974); Dickens' shortcomings as a campaigner are exposed. The 1842 visit and its aftermath are well discussed by George Ford, reviewing the third volume of *Pilgrim* (*Dkn*, 1975), in the Penguin edition of *American Notes* (1972), and by Steven Marcus in *Dickens: From Pickwick to Dombey* (1965). The 1867–68 visit is related to the 1842 one by Peter Bracher (*DiS*, 1969) and by Philip Collins (in *Abroad in America*, ed. Marc Pachter, 1976). Ada Nisbet has long been working on Dickens (and his British contemporaries) and America; her book will be much welcomed. Yamilè Morsiani's *Dickens e l'America* (Bologna, 1963) contains little that is new.

How America influenced Dickens' outlook has yet to be fully explored. In "Dickens the Citizen" (*Politics in Literature in the 19th Century*, Lille, 1974) Collins assesses his political stance; confining himself here to Dickens' nonfictional writings, he argues that Dickens was less radical and less clear-sighted than other commentators have maintained. (In the same collection, Jacob Korg usefully discusses "Society and Community in Dickens.") Il-liberal and unradical he certainly was over the Indian mutiny (William Oddie, *Dkn*, 1972). Ludwig Borinski argues that the contemporary politi-cian to whom he was closest was the unalarming Lord John Russell ("Dick-ens als Politiker," *NS*, 1973). Certainly he knew little about Chartism or Christian Socialism, as Peyrouton shows, but the Chartists' opinions of him are of some interest (*Dkn*, 1964, 1962). His earlier political development is traced by Michael Goldberg in "From Bentham to Carlyle" (*JHI*, 1972), but R. D. McMaster, discussing some opposed views about Dickens' politics, notes the paradox that, in the politicized 1960s, interest in Dickens' re-formism declined rather than quickened (*NCF*, 1971). His views on the Empire are thoroughly surveyed by Donald H. Simpson (*LNRCS*, 1970). His politics remains, however, a largely unmapped area, the subject still for travelers' tales that will be most convincing to readers who know least about Victorian politics. The historical amateurishness of too many interpreters of Victorian literature has moved a real historian, John Vincent, to the sar-donic comment that "There is history, and there is Eng Lit history. The latter genre . . . exists in a world all its own" (*Listener*, 22 Mar. 1973).

Some of Dickens' personal relationships have been well surveyed. Sybilla Jane Flower's account of his friendship with Bulwer-Lytton includes a notable assessment, by Lytton in 1869, of the author and the man (*Dkn*, 1973; see also the 1970 catalogue *Dickens Centenary Exhibition at Kneb-worth House*). Many of Carlton's essays (above) are on friendships dating from Dickens' early life. His contacts with such disparate contemporaries as Hans Andersen, Queen Victoria, Captain Marryat, and the *Punch* set have been described (*Dkn*, 1966, 1975; *DSA*, 1972; *DiS*, 1967), and Fielding has commented further on his friendship with Miss Coutts (*Dkn*, 1965). Patrick Waddington describes his acquaintance with Turgenev and with Pauline Viardot, the soprano they admired (*NZSJ*, 1974). There are interesting let-ters about Dickens and his family, by the Lehmanns and their relatives the Willses and the Chamberses, in John Lehmann's *Ancestors and Friends* (1962). How he appeared in the unpublished and destroyed portion of the Macready diaries is recalled by Macready's granddaughter (*DiS*, 1966). Drawing largely on unpublished materials, Wagenknecht traces the Long-fellow-Dickens acquaintance in his *Scandalmongers* volume. Arthur A. Adrian's *Mark Lemon: First Editor of "Punch"* (1966) is one of several

recent biographical studies of Dickens' friends and associates that clarify
and illuminate his involvement with his society (see review in *DiS*, 1967).
The Dickensian has lately made a practice of reviewing similar biographies
that bear upon Dickens. Studies of Dickens' relationships with his illustrators are mentioned below. New information about his sons' relationships
with him and about their later history appears in Mary Lazarus' *A Tale of
Two Brothers* (1973), on Alfred and Edward in Australia; see also the
Dickensian Australian Issue (1972). Alfred's school friends, when visiting
Gad's Hill, always made some such remark as "By Jove, Dickens, your
governor is a stunner and no mistake"—a verdict that might be extended
beyond his function as host. A great-grandson, Eric Dickens Hawksley, recalls Katey and Henry and Auntie Georgie (*Adam*, 1971). Further recollections of Dickens' offspring, though of dubious authenticity, appear in W.
Harrison Culmer's *Billy the Cartwheeler: "The Last of the Dickens Boys"*
(1970).

Dickens' most important friendship has been brilliantly and sensitively
analyzed by James A. Davies in "Forster and Dickens: The Making of
Podsnap"—much the best study of this relationship and a substantial addition to our understanding of Dickens. It appears in a Commemorative Issue
of the *Dickensian* (1974) honoring the centenary of the *Life of Dickens*.
This issue also includes Anthony Burton's essay on Forster as an amateur
actor with Dickens and Fielding's survey of Forster's novel criticism. Fielding explores its theoretical bases and notes Forster's objectivity when reviewing friends such as Dickens and Lytton. (Forster's range as a reviewer
and the critical qualities of the *Life of Dickens* are discussed elsewhere by
Tillotson, *Dkn*, 1972, and Monod, in *English Studies Today*, 4th ser.,
Rome, 1966. Monod concludes that, despite many shortcomings, Forster is
far from negligible; and Monod's judgment on this and other matters com-
mands respect, for he has been described as "the reader who has, in some
ways, come closer to Dickens than any since Forster"—Fielding, *Dkn*, 1969,
p. 50.) But Alec Bryce, continuing an argument he began elsewhere (*DSN*,
1972), shows that much of the criticism in the *Life* is scissors-and-pasted
from reviews in the *Examiner*, many of which Forster did not write (*Dkn*,
1974). This discovery, coming hard upon the *Pilgrim* editors' demonstration
that Forster's "improvements" upon the text of Dickens' letters cited in the
Life included creating phrases to enhance his own importance, raises questions about his literary ethics—which must, however, be regarded in the
context of the 1870s, not the 1970s. Bryce's arguments endanger much of
the case that Collins erected on the assumption that Forster wrote most of
the *Examiner* critiques, in "Dickens' Self-Estimate" (in Partlow, 1970), and
render doubtful some of the attributions of authorship of *Examiner* items
reprinted in Collins' *Dickens: The Critical Heritage*. Forster's procedures
and merits as a biographer are fully discussed by the *Pilgrim* editors (I,
xi–xxii) and in essays on his lives of Goldsmith and Swift (*Dkn*, 1974–75).
The reception of the *Life* is presented in *Dickens: The Critical Heritage*
and in the seventy letters that Forster received after its publication (Carl-

ton, *Dkn*, 1962). These letters, and many other important Forster papers, are now in the Victoria and Albert Museum (*Dkn*, 1971). The only new reprint of the *Life*, the Everyman edition (ed. A. J. Hoppé, 1966), is sadly deficient (see *TLS*, 6 Apr. 1967), but Bryce is preparing a new critical edition. Davies is working further on Forster's relationships with Dickens and others, with a book-length study in prospect.

Dickens' relationship with Carlyle has also received much attention of late, but this important topic, together with other studies of Dickens' reading and of his literary relationships, is discussed below (Special Aspects). One common surmise about his reading can now, presumably, be ended: he had not, he said in the 1860s, read *Jane Eyre* or *Wuthering Heights*, "as he disapproved of the whole [Brontë] school." This comment appears in a fascinating and wide-ranging account of conversations with him, by an unidentified recorder, discovered by Jerome Meckier (*Dkn*, 1975). Several other such manuscript (or forgotten) reminiscences of Dickens have been printed, all of which add useful detail to our knowledge of his demeanor and opinions and of the impression he created—accounts of him as a boy, by J. H. Stocqueler; in 1843, by two Frenchmen who interviewed him; and in 1867, by an American clergyman (*Dkn*, 1966, 1963, 1967). The most illuminating, and the most critical, of such accounts is J. T. Danson's (Fielding, *Dkn*, 1972). Danson, a colleague of Dickens on the *Daily News*, offers a severe assessment of Dickens' editorial abilities and indicates that he had seen enough of Dickens to understand why Dickens' marriage later collapsed and why Dickens became so unhappy. Using many earlier accounts of Dickens' conversations, Collins discusses his range, manner, and style as a conversationalist (*Dkn*, 1963), and in "Dickens in 1870" (*TLS*, 4 June 1970) he describes Dickens' final months as containing, in many ways, an epitome of his interests.

Two of Dickens' supplementary careers have received new attention, his work as a magazine editor and as a public reader. His "conducting" of *Household Words* is fully discussed by Stone (see Minor Writings, above) and by Anne Lohrli in her *Household Words . . . Table of Contents* (1973). Lohrli prints the Office Book, which identifies who wrote what, and adds a 275-page gazetteer of the contributors, which greatly enlarges our knowledge of these colleagues and associates of Dickens and what they thought of him. Deborah Thomas has identified and discussed the contributors to his two magazines' Christmas Numbers (*Dkn*, 1973–74). In a series of essays, Collins has discussed the establishment of Dickens' two weeklies and his involvement in them (*Dkn*, 1965; *VPN*, 1968, 1970) and has speculated about why he failed, despite several promises, to write for the *Edinburgh Review* (*RES*, 1963). Fielding, in several places, has questioned the general assumption that Dickens agreed with everything he published in his magazines (e.g., *Dkn*, 1973). Angus Easson discerns a "double standard"—"his standards in journalism [but not in fiction] were determined not primarily by artistic but circulatory considerations" (*Dkn*, 1964, p. 104)—though I would see, not two standards here, but one and a half. Several graduate dissertations on Dickens as editor have been written, but so far no book. Articles and dissertations on Dickens as journalist and editor are listed in *The Nineteenth-Century Periodical Press in Britain: A Bibliography of Modern Studies* (comp. Lionel Madden and Diana Dixon, *VPN*, Supp., 1975), and the annual checklist in the *Victorian Periodicals Newsletter* should be consulted for further items about him, his colleagues, and competitors. J. S. Ryan's *Charles Dickens and New Zealand* (Wellington, 1965) reprints *Household Words* articles about that country and traces other Dickens connections with it.

Raymund Fitzsimons' *The Charles Dickens Show* (1970) is a lively, though unscholarly, account of Dickens' adventures as a public reader. New information about this phase of his life appears in Collins' edition of the *Readings* (above), and Collins writes more fully elsewhere about connections between the reader and the novelist (*SNNTS*, 1969; *DSA*, 1974). Accounts of Dickens on tour appear in the *Dickensian* (1969) and the *Pennsylvania Magazine of History* (1974). Emlyn Williams casts a professional eye on Dickens as a performer (in Tomlin, 1969). Michael Slater writes about the *Bastille Prisoner* script Dickens prepared but never performed (*EA*, 1970). One inspirer of Dickens' platform career, who also affected his early writing, is discussed in Ana Laura Zambrano's "Dickens and Charles Mathews" (*MSpr*, 1972). The relation of Dickens' various subsidiary activities—journalistic, histrionic, philanthropic, etc.—to his fiction is the concern of "How Many Men Was Dickens the Novelist?" where Collins argues against those purist critics who regard the novelist as distinct from the journalist (etc.) or who seek to abstract him from his age (in Amalric, 1973). This is a topic to which Fielding often returns: "No doubt there is a continuity between Dickens' experience in journalism and the world of his imagination, though it is rash to try to define it too sharply" (*VS*, 1968, p. 242). Another of Dickens' activities has lately been investigated, in relation to his art, in Fred Kaplan's *Dickens and Mesmerism: The Hidden Springs of Fiction* (1975). Kaplan enlarges our knowledge of Dickens' mesmeric powers and relates his activities to current experimentation in, and beliefs about, "animal magnetism," but Kaplan is less convincing when he asserts the ubiquitous presence of mesmerism in the novels.

One area of Dickens studies remains unreconstructed and unprofessionalized—the topographical, that favorite resort of old-tyme Dickensians. It is still at the *Week's Tramp in Dickensland* or Percy Fitzgerald's *Bozland* stage: critically innocent and generally amateurish and unreliable in scholarship. Not much has been done lately in this area; a sample centenary batch was reviewed in the *TLS* (4 June 1970), to which might be added C. H. Bishop's *Charles Dickens in Folkestone* (1970) and Paul-Emile Schazmann's well-produced *Charles Dickens in Switzerland* (1972). An essential book remains to be written about Dickens' selection, transmogrification, and artistic use of place in his fiction, by a student more sophisticated than has yet been drawn to this topic—a student with a thorough knowledge of Dickens' England, a historical imagination, an intimacy with the novels, and strong legs. Also, as John Butt remarked, "Isn't it time that someone interested in Dickens' craftsmanship salvaged some of the accumulation of old-fashioned Dickensians who established the originals of certain characters . . . and placed this material in the larger context of the shaping faculty of imagination at work?" (*NCF*, 1964, p. 91). It is indeed absurd that the only full-length study of this fascinating and important topic is Edwin Pugh's *The Charles Dickens Originals* (1913); it is as if we still relied, for our knowledge of Shakespeare's sources, upon Mrs. Lennox (1753–54). How much can be learned, biographically and critically, from a more sophisticated approach Harry Stone demonstrates in his "Woman in White" essay on Miss Havisham's ancestry (see below). Lauriat Lane, Jr., reflects upon the current "Theory and Practice of Dickensian Source Study" (*DSN*, 1973).

Poets' laundry bills are the stock example of trifling literary research, but perhaps novelists' bank accounts may be admitted as a worthwhile topic. Certainly M. Veronica Stokes's admirably detailed study of Dickens' account with Coutts & Co. touches a remarkable number of aspects of his personal, professional, and public life (*Dkn*, 1972). Robert L. Patten's *Dickens and His Publishers* (forthcoming) will greatly amplify our knowledge of his sales, finances, and professional career, matters about which he has already written usefully (appendix to Collins' *Dickens: The Critical Heritage*; *SEL*, 1970).

Some odd aspects of Dickens are discussed in articles published in the appropriate special-interest journals during the centenary. Although many of these are only peripheral contributions to scholarship, their sheer quantity testifies to Dickens' continuing special status in the mind of the English-speaking world (for no other literary centennial could command such miscellaneous attention) and reminds us that he touched the life of his times and the paraphernalia of our civilization at many points. To cite a few examples: E. Gaskell, compiler of *Dickens and Medicine*, the excellent catalogue of the Dickens Centenary Exhibition at the Wellcome Institute of the History of Medicine, writes on "Dickens and Medico-Social Reform" (*JAMA*, 1971). His knowledge of, and taste in, painting and music are discussed in the appropriate journals (Graham Reynolds, *Apollo*, 1970; Charles Cudworth, *MT*, 1970; cf. Lillian M. Ruff, "How Musical Was Dickens?" *Dkn*, 1972). Philip Hobsbaum contributed "Dickens and the Jews: A Centennial Essay" to *Jewish Affairs* (1971), and the *London Magazine* turned its attention in June 1970 to "Dickens and Cricket." Dickens' concern with time was conspicuous enough for a lampoonist of *Dombey and Son* to imagine respectable artisans perambulating the streets before Paul's funeral "carrying cuckoo clocks—emblems of the fleeting nature of time" (*The Man in the Moon*, March 1847), and Frederick R. S. Rogers discusses this preoccupation professionally, if narrowly, in "Dickens and Horology" (*Antiquarian Horology*, 1970). A bibliographical checklist of items on "Law and Society in the Life and Works of Charles Dickens," to mention another recurrent interest, appears in the *Record of the Association for the Bar of the City of New York* (comp. Anthony P. Grech, 1972). Students willing to extend the term "practical criticism" to include eating Inimitable meals are given guidance and recipes in Helen Cox's *Mr. and Mrs. Charles Dickens Entertain* (1970; cf. Margaret Lane, "Mrs. Beaton and Mrs. Dickens," in her *Purely for Pleasure*, 1966). Blake—now a reference, de rigueur, when discussing Dickens—here provides a timely utterance: "Enough! or Too much."

General Criticism

Two distinguished visitants to Dickens studies might be quoted as rival epigraphists for this section. Alfred Harbage, proceeding from the known to the relatively unknown (for him) in his brilliant study of "the Shakespeare-Dickens analogy," read Dickens critics extensively for the first time and was "impressed by how good they are" (*A Kind of Power*, 1975). The redoubtable J. C. Maxwell, fittingly editor of *Notes and Queries*, seeking to praise (though with reservations) one recent book on Dickens, remarked that at least it contrasted with "the loads of pretentious silliness that have been heaped on Dickens in recent years" (*N&Q*, 1976). Both judgments, I think, are justified. The years under survey have produced a great deal of intelligent and thoroughly professional critical work—far more indeed than the equivalent dozen or so years before Ada Nisbet made her assessment for the Stevenson *Guide*, though since 1962 (her cutoff date) there have been no single studies so liberating or suggestive as several by renowned critics who were active then, such as Edmund Wilson (1941), Humphry House (1941), Lionel Trilling (1953), and Hillis Miller (1958). Maxwell's point stands, however: call such otiose and obtuse criticism as he has in mind professionalized, perhaps, instead of professional. "Are there really no limits to our freedom of interpretation?" protests one reviewer of a batch of Dickensiana (A. G. Hill, *EIC*, 1965). An Augustan protest sometimes comes to mind, Pope's

> Pains, reading, study are their just pretense,
> And all they want is spirit, taste, and sense.

What Pope would call a "perfect judge" of Dickens is suggested by the terms used about Barbara Hardy by two of her reviewers. She "passes the essential test of a Dickens critic," writes W. W. Robson: "she shows humaneness and humanity" (*Dkn*, 1969). Most academic critics, says Angus Wilson, are "somewhat ashamed of good sense, wrapping it up in jargon of one sort or another," but she always displays "modest good sense" (*Dkn*, 1971). The critical qualities Hardy admires appear in two of her reviews. Of one commentator she writes that "like so many highly imaginative critics, especially critics of Dickens, he hates the obvious answer" (*MLQ*, 1966). Writing about another, Northrop Frye, she suggests other desiderata in a Dickens critic: his essay on Dickens' comedy has humour, lack of solemnity, wit; it is "congenial as well as brilliant" (*Dkn*, 1969). A critic may be worth his salt who cannot match all these standards, but some commentators might have written better and more aptly had they shown more respect for these qualities. Inevitably, not all the items mentioned below are equally congenial to me; some earn respectful attention, though I personally find them innutritious, because other judges—better judges maybe—than myself have commended them. The critical books of the years since 1962 that remain most valuably in my memory are, I might state, those by Garis, Marcus, Stoehr, Monod, Smith, E. D. H. Johnson, Angus Wilson, the Leavises, Hardy, Carey, and Stewart.* It may also be useful to list here some recent surveys of Dickens criticism, many of which offer judgments alternative to mine. Essays or review articles presenting a view of current criticism include those by Robert Garis (*VS*, 1964), A. G. Hill (*CritQ*, 1965), Edgar Rosenberg (*Dkn*, 1969), Lauriat Lane, Jr. (*SNNTS*, 1969), Dieter Mehl (*Archiv*, 1969), Anthony Burton and George Ford (*Dkn*, 1970), George Wing (*Ariel*, 1970), John Carey (*Listener*, 28 May 1970), John Holloway (*Encounter*, 1970), R. D. McMaster and Grahame Smith (*NCF*, 1971), Stephen Wall (*EIC*, 1971), Maria Bachman (*SAP*, 1972), and Martin Price, welcoming this excellent new habit of "Taking Dickens Seriously" (*YR*, 1972). Notable centennial essays on Dickens' critical reputation include Steven Marcus' "Dickens after 100 Years" (*NYTBR*, 7 June 1970) and Harry Levin's "Charles Dickens 1812–1870" (*ASch*, 1970; rpt. in his *Grounds for Comparison*, 1972); and Philip Hobsbaum in his *A Theory of Communication* (1970) offers a spirited survey of earlier criticism.

To help the reader through the considerable mass of critical material surveyed here, I am using the following broad headings under General Criticism: Anthologies and Collections; Introductory Studies; and Major Studies (the main critical books on the novelist). I then go on to discuss criticism of Special Aspects—Characterization, Plot and Narration, and so on—and finally I turn to Studies of Individual Novels, which many readers may find the most useful section.

Anthologies and Collections

Dickens figures in most of the series of critical anthologies that have lately proliferated—volumes edited by William Ross Clark (Discussions of Literature, 1961), Martin Price (Twentieth Century Views, 1967), A. E. Dyson (Modern Judgments, 1968), Stephen Wall (Penguin Critical Anthologies, 1970), and Collins (Critical Heritage, 1971). The Ford and Lane *Dickens Critics* (1961) has been reprinted in paperback (1966). There are nine good Dickens items in Ian Watt's anthology *The Victorian Novel: Modern*

---

* To check whether my judgment is eccentric here, I asked colleagues from several countries to name the dozen critical books of these years that they would select and was pleased (and surprised) to find how closely their lists coincide with mine. Their addenda comprise the books on Dickens by Earle Davis, Axton, Kincaid, Sucksmith, and Lucas.

Essays in Criticism (1971). Edgar Rosenberg writes trenchantly about what this anthology phenomenon portends (*Dkn*, 1969). Arguably, publishers are overimpressed by the latest in wisdom (see *TLS*, 25 July 1968), and few anthologies find any reprintable wisdom outside the Anglo-Saxon world. Lionel Trilling's essay on *Little Dorrit*, reprinted in five of these anthologies, is the editors' favorite item, and Hillis Miller their other favorite critic. The other scholars most represented are Humphry House, Kathleen Tillotson, Angus Wilson, George Ford, and Dorothy Van Ghent—and this seems just (Edmund Wilson's and F. R. Leavis' essays were not available for reprinting). Of the "modern" anthologies, Dyson's has the most stimulating introduction. The Penguin and Critical Heritage volumes stand apart, in accordance with their series' policies. Wall prints representative items from 1836 to 1968 and includes many statements by Dickens himself. This anthology will give the newcomer to Dickens studies the best quick sense of the field, though, with some 150 items packed into 551 pages, the extracts are generally brief. The Critical Heritage volume is confined to Dickens' contemporaries, 1882 being its terminal date. Both these volumes contain substantial editorial assessments of Dickens criticism. The bibliography in Collins' anthology lists further studies in Dickens' reputation, and headnotes to his sections discuss the critical reception of individual novels. Other volumes in the Critical Heritage series—those, for instance, devoted to Thackeray, Wilkie Collins, and Gissing—contain many comparisons with Dickens. Anthologies dealing with individual novels are noted in the final section below.

Many collections of new essays have appeared, mostly occasioned by the centenary. The main items they include are mentioned in the appropriate sections below, but it may be convenient to list the anthologies here, with their editors (whose introductions often comment usefully on "the state of the art"). Some have already been mentioned, to exemplify the international aspect of Dickens' fame. Collections include *Charles Dickens 1812–1870* (ed. E. W. F. Tomlin, 1969); *Charles Dickens: Sein Werk im Lichte neuer deutscher Forschung* (ed. Heinz Reinhold, Heidelberg, 1969); *Dickens 1970* (ed. Michael Slater, 1970); *Dickens the Craftsman: Strategies of Presentation* (ed. Robert B. Partlow, Jr., 1970); *Dickens Memorial Lectures*, by Kathleen Tillotson, Sylvère Monod, and Angus Wilson (*Dkn*, Supp., 1970); *Charles Dickens 1812–1870: Homenaje en al primer centenario de su muerte* (Mexico City, 1971); and *Studies in the Later Dickens* (ed. Jean-Claude Amalric, Montpellier, 1973). Special numbers were devoted to him in the following journals: *Europe* (ed. Pierre Gamarra, 1969); *Studies in the Novel* (ed. James W. Lee, 1969); *The Dickensian*, "Dickens and Fame 1870–1970" (ed. Michael Slater, 1970); *Etudes Anglaises* (ed. L. Bonnerot, 1970); *Nineteenth-Century Fiction* (ed. Ada Nisbet with Blake Nevius, 1970; rpt. as *Dickens Centennial Essays*, 1971, but with Miller's essay on *Sketches by Boz* substituted for his "Dickens' Comic Art"); *Eigo Kenkyū: The Study of English* (Tokyo, 1970); *Hiroshima Studies in English Language and Literature* (ed. Michio Masui, 1970); and *Adam* (ed. Miron

Grindea, 1971). Journals containing a number of essays, by way of centennial salute, included the *TLS* (4 June 1970), *Le Monde* (13 June 1970), and *Kansas English* (1970).

Introductory Studies

Ada Nisbet's imprimatur in the Stevenson *Guide* must be renewed: Fielding's *Charles Dickens: A Critical Introduction* (1958; rev. ed., 1965) is still "the best brief introduction to the work and life of Dickens, sound in its facts and astute in its criticism." In its 1965 revision—mainly an enlargement of the critical sections—it merits *English Men of Letters* status (if that defunct, but classic and beloved, series may be invoked). Its leading rival is E. D. H. Johnson's *Charles Dickens: An Introduction to His Novels* (1969), which, though not the major study that its author is manifestly equipped to write, more than fulfills its professed function and can suggest new lines of thought, or widen old ones, for readers well beyond an introductory stage. Johnson—whose felicity in quotation and analysis should delight any reader, aesthetically and intellectually—proceeds in an old-fashioned way, as he admits, presenting Dickens biographically and in his times, with chapters on his narration, characterization, and setting. I rejoice to concur with Richard D. Altick, who found this "the most succinct treatment I know of Dickens' artistry," offering "masterpieces of criticism" yet being "comfortable reading" (*Dkn*, 1970). Other introductory studies from which the specialist may learn include the two British Council pamphlets (1968), Trevor Blount's *Dickens: The Early Novels* (but see Steven Marcus in *Dkn*, 1969) and Barbara Hardy's admirable *Dickens: The Later Novels*; Martin Fido's *Charles Dickens* (1968) and his pleasantly illustrated *Charles Dickens: An Authentic Account of His Life and Times* (1970), the title of which reproved his confrères more sharply than his contribution to the art quite warranted; George Wing's *Dickens* (1969); A. H. Gomme's *Dickens* (1970); and Philip Hobsbaum's *A Reader's Guide to Charles Dickens* (1973), which includes an intelligent discussion of Dickens' nonfiction.

Major Studies

Sylvère Monod's notable *Dickens romancier* (1953) has been revised, expanded, and translated as *Dickens the Novelist* (1968). Monod still considers Dickens "At the Top" when writing *David Copperfield*, but the aftermath is no longer summarized as "La Dispersion" but is more encouragingly entitled "Renewals." The treatment of the later Dickens remains, however, disproportionately brief; Monod writes more adequately about the later novels in essays published elsewhere. His book was "a protest against the often-expressed view that Dickens was a negligible craftsman"—a view more widespread in 1953 than later—and he was the first scholar to publish a study that made extensive and effective use of Dickens' manuscripts and proof sheets, which provide part of his evidence of Dickens' craftsmanship. By 1970, a title such as *Dickens the Craftsman: Strategies of Presentation* (ed. Partlow) had become commonplace: but in 1963 there was still, argued Earle Davis, "a gnawing need for intense study of the artistry and craftsmanship of Dickens." Davis' book *The Flint and the Flame: The Artistry of Charles Dickens* (1963) is at its best on some of the literary and theatrical sources of Dickens' art, notably stage farce, melodrama, and the acting of Charles Mathews, and is interesting about Wilkie Collins' alleged influence on Dickens; but, though instructive, the book lacks critical edge, and it is marred by errors and an incomplete command of the relevant scholarship. A much more striking "Reassessment of the Novels" is Robert Garis' *The Dickens Theatre* (1965), though one of its aims—in reaction against such influential but "eagerly misdirected" interpretations as Edmund Wilson's and Hillis Miller's—was "to restore something like the popular understanding of Dickens." Garis' book is not about the actual theater, but about Dickens and his characters as brilliant and ostentatious performers—the characters "enacting their loud and distinct natures," and the narrator, a self-exhibiting master of language, performing in "a theatre created by the insistent and self-delighting rhetoric of his voice." After arguing his general case, Garis devotes the second half of his book to some distinguished essays on five of the later novels—though, as often in critical books that state a case, the particular studies seem only incidentally related to it. "There is always," writes Q. D. Leavis, "a smart Dickens book in vogue with the academics and literary journalists, and those favored at the moment seem to be Garis and Dabney" (*Dickens the Novelist*, 1970). I had not noticed this, and doubt it; but her reservations about Garis should be consulted, as should George Ford's respectful but critical review (*DiS*, 1966), William Burgan's (*VS*, 1966), K. J. Fielding's (*Dkn*, 1965), and Martin Green's (*KR*, 1965—"the moral interests of this criticism are very strong, and very fully integrated into the aesthetic"). Sundry reviews of notable, or contentious, general studies are cited thus, to spread the load of judgment.

Steven Marcus' *Dickens: From Pickwick to Dombey* (1965) might seem a likelier target for Q. D. Leavis' strictures. Harry Stone, in a review article that acknowledges the book's many merits, sees it nevertheless as "a book of the hour for the reader of the hour," presenting a modish Dickens "congenial to our souls," an existentialist, a psychoanalytic novelist, and so on (*KR*, 1965). Marcus' book received a notably mixed reception, ranging from the severe (Barbara Hardy, *VS*, 1966) to the highly encomiastic (Fielding, *DiS*, 1965; see also John Butt, *Dkn*, 1965; Edgar Johnson, *NCF*, 1965; Pamela Hansford Johnson, *Listener*, 18 Mar. 1965); all agree it is a noteworthy study, and the more challenging because it was still rare for the novels of Dickens' first decade as an author to attract such sophisticated and enthusiastic attention. Besides a lively and communicative literary intelligence, Marcus' special qualities include an excellent command of Victorian literature and history—his study of Engels' Manchester (1974: see below) attests the latter and is of great interest for students of Dickens—and of both

Freudian and Marxist theory. Marcus promises a follow-up volume on the later Dickens. Another intelligent study, more heavily dependent upon Freud, is Taylor Stoehr's *Dickens: The Dreamer's Stance* (1965). Dickens is a "dreamer" in the sense that his literary manner is akin to Freud's notion of dreamwork, though "Dickens is neither realist nor fantast, but something in between"—and he is a Victorian dreamer, not a timeless one. The core of the book is an interpretation of six of the "dark" novels as if they were dreams; there is much of interest on Dickens' double plots, his use of disguise, condensation, displacement, etc., and the relevance (in the dream pattern) of details that may otherwise appear otiose or irrelevant. Even readers unconvinced by Stoehr's theoretical structure (like Barbara Hardy, *MLQ*, 1966) find dark places made light here (see Fielding, *Dkn*, 1966; Alexander Welsh, *VS*, 1966; Michael Steig, *L&P*, 1965). H. M. Daleski finds a different organizing principle in the novels; taking a hint from Marcus, he argues in his *Dickens and the Art of Analogy* (1970) that Dickens has "an analogical imagination." Studying eight novels, he attempts to identify the "focus" of each and to indicate Dickens' development. In reaction against some of the subtleties of recent criticism, he discovers "a traditional Dickens who is preeminently concerned with money and love" (and he is arguably fresher and more convincing on Dickens' presentation of these themes than on the analogical structure).

Of the many centenary books, two of the most impressive are examples, not of new ways of looking at the novels, but of critical intelligence applying itself, along familiar lines, to the texts and their author—Angus Wilson's *The World of Charles Dickens* (1970) and F. R. Leavis and Q. D. Leavis' *Dickens the Novelist* (1970). Wilson's approach to Dickens' (imaginative) world is biographical, an inquiry into how the novels were fed by his public and private life, and he sees Dickens as a most complex and interesting man, full of contradictions and strangenesses that are reflected in the works; but his is a Dickens akin to the common reader's, who is right (he avers) to see Dickens as "above all funny" but, next to that, as compassionate. "Wilson has a novelist's feel for signs and evidence" (Denis Donoghue, *NCF*, 1972); some fresh biographical interpretations emerge, and Wilson feels his way into the problems Dickens experienced as a constantly but unpredictably developing novelist. Topics treated particularly well include Dickens' women, children, politics, and visual sense. Though showing both an intimate knowledge of Dickens and a profound sympathy for him, Wilson is severe about his lapses and limitations. John Carey finds this book disappointing (*Listener*, 28 May 1970), but most reviewers have been enthusiastic (Fielding, *Dkn*, 1970; Monod, *DSN*, 1971). It is sumptuously and intelligently illustrated. In *Dickens the Novelist*, the Leavises generally eschew biographical information ("our perhaps unfortunate knowledge of Dickens' life"). Most of the book consists of chapters—some of monograph length—on "the six great novels": F. R. Leavis on *Dombey, Hard Times,* and *Little Dorrit*; Q. D. Leavis on *Copperfield, Bleak House,* and *Great Expectations.* They have the intellectual edge one would expect; the approaches taken are described under Novels. The earlier novels are not valued highly, and the comic Dickens is not strongly in evidence. High claims are made for the flexibility and subtlety of Dickens' art, his understanding of how the mind works and expresses itself in speech, "the truth of his understanding of the nature of the age in which he lived," and his capacity for profound and effective thought about life (which is "indistinguishable from his genius as a novelist")—"the thinking intelligence directed to a grasp of the real." Reviewers' pleasure at such strongly argued enthusiasm from two highly influential critics, many of whose earlier pronouncements on Dickens had been cool, was tempered by regret that the Leavises never mention their previous shortcomings but castigate every commentator in sight, except for Tolstoy and Lord Brain, and seem unaware of, or obtuse about, much relevant discussion. Ford in a review article (*NCF*, 1971) finds "a lack of a sense of professional responsibility" in such errors of omission and commission and notes how much of the case they are arguing was anticipated by Edmund Wilson, about whom they are scathing. Controversies appear in the *Listener* (John Carey, 29 Oct. 1970; Ian Watt, 11 Mar. 1971; sundry correspondence, and a substantial reply by Q. D. Leavis, 8 Apr. 1971) and the *TLS* (C. P. Snow and others, from 9 July 1970). Other notable assessments of this important and contentious book include Barbara Hardy's (*NewS*, 9 Oct. 1970), Monod's (*EA*, 1971), Fielding's (*DSN*, 1971), W. W. Robson's (*Dkn*, 1971), and J. M. Blom's "*Dickens the Novelist* and the History of Dickens Criticism" (*DQR*, 1974). Fielding suggests that readers should "disregard what its authors say of themselves, as well as nearly everybody else" but pay respectful though "yes but—" attention to whatever they say about Dickens.

Barbara Hardy's brief study—"succinct and decisive," as one reviewer puts it—*The Moral Art of Dickens* (1970), mainly a compilation of earlier essays, is less successful in fulfilling the promise of its title than in adumbrating an approach to Dickens and in suggesting the mistakenness of some recent alternative approaches. Dickens, she maintains, suffers more than, say, George Eliot or Conrad from "the critical fictions of total relevance and covert symbolic form, for he is especially close to the explicit and under-distanced modes of acting, oratory, and journalistic address. It seems important, therefore, to stress both his failures and successes." She explores the latter contrast in a notably elegant essay, "The Complexity of Dickens," in Slater, 1970, refreshing at a time when admiring Dickens has too often persuaded critics to forget his weaknesses. Her chapters on "The Change of Heart in Dickens" provide the most sustained exploration of her "moral art" theme; the essays on *Pickwick, Chuzzlewit, Copperfield,* and *Great Expectations* that follow are stimulating and often astringent, but they fail to constitute a case. Angus Wilson takes up her argument interestingly (*Dkn*, 1971). Dickens, Barbara Hardy argues, was not very sensitive to Nature or God, his language being at its weakest and flattest when dealing with aesthetic or religious feeling; A. E. Dyson, by contrast, maintains in his *The Inimitable Dickens: A Reading of the Novels* (1970) that Dickens was "a deeply religious writer" and indeed "found his real energy in religion." Politically, Dyson's Dickens is a "radical-conservative," "in no perceptible way left-wing." As the book's title advertises, this is an enthusiastic presentation of an "exuberant" old-style Dickens; Dyson combats doughtily various modernizing views. With chapters on a dozen novels, he stresses Dickens' comic powers, vigorous even in the "dark" years, besides his vision of "the tragic world of Christian belief." John Lucas' tough-minded *The Melancholy Man: A Study of Dickens' Novels* (1970) presents a very different Dickens—more aware of social change, more disturbed, more penetrating (wiser than George Eliot, indeed "far and away the most intelligent of all English novelists"), a Dickens who was the conscience of his age but whose art suffers from clashes between the entertainer and the great truth teller in him. The difference between Dyson's and Lucas' Dickens can be partly accounted for by the fact that Dickens is "well worth stealing" and is remarkably susceptible of being reinterpreted in the image of his commentators. This is a recurrent phenomenon in Dickens criticism—George Orwell began his essay on Dickens (1940) by commenting upon it—and we should all beware. Dyson, a polemicist in extraliterary matters, is a decidedly conservative radical; Lucas (see *Literature and Politics in the Nineteenth Century*, 1971, which he edited) shares a "political viewpoint" from which Marx, Engels, and Lukács loom large. Lucas surveys all the novels, though concentrating on about half of them; he is at his most original on the earlier novels, about which there are more new things to be said. This is "an ideal book for any group of advanced students to have on hand to show them how to read, to argue about, and to appreciate Dickens" (Fielding, *Dkn*, 1971).

Most of the postcentennial critical studies are dealt with in the next section. That leaves two lively books to describe here, both of which are also mentioned below for their special concern with various topics: Alexander Welsh's *The City of Dickens* (1971) and John Carey's *The Violent Effigy: A Study of Dickens's Imagination* (1973; Amer. ed., 1974, retitled *Here Comes Dickens: The Imagination of a Novelist*). Welsh's is a book of much wider ambition and achievement than its title suggests; only its first third is concerned with Victorian London, for he also has in mind the Celestial City as an expression of religious and moral values. The final section, "The Bride from Heaven," treats of heroines ("The Spirit of Love and Truth"), the hearth, and death—a far cry, apparently, from the opening chapters about "The City as a Problem" and "Public Opinion and Policemen," but Welsh argues the profound interconnection between all these (and other) matters. Thus, "The worship of hearth and home . . . is not fully explicable without the pressures that the modern city has brought to bear upon it." This is a book of considerable wit, learning, and sophistication, and "the most sustained and intelligent attempt" (James Kincaid argues, *DSN*, 1972) to mediate between "two camps in Dickens criticism," the Honorary Colonels of which might be Humphry House and Hillis Miller. Raymond Williams sees it as raising "a fundamental problem of method in literary studies which offer to include a study of institutions" (*Dkn*, 1972). Carey's book is certainly the most entertaining recent book on Dickens: "Unlike any other recent Dickens critic John Carey manages to join styles with Dickens without producing a painful sense of falling" (Barbara Hardy, *Dkn*, 1975). A rare achievement indeed: frequenting the greatest English humorist has not made his commentators conspicuously more adept than, say, Milton's at managing a lightness of touch even when being (to use the Victorian phrase) deeply in earnest, as Carey almost always is. (He sometimes makes irresponsible jokes, quite good ones but not altogether what we expect from the Merton Professor of English in the University of Oxford.) As the oxymoron of Carey's English title *The Violent Effigy* suggests, he is concerned with the fact that "it is Dickens's gift to react to things in contradictory ways" and that such confusions "greatly strengthen him as a novelist in that he can appeal to those deep and never-quite-extinguished responses which make liberal intellectuals feel queasy." Hence Dickens' balancing or undercutting his Little Nell with a Quilp; hence Carey's opening his book with chapters on two of Dickens' conflicting preoccupations, "Violence" and "Order"; hence, too, his assertion that Dickens' imagination is most fully engaged in a "border country between people and things." Barbara Hardy's brilliant review (*Dkn*, 1975) of this "brilliant and unsettling book" should be consulted, and Garrett Stewart's fine book (1975), discussed below, offering a complementary view of Dickens' imagination (see Collins, *TLS*, 19 Sept. 1975), may usefully be contrasted with it. It is pleasant that this section can end on a book both funny and unsettling; few are either, fewer are both.

Many other considerable books might have been discussed in this section, but it seems tidier to describe them below under Special Aspects or Novels, though they bear so broadly upon Dickens' mind and art that any student needing a guide such as this should be aware of them. These include the studies by Mark Spilka (1963), Donald Fanger (1965), William Axton (1966), Ross Dabney (1967), Archibald Coolidge (1967), Grahame Smith (1968), G. L. Brook (1970), H. P. Sucksmith (1970), James Kincaid (1971), Sylvia Manning (1971), Michael Goldberg (1972), William Oddie (1972), Randolph Quirk (1974), Alfred Harbage (1975), and Garrett Stewart (1975). Others too perhaps, because a surveyor of this field other than myself might also have listed here Stanley Gerson (1967), Christopher Hibbert (1967; see above), Joseph Gold (1972), and Fred Kaplan (1975; see above), who certainly have done the state of Dickens studies some service, and I know it, or indeed Robert F. Fleissner (1965), Bert Hornback (1971), or Arthur Washburn Brown (1971).

Studies of Special Aspects

The special aspects surveyed here are as follows: characterization; plot and narration; imagery and symbolism; style and language; comedy, humor, and satire; illustrations; serialization; Dickens and society; London; industrialism; women; religion; literary predecessors, contemporaries, and successors (an untidy grouping); and notable critics criticized. These are manifestly rough-and-ready and overlapping categories, and there might have been many more, but they are not, I hope, altogether arbitrary. To have things in their right places was one of the diurnal passions of Dickens' life, and his commentators and bibliographers should brace themselves for a sharp look from those brilliant martinet eyes when they join him in the afterlife (above).

Characterization

Most writings on Dickens bear somehow upon his characterization but, of the general studies, those by Robert Garis (1965), William Axton (1966), Barbara Hardy (1970), F. R. and Q. D. Leavis (1970), John Carey (1973/74), and Garrett Stewart (1975) contain arguments—widely disparate in their tendency—that are notably suggestive. There have been many special studies. W. J. Harvey's admirably unfussy exercise of intelligence, *Character and the Novel* (1965), incorporates as its main discussion of Dickens his chapter on *Bleak House* in Gross and Pearson's *Dickens and the Twentieth Century* (1962) but includes many further perceptions. Thomas Kelly's "Character in Dickens' Later Novels" (*MLQ*, 1969) defends him against reductive assertions that he sees only where the clock's fingers are pointing and has, or conveys, no knowledge of the mechanism: "he represents truths about buried character no less important than those which engaged George Eliot and Henry James—truths that can be recovered only if we learn to take Dickens on his own terms." Patrick Swinden, too, in his *Unofficial Selves: Character in the Novel from Dickens to the Present Day* (1973), finds Dickens subtle and resourceful in the revelation of character: "The variety of Dickens's characters is matched by the variety of his modes of characterizing them and the relationships which obtain between one and another of them, and between all of them and the reader." This is an outstanding essay, as is Barbara Hardy's "Dickens and the Passions" (*NCF*, 1970), which discriminates between his stronger and weaker suits (he's less good on the tender passions, she argues). J. B. Priestley (in Tomlin, 1969) regards him as a mythopoeic genius, akin not to Jonson but to Shakespeare. William F. Hall distinguishes between two modes of caricature and argues that caricature can be both subtle and complex (*UTQ*, 1970), and V. S. Pritchett discusses Dickens' comic characterizations in *George Meredith and English Comedy* (1969). Bernd-Peter Lange's *Das Problem der Charakterentwicklung in den Romanen von Charles Dickens* (Berlin, 1969) is a thorough survey.

"Psychoanalytic criticism has come to be an accepted, and perhaps inevitable, technique for the examination of Dickens' works," says Michael Steig in a review article (*L&P*, 1965). Two pioneers in this area, Leonard F. Manheim and Warrington Winters, have written further such studies: Manheim on his women (*TSLL*, 1965), on the death instinct in his later novels (*Hidden Patterns*, ed. Leonard Manheim and Eleanor Manheim, 1966), on his children (*SNNTS*, 1969), and on "multiple projection" in *A Tale of Two Cities* (*DSA*, 1970); Warrington Winters on the pursuit theme (*VN*, 1963), on "The Death-Hug in Dickens" (*L&P*, 1966), and on particular novels—*The Old Curiosity Shop* (*Dkn*, 1967), *Our Mutual Friend* (*NDQ*, 1966), and *Hard Times* (*DSA*, 1972). Winters particularly commends a neglected pioneer study, S. Sprigge's *Physic and Fiction* (1921). Manheim founded *Literature and Psychology*, which has contained similar studies of Dickens by Michael Steig (1965), Ana Laura Zambrano (1972), and Branwen B. Pratt (1974). Charles Kligerman writes on "The Dream in Dickens" (*JAPA*, 1970). The general studies by Mark Spilka (1963), Steven Marcus (1965), and Taylor Stoehr (1965) depend heavily on psychological theories. Arthur Washburn Brown's *Sexual Analysis of Dickens' Props* (1971) moved reviewers to unwonted hilarity (Martin Dodsworth, *Dkn*, 1972; Lawrence Senelick, *DSN*, 1973), and Russell M. Goldfarb's chapter on "Orphans, Incest and Repression" in Dickens (*Sexual Repression and Victorian Literature*, 1970) was also severely criticized (Albert D. Hutter, *DSN*, 1973). A Jungian-Neumannian interpretation of Mrs. Gamp as the Magna Mater is recorded below (see Novels), and further essays of Freudian, Kleinian, and other such bents are noted in that section. Many of these studies, and of the more general ones, relate of course not only to the characterization but also to the narration, the props, and the novelist himself, though, as Ian Watt remarks after dabbling in some Freudian analysis, it is not clear just what critical advantages would accrue if it could be established that Dickens himself was an oral-erotic character (*DSA*, 1974).

Another approach may be considered here that spans characterization, narrative, and style—Dickens as a master of the grotesque. Arthur Clayborough's *The Grotesque in English Literature* (1965), which has an excellent chapter on the psychological implications of grotesque art, concludes with a substantial and profound chapter on Dickens (well summarized by Robert Hamilton, *Dkn*, 1966). Edgar Rosenberg (*Dkn*, 1970) commends Georg Seehase's *Charles Dickens: Zu einer Besonderheit seines Realismus* (Halle, 1961) as a brilliant study of Dickens' grotesque, though he finds it also erratic and overladen with "Marxist party-lining pish-posh." Dickens' grotesque imagination "offers a new reading of the world," Peter Steele argues (*Quadrant*, 1973). Other examples of this approach include Michael Steig's "Structure and the Grotesque in Dickens" (*CentR*, 1970), Donald Fanger's discussion of his "urban-grotesque" (*Dostoevsky and Romantic Realism*, 1965), Axton's *Circle of Fire* (see below), and studies of grotesque elements in *Great Expectations* by Nils-Göran von Lempruch (*ModSp*, 1973) and Christian W. Thomsen (*Anglia*, 1974). In his *Carlyle and Dickens* (1972) Michael Goldberg has a useful chapter on these authors' respective uses of the grotesque, and he refers to further recent discussions.

Finally, studies of categories of characters should be mentioned. Angus Wilson has memorably discussed Dickens' children (in Slater, 1970) and villains (*Listener*, 28 May 1970): for other views see John Carey (1973/74) on Dickens' "plastic" or "manufactured" children; Leonard Manheim on some inadequacies in his apprehension of childhood (*SNNTS*, 1969); I. W. Kreutz's rather chirpy, if not silly, essay "Sly of Manner, Sharp of Tooth: A Study of Dickens' Villains" (*NCF*, 1968); and Jonathan Miller on the terrific in Dickens (*Listener*, 28 May 1970). Leonard Manheim notes Dickens' fascination, as man and author, with fools, madmen, and psychopathic states (*DSA*, 1972). In "Dickens' Storytellers" (*Dkn*, 1973; rpt. in *Tellers and Listeners*, 1976), Barbara Hardy shows how many of Dickens' major characters are compulsive anecdotalists or reminiscers, and she educes the significance of this. Harry Levin discusses "two archetypal figures" in the novels—the orphan child and the surrogate father, an uncle or avuncular elder (*The Worlds of Victorian Fiction*, ed. Jerome H. Buckley, 1975). Another category of characters is surveyed below—see Women.

Plot and Narration

Dickens is the novelist most cited in John R. Reed's enterprising *Victorian Conventions* (1974), which throws much light on his kinship with his contemporaries in popular fiction. David Goldknopf, too, in his *The Life of the Novel* (1972), is illuminating about Victorian plotting, use of coincidence, etc., and Robert A. Colby explores, with impressive scholarship, Dickens' handling of one stock situation, that of "the fortunate foundling" (see *Oliver Twist* below). "Every writer of fiction," said Dickens, ". . . writes, in effect, for the stage," and William Axton in his *Circle of Fire: Dickens' Vision and Style and the Popular Victorian Theater* (1966) provides the fullest exploration to date of his manifold debt to the drama of his day. Axton distinguishes the various current genres of drama, examines the theatrical elements in four Dickens novels, and concludes with chapters on "Grotesque Scene," "Burlesque People," and "Melodramatic Narrative." Valerie Purton's "Dickens and 'Cheap Melodrama' " (*EA*, 1975) adds a note on the latter topic. Axton's enjoyable book measures up to its important subject; Michael C. Kotzin's *Dickens and the Fairy Tale* (1972) misses its chance on another aspect of the genesis of Dickens' art, one that everyone mentions but that had not previously been treated at book length. Though useful in tracing recurrent fairy-tale patterns in Dickens, the discussion is superficial: see the review by Harry Stone, author of important essays in this field (*Dkn*, 1973). Another critic who has specialized in this approach is Shirley Grob (see Novels below). Katherine M. Briggs writes well about folklore situations, materials, and atmosphere in the novels (*JFI*, 1970). Dickens' relation to a more recent urban folklore form, the detective novel, is traced by Julian Symons and others (see Literary . . . Successors below).

According to Northrop Frye, Dickens writes "not realistic novels but fairy tales in the low mimetic displacement," and their structure is that of New Comedy (see Humor below). Frye offers many perceptive suggestions about Dickens' plotting. Ioan Williams, however, in his *Realist Novel in England* (1974), argues that recent criticism overemphasizes the fantastic element in

Dickens at the expense of the realistic. Kenneth Graham discusses Dickens in relation to the debate about realism in his *English Criticism of the Novel 1865–1900* (1965); J. T. Flibbert shows how he figured in the French debate (*CL*, 1971), and Heinz Reinhold how he appeared in other areas of the debate (see Notable Critics below). On this topic, Reinhold commends Herbert Foltinek's *Vorstufen zum victorianischen Realismus: Der englische Roman von Jane Austen bis Charles Dickens* (Vienna, 1968). In "Dickens's Plot of Fortune" (*REL*, 1965), Stephen Wall argues that Dickens' plots, too often considered a liability, at their best "express or at least educe an important part of the novels' meaning."

Regarded by K. J. Fielding as "the best critical work on Dickens of the centenary year, and the best study of its kind there has ever been of Dickens" (*VS*, 1970), Harvey Peter Sucksmith's *The Narrative Art of Charles Dickens: The Rhetoric of Sympathy and Irony in His Novels* (1970) is a wide-ranging study of Dickens' rhetoric ("the technical means whereby, through structure, effects are created and vision focussed"), and it demonstrates that Dickens was a conscious artist. Sucksmith is acute on the structure of the novels, but his book is at its most original in its extremely thorough use of Dickens' manuscripts. Surprisingly many of the finest touches in familiar passages turn out to be revisions or afterthoughts. Sucksmith also explores Dickens' concept of narrative art by quoting his remarks —more numerous than is often recognized—on fictional technique. (Harry Stone, whose large assembly of such remarks, *Dickens on Dickens*, is awaited, cites and analyzes his dicta on "the uses of literature," *Dkn*, 1973.) Another notable study of Dickens' narrative methods, in relation to his leading contemporaries', appears in J. Hillis Miller's *The Form of Victorian Fiction* (1968), a book destined to revolutionize criticism, in E. D. H. Johnson's judgment (*NCF*, 1969). Herbert Howarth's "Voices of the Past in Dickens and Others" (*UTQ*, 1972) is another essay of notable quality. Dickens' affinities with film technique have been explored by Ana Laura Zambrano (see Novels below) and by Graham Petrie in "Dickens, Godard and the Film Today" (*YR*, 1975). Not only has Dickens had a powerful influence on film technique but also, Petrie argues, he remains a model for the art of film, which has not yet fully assimilated his innovations in narrative method. Zambrano notes Eisenstein's debt to Dickens (*Style*, 1975).

Imagery and Symbolism

Robert Barnard's *Imagery and Theme in the Novels of Dickens* (1974) begins: "Imagery is as vital a part of a Dickens novel as irony is of a Jane Austen novel. It helps to create his world and to shape the reader's view of it." Studies in this area have been plentiful. Barnard offers a careful if somewhat predictable account of the source of Dickens' imagery and, through an analysis of selected novels, indicates his growing skill in using images organically. Another book-length study, Hans-Dieter Gelfert's *Die Symbolik im Romanwerk von Charles Dickens* (Stuttgart, 1974) is a sophisticated, highly original, and distinguished work, by Edgar Rosenberg's account (*Dkn*, 1976). Gelfert, Rosenberg reports, sees Dickens' figurative and symbolic language as corresponding to the essential plot content of the novels. Defining symbolism as the interplay of steadily recurrent image clusters with equally recurrent "thematic constellations," Gelfert argues that Dickens' most persistent concerns are problems of isolation, self-estrangement, and heteronomy—problems expressed through three recurrent *grundsymbole*, the prison, water, and the legacy. (Barnard's list of *grundsymbole* features London, crime, wealth, and prisons.) Roselee Robison's "Time, Death and the River in Dickens' Novels" (*ES*, 1972) is another impressive discussion of his water imagery. Another familiar topic, his fire imagery, is discussed by B. F. Fisher iv and J. Turow (*RLV*, 1974). "The new look of Dickens criticism in France today," Sylvère Monod writes (*DSN*, 1971) is heavily dependent on Lucien Pothet's recent work, a good sample of which is his essay "Sur quelques images d'intimité chez Dickens" (*EA*, 1970). Lionel Stevenson found this impressive (*DSN*, 1971), but Sheila Smith regards this nouvelle vague as a lit-crit game, out of touch with common sense (*Dkn*, 1971).

Nineteenth-Century Fiction has carried three outstanding essays in this area: Jerome Thale's "The Imagination of Charles Dickens: Some Preliminary Discriminations" (1967), Samuel M. Sipe's "The Intentional World of Dickens' Fiction" (1975), and James E. Marlow's "Memory, Romance and the Expressive Symbol in Dickens" (1975). Thale, seeing Dickens as *the* great symbolic novelist, regards description as the foundation of his symbolic art. He seeks to relate the representational to the symbolic aspects of Dickens' descriptions and to distinguish between his various modes of description—the reportorial, enumerative, selective, atmospheric, metaphoric, familiar hyperbolic—but the effect is altogether less Polonius-like than this summary suggests. Sipe, developing one of Thale's suggestions, concentrates upon metaphors of transformation and upon Dickens' concern with both the man-made and the natural. Marlow explores another dichotomy, expressed through his symbolism, that between Dickens' impulses both to reconcile the reader to the world and to encourage escape from it into fanciful, fairy-tale, or supernatural metalevels. John Holloway's "Dickens and the Symbol" (in Slater, 1970) contrasts various ways of regarding and evaluating this element in the novels.

Many essays listed below under Novels bear on these topics, as of course do many of the general studies above, notably Daleski's (1970) and—challenging the view that Dickens should be regarded as a seriously symbolic or prophetic author—Garis' (1965) and Carey's (1973/74). The discovery that Dickens is a symbolic novelist, Garis remarks sardonically, "has apparently exempted his critics from even the most elementary standards of relevance." According to Carey, not symbolism but simile is Dickens' forte: "The exuberance of his similes is equalled only by their precision. . . . His similes remake the world." A. H. Gomme, too, in his *Dickens* (1970) argues that the symbolism has been overrated; most of the novels are damaged, he says, by forced symbolism, and "quite a lot of Dickens's symbols remain inert." Collins, in a presidential address (*DSN*, 1976), suggests that the routine essay on imagery—probably the favorite critical genre today—is too facile.

Style and Language

"Dickens' own characters become stylists with him, and a passion for expression is diffused through every level of his writing," Garrett Stewart writes in his *Dickens and the Trials of Imagination* (1975), one of the most perceptive—and best-written—recent studies of Dickens' imaginative cast of mind and creative handling of language. Stewart offers excellent analyses both of the characters as stylists and (often) as people with vivid imaginations and of Dickens' various narrative styles, including his less felicitous ones. He rightly notes, too, the important element of verbal fun—nonfunctional because "inutility is often the point of Dickens' word-play"; it betokens "a spirit of truancy and trifling" in healthy protest against a utilitarian world. Robert Garis' book (1965), too, is splendid on Dickens' eloquence and verbal stunts; and in the Leavises' book (1970)—which is contemptuous of Garis'—assertions about Dickens' "Shakespearian use of the language" rise well above the level of hopeful gesture at which such phrases commonly remain. George Ford in his "Dickens and the Voices of Time" (*NCF*, 1970) examines what Graham Greene has called his "secret prose" and discusses the interaction between Dickens' private and public voices. Another brilliant essay is Ian Watt's "Oral Dickens" (*DSA*, 1974), which ranges from Dickens' mastery of the spoken word to his mastery of food and drink as literary topics and points out the (Freudian) connections between them. Collins' edition of the *Public Readings* (1975) has stimulated reviewers to discuss the relation between Dickens' writing and the spoken word (a matter on which Collins offers inadequate editorial suggestion) and may provoke further thought on these lines. Little has been written about the relevance of the reading aloud of Victorian fiction, but useful suggestions occur in Elliot M. Shrero's "Intonation in Nineteenth-Century Fiction" (*QJS*, 1974), which compares Dickens with Henry James as heard novelists; and Collins in his *Reading Aloud: A Victorian Métier* (1972) ruminates and anecdotalizes about this phenomenon. How many of Dickens' most ear-satisfying cadences result from second thoughts in his manuscripts becomes apparent in Sucksmith's book (1970).

Dickens' earlier and later styles have been studied by Richard J. Dunn (*Dkn*, 1966) and Ludwig Borinski (in Reinhold, 1969). Reinhold's collection also contains essays by Helmut Viebrock on the relation between Dickens' syntax and his style and by Wilhelm Füger on Dickens' tactics in opening his novels. Talbot Penner considers early stylistic influences (*Dkn*, 1968), and Park Honan defends Dickens in regard to a tic most prominent in his earlier work, his fondness for metrical prose (*VN*, 1965). William Axton's book (1966) considers theatrical influences on his style. W. A.

Ward's "Language and Charles Dickens" (*Listener*, 23 May 1963; rpt. in *Literary English since Shakespeare*, ed. George Watson, 1970) sees liveliness as Dickens' most characteristic quality and uses Pecksniff as a prime instance. David Lodge's notable *Language of Fiction* (1966) has a chapter on Dickens, "The Rhetoric of *Hard Times*," and William Cappel analyzes *Great Expectations* in like mode (*Style*, 1970). Three other outstanding essays are commended: David Parker's on Dickens' archness ("a knowingness, a calculated mock-pomposity that at its best delights all readers. At its worst it degenerates into mere facetiousness . . . ," *Dkn*, 1971) and two already referred to—Jerome Thale's discrimination among his modes of description and how they relate to his imaginative vision (*NCF*, 1967) and Samuel M. Sipe's essay, "The Intentional World of Dickens' Fiction" (*NCF*, 1975), on how his "metaphors of transformation provide a crucial insight into the ontology of his fictional world." To my disadvantage, I have not seen Ian Milner's "Dickens' Style" (*PP*, 1974).

Of more strictly linguistic studies, G. L. Brook's *The Language of Dickens* (1970) is the most comprehensive discussion of his slang, substandard grammar, choice of proper names, and their contribution to his literary craftsmanship.* What Dickens offers to students of language is best displayed in Stanley Gerson's exacting monograph, *Sound and Symbol in the Dialogue of the Works of Charles Dickens* (Stockholm, 1967). Randolph Quirk's well-known earlier essays (1959, 1961) are revised and expanded in his *The Linguist and English Literature* (1974; and see also his "The Language of Charles Dickens," *LeL*, 1961). His treatment of the topic is less comprehensive but more sophisticated than Brook's. Norman Page's *Speech in the English Novel* (1972) contains a lively chapter on Dickens, and he and Gerson have written elsewhere on details of Dickens' linguistic usages (*Dkn*, 1965, 1966, 1968, 1969, 1971; *CS*, 1969; on Cockney dialect in Dickens, Page's topic in *ES*, 1970, see also P. J. Keating's *The Working Classes in Victorian Fiction*, 1971, Ch. x; on Dickens' creation of names, *ModSp*, 1975). Page's book refers to several useful unpublished dissertations.

Comedy, Humor, Satire

"Dickens is essentially a comic writer," John Carey maintains in his book (1973/74): when his humor fails, "his imagination seldom survives it for more than a few sentences." Few critics would go that far, but Carey's book, with Garrett Stewart's (1974), is one of the general studies with most to say on this topic. The one essential recent discussion is Northrop Frye's "Dickens and the Comedy of Humors" (*Experience in the Novel*, ed. Roy Harvey Pearce, 1968; rpt. in Frye's *The Stubborn Structure*, 1970), which sees Dickens in the New Comedy tradition, from Plautus and Terence to Jonson and Molière—"The main action is a collision of two societies which we may call for convenience the obstructing and the congenial society. . . .

---

* This paragraph was drafted by my colleague K. C. Phillipps, author of *Jane Austen's English* (1970) and of *Thackeray's English* (forthcoming).

All the stock [New Comedy] devices, listed in Greek times as laws, oaths, compacts, witnesses, and ordeals, can be found in him." This is a totally underlinable essay, where one is only in danger, like Troilus, of losing distinction in one's joys. Matthew Hodgart, in his *Satire* (1969), also has a few suggestive pages on Dickens as "the greatest of all natural humorists" (in the old Humors sense). Other notable essays include Barbara M. Gross's (*WHR*, 1963); Margaret Ganz's lively protests against the recent neglect of Dickens' humor and of his simple playfulness (*DSA*, 1970; *VS*, 1971; *DSA*, 1975, on *Pickwick*); Walter Allen's "The Comedy of Dickens," which recognizes the "black comedy" in his novels but is vivaciously polychromatic in celebrating the other colors (in Slater, 1970); Hillis Miller's on the special qualities of Dickens' earlier comic art (*NCF*, 1970); Donald Fanger's comparison with Gogol (in *Veins of Humor*, ed. Harry Levin, 1972); W. W. Robson's lecture (see below, under *Nicholas Nickleby*); and, I am assured, K. H. Wagner's (*NsM*, 1970).

Two considerable books have been produced in this area, James R. Kincaid's *Dickens and the Rhetoric of Laughter* (1972) and Sylvia Bank Manning's *Dickens as Satirist* (1971). "Even if there *is* genial or harmless laughter, I think it is very rare in Dickens," writes Kincaid, and Margaret Ganz (*DSN*, 1973) will not have been his only reader to find such a view too solemnly purposive, nor will his assessment of the world of *David Copperfield* (noticed below) as "grim" with "almost no pure mirth present" command universal assent. But his book is full of perceptive and challenging evaluations; like Angus Easson (*N&Q*, 1975), "I find much here of interest and value, but cannot go along with the book's basic critical stance." Carey's book, written wittily and showing a fuller capacity to be amused, inspires more confidence in this respect, for reasons that Longinus indicated. Sylvia Manning's book explores Dickens' originality by distinguishing his aims and procedures from those of classical satire and shows the developments in his narrator persona and in his choice of satirical butts. She is amplest and strongest on the later novels. For some pertinent objections to her critical terminology and procedures, see Edgar Rosenberg (*ELN*, 1975) and Rachel Trickett (*Dkn*, 1972). Like Kincaid, she is often most valuable in perceptive analysis of verbal detail, independent of the larger case being argued.

Illustrations

More work of high quality on Dickens and his illustrators has been produced in the past decade or so than in the century preceding, though the results have not yet permeated his commentators' consciousnesses. The specialists in this line have demonstrated, in convincing detail, how integral a part of the novels—or most of the novels—the illustrations are and how deeply collaborative was Dickens' relationship with his illustrators, whose efforts (it now appears abundantly) were not confined to merely picturing moments in his text, but, with or without his full knowledge or encouragement, went further, intelligently reinforcing, amplifying, and clarifying the moral and thematic implications of the moments selected for illustration. These commentators have advanced well beyond the commonly accepted notion that Dickens' are the only adult English novels, except perhaps Thackeray's, whose original illustrations have a classic status—that Pickwick and Pecksniff and Micawber, for instance, are inseparable from Phiz's depictions of them. The relationship of the illustrations, frontispieces, and cover designs to the text is, it has been argued, hardly less close than Blake's graphics are to his poems. Michael Steig, the most prolific and one of the most learned and persuasive of the students of the illustrations, has even argued that the illustrated novel of this period should be recognized as a subgenre of fiction: "To read an illustrated novel as though it had no illustrations is to distort it. . . . The use of emblematic details links the illustrator to the novelist in a special way. . . . He becomes a collaborator with the novelist in more than mere mimetic representation" (*DSA*, 1973); and he contends here and elsewhere that Phiz has never had his deserts as Dickens' collaborator. Q. D. Leavis, arguing similarly that the illustrations of the novels up to *Bleak House* "are a unique addition to the text . . . indispensable even to us, the highly-trained modern reader, in interpreting the novels correctly," adds that "this is true of no other English novelist" (*Dickens the Novelist*, p. 336). But most critical studies still ignore, or give only perfunctory attention to, the fact that Dickens' novels are illustrated, though enough has been shown to make any commentator who is visually ill educated realize that there is a sizable gap in his competence. Future Dickens studies are likely to recognize more constantly that his art is, agreeably to the 1970s, a multimedia or (more precisely) a dual-media one.

Q. D. Leavis' chapter on "The Dickens Illustrations: Their Function" is the most substantial discussion in a critical book, and she is perceptive in her comments both on individual plates and on the nature and development of Dickens' collaboration with his illustrators. But it is, perhaps, symptomatic of the critical failure I have mentioned that even she hives off her remarks on the illustrations into a separate chapter: for, if the illustrations are really "indispensable," the place to discuss them should surely have been in the critical analyses of the novels in earlier chapters. Few critics, however, have yet consistently shown how this dual-media discussion should be conducted; almost all remarks about the illustrations occur in specialist essays. Robert L. Patten's essay on the *Carol* (*DSA*, 1972) is one honorable exception to this stricture. One book has been written on the subject, John Harvey's *Victorian Novelists and Their Illustrators* (1970), mostly about Dickens, particularly in his relation with Browne, and it is admirable (see reviews by Anthony Burton, Richard A. Vogler, and Charles B. Gullans, *Dkn, VS, NCF,* all 1971). Harvey, like Steig and others to be mentioned, enjoys the advantage over Q. D. Leavis of having a fuller technical knowledge of art history, but the conclusions that most of them reach have a common tenor: an increasing respect for Browne as an illustrator, capable of responding to Dickens' developing art, at least up to *Bleak*

House, with *Dombey* and *Copperfield* generally being seen as the climax of their collaboration; the importance, in the Cruikshank and Browne illustrations, of the inheritance from Hogarth and, to a lesser extent, from Gillray and Rowlandson—an artistic tradition that also profoundly affected Dickens' imaginative habits, for, as John Dixon Hunt says (see below), Dickens "drew upon and was conditioned by the same graphic traditions that gave him his illustrators"; the function of the illustrations, not merely to give a visual equivalent to episodes from the novels, but also to provide a running commentary upon their moral significance and to hint at future plot developments and dominant themes; the illustrations' allusiveness both to earlier engravings in their graphic tradition and to topical events and personalities; and the comparative irrelevance of the illustrations to the later novels by Stone and Fildes, characteristic of the emerging school of graphic design that had no vital connection with Dickens' mode of seeing and writing.

Jane Rabb Cohen has written extremely thorough and judicious accounts of Dickens' relations, personal and professional, with Cruikshank, Seymour, Cattermole, and Fildes (*HLB*, 1969, 1971; *DSA*, 1970; *DiS*, 1967). In these and other recent studies, more credence than before is given to Seymour's and Cruikshank's claims to have originated important elements of *Pickwick* and *Oliver Twist*. On the latter, see also Vogler's pamphlet for the UCLA Dickens Centenary *Oliver Twist* Exhibition (1970), his essay "*Oliver Twist*: Cruikshank's Pictorial Prototypes" (*DSA*, 1972), and his contribution to *George Cruikshank: A Revaluation* (ed. Robert L. Patten, 1974), an entirely enjoyable volume (see Peter Conrad, *TLS*, 26 July 1974), which includes other essays relevant to Dickens by Harvey, Steig, Anthony Burton, Harry Stone, E. D. H. Johnson, and Ronald Paulson. Louis James, another contributor to Patten's book, refers elsewhere to Dickens' relations with Seymour (*DSA*, 1970). Dickens' older and fundamental relationship with Hogarth is convincingly examined by Harry P. Marten (*SNNTS*, 1974), and this is one of John Dixon Hunt's topics, too, in his fine essay "Dickens and the Traditions of Graphic Satire" (in *Encounters*, ed. Hunt, 1971).

Cruikshank's illustrations for *Oliver Twist* are "very poor," writes Sylvère Monod with blithely iconoclastic candor (*DSA*, 1974)—a refreshing minority report, though various critics regard him as a less satisfactory illustrator (though a greater artist) than Browne, an exception here being the distinguished present-day illustrator Nicolas Bentley, who, surveying "Dickens and His Illustrators," gives the palm to Cruikshank (in Tomlin, 1969). Cruikshank's work, particularly on *Sketches by Boz*, is submitted to a remarkable analysis by Hillis Miller (see *Sketches by Boz* below), which has been described by Jane R. Cohen as "a landmark for scholars of Dickens' earliest work and illustrator" and "a model for future study of Dickens' books" (*Dkn*, 1972, p. 60). For other notes on the *Oliver Twist* illustrations, see Brian Cobb (*Listener*, 22 July 1965) and Steig (*Ariel*, 1973). Patten has written about some *Pickwick* plates (*ELH*, 1967, 1969; *Dkn*, 1970), notably "an astonishingly detailed interpretation" (Slater, *Dkn*, 1970, p. 228) of the one showing Mr. Pickwick in the pound. Dickens' experiment in the *Clock*

—"Woodcuts Dropped into the Text"—is discussed by Joan Stevens (*SB*, 1967), and Steig accounts for disparities in the depiction of the Marchioness there (*DiS*, 1966). Steig's writings on the ensuing novels are numerous and lively—on *Chuzzlewit* (*DSA*, 1972), on *Dombey* (*ELN*, 1969; *DSA*, 1970; *Dkn*, 1971), on *Copperfield* (*HSL*, 1970; *DSN*, 1971), and on *Bleak House* (*DiS*, 1968; *HLQ*, 1972). The last mentioned of these essays—"The Critic and the Illustrated Novel: Mr. Turveydrop from Gillray to *Bleak House*"— contains one of Steig's best general discussions of the "aesthetics of the Dickens-Browne novel" and of Browne's brilliant insights into the meaning of the text. In "Emblems in Victorian Literature" (*HSL*, 1970), John R. Reed compares Dickens with his contemporaries in this regard. The Clarendon edition of the novels gives special attention to the illustrations, providing an appendix on them in every volume. Margaret Cardwell, editor of its *Edwin Drood*, gives further information about the *Drood* engravings in the *Dickensian* (1970, 1973, 1975). Analogues to the *Bleak House* cover design are noted by J. R. Tye (*Dkn*, 1969). Anthony Burton notices recent exhibitions of Maclise and Cruikshank in their bearings upon Dickens (*Dkn*, 1972, 1974), and Graham Reynolds in his "Charles Dickens and the World of Art" (*Apollo*, 1970) offers an excellent brief analysis of Dickens' taste in contemporary art, using as evidence his own purchases in this area, his friendships in the artistic fraternity, and his moving from Cruikshank and Browne to Marcus Stone, Charles Collins, and Luke Fildes as his chosen illustrators. Interest in this area of Dickens studies was evinced by the MLA's holding a seminar on "Dickens and the Graphic Arts" (see Deborah Thomas' report, *DSN*, 1973). Finally, it should be mentioned that Frederic Kitton's pioneer work *Dickens and His Illustrators* (1899) has been reprinted (Amsterdam, 1972), that Jane Rabb Cohen and Robert Patten have books on the stocks that should supersede it, that a checklist of the present whereabouts of the original drawings to which Kitton refers is now being compiled (see *Dkn*, 1972), and that Steig has a book forthcoming on "Phiz."

Serialization

The major book-length work on this subject, Archibald C. Coolidge, Jr.'s *Charles Dickens as Serial Novelist* (1967), is a valuable pioneer study, despite many embarrassing puffs by the author and his publishers. It raises important questions about the pattern of Dickens' serial installments and about his plotting and his unifying devices (see discussion by Fielding, *Dkn*, 1967). Briefer studies of this topic include Joan Stevens' *Some Nineteenth-Century Novels and Their First Publication* (Wellington, N.Z., 1961), John Butt's in his *Pope, Dickens and Others* (1969), and William Axton's (*UTQ*, 1967), Stevens using *Copperfield* and Butt using *Chuzzlewit* and *Little Dorrit* as their main instances. Stevens' booklet is the handiest primer on this topic. How the early Dickens relates to his predecessors in serial publication—a topic hitherto neglected—has been studied by Lance Schachterle (*DSA*, 1974; see also his "*Bleak House* as a Serial Novel," *DSA*,

1970), Robert L. Patten in his *"Pickwick Papers* and the Development of Serial Fiction" (*RUS*, 1975), and Donald Hawes (*DSA*, 1972). Patten's particularly thorough and illuminating essay surveys the history of part-issue publication from the late eighteenth century onward and relates it to technological developments in printing and distribution. Edgar Rosenberg notes Dickens' habit of continuing to plan in monthly installments even when publishing weekly (*DSA*, 1972). J. D. Jump in his distinguished lecture "Dickens and His Readers" includes the effects of serialization among the relationships that he examines (*BJRL*, 1972). I have not seen Daniel Fader's *The Periodical Context of English Literature 1708–1907* (1971), which has a chapter on Dickens; it is reviewed, unfavorably, by Lance Schachterle (*DSN*, 1973).

Dickens and Society

"It is high time for a revaluation of Dickens' position with regard to the society of his day," writes Monod, noting some wide disparities in current assertions on this subject (*DiS*, 1965). According to Robert Garis, in an important discussion of Dickens criticism (*VS*, 1964), such difficulties arise partly because "modern intellectuals wear their alienation almost with pride," and because "a vaguely Marxist analysis of Victorian thinking" discourages serious and actively discriminating criticism. Northrop Frye similarly detects a current overemphasis on "everything in Dickens, real or fancied, that is darkly and ambiguously ironic, or hostile to Victorian social standards" (*The Stubborn Structure*, 1970). The most substantial recent study is Grahame Smith's *Dickens, Money and Society* (1968), which includes an excellent discussion of "The Man and His Times" and useful comparisons with several literary contemporaries. For Raymond Williams, Smith's is "one of the three or four essential books on Dickens and on the nineteenth-century novel" and a needed corrective to Humphry House and other critics in the liberal-reformist tradition (*Dkn*, 1969), but another reviewer was less convinced: "Mr. Smith's Dickens is another lonely pacer of Dover Beach, and certainly not recognizable as the involved, immersed editor of *Household Words*" (*TLS*, 13 Nov. 1969). Money also provides the way into an analysis of Dickens' values in Ross H. Dabney's elegant little book about mercenary and unmercenary marriage, *Love and Property in the Novels of Dickens* (1967).

Whether Louis Cazamian's pioneer study *The Social Novel in England 1830–1850* (trans. Martin Fido, 1973), in which Dickens' outlook is described as "la philosophie de Noël," deserves its classic status is discussed by Sylvère Monod and P. J. Keating (*Dkn*, 1973; *DSN*, 1974). Important recent essays on Dickens as a social novelist include Raymond Williams' "Social Criticism in Dickens: Some Problems of Method and Approach" (*CritQ*, 1965) and "Dickens and Social Ideas" (in Slater, 1970), and John Holloway's "Dickens' Vision of Society" (*Listener*, 25 Feb. 1965; rpt. in *The Novelist as Innovator*, ed. Walter Allen, 1966). Williams and Holloway analyze Dickens' originality in integrating his social vision and ideas into his art. John Lucas' book on Dickens (1970) is strong on this topic, too. Elsewhere, in "Dickens and [Matthew] Arnold" (*RMS*, 1972), Lucas uses the comparison with Arnold's social and literary outlook as a means of demonstrating Dickens' greater awareness, intelligence, and artistic richness; Arnold looks "precious and limited" beside Dickens. Richard A. Levine explores the "two nations" theme in Dickens (*SNNTS*, 1969), R. D. McMaster his growing pessimism about society (*EA*, 1970), Richard Faber (rather superficially) his concern with social class (*Proper Stations*, 1971), and Robin Gilmour the relationship between the gentleman and the self-made man in the novels ("Dickens and the Self-Help Idea," in *The Victorians and Social Protest*, ed. J. Butt and I. F. Clarke, 1973). Everett Knight in his *Theory of the Classical Novel* (1970) sees Dickens as "of all the classical novelists the most flagrantly and unrepentantly middle class," with many consequential limitations. Studies of his politics are mentioned above under Biography, and many relevant studies relating to particular novels are discussed below.

London

"He describes London like a special correspondent for posterity," Walter Bagehot memorably remarked in his essay on Dickens (1858). How perceptive, wide-ranging, and sagacious a "correspondent" he was and how central to his art was his concern with urban (and specifically metropolitan) life have been widely discussed. Raymond Williams has written well, if repetitively, about Dickens' essentially urban sensibility in the *English Novel from Dickens to Lawrence* (1970), *The Country and the City* (1973), and in reviews in the *Dickensian* (1969, 1972). Other distinguished studies of this theme are Donald Fanger's section on "Representing London," in his *Dostoevsky and Romantic Realism: A Study of Dostoevsky in Relation to Balzac, Dickens and Gogol* (1965; and most comparisons between Dickens and Balzac [see below] refer to their presentations of their metropoles), Alexander Welsh's *The City of Dickens* (1971), Peter Conrad's *The Victorian Treasure-House* (1973), and Alan Burke's "Strategy and Theme of Urban Observation in *Bleak House*" (*SEL*, 1968). Volker Klotz in his *Die erzählte Stadt* (Munich, 1969) compares Dickens' earlier and later presentations of urban living. P. J. Keating's *The Working Classes in Victorian Fiction* (1971) contains much about the literary tradition in which Dickens participated; his Cockneys' idiom—the topic of Keating's final chapter—is discussed by Norman Page and others (see Style and Language above). Christopher Hibbert is informative about Dickens' knowledge and artistic use of London in his *The Making of Charles Dickens* (1967) and in Tomlin, 1969. That Dickens' ideal was suburbanism—that he was anticity but no pastoralist—is argued by Coral Lansbury (*DSN*, 1972).

The serious study of English urban history, which has an obvious relevance for Dickens students, is virtually the invention of the past two decades, and *The Victorian City: Images and Realities* (ed. H. J. Dyos and Michael Woolf, 1973), which includes an essay by Collins on Dickens and London, was immediately recognized as a monumental contribution to both urban and Victorian studies (see Welsh, *VS*, 1974). Other works edited by Dyos are important for the student of Dickens' main locale—*The Study of Urban History* (1968), *The Urban History Yearbook* (1974–   ), and a reprint (1973) of a very convenient gazetteer, *Collins' Illustrated Atlas of London* (1854). The latter appears in the Victorian Library (Leicester Univ. Press), a series of reprints that includes many other items of relevant topographical and social interest. *Dickens' Dictionary of London* (comp. Charles Dickens, Jr., 1879; rpt. 1973) is also handy for readers of the novels, and Aldon D. Bell's *London in the Age of Dickens* (1967) is useful too, though it does not aspire to be the major work on Dickens and his London that remains so much to be desired. Of the many recent scholarly books on Victorian London, these are particularly helpful for Dickensians: J. J. Tobias' *Crime and Industrial Society in the Nineteenth Century* (1967—I wish that it had been available when I wrote *Dickens and Crime*), Gareth Stedman Jones's *Outcast London: A Study in the Relationship between Classes in Victorian Society* (1970), Francis Sheppard's *London 1808–1870: The Infernal Wen* (1971), and B. I. Coleman's anthology *The Idea of the City in Nineteenth Century Britain* (1973). Of more limited studies, the catalogue of an exhibition at the Guildhall Art Gallery, *Charles Dickens and His London* (1962), and Graham Prettejohn's *Charles Dickens and Southwark* (1974) should be mentioned. Jacob Korg's *London in Dickens' Day: A Book of Primary Source Materials* (1960) is a stimulating companion to the novels.

Industrialism

Louis Cazamian's pioneer study of *The Social Novel in England 1830–1850* (1903) has at last been translated (by Martin Fido, 1973), but no successor of comparable ambition has appeared. Dickens features prominently in several useful studies, such as Herbert L. Sussman's *Victorians and the Machine: The Literary Response to Technology* (1968), Ivanka Kovačević's *Fact into Fiction: English Literature and the Industrial Scene 1750–1850* (1975, an anthology with a monograph-length introduction), and Steven Marcus' *Engels, Manchester and the Working Class* (1974; see discussion in *VS*, 1975). Sheila M. Smith discusses the relation between fact and fiction in the treatment of industrialism in the Victorian novel (*RMS*, 1964; *RES*, 1970). Dickens' ambivalence toward the factory system and related topics are explored in a notable series of essays by Patrick Brantlinger (*VS*, 1969; *NCF*, 1971; *Criticism*, 1972), and there has been a lively controversy about what Mr. Rouncewell the Ironmaster portends (*EIC*, 1965, 1967, 1971, 1973, by Trevor Blount, David Craig, and Anne Smith; see also Ivan Melada, *The Captain of Industry in English Fiction 1821–1871*, 1970). K. J. Fielding and Anne Smith in their notable essay "*Hard Times* and the

Factory System: Dickens vs. Harriet Martineau" (*NCF*, 1970) detect a shift in Dickens' views in the early 1850s. Kovačević, too, contrasts Dickens and Martineau in her "The Ambivalence of a Generation" (in *Zbornik Radova* . . . , Belgrade, 1969). Another discussion of *Hard Times*, with wider implications, is David Craig's Marxist study, *The Real Foundations: Literature and Social Change* (1973). Extracts from Dickens are prominent in the Open University's "collection of readings" *Industrialism and Culture 1830–1914* (ed. Christopher Harvie et al., 1970; rev. 1975), an anthology of exemplary range and suggestiveness that provides an admirable context within which Dickens' mixed—complex or muddled—responses to industrialism may be placed and better understood.

Women

Dickens' heroines have continued to puzzle, where they do not bore, his commentators, though Esther Summerson has enjoyed a remarkable amount of respectful attention (see *Bleak House* below), and Dickens inevitably features in the recent books on women in Victorian fiction, though he is some way from being the hero of Kate Millett's *Sexual Politics* (1969) or Françoise Basch's *Relative Creatures* (1974). The only monograph-length study, Sylvia L. Jarmuth's *Dickens' Use of Women in His Novels* (1967), is a pedestrian survey; Michael Slater, whose *Dickens and Women* is forthcoming, has a crucial topic to make his own. Hillis Miller, at the MLA seminar on this subject, made some excellent suggestions (*DSN*, 1974), and there have been several good essays—Jane W. Stedman's on Dickens' child-wives and Sylvia Manning's on his January-and-May marriages (*Dkn*, 1963, 1975), Margaret Lane's "Dickens on the Hearth" and Pamela Hansford Johnson's "The Sexual Life in Dickens' Novels" (in Slater, 1970), and Harry Stone's on the love patterns in the novels (in Partlow, 1970). Carol Munn discusses Dickens and Gissing as "radical feminists" (*GN*, 1972), and Leonard Manheim adopts a psychological approach in his "Floras and Doras: The Women in Dickens' Novels" (*TSLL*, 1965). The most comprehensive, sophisticated, and learned account of Dickens' heroines is Alexander Welsh's in his *The City of Dickens* (1971); its section on "The Bride from Heaven" makes better sense than has any previous study of why so intelligent a man as Dickens makes such a fuss about Agnes and her like. Women decidedly unlike Agnes predominate in Steven Marcus' *The Other Victorians* (1966), which contains interesting references to Dickens. Heinz Reinhold discusses Dickens' early heroines, and heroes, as seen by nineteenth-century German critics, in *Grossbritannien und Deutschland: Europaische Aspekte der politisch-kulturellen Beziehunge* . . . (ed. Ortwin Kuhn, Munich, 1974). There are chapters on Dickens (which I have not seen) in Katharine Moore's *Victorian Wives* (1974), Rosalind Miles's *The Fiction of Sex* (1974), Carolyn Heilbrun's *Toward a Recognition of Androgyny* (1973), and Elizabeth Hardwick's *Seduction and Betrayal* (1974).

Religion

Remarking that we need a book on Dickens and Christianity, John R. Wilson in his "Dickens and Christian Mystery" (*SAQ*, 1974) argues that Dickens was a hesitant Christian, only half believing in the reality of the supernatural. A number of doctoral theses have been written on Dickens and religion, but no full-length study has been published, though one such thesis, Norris F. Pope's formidably learned "Charitable Activity and Attitudes in Early Victorian England, with Special Reference to Dickens and the Evangelicals" (Diss. Oxford 1975) provides another reminder of how much is to be discovered in this area—how, for instance, Dickens had much more in common with the Evangelicals than his fictional presentations of such religionists would suggest. It awaits publication. Valentine Cunningham has a valuable chapter on Dickens and the anti-Dissenting tradition in his *Everywhere Spoken Against: Dissent in the Victorian Novel* (1975), and Heinz Reinhold shows how many pious Victorian readers were upset by his religious and moral attitudes (in Reinhold, 1969). Peyrouton, in some notes on *The Life of Our Lord*, discusses Dickens' religious position, and Archibald C. Coolidge describes it as latitudinarian (both *Dkn*, 1963). Perhaps the best discussion of this topic occurs in Alexander Welsh's *The City of Dickens* (1971); Michael Slater, reviewing it, remarks that there is now no excuse for "the easy generalisations about Dickens and religion that have been made all too often" (*VS*, 1972). John Carey is provocatively irreverent about Dickens' religion, or religiosity (*Listener*, 25 May 1970, and in his book, 1973/74). Avrom Fleishman, in a critique of fashionable attempts to see Dickens as an apocalyptic writer, argues well that he should be framed within the religious, as well as the literary and philosophical, currents of his time, not of ours (*MLQ*, 1973). Welsh, Cunningham, and Pope indicate how this may best be done.

Bert G. Hornback's *Noah's Arkitecture: A Study of Dickens' Mythology* (1972) and Joseph Gold's *Charles Dickens, Radical Moralist* (1972) propose a much more God-intoxicated Dickens than other commentators have yet done. They review each other respectfully (*DSN*, 1973), Hornback finding Gold brilliant and Gold labeling Hornback's book "an important contribution to the field" and commenting, "It is the right kind of thing and contains a central truth about the way Dickens wrote"—though he suggests reservations about details ("it is hard to see how [Noah Claypole] has much in common with his Biblical namesake"). Gold was, however, "willing to bet that a good many reviewers will feel less kindly towards the book than I do." He wins his bet. I for one regard both these books as being, whenever they touch on religious matters, just such pretentious silliness as J. C. Maxwell complained of (above; see *TLS*, 27 April 1973 and 25 Jan. 1974). Hornback maintains that Dickens' basic mythology is "one of new beginnings, a Genesis mythology. The recurring mythic symbols are the days of the Creation, Eden, the Flood, Noah's Ark, and the tower of Babel." As Gold says, no one "has ever proposed quite as boldly so systematic a reading of

Dickens," and I find this an inappropriate system anyway. Gold's book, too, is ingenious in discovering in Dickens highly improbable biblical references and a theology as private as Blake's mythology, playing those dreary alphabet games (Jerry Cruncher as a parody of Jesus Christ: same initials, of course), and generally "placing Dickens in a great cat's-cradle of approved ideas and values" (*YWES: 1973*, p. 346). Dickens might have been surprised, too, to learn that the struggle of all his heroes is "to apprehend a great Divine system and their relation to it." But, for a more favorable view of these two books, see the reviews noted above—and Gold, it should be added, has more valuable insights to offer when his argument proceeds on a secular plane, for Dickens was indeed a moralist and some kind of radical.

Literary Predecessors, Contemporaries, and Successors

There have been many essays on Dickens' reading, its influence on his works, his relationship with his literary contemporaries, and his later influence, but no comprehensive study exists of any of these matters. R. C. Churchill's *Bibliography* (1975) has a useful if sketchy section on "Critical Comparisons," listing items on sixty-odd authors from Aristophanes to Orwell with whom Dickens has been juxtaposed. The extent of his reading has been surveyed by Collins (*Dkn*, 1964), who later remarks (in *TLS*, 25 Dec. 1970) how much we need a thorough study of this topic, to which many recent books have contributed suggestions. The books he reviews in the 1970 article contain arguments or surmises about Dickens' reading of Pope, Chatterton, Wordsworth, Austen, Crabbe, "Monk" Lewis, the "Tales of Terror" in *Blackwood's*, Tennyson, Lytton, Disraeli, Hawthorne—and did he read Blake, his affinities with whom F. R. Leavis and others have noted? The 1844 inventory of his library (to be appended to *Pilgrim*, Vol. IV) may throw some light on such questions.

Some useful work has been done on Dickens' childhood reading, notably by Jane W. Stedman on *The Tales of the Genii* (*Dkn*, 1965), by Trevor Blount on *The Terrific Register* (*DSA*, 1970), and by Gillian Thomas on *The Portfolio*, in which the most frequent subject was apparently the French Revolution, complete with guillotinings and buryings alive (*Dkn*, 1972). Dickens' affinities with his most illustrious predecessor have been ineptly studied by Robert F. Fleissner (*Dickens and Shakespeare: A Study in Histrionic Contrasts*, 1965; see Collins, *NCF*, 1967) and explored with predictable skill by Alfred B. Harbage, whose *A Kind of Power: The Shakespeare-Dickens Analogy* (1975) is as delightful as it is learned and critically suggestive. How Dickens and other Victorians used Shakespeare is discussed by Herbert Howarth (*DR*, 1972), and Jerome Meckier notes the influence of *King Lear* in particular (*SAQ*, 1972). Another influence on the early Dickens, that of *Don Quixote*, is reassessed by Steven H. Gale (*ACer*, 1973). His affinities with Sterne, Smollett, and Rousseau have been discussed (Roselee Robison, *UTQ*, 1970; Q. D. Leavis, *Dickens the Novelist*, 1970; Francesco Casotti, *RLMC*, 1969). The Gothic novel has been seen as an influence on him (Archibald C. Coolidge, *Dkn*, 1962; Larry Kirkpatrick, *VN*, 1967), and his art has been compared and contrasted with Scott's (Edgar Johnson, *VN*, 1965; Alexander Welsh, *NCF*, 1967; Peter-Jurgen Rekowski, *Die Erzahlhaltung in den historischen Romanen von Walter Scott und Charles Dickens*, Bern, 1975). His relationship to the Romantic tradition was the subject of a Dickens Society seminar (*DSN*, 1972); his affinities with various Romantic authors have been discussed—Wordsworth (John P. Farrell, *KE*, 1970; John Speirs, *Poetry towards Novel*, 1971), Lamb (Peter A. Brier, *CLB*, 1975), De Quincey (Christopher Herbert, *VS*, 1974), and Byron (M. L. Allen, *ES*, 1966; William R. Harvey, *NCF*, 1969); and R. D. McMaster considers his use of Romantic primitivism and of the Regency dandy figure (*SNNTS*, 1969). I have mentioned Blake above, though less often than most other commentators. The well-worn topic of Washington Irving's influence on the early Dickens has proved susceptible of fresh illumination from Malcolm Andrews and Katherine Carolan (*Dkn*, 1971; *DSN*, 1973). Less plausible accounts of his reading and the uses to which he put it include Annabel Endicott's surmise that *Astrophel and Stella* lies behind Pip (*Dkn*, 1967) and Annabel M. Patterson's extravagant suggestion that *Our Mutual Friend* is underpinned by *The Compleat Angler* (*DSA*, 1970). Further studies of the influence of his reading upon particular novels are mentioned below.

His most important literary relationship with a contemporary has received much attention; both Michael Goldberg's *Carlyle and Dickens* (1972) and William Oddie's *Dickens and Carlyle: The Question of Influence* (1972) describe the friendship of the two men and attempt the difficult task of assessing Dickens' ideological, stylistic, and narrative debts to Carlyle. Noting that the two books' virtues are complementary, G. B. Tennyson writes, "Both add immeasurably to our understanding of what is by any account one of the most important and illuminating literary relationships in the entire nineteenth century" (*NCF*, 1973). Fielding, in a review article, adds further important suggestions (*Dkn*, 1973); there are other notable reviews by Charles R. Sanders, Richard J. Dunn, and George Ford (*NCF*, 1973; *DSN*, 1973; *SNNTS*, 1974). The impact of Carlyle on various of Dickens' works has been discussed: *The Chimes* (Slater, who also notices Jerrold's influence here, *NCF*, 1970; Rodger L. Tarr, *NCF*, 1972; Sheila M. Smith, *VS*, 1974), *Bleak House* (Tarr, *SNNTS*, 1971; Blair G. Kenney, in a detailed and convincing comparison with *Past and Present, Dkn*, 1970), and *Hard Times* (a controversy between Dunn and Tarr, *DSN*, 1971, 1972). Sheila Smith's essay is of special importance. Two Dickens heroes, Martin Chuzzlewit and David Copperfield, have been studied from a Carlylean angle (Samuel G. Barnes in *The Classic British Novel*, ed. Howard M. Harper et al., 1972; Allan C. Christiansen, *SNNTS*, 1971; Dunn, in Partlow, 1970). "Dickens and Carlyle" was a topic at the Dickens Society's 1974 meeting (*DSN*, 1975); one of the participants, George Ford, discusses the stylistic affinities of the two authors in *Carlyle Past and Present* (ed. Fielding and Tarr, 1976).

Other studies of Dickens' relationships with, and influence on, his Anglo-

Saxon contemporaries include notes by Michael Steig and Katherine Carolan on Thackeray (*NCF*, 1970; *SSF*, 1974) and essays by Robert Lee Wolff on Bulwer-Lytton (*Strange Stories*, 1971), by Donald Hawes on Marryat (*DSA*, 1972), by H. Crago on George MacDonald (*DiS*, 1969), by Benjamin Franklin Fisher IV on Poe (*PoeS*, 1973), and by J. M. Ridland, J. H. Gardner, and N. C. Mills on Twain (*NCF*, 1965; *MP*, 1968; *PMLA*, 1969; *JAmS*, 1970), Gardner's *PMLA* essay being the most substantial treatment. Gardner has also traced Dickensian elements in other American authors—Bret Harte (*CRevAS*, 1971), W. D. Howells (*MFS*, 1970), and Frank Norris (*ELWIU*, 1974)—and Edward Passerini has seen Dickens in relation to Hawthorne (*DiS*, 1966). Dickens' influence on Australian literature has been discussed by Coral Lansbury (*MLS*, 1971) and Stanley Gerson (*Dkn*, 1972). Barbara C. Gelpi has noted his influence on Victorian autobiography (in *The Worlds of Victorian Fiction*, ed. Jerome H. Buckley, 1975), and his influence on various late Victorian authors has received attention—Gissing (M. K. Choudhury, *IJES*, 1973), Shaw (Harold and Jean Brooks, *Dkn*, 1963; Michael K. Goldberg and Martin Quinn, *ShawR*, 1971, 1974), and Conrad (J. Walton, *NCF*, 1969; Norman Page, *Conradiana*, 1973). Walton's essay concerns Dickens' contribution to the detective novel genre, a topic also discussed by Paul G. Buchloh (in *Der Detektivroman*, ed. Buchloh and Becker, Darmstadt, 1973), Julian Symons (in *Mortal Consequences*, 1972), George Wing (*SEL*, 1973), and Albert D. Hutter and Mary W. Miller (*MDAC*, 1973). His influence on his German contemporary Wilhelm Raabe has been assessed by H. R. Kleineberger (*OGS*, 1969). Later authors seen as indebted to Dickens include Faulkner (Joseph Gold, *DR*, 1969; C. Hines Edwards, *NMW*, 1974; Louis Berrone, *Dkn*, 1975), Sinclair Lewis (Robert F. Fleissner, *BNYPL*, 1970, and *SLN*, 1971), Erich Segal (Mark Spilka, *SoRA*, 1972), T. S. Eliot (William Empson, *EIC*, 1972), Dylan Thomas (Walford Davies, *EIC*, 1968), and James Joyce (Fred Kaplan, *NCF*, 1968, who lists many other Dickens-Joyce studies; Ann B. Dobie, *NCF*, 1971). An essay on Dickens, written by Joyce in 1912, has recently come to light (*CdS*, 25 Sept. 1975; *New York Times*, 19 Sept. 1975; *JML*, 1976). A conventional performance for the 1912 centenary, it shows no great insight into Dickens, characterizing him as "the great Cockney," secure in the affection of the English, and certainly very influential on the English language, but inferior to Thackeray at his best.

In "Dickens and Melville: Our Mutual Friends" (*DR*, 1971) Lauriat Lane, Jr., notes some concerns and literary inheritances common to both writers, and Pearl Chester Solomon writes more fully, and very perceptively, on this in her *Dickens and Melville in Their Time* (1975), noting how utterly different was their handling of similar topics and relating this to differences in their cultures as well as in their literary personalities. There have been several such "Mutual Interpretations," to cite the subtitle of Mark Spilka's interesting *Dickens and Kafka* (1963). Spilka's book offended some by its Freudianism (Ruth Mateer, *EIC*, 1965), others by its assuming "the familiar picture of modern urban, industrial and bureaucratic society," with society as "a bad father" (Hillis Miller, *NCF*, 1964), and others because they regarded its subject as factitious and overdone. Victor Hugo would provide a more relevant if less fashionable comparison, A. G. Hill argues (*CritQ*, 1965); Dickens' similarities to Kafka are marginal, contends Denis Donoghue, his relation to Wordsworth more central (*NCF*, 1970). Eleanor Tate's argument that *The Castle* is much indebted to *Great Expectations* points out a more direct influence (*SoRA*, 1974; see also Anna Katona, *DSN*, 1973). The relationship between Dickens and Dostoevsky, familiar since Edmund Wilson (though Gissing had made the point in 1898), has been further studied by Alexandra Wexler (*DRund*, 1962), Angus Wilson in a brilliant lecture (*Dkn*, Supp., 1970), and N. M. Lary in his judicious *Dostoevsky and Dickens: A Study of Literary Influence* (1973). Q. D. Leavis invokes Tolstoy's learning from Dickens as the entry into her "Case for a Serious View of *David Copperfield*" (*Dickens the Novelist*, 1970), and Tom Cain argues that Tolstoy's debt to Dickens in *War and Peace* is even more extensive than she remarks (*CritQ*, 1973; see also Henry Gifford, *FMLS*, 1968). Dickens is seen in relation to several great contemporaries in Donald Fanger's excellent study in comparative literature *Dostoevsky and Romantic Realism: A Study of Dostoevsky in Relation to Balzac, Dickens and Gogol* (1965), and Fanger returns to Dickens and Gogol in "Energies of the Word," in *Veins of Humor* (ed Harry Levin, 1972). Dickens never read a word of Balzac, Wilkie Collins was sure (*Dkn*, 1976, p. 48), but comparisons between the two novelists have proved suggestive. Besides Fanger's, these include Graham Hough's in an essay on the nineteenth-century intelligentsia (*Listener*, 23 May 1968), Bernard N. Schilling's of their respective attitudes to "This Harsh World" (*Adam*, 1969), Cesare Pavese's (in his *American Literature*, trans. Edwin Fussell, 1970), C. P. Snow's (in Slater, 1970), and Arnold Kettle's "Balzac and Dickens" (in *The Modern World, II: Realities*, ed. David Daiches et al., 1972). Essays by Margaret Sobel and Arnold I. Weinstein, on comparisons between particular novels, are mentioned below. A less familiar comparison is Cyril Pearl's "Mr. Dickens and Mr. [G. M. W.] Reynolds" (in his *Victorian Patchwork*, 1972).

Notable Critics Criticized

Attacking the critical "distortions" of Edmund Wilson, Lionel Trilling, J. Hillis Miller, and other influential figures in the reinterpretation of Dickens, Robert Garis argues, "Intelligent and sophisticated readers will not in fact find what they have been sent back [by these critics] to Dickens to find" (*The Dickens Theatre*, 1965). Garis' book, like the Leavises' (1970) and John Carey's (1973/74), contains some salutary challenges to recent orthodoxies, and R. C. Churchill in his *Bibliography* (1975) enjoys pointing out how many "new insights" of modern criticism were anticipated by earlier and now neglected commentators. Studies of Dickens' recent critical reputation by Collins and Ford (*Dkn*, 1970) and by Lauriat Lane, Jr. (*SNNTS*, 1969) are mentioned above, as are a number of review articles, but there have been no extended assessments of the nature and quality, and the influence, of the major critical texts in this field. It is time that such pioneers of modern Dickens studies as Edmund Wilson, Humphry House, and Hillis Miller were subjected to a critical examination more considered than at-the-time reviews and later off-the-cuff (and often querulous or polemical) judgments. George Orwell's apprehension of Dickens has been reassessed by Wayne Warncke (*SAQ*, 1970), soberly though untrenchantly, but it is only the long-dead Dickens critics that have occasioned much scholarly discussion.

Besides the editorial remarks in the Penguin and Critical Heritage anthologies (see above), there have been such studies of individual critics as Charles Mauskopf's "Thackeray's Attitude towards Dickens' Writings" (*NCF*, 1966). In *Gissing's Writings on Dickens: A Bio-Bibliographical Survey* (1969) Pierre Coustillas reprints two important uncollected items, besides presenting and discussing other evidence of Gissing's preoccupation with his more cheerful predecessor. How Dickens appeared to George Moore and other such naturalist authors is discussed by Heinz Reinhold (in Reinhold, 1969), who has further such studies forthcoming. In a spendid newly discovered letter of 6 Sept. 1906 (rpt. *Dkn*, 1973), G. B. Shaw congratulates and corrects G. K. Chesterton on his *Charles Dickens* (1906), which has lately been reprinted (1965) with an intelligently applausive introduction by Steven Marcus. Sylvère Monod is another "Unrepentant Chestertonian" (*DSA*, 1974), and a hereditary one, for his father "Maximilien Vox" was Chesterton's leading champion in France. R. C. Churchill too has urged the merit of G. K. C. as a Dickens critic (*DSN*, 1974). But, all told, there has been but thin appraisal of the critics who have mattered most in both earlier and more recent attempts to comprehend Dickens. Is it true, for instance, that Edmund Wilson's "Dickens: The Two Scrooges" has been "one of the most disastrous obstacles to getting Dickens' novels read responsibly" ever since 1941, his essay being a "crudely journalistic" effort based on "wild travesties of Dickens's novels and character," or is Q. D. Leavis here (*Dickens the Novelist*, 1970) being unjust or intemperate? Most such decisive pronouncements about Dickens' major interpreters remain at this level of vigorous assertion, with little or no supporting argument adduced. We need more reassessments of Wilson, and other such formative critics, of the caliber of Monod's and Fielding's discussions of John Forster's qualities (see above).

Studies of Individual Novels

Sketches by Boz

The imaginative quality of the early Dickens is superbly analyzed by J. Hillis Miller in his crucial lecture "The Fiction of Realism: *Sketches by Boz, Oliver Twist*, and Cruikshank's Illustrations" (in *Charles Dickens and*

George Cruikshank, 1971; also in Nisbet and Nevius, 1971). Virgil Grillo, too, in his *Charles Dickens' Sketches by Boz: End in the Beginning (*1974) shows how much of the later Dickens—not only content, but rhetoric, form, vision, and thinking about the world—is implicit thus early in his career, though it is in the sketches that his originality best appears, the stories often being derivative and weak (a point also made by Frederic S. Schwarzbach, *Dkn,* 1976, and Harvey P. Sucksmith, *NCF,* 1971). Duane DeVries, whose *Dickens's Apprentice Years* appeared in 1976, has shown Dickens improving his skills, in his early revisions of some items (*DSA,* 1970); and Margaret Ganz analyzes his characteristic humor, already present in his first book (*Genre,* 1968). Heinz Reinhold discusses "The Drunkard's Death" in his essay on madness in Dickens (in Reinhold, 1969). Collins notes one preoccupation of these sketches, which continues throughout Dickens' life, in "Dickens and Popular Amusements" (*Dkn,* 1963), and Malcolm Morley discusses some of the essays about theaters (*Dkn,* 1963, 1964). The factual background to another early work, "The Mudfog Papers," is explored by G. A. Chaudhry (*Dkn,* 1974). There is still no edited reprint of the *Sketches.*

Pickwick Papers

Dismissed in the Leavises' book simply as "the callow" (p. 280), *Pickwick* has continued to impress other recent critics more favorably: "one of the most remarkable works ever written" (Walter Allen), "the greatest of Dickens' mysteries" (Steven Marcus), or even, most boldly in our joyless literary climate, as "one of the funniest books ever written" (Rachel Trickett, complaining of critics who discuss the novel without recognizing this fact: "Since *Pickwick Papers* has now been shown to possess a theme," she remarks sardonically, "it can hold up its head in company with those dark analyses of urban Victorian society, *Little Dorrit* and *Our Mutual Friend,*" and she offers excellent brief advice about how, and how not, to read this novel—*Dkn,* 1973, p. 119). As Barbara Hardy notes, "Reading, as opposed to reading into, those 800 pages is a very bumpy and fragmented experience," and she confesses, "I have often found that in attempting to give some account of its many features, I have succeeded in forgetting and neglecting much that seems striking when actually reading the book" (*The Moral Art of Dickens,* pp. 84, 82). Laughter holding both his sides is not, indeed, an eminent presence, or even the acknowledged offstage presiding genius, in recent Pickwickiana: but, inhospitable to many current critical procedures as this novel may seem, it has occasioned much more discussion than any of the other novels before *Copperfield.*

The interpolated tales, and the question of their relevance to the novel overall, have attracted much more attention than their literary quality merits (William Axton, *SEL,* 1966, rpt. in his *Circle of Fire*; Patten, *DiS,* 1965, *ELH,* 1967, *DSN,* 1970; H. M. Levy and William Ruff, *DiS,* 1967, *Dkn,* 1968; Heinz Reinhold, *Dkn,* 1968, rpt. with additions in Reinhold, 1969; Robert E. Lougy, *NCF,* 1970; Christopher Herbert, *NCF,* 1972; Karl L.

Klein in *Miscellanea Anglo-Americana: Festschrift für Helmut Viebrock*, Munich, 1974; Horst Wagner, *Arcadia*, 1974). The burden of these articles generally is that the interpolated tales are more relevant and/or better than has been recognized. Another German critic, Volker Neuhaus, discusses the novel as an *Archivroman* in his *Typen multiperspektivischen Erzählens* (Literatur und Leser, Cologne, 1971). Mary Colwell writes judiciously on "Organization in *Pickwick Papers*" (*DiS*, 1967), relating Dickens' tentatives here to his subsequent development. Mr. Pickwick's Innocence and his alleged education by Experience are discussed by James R. Kincaid and Philip Rogers (*NCF*, 1969, 1972), and Sam Weller's character is sketched by Gwenllian L. Williams (*Trivium*, 1966). The Fat Boy, it appears, is "a remarkably detailed description of a condition [the Kleine-Levin syndrome] so rare that only 26 cases have so far been recorded in medical literature," observes Peter G. Jones in the *Australian Paediatric Journal*, 1972, and he notes other instances of Dickens' skills in medicosocial areas (see *Dkn*, 1972, p. 201). Other well-conducted inquiries include studies of the illustrations (Patten, *ELH*, 1969, *Dkn*, 1970; Jane Rabb Cohen, *HLB*, 1971), possible literary prototypes of Mr. Pickwick (Dr. Syntax?—B. C. Saywood, *Dkn*, 1970; My uncle Toby?—Roselee Robison, *UTQ*, 1970), the theatrical origins of some characters and episodes (Earle Davis, *The Flint and the Flame*, 1963), the identity of the mad huntsman seen in the Fleet (Harvey P. Sucksmith, *Dkn*, 1972), and the significance and factual background of imprisonment for debt in *Pickwick* (Angus Easson, *Dkn*, 1968). Harry Levin, seeing *Pickwick* as "Dickens' pivotal work," relates its hero to other avuncular figures in the novels (*The Worlds of Victorian Fiction*, ed. Jerome H. Buckley, 1975). Stephen C. Gill writes a note on the style (*MLR*, 1968). Patten gives a detailed and illuminating account of the place of *Pickwick* in the history of serial publication (*RUS*, 1975), and Louis James discusses plagiarisms of it (in his *Fiction for the Working Man*, 1963, and *DSA*, 1970), a topic fully and admirably treated in Mary McGowan's "*Pickwick* and the Pirates" (Diss. London Univ. 1975). The novel's reception in 1836–37 is reexplored by J. Don Vann (*Dkn*, 1970). Of the five recent paperback editions surveyed by Peter L. Shillingsburg (*DSN*, 1973), Patten's emerges as the only satisfactory one (Penguin, 1972). All these items are competent and useful (if some are rather flat-footed) but—except for students of these particular aspects—not indispensable. How banal the more routine items can get may be illustrated by one essayist (not named above) who thinks it "a point worth making" that "the domestic economy of Pickwick's Goswell Street apartment contrasts with that of other interior establishments in the novel, especially those of the Fleet Street Prison [sic]." A footnote is appended: "There has been a focus in Dickens criticism on interior establishments and their significance as symbols"; references duly follow. Five pages of Kenneth Rexroth's *The Elastic Retort* (1973) suggest more adventurous thoughts. Edgar Rosenberg (*Dkn*, 1970) refers to a neglected essay on *Pickwick* by Jan Kott, available in both German and Polish.

"Where is the critical handle for such a work of genius to be found?" asks

Steven Marcus ("Language into Structure: *Pickwick* Revisited," *Daedalus*, 1972; rpt. in his *Representations*, 1975). Marcus, who had written well about *Pickwick* in his earlier book (1965), uses as "handle" the spectacular linguistic inventiveness that Dickens develops here. Barbara Hardy discusses the importance of jokes, comic wit, and the mixture of the comic and the macabre in the novel, and, like Rachel Trickett, questions the wisdom of many recent ambitious reassessments ("if we follow up the moral interpretations closely and logically, [*Pickwick*] falls apart under the strain of such inappropriate investigation," *The Moral Art*, p. 92). The nature of the comedy is analyzed by Alexander Welsh in "Waverley, Pickwick and Don Quixote" (*NCF*, 1967). These three essays provide useful starting points for thought about *Pickwick*. Welsh elsewhere uses Kierkegaard, an author not often juxtaposed with Dickens, to illuminate this novel, seeing "Samuel Pickwick, victim of circumstances, in the light of a Kierkegaardian joke" (*Novel*, 1975). Finally, two critical *jeux d'esprit*—first, "*Pickwick Papers* Rewritten," by Robert Graves (*MHRev*, 1973): Graves, who produced in 1933 an "improved" version of *Copperfield*, unfortunately got stuck after rewriting only two chapters of *Pickwick*. The novel received quizzical attention, too, in *Fifty Works of English Literature We Could Do Without*, by Brigid Brophy et al. (1967).

Oliver Twist

The best introductions in the eight recent reprints very thoroughly discussed by Patten (*DSN*, 1972) are, he judges, Hillis Miller's (Rinehart, 1962) and Angus Wilson's (Penguin, 1966). Another good general essay is Slater's on the extraordinary mixture of satirical, documentary, and fabular elements in the novel (*Dkn*, 1974: an *Oliver Twist* issue, which also contains essays on the novel's stage history and Shakespearean echoes). The fabular elements are further discussed by Kenneth C. Frederick (*CE*, 1966), Joseph M. Duffy, Jr. (*ELH*, 1968), John Ferns (*QQ*, 1972), and Robert A. Colby, whose *Fiction with a Purpose* (1967) has a fascinating chapter, "*Oliver Twist*: The Fortunate Foundling," which sees Oliver in relation to thirty minor novels of the period dealing with orphans and such. (Malcolm Andrews raises interesting questions about Colby's methodology, *Dkn*, 1968.) See also Nina Auerbach's "Incarnations of the Orphan" in novels (*ELH*, 1975). Patten explores the novel's moral pattern—the conflict between self-interest and compassion in a capitalist environment (*SNNTS*, 1968)—and Lothar Cerny sees the novel as a critique of Utilitarianism (in *Studien zur englischen und amerikanischen Sprache und Literatur*, ed. Paul G. Buchloh et al., Neumünster, 1974); but A. F. Dilnot in "Dickens' Early Fiction and the Idea of Utility" (*SoRA*, 1975) argues that he was in closer sympathy with Utilitarianism and the commercial ethic than we like to think. Some loose ends in the narrative are pointed out by Colin Williamson (*NCF*, 1967). The novel's contribution to the art of serialization is demonstrated by Lance Schachterle (*DSA*, 1974), and Kathleen Tillotson, editor of the

Clarendon edition, has written about the three-volume edition (*Library*, 1963). On Cruikshank's alleged contribution to the story, see Illustrations, above. Barry Westburg, in an essay I could make nothing of, " 'His Allegorical Way of Expressing It': Civil War and Psychic Conflict in *Oliver Twist* and *A Child's History*" (*SNNTS*, 1974), sees confessional elements in the novel and starts from the improbable point that Oliver Twist's name recalls Oliver Cromwell, whose contemporaries included a Brownlow, a Claypole, and an Admiral Monk(s). Alphabet-game critics have not yet remarked that Oliver has the same initials as the Old Testament, but somebody will.

Norman Longmate's *The Workhouse* (1974) is a substantial contribution to the recent controversy about "How cruel was the Poor Law?" How Mr. Bumble chimed with contemporary opinions about the Poor Law, and jokes about beadles, is shown by Paul Schlicke (*Dkn*, 1975). Another relevant background area is surveyed by J. J. Tobias in his *Crime and Industrial Society* (1967). Elsewhere, Tobias argues that Ikey Solomons was not the original of Fagin, as is generally assumed (*Listener*, 3 Apr. 1969; *Dkn*, 1969; *Prince of Fences: The Life and Crimes of Ikey Solomons*, 1975). Dickens' interest in crime, at another level, appears in his addiction to "Sikes and Nancy," the text of which is now made generally available in Collins' edition of the *Public Readings* (1975), where Dickens' performance of this item is described at some length.

Nicholas Nickleby

Slater, whose Penguin edition is forthcoming, wrote a monograph, "The Composition and Monthly Publication of *Nicholas Nickleby*," with extra illustrations, to accompany the Scolar Press facsimile of the part issue (1973). This Dickens-at-Work-type study, which "immediately and decisively established itself as the most comprehensive, sound and cogent introduction to the novel" (*TLS*, 22 June 1973), refers to what little scholarly work has lately been done on this novel. W. W. Robson's lively "Talk about *Nicholas Nickleby*" (*PMLPS*, 1967–68) finds the novel very faulty, lacking in poetry and atmosphere, and poor in its pathos and melodrama: "everything that is good in [it] is humorous," though, Robson adds, this is "not *generally* true of Dickens." Other general studies of the novel include John R. Reed's of its "moral form" (*PLL*, 1967). Jerome Meckier's of the serialization (*DSA*, 1971), and Richard Hannaford's of the fairy-tale references, played off against "a dull and ugly commercial world" (*Criticism*, 1974). G. D. Wing writes about Ralph Nickleby (*Dkn*, 1968), and Leslie M. Thompson and Michael Slater about Mrs. Nickleby (*SNNTS*, 1968; *Dkn*, 1975). There are stimulating chapters about the novel in the books by Monod, Marcus, and Lucas; but, all told, it is a thin haul. *Nicholas Nickleby* is not the sort of novel we now find it easy to write about.

Master Humphrey's Clock

The *Clock* mechanism, in its creaky entirety, has been most perceptively examined by Malcolm Andrews (*Dkn*, 1971), and Joan Stevens and Jane Rabb Cohen have added useful footnotes about the illustrations (*SB*, 1967; *DSA*, 1970). Neither constituent novel has attracted major attention. The most suggestive general studies of *The Old Curiosity Shop* are those by Monroe Engel, who inquires in what sense it is "A Kind of Allegory" (in *The Interpretation of Narrative: Theory and Practice*, ed. Morton W. Bloomfield, 1970), and Jerome Meckier on the matters appropriate to the *Journal of Narrative Technique* (1972). Frank W. Gibson also has discussed the novel as an allegory of virtue and vice, both individual and social (*Dkn*, 1964). Angus Easson, editor of the useful Penguin edition (1972), has described the novel "From Manuscript to Print" and has rescued many interesting jettisoned passages (*DSA*, 1970), and Patten has used a reexamination of Dickens' initial difficulties in composing the novel as a way into a substantial analysis of its artistry (in Partlow, 1970). Time, an appropriate topic in the *Clock*, is considered by Philip Rogers (*NCF*, 1973) and by Stephen Franklin (*DSA*, 1974). The parentage and iconography of the Marchioness have received attention (Easson, *MLR*, 1970; Steig, *DiS*, 1966), and Dick Swiveller figures prominently in Garrett Stewart's admirable *Dickens and the Trials of Imagination* (1974). But Quilp has compelled the imagination of more commentators. "Quilp source-hunting continues unabated" (*Dkn*, 1972): hunters include Robert Simpson McLean (*VN*, 1968; *NCF*, 1971), Toby A. Olshin (*NCF*, 1970), and G. M. Watkins and Rachel Bennett, who respectively discern Grimaldi and Mr. Punch behind Quilp's self-delighted anarchic wickedness (*N&Q*, 1971; *RES*, 1971). Quilp is further discussed by Steig (*CLS*, 1969) and Branwen Pratt (*HSL*, 1974), in whose "dissenting view" Dickens' portrayal is often ambivalent and ultimately compassionate. Some literary sources of the novel are suggested by Malcolm Andrews and Patrick Diskin (*N&Q*, 1971, 1974). Dickens' intentions about Little Nell are studied, from the manuscript, by Stanley Tick (*PCP*, 1974). The familiar topic of how the pathos of Little Nell was then, has since been, and now should be taken is discussed by Laurence Senelick (*DiS*, 1967), and inevitably she figures prominently in Collins' lecture on the Victorians and tears, *From Manly Tear to Stiff Upper Lip* (Wellington, N.Z., 1974). Not death merely, but suicide, is at the center of the novel, in Warrington Winters' psychological account, "*The Old Curiosity Shop*: A Consummation Devoutly to Be Wished" (*Dkn*, 1967): at one point, after complex arguments, Winters declares, "We see, in short, the suicide of John-Charles Dickens even before they departed [from Chatham] for London" (p. 179), and on the next page, noticing that no women are present at Little Nell's funeral, he asks, "Shall we say that Dickens here excluded his own mother from his funeral?" Like Brutus—but Buzfuz should have said it—I pause for a reply. Any reply would, presumably, point out that at this period women did not attend funerals: see John Morley's *Death, Heaven and the Victorians* (1971), which contains much that is relevant to Dickens' deathbed sentiment. Little Nell is "Revisited Again" in *Literature and Psychology* (1965) by Michael Steig. Hans Mayer's essay on the novel in his *Aussenseiter* (Frankfurt, 1975) has been commended to me.

The best recent discussions of *Barnaby Rudge* occur in the books about Dickens by Marcus—"no study of the novel has thrown a better light on it," Fielding remarks (*DiS*, 1965, p. 147); by Dyson, Angus Wilson, and Lucas; and in Gordon Spence's Penguin edition (1973). Most of these maintain that the novel is neglected and will repay more serious attention, Wilson seeing it as "the turning point in Dickens' growth from an extraordinary to a great novelist" (in Slater, 1970, p. 199). Hugh of the Maypole, whom Wilson finds one of the most moving characters in Dickens, is the subject of Monod's essay "Rebel with a Cause" (*DiS*, 1965), which raises important issues about the novel and about Dickens' attitude to society. Marcus sees *Barnaby Rudge* as primarily a study in relations between fathers and sons; most studies have concentrated on its social and political content and on its interpretation of history and its relation to the problems of England in 1840 (Anthony O'Brien in a notably intelligent discussion of its form and political implications, *DiS*, 1969; Avrom Fleishman in his *The English Historical Novel*, 1971; Steig, *DSN*, 1973; Spence, *Dkn*, forthcoming). Paul Stignant and Peter Widdowson in their elaborate discussion "*Barnaby Rudge*—A Historical Novel?" in *Literature and History*, 1975, raise questions, central to this new journal, about the relations between fiction and the "history" both of the time of publication and of the period setting. Thomas J. Rice is illuminating about the novel's political background (*DSN*, 1973) and its ancestry (*NCF*, 1975). Possible sources of its episodes, in Shakespeare and Fielding, are discussed by M. Rosario Ryan (*English*, 1970) and Roger Robinson (*AUMLA*, 1973), and the novel's relationship with Lord Chesterfield is reexplored by Myron Magnet (*BNYPL*, forthcoming).

Martin Chuzzlewit and *American Notes*

Some studies of Dickens' American experiences are mentioned under Biography above; see also Louise Crow, "Dickens as a Critic of the U.S.A." (*MQ*, 1974). In his "Sources of Dickens' Comic Art: From *American Notes* to *Martin Chuzzlewit*" (*NCF*, 1970), Miller compares fact with fiction as a way of identifying some special qualities of Dickens' comic vision ("the metamorphosis of people into mechanically animated objects"). The best general studies of the novel are in Marvin Mudrick's and P. N. Furbank's introductions to their editions (Signet, 1965; Penguin, 1968), and in chapters in the books by Marcus, Lucas, Dyson, Daleski, and Stewart. Barbara Hardy in her book (1970) challenges some recent reinterpretations of this novel. Its serial publication is discussed by John Butt *(Pope, Dickens and Others*, 1969), and its illustrations by Steig (*DSA*, 1972). Steig maintains that Tom Pinch is the most fully developed character in the book (*SNNTS*, 1969), and Jerry C. Beasley extends this argument, also seeing him as its most important character (*Ariel*, 1974). So much the worse for the book, if so. Steig, incidentally, draws attention to a hair-raising extended sexual pun: Mary "touched his organ, and from that bright epoch, even it, the old companion of his happiest hours, incapable as he had thought of elevation, began a new and deified existence" (Ch. xxiv). But the most enjoyable essay about the novel is Veronica M. S. Kennedy's "Mrs. Gamp as the Great Mother: A Dickensian Use of the Archetype" (*VN*, 1972), a hilarious example of "mythologically oriented criticism." Everything falls into place: Mr. Gamp's wooden leg (he was "the maimed king or lame god so often associated . . . with a mother goddess"), the pickled salmon ("the mother goddess is often associated with sacred fishponds"), and so on, for 5,000 words. Old Martin Chuzzlewit performs the functions of a deity, in Stuart Curran's "The Lost Paradises of *Martin Chuzzlewit*" (*NCF*, 1970); other religious affiliations of the novel are discussed by Joseph Gold (*DSA*, 1970) and by Branwen B. Pratt (*NCF*, 1975), who sees Young Bailey as a fertility god.

Mrs. Gamp's diction is well discussed by Norman Page (*CS*, 1969) and W. J. B. Owen (*Dkn*, 1971), and Pecksniff's by W. A. Ward (*Listener*, 23 May 1963). Carl Woodring examines the strategies of character depiction, here more internal than in earlier Dickens novels ("Change in *Martin Chuzzlewit*," in *Nineteenth-Century Literary Perspectives*, ed. Clyde de L. Ryals, 1974), and Richard Hannaford discusses the conflict between irony and sentimentality (*VN*, 1974). That the novel is more unified than is generally recognized is argued by Curran (above) and by John S. Whitley (*PMASAL*, 1965). Dickens' dislike of America's great open spaces is perceptively analyzed by Coral Lansbury (*DSN*, 1972). Little has been written about *American Notes*, except in relation to *Chuzzlewit* (though see Peyrouton above). Fielding and Peter Bracher have written about its reception in 1842 (*MLR*, 1964; *DiS*, 1969). The Penguin edition (1972) is useful, and its introduction contains a suggestive account of the book's artistry, and Bracher has described the race to reprint it in the United States (*PBSA*, 1975).

Christmas Books and Stories

Until recently, surprisingly little effective criticism has been devoted to the Christmas Books and Stories, perhaps because they had embarrassing associations with an unfashionable Chestertonian Dickens, or perhaps because the *Carol* (at least) "is one of those things, like one's front doorknob, which has become too familiar to be really seen" (Alfred Harbage, *A Kind of Power*, 1975, p. xii). Two admirable general accounts of the Christmas Books have lately appeared: John Butt's in his *Pope, Dickens and Others* (1969) and Slater's (*Dkn*, 1969), part of which is used in his Penguin edition (1971). The meaning of Dickens' special interest in Christmas, in his life, art, and editorial work, has been discussed by Collins (*EA*, 1970), by Patten (*DSA*, 1972), and by Katherine Carolan, who has contrasted Dingley

Dell with Cloisterham and other later Christmases (*DSN*, 1973; *DR*, 1972). Deborah A. Thomas has written about Dickens' magazines' Christmas Numbers and his contributions to them (*Dkn*, 1973; *DSN*, 1975), and she reprints some of these contributions in her anthology, *Dickens: Selected Short Fiction* (Penguin, 1976). John Butt discusses the relation between Gabriel Grub and Scrooge (above); the latter has been the subject of controversy in *PMLA* (Gilbert vs. Cox, 1975). Slater has written about the composition of *The Chimes*, the influence that Carlyle and Jerrold had on it, and its topicality (*DiS*, 1966; *NCF*, 1970; and his *Dickens 1970*, 1970). Edward Wagenknecht has also written well about Dickens at work on *The Chimes* (*Dickens and the Scandalmongers*, 1965). The place of the Christmas Books in Dickens' artistic development is assessed by Kathleen Tillotson in "The Middle Years from the *Carol* to *Copperfield*" (*Dkn*, Supp., 1970), a notably acute lecture; Carolan discusses the relation of the Christmas Books to *The Battle of Life*, and Monod their relation to *The Haunted Man* (*Dkn*, 1973, 1972). Nelly Stéphane discusses the differences between the Christmas Books and the Christmas Stories (*Europe*, 1969). Collins, in his edition of the *Public Readings* (1975), notes the Christmas writings' prominence in Dickens' repertoire and also gives unusual attention to them in his *Dickens: The Critical Heritage*. The *Carol* is, with *Bleak House*, Michael Steig's main example of "Dickens' Excremental Vision" (*VS*, 1970): Scrooge's miserliness is so constantly expressed in constipatory terms that the office "stool" upon which he sits takes on quotation-mark significance. Finally, whatever Mr. Filer had instead of a heart would have been gladdened by the news that the *Carol* has gone through the computer, for research into "Collocations and Their Relevance in Lexical Studies" (in *The Computer and Literary Studies*, ed. A. J. Aitken et al., 1973). The mean sentence length in the *Carol*, it turns out, is 14.03 words.

Dombey and Son

There remains a critical consensus that, as Edgar Johnson remarked in 1952, *Dombey* is Dickens' first mature masterpiece: "the first major novel," as F. R. Leavis affirms (*SR*, 1962; rpt. in *Dickens the Novelist*). The most important reassessments, in essay form, are those by Stone, Lucas, Donoghue, and Williams, detailed below. Dickens' attitude here to social and economic change has been much discussed, the railway inevitably often providing a focus for the argument. Major contributions are John Lucas', subtitled "Past and Present Imperfect" (in *Tradition and Tolerance in Nineteenth-Century Fiction*, by David Howard et al., 1966); Steig's "*Dombey and Son* and the Railway Panic of 1845" (*Dkn*, 1971); Raymond Williams' introduction to the Penguin edition (1970; mostly rpt. in his *The English Novel from Dickens to Hardy*, 1970); and Harland S. Nelson's "Staggs's Gardens: The Railway through the Dickens World" (*DSA*, 1974). Denis Donoghue discusses this issue, and much else, in a distinguished essay (*NCF*, 1970). The novel's artistic unity and symbolism have been well discussed by Stone (his essay, "The Novel as Fairy-Tale," *ES*, 1966, has a wider range than its title suggests) and William Axton (*PMLA*, 1963; *ELH*, 1964), and its narrative method by Janice Carlisle (*JNT*, 1971). Barbara Lecker, concentrating on the nautical characters, challenges Lucas' and Stone's interpretations (*Dkn*, 1971). The real-life original of one nautical figure, Captain Cuttle, is discussed by William J. Carlton (*Dkn*, 1968); Q. D. Leavis notes his affinities with Smollett's seadogs and points out Dickens' greater artistic sophistication (*Dickens the Novelist*). Mr. Dombey is the character who has attracted most attention, being the subject, or a subject, of essays by Steig (*CentR*, 1970); Henri Talon (*DSA*, 1970); Ian Milner, who sees Dombey's role as a test case for Dickens' art (*NCF*, 1970); and Margaret Sobel, who compares him with another fictional father, Père Goriot (*RUS*, 1973). Collins has compared the interpretations of the novel's original readers with modern views (*Dkn*, 1967). T. B. Tomlinson's "Dickens and Individualism: *Dombey and Son* and *Bleak House*" (*CR*, 1972), which I have not seen, has been praised (*Dkn*, 1973). Stanley Tick (*MLQ*, 1975) argues that the novel's themes are imperfectly rendered.

Richard A. Levine, reviewing paperback editions, commends Edgar Johnson's (Laurel, 1963) and Raymond Williams' (Penguin, 1970), though Williams' introduction—which contrives not to mention Paul Dombey, let alone Cuttle, Bagstock, Toots, Blimber, and many other notable characters and narrative strains—presents an extremely partial view. Alan Horsman's Clarendon edition (1974) is, of course, textually authoritative and has an admirable introduction and appendixes. The number plans, published there, are also discussed by Paul D. Herring (*MP*, 1970). For further references, see the sections under Editions and Illustrations (above).

David Copperfield

The most substantial and comprehensive discussion is in Sylvère Monod's *Dickens the Novelist* (1967), which has a hundred pages entitled, unfashionably, "At the Top: *David Copperfield*." Q. D. Leavis' chapter in her and her husband's book (1970) contains many challenging revaluations of elements in this novel, including the best recent argument for seeing the adult David as no less well imagined and significant than his child self. Other books on Dickens with notable chapters on *Copperfield* include Dabney's and Angus Wilson's. Wilson's account may be contrasted with Q. D. Leavis' for, though adulatory about the boy David, Wilson is severe about the man. There are good general essays by Stone ("Fairytales and Ogres: Dickens' Imagination in *David Copperfield*," *Criticism*, 1964), Horst Oppel (in his collection *Der englische Roman vom Mittelalter zur Moderne*, Düsseldorf, 1969), and C. B. Cox ("Realism and Fantasy in *David Copperfield*," *BJRL*, 1970); and an illuminating brief preface by Cesare Pavese, translated in his *American Literature: Essays and Opinions* (1970). Oppel also writes about time and narrative technique in this novel, in Reinhold's collection (1969). James R. Kincaid has written a series of essays on *Cop-*

berfield (*DiS*, 1965, 1966; *NCF*, 1968; *SNNTS*, 1969) that I can only find perversely ingenious; David is seen as an "easy prey for the soft, subtle influence of Agnes," whose keys are those of a jailor as much as of a Little Housekeeper; "almost no pure mirth is present" in a novel whose "world is so grim . . ." (etc.). Nor am I much nourished by Stanley Tick's arguments that Mr. Dick is "an image of the author himself" and (of course) an "organic metaphor, a figure . . . in part defining the novel" (*NCF*, 1969).

Joan Stevens demonstrates succinctly how the serial mode of publication affected the novel's construction and reception (*Some Nineteenth-Century Novels and Their First Publication*, Wellington, N.Z., 1961), and Milton Millhauser argues that Dickens changed his mind as he wrote it serially (*NCF*, 1972). The relation between the novel and its author's personality and experience has been discussed by Stanley Tick (*BuR*, 1968), Vereen Bell (*SEL*, 1968), Collins (*E&S*, 1970), and Angus Easson (*L&H*, 1975), Easson's essay being the most cogent. The "originals" of various characters and places in the novel have continued to fascinate contributors to the *Dickensian* (Collins, 1965; William Oddie, 1967; P. F. Skottowe, 1969). Possible literary influences upon *Copperfield* have been most fully assessed by Earle Davis in his *The Flint and the Flame* (1963), and useful footnotes are provided by Lawrence Poston (*Dkn*, 1971) and Ivanka Kovačević, writing in English in *Filološkog Pregleda* (Belgrade, 1970). Most essays on the novel have, rightly, centered on David. Robin Gilmour's "Memory in *David Copperfield*" (*Dkn*, 1971) is outstanding, and Michael Black's chapter on "David Copperfield: Self, Childhood and Growth" (in his *The Literature of Fidelity*, 1975) is a sensitive account of more aspects of the novel than its title suggests. As bildungsroman and as a "Portrait of the Artist as a Young Man," *Copperfield* is admirably treated in Jerome H. Buckley's *Season of Youth* (1974) and Maurice Beebe's *Ivory Towers and Sacred Founts: The Artist as Hero in Fiction* (1964). Edward Hurley, too, considers "Dickens' Portrait of the Artist" (*VN*, 1970)—but Collins, in his 1977 monograph on the novel, argues (as Angus Wilson does in his *World of Charles Dickens*, 1970) that Dickens entirely fails to imagine David as a novelist. David as the novel's narrator is a more promising subject. Hillis Miller has cogitated with his usual difficult brilliance on "First-Person Narration in *David Copperfield* and *Huckleberry Finn*" (in *Experience in the Novel*, ed. Roy Harvey Pearce, 1968, where Fielding, too, writes well about memory and the past in this novel). Roger Gard, Janet H. Brown, Felicity Hughes, and George Worth have contributed useful but less spectacular essays on this subject (*EIC*, 1965; *DSA*, 1972; *ELH*, 1974; George Goodin, ed., *The English Novel in the Nineteenth Century*, 1972). Of recent psychological approaches to this favorite novel of Freud's, the most notable are Mark Spilka's in his *Dickens and Kafka*, 1963, E. Pearlman (*AI*, 1971), and Max Vega-Ritter's impressive "Etude psychocritique" (in Amalric, 1973).

David's womenfolk are most profoundly analyzed in Alexander Welsh's learned, suggestive, and amusing discussion of "The Bride from Heaven" in his *The City of Dickens* (1971). John Carey's book (1973/74) has a chapter

on "Dickens and Sex," which includes some apposite jokes and remarks.
Jane W. Stedman sees Dora as one of a series of Dickensian child wives
(*Dkn*, 1973). Steerforth's character and role in the novel are discussed by
Monod (*AdUP*, 1967). Dickens' presentation of Micawber is finely analyzed
by Bernard Schilling (in *The Comic Spirit*, 1965), William Oddie (*Dkn*,
1967), William F. Hall (*UTQ*, 1970), and Alfred Harbage (in his *A Kind of
Power*, 1975). Jean-Paul Martin writes about social class in this novel, in
Annales Littéraires de l'Université de Besançon (Paris, 1971). Bert G.
Hornback makes some interesting points about the Micawber family in
"Frustration and Resolution in *David Copperfield*" (*SEL*, 1968).

Bleak House

My remarks on items about *Bleak House* must be terse, since this has
lately been the most written about of the novels. There are two anthologies
of criticism (ed. Jacob Korg, Twentieth Century Interpretations, 1968, and
ed. A. E. Dyson, Casebook Series, 1969) and three introductory booklets (by
Peter Daniel, 1968; Philip Collins, 1971; and Grahame Smith, 1974). The
respective aims and merits of these compilations and booklets are discussed
by Trevor Blount (*Dkn*, 1970–71), Norman Friedman (*DSN*, 1973), and
Robert Newsom (*Dkn*, 1975). There are notable introductory essays by
Geoffrey Tillotson to the New American Library edition (1964) and by J
Hillis Miller to the Penguin (ed. Norman Page, 1971). Duane DeVries
edition (Crowell Critical Library, 1971) contains much useful ancillary
matter. The number plans have been published, with an admirable analysis
of the process of composition, by Harvey P. Sucksmith (*RMS*, 1965). The
alternative titles for the novel are discussed by Ford (*Dkn*, 1969), the print
ing of it by Monod and DeVries (*Dkn*, 1969, 1970), and the serialization by
Lance Schachterle (*DSA*, 1970).

Possible literary influences upon various characters or incidents have been
much canvassed: Carlyle (Blair G. Kenney, *Dkn*, 1966; Rodger L. Tarr
SNNTS, 1971), the Brothers Grimm (Joseph T. Flibbert, *VN*, 1969), Bun
yan (Paul Delany, *DSN*, 1972), Bulwer-Lytton (Edwin M. Eigner, *NCF*
1969), Sydney Smith (Robert S. McLean, *VN*, 1970), Mayhew (Richard J
Dunn, *NCF*, 1970), and Gothic fiction (Ann Ronald, *DSN*, 1975). Stephen
Gill has noted the high incidence of quotations and allusions and their
importance as a structural device (*NCF*, 1967). Susan Shatto's thesis (cited
above) annotates these; she has published some samples (*DSN*, 1975), and in
a more recent essay (*YES*, 1976) she relates the Megalosaurus on the open
ing page to mid-nineteenth-century geology. The role of society in the novel
is explored by Joseph I. Fradin (*PMLA*, 1966). What F. S. Schwarzbach, in
an explication on "the East Wind" reference, has called "the inspired
topicality of *Bleak House*" (*DSN*, 1975) has been eminently the province of
Trevor Blount in a series of scholarly articles. Along with other critics
mentioned below, he has written on the background of Jo and Tom-all
Alone's (*MP*, 1965; *MLR*, 1965; on Jo, cf. Winifred J. Peterson, *Dkn*, 1964

ınd Edward J. Passerini, *DiS*, 1965); the facts and symbolism of Chancery (*DiS*, 1965; *Dkn*, 1966; cf. Douglas Hamer, *N&Q*, 1970); the graveyard satire (*RES*, 1963; cf. K. J. Fielding and A. W. Brice in Partlow, 1970); the Chadbands and Dickens' view of Dissenters (*MLQ*, 1964; cf. Valentine Cunningham's excellent discussion of the "Chadband stereotype" and its literary origins in his *Everywhere Spoken Against: Dissent in the Victorian Novel*, 1975); Guster's origins (*DiS*, 1967); and the importance of place in the novel (*Dkn*, 1965). Blount has also seen Sir Leicester Dedlock in relation to Mr. Turveydrop (*NCF*, 1966) and Mr. Rouncewell (*EIC*, 1965). His view that Dickens is no more sympathetic to "the new acquisitiveness" represented by the Ironmaster than to the Dedlock paternalism has been applauded by David Craig (*EIC*, 1967) but effectively disputed by Anne Smith (*EIC*, 1971, 1973). H. P. Sucksmith "rehabilitates" Mr. Rouncewell, partly through his association with Wat Tyler (a Good Man and a Good Thing, in *1066 and All That* and *A Child's History of England* terms), but also with reference to Dickens' political position in the 1850s (*DSA*, 1975).

Spontaneous combustion—its scientific warrant, its appearances in literature, and its function in the novel—has been much discussed (Timothy Shaw, *CLife*, 19 June 1969; Elizabeth Wiley, *Dkn*, 1962; Donald Hawes, *DSA*, 1972; George Perkins, *Dkn*, 1964; Blount, *DSA*, 1970; Janice Nadel-half, *SNNTS*, 1969). E. Gaskell, a historian of medicine, shows that Dickens was less foolish than one had thought for believing then in spontaneous combustion (*Dkn*, 1973). Other scientific, and cosmic, dimensions of the novel are well discussed by Ann Y. Wilkinson in her nicely entitled essay "*Bleak House*: From Faraday to Judgment Day" (*ELH*, 1967). Fire, one of the elements she discusses, appears in Joseph Brogunier's essay on "the funeral pyre" awaiting Chancery (*Dkn*, 1965), and "The Cosmic Point of View" is also taken by Anthony Farrow (*Cithara*, 1974). The novel's concern with contemporary politics, and with the Woman Question controversy, is explored by Collins and Ellen Moers (*Dkn*, 1974, 1973), and Borrioboola-Gha provides the title for Howard J. Pedraza's book (1969) about the first British settlement in Nigeria. Collins has also discussed the novel's topicality, and the average man's reactions implicit in it, through a comparison with current *Punch* jokes (*DiS*, 1967). The Skimpole–Leigh Hunt affair has been reexplored, with fresh evidence, by Fielding (*Dkn*, 1968), James A. Davies (*RES*, 1968), and Brahma Chaudhuri (*DSN*, 1975); and other bearings on Skimpole have been taken by Richard J. Dunn (*DiS*, 1965) and Donald H. Erickson (*JEGP*, 1973). Other characters attracting critical attention include Inspector Bucket (Collins, *Dkn*, 1964; Michael Steig and F. A. C. Wilson, *PMASAL*, 1965, and *MLQ*, 1972) and Mr. Tulkinghorn (Elliott B. Gose, *Imagination Indulged*, 1972; Eugene F. Quirk, *JEGP*, 1973).

The character much the most written about, however, is Esther Summerson. "I see you understand me! I see you understand me!" exclaimed Dickens in 1867 to an American visitor, his face taking on "a pensive, tender aspect" in appreciation of his visitor's enthusiasm over this example of his

"insight into the heart of woman" (G. D. Carnow, *Dkn*, 1967, pp. 117–18)
The Inimitable ghost must have spent many happy moments lately in the
Celestial Library. "In the chorus of critical praise lavished upon *Bleak
House*, few voices have been raised in defence of Esther Summerson,'
wrote Mary Daelher Smith (*VN*, 1970, p. 10)—but where could she have
been living not to have heard the numerous chorus lately singing Esther's
praises fortissimo, with few but Angus Wilson (*NCF*, 1967), Monod (*DiS*
1969), and Collins (booklet, 1971) sticking to the old-fashioned guns, which
used to sound so victorious? Articles with titles like "Esther Summerson: A
Plea for Justice," "In Defense of Esther Summerson," or "Esther Summerson
Rehabilitated" have overwhelmed the opposition—"Only they come too
short," as later defenders have Regan-like impugned the inadequacy of the
tentative Gonerils who preceded them: even such defenders as Tom Mid
dlebro' (*QQ*, 1970) and Martha Rosso (*Dkn*, 1965) tend to patronize her
complains Crawford Kilian (*DR*, 1974). Of all Dickens' characters, Esther
has been revalued upward most remarkably; the only comparable whirligig
of time is the more easily explicable devaluation of Little Nell, traced in
Ford's disconcerting chapter about critical lemmingism, "Little Nell: The
Limits of Explanatory Criticism," in *Dickens and His Readers* (1955). The
credibility and fascination of Esther's character, and/or her efficacy as a
narrator, have been celebrated by—besides the above-named—A. E. Dyson
and Q. D. Leavis in their books on Dickens (both 1970), W. J. Harvey in his
Character and the Novel (1965), Richard J. Dunn (*Dkn*, 1966), Dori
Stringham Delespinasse (*NCF*, 1968), Alex Zwerdling, very persuasively
(*PMLA*, 1973), Gordon D. Hirsch and Lawrence Frank (*DSA*, 1975), Craw
ford Kilian (*DR*, 1974), and William Axton (*MLQ*, 1965). Axton has
usefully demonstrated the relevance of Esther's nicknames (*Dkn*, 1966).

"Famous as it is, the whole symbolic apparatus of *Bleak House* seems to
me to be attached to the narrative by factitious contrivance," Ando
Gomme remarks in a discussion of Dickens' "forced symbolism" (*Dickens*
1971, p. 49)—a refreshing challenge to the consensus of admiration about
the novel's symbolism and imagery (e.g., Cynthia Dettelback, *Dkn*, 1963
Susan Moth, *DiS*, 1965; William Axton, *NCF*, 1968; Philip M. Weinstein
DiS, 1968; Alice Van Buren Kelley, *NCF*, 1970). Axton refers, dauntingly, t
"the half-a-hundred excellent recent studies employing this approach" (p
349, n., q.v., but stretch your concept of excellence). The visual imagery of
Bleak House, its illustrations and cover design, have been analyzed by Stei
(*DiS*, 1968; *HLQ*, 1972) and J. R. Tye (*Dkn*, 1973). *Bleak House* has bee
selected by John Lucas to demonstrate Dickens' considerable superiority
over Matthew Arnold as an informed and intelligent critic of Victoria
England (*RMS*, 1972). In "The Irrelevant Detail and the Emergence of
Form" (in *Aspects of Narrative*, ed. J. Hillis Miller, 1971) Martin Price de
velops an argument about the function of the Sol's Arms group with
brilliance that quite occludes Collins' climactic flourish about another
hostelry in this novel, Mr. Grubble's Dedlock Arms (booklet on *Bleak
House*, 1971). The novel also looms large in "Dickens' Excremental Vision,

Michael Steig's entertaining piece about "the pervasiveness of shit in the smell, sight, and feel of life in [mid-Victorian] English cities" (*VS*, 1970).

Divergencies in approach to *Bleak House* by major representative critics have been analyzed by Lauriat Lane, Jr. (*SNNTS*, 1969). The most significant subsequent reassessments of the novel, besides the monographs mentioned above, are Albert J. Guerard's (*SoR*, 1969), Q. D. Leavis' (*Dickens the Novelist*, 1970), and D. W. Jefferson's (*E&S*, 1974). Alan Burke's and Ian Ousby's essays on its narrative strategies also impress me (*SEL*, 1968; *NCF*, 1975). General essays from outside Anglo-Saxony that have been admired include Heinz Reinhold's (in *Der englische Roman im 19. Jahrhundert: Interpretationen*, ed. Paul Goetsch et al., 1973), Kiochi Miyazichi's in his *Study of Two of Dickens' Later Novels*, Tokyo, 1971), and M. Nersesova's book-length study (Moscow, 1972; reviewed by Lawrence Senelick, *Dkn*, 1973). Another book-length study, by Collins, is forthcoming.

Hard Times

Monod has studied the novel's composition and revision (*Dkn*, 1968) and with Ford has edited the Norton edition (1966), which Anne Smith, surveying seven editions (*DSN*, 1973), praises the most highly, though she also commends Raymond Williams' Introduction to the Fawcett Premier edition (1966). The Norton edition appends much background and critical material. Another critical selection is Paul Edward Gray's (Twentieth Century Interpretations, 1969). There are booklets by Graham Handley (1969) and Augustine Martin (1974), but much the best of such introductory studies is Angus Easson's *Hard Times: Critical Commentary and Notes* (1973). The origin of "the Gradgrind school" has been found, in the economics-teaching Birkbeck Schools, by Robin Gilmour (*VS*, 1967), who writes elsewhere about the educational theme (*Dkn*, 1967) and the "self-help idea" in this novel (*The Victorians and Social Protest*, ed. J. Butt and I. F. Clarke, 1973). In an important essay, "Disinterested Virtue: Dickens and [J. S.] Mill in Agreement" (*Dkn*, 1969), Edward Alexander, like Gilmour, finds Dickens' understanding of his society deeper than he is often given credit for. Melvyn Haberman explores the conditions that Utilitarianism helps to create and their influence upon human relationships, in "The Courtship of the Void: The World of *Hard Times*" (*The Worlds of Victorian Fiction*, ed. Jerome H. Buckley, 1975). The Benthamite dimension of the novel is one of Anny Sadrin's topics in her "Plea for Gradgrind" (*YES*, 1973); and the childhood theme appears in Edward Hurley's "A Missing Childhood [Louisa's] in *Hard Times*" (*VN*, 1972), in Daniel P. Deneau's essay on the brother-sister relationship (*Dkn*, 1964), and in Warrington Winters' far-fetched argument about the autobiographical matrix of the novel––its "lost childhood" being Dickens' own (*DSA*, 1972).

Fielding, who discusses the educational theme in "*Hard Times* and Common Things" (in *Imagined Worlds*, ed. Maynard Mack and Ian Gregor, 1968) and writes a fine note on the peculiarity of this novel in the oeuvre (*Dkn*, 1967), turns to the industrial theme in his essay (with Anne Smith) about its reflection of the current factory controversy (*NCF*, 1973; cf Carnall, below) and elsewhere discusses "the martyrdom of Stephen" (*JNT* 1972). Jacques Carré analyzes the presentation of "le prolétariat industriel" (in *Hommage à Georges Fourrier*, 1973). Other essays concerned largely with the industrial theme are Ronald Berman's admirable note on "the human scale" in *Hard Times* (*NCF*, 1967), Jiro Hazama's comparison with *The Chimes* (*RRCU*, 1968), Jerome Meckier's argument that it is an anti industrial dystopia (in *The Novel and Its Changing Form*, ed. R. G. Collins, 1972), Ivan Melada's discussion of Bounderby (in his *The Captain of Industry in English Fiction 1821–1871*, 1970), and the Marxist essay by David Craig (editor of the Penguin edition, 1969), "*Hard Times* and the Condition of England" (in his *The Real Foundations: Literature and Social Change*, 1973). For other relevant essays, see Industrialism above. A number of essays comparing Dickens with Mrs. Gaskell further explore this topic notably Geoffrey Carnall's illuminating essay "Dickens, Mrs. Gaskell and the Preston Strike" (*VS*, 1964), Angus Easson's introduction to the Oxford English Novels edition of *North and South* (1974), Dorothy Collin's essay (*BJRL*, 1971), and David Smith's comparison with *Mary Barton* (*Mosaic* 1972); see also Norman Page (*N&Q*, 1971) and Ralf Normann (*FT*, 1971) A related topic is the novel's indebtedness to Carlyle, discussed in recent studies of the two writers (see above) and in an exchange between Richard J. Dunn and Rodger L. Tarr (*DSN*, 1971–72). The circus offset against the Coketown way of life has received little attention, but Collins' "Dickens and Popular Amusements" (*Dkn*, 1965) is relevant.

Two particularly good essays on the rhetoric of the novel have appeared David Lodge's in his *Language of Fiction* (1966) and Robert Green's "*Hard Times*: The Style of a Sermon" (*TSLL*, 1970). The tactics of its opening page are analyzed by Stanley Tick (*VN*, 1974). "Fancy," a theme of these essays, is critically assessed in another fine essay, David Sonstroem's (*PMLA* 1969), and the imagery in several essays—J. Miriam Benn's (*DSA*, 1970) Mary Rose Sullivan's (*VN*, 1970), and most substantially in George Bornstein's (*NCF*, 1971). Anny Sadrin's "The Perversion of Desire" is a study of irony as a structural element in the novel (in Amalric, 1973). Performance or poetry? The romance as radical literature? Facts or fantasy? A fairy tale with realistic elements?—these are some of the questions raised about what kind of a fiction this is (see Alan P. Johnson, *DiS*, 1969; Robert E. Lougy *DSA*, 1972; Anne Sedgley, *CR*, 1973; Inge Leimberg, *GRM*, 1973; Koichi Miyazaki, *A Study of Two of Dickens' Later Novels*, Tokyo, 1971). Other such studies include A. E. Voss's on its theme and structure (*Theoria*, 1964 and A. Bony's "Réalité et imaginaire dans *Hard Times*" (*EA*, 1970). William J. Palmer argues that the novel should be seen as "a fable of personal salvation" (*DR*, 1972). F. R. Leavis' influential way of reading the novel (*The Great Tradition*, 1948; rpt. with minor alterations and additions i *Dickens the Novelist*, 1970) has been challenged by David H. Hirsch (*Criticism*, 1964) and Geoffrey Johnston Sadock (*DSA*, 1972). David Goldknopf

1as a sharply critical chapter on the structure of *Hard Times* in his *The Life of the Novel* (1972). "The critical history of *Hard Times* is astonishing, 1nd it is quite an education to contemplate it," writes Monod in his "*Hard Times*: An Un-Dickensian Novel?" (in Amalric, 1973). His judicious essay 3s an education to read, not least for its concluding words: he has read the 10vel some twenty times, typed out its text, edited and annotated it—"And et I feel that I have only just discovered some of its beauties."

References to two essays came to hand too late for me to be able to onsult them—Edwin J. Heck's "*Hard Times*: The Handwriting on the 'actory Wall" (*EJ*, 1972) and P. T. Stapleton's "*Hard Times*: Dickens' :ounter Culture" (*CH*, 1973). Frederic Jameson gives a Structuralist ac- ount in his *Prison-House of Language* (1972): the novel's idea content is 'formulated . . . in terms of a binary opposition."

Little Dorrit

For F. R. Leavis, this is "one of the very greatest of novels," certainly)ickens' greatest, and one that triumphantly demonstrates his poetic power, is mastery of the inner life (a match for Henry James's), and his pro- undity of thought, "an affair of the thinking intelligence directed to a rasp of the real" (*Dickens the Novelist*). His is the most forceful and istinguished new study of this novel, which otherwise has attracted less nteresting attention than several other of Dickens' mature novels. William 3urgan praises the two recent paperback editions (Penguin, ed. John 1olloway, 1967; Odyssey, ed. R. D. McMaster, 1969), though contrasting 1eir critical styles. McMaster prints the number plans, which Paul D. Her- 'ng analyzes thoroughly (*MP*, 1966). John Butt describes the serialization °ope, *Dickens and Others*, 1969). The mystery elements in the plotting are 1alyzed by the Russian formalist critic Viktor Shklovsky, in *Readings in* :ussian *Poetics* (ed. Ladislav Matejka et al., 1971). Fielding, in *Experience* ι *the Novel* (ed. Roy Harvey Pearce, 1968), sees this as "very much a ovel of the past, of memory, . . . as saturated with a sense of past Time as *opperfield*": and its concern with time has also been analyzed by Mike 1ollington and R. Rupert Roopnaraine (*The English Novel in the Nine- -enth Century*, ed. George Goodin, 1972; *DSA*, 1974).

The prison continues to provide the most frequent approach to this ovel, with new points being made by Marie Peel (*B&B*, 1972), Koichi 1iyazaki (SEM, No. 12, 1973), T. N. Grove on Arthur Clennam's psycho- •gical prison (*MLR*, 1973), and Jerome Beaty, who sees the prison image as ubsumed by a larger, and quite different, cosmological view" (*Nineteenth- entury Literary Perspectives*, ed. Clyde de L. Ryals et al., 1974). Beaty's say is of particular importance. Angus Easson compares Mr. Dorrit with a milar real-life inmate of the Marshalsea, shows that Dorrit could never ιve become the respected "Father" of that place, but argues that Dickens as artistically justified in this departure from local probabilities (*DSA*, 174). Future commentators on the prison imagery should take account of

John Carey's argument that, though "multiplied relentlessly," it become
trite and cannot bear the weight imposed upon it by modern criticism
(*Here Comes Dickens*, pp. 113–17). The prison imagery should be seen a
supplemented by images of sickness, poison, and infection, Edwin B. Barret
argues (*NCF*, 1970), and Jerome Meckier (*DiS*, 1967) and Robert Barnard
(*ES*, 1971) have also surveyed these not unfamiliar fields of imagery. Rich
ard Stang uses a single metaphor to show how highly integrated the novel i
("*Little Dorrit*: A World in Reverse," in Partlow, 1970). Burgan has writ
ten well about the settings of the action in England (*TSLL*, 1973) and Ital
(*NCF*, 1975), and David Gervais on the locations' being even more vivi
than the characters ("The Poetry of *Little Dorrit*," *CQ*, 1969). Burgan
writes elsewhere (*MLQ*, 1975) about pastoral settings in this novel and others

Two admirable essays on the social bearings of the novel are William
Myers' "The Radicalism of *Little Dorrit*" (in *Literature and Politics in th
Nineteenth Century*, ed. John Lucas, 1971) and Grahame and Angela
Smith's "Dickens as a Popular Artist" (*Dkn*, 1971), which centers on Mer
dle. For Myers, the novel is, "in its complex rejection of violent insurrection
against the social system, an astonishingly courageous statement of political
despair." In this wide-ranging and tough-minded essay, Myers pays special
attention to Mr. Meagles, another and simpler view of whom is taken by
Stanley Tick (*DSA*, 1974). The Smiths' essay traces the origins of Merdle i
real life and in popular iconography, raising important questions about
Dickens' originality in handling this popular theme of a financial magnate
crash and about the way this profoundly creative genius integrates such
topicalities into the life of the book. Other valuable essays on the Merdle
and money themes are Easson's "Finance and Religion in *Little Dorrit*"
(*LonR*, 1968) and N. N. Feltes' on Dickens' response to the new limited
liability form of capitalism (*VS*, 1974). Another social manifestation in th
novel, the Circumlocution Office, is studied by John D. Jump (*CS*, 196:
and C. P. Snow, who argues that Dickens was unfair to the Civil Service (i
Slater, 1970).

Even such a highly organized novel as this, I read lately in a graduat
dissertation, "bears residual traces of the earlier mode, as with Mr. F's Aun
who is defiantly irreducible to any pattern of significance." Little did th
candidate know!—for Alan Wilde in his "Mr. F's Aunt: The Analogic
Structure of *Little Dorrit*" (*NCF*, 1964) argues that she is "at the heart
the book." A year later, in the same journal, Vereen M. Bell in "Mr
General as Victorian England" adopts exactly the same approach: here is
character neglected by the critics (Wilde says the same of Mr. F's Aunt); ye
she provides comic relief (and, says Wilde of his lady, "it may seem prete
tious to take her too seriously"), but Mrs. General has "a thematic functic
as well" and embodies "one of Dickens' most mature and enlightened mor
observations." Mr. F's Aunt, similarly, ends up "nearly pure symbol." Bo
essays are competent and intelligent; both illustrate a way we live now,
academic critics. Other worthwhile studies that start from characters b
widen outward include Easson's of John Chivery (*DUJ*, 1975), Harvey

Sucksmith's of the originals of Rigaud (*Dkn*, 1975), Avrom Fleishman's "Master and Servant in *Little Dorrit*" (*SEL*, 1974), and Kathleen Woodward's "Passivity and Passion," about the women in the novel (*Dkn*, 1975). Finally, J. C. Reid's intelligent and provocative introductory study *Dickens: Little Dorrit* (1967) may be recommended, as may Douglas Hewitt's salutary discussion, in his *The Approach to Fiction* (1972), of good, arguable, and bad ways of reading *Little Dorrit*, exemplified by four possible interpretations of its Iron Bridge episodes.

A Tale of Two Cities

Why this novel was unpopular in 1859, and has since been so, among readers who generally admire Dickens is discussed by Heinz Reinhold (in Reinhold, 1969). It remains much the least admired and least discussed of the later novels, though a standard text in schools—R. D. McMaster reviews thirteen recent paperback editions (*DSN*, 1972). He finds Edgar Johnson's (Signet, 1963) and George Woodcock's (Penguin, 1970) the most satisfactory, though expressing reservations about both; Monod reviews the Penguin edition severely (*Dkn*, 1971). There is a useful collection of essays, in the Twentieth Century Interpretations series, ed. Charles E. Beckwith (1972), with suggestions for further reading, and Ralph W. V. Elliott's *A Critical Commentary on Dickens's* A Tale of Two Cities (1966) is a sound introductory booklet. The origins of the novel in Dickens' reading are discussed by Oddie and Goldberg in their books on Dickens and Carlyle, and by Beth R. Arnold (*Dkn*, 1967), Gillian Thomas (*Dkn*, 1972), and Collins, who shows how long Dickens' imagination had been haunted by elements of this novel (*DSA*, 1972). Its connections with recent events at home and in India are argued by Nicholas Rance in his *The Historical Novel and Popular Politics in Nineteenth-Century England* (1975) and by Oddie (*Dkn*, 1972). Leonard Manheim sees it rather as a projection of Dickens' psychic conflicts (*DSA*, 1970). Its relation to its genre is assessed by Bernd-Peter Lange (*GRM*, 1970) and Avrom Fleishman in his *The English Historical Novel* (1971), and Robert Alter examines "how Dickens visualized history in a more or less ordered symbolic scheme" (*Novel*, 1969). Michael Gregory writes about some speech usages (*REL*, 1965).

The critic most given to seeing this novel steadily and seeing it whole, instead of in some special aspect, is (appropriately enough) Monod, whose *Dickens the Novelist* contains a judicious assessment of its strengths and limitations. He particularly admires its stylistic qualities (in Partlow, 1970) and elsewhere discusses "Dickens' Attitudes" (*NCF*, 1970)—not his ideological but his narratorial attitudes, this being one of Monod's important series of essays on the author-reader relationship in Victorian fiction. His most comprehensive study is "*A Tale of Two Cities*: A French View" (*Dkn*, Supp., 1970), which both reassesses the novel and relates it to Dickens' personality and outlook. "However intensely one may dislike many aspects," he begins one of these essays; another argues that it "collapses in the final third" into "utter unreality." He has come to think better of it than he did, he says, but he stops short of enthusiasm; indeed, elsewhere candor overcomes him—this is "the only Dickens novel that I have no wish to read again soon and often" (in Amalric, 1973). As Samuel Johnson remarked, about Shakespeare, "We must confess the faults of our favourite, to gain credit to our praise of his excellencies."

Great Expectations

As a candidate for the most discussed of Dickens' novels, *Great Expectations* rivals or surpasses *Bleak House.** Criticism was well surveyed by Monod in his review of the Leavises' book (*EA*, 1971); riled, as others were, by Q. D. Leavis' peremptory chapter title "How We Must Read *Great Expectations*," he added a "Note bibliographique, ou Comment on *peut lire Great Expectations*' " indicating the range of defensible interpretations. There is a useful anthology, *Assessing* Great Expectations (ed. Richard Lettis and William E. Morris, 1960), and introductory booklets by R. George Thomas (Studies in English Literature, 1964: not very good), John Barnes (1966), and Graham Martin (two Open University texts, 1973: *A Study Guide to* Great Expectations and a follow-up entitled *Great Expectations*; see review by Robin Gilmour, *Dkn*, 1974). Martin's amply illustrated and intelligently devised studies provide the best stimulus to further thought. Other useful introductions are Monod's in his translation *Les Grandes Espérances* (1959), R. D. McMaster's in the Odyssey edition (1965), Angus Wilson's in the Signet edition (1963), and Elizabeth Drew's in her *The Novel: A Modern Guide to Fifteen English Masterpieces* (1963). Duane DeVries surveys paperback editions (*DSN*, 1974). The Bobbs-Merrill Library of Literature reprint, edited by Louis Crompton (1964), contains useful maps. Edgar Rosenberg, editor of the forthcoming Norton Critical Edition, writes extensively about the problems involved in that project and about many aspects of the composition, publication, and craft of the novel (*DSA*, 1972; *Dkn*, 1973), the first of these essays being indeed "massive and concrete," as Herbert Pocket overkindly described Mr. Wopsle's Hamlet.

The revised ending has been much discussed, Q. D. Leavis (whose essay was never marred by underemphasis) finding it "incomprehensible" that some critics prefer the original. Among those who share her conclusions, though for different reasons, are M. W. Gregory (*EIC*, 1969), Kurt Tetzeli von Rosador (*NS*, 1969), and Robert A. Greenberg (*PLL*, 1970). Milton Millhauser's is perhaps the best all-round discussion of what he calls "the

---

* When this section was due to go to press, Professor Edgar Rosenberg had occasion to read a copy of it and, though generally in agreement with my emphases, kindly gave me a list of forty or fifty further items that I might wish to consider for inclusion. Some of these I had deliberately omitted, but most of them were simply unknown to me. "I hope you've got a researcher," he concluded—but I haven't; and it was too late for me to consult more than a handful of these new items, and I was able to insert only a few extra references. I mention this both to thank Professor Rosenberg and to apologize for the omission of items I have not read—but more to indicate the high degree of fallibility inevitable in a chapter such as this on an author so much discussed, unless it were written by a person (who, I hope, does not exist) whose sole mission in life is reading current writings about Dic   ns.

three endings," the novel being effectively over before either of the disputed endings operates as the "final formality" (*DSA*, 1972); a similar argument is presented by Martin Meisel (*EIC*, 1965; see also John T. Smith, *Thoth*, 1971, and V. J. Emmet, *N&Q*, 1973). Edward M. Eigner inquires what "good reasons" Bulwer-Lytton gave for rejecting the original ending (*NCF*, 1970), and William H. Marshall considers the conclusion as "the fulfillment of myth" (*Person*, 1963). Features of the narration are discussed by Robert B. Partlow, Jr. (*CE*, 1961), Philip L. Marcus (*DiS*, 1966), Peter Wolfe (*SAQ*, 1974), and Ana Laura Zambrano (*HSL*, 1972). Walter Killy considers the fairy-tale elements of the novel (in his *Wirklichkeit und Kunstcharakter*, 1963), Jean-Claude Amalric the allegorical quality (in Amalric, 1973), and Christian W. Thomsen the grotesque (*Anglia*, 1974). Critics have not done justice to the comic elements in the novel or to Pip's awareness of the comic side to his situation, Henri Talon argues in an excellent essay (*VN*, 1972), and he has also written well about its "Space, Time and Memory" (*DSA*, 1974). Another distinguished *angliciste*, Henri Fluchère, has written a suggestive general essay on the novel (*Europe*, 1969). Family relationships in the pattern of the story are discussed by Vereen M. Bell (*VN*, 1965) and Alan Lelchuk (*SR*, 1970).

The imagery has been subjected to the usual kind of attention (see Joseph A. Hynes, *ELH*, 1963; Jack B. Moore, *Dkn*, 1965; William H. New, *DiS*, 1967; Robert Barnard, *DSA*, 1970; Donald H. Erickson, *IllQ*, 1970; J. W. Crawford, *RS*, 1971; and John P. McWilliams, *DSA*, 1972). Another familiar gambit, the "doubling" of characters, has been further used by Richard J. Dunn (*Dkn*, 1967), Barry D. Bort (*VN*, 1966), and Karl P. Wentersdorf (*NCF*, 1966). "The contrasts between Orlick and Herbert are manifold," Wentersdorf incontestably remarks, but he is elsewhere bolder: '*Pepper* is unmistakeably an echoic version of *Pip* and *Pirrip*," etc. Barbara Hardy writes about food and feasting in the novel (*The Moral Art of Dickens*, 1970), as does Thomas L. Watson (*Essays in Honor of Esmond Linworth Manilla*, ed. Thomas A. Kirby, 1970). A. L. French considers the motif of beating and cringing (*EIC*, 1974). Pip's role in the novel has been explored by Christopher Gillie (*Character in English Literature*, 1965), Patricia R. Sweeney (*Dkn*, 1968), Albert D. Hutter (in *Psychoanalysis and Literary Process*, ed. Frederic Crews, 1970), and Edward W. Said (in *Aspects of Narrative*, ed. J. Hillis Miller, 1971), Said's essay being notably acute. The functions of other characters have been analyzed: Wopsle by James D. Barry (*Dkn*, 1968), Estella by Lucille Shores (*MSE*, 1972), Wemmick by N. C. Peyrouton (*DiS*, 1965) and Lawrence Jay Dessner (*Ariel*, 1975), and Jaggers by Andrew Gordon (*DiS*, 1969) and Anthony Winner (*DSA*, 1974). A. F. Dilnot defends Jaggers as a man of benevolent wisdom (*EIC*, 1975). G. d'Hangest writes about the characterization (*EA*, 1971). Alleged originals for Miss Havisham pop up everywhere, from Australia to the Isle of Wight, but the most reliable information occurs in essays by Martin Meisel (*PMLA*, 1966) and Harry Stone, whose "Dickens' Woman in White" (*VN*, 1968; exp. and rev. in Tomlin, 1969) is one of the most thorough and thoughtful explorations of the origins of a Dickens character in the novelist's memories, reading, and imagination. The novel's cinematic qualities are considered by Ana Laura Zambrano (*HSL*, 1972; *LFQ*, 1974).

Of general essays about the novel's quiddity, George Levine's on "Communication in *Great Expectations*" (*NCF*, 1963) is the most suggestive; William Axton's (*DSA*, 1972), Mordecai Marcus' (*VN*, 1964), Ann B. Dobie's (*NCF*, 1971), Roselee Robison's (*QQ*, 1971), and Diderik Roll-Hansen's "Characters and Contrasts in *Great Expectations*" (in *The Hidden Sense*, ed. Marie-Sofie Røstvig et al., Oslo, 1963) may also be mentioned. Wayne Shumaker offered a commentary along anthropological Lévi-Strauss lines in his *Literature and the Irrational* (1960). The bildungsroman structure of the work is discussed in Jerome Buckley's *Season of Youth* (1974). There are useful footnotes on minor points: on "bringing up by hand" (Charles Parish and Robert J. Finkel, *NCF*, 1962, 1966), on Pip's age (Daniel P. Deneau, *Dkn*, 1964), on the Finches of the Grove (Isobel Murray, *N&Q*, 1971), and on the novel's relation to its author (Collins, *DSA*, 1972); but on the last subject the best and fullest treatment remains Ada Nisbet's "The Autobiographical Matrix of *Great Expectations*" (*VN*, 1959). Comparisons have been made with *The Great Gatsby* (Edward Vasta, *Dkn*, 1965), *Huckleberry Finn* (J. M. Ridland, *NCF*, 1965, and Nicolaus C. Mills, *JAmS*, 1970), *The Trial* (Richard Pearce, *Stages of the Clown*, 1970), and *Père Goriot* (Arnold L. Weinstein, *Vision and Response in Modern Fiction*, 1974). Nina Auerbach compares Pip with other fictional orphans (*ELH*, 1975).

Our Mutual Friend

There is less agreement about the status of *Our Mutual Friend* than about that of any of Dickens' other mature novels. For some critics, such as Q. D. Leavis, it shows a decided breaking-down of Dickens' powers, and Fielding argues that there is no drive behind the story; for others, such as Daleski, it is one of the most poetic of the novels and one of the greatest and most subversive English novels of the century. Angus Wilson, who detects "many dead passages" in it, finds it nevertheless "a book of strangely subtle psychological nuances, of moments, glances, asides that mean more than the whole, in short a novel before its time," but he adds a warning: it "passes with flying colours the sort of abstracting trial that modern criticism tends to make of a novel. . . . Yet criticism must test a work not only in retrospect but in the reading"—and here, he maintains, *Our Mutual Friend* falls short of the other later novels (*The World of Charles Dickens*). In his book (1970), A. E. Dyson discovers "a real recovery of Dickens' great comic form" in *Our Mutual Friend*. Philip Hobsbaum, in "The Critics and *Our Mutual Friend*," surveys "the remarkable range" of valuation of it, "even in modern times" (*EIC*, 1963).

Some problems Dickens met in writing the novel are discussed by F. X. Shea (*Dkn*, 1967; *PLL*, 1968), and the real-life originals or analogues of Podsnap and Gaffer Hexam are described by James A. Davies and Collins (both *Dkn*, 1974). The actuality and the popular emblematic significance of dustheaps are reexplored by Harvey P. Sucksmith (*EIC*, 1963)—and did Dickens owe something here to Henry Mayhew (*NCF*, 1965, 1969; see Anne Humpherys, *DSA*, 1975)? Annabel M. Patterson's contention that *The Compleat Angler* lies behind the novel (*DSA*, 1970) strikes me as more ingenious than valid, but her discussion of the fishing motif has impressed another reviewer as notable (Daleski, *NCF*, 1972). Gibbon is a classic author certainly present here, and Norman Page writes amusingly about Dickens' cavalier way of using him (*Dkn*, 1972). Stanley Friedman traces "The Motif of Reading" in the novel (*NCF*, 1973), and Richard D. Altick expands on this idea in his important essay "Education, Print and Paper in *Our Mutual Friend*" (in *Nineteenth Century Literary Perspectives*, ed. Clyde de L. Ryals et al., 1974), showing how topical these concerns were in the aftermath of the 1863 Revised Code, etc.

The novel's opening has been particularly well analyzed. John M. Robson uses the techniques of classical rhetoric to study the first number, and he thereby illuminates Dickens' verbal art considerably (*DSA*, 1974). Jean-Marie Baïssus is shrewd and thorough in his "L'Adjectif dickensien: Essai d'analyse sémantique des procédés stylistiques dans le chapitre 1 de *Our Mutual Friend*" (in Amalric, 1973); and Hillis Miller has brilliantly analyzed the Veneerings' dinner party, in *The Form of Victorian Fiction* (1968; see also Miller's afterword to the New American Library edition of the novel, 1964; rpt. in *The Victorian Novel: Modern Essays in Criticism*, ed. Ian Watt, 1971). U. C. Knoepflmacher, too, in his essay on this novel, "Fantasy as Affirmation" (in *Laughter & Despair*, 1971), remarks how in the opening pages "Dickens continually deludes his reader and denies him the security he seeks"; and, to revert to the concerns of my earlier paragraph, Knoepflmacher characterizes this novel as "idiosyncratic, difficult and different," with Dickens going "far beyond Thackeray's efforts to come to terms with the instability of Vanity Fair"; so small wonder, he argues, that Dickens' contemporaries did not appreciate its vitality: "In their failure to recognize that he had intentionally portrayed the debility of an age, they dismissed the work as that of a debilitated novelist." New ways of regarding the novel are proposed by Masao Miyoshi (it is about "nothing less than the whole problem of identity in a world where things—and men—are not always what they appear to be," *The Divided Self*, 1969), by G. W. Kennedy ("a character's name is the key symbolic contact-point between the public world of language and society and the individual realm of moral responsibility," *NCF*, 1973), and by William J. Palmer (it is "an existential novel dealing with the struggles of the central character to place, in Sartre's terms, existence before essence," *PMLA*, 1974). Ray J. Sherer, like A. E. Dyson, is impressed by the novel's abundant comic invention (*TSLL*, 1971); Richard J. Dunn explores its "tragic-comic grotesque" elements (*SNNTS*, 1969). The imagery is surveyed by Kenneth Muir (*E&S*, 1966) and the symbolism by Jennifer Gribble (*EIC*, 1975) and by Avrom Fleishman in a suggestive essay about the urban and rural landscapes (in Amalric, 1973). Norman Page discusses Lizzie's speech habits (*Dkn*, 1969), and John R. Reed often cites examples from this novel in his fascinating *Victorian Conventions* (1975).

Horst Oppel includes an essay on this novel in his book of *Interpretationen* (1965). Paperback editions are surveyed by Benjamin Franklin Fisher IV (*DSN*, 1974).

The novel would have been read much more widely had T. S. Eliot used "He do the Police in different voices" as the title for *The Waste Land* (think how we all read *Heart of Darkness* because of "The Hollow Men"). Donald Gallup's revelation that this had been the working title of the manuscript (*TLS*, 7 Nov. 1968) was followed by a long correspondence about the bearings of *Our Mutual Friend* on the poem.

Edwin Drood

"Dickens's last laboured effort, the melancholy work of a worn-out brain," Wilkie Collins lamentably judged it; but recent Dickens critics seem to have worn out their brains by the time they arrive at 1870. The old breed of Droodians has almost died out, leaving no alternative critical regime; traditional Droodiana techniques flicker interestingly only in Arthur J. Cox's articles (*Dkn*, 1962; *DiS*, 1966, 1967; *MDAC*, 1972) and in Sir Felix Aylmer's lively *The Drood Case* (1964), which posits, with wild but ingeniously argued implausibility, that John Jasper was a good man, and no murderer, and that Rosa loved him—but Aylmer's exploration of the Middle Eastern bearings of the novel, and other incidentals, have carried more conviction (see *TLS*, 5 Nov. 1964, and Fielding, *NCF*, 1966). More orthodox studies are Charles Mitchell's "*Edwin Drood*: The Interior and Exterior of Self" (*ELH*, 1966) and Paul Gottschalk's "Time in *Edwin Drood*" (*DSA*, 1970), and the origins of Deputy's "Widdy widdy wen" have been learnedly controverted (*Dkn*, 1971). But the most substantial reexaminations of the novel have been in Angus Wilson's introduction to the Penguin edition (1974) and in reviews of that and the Clarendon edition (by Wilson and by J. I. M. Stewart, *Dkn*, 1973, 1974, and by Edgar Rosenberg, *DSN*, 1974). There are useful minor comments on the origins of the Princess Puffer (Collins, *Dkn*, 1964), the prevalence of artists in the novel (Jane Rabb Cohen, *DiS*, 1967), and its historical significance in detective fiction (George Wing, *SEL*, 1973). Richard D. Altick suggests that the notorious Constance Kent case may have influenced the Drood murder case in his *Victorian Studies in Scarlet: Murders and Manners in the Age of Victoria* (1970), which has much about Dickens' persistent interest in murder. What, in 1870, seemed vulnerable in it appears in a contemporary lampoon, "The Mysterious Mystery of Rude Dedwin," reprinted with commentary by Peyrouton (*Dkn*, 1966). Paul A. Wellsby's *Rochester Cathedral in the Time of Dickens* (1976) provides useful background information.

Minor Writings

Few of the minor writings have attracted much attention except the Christmas Books and Stories, studies of which have been mentioned above.

Dickens' work as an essayist—an underregarded art nowadays—is discussed by Robert Hamilton (*Dkn*, 1968), and Deborah A. Thomas pays attention to it in her *Dickens: Selected Short Fiction* (1976). Elsewhere she gives a sophisticated account of "George Silverman's Explanation" (*DSA*, 1974), the only Dickens short story to be much discussed lately. Q. D. Leavis sees it as one of Dickens' "best-written and most accomplished, as well as one of his most significant works" (*Dickens the Novelist*, p. 282). Like Barry D. Hart and Dudley Flamm (*Dkn*, 1964, 1970), she discusses it in relation to *Great Expectations*. But still "the short stories in general have been neglected by critics," as Ada Nisbet reported in 1964. These and other minor works await adequate critical, editorial, and biographical attention. Was it need, or cupidity, or a sense of duty, or sincere, if ill-judged, artistic adventurousness that induced Dickens in his maturity to write "Tom Tiddler's Ground" and "A Holiday Romance"? Or do these and other short narratives have unrecognized importance? What light, anyway, do these items throw upon the major works then being written? And how much brilliant writing lies neglected in the little-read essays? "A Flight," for example, is a tour de force, but it has rarely attracted any attention. And, again, how do these essays, the humdrum as well as the remarkable, relate to the novels? And, supposing that not even the most sympathetic and resourceful of critics can discover any substantial merits in Dickens' plays, can anything be added to Marvin Rosenberg's explanation (*JEGP*, 1960) of Dickens' failure in this area, surprising as it is in the classic English novelist with the greatest instinctive knowledge and love of the theater?

"The more you want of the master, the more you will find in him," exclaimed the gasman in Dickens' public-reading entourage after the great man had triumphantly surmounted a crisis. Dickens has proved susceptible to most of the current modes of criticism, including—his art being so poetical and so akin to the dramatic—those originally developed in the discussion of poetry or poetic drama. Thus F. R. Leavis' essay on *Hard Times*, which (he claims in *Dickens the Novelist*) "marked a new approach both to Dickens (and effected a revolution in Dickens criticism) and to the art of the novel generally," opened a *Scrutiny* series entitled "The Novel as Dramatic Poem." Critics less talented than Leavis have sometimes proceeded as if Dickens' works *were* poems or something other than novels, instead of novels resembling poems in some important, though limited, respect. The ahistorical nature of some favorite modern critical approaches has certainly encouraged critics to discover in Dickens, or to impose upon him, meanings that he could not possibly have envisaged, and, though we have been warned about the Intentional Fallacy, we may sometimes feel that Dr. Johnson's warning is more apposite: "Truth, Sir, is a cow which will yield such people no more milk, and so they are gone to milk the bull." William E. Fredeman has protested forcefully against the metamorphoses to which Dickens, like Tennyson, has lately been subjected, "the design of

which is to transform Victorian caterpillars into modern butterflies"
(*BJRL*, 1972), and Collins makes this a theme of his presidential address to
the Dickens Society (*DSN*, 1976). Dickens has many reputations, as Fielding
remarks:

> . . . and now that his triumph as a novelist is conceded we hear rather less of
> him as a social critic, a journalist, and as a leading figure of his time . . . but
> we cannot understand him unless we see how, even as a writer of fiction, he
> refused to keep simply to the world of his imagination.   (*VS*, 1968, p. 227)

Mention has already been made of various social, cultural, and ideological contexts in which Dickens can profitably be seen but that have been
inadequately studied—politics, religion, popular journalism, the literature
of his day, the Woman Question, London, and topography generally.
Though in the most important sense "not of an age but for all time,"
Dickens was, more intricately than Shakespeare, "of an age" (and of a
place, too). We risk misinterpreting him whenever we forget this—and who
knows how much of his meaning we are missing for lack of the requisite
contextual studies and of annotation on an adequate scale? There is, perhaps, a disproportion between the plenitude of imaginative interpretations
of Dickens, which include—sometimes very cogently—meanings he is most
unlikely to have intended, and the relatively few attempts to establish, at the
unspectacular annotatory level, meanings that he must have intended and
that his original readers, unlike us, must have caught. (I tried to indicate
this distinction briefly, in Amalric, 1973, by contrasting two interpretations
of the "great Cross on the summit of St. Paul's Cathedral" passage, in *Bleak
House*, Ch. xix.) Hence the attractiveness of the Shakespeare Institute's
Dickens project, mentioned above, and of Robert Patten's adumbration of a
similar superannotated edition (*DSN*, 1971), despite John Butt's formidable contention that annotation cannot satisfactorily be attempted until
standard works have been written on Dickens' London, his English, his
"originals," etc. (*English Studies Today*, Bern, 1961). Also, impossible
though it is for Dickens students to keep up with current work about him, it
is desirable that some of them keep up with some of the many notable
developments in Victorian historiography; the increasing sophistication of
urban history was mentioned above, as one example. The student of Dickens can never know too much about Dickens' England—and, in the recent
vogue of Victorian studies, more is becoming known about his England
every day.

Some areas of his biography that would repay further investigation have
been noted above: for instance, his early life and his reading, and maybe his
relationship with Ellen Ternan (precise knowledge of this is still scanty).
"He mixed with the *élite* that shared the finest culture of the age," to quote
F. R. Leavis again, here speculating about Dickens' awareness of Romantic
poetry (*Dickens the Novelist*, p. 228). Yes and no, I would incline to say,
and doesn't this make Dickens sound more like George Eliot than he was?

Certainly, however, we need a study more sophisticated than J. W. T. Ley's useful compilation *The Dickens Circle: A Narrative of the Novelist's Friendships*, one that can draw upon information not available to Ley in 1918—but his remains the fullest study on this subject, as does Edwin Pugh's of *The Charles Dickens Originals* (1913). That such obsolete and amateurish works on major topics remain unreplaced is as amazing as it was for me to find, in 1962, so rich and central a topic as "Dickens and Crime" virtually untouched by any scholar who could display a few basic skills in this area. Many other notable "Opportunities for Research" are suggested by W. F. Axton (*DSN*, 1971); and Jerome Meckier's useful report on "Research in Progress" (also in *DSN*, 1971) indicates what was then known to be cooking, mainly in the United States, and, by its silence on many important topics, may reassure future researchers that much significant investigation still awaits a competent and industrious hand. To specify one tiny example: How did Dickens vote in General Elections? Wisely, and therefore as radically as was possible, we are likely to assume; but, if anyone has checked the record in the pollbooks (which are extant), he has kept his discoveries to himself, so far as I know. How many votes, indeed, did Dickens have? And, contemptuous of Parliament, did he bother to vote at all? And when there were two Liberal candidates—and one would expect him to vote Liberal— for which, if either, did he vote, and why? Is it not curious (to continue in this questioning vein) that nobody, apparently, knows the answer to such simple and basic questions about how one of the most politically concerned of English novelists behaved politically?

It is relatively easy to descry such gaps in our factual knowledge of Dickens, but less easy to write a shopping list of critical desiderata. Certainly a lot of central topics, though widely discussed, still await discussion at a level, possibly falling short, indeed, of a classic treatment (one hopes, but cannot plan, for that), but providing an authoritative starting point for further thought over the next decade or next generation. Thus, while the pages above on Characterization, on Style and Language, and on Comedy, Humor, Satire—all basic critical issues—record many competent items, and a number of brilliant ones, in none of these areas (I think) is there a decisive study to which students may be referred because, by general consent, it constitutes a basic, essential, and comprehensive analysis. The same could, indeed, be said of most of the "special aspects" surveyed in the Criticism section. Grateful though we all must be, for instance, for many general essays on Dickens' characterization and for many more particular essays on individual characters, there is no study that, while recognizing the paramount importance of Dickens' achievement in imagining and projecting his classic "Dickens characters," also pays due attention to his other modes of apprehending and presenting character—for Little Nell, Pip, Krook, Mr. Dombey, Maggy, and Mr. Dorrit are creations as uniquely Dickensian as his more acceptably "Dickensian" creations such as Pickwick, Pecksniff, Micawber, Chadband, and Mrs. Gamp.

This failure to recognize the multifarious (and also the persistently uneven) quality of Dickens' achievement has been the most obvious weakness of recent criticism of his work. Rupert Crawshay-Williams, in his admirable essay on philosophical tendencies, *The Comforts of Unreason* (1947), has a usefully minatory chapter on "the comforts of Unifying Formulae." Dickens, it should never be forgotten, is splendidly resistant to the critical unifying formula. *"Isms!"* he exclaimed in a letter of 27 April 1844. "Oh for a world without an ism." His critics should take the tip, and some of them have done so. Margaret Ganz, commending Barbara Hardy's animadversions on that "super-criticism which blurs analysis in re-creation," has protested vigorously against the "trend which has tended to impose on the sprawling imagination of Dickens' fiction an order not only intellectually or ideologically but academically inspired . . . [and which] has removed us remorselessly from the sights, sounds, smells and shapes of the text" (*VS*, 1971, p. 234). Across the Atlantic, another critic writes:

> One is naturally suspicious of critics who start their treatment of a complicated work of art with the announcement that it is "about" some one, usually faintly surprising, thing. Thus [someone] writes: *"David Copperfield* is a novel about worldly prudence; and conversely, about the dangers of imprudence and trust." This tactic may derive from recent writings about Shakespeare (always a resonance around Dickens), but when it has ceased to shock into the reconsideration of ideas of "comic relief," etc.—which it has—it has done its work. (Roger Gard, *EIC*, 1965, p. 320)

Dickens has indeed been subjected to far too much reductive tidying-up.

A sagacious phrase and notion from a major Victorian critic, citing a majestic author, may suggest, not an agenda for future Dickens critics, but the spirit in which they might hope to conduct their inquiries. "To handle these matters [of poetical criticism] properly there is needed a poise so perfect that the least overweight in any direction tends to destroy the balance," Matthew Arnold wrote in his *On Translating Homer: Last Words* (1862), where he was arguing against the insensitive pedantry of Francis Newman:

> Temper destroys it, a crotchet destroys it, even erudition may destroy it. To press to the sense of the thing itself with which one is dealing, not to go off on some collateral issue about the thing, is the hardest matter in the world. The "thing itself" with which one is here dealing, the critical perception of poetic truth, is of all things the most volatile, elusive, and evanescent; by even pressing too impetuously after it, one runs the risk of losing it. The critic of poetry should have the finest tact, the nicest moderation, the most free, flexible, and elastic spirit imaginable; he should be indeed the "ondoyant et divers," the *undulating and diverse* being of Montaigne.

The terms of Arnold's specification of the ideal critic (and "poetic criticism" may well embrace Dickens, though Arnold himself had a "crotchet" that prevented his seeing this) must wring the withers of most Dickens commentators, for it is "the hardest matter in the world"—or one of the harder tasks in the useful if minuscule world of literary criticism—to be and to remain as intellectually "ondoyant et divers" as Dickens' extensive, extraordinary, and *"undulating and diverse"* creative achievement demands.

WILLIAM MAKEPEACE THACKERAY

Robert A. Colby

"The status of Thackeray is perhaps more equivocal than that of any major Victorian novelist," began the essay by my distinguished predecessor, the late Lionel Stevenson. He pointed in evidence to the central paradox of Thackeray's present-day reputation: while he maintains a place alongside Dickens in literary histories, his reputation among modern critics is not so secure. A further anomaly in the early 1960s was the relative inaccessibility of Thackeray's works. "Among his major novels, only two [*Vanity Fair* and *Henry Esmond*] have been made available in the paperback editions which are the current gauge of academic respectability in the United States," Stevenson observed.

Although Thackeray remains something of a colossus in the shade, his position is not quite what it was when Stevenson wrote. There is no doubt that his general readership has been declining since the turn of the century, but there are signs of a shifting climate in academia. More of his books have been brought back into print lately, so that, while *Vanity Fair* and *Henry Esmond* continue to draw the largest splash of critical ink, other works, both before and after these masterpieces, are beginning to be recognized as worth reading. The attribution of anonymous pieces has undergone fresh scrutiny. Attempts have been made, fitful and faulty though they may be, to edit some of the novels by modern principles—an indication of dissatisfaction with the received texts (rubbing off perhaps from the enterprise of the Clarendon Dickens and, on American soil, of the Center for Editions of American Authors). We still neither *read* nor *see* Thackeray's books quite as his first readers did, but our attention is being drawn more to their original formats and trappings, and the reciprocity of text and illustration is coming to be appreciated in our visual age.

Furthermore, anachronistic as much of the criticism of his principal novels continues to be, Thackeray's career is being recovered more and more in the context of his times—an essential step toward true appreciation and evaluation. To be sure, the centenary of his death came and went in 1963 (the year before the publication of the forerunner to this volume) with only a portion of an issue of one journal, *Nineteenth-Century Fiction* (Dec.), to mark the occasion, by contrast with the fanfare that commemorated his erstwhile contender "at the top of the tree" in 1970. But 1975 marked something of a banner year, with the emergence of an entire issue of the journal *Costerus* (NS 2, dated 1974) devoted to "the presentation of new research and better formulated procedures for the understanding of Thackeray's literary achievement"* and the launching of a *W. M. Thackeray Newsletter*, with headquarters at Mississippi State University. Both publications are edited by an energetic Thackerayan of the new generation, Peter L. Shillingsburg. There is indication too of a flurry in the graduate schools, with some sixty doctoral dissertations registered since 1964 in *Dissertation Abstracts*. All of this, if it does not necessarily presage a popular revival, suggests that this much misunderstood and sometimes underrated "Gentle Censor" of his age has something also to say to ours and may now be standing on more solid ground than he was in the previous decade.

Manuscripts and Special Collections

Like the work of most other writers represented in this volume, Thackeray's novels cry out for editing, but the future editor who wants to go back to manuscript will have to make bricks without straw. Lacking a literary executor such as Dickens had with Forster, or a repository like the Victoria and Albert Museum, Thackeray's literary remains have suffered unusual scatter. Of the greater novels, only *Henry Esmond* is reasonably intact, as well as in one place (Trinity College, Cambridge). About two thirds of *The Virginians* is left in the form in which it went to the printers (Morgan Library); a little more than half of *The Newcomes* (mainly at Charterhouse School, with other blocks of chapters in the Berg Collection); twelve chapters of *Vanity Fair* (Morgan Library; stray pages in various other libraries); and only fragments of *Pendennis*, strewn among several repositories. One of the curiosities of Thackeray's survival is that his most popular novel is among the most poorly preserved, while those least read, the *Cornhill* group, are among the best preserved: the bulk of *The Adventures of Philip* is available virtually in one piece in the Huntington Library; and the Morgan Library has practically all of *Lovel the Widower*, including Thackeray's original pen-and-ink drawings, and all but one chapter of the half-told *Denis Duval*.

An attempt at an inventory has been made by Robert A. Colby and John

* The individual contributions, divided among textual and bibliographical problems, source materials, literary background, and illustration, are taken up in appropriate sections of this essay.

A. Sutherland in "Thackeray's Manuscripts: A Preliminary Census of Library Locations" (*Costerus*, 1974). Those in pursuit are directed therein to leading repositories of manuscripts, and in some instances proof sheets, of (1) the novels and other principal prose works, (2) uncompleted, late posthumous publications, (3) poems, (4) various unpublished pieces, (5) diaries, notebooks, (6) correspondence.* The holdings of some twenty libraries, mainly in America, are reported in this census, along with three private collections.

Apart from the repositories cited in this census, which concentrates on primary sources, the Metzdorf Collection purchased by the University of Texas in 1966 merits special mention for its abundance of first editions and association copies that await study and assessment. Since then the University of Rochester Library has received a collection of Thackeray family papers from the Metzdorf estate, which includes drawings, photographs, and letters principally by Thackeray and his daughter Anne. The Robert H. Taylor Collection at Princeton, partially recorded in the aforementioned issue of *Costerus*, is still in the process of being catalogued. The Beinecke Library at Yale has in recent years added to its vast Thackeray holdings several presentation copies of first editions (*YULG*, 1975), as well as proof sheets, in various stages, of *The Roundabout Papers* and *The Four Georges*. The Mitchell Memorial Library at Mississippi State University now owns several items of peripheral interest to Thackeray scholars, including notebooks compiled by M. H. Spielmann and Anthony Walker (*ThN*, 1975). The two largest collections of unpublished letters appear to be in the Fales Library of New York University and in the Metzdorf Collection of the University of Texas.

As Colby and Sutherland observe in their census, "the Thackeray scholar must be prepared to be peripatetic and/or a tireless correspondent."

Bibliography

There is nothing like a complete bibliography of Thackeray—descriptive or enumerative. The record has to be pieced together from the pioneering efforts of R. H. Shepherd and C. P. Johnson, from bibliographical appendixes (e.g., the chronological listing of Thackeray's *Works* in order of their first appearance in book form, prepared by W. J. Williams for Vol. XIII of the Biographical Edition; Lewis Melville's notes to the sets issued by Macmillan), and from scattered documents—principally inventories of private libraries and catalogues of library exhibitions, a number of which were noted by Stevenson.

Henry Van Duzer's *A Thackeray Library* (1919), the most extensive and best-known list from a private collection, has been reissued by Kennikat Press (1965) with a judicious introduction by Lionel Stevenson, pointing out its scholarly deficiencies but indicating why it will have to continue to

---

* A few additional locations of Thackeray letters are indicated by H. W. McCready in "Towards a Checklist of MS. Resources for Victorian Periodicals" (*VPN*, 1974).

serve faut de mieux. Van Duzer, however, was but one of several wealthy amateurs drawn to Thackeray earlier in the century. The *Valuable Library of Frederick S. Dickson,* sold at auction in Philadelphia on 28–29 March 1913, included not only first editions of Thackeray's works but also books to which Thackeray contributed and in which he is mentioned, along with translations, illustrations, and portraits.* Over a period of thirty-five years another devotee, Major William Lambert, assembled a precious collection of manuscripts, correspondence, and drawings by and portraits of Thackeray (his efforts were facilitated by his direct access to the author's heirs). The catalogue of the sale of his Thackerayana by the Metropolitan Art Association of New York (1914) constitutes another valuable bibliographical source. The first editions of Dickens and Thackeray amassed by George Barr McCutcheon, author of *Graustark,* are characterized in the foreword to the sales catalogue published by the American Art Association (1926) as "One of the finest collections of these two writers that has ever been brought together." McCutcheon was attracted in particular to the early publications and to out-of-the-way periodicals Thackeray contributed to. In the next decade *The Library of the Late Hon. D. Phoenix Ingraham,* an eminent Justice of the Supreme Court of New York, was proclaimed as a rival to that of Van Duzer in the catalogue issued at its dispersal by the American Art Association (1936).

These collections, alas, are scattered to the winds, like Thackeray's literary remains in general. Some items are traceable to various research libraries (e.g., Ingraham—Berg Collection; Lambert—Morgan, Huntington, Rosenbach), but thorough tracking down remains to be done.

Two retrospective bibliographies issued over the past decade are handy, though not all-encompassing. Lionel Stevenson has updated the section on Thackeray for *NCBEL,* III, 1800–1900 (1969), which consists of nine closely packed columns divided into Bibliographies, Collections, Publications, Letters, and Criticism, Comment. There are lacunae, notably in catalogues of private libraries, editions of the collected works, and posthumous publications, but, all in all, this is the longest checklist easily available. Stevenson's record is extended partially by Arthur Pollard's essay on Thackeray (originally drafted by the late Geoffrey Tillotson) in *The English Novel: Select Bibliographical Guides,* ed. A. E. Dyson (1974). The *MLA International Bibliography* having fallen behind in its publication schedule, scholars lean more on the annual Victorian bibliography (*VS*) to keep up-to-date, bolstered by the semiannual "Recent Publications: A Selected List," compiled by Arthur E. Minerof for the *Victorian Newsletter,* and the annual review article in the fall issue of *Studies in English Literature,* under rotating editorship.

---

* Dickson, of course, is remembered for his bibliography, appended to James Grant Wilson's *Thackeray in the United States* (1904). Unknown apparently, certainly unused, five notebooks in his hand rest on the shelves of the reference room in the Beinecke Library. Here are painstakingly recorded publications both by and about Thackeray, from his boyhood letters and earliest identified contributions to school magazines, to posthumous publications, extending to the year 1900. Pruned of its ephemera and erroneous attributions, this list could serve as the basis for an enumerative bibliography.

Thackeray is woefully in need of a bibliographer, or ideally of a pool of bibliographers, who can bring to his variegated canon the requisite kinds of competence—textual, bibliophilic, historical, critical, artistic.

Journalism Attribution

"After dinner he was sitten over his punch, when some of our gents came in; and he began to talk and brag to them about his harticle, and what he had for it and that he was the best cricket in Europe . . . ," are the immortal words of Miss Barbara at Morland's Hotel, where Mr. Michael Angelo Titmarsh has taken up temporary residence ("A Pictorial Rhapsody: Concluded," *Fraser's*, July 1840). As is well known, Thackeray was sought out as a "good hand for light articles," and he welcomed such opportunities until he reached the hearts and pocketbooks of the common novel reader. As a "cricket," he chirped widely and pseudonymously to an extent not fully known to this day. "Obviously, a good deal of already identified material must be sought in the files of the sometimes obscure journals that Thackeray wrote for," Lionel Stevenson observed, predicting at the time that "probably there is further material yet to be discovered." Not surprisingly, more fugitive items have come to light lately, which, if not of the significance of the *Morning Chronicle* reviews identified and published by Gordon Ray (1955; paperback, 1966), are interesting to students of Thackeray's mind.

Discovered in the files of the National Library of Calcutta, six pieces contributed by Thackeray to the *Calcutta Star* from August 1844 to 21 August 1845 (under the signature SQUAB) are reprinted for the first time in the issue of *Nineteenth-Century Fiction* (1963) observing the centenary of his death. These so-called "Letters from a Club Arm-Chair" are ably edited by Henry Summerfield, who unearthed them. Here Thackeray brings the real-life Colonel Newcome up on such topics of the day as the Irish problem, the Maynooth grant, and the railway mania. In "Thackeray as Historian: Two Newly Identified Contributions to *Fraser's Magazine*" (*NCF*, 1967), Geoffrey C. Stokes, on the basis of evidence in letters, adds to the list of probable items two reviews related to Thackeray's interest in French culture, "Le Duc de Normandie" and "Gisquet's *Memoirs*." Fortunately these items were discovered in time to be registered in Volume II of *The Wellesley Index*.

Generally, however, there has been more loss than gain. Fresh work on attribution stimulated by *The Wellesley Index* has led to a restirring of the muddy waters of Thackeray's magazine canon. In "Thackeray's Contributions to *Fraser's Magazine*" (*SB*, 1966), Edward M. White, employing Walter Houghton's criteria of external evidence, subjects this least firmly established body of Thackeray's review writing to the most rigorous investigation it has ever had. The more than one hundred pieces that have been assigned to Thackeray by one bibliographer or another are here reduced to a hard core of about fifty, with a few others tentatively accepted, the rest cast into a bin of "disallowed attributions." The most important of White's rejections, a review entitled "Hints for a History of *Highwaymen*" (*Fraser's*, 1834), assigned to Thackeray as early as 1888 by C. P. Johnson, has since been proved to be not by Thackeray, on the basis of biographical evidence in the article itself (*WI*, II, 341; fuller documentation than that printed in the *Index* is on record for this and other articles in the files in the Wellesley College Library). Most other uncollected *Fraser's* pieces remain suspect. (White's "disallowed attributions" are left unascribed in the *Fraser's* section of *WI*, II.)

Deattribution of articles has also been the net result of the editors' research in regard to *The Foreign Quarterly Review*, the other major journal with which Thackeray was connected that is covered in the *Index*. Two pieces included among Thackeray's writings in *The New Sketch Book*, ed. Robert S. Garnett (London, 1906)—the reviews of Dumas's *Celebrated Crimes* and of Charles Gutzkow's *Paris* (*WI*, II, 165)—have been reassigned to others, and "Balzac on the Newspapers of Paris" has been questioned. Although never canonized in any of the editions of Thackeray's works, most of the other essays gathered together in *The New Sketch Book* have gained general acceptance on the basis of references in Thackeray's correspondence or of internal evidence (such as analogies with his novels). Unfortunately no new articles have been revealed by *The Wellesley Index*, although it is assumed that not all of Thackeray's contributions to the *Foreign Quarterly Review* have been identified to this day.*

Work is still going on. In "Thackeray and the *National Standard*" (*RES*, 1972), Donald Hawes traces the background and history of Thackeray's first journalistic venture, incidentally attributing to him reviews in addition to those reprinted in the Oxford edition. More recently a French scholar, Jean Guivarc'h, in "Deux journalistes anglaises de Paris en 1835 (George W. M. Reynolds et W. M. T.)" (*EA*, 1975), confirms what has long been suspected —that Thackeray was among the contributors to *The Paris Literary Gazette*, edited at this time by Reynolds. Guivarc'h lists five articles signed "W. M. T." and reprints one of them for the first time ("England," a literary letter intended for Thackeray's countrymen vacationing abroad). Obviously much is left to be done in the area of attribution.

Editions: Collected Works

From 1867, the year when the Smith & Elder edition was launched, to 1911, the centenary of his birth, Thackeray's collected works were issued, both in England and America, in a stream of publishers' sets—"de luxe" and cheap,

---

* Volume III of *The Wellesley Index* will include four journals associated with Thackeray: *Ainsworth's Magazine, The New Monthly Magazine, The Westminster Review,* and *The British and Foreign Review*. For the first three, Thackeray's contribution seems to be fully identified. In *The British and Foreign Review*, one article identified by Lila Winegarner (*JEGP*, 1948), a review of Lord Brougham's speeches (April 1839), is now established on external evidence. A second, "Manners and Society in St. Petersburgh" (Jan. 1839), will be listed as "probable." A third and tentative attribution by Winegarner, a review entitled "Tytler's Reigns of Edward VI and Mary," has been reassigned to another writer.

some attempting to reproduce his illustrations, others with new illustrations, and in a variety of formats. None, unfortunately, is either authoritative or definitive, but several are of special value to the student of Thackeray for certain subsidiary features, apart from text, and should be given preference among the so-called library editions that abounded in the heyday of his popularity.

Pride of place has generally been given to the Biographical Edition (Smith & Elder, 1898–99, 13 vols.; issued simultaneously in America by Harper) and to its offshoot, the Centenary Biographical Edition (1911, 26 vols.), both derived from the earlier Smith & Elder editions. Before Gordon Ray's monumental edition of the letters and his two-volume biography, the introductions by Anne Thackeray to these editions constituted a chief primary source, both for their background information and for their quotations from letters that had not then been published. They retain their value for their hints at Thackeray's sources, as well as for their glimpses into his working habits. Other features of the Biographical Edition are the graphics (sketches and doodles, portraits), the biographical sketch by Leslie Stephen (corrected from the *DNB*), and the chronological bibliography prepared by W. J. Williams. Although no more reliable from the textual standpoint, the Centenary Biographical Edition is superior to its predecessor in a number of ways: the augmentation of Anne Thackeray's introductions; the addition of posthumous pieces; the reproductions of Thackeray's pictorial initials, as well as the cuts and plates; and the inclusion of wrappers from the books issued in monthly parts. It is evident, moreover, from the correspondence of Anne Thackeray and her daughter Hester Fuller with W. J. Williams (Parrish Collection, Princeton) that much thought went into such matters as the juxtaposition of related works in the various volumes, the authentication of unsigned pieces, the selection of portraits, and the placement of illustrations.

More useful for the study of Thackeray's text, though not so full, is the Oxford Thackeray (1908, 17 vols.) prepared under the supervision of George Saintsbury, with collations by F. S. Hall. The textual notes appended to each volume listing various changes and deletions provide the closest approach we have to a variorum edition, though more recent scholarship has found this work neither complete nor thoroughly accurate. (It is taken for granted here, for example, that the various cuts from edition to edition were made by Thackeray, a matter now in dispute. See in particular the essays by Peter Shillingsburg and Gerald Sorensen in *Costerus*, 1974, discussed below in connection with reprints of individual novels.) Saintsbury's unusual arrangement of volumes—beginning with the "magazinery" and other "small potatoes" instead of with *Vanity Fair*—is more helpful than other editions in enabling us to trace Thackeray's development as a writer.

From the graphic standpoint, the outstanding set is the Harry Furniss Centenary Edition (Macmillan, 1911, 20 vols.) with its "artist's prefaces" by Furniss, evaluating Thackeray's accomplishment in drawing and illustrating. Its contents include papers by Thackeray on both art and literature that were not previously reprinted (Vols. xii and xiii), as well as the text that Thackeray provided for his friend Louis Marvy's *Sketches after English Landscape Painters*. One feature devotees are likely to resent is Furniss' "correcting" and updating of Thackeray's original illustrations. Textually the Furniss Edition is noteworthy for reprinting the first versions of the novels (except for *Barry Lyndon*)—a carryover from the earlier Macmillan editions, along with the valuable textual introductions by Lewis Melville.

Reprints: Individual Works

Like most other Victorian novelists, Thackeray has not been well served by the reprint industry—many of the student texts issued over the past two decades perpetuating, in some instances compounding, errors of the past.

A convenient starting point for assaying this situation is Gerald C. Sorensen's "Thackeray Texts and Bibliographical Scholarship" (*Costerus*, 1974). Sorensen points out the various impediments to the production of "sound texts," either "definitive" or "practical," beginning with the haphazard survival of the manuscripts, complicated by the lack in many instances of proof sheets, the disappearance of many of Thackeray's working notes and sketches (referred to by Anne Thackeray in the Centenary Biographical Edition), our inadequate knowledge of the relationship between American editions and English prototypes, and the arbitrary choice of copy-text by editors of scholarly reprints.

The strands in our present textual cat's cradle are expertly disentangled by Peter Shillingsburg in "Thackeray's Texts: A Guide to Inexpensive Editions" (*Costerus*, 1974). This "consumers' report" on the range of paperbacks and other cheap editions should be examined carefully by any editor or teacher of Thackeray. The charts (including a genealogical tree for *Vanity Fair*) are especially useful. The rigorous criteria that Shillingsburg sets up for judging both the text and the critical apparatus of "practical editions" are not wholly met, sad to say, by any of those available to us. Some highlights of the present reprint situation are discussed below.

Early Works

A quirk of recent reprint publication is *A Shabby Genteel Story*, brought out jointly by Scolar Press in England and New York University Press (1971)—a photoreproduction of the unauthoritative 1879 edition, sans introduction, notes, or apparatus of any sort—a pointless production, in short.

For *Barry Lyndon* there are now two principal student editions. The paperback edited by Robert L. Morris for the Bison Book series of the University of Nebraska Press (1962) is derived ultimately from the 1856 revision, *The Memoirs of Barry Lyndon*, which reprints (incompletely) in an appendix the passages cut out from the original *Fraser's* version of 1844. The later hardcover critical edition prepared by Martin J. Anisman for the Gotham Library of New York University Press (1970) goes back to the superior serial version for its copy-text, indicating by brackets and footnotes changes made in 1856. Fundamentally, Anisman's is the sounder approach, but by critical consensus his editing is slipshod (see Shillingsburg's review *PBSA*, 1972; *TLS*, 5 Nov. 1971), and the annotation, in my opinion, is perfunctory. However, Anisman gives us some idea of how this best of Thackeray's minor novels originally read.

Three recent reprints, all based on *The Memoirs of Barry Lyndon* of 1856, make no bibliographical contribution: a hardcover in Cassell's Dufour Editions, First Novel Library (1967), with an appreciative, if sometimes wrongheaded, introduction by Lord David Cecil; a paperback issued by Futura Publications (1974), introduced by Mollie Hardwick, intended evidently as a tie-in with the then forthcoming film version advertised on its back flap. All that is offered by the Penguin edition (1974) is an idiosyncratic foreword by the novelist J. P. Donleavy.

Vanity Fair

The Riverside edition of Thackeray's most popular novel, edited by Geoffrey Tillotson and Kathleen Tillotson, came out in time (1963) to be saluted by my predecessor. It continues to tower above all other student texts, though it must be added that searching bibliographical appraisal has since diminished its claim to definitiveness. The Tillotsons' choice of copy-text has been challenged (by Shillingsburg and Sorensen in *Costerus*, 1974), some of their emendations have been questioned (*TLS*, 28 Nov. 1963), and omissions have been pointed out, resulting from their reliance on a photocopy of the manuscript (by Joan Stevens in *AUMLA*, 1964). It is unfortunate too that Thackeray's historiated initials are not reproduced. Nevertheless, for its contextual scholarship and copious annotation, it remains "the best buy" (Shillingsburg's phrase).

The only recent reprints within hailing distance of the Riverside are those produced by the Penguin English Library (1968), with an introduction by J. I. M. Stewart, and the Odyssey Press (1969), with an introduction by F. E. L. Priestley. Although it takes its point of departure from the Riverside, the Penguin is not nearly so scrupulous about textual matters, presenting us with a text that might politely be described as eclectic. It has its rewards, however: the gracefully written, if at times condescending, introduction by Stewart and the notes, mainly defining obscure phrases and identifying persons and titles. The Odyssey Press reprint is unannotated and, from the textual standpoint, retrograde, merely photoreproducing the first edition, with no record of changes. It justifies itself by providing what the Penguin lacks—Thackeray's illustrations, plates and initials being reproduced here in their entirety.

Pendennis

Until recently the only readily accessible cheap edition of Thackeray's second major novel was in the Everyman Library (1910; reissued 1954, with an introduction by M. R. Ridley)—a corrupted version of the text in the Biographical Edition, itself of no authority.

The Penguin English Library *Pendennis* (1972), edited by Donald Hawes, attractively decked out in a Cruikshank wrapper, furnishes more guidance to the student than has hitherto been available, though it does not go very far toward establishing the text. A note on the text calls attention to some—but by no means all—of the changes made for the 1856 edition, on which the Penguin is based. Hawes's assumption that this revised version is an "improvement" will be contested by many a Thackerayan who prefers the ampler one of the monthly parts and the first book edition. A virtue of this text is that the monthly-part division is indicated, and Hawes's notes are helpful, even if they fall short of the most painstaking scholarship. Alas, no "Author's own candles." (For this reason one should hunt up the *Pendennis* in Macmillan's Illustrated Pocket Thackeray, 1906, which, like this whole set, reprints the first edition and reproduces all the initials, cuts, and plates.)

The most intensive effort thus far at a definitive edition is Peter Shillingsburg's unpublished doctoral dissertation "The Text of Thackeray's *Pendennis*" (Univ. of South Carolina 1970)—based on a machine collation of five copies (three sets of parts, two book issues) and examination of five other copies. Pending publication of his thesis, Shillingsburg's findings can be sampled in two articles: "The First Edition of Thackeray's *Pendennis*" (*PBSA*, 1972) and "Thackeray's *Pendennis* in America" (*PBSA*, 1974).

Henry Esmond

The most thoroughly annotated school text of Thackeray's second most popular novel, that of T. C. and W. Snow (Oxford, 1909; rev., 1915), which traces much of Thackeray's historical scholarship, is unfortunately out of print. Also inaccessible is the John Bell Henneman edition (Macmillan, 1923).

The post–World War II boom brought forth a succession of inexpensive reprints: Modern Library (1950), with an introduction by Gordon N. Ray; Harper's Modern Classics (1950), introduced by Lionel Stevenson; Holt, Rinehart and Winston (1962), introduced by G. Robert Stange; Washington Square, Collateral Classic (1966), introduced by Edward R. Easton; the Penguin English Library (1970), edited by John Sutherland and Michael Greenfield; Pan Classics (1974), with introduction and notes by Gilbert Phelps.

Of these reprints, two can be singled out for their attempts to grasp the textual nettle. In the Holt, Rinehart and Winston edition (loosely based on the revision of 1858), Stange has inserted "A Note on the Composition and Text of the Novel," useful, though misleading in some details, as Shillingsburg points out, on the transmission of the text. The Penguin English Library is the only student text to have made use of the manuscript at Trinity College, Cambridge, described in one of the prefatory notes, but only one of a number of omitted passages is mentioned, none of the substantive changes is accounted for, and no collation has been attempted with printed text. Like the Holt, Rinehart and Winston edition, the Penguin is based on the 1858 revision on the assumption that it was "the last text to be supervised by the author," a claim without support. On the credit side are Sutherland's scholarly introduction and notes, some of which correct Thackeray's factual errors.

Other Novels

Beyond *Esmond* the pickings are slim. For *The Newcomes* we must make do with the reissue of the Everyman edition, with an introduction by M. R. Ridley (1962; also in paperback). Likewise with *The Virginians* (1961; paperback). The only bibliographical advance of these over the previous Everyman editions is the indication of the monthly-part divisions. In connection with the later novel, mention should be made of Sorensen's unpublished doctoral dissertation, "A Critical Edition of . . . *The Virginians*" (Univ. of Minnesota 1966), the first systematic, if partial, comparison of the manuscript, bound parts, parts in wrappers, first book publication, and 1863 cheap edition, with the object of establishing the text. (In his "Thackeray's Texts and Bibliographical Scholarship," cited above, Sorensen gives his reasons for adopting the first edition as copy-text. For comment on Sorensen's work, see Edgar Harden, "The Growth of *The Virginians* as a Serial Novel: Parts 1–9," *Costerus*, 1974.)

The only one of Thackeray's Christmas Books readily available is *The Rose and the Ring*. The Morgan Library has brought out a facsimile of the manuscript in their possession, reproducing Thackeray's original drawings and introduced by Gordon Ray (1947). Intended as a Christmas gift book, it is a luxury. Unfortunately the inexpensive alternative is a reprint in Dent's Children's Illustrated Classics (1959), pleasantly introduced by Roger Lancelyn Green, but making mincemeat of the tale itself by failing to match up pictures to text according to Thackeray's careful arrangement. (See Joan Stevens, "A Fairy Tale Mishandled," *AUMLA*, 1965.)

Gerald Sorensen points to the need for "collation by team and by machine" if we are ever to have definitive editions of Thackeray's novels, individual or collected. A clearing through our dense, dark thicket of accumulated error now presents itself in the form of a projected edition of Thackeray's complete works. We are promised by the general editor, Peter Shillingsburg, that this edition "will be prepared according to the most rigorous of modern editing standards" (*ThN*, 1975). The edition is to follow a chronological order, presenting Thackeray's work in its "earliest complete form," a departure from most of its predecessors. Volume 1 is scheduled for 1979, to be followed by one or two volumes per year, eventually reaching (with the inclusion of the complete journalism and the drawings, published and unpublished) approximately twenty-three volumes.

Critical Reception and Reputation

A prime desideratum singled out by Stevenson was a history of Thackeray's reputation. The most comprehensive survey, unfortunately unpublished, is Sara Carruth's doctoral dissertation "Thackeray's Reputation in England, 1840–1903" (Univ. of Chicago 1958). Carruth has made a judicious survey of the reviews, divided into periods dominated by key works. Among her conclusions is that a "lag in literary taste" set in by the end of the century, Thackeray's esteem growing with the general public while dissatisfaction of the sort that has carried over to the present day was sounded among critics. An epilogue chapter, "Thackeray in the Twentieth Century," assesses the reasons why he has failed to "come back," despite the plethora of scholarship on him.

The past decade has produced two reference works that provide data for further study of the reputation. Dudley Flamm's *Thackeray's Critics: An Annotated Bibliography of British and American Criticism, 1836–1901* (1966) draws on Carruth's dissertation as well as on the pioneering bibliography of F. S. Dickson. It consists of excerpts from seven hundred items —reviews, essays from critical books, introductions to collected works— arranged in a year-by-year chronology. Flamm has cast his net wide, taking in obscure journals and newspapers, including reviews of the nonfiction prose as well as novels. Items that he considers "of particular critical and/or historical interest" are asterisked (but with no criteria indicated), and detailed indexes are provided. An introductory essay attempts to place Thackeray in the tradition of realism and charts the course of his reputation to its peak at the turn of the century. Omissions in Flamm's record have been cited by Sara Carruth (*MP*, 1969) and by Geoffrey Tillotson (*MLR*, 1970), and others undoubtedly will be turned up by further research,* but all in all this is the most extensive conspectus of criticism available.†

A critical retrospect is offered from another vantage point in *Thackeray: The Critical Heritage*, edited by Geoffrey Tillotson and Donald Hawes (1968). Here are gathered together fifty-six items—contemporaneous reviews from periodicals, together with other documentary material (such as ex-

---

* One I have noted is "Mr. Thackeray's Satire" (*Spectator*, 1861), attributed to its co-editor Richard Holt Hutton, the most extended review I have seen of the rarely noticed novel *the Widower*. On the other hand, Sara Carruth points out that for the period 1836–63 Flamm lists ninety-seven items in addition to those cited in her dissertation.

† Flamm's record is carried forward by John C. Olmsted's *Thackeray and His Twentieth-Century Critics: An Annotated Bibliography of British and American Criticism, 1900–1975*, published by Garland too late for notice in this essay.

cerpts from letters), tracing Thackeray's critical fortunes from 1837 to 1879. In line with other volumes in this well-known series, there is useful editorial apparatus, such as identifying headnotes (rather sparse), explanatory footnotes, and indexes of names, titles, and topics. On the whole the twofold aim is fulfilled: to rescue some "forgotten worthies" (including American reviewers) and to place in context some of the better-known critics. Inevitably, as with any selection, one can carp at what has been left out. A more glaring gap is the neglect of the slight but wistfully charming *Lovel the Widower*, the unfinished but significant *Denis Duval*, and all the nonfiction prose except for *The Paris Sketch Book*.

The history of Thackeray's reputation both in England and America remains then in the annal and chronicle stage, with his Continental reception still completely untouched.

General Criticism

In their introduction to the Critical Heritage volume, Tillotson and Hawes assert that "our red-hot views are those of at least some of our great-grandparents. Our discoveries are rediscoveries." Amid the fresh light cast by the newer criticism, it is true, lurk the shadows of old bugaboos—the "intrusive" commentary, the "indifferent" workmanship, the alleged intellectual superficiality, the perverseness and contradictoriness—that call to mind the likes of William Caldwell Roscoe and Nassau Senior. There are, however, perceptible shifts of attitude. In his own day Thackeray's detractors were often repelled by his cynicism, whereas nowadays those who do not take to him are more prone to react against his sentimental side. On the other hand, our psychoanalytic age is more receptive to the "mixed" characters that disturbed those hot for certainties during Thackeray's lifetime. (One quickly loses count of the current articles on "moral ambiguity" in *Vanity Fair, Pendennis*, etc.) Thanks to the labors of Gordon Ray, modern critics write with a greater knowledge of Thackeray's life than was available to his fellow writers and journalists, but in general they move on a narrower gauge, less cognizant of his work as a whole. Even among Thackeray's most ardent latter-day admirers, one still senses a note of apology, suggesting a felt need to "sell" him to this generation of students and readers.

"I have tried to represent the best twentieth-century criticism . . . but I have not tried to conceal that the twentieth-century has often been impatient or even hostile to Thackeray," candidly declares Alexander Welsh in his introduction to *Thackeray: A Collection of Critical Essays* (1968). This volume in the Prentice-Hall series gathers together conveniently some of the better-known spokesmen for our century, both admiring (G. K. Chesterton, John Dodds, Kathleen Tillotson, Gordon Ray) and qualified (Percy Lubbock, J. Y. T. Greig, Mario Praz, Georg Lukács). Apparently aligned with the second group, editor Welsh gives with one hand, praising Thackeray as "a brilliant master of language," while taking away with the other, judging him to be "an artist . . . careless and amateurish in part." He pays tribute nevertheless to Thackeray's moral power as "a veritable student of human botching and repenting."

Perhaps in reaction against the sniping campaign waged throughout the first decades of this century, most recent students of Thackeray veer toward this side of idolatry, while subjecting him to closer analysis. The first of the new-wave (i.e., post–Geoffrey Tillotson) monographs, John Loofbourow's *Thackeray and the Form of Fiction* (1964), is stimulating on Thackeray's growth as a parodist, even if it treats the novels rather abstractly as out-growths of such neoclassic genres as pastoral and mock epic. Loofbourow's approach works best for *Henry Esmond* (to which he devotes four of his nine chapters), probably because it is the most stylized of Thackeray's novels; but to make it the summit of Thackeray's achievement, as he does, is to distort the perspective. A decided drawback of Loofbourow's book is its opaque writing, especially unfortunate in a study that lays so much stress on Thack-eray's "witty poetry" and "the expressive elements" of his language.

The only other substantial purely critical study of Thackeray published during the past decade is Juliet McMaster's *Thackeray: The Major Novels* (1971), overly defensive at times, but sensible and sensitive, if not exactly startling. As its title indicates, her book is pretty much confined to the "big four" (though, unlike most critics, she has some good words in passing for *The Adventures of Philip*). The best chapter is that on the unjustly ne-glected *The Newcomes* (the most "moving" of the novels in the author's opinion); the poorest, to my mind, that on *Henry Esmond*, in which her striving for originality leads to perverseness. The last chapter, entitled "Ambivalent Relationships," is rather heavily Freudian. A word should be said, by the way, for the attractive design of this book, imitative of a Vic-torian album.

Several briefer studies are of varying usefulness as introductions. Ioan M. Williams' *Thackeray* (1968) in the Literature in Perspective series, in-tended as a vade mecum to "the ordinary man who reads for pleasure," is informed on its elementary level, offering succinct biography and straight-forward critical commentary, written without tendentiousness and out of genuine admiration for its subject. (An earlier example worth mention is Laurence Brander's judicious and well-written pamphlet *Thackeray* (1959) in the Writers and Their Work series.) James H. Wheatley's *Patterns in Thackeray's Fiction* (1969) vaults valiantly through the canon (including the *Fraser's* period) in fewer than 150 pages. The result, perhaps inevitably, is tenuousness and vaporous generalization. Wheatley, however, has read Thackeray intelligently, noting among his "patterns" the recurrence of naïfs as concrete universals—a topic worth pursuing. Barbara Hardy's *The Exposure of Luxury: Radical Themes in Thackeray* (1972) is gracefully written, with some penetrating observations on Thackeray's "symbols of class and money." Like most other current critics, however, Hardy is con-cerned more with relating Thackeray to our times than to his own, and, lacking any overall conceptual framework, her book does not extend far beyond intelligent appreciation. Jack P. Rawlins' monograph *Thackeray's Novels: A Fiction That Is True* (1974) is little more than an attenuated essay built on the dubious premise that Thackeray rejected "current literary forms" as inadequate but failed to find a "suitable alternative." This scarcely does justice to Thackeray's eclecticism or to the "accretive" faculty that contemporaries made much of.

In a class by itself is John A. Sutherland's *Thackeray at Work* (1974), based on the closest analysis to date of the extant manuscripts. Because of the scrappiness of these materials, Sutherland's book inevitably falls short of the analogous landmark study of Dickens by John Butt and Kathleen Tillotson. Significantly, his strongest chapters are those on *The Virginians* and *Denis Duval*, where Thackeray's process of revision is most readily traceable. Sutherland's general thesis is that "'our author is a novelist of genius, but one whose genius is of a peculiarly spontaneous and easy-going nature." Along these lines he argues (in his most controversial chapter) that *Henry Esmond*, contrary to received opinion, was largely a work of improvisation. Yet with *The Newcomes* he is at pains to demonstrate (pace Henry James) Thackeray's careful planning. By turns brilliant and provoking, *Thackeray at Work*, whatever its deficiencies of method and contradictions, is a ground-breaking book. (An especially penetrating review is that of Edgar Harden, *NCF*, 1975; see also Ruth apRoberts' review article, *Costerus*, 1974.)

Recent studies, with all their valuable aperçus, have not exactly displaced the old landmarks. We can be thankful, therefore, for the industry of the reprint mills that have made accessible such standbys as Adolphus A. Jack's *Thackeray: A Study* (1895; 1970); Albert S. G. Canning's *Dickens and Thackeray Studied in Three Novels* (1911; 1967); Saintsbury's *A Consideration of Thackeray* (1931; 1968); John Dodds's *Thackeray: A Critical Portrait* (1941; 1963); Lambert Ennis' *Thackeray: The Sentimental Cynic* (1950; 1970); J. Y. T. Greig's *Thackeray: A Reconsideration* (1950; 1967); and Geoffrey Tillotson's *Thackeray the Novelist* (1954; 1974). New libraries have access also to two early summings up by fellow novelists: James Hannay's *Studies on Thackeray* (1868; 1970) and Anthony Trollope's *Thackeray*, in the English Men of Letters series (1879; 1968).

Studies of Individual Works

Early Works

T. O. Beachcroft in *The Modest Art* (1968) glances at Thackeray's abilities in the short story, mainly to suggest this as a desirable subject for further study. Otherwise, critics of Thackeray continue to neglect the "comicalities and whimsicalities" of his magazine apprenticeship, the single exception being Robert L. Bledsoe's "Fitz-Boodle among the Harpies: A Reading of 'Denis Haggarty's Wife' " (*SSF*, 1975), a brief exploration of its "simplistic morality" and point of view. The wicked "Miss Cat," however, has exerted her fascination. Nicholas A. Salerno in "*Catherine*: Theme and Structure" (*AI*, 1961) dwells on its oedipal elements as manifested in the heroine's supposed incest with her son. Robert A. Colby's "*Catherine*: Thackeray's Credo" (*RES*, 1964) relates it to an early *Fraser's* article once attributed to Thackeray, "Hints for a History of Highwaymen," and to popular fiction of the 1830s apart from the Newgate School. John Christopher Kleis's "Dramatic Irony in Thackeray's *Catherine* . . ." (*VN*, 1968) concentrates mainly on the nuances of tone of its persona Ikey Solomons, who gives a further fillip to the irony of the story by being himself a criminal in prison. In "The Two Voices in Thackeray's *Catherine*" (*NCF*, 1974), Frederick C. Cabot compares it with its prototypes among eighteenth-century ironical fictitious memoirs and finds an essential and unresolved conflict here between Thackeray as satirist and moralist.

Recent comment on *Barry Lyndon* is relatively scarce, even in critical monographs. The introductions to the critical editions by Morris and Anisman (see above under Reprints) are informative, but both approach this most tongue-in-cheek of Thackeray's tales rather humorlessly, missing much of its bite and innuendo. Robert A. Colby's "*Barry Lyndon* and the Irish Hero" (*NCF*, 1966) relates this picaro from Dublin to the stage Irishman and various fictional stereotypes of the time, as well as to contemporaneous Irish politics. The most extended treatment is to be found in Eugene Hollahan's dissertation "Thackeray's *Barry Lyndon*: A Study of Genre, Structure, Background, and Meaning" (Univ. of North Carolina 1969), which appends a useful list of the articles in *Fraser's Magazine* that appeared alongside it. The only other piece that has come to notice relating to the pre–*Vanity Fair* period is Katherine Carolan's "Dickensian Echoes in a Thackeray Christmas Book" (*SSF*, 1974), identifying humorous details carried over from Dr. Blimber's school in *Dombey and Son* to the academy in *Dr. Birch and His Young Friends*.

Vanity Fair

A convenient retrospect of modern criticism through 1965 is provided by *Twentieth Century Interpretations of Vanity Fair*, ed. Michael G. Sundell (1969). Assembled here are many of the frequently cited critics, some of whom (G. Armour Craig, Geoffrey Tillotson, Joseph E. Baker) have already been commented on by my predecessor. A number of the selections (e.g., those by Frank W. Chandler, Percy Lubbock, E. M. Forster, Edwin Muir, Walter Allen, E. M. W. Tillyard) are excerpts from standard critical books that deal with Thackeray incidentally, in relation either to theories of the novel or to genre study. An especially well written later essay is A. E. Dyson's "An Irony against Heroes" (rpt. from *CritQ*, 1965), which fixes the moral world of Becky and the Crawleys within the pecking order and status seeking depicted in *The Book of Snobs*. Sundell himself contributes a shrewd introduction.

Although, according to the latest statistical summary, Thackeray ranks fifteenth quantitatively among Victorian authors to whom scholarly writing has been devoted (accounting, for example, for but one sixth of the number of items credited to Dickens; see Robert C. Slack's introduction to the decennial cumulation, *Bibliographies of Studies in Victorian Literature, 1955–64*—1967), *Vanity Fair* by now must be near the top when it comes to individual novels. The plethora precludes anything more than trend spotting here.

The gestation and the stages of composition of Thackeray's first popular success continue to baffle investigation, but ingenious guesswork goes on. In "A Date for the Early Composition of *Vanity Fair*" (*ES*, 1972), John Sutherland pushes it back to early 1845 on the basis of an echo of an 1844 novel by G. P. R. James in "The Night Attack" parody. In a later article, "A *Vanity Fair* Mystery: The Delay in Publication" (*Costerus*, 1974), Sutherland suggests, on the basis of revisions in manuscript and in proof, reasons for the nine-month hiatus between the scheduled date for the appearance of the first number and its actual debut. In "Thackeray at Work: The Significance of Two Deletions from *Vanity Fair*" (*NCF*, 1963), Myron Taube tries to account for a change made by Thackeray in manuscript relating to Miss Horrock's relationship with Sir Pitt, drawing a belated rebuttal from Peter Shillingsburg, "Miss Horrocks Again" (*NCF*, 1973). Attention has been directed to details of the novel's stylized format. In "The Puppet Frame of *Vanity Fair*" (*ELN*, 1968), Myron Taube contends that this device was an afterthought (ignoring, however, the recurrence of the puppetry motif in *Punch*, present from its inception). The origin and explication of the "Before the Curtain" prologue have been taken up by W. Eugene Davis, Joan Stevens (both in *NCF*, 1968), Roger B. Wilkenfeld (*NCF*, 1971), and John Sutherland (*N&Q*, 1972). Edgar Harden's "The Discipline and Significance of Form in *Vanity Fair*" (*PMLA*, 1967) is a painstaking analysis of the parallels and linkages among the monthly parts, which should lay to rest forever the charge that the novel is loosely constructed. The most detailed account of its economic fortunes, gleaned from a study of the publishing records, is Robert L. Patten's "The Fight at the Top of the Tree: *Vanity Fair* versus *Dombey and Son*" (*SEL*, 1970). (For comparison of Thackeray's earnings from *Vanity Fair* with those from later novels published in parts, see Peter Shillingsburg's "Thackeray and the Firm of Bradbury and Evans," *VSAN*, 1973).

The bulk of writing on *Vanity Fair* has been concerned with various modes of interpretation. D. J. Dooley in "Thackeray's Use of Vanity Fair" (*SEL*, 1971), taking issue with Joseph Baker (*NCF*, 1958), aligns Thackeray's meaning of the phrase with Dr. Johnson rather than with Bunyan. Edgar Harden in "The Fields of Mars in *Vanity Fair*" (*TSL*, 1965) and in "The Function of Mock-Heroic Satire in *Vanity Fair*" (*Anglia*, 1966) demonstrates how its imagery unites war, children's games, the maneuverings of the marriage market, and the world of getting and spending. Articles explicating Thackeray's authorial role tend to overlap one another, with some differences in emphasis or detail: Ann Y. Wilkinson's "The Tomeavsian Way of Knowing the World . . ." (*ELH*, 1965); Michael J. Tolley's "The Teller and the Tale" (in *Approaches to the Novel*, ed. John Colmer, 1967); Harriet Blodgett's "Necessary Presence: The Rhetoric of the Narrator . . ." (*NCF*, 1967); Roger M. Swanson's "*Vanity Fair*: The Double Standard" (in *The English Novel in the Nineteenth Century*, ed. George Goodin, 1972). Wolfgang Iser's chapter on *Vanity Fair* in his *The Implied Reader* (1974) stresses Thackeray's function as mediator, his ability to activate his audience's critical responses, so that the reader becomes in effect a collaborator. Other articles center on the principal characters. Myron Taube's "The George-Amelia-Dobbin Triangle in the Structure of *Vanity Fair*" (*VN*, 1966) brings out the careful planning that went into the development of this relationship. Neal B. Hurston's undermining of Thackeray's sentimental heroine in "A Brief Inquiry into the Morality of Amelia . . ." (*VN*, 1966) can be balanced against Katherine M. Rogers' "A Defense of Amelia" (*TSLL*, 1970). Andrew Von Hendy in "Misunderstanding about Becky's Characterization . . ." (*NCF*, 1963) defends not Becky's morality but the "moral realism" of Thackeray's characterization of her; Leslie M. Thompson, however, puts in a word for this tarnished lady herself in "Becky Sharp and the Virtues of Sin" (*VN*, 1967).

A number of critics have addressed themselves to the apparent hopelessness of Thackeray's view of the world in *Vanity Fair*. In a chapter of his *Laughter & Despair* (1971) U. C. Knoepflmacher surprisingly contends that Thackeray, unlike his fellow novelists, "refuses to impose a moral order on the erratic universe he portrays." Bernard J. Paris' chapter on *Vanity Fair* in his *A Psychological Approach to Fiction* (1974) examines its characters' various adjustments to life in the light of Karen Horney's theories of neurosis—without much illumination. A kind of rhapsode on despair is Robert Lougy's eloquent "Vision and Satire: The Warped Looking Glass in *Vanity Fair*" (*PMLA*, 1975), extending Thackeray's indictment beyond his own society to take in "the diseased structure of civilization itself." Anne-Marie Dibon in her "Form and Value in the French and English 19th-Century Novel" (*MLN*, 1972) selects as her test cases *Vanity Fair* and *Le Rouge et le noir*, both "novels of ambition" exposing the corrupt values of their respective societies. In this long and challenging essay, she draws on, and takes issue with, the socioliterary theories of René Girard, Georg Lukács, and Lucien Goldmann.

"We can probably stand for a moratorium on discussion of the narrative brilliance of *Vanity Fair*," proposes Michael Sundell in a review article "Thackeray Criticism: Its Fortunes and Misfortunes" (*SNNTS*, 1972). Without going to this extreme, one may put in a plea for more attention to the literary and cultural background of this richly topical fictional panorama. Some steps in this direction are Myron Taube's "The Parson-Snob Controversy" (*VN*, 1968), which brings to bear the infighting among the *Punch* circle; John K. Mathison's "The German Sections of *Vanity Fair*" (*NCF*, 1965), showing how these episodes set off the limitations of the

English bourgeois mind; Kenneth L. Moler's "Evelina in Vanity Fair: Becky Sharp and Her Patrician Heroes" (*NCF*, 1972), a fresh look at Jos Sedley, Sir Pitt Crawley, and Lord Steyne as deteriorations of the Richardson-Burney model "Christian gentleman"; and Robin Sheets's "Art and Artistry in *Vanity Fair*" (*ELH*, 1975), contrasting three different attitudes toward art as exemplified by Becky, Dobbin, and the narrator.

Pendennis

This most personal of Thackeray's large novels has long interested aficionados for its autobiographical elements and psychologically minded readers for its manifestations of Victorian "momism," but it is now gaining increasing recognition as a novel of ideas. Martin Fido's "The History of *Pendennis*: A Reconsideration" (*EIC*, 1964), while supercilious in tone and modernist in predilection, acknowledges Thackeray's remarkable ability to represent phenomena from a variety of angles and diversity of points of view. The chapter in Robert A. Colby's *Fiction with a Purpose* (1967) entitled "Arthur Pendennis and the Reformed Coxcomb" concentrates on its literary context—the fashionable novels and bildungsromane in vogue at the time, which it parodies, imitates, and improves upon. In some respects J. I. M. Stewart's introduction to the Penguin English Library reprint (1972) is complementary, making a pointed contrast between *Pendennis* as an author's bildungsroman and a twentieth-century counterpart, Joyce's *Portrait of the Artist as a Young Man*. The pervasive metaphor of the stage and role playing is explored by Edgar Harden in "Theatricality in *Pendennis*" (*Ariel*, 1973), distinguishing the false theatricality displayed by a number of the characters from the more constructive function of the histrionic art "to dramatize genuine feelings of sympathy and love." Harden's "The Serial Structure of Thackeray's *Pendennis*" (*RUO*, 1975) analyzes the connections and cross references binding together the monthly parts, showing that the first half of the novel is more tightly knit than the second.

Henry Esmond

Traditionally praised as his most carefully wrought book, its hero generally regarded as his noblest hero, and its denouement as a celebration of true marital bliss, Thackeray's most widely read historical novel has been subjected latterly to critical scrutiny that challenges all these assumptions. John Sutherland, in the chapter devoted to *Esmond* in his aforementioned *Thackeray at Work* (significantly entitled "The Virtues of Carelessness"), along with his article on Chapter xi, "Thackeray's Patchwork . . ." (*YES*, 1971), pokes holes in its chronology, exposes inconsistencies, and finds various evidences of changes in direction. These discrepancies fortunately do not impede the narrative flow for those innocent of them or, as Sutherland admits, diminish the author's accomplishment. Other attempts at "new" interpretations are more ingenious than convincing. Juliet McMaster is hard put in the chapter on *Esmond* in her *Thackeray: The Major Novels* to establish that the hero's account of himself is unreliable and self-serving; John Hagan in " 'Bankruptcy of His Heart': The Unfulfilled Life of Henry Esmond" (*NCF*, 1972) holds, in the face of Henry's own explicit testimony, that he is really disillusioned with Rachel, as Dobbin is with Amelia.

Distinctly not iconoclastic is Robert Bledsoe's "*Sibi Constet*: The Goddess of Castlewood and the Goddess of Walcote" (*SNNTS*, 1973), which traces the fulfillment of Esmond's "complex search for self-consistency," rewarded by Rachel, who evolves into his "complete kinswoman." Along similar lines is Edgar Harden's "Esmond and the Search for Self" (*YES*, 1973), a quest culminating in the discovery of "the impotence of human desire as it is revealed by the development of personal, familial, and national history." In his *The Form of Victorian Fiction* (1968), J. Hillis Miller sees in *Esmond* a "primordial Oedipal situation reforming itself over and over with different dynamic structures," taking rather solemnly what Thackeray (through Henry) makes a joke of in the mock *Spectator* paper that Miller cites. Two rarefied essays in philosophical interpretation are Stephen Bann's "L'Anti-Histoire de Henri Esmond" (*Poétique*, 1973) applying Roland Barthes's theories of plenum and vacuum to its view of the past; and Elaine Scarry's "*Henry Esmond*: The Rookery at Castlewood" (UWLM, No. 7, 1975), which sees the hero as solipsistic and the author as a manipulator of the narrative "to demonstrate that personal truths are as elusive and illusory as the objective truths Esmond rejects."

Back on terra firma are a few studies of historicoliterary background. The treatment of *Esmond* in Avrom Fleishman's *The English Historical Novel* (1971) is smoothly written, but superficial. No historian is cited besides the well-worn Macaulay, and Thackeray is placed in the stream of European historical fiction (such as *The Charterhouse of Parma* and *War and Peace*) rather than among the contemporaneous English novelists we know he read. Far better informed on Thackeray's immediate forebears is James C. Simmons' *The Novelist as Historian* (1975), which compares Thackeray with his predecessors Scott and Bulwer, along with numerous lesser-known figures, relating them to developments in nineteenth-century historiography. A short piece by Simmons, "Thackeray's *Esmond* and Anne Manning's 'Spurious Antiques' " (*VN*, 1972), calls our attention to the vogue of the time for quaint feigned memoirs of the kind imitated by Thackeray. In "Thackeray's Notebook for *Henry Esmond*" (*Costerus*, 1974), John Sutherland deciphers some of the cryptic jottings in this neglected source owned by the Manuscript Division of the New York Public Library, an indication that work remains to be done in tracking down Thackeray's historical research—even after the investigations of the Snows and R. S. Forsythe.

The Newcomes

Thackeray's *Familienroman* has been accorded increasing respect in critical monographs, notably by Juliet McMaster. Jean Sudrann's outstanding and beautifully written " 'The Philosopher's Property': Thackeray and the Use of Time" (*VS*, 1967) sees the novels as a series of "collocations of past and present, reminders of time–the preserver and time–the destroyer," culminating with *The Newcomes*, which moves from "the destiny of a single man" (as with *Pendennis*) "to encompass the fate of society itself." The mythic analogy of R. D. McMaster's "The Pygmalion Motif in *The Newcomes*" (*NCF*, 1974) seems strained, but this is a suggestive essay nevertheless, centering on the artistic sensibility represented by Clive and other figures in the novel and the pervasive tragedy of self-delusion. A more textual-bibliographical approach is Edgar Harden's "The Challenges of Serialization: Parts 4, 5, and 6 of *The Newcomes*" (*NCF*, 1974), which accounts for some of the additions and deletions that Thackeray made in manuscript to resolve problems he encountered in serial publication. The manuscript, more nearly intact than that of *Vanity Fair*, offers further opportunities for the textual editor and students of Thackeray's workmanship. We need also to see *The Newcomes* more as a representative novel of the 1850s. Meanwhile, critical revaluation of this domestic tragedy seems on the way to restoring it to the esteem it enjoyed in Thackeray's lifetime.

Later Novels

Among the widely ignored and often maligned works of Thackeray's silver age, *The Virginians* has attracted most attention during the period under review, with a number of students regarding it as a worthy novel in its own right rather than as an inferior sequel to *Esmond*. In the introduction to his dissertation (see above under Editions), Gerald Sorensen makes a strong case for the vitality of its characterization and its validity as social history. He sees George and Harry Warrington as complementary sides of Thackeray's own temperament, as well as representative figures in the Anglo-American clash of cultures, the underlying theme of the novel. William Grant's semipopular "A Thackeray Novel about the Old Dominion" (*VC*, 1972) praises its historicity while calling attention to a few gaffes (such as placing the maple season in the fall). Dennis Douglas utilizes *Carpezan*, the historical drama composed by George Warrington, as a springboard for a learned if unfocused discussion of "Thackeray and the Uses of History" (*YES*, 1975), which expands on Thackeray's antiromanticism. Edgar Harden applies his methods of textual criticism in "The Growth of *The Virginians* as a Serial Novel: Parts 1-9" (*Costerus*, 1974), an extensive though tentative exploration of its development from manuscript to printed monthly parts, based on evidence from the torso remains in the Morgan Library. (This and analogous articles by Harden mentioned earlier are to be incorporated into his book on the effects of serialization on Thackeray's workmanship.) Harden's study of the manuscript revisions of *The Virginians* stresses the improvements Thackeray made in his narrative, while John Sutherland in his corresponding chapter in *Thackeray at Work* dwell more on what went wrong with Thackeray's original conception, though h also points out how the presumed transatlantic audience for the novel may have guided the author's hand.

The Adventures of Philip is referred to by McMaster and Hardy in their monographs and discussed in connection with Thackeray's realism by Jack Rawlins in *A Fiction That Is True*. Commentary on Thackeray's last completed novel is otherwise confined to Sutherland's brief examination of the portion of the manuscript in the Beinecke Library (*YULG*, 1974). *Denis Duval* has been passed over except for Sutherland's study of its composition in *Thackeray at Work*. Critics have yet to appreciate the importance of this vigorous, though aborted, adventure story, deliberately written against the grain, in completing the curve of Thackeray's development. Nobody has put forward *Lovel the Widower* as a neglected masterpiece, but who knows what time's whirligigs will bring in? There are signs that the later novels are emerging from neglect—for example, Ina Ferris' "Fictions by Pendennis: Narrative and Self in Thackeray's Later Novels" (Diss. Univ. of California, Los Angeles, 1975), an examination of *Lovel the Widower* and *The Adventures of Philip* as innovative "inward-turning works," and James R. Gross's "Technique in Thackeray's Later Novels" (Diss. Duke 1968).

Background, Influences, Ideas

It has long been recognized that Gordon Ray's edition of Thackeray's *Letters and Papers* is incomplete. A few additional letters have been published subsequently in *Notes and Queries* and other journals (see the annual Victorian Bibliography in *VS*) filling in some lacunae in Thackeray's life and the publishing history of his books. Enough unpublished letters have accumulated in libraries (see Manuscripts and Special Collections above) to make highly desirable a supplementary volume to Ray's set.

With Thackeray biography, time seems to have borne out Lionel Stevenson's judgment that Gordon Ray's monumental work "undoubtedly . . . will remain the basic source of information, for further revelations are unlikely to occur." The only recent biography, Audrey Curling's *The Young Thackeray* (1966), a slim monograph derived mainly from Ray, stresses Thackeray's precocity, as is appropriate for its presumed teen-age audience. Scholarly concentration has been on various phases of Thackeray's literary life and mental history.

Some new light has been cast on his relations with fellow writers. In "Thackeray vs. Disraeli" (*QR*, 1964) David E. Painting defends the basic authenticity of Disraeli's caricature, St. Barbe in *Endymion*, and attributes the rancor mainly to Disraeli's reaction against Thackeray's anti-Semitism. In "Michael Angelo Titmarsh and the Knebworth Apollo" (*Costerus*, 1974), Anthea Trodd analyzes Thackeray's various attacks on Bulwer over a ten-year period, relating them to specific literary issues. In another contribution to this volume, "History *versus* Fiction: Thackeray's Response to Macaulay," Jane Millgate recapitulates a reciprocal influence beginning with Thackeray's reviews of the historian's essays in the early 1840s, extending to Macaulay's death while Thackeray was editor of *Cornhill*. In "The Carlyles and Thackeray" (*Nineteenth-Century Literary Perspectives*, ed. Clyde de L. Ryals, 1974), Charles Sanders, drawing on the Carlyle letters being edited at Duke University, traces a friendship that moved on an "uneasy, uncertain, irregular course" over the entire span of Thackeray's literary career. In *Yesterday's Woman: Domestic Realism in the English Novel* (1974), Vineta Colby touches on the influence of Mrs. Gore. Two recent articles bear on the *Punch* period: Richard Kelly's "The Birth of a Snob: Douglas Jerrold, William Makepeace Thackeray, and the 'Jenkins Papers' " (*SatireN*, 1970); and Janice Nadelhaft's "*Punch* and the Syncretics . . ." (*SEL*, 1975), on the literary background of Thackeray's first contribution to this comic weekly.

Several critics have attempted to probe Thackeray's sensibility. Myron Taube in "Thackeray and the Reminiscential Vision" (*NCF*, 1963) considers the traumatic experiences of 1840–41, particularly Isabella's insanity, significant in his shift from satirist to moralist. John Sutherland argues (not very persuasively) in "The Inhibiting Secretary in Thackeray's Fiction" (*MLQ*, 1971) that his practice of dictating his later novels to his daughters made for reticence in sexual matters. Sylvère Monod in " 'Brother Wearers of Motley' " (*E&S*, 1973) assesses Thackeray's relationship with his readers as sometimes, in *Pendennis*, for example, "shifting and fragmentary," at other times "more stable, less impish," notably in *Esmond*, which, Monod believes, appeals more to modern readers for that reason. Winslow Rogers contends in "Thackeray's Self-Consciousness" (*The Worlds of Victorian Fiction*, ed. Jerome H. Buckley, 1975) that because of Thackeray's deliberate repudiation of fictional devices, and owing to contradictory attitudes growing out of an essentially pluralistic philosophy, "no event in a Thackeray novel can have a stable meaning; no character can be finally known."

In "Thackeray and the Plight of the Victorian Satirist" (*ES*, 1968), Chauncey C. Loomis, Jr., represents the author as struggling against a built-in antipathy to satire among contemporaneous readers and critics. Another view of the light side of Thackeray's genius—his spontaneous gift for mimicry—is delightfully set out by Robert Kiely in "Victorian Harlequin: The Function of Humor in Thackeray's Critical and Miscellaneous Prose" (*Veins of Humor*, ed. Harry Levin, 1972). In "Music in the Victorian Novel" (*KR*, 1963), D. J. Smith glances at Thackeray's representations of musicians as indicative of attitudes of the period toward performing artists, particularly in *The Book of Snobs* and *The Newcomes*. Richard Faber in *Proper Stations* (1971) makes much of Thackeray "as a social classifier as [well as] a moral one." More serious themes in the novels are dealt with in John Sutherland's "Thackeray as Victorian Racialist" (*EIC*, 1970), asserting that his "views hardened" with the years; and in Laurence Lerner's "Thackeray and Marriage" (*EIC*, 1975), which explores the continuous "tension between two ideals"—romantic marriage and the *marriage de convenance*—concluding that the author finds virtues and faults in both.

Commentary on Thackeray's literary ideas is relatively scarce. In "Thackeray's Attitude towards Dickens's Writing" (*NCF*, 1966) Charles Mauskopf indicates that privately Thackeray was more critical of his rival, particularly of Dickens' lack of realism, than he was in public pronouncements. In a later article, "Thackeray's Concept of the Novel: A Study of Conflict" (*PQ*, 1971), Mauskopf, concluding that Thackeray attempted the impossible by trying to reconcile realism with moral teaching, poses what is really a false dilemma. A well-documented sketch of the culmination of Thackeray's career as man of letters, including reactions to and by late associates, is offered in Spencer L. Eddy's *The Founding of the Cornhill Magazine* (BallSM, No. 19, 1970).

Thackeray Abroad

Translations

A constant traveler and a cultural cosmopolite during his lifetime, Thackeray has been a continuous presence on what he once dubbed "the incontinent." It is impossible to detail here the translation history of his novels in Europe, except to note such surprises as *The Ravenswing* in France (1871), *Catherine* (1870) and *The Great Hoggarty Diamond* (1850) in Sweden, *Rebecca and Rowena* in Russia (1849), and the publication of the collected works in Dutch as early as 1868. As with other popular Victorian novelists, the Leipzig firm of Baron Tauchnitz made Thackeray's works available in English to European readers in their Continental editions.

Leaping forward to the 1960s, we discover that *Vanity Fair* remains the favorite with foreign readers, as with English and American. Some thirty translations are registered for this decade, ranging over Western Europe, Scandinavia, the Slavic countries, Brazil, and China (*Fu Hua Shih Chiai* is its title in Taipei).* *The Book of Snobs* is a not very close second, with ten translations on record: Denmark, France, Hungary, Italy, Romania, Yugoslavia, and two each from Belgium and Germany. On the basis of the raw data there is no accounting for tastes. Why there should be only three new translations of *Henry Esmond* recorded for the 1960s (two in Germany, one in Romania) as against six of *The Great Hoggarty Diamond* (two in Sweden, apparently its most steady customer, and one each in France, Hungary, Portugal, and the USSR) is anybody's guess. *Pendennis* seems to have been translated recently only in Hungary, France, and Italy (where it is known as *Addio, Pendennis!*). *The Virginians* has been offered to the reading public of Budapest—successfully, to judge by its reaching a second edition. *The Rose and the Ring* is available to "Children Great and Small" in France, Italy, Romania, and the Soviet Union. It is easy to understand

---

* My figures are gleaned from the annual *Index Translationum*, which had not extended beyond 1973 at present writing.

why *The Kickleburys on the Rhine* found a translator in Germany, but why two versions of *The Yellowplush Papers* there? And what has attracted the Dutch to *A Little Dinner at Timmins*? We could use a comparatist to account for some of these apparent fortuities.

Scholarship

France, practically a second homeland for Thackeray throughout his literary life, has kept his memory alive, though unfortunately the landmark analytical study *W. M. Thackeray: L'Homme, le penseur, le romancier* (1932) by Raymond Las Vergnas, the doyen of French Thackerayans, languishes untranslated and out of print. During the postwar period Las Vergnas translated *Henry Esmond* and *The Book of Snobs* and contributed a preface to a translation of *Pendennis*. A student of Las Vergnas, Raymond Maître of the Université de Rennes, has completed a dissertation, "Thackeray et la France," out of which comes his article, "Nouvelles sources françaises de Thackeray" (*EA*, 1964). Here Maître reveals further indebtedness to Charles de Bernard and brings to light the research Thackeray did in the *Archives de la Police de Paris* for *The Paris Sketch Book*. From the Université de Toulouse comes Jean Lozes' "Le Snob et le gentleman" (*Caliban*, 1971), an attempt to define Thackeray's ethical ideal. Otherwise, French students of Thackeray seem attracted mainly to modern structuralist-phenomenological approaches. Max Véga-Ritter of the Centre d'Etudes et de Recherches Victoriennes et Edouardiennes (Montpellier) has completed a dissertation on "Le Crise de l'initiation . . ." in Dickens and Thackeray. "In more ways than one Thackeray poses the problem of man's relationship to woman in a society hungry for money, status, and power," according to his formulation. Maurice Chrétien of the Université de Lyon II is at work on a dissertation, begun under the late Henri Talon, entitled "Individu et societé dans l'œuvre de W. M. Thackeray." A portion, "La Relation mère-fils dans *Pendennis*," has appeard in *Confluents* (1975).

"Thackeray semble décidément revenir à la mode," affirmed a French reviewer, Pierre Arnaud in *Mercure de France* (1964), commenting on translations of *The Great Hoggarty Diamond*, *The Book of Snobs*, and *The Rose and the Ring*. During the zesty sixties this may have seemed true, but present indications are that this upsurge has lost momentum. Professors report widespread ignorance of Thackeray on the part of students, a paucity of new scholarly activity, and a lack of enterprise among publishers who may have been scared off, as suggested by one professor, by the flop of the most recent *Pendennis*. "I feel like a thin voice crying from a Thackerayan desert," writes one of France's eminent Victorian scholars, Sylvère Monod; "It is a great pity, for our students seem to show a great deal of interest when Thackeray is placed on their syllabus."

From Eastern Europe the Thackerayan best known, and most accessible, to the English-speaking world is the Czech scholar Lidmila Pantůčková. Several monograph-sized articles contributed by her to *Brno Studies in En-*

glish (Universita J. E. Purkyné) represent the most thorough investigation to date of Thackeray as a reviewer of, or commentator on, other writers: the first, on his contributions to *The Morning Chronicle* (1960), was followed by "The Aesthetic Views of W. M. Thackeray" (1966), which tries to define his credo of realism; "Thackeray as a Reader and Critic of French Literature" (1970); and a double number entitled "W. M. Thackeray as a Critic of Literature" (1972), which brings together his views on English writers, both eighteenth-century and contemporary, and concludes with sections on poetry, theater, and nonfiction. Her most interesting, though controversial, arguments are on Thackeray's reactions to French writers, enhanced by her background in European scholarship and her comparatist point of view. If Pantůčková has not produced the synthesis of Thackeray's literary ideas that we could wish for, her exhaustive culling of his opinions amounts virtually to an index of his reading. An undercurrent of Marxist ideology is detectable in some of her pronouncements, along with those of the Russian critics she cites, who apparently conceive of Thackeray as a bourgeois radical, a Chartist in all but name. A further peep behind the Iron Curtain is offered by B. Alexandrov's "Thackeray in Russia" (*SovL*, 1963). He indicates considerable enthusiasm there, along with the startling news that the first full Soviet collection of Thackeray's works was then under way. We are still waiting.

There are glimmerings of interest in Thackeray from the other side of the world. An Arabic scholar, Rida Hawari of the University of Riyad (Saudi Arabia), has contributed an erudite inventory of "Thackeray's Oriental Reading" (based on an Oxford thesis) to a French journal (*RLC*, 1974). Hawari considers this extensive reading, as well as Thackeray's visit to the Orient itself, to have had "a profound effect on the man and his work." A scholar from India, Jaswant Singh, editor of the journal *Literary Studies* (Ambala City, Haryana), plans to honor Thackeray in the country of the author's birth by devoting a special issue to him. All in all, sufficient material seems to have accumulated to make feasible a study of Thackeray's foreign image.

Thackeray as Illustrator

"The duet between the eye and the mind, between the work and the figure," so active throughout much of Thackeray's writing, as noted by one of his friends and admirers, Dr. John Brown,[*] has engaged the attention of a number of Thackeray scholars lately. Despite evidence that Thackeray was concerned with the integrity of picture and text, this feature of his work has not been fully realized in most publications of his books, either in our time or, as pointed out by Joan Stevens (*REL*, 1965), in the Victorian period. Fortunately, critics have been emerging who bring historical background or

---

[*] *North British Review*, Feb. 1864, p. 255; quoted in Joan Stevens, "Thackeray's 'Vanity Fair'" (*REL*, 1965, pp. 19–20).

technical competence to the too long postponed study of Thackeray's illustration.

In the chapter of his *Victorian Novelists and Their Illustrators* (1971) devoted to Thackeray, J. R. Harvey places him in a satiric tradition beginning with Hogarth and continued by Gillray and Cruikshank. Much rightly is made here of the influence of Hogarth's moral parables, and subsequently of the *Punch* style of decorated initials, but nothing of the emergent genre art of the 1830s and 1840s to which Thackeray was exposed both as art student and art critic. Harvey generally scants the cuts and plates in favor of the initials, considering Thackeray at his best as caricaturist. He assumes, furthermore, that Thackeray did nothing of consequence as an illustrator before *Vanity Fair*, and the chapter tapers off with *The Virginians*, so that Harvey's treatment is rather truncated.

Joan Stevens, working from a wider historical base than Harvey, has studied Thackeray's iconography closely. In an illustrated article, "A Roundabout Ride" (*VS*, 1969), she reconstructs an equestrian tour Thackeray took to gather material for his *Punch* series "Travels in London," which he also utilized shortly afterward to give authenticity and specificity to various locales in *Vanity Fair*. In "*Vanity Fair* and the London Skyline" (*Costerus*, 1974) she adopts the point of view of those who read the novel in monthly parts, pointing out recurrences in the initials of figures first depicted on the yellow wrapper (such as clowns and children playing war). By means of illustrations she demonstrates in particular the immediate topicality of the locale and the monuments represented on the cover, as well as their historical connection with the period of the novel. Her "Thackeray's Pictorial Capitals" (*Costerus*, 1974; rev. from *AUMLA*, 1969) considers vignettes drawn not only for *Vanity Fair* but also for *Pendennis*, *The Virginians*, *Lovel the Widower*, and *The Adventures of Philip*. This substantial article suggests the range of purposes these serve—literal, symbolic, evocative.

A different approach to Thackeray's artistry is offered by Anthony Burton in another essay in *Costerus*, "Thackeray's Collaborations with Cruikshank, Doyle, and Walker." Drawing on the collections of the library in the Victoria and Albert Museum, of which he is a staff member, Burton distinguishes the work of the three artists who worked with Thackeray at, respectively, the early, middle, and late stages of his career, pointing up also differences in their various relationships with him. Burton brings welcome technical background to this stimulating account but goes too far in downgrading Thackeray, not only as artist, but as critic.

Still another essay in *Costerus*, Patricia Sweeney's "Thackeray's Best Illustrator," surveys the various attempts artists have made to supply fresh candles to illuminate Thackeray's verbal pictures—from Gerald du Maurier (who designed curious white-on-black drawings for the originally unillustrated *Henry Esmond*) to the limited editions of the 1950s. Finding that others have invariably distorted Thackeray's intentions, or that something is lost by their "improvements," she concludes that the best choice of illustrator for a modern edition is Thackeray himself.

The graphic aspect of Thackeray's imagination is clearly one open to further investigation. So far we have only the vaguest notion of how he was influenced by changes in techniques of illustration during the Victorian period, the differences between his original designs and their execution by others, the shifts in modes of illustration from his early novels to his later ones. A formidable bibliographical problem that remains is the authentication of numerous separate drawings attributed to Thackeray now stored in library collections. Enlightenment along these lines is promised by the doctoral dissertation near completion by Nicholas Pickwoad at Oxford University entitled "Thackeray and His Illustrators." An appendix to this thesis is to include a complete list of drawings that Thackeray did for publication, with a discussion of some of the forgeries of his work.

Thackeray on Stage and Screen

In view of his own lifelong relish for the theater, Thackeray would probably have been disappointed in the sparsity of dramatizations of his novels. *Vanity Fair* has been the most frequently staged. The best version is Langdon Mitchell's *Becky Sharp* (1899), commissioned as a vehicle for Mrs. Fiske, who appeared in the title role time and again, playing it in repertory as late as 1931. A rival English version by Robert Hichens and Cosmo Gordon-Lennox (1901) with Marie Tempest as the star did not prove as durable. Mitchell's other Thackeray adaptation, *Major Pendennis* (1916), in which John Drew scored a personal success, is less famous. *Colonel Newcome* by Michael Morton (1906) held the stage off and on until about 1920. In the 1940s two new versions of *Vanity Fair* had brief stage lives, one by Jevan Brandon-Thomas, produced in Edinburgh (1944), the other by Constance Cox, produced in London (1946). (The history of these and other productions can be reconstructed through the excellent resources of the Theatre Collection, New York Public Library at Lincoln Center.)

On record are British film versions of *Pendennis* (1916) and *The Newcomes* (1920, retitled *Colonel Newcome, the Perfect Gentleman*). *Vanity Fair* was first filmed at full length in America in 1915 by the Thomas Edison Company. Again Mrs. Fiske was the star, but this time in what was billed as "an entirely new scenario" by Sumner Williams, which drew on the original source more fully than had the Langdon Mitchell play. Two more silent film versions followed, one in England (1922) and the other in America (1923). Better remembered is the sound film version *Becky Sharp* (1935); using the Langdon Mitchell play as its main source, it fixed Miriam Hopkins as Becky in the minds of moviegoers of that generation and made history as the first full-length photoplay in Technicolor. It can still be seen occasionally in film revival houses or on television. In 1956 plans were set afoot by David Selznick to produce another version, based on a script by the playwright-teacher Louis Coxe, to star Jennifer Jones—a project that fell through for reasons unknown. The scenario, however, is preserved in typescript in the Houghton Library, together with Selznick's shrewd, literate commentary on it to Coxe's agent. Selznick expresses a deep respect for Thackeray and Dickens, regarding them as better cinematic material than modern novelists like Hemingway and Fitzgerald. Among his pieces of advice to the adapter of *Vanity Fair* (which he likened to *Gone with the Wind*) was not to "soften or sweeten Becky Sharp," advice that should have been taken by the producers of the 1967 BBC Masterpiece Theatre version on television (shown in America in 1972) unfortunately dominated by the sentimental interpretation of Susan Hampshire. It was in fact a complete botch—miscast throughout, cut to the point of incoherence, listlessly directed, tackily produced. Umbrage must be taken for other reasons at the last of the Thackeray film adaptations to be considered—Stanley Kubrick's spectacular eleven-million-dollar *Barry Lyndon* (1975). Hailed for its beauty and painterly quality, it nevertheless moves like a dirge, completely out of the spirit of Thackeray's rollicking satire. Thackeray, in short, has not fared well in the media.

The combined labors of scholars bringing a variety of approaches—bibliographical, textual, contextual, critical, iconographical—to Thackeray's immense canon are opening up new areas of his versatile imagination. We have become increasingly sensitive, as a result, to those complexities pointed out by Lionel Stevenson at the end of his essay in the earlier *Guide*, the "multiple levels of irony . . . elusive changes of tone, with all their implications about the relativity of truth." Somehow, however, the whole man has eluded our grasp in the midst of our searches, like Proteus, to whom he was likened in his lifetime. Although as far back as the 1860s David Masson spoke of "a more constant element of doctrine" in Thackeray's writings, a "more distinct vein of personal philosophy than could be found in the work of most other novelists," we continue to view Thackeray piecemeal and in an artificially foreshortened way. One way to set him in proper perspective is to direct our attention more to *all* his work, early and late, as Stevenson advised, to the "chronicles of small beer" as well as to the epical novels that grew out of them. We need also to see Thackeray as the polymath his contemporaries recognized rather than exclusively as the "wit with no head above my eyes" that he disingenuously called himself. There will probably be no need to rewrite his biography in our century, but the life of his mind still is relatively unexplored—despite the many records extant of his reading. A further avenue of research is suggested by the fact that, next to Trollope and Dickens, Thackeray is the author among all those represented in this volume most frequently cited in Myron Brightfield's four-volume compendium *Victorian England in Its Novels*. Here is further testimony that Thackeray has to be seen in relation to his original cultural environment if his novels are fully to come to life for us. Perhaps in our age of specialization it is no longer possible to restore what Geoffrey Tillotson has called "the Thackerayan oneness." But surely it is worth the try.

ANTHONY TROLLOPE

Ruth apRoberts

The challenge of Trollope studies is still, as Donald Smalley put it in the Stevenson *Guide,* a challenge to define the very qualities of the man, both as writer and as personality; but it is much more widely appreciated now than in 1962. A good deal of published work since 1962 is rather different in kind from the earlier: there is less of the general overview and more dealing with specific novels; there is still much on Barsetshire and much more on the non-Barsetshire; there is less of the amateur cultist and more of the professional critic. A cursory quantitative survey of dissertations is an index of increasing academic interest: about twenty before 1962, about fifty-five since. Some of this academic work is plodding stuff, where the field is worked because it is neglected rather than because it is understood; but there has been considerable enlightened scholarship, and time will sift it out.

Bibliography

Three welcome reprints have appeared: Michael Sadleir's classic and exemplary *Trollope: A Bibliography* (1928; rpt. 1964), Mary Leslie Irwin's *Anthony Trollope: A Bibliography* (1926; rpt. 1968), and, for secondary material, Rafael Helling's *A Century of Trollope Criticism* (1956; rpt. 1967). Otherwise, the usual bibliographical resources may be supplemented by Phillip Holcomb's unpublished doctoral dissertation, "A Study of the Critical Responses to Anthony Trollope's Novels with an Annotated Bibliography of Criticism, 1920–1968" (1971), which has 521 items. David Skilton's *Anthony Trollope and His Contemporaries* (1972) includes the largest bibliography to date of criticism and reviews of Trollope's own time. Before his premature death in 1968, Bradford A. Booth was working on the Trollope chapter for *The English Novel: Select Bibliographical Guides,* ed. A. E. Dyson (1974). Dyson made a few additions to update the chapter, and we are glad to have this late overview from Booth, who did so much for

Trollope studies. It is good to have his incidental critical remarks, his thoughtful assessments of scholarship, and an interesting list of "Background Reading." More recently, we have a useful survey in Hugh H. Hennedy's "Trollope Studies 1963–1973" (*BStM*, 1975). It includes evaluations of most of the prefaces, forewords, and afterwords to editions of the novels, and—as a bonus—evaluations of many of the dissertations. Hennedy sums up: "The fact is that even though not everyone has heard the news, the days of apology are over." Amen.

Donald Smalley makes a distinguished addition to the Critical Heritage series with his *Anthony Trollope* (1969). His task was formidable: forty-seven novels eliciting copious reviews from a myriad of journals. He organizes and condenses well-chosen excerpts from all this material under the headings of each novel, frequently setting off the critical response against Trollope's own self-critique in the *Autobiography*. Smalley's introduction is a valuable survey benefiting from his reading of this vast array of materials. "Trollope," he says, "had followed the advice of Horace only too well. He had hidden his art." This surely is the central irony of Trollope criticism; he is so good that he makes it seem easy—hence the condescension.

Students as well as general readers will find the book invaluable, and will be reminded that contemporary insights have often been anticipated in the older criticism. Smalley even has a useful index for special interests: for Women's Studies: "feminine heart, skill in portraying"; for the antihero: "heroes and heroines, unheroic"; for value judgments: "genius, possession of a kind of," and so on. He includes a broad sampling of anonymous reviewers, often recording his informed hunches about authorship. He records the famous and important comments by such as Hawthorne, Fitzgerald, and Browning, as well as a generous selection from R. H. Hutton, whom Trollope considered his most "observant" critic. He covers both early Henry James and late, tracing the interesting movement from condescension to frank and discriminating admiration. In his later analysis, James finds Trollope one of the most "trustworthy" of the writers "who have helped the heart of man to know itself."

David Skilton's *Anthony Trollope and His Contemporaries* (1972) constitutes a supplement to Smalley: where Smalley is selective, Skilton is copious. And Skilton surveys, besides criticism and reviews, contemporary theory and economics of fiction, with a special section devoted to R. H. Hutton on Trollope. This book will be a useful prolegomenon to all Trollope studies.

The Canon, Letters, Manuscripts

Probably the greatest Trollope news of the decade is the first publication of his book-length *New Zealander* (1972), that peculiar venture into the Carlylean mode that gave Longmans' reader such a turn when submitted after the publication of *The Warden*. Ably edited and introduced by N. John Hall, it casts invaluable new light on Trollope himself, for here Trollope surveys the whole "Condition of England," under various heads, and reveals his views and concepts discursively, as he does not in the novels. Ruth apRoberts believes Trollope used some of this unpublished material ironically in the American Senator's lecture to the British public (review of *The New Zealander, NCF*, 1973). Hall also prints an odd minor item in *Salmagundi: Byron, Allegra, and the Trollope Family* (1975), the kernel of which is Frances Trollope's poem on the burial of Byron's daughter Allegra. The manuscript of the poem, our earliest example of Trollope's handwriting, is valuable for his own notes on the poem, which reveal him as a more literary and sophisticated nineteen-year-old than the *Autobiography* implies. *Nineteenth-Century Fiction* will soon present, under Hall's auspices, "Trollope's Commonplace Book, 1835–40," which has great biographical value. The young man who in musing on Pope's *Essay on Man* can refer to God as "Pope's Client" cannot be quite the dull clod he says he was. In "An Unpublished Trollope Manuscript on a Proposed History of World Literature" (*NCF*, 1974), Hall prints another manuscript tentatively dated 1840, which reveals the portrait of the artist as a young encyclopedist. Trollope envisaged a mammoth history of *everything* written: poetry, history, theology, fine arts, fiction, and all the sciences.

Hall is preparing a new edition of the *Letters*, considerably expanded. The following items give a preview: Bradford A. Booth, "Author to Publisher, Anthony Trollope and William Isbister" (*PULC*, 1963); P. D. Edwards, "Trollope to Gladstone: An Unpublished Letter" and "Trollope and the Reviewers: Three Notes" (both *N&Q*, 1968); Joan Stevens, "An Unrecorded Trollope Letter" (*N&Q*, 1970); N. John Hall, "Letters of Thomas Adolphus Trollope to Henry Merivale Trollope, 1882–1892" (*UPLC*, 1973) and "Trollope's 'Hobbledehoyhood': A New Letter" (*N&Q*, 1974); and Mary Hamer, "Forty Letters of Anthony Trollope" (*YES*, 1973).

Hamer describes another important manuscript in "The Working Diary of *The Last Chronicle of Barset*" (*TLS*, 24 Dec. 1971), which not only reveals the artist at work but records details of his contributions to periodicals. In "Trollope in Holland" (*N&Q*, 1966), John E. Dustin describes a Trollope contribution (identified by Walter E. Houghton) to the *Cornhill* that shows him as amateur art critic. Helen G. King in "Trollope's Letters to the *Examiner*" (*PULC*, 1966) notes the historical importance of his reports on Ireland.

The Osprey Guide to Anthony Trollope by Michael Hardwick (1974) was sadly announced in *TLS* with the headline "Not Even a Map," and the good old Gerould *Guide* (1948; rpt. 1970) was rightly declared to be still the best (*TLS*, 18 Jan. 1974).

For the location of manuscripts of novels, the master list is Appendix B to Gordon Ray's important "Trollope at Full Length" (*HLQ*, 1968), the two major collections being those of Yale University and of Robert H. Taylor of Princeton, New Jersey. Ray's list is still substantially correct and complete, except that *The Way We Live Now* is known to be extant but in limbo. James Thorpe in "Writers at Work: The Creative Process and Our Views of Art" (*HLQ*, 1967) mentions the Huntington Library Trollope holdings. The files of *Nineteenth-Century Fiction*, for now and for the old days when it was *The Trollopian*, will yield information about collections and collectors. Andrew Wright's readable and substantial survey in "Anthony Trollope as Reader" (in *Two English Novelists*, 1975) culls information from fugitive and forgotten pieces and thereby, as he says, "offers a catalogue of possibilities, or a table of contents, to a vast quantity of materials." He is widely informed on libraries, collections, projects, and clues to finding out more, and his learning and insight also contribute richly to our sense of the man and his work. Further possibilities will emerge in Richard H. Grossman and Andrew Wright's "Anthony Trollope's Libraries" (*NCF*, 1976).

Reprints, Editions, Biography

Such is the need and such the difficulty of getting the works complete that the librarian E. V. Corbett indicates in "Anthony Trollope" (*NewS*, 1966) where to locate some hard-to-find items in London libraries and deplores, as do we all, the incompleteness of the list in print. Trollope has never been merely an academic interest, and so searchers may often do well to check public libraries as well as academic ones.

The travel books are freshly available. Penguin brought out a *North America* (1968) edited by Robert Mason and shortened to one third of the original. The annotation is not careful, and the excellent 1951 edition by Smalley and Booth remains the standard one. *The West Indies and the Spanish Main* and *South Africa* were reprinted in 1968 and another *South Africa* in 1973, with an introduction by J. H. Davidson. In 1966 Hume Dow brought out a good shortened form of *Trollope's Australia* (previously, in 1949, Marcie Muir had made a selection and commentary, *Anthony Trollope in Australia*); and now we have a full scholarly *Australia* edited by P. D. Edwards and R. B. Joyce (1967; with the New Zealand parts omitted).

Trollope's character sketches *Clergymen of the Church of England*, originally in the Pall Mall Gazette, were reprinted in the Leicester Press Victoria Library (1974), with an introduction by Ruth apRoberts that gives cursory historical background for the general reader and suggests the significance of the essays for the study of the novels. In considering the connections with clergymen in the novels, she proposes some critical lines: the two clergymen in *The Way We Live Now* may represent some Arnoldian concepts, for instance. Trollope's valuable *Thackeray* (English Men of Letters series), reprinted in 1968 and 1973, may be of special interest now for what is still an excellent appreciation of *Barry Lyndon*.

But the novels themselves are the thing. The hopes for a complete edition that Gordon Ray expressed in 1968 ("Trollope at Full Length," *HLQ*) have been sadly dashed. Lately, however, after letting many titles lapse, Oxford— whose World Classics series has long had the best Trollope list, as many as thirty-five titles in 1950—has announced the return of *The Three Clerks, The Claverings, The Vicar of Bullhampton, The Kellys and the O'Kellys,* and *He Knew He Was Right.* Meanwhile, some notable reissues have come out: *An Eye for an Eye,* as the first volume of the Doughty Library series (1966); from Australia a reprint of *He Knew He Was Right* introduced by P. D. Edwards (1974); and in America *The Way We Live Now* edited with some textual corrections (without benefit of ms) by Robert Tracy (1974). Penguin gives us *The Last Chronicle of Barset,* introduced by Laurence Lerner (1967); *The Eustace Diamonds,* introduced by Stephen Gill and John Sutherland (1969); *Can You Forgive Her?* introduced by Stephen Wall (1974); and *Phineas Finn,* introduced by John Sutherland (1974). The Gill, Sutherland, and Wall introductions are particularly fine. There are River-side editions of *The Last Chronicle of Barset,* introduced and edited by Arthur Mizener (1964), and of *The Warden* and *Barchester Towers,* both in one volume, introduced and edited by Louis Auchincloss (1966). Chatto and Windus reprinted *John Caldigate* in 1972, and Oxford World Classics *Mr. Scarborough's Family* in 1973. In all, of the forty-seven novels, about twenty-five are listed as in print. The most admired and wanted of the scarce ones is probably *The Macdermots of Ballycloran.*

The BBC Television Palliser series happily drew forth a special Oxford reprint of the six Palliser novels, with notes, a Who's Who, and cross references by R. W. Chapman. Less happy is Michael Hardwick's abridged version of them all run together, *The Pallisers* (1974), amounting to about one tenth of the original—to what end, and for whom, one wonders. *The Oxford Companion to English Literature* summaries are much shorter, and masterly.

Someone should make a checklist of translations of Trollope's novels. A quick survey reveals, not surprisingly, that *The Warden* and *Barchester Towers* are the most translated. It is somehow remarkable, however, to find *An Eye for an Eye* in Flemish (1955) and *The Three Clerks* in Hebrew (1958). The foreign view can be illuminating, and even a title can suggest a critical approach: one Italian version of *The Warden* is *Gli scrupoli di Mister Harding* (1952), and another is *Un caso di conscienza* (1951).

Sadleir's *Trollope: A Commentary* is still the best biography, with all its many merits—and its few though vitiating faults, such as a pervading sense of cultism and that trace of condescension that Paul Elmer More noted when the book came out ("My Debt to Trollope," *The Demon of the Absolute,* 1928). James Pope Hennessy's *Anthony Trollope* (1971) brings together a great deal of material, a little of which is new, an interesting selection of illustrations, a good deal of Irish background, and the claim that Pope Hennessy's grandfather was the original of Phineas Finn (but there have been other claimants). It is hard, nevertheless, to see why such a derivative book was written. Pope Hennessy occasionally finds something to admire and makes an occasional perceptive comment, but he can hardly have felt any mastery of his subject—he confesses so often to being astonished, puzzled, exasperated, and irritated. And yet he feels justified in psychologizing and tells us about Trollope's subconscious. Important statements of fact go undocumented, the literary criticism is naïve, and the structure of the book is unwieldy.

When the new *Letters* are out, and some critical consensus takes form, as seems imminent, there will be room indeed for a good critical biography. Because Trollope is so much *homme engagé*, our expanding knowledge of Victorian history—Ireland, the Civil Service, the Church, politics, the women's movement, and the way people lived—will be particularly valuable to his biography.

General Criticism

From where we stand now, A. O. J. Cockshut's *Anthony Trollope: A Critical Study* (1955, rpt. 1968) looks increasingly important in that it initiated a new kind of Trollope criticism, which assumes his greatness and proceeds with sophisticated academic analysis. Not that Cockshut appears any more "right" than before—indeed, the book is generally considered oversophisticated, over-Freudian, and idiosyncratic in its evaluations and its claim for a "progress toward pessimism." But Cockshut drew attention to the richness of long-overlooked and undervalued novels, recorded frequent brilliant insights, and proved stimulating and provocative. If he is felt to be wrong, any valid rebuttal had better be scrupulously scholarly.

The new perspective brings to light from the past a few neglected items that may now appear valuable: the bibliographies neglect the old *Revue des Deux Mondes* critiques, though Smalley lists them in the Critical Heritage volume: Émile Montégut, "Le Roman religieux" (1855; on *The Warden*) and "Le Roman des moeurs" (1858; on *Barchester Towers* and *Doctor Thorne*); and E. D. Forgues, "Une Thèse sur le mariage en deux romans" (1860; on *The Bertrams* and *Castle Richmond*). These are valuable for the foreign point of view and the foreign concept of "roman des moeurs." Helen Darbishire's old but good general critique of Trollope's psychological realism is available in *Somerville College Chapel Addresses* (1962). Gerald Warner Brace works in the older mode of general appreciation in "The World of Anthony Trollope" (*TQ*, 1961); himself a novelist, he writes a graceful essay of judicious praise specific enough to be suggestive to the scholar: Trollope is unmatchable for the power of invention and is like Dumas and Balzac in this respect; the *Autobiography* offers "the most reliable advice to writers that I know of."

A little post-Cockshut scuffle took place in *PMLA*. John Dustin ("Thematic Alternation in Trollope," *PMLA*, 1962) proposes a classification of the novels according to theme: in type A, a heroine must make a choice of suitors and an inheritance is involved; in type B, a hero makes an error of moral judgment and must find his way out of difficulties. Types A and B alternate in Trollope's career so long as he writes "mechanically"; type C breaks the pattern with variety and profundity and the "darkness" that Cockshut sees in the late novels. William Cadbury takes issue with Dustin in "Shape and Theme: Determinants of Trollope's Forms" (*PMLA*, 1963). He himself puts the novels in pairs according to shape, then in different pairs according to theme, and then in different sets according to type—epic, romance, or picaresque (Mark Robarts is a picaro)—concluding that there is variety that resists Cockshut's light-dark classification and that Trollope generally has moral insights throughout.

It was a red-letter day for Trollope scholarship when Gordon N. Ray delivered an address, "Trollope at Full Length," at the Huntington Library (*HLQ*, 1968). Ray has some interesting quantitative studies to buttress his point that it is the big novels that are the most characteristic and the best. He explains how the novels may be rated according to length from one to five units, with only five reaching the five-unit or seventy-thousand-word measure: *Orley Farm, Can You Forgive Her?, The Last Chronicle, He Knew He Was Right*, and *The Way We Live Now*. In these, and in the others that approach them in length, "A whole society has been created, and the figures of the main plot gain salience and reality from being seen in relation to so many other characters and against a background so comprehensively depicted." *Mr. Scarborough's Family*, for instance, has three subplots besides the main, as well as characteristic "little tales" or graphic character sketches, which all add to the total effect of "expanding novel." His method is amplification in breadth, with well-timed shifts from one plot to another; in fact "he made himself a great master of the contrapuntal novel before anyone had thought of the term." His subject is life in society, and Ray acclaims R. H. Hutton's appreciation of Trollope's characters as "social combatants." In an overview of Trollope's career, Ray notes the marks of slapdash characteristic of the novels of the 1840s and 1850s—and yet, for vigor and brilliance, *Barchester Towers* and *Doctor Thorne* are among the best. But, as Trollopians all agree, it is a pity to know only the early style, to miss "the easy narrative mastery, the nice balance of judgment, and the harmony of tone" that were to come. Trollope was "a great, truthful, varied artist, who wrote better than he or his contemporaries realized, and who left behind him more novels of lasting value than any other writer in English."

The same year, 1968, saw the publication of Robert Polhemus' *The Changing World of Anthony Trollope*, which did not meet with a favorable reception. Imprecise and confused as it is, it nevertheless has passages that embody a just insight or stimulating suggestion. And Polhemus has a good sense of Trollope's plain style, natural dialogue, and phenomenal breadth of sympathy.

J. Hillis Miller's *The Form of Victorian Fiction* (1968), important for general theory, must be considered here for a radically new approach to

Trollope. In Miller's view, the common formal element in the great Victorian novels is the omniscient narrator, playing the role of the "collective mind," and the narrator of Trollope's novels is the best example. The narrator watches the characters with a sympathy "that insinuates itself into the reader's mind to the point of identification." Trollope speaks far less as an individualized moralizing narrator than Thackeray or George Eliot does, more as a part of the community that is the ground of being of his characters. "His fiction concentrates with admirable consistency on the question of what constitutes authentic selfhood." Taking *Ayala's Angel* as his base, Miller explains that the most important commitment of the self is falling in love. This is, for Trollope, the absolute in his world of relativity. It is, moreover, gratuitous. Some scholars may feel Miller's disappearance-of-God theme is pushed rather far when he says that "interpersonal relations replace religious experience for Trollope." And yet, as Miller develops the point, he is clearly claiming something legitimate about Trollope's sense of society: that we make ourselves in relationship to others, and that these sustaining relationships are what generate the validity and meaning of life. As structuralist, Miller draws what is to my mind a valid analogy with linguistic process: "The source of meaning which makes language possible can be located in no single word, but only in the interaction of words in syntactical patterns." The novel, then, "might be defined as the poetry of interpersonal relations," and Trollope, of all the Victorians, is the most *accepting* of this social syntax (if Miller will permit my development of his figure) and is therefore, in a way, the exemplary narrator.

Another new approach to the novel that has some points in common with Miller's is James Gindin's *Harvest of a Quiet Eye: The Novel of Compassion* (1971), and he too takes Trollope as exemplary. The "novel of compassion," he says, although not quite new—and he cites Chaucer and Jane Austen—really asserts itself and develops as a "tradition" after about 1875, notably with Trollope's later novels from *The Last Chronicle* through *Ayala's Angel*. These novels reject the universal, the paradigmatic, and the allegorical and turn to the particular and experiential; they deny formal moral absolutes and "present experience from which no guide or lesson can be extrapolated." For a critic who makes much of Trollope's "particularity," Gindin makes perhaps too many generalizations about his themes and types and gives us too many plots. But he argues soundly that Trollope's novels rely on "density of social characterization, completeness, to demonstrate the world's complexity"; that his skepticism guards him against sentimentality, the inherent danger of this genre; that Trollope's acceptance of the unjust, unsystematic world yields his characteristic compassion; and that his world is more "free and flexible" than Dickens' or George Eliot's, and ultimately more mysterious. One might observe a common thread running through the work of Ray, Miller, and Gindin—a celebration of Trollope's plenitude: the novel of full length, multiple interactions, and density leading to something like a Carlylean sense of wonder.

By way of new short general introductions, we have P. D. Edwards' *An-*

thony Trollope (1968) and Alice Green Fredman's *Anthony Trollope* (1971). Edwards' is in the Profiles in Literature series, and its method of illustrative extracts is particularly useful for Trollope, since his work is so large and so various. Fredman's pamphlet, one of the Columbia Essays on Modern Writers, is a just and thoughtful general introduction. She partakes of, and gives informed expression to, the newer, more respectful criticism, observing that Trollope is not only a highly representative Victorian but also the most "modern," in introducing atypical characters, in depth psychology, and in "moral relativism, describing strangely disconcerting situations and problems."

Ruth apRoberts' *The Moral Trollope* (1971; in England, *Trollope: Artist and Moralist*) claims a connection between Trollope's art and his moral concerns. She believes that what Lord David Cecil calls an absence of style is for the most part a highly efficient, plain mode of writing that recalls Swift's. She declares that we need a new aesthetics for this novelist so little served by older systems and values and proposes a theory of the novel as "casuistry." She finds a basis for this in Cicero, using the neglected two-volume *Life and Works of Cicero* that Trollope published in 1880; she explores casuistry as a tradition in the Anglican Church, connecting seventeenth-century divines with Whewell, Grote, and Maurice. The center of a Trollopian novel is a case of conscience or a moral dilemma; he practiced something like "situation ethics" and developed a "situation aesthetics" for it. Walter Bagehot's *The English Constitution* helped Trollope develop the dilemmas and ironies of his political novels (Asa Briggs first made this important Bagehot-Trollope connection in *Victorian People*, 1954; rpt. 1963). Finally, in the Victorian age it is Trollope who best maintains the humane classical English novel. It may seem that apRoberts is cavalier in dismissing precedent scholarship, and yet maybe it was as well to strike out on a new line unimpeded by many negative arguments.

Professional writers frequently comment on Trollope in general: the student will want to turn to Rebecca West's *The Court and the Castle* (1957), Frank O'Connor's *The Mirror in the Roadway* (1956), Louis Auchincloss' *Reflections of a Jacobite* (1961), V. S. Pritchett's *The Working Novelist* (1965), and Virginia Woolf's *Collected Essays* (1966). It is often disappointing to find such generalizations made on a limited knowledge of the works. Auden reviewed Pope Hennessy's biography (*NY*, 1972), but he too was insufficiently informed, and one is obliged to see this review as an act more of friendship than of criticism.

But C. P. Snow's work is another matter entirely. He writes out of a wide knowledge and professional respect in *Trollope: His Life and Art* (1975). The book is a handsome one with many out-of-the-way pictures. It is often felt that Snow has something in common with Trollope, which could be called, loosely, realism and, more specifically, a keen curiosity about how things get done in society. Both bring actual institutional experience to their art. But otherwise they are quite far apart: whereas Snow habitually takes shelter behind a persona-narrator who is often mannered or slack in style, Trollope is frank, incisive, and ironically humorous. Snow, one senses, feels both the fellowship and the differences. Nigel Dennis in his review (*NYRB*, 1975) said all the negative things about the book very pungently; one might wish he would give us more of the benefit of his own obviously refined understanding of Trollope. But Snow's book has the merits of modesty and informality, some useful new biographical material on Trollope's Post Office work, some valuable ideas about Trollope's dialogue, and some good analysis of Trollope as a psychological novelist. This psychological analysis he anticipated in an earlier essay, "Trollope: The Psychological Stream" (*On the Novel: A Present for Walter Allen*, ed. B. S. Benedikz, 1971). It is the characters' mental processes, says Snow, that constitute Trollope's central concern. The challenge of representing the stream of consciousness, which is "probably not always a stream, and only partly, in the strictest sense, conscious," Trollope met in his own distinguished way, which Snow compares with Stendhal's, Dostoevski's, Proust's, and Joyce's.

The social historian J. A. Banks writes of the extent to which Trollope may be taken as "the mirror of his age" in "The Way They Lived Then: Anthony Trollope and the 1870's" (*VS*, 1968). Banks reminds us that in his study *Prosperity and Parenthood* (1954) he considered the later novels too much affected by personal and economic depression. He now believes he was overinfluenced by the gloom of *The Way We Live Now* and by the Stebbinses' biography and that the whole range of novels is solidly informative, especially about norms and standards of conduct. *The Way We Live Now* illustrates a general ignorance and mistrust of the stock market, and Trollope exploits his own mistrust in the novel. Banks modifies Asa Briggs's account of Trollope at some points, ranging over politics, economics, manners, marriage, and feminism. His knowledge of the novels and the scholarship is broad and deep, and the essay illustrates how a just artistic sense of the novel can help in determining its historicity and how the historian in turn can help the literary critic. E. W. Martin in *Country Life in England* (1966) uses passages from Trollope (and Gaskell and Dickens) for their historicity.

As late as 1964, Laurence Lerner in "Trollope the Entertainer" (*Listener*) speaks of "dreadful competence" but nevertheless reads Trollope for escape. Trollope was so naïve that he did not even know that Trevelyan in *He Knew He Was Right* was "mentally ill." Kathleen E. Morgan, however, defends "The Relevance of Trollope" (*English*, 1967) in the days when "relevance" was relevant. In "Trollope and the Modern Reader" (*MR*, 1962) Clara Claiborne Park defends Trollope against Leavis' dismissal. Trollope's message is "agree or crack up"; we, with less convention left to agree to, are more inclined to crack up. In a chapter on Trollope in *The Victorian Debate: English Literature and Society* (1968), Raymond Chapman finds Trollope "strangely silent on the real challenges." Where Chapman considers Trollope paradoxical, one might suspect that the critic has not come to grips with his subject. Sheila M. Smith considers "Anthony Trollope: The Novelist as Moralist" (*Renaissance and Modern Essays . . . ,* ed. G. R. Hibbard, 1966) and seems surprised to find he is not simply a purveyor of moral clichés. Raymond Williams says very briefly (*The English Novel from Dickens to Lawrence*, 1970) that Trollope is good at "unity of tone" and other mere matters of art while George Eliot is infinitely superior because she questions values. William Myers in "George Eliot: Politics and Personality" (*Literature in Politics in the Nineteenth Century*, ed. John Lucas, 1971) cites Trollope as a "merely" conventional writer to show the superiority of both George Eliot and Dickens on politics. Roger L. Slakey in "Trollope's Case for Moral Imperative" (*NCF*, 1973) takes issue with those who have found him a moral relativist: Cockshut, Polhemus, and apRoberts. These critics may be unguarded on this matter at some points, but Slakey may be culpably absolute himself in professing to know for certain the moral of *Mr. Scarborough's Family*, that peculiar novel whose essence is to be problematical.

In "'Be Ye Lukewarm!': The Nineteenth-Century Novel and Social Action" (*BMMLA*, 1973), James R. Kincaid proposes that the nineteenth-century novel "asserts the impossibility of effective or meaningful external response"; evidence is drawn from Austen, Dickens, George Eliot, Butler, and Wilde, while Trollope, surprisingly, occupies the extreme position, saying, "In this world the man that is in the wrong almost invariably conquers the man that is in the right." Hardy's *Jude* is conclusive, and little Father Time has the last word. The case is brightly argued, but few critics would agree with Kincaid that Mr. Harding's virtue is in vain, "without descendants or followers . . . or influence." In another article, "The Forms of Victorian Fiction" (*VN*, 1975), Kincaid proposes that the Victorian novel combines "open" and "closed" form; Trollope's "intrusions," called so by the "obtuse" Henry James, are essential. The closed plot of Trollope—closed because we know in advance that Eleanor is not going to marry Mr. Slope (or whatever)—is "pried apart" when Trollope comments on his art, reminding us that this is only art. "But at the very same time this very tradition has controlled the plot, and Trollope has managed to complicate that tradition without at all subverting it." How surprised old Hugh Walpole and Elizabeth Bowen would have been at all this! It is believed that Kincaid is about to throw down the gauntlet in "Bring Back *The Trollopian*" (*NCF*, originally *The Trollopian*, 1976). This is the hour of challenge for Trollope criticism, to declare his greatness and his quiddity. Perhaps Kincaid is the man.

Marvin Mudrick, at any rate, is not. In "Looking for Kellerman" (*The Theory of the Novel*, ed. John Halperin, 1974) he laments that the critic must read quite a lot of those many Trollope novels, "worse luck," before criticizing. But he goes ahead anyway.

It is good to conclude this survey of general assessments with the wisdom of Richard Harter Fogle's "Illusion, Point of View, and Criticism" in the same collection. Fogle draws attention to the anomaly that, while James (and his school) deplore authorial intrusion, it is nevertheless Trollope who is the realist par excellence, as Hawthorne witnesses, as Beerbohm witnesses, and as Fogle himself witnesses. Those readers who like Trollope for escape or period charm, though harmless and good-natured folk, miss the real value. To Fogle's mind "Trollope is more sure-footed than any of his great contemporaries. Thackeray sometimes hectors, sometimes whines at us, George Eliot is too steadily intense, and immoderate Dickens over-persuades." Trollope can afford to play with intrusion; his "illusion is so strong that it can be doubted without harming it—its exposure is in reality a reinforcement."

Studies of Special Aspects

Style

There is an old commonplace that Trollope has no style. Geoffrey Tillotson, however, writing about "Trollope's Style" (*BSTCF*, 1961; rpt. *Mid-Victorian Studies*, 1965), declares it is like Dr. Johnson's and has art and efficiency that enable Trollope to "master complexity." David Aitken in "'A Kind of Felicity': Some Notes about Trollope's Style" (*NCF*, 1966) compares the style to Jane Austen's and to Macaulay's but concludes that its main characteristic is to draw attention to the matter rather than the manner. Norman Page considers "Trollope's Conversational Mode" (*ESA*, 1972), taking off from W. P. Ker's assertion that Trollope is better than Balzac in dialogue. He too notes the Austen debt and says Trollope is a dramatist. Page uses mostly *The Last Chronicle*, which offers a wide range, including Johnny Eames's hackneyed slangy mode, Madalina Desmolines' romantic silliness, Josiah Crawley's Authorized Version grandeur, sometimes tragic, sometimes in sharp and hilarious contrast with Mr. Toogood's cockney-sparrow "right as a trivet." Besides mastering scores of styles in context, Trollope has also a delicate mastery of "inner speech"—what Snow was to call "psychological streaming." George Watson considers "Trollope's Forms of Address" (*CQ*, 1973), noting Trollope's special expertise in dialogue and "a linguistic self-consciousness hard to parallel" in nineteenth-century English fiction. A short discussion of how Trollope's plentiful use of Shakespeare allusions contributes to his "ease and pleasantness" is in Herbert Howarth's *Voices of the Past in Dickens and Others* (1972).

Helmut Klinger's "Die Umschreibung als Stilmittel in den Romanen Anthony Trollopes" (*WBEP*, 1973) is a full and authoritative study. He agrees with Aitken and approves the earlier claim of Hugh Sykes Davies (see the Stevenson *Guide*, p. 207) that the skillful use of humble "adversatives"—"but," "though," etc.—are Trollope's means to function as a casuist, exploring relations between principles and practice. Klinger cites the quiet antitheses: Lizzie Eustace debates with herself about whom she should fall in love with, but "in truth," says Trollope, "she had no heart to give." Josiah Crawley in his interior monologue asserts his humility in suffering, and Trollope with a quiet "though" clause reveals the man's perverse pride. This counterfoiling style is Trollope's means to distancing and irony, and it mediates the important principles that constitute his authorial personality. That personality, says Klinger, holds the novels together and accounts for Trollope's success in realizing his problematical and extraordinary characters.

No one can say anymore that Trollope has no style, for there is a book about it, a good new book in the Language Library series: John W. Clark's *The Language and Style of Anthony Trollope* (1975). From an abundance of evidence, attractively marshaled, Clark draws valuable conclusions: for instance, that Trollope's "literary" archaisms are rare after 1866, virtually nonexistent after 1873; that his "playful" language is heavily concentrated between 1856 and 1860, rare after 1868; that facetious names are unevenly distributed, with a slight tendency to average fewer in later novels; that Latin tags are roughly steady in incidence; and so on. Clark takes up the nonstandard English: provincial, urban-uneducated, Scots, Irish-English, Australian, and American; the "Ornaments—Mostly Bad"; and literary allusions. In general, Clark concludes that Trollope's style is "remarkably uniform from beginning to end; uniformly easy, flowing, clear, plain, unlabored, unaffected, unmannered, and above all, businesslike"; it is surprisingly "modern," or "timeless." "His vocabulary is copious and precisely used," and sentences are balanced, within themselves or in pairs, and marked by use of adversative conjunctions. Paragraphs are long and rhetorically well organized. Clark has not bothered with the recent scholarship on Trollope's style—a pity, as it would not have taken him long. And the book unfortunately lacks an index. But it is written with elegance and zest and can be read with pleasure.

Specific Topics

R. L. Agnew in "A Novelist Who Rode to the Hounds" (*CLife*, 1974) writes that Trollope generally knows his subjects very well, but the subject of hunting especially. He admires in particular the run from Craigallon Gorse in *The Eustace Diamonds* and the scenes in *The American Senator* where the Senator tries to understand this irrational amusement. The *Hunting Sketches*, those "characters" Trollope did for the *Pall Mall Gazette*, are much admired, too. Richard Gill in *Happy Rural Seat: The English Country House and the Literary Imagination* (1972) observes that, among English novelists, Trollope has the most country houses but does the least with them. William A. West takes up the important subject of Trollope's classical studies in "Trollope's Cicero" (*Mosaic*, 1971) and finds that his writings about Rome can shed light on the novels. In his Roman history Trollope finds his way to an ideal—Cicero—just as in the novels he finds his way to an ideal—Palliser.

Relations to Others

N. John Hall surveys a relationship in a brief compass in "Trollope and Carlyle" (*NCF*, 1972), and Ruth apRoberts makes a wider study linking the two in a forthcoming essay for the Sanders Festschrift to be published at Duke (ed. John Clubbe).

In an original and important essay Donald D. Stone explores another relationship: "Trollope, Byron and the Conventionalities" (*The Worlds of Victorian Fiction*, 1975). "Byron haunts Trollope's characters with such frequency," Stone demonstrates, that we can see that Trollope is rejecting Byron in his way, just as Carlyle and Arnold did in theirs; his way is to define and discriminate aspects of Byronism through his characters, with surprising frequency, variety, and precision. Stone's knowledge of Trollope is wide and profound.

We are indebted to Stephen Wall for broaching a significant comparative study with "Trollope, Balzac, and the Reappearing Character" (*EIC*, 1975). In the *Comédie Humaine*, he reminds us, there are 2,472 characters, of which 460 appear in more than one novel. Of Victorian novelists, Thackeray is the first of note to "interconnect" novels in something like this way. Is Trollope in his "interconnecting" merely developing a Thackerayan ploy, or is he, as Mrs. Humphry Ward suggested, following the example of Balzac? There is not much to go on, Wall observes, to demonstrate any real Balzacian influence. Wall considers that the interconnecting grows rather out of Trollope's youthful habit of serial fantasizing, more and more "subjected to a kind of novelistic discipline," and developing into his "secure creativity." Trollope "proceeds empirically, without benefit of Balzacian theory." The essential point is that "Trollope writes not as an anatomist of society, but as a participant in it." Wall concludes: "Since in Balzac reappearance is underpinned by explicit ideas about society and human nature, it strikes us as a form of knowledge. In Trollope, reappearance seems rather to be due to a creative form of love." The germ of another comparative study may lie in Patrick Waddington's short note, "Turgenev and Trollope: Brief Crossings of Paths" (*AUMLA*, 1974).

The Woman Question

In his own time, Trollope's readers were often astounded at his knowledge of female behavior and psychology, and so it is not surprising that in this era of Women's Studies one looks to Trollope. Margaret Hewitt in "Trollope: Historian and Sociologist" (*BJS*, 1963) observes that the Woman Question weighs heavily in his writing, that he is a faithful recorder, and that he deliberately makes patterns for women to copy. All his spinsters are peculiar, she says, and Miss Thorne is a crank. But some of us might refuse to call Miss Thorne a crank and might find Miss Todd or Priscilla Stanbury legitimate role models as spinsters. Hewitt seems to be trying to rally Trollope's women to rebel against him and Victorian convention; she ends with a real banner waver from Wollstonecraft. David Aitken argues that Trollope was consistently proconvention, altogether against women's rights and in favor of male supremacy ("Trollope on 'the Genus Girl,'" *NCF*, 1974). But he makes the error of mixing Trollope's own statements with his characters', and in a fatal footnote accuses Trollope of inconsistency. He concludes by saying that what we like about Trollope and his women is that they transcend his theory of women—which is as much as to say the theory was not really there in the first place.

Pamela Hansford Johnson writes on "Trollope's Young Women" (*On the Novel: A Present for Walter Allen*, ed. B. S. Benedikz, 1971). Earlier she did a half-page general essay on him ("Anthony Trollope, an Odd Fish," *NYTBR*, 1965) but now finds him less of an odd fish and more of a good novelist. "Of all the English novelists of the late nineteenth century, Trollope had the sharpest appreciation of women in their thoughts, actions, speech-rhythms and in their domestic routines." Ruth apRoberts in a forthcoming essay on "Emily and Nora and Priscilla and Dorothy and Jemima and Carry" (*The Victorian Experience: The Novel*, ed. Richard Levine) relates *He Knew He Was Right* to the contemporary parliamentary speeches of Mill on women's rights.

Studies of Individual Works

Works Other than Novels

An Autobiography has been generally neglected, except for routine descriptions in introductions and histories. Wayne Shumaker's study (*English Autobiography*, 1954) remains the only important treatment. He takes it as "The Mixed Mode": whereas J. S. Mill's *Autobiography* is expository and George Moore's is narrative, Trollope stands midway—reflective in part, active in part. H. N. Wethered in *The Curious Art of Autobiography* (1956) gives only a brief description and some extracts. Roy Pascal in *Design and Truth in Autobiography* (1960) says that Trollope shows how *not* to do it. There must be more to say about this remarkable example of the genre. Certainly it continues to be read.

There has been some interest in Trollope's travel books, chiefly J. H. Davidson's "Anthony Trollope and the Colonies" (*VS*, 1969). Davidson notes that Trollope "alone among the eminent Victorians went to all the major groups of colonies and wrote separate books about them." In a survey of all these, he traces some change of attitude on Trollope's part and relates the books to his career and his novels. *The Fixed Period*, he believes, reflects some views of Trollope's on the annexation of the Transvaal. He finds the travel writing generally perfunctory and the thinking hardly sustained or systematic. But, illogically, he finds the books both vivid and "unique."

The occasion of the Penguin publication of the shortened *North America*, ineffectually edited by Robert Mason (1968), drew forth one of those *TLS* epistolary dialogues, with Arnold Goldman taking the offensive: he says the text "has been thinned to inanity" (*TLS*, 28 Nov., 5, 12, 19 Dec. 1968). V. S. Naipaul in "Trollope in the West Indies" (*Listener*, 1967) records his enjoyment of *The West Indies and the Spanish Main*. Trollope can hardly be called racist, Naipaul believes. The Victorians felt free to express their prejudices as such, and the book is a frankly personal record that catches Trollope's forthrightness. His disgust at the laziness of the blacks came from his own high sense of duty and his "Civil Servant's sense of what helps to balance a budget." C. P. Snow thinks *The West Indies* his best travel book. Iva G. Jones believes the book did harm ("Trollope, Carlyle, and Mill on the Negro: An Episode in the History of Ideas," *JNH*, 1967). Trollope's views were those of the *Times*, and the book got a good press and gave him a reputation; it also contributed to the vicious stereotyping of the Negro as intellectually inferior and lazy. Trollope is usually humane, says Jones, but on this subject he and Carlyle are similarly intolerant, and Mill in contrast all the more conspicuously just. *How the 'Mastiffs' Went to Iceland*, Trollope's pleasant trifle recording a social jaunt, has been translated into Icelandic, Richard F. Tomasson tells us in "Iceland on the Brain" (*ASR*, 1972), which records various famous visitors to Iceland.

On the occasion of an Australian reprint of *Harry Heathcote of Gangoil* (1963), P. D. Edwards writes a review essay (*ALS*, 1963). Edwards observes that, as generally agreed, this is not first-rate Trollope—he hated doing the Christmas Story, for which genre this was written. But Edwards finds him pretty well informed on the Australian way of life, though Trollope's bias in favor of the gentleman settler, which his son Fred was, is rather too conspicuous, Edwards says, in his obvious dislike for the convict and the free selector. In *John Caldigate*, a far superior novel, the picture of Australian life is accurate and much more lively as well; and the Australian element is used, as the American element is used in *Doctor Wortle's School*, to formulate a moral challenge to the older civilization. Coral Lansbury in an interesting study of the nineteenth-century image of Australia in English literature (*Arcady in Australia*, 1970) includes a brisk survey of Trollope's views on Australia, Australia's views on Trollope, and his uses of Australia in his fiction.

On the subject of the short stories, Wendell V. Harris reminds us that Trollope wrote short stories more constantly and collected them more regularly than the other Victorian novelists ("English Short Fiction in the Nineteenth Century," *SSF*, 1968). Like other contemporary English specimens of the genre, they are generally not the "true short story"; that is, they do not measure up to Poe's theory and art. For Trollope, "consistent and uninspired competence" is the keynote, says Harris. Further, closer consideration is given to this matter by Donald D. Stone in "Trollope as a Short-Story Writer" (*NCF*, forthcoming).

The Irish Novels

Trollope's first published novel, *The Macdermots of Ballycloran*, takes us into a consideration of his Irish novels. E. W. Wittig gives a good survey in "Trollope's Irish Fiction" (*Éire*, 1973). The early *Macdermots* is an excellent tragedy and excellent in its Irishness. From then on the Irish mode deteriorates: *The Kellys and the O'Kellys* is a mere novel of manners in the tradition of the early Lever; *Castle Richmond* falls apart; the late, unfinished *Landleaguers*, although it has some touches of the strength of *The Macdermots*, is essentially mere melodrama and is vitiated by Trollope's now one-sided protest against Gladstone's policies. In the Phineas Finn novels, the hero's Irishness doesn't matter, but Fitzgibbon is a fine self-parodying stage Irishman. *An Eye for an Eye* succeeds in playing off romance against reality, and the young Englishman against Irish society. Wittig may seem at times to overvalue the historicity at the expense of the art, but perhaps there is indeed a high correlation in these novels. In an older survey, "Anthony Trollope and Ireland" (*DM*, 1955), Constantia Maxwell gives more praise to *The Landleaguers* than Wittig does. She finds that it has an intelligent sympathy for the two parties. A more popular survey for magazine readers in English country houses was done by Ian Stewart ("Go West, Young Man: Anthony Trollope's Early Days in Ireland," *CLife*, 1971). Stewart too notes the seriousness and excellence of *The Macdermots*. Doris Asmundsson, who finds Barset and its clergy culturally remote, acclaims *The Macdermots* as powerful and also "relevant," dealing with racial oppression, terrorists, exploitation of the poor, violence, etc. ("Trollope's First Novel: A Re-examination," *Éire*, 1973). She agrees with Hugh Walpole that Feemy is one of Trollope's finest heroines, and finds that the novel has the inevitability and pathos of *The Cherry Orchard* and *Absalom, Absalom!* She notes that it anticipates by thirty years the powerful social criticism of *The Way We Live Now*.

R. C. Terry acclaims *The Macdermots* as "the most neglected first novel of any English author of recognized achievement" and proceeds to some valuable textual study ("Three Lost Chapters of Trollope's First Novel," *NCF*, 1972). *The Macdermots* was first published in 1847, and, when republished between May 1860 and February 1861 (Sadleir gives an earlier date), three chapters had been excised from Volume III, improving unity and pace. Terry's examination reveals the artist at work and prepares the ground for a much desired good edition. E. W. Wittig expands and modifies Terry's work ("Significant Revisions in Trollope's *The Macdermots of Ballycloran*," *N&Q*, 1973). Mary Hamer extends the study to *The Kellys and the O'Kellys* ("Chapter Divisions in Early Novels by Anthony Trollope," *N&Q*, 1973) and finds that "Trollope was consciously experimenting with chapter divisions, presumably recognizing their structural significance."

Castle Richmond will remain distasteful to many readers for Trollope's apparent view of the famine as a warrant of God's *mercy*, but Hugh Hennedy rightly believes it deserves critical attention anyway ("Love and Famine, Family and Country in Trollope's *Castle Richmond*," *Éire*, 1972). He sees a "key parallel" between the two parts generally thought of as badly split: just as the Molletts are bleeding the Castle Richmond family dry by blackmail, so the middle-class Irish have bled the peasantry.

The Barsetshire Novels

Historical background studies of *The Warden* and *Barchester Tower* continue. Thomas B. Lundeen in "Trollope and the Mid-Victorian Episco pate" (*HMPEC*, 1961) says that, although Trollope knew more abou clergymen than he pretended, he errs in *Barchester Towers* at two impor tant points: one, at no time in the nineteenth century did a son succeed hi father in a bishopric—so the Archdeacon was oversanguine; two, the prac tice was to delay a month in filling an episcopate vacant by death—so th Archdeacon need not have been so hurried. The article has valuable infor mation, but it is critically naïve. G. F. A. Best in "The Road to Hiram Hospital" (*VS*, 1961) gives a good deal of useful historical backgroun (marred by the consistent misspelling of "Grantly"). Carol Ganzel argue that the origin of *The Warden* was a series of letters in the *Times* o simony in a Cornish town (*NCF*, 1967), and Bradford Booth (*The Englis Novel*, 1974) finds that this theory squares with a good many of the fact Increased interest in Trollope brings back to light Joseph E. Baker's chapte on Trollope in *The Novel and the Oxford Movement* (1932); Trollope a novelist, Baker says, is the essential High and Dry Anglican. "Anthon Trollope and the Church of England" (*CQR*, 1962) is a readable essay b Paul A. Wellsby, who took the advice of Bishop Edward King: "Read goo novels. You will thus travel into circumstances, and conditions, and situa tions of life." Wellsby, now that he has read about forty Trollope novels, sorry that there are so few left. He brings a wide knowledge of churc history to a perceptive statement of Trollope's position. Trollope deprecat theology and believes that the taking of holy orders is crippling to a man mentality, but he considers himself nevertheless a loyal son of the Church England. Wellsby has made good the Bishop's advice, with a keen apprec ation of Trollope's "situations."

M. S. Bankert gives us more insight into background in "Newman in th Shadow of Barchester Towers" (*Renascence*, 1968) and shows a nice critic sense of the novel, affirming that it is none the less serious for its humor. I Proudie, Bankert sees the combination of Low Church with Latitudinaria —like Hampden, who was appointed to the See of Hereford in 1847 an anathematized by both Newman and Pusey. In Arabin he sees something Matthew Arnold and of Newman's disciple Isaac Williams. James M. L insists on Trollope's knowledge of contemporary ecclesiastical issues ("Tro lope's Clerical Concerns: The Low Church Clergyman," *HSL*, 1969) an refers us to Trollope's *Clergymen of the Church of England* for the mot "In the religion of the day, moderation is everything." Frederick F. Jills in "The 'Professional' Clergyman in Some Novels by Anthony Trollop (*HSL*, 1969) reflects the professional view of an Episcopalian priest an finds Trollope well informed indeed on the doctrine, traditions, and pra tices of the Church of England of his time—here is ecclesiastical learni combined with an intelligent and delighted reading of Trollope. Critics

Trollope who claim that he is a casuist will be particularly satisfied with another professional view: Dayton Haskins, S.J., in "Awakening Moral Conscience: Trollope as Teacher in *The Warden*" (*Cithara*, 1973) gives us the spectacle of a Jesuit demonstrating casuistry, and it is an excellent demonstration. Against the background of Bentham and Mill, he exhibits *The Warden* teaching with "speaking pictures" that "even a simple moral decision is extremely complex; and in this way the novel quickens our sense of the richness and complexity of human freedom."

For the art of Barchester, the bibliography grows rapidly. M. A. Goldberg finds in *The Warden* an equipoise to balance the social and political equipoise of the time ("Trollope's *The Warden*: A Commentary on the Age of Equipoise,'" *NCF*, 1963; rpt. in *The Victorian Novel: Modern Essays in Criticism*, ed. Ian Watt, 1971). With a kind of satire like Jane Austen's and a sympathy for all parties, Trollope achieves a stability in the fiction that is parallel to contemporary political stability. Harding's virtue is neither Shaftesbury's benevolence, nor Paine's radicalism, nor Mill's Utilitarianism; it is rather a virtue of quietude and compromise. Louis Kronenberger in *The Polished Surface: Essays in the Literature of Worldliness* (1969) has an essay on Trollope that harks back to the older school: ". . . not a master psychologist . . . mere storyteller." This could be indexed under Smalley's rubric for limited praise: "genius, a kind of." David Shaw is most explicit on the Austen link ("Moral Drama in *Barchester Towers*," *NCF*, 1964). In both *Emma* and *Barchester Towers* the central characters (Emma and Eleanor) move through deception and illusion to self-knowledge. Austen has "progressive moral action," while Trollope is episodic and fragmentary, working through situation and speech patterns. By "intrusion," Trollope achieves "a species of dramatic irony that is often so bland and dry that we may almost miss its artistry." Samuel F. Pickering, Jr., swells the chorus of defense of "intrusion" ("Trollope's Poetics and Authorial Intrusion in *The Warden* and *Barchester Towers*," *JNT*, 1973) and defines the poetics as different from that of the religious tracts and of Dickens, Carlyle, and the Pre-Raphaelites. William Cadbury also finds art in the narration ("Character and Mock Heroic in *Barchester Towers*," *TSLL*, 1964). The occasional mock-epic projection of the narrator is a device for distancing and preventing the "too great illusion of reality." Cadbury makes the interesting observation that the virtues of *Barchester Towers* are different from those of the other novels. Although the novel starts on the inside, with the archdeacon's psychological processes, we move to the outside. Once we know the Archdeacon for what he is, a good man, we can be the better amused. The characters are now seen from the outside; in Kenneth Burke's phrase, they "dance an attitude."

U. C. Knoepflmacher puts "*Barchester Towers*: The Comedy of Change" first in his *Laughter & Despair: Readings in Ten Novels of the Victorian Era* (1971) primarily to demonstrate the fictiveness of fictions. If even Trollope, often called the most photographic Victorian novelist, observes that there is "no mental method of daguerreotype or photography" for novelists, we are the more inclined to remember that the novelist's world is invented. And this novel comes best at the beginning because its "traditional comic form" serves best to gauge the innovations of the others. Behind Trollope stand Fielding, Goldsmith, Smollett, Sterne, Johnson, Addison, Steele, Austen, and even Swift and Pope. Knoepflmacher applies an interesting notion of concentric circles: at the heart lies Ullathorne Court, the most unchanging element; then Barchester, where things move, but with resistance; outside spins the world at large—London, Westminster, the press; still outside that is the chaotic actuality to which reader and novelist both belong, and the novelist reduces that chaos for the reader and disposes of it with laughter.

James R. Kincaid finds *Barchester Towers* not only "one of the warmest of all the great English comic novels, but also one of the subtlest" ("*Barchester Towers* and the Nature of Conservative Comedy," *ELH*, 1970). Trollope writes in the tradition of Jane Austen and shares many of her values but is yet more conservative. Along with the benignity, there is an implicit distrust of the young, and a vision, more troubled and complex than Austen's, that recognizes the impossibility of its own norms. How remarkably unconventional it is, Kincaid points out, to have such a figure as Mr. Harding as the center! The theme is the fight, and in each contest the winner is the one who does not try, indicating thereby a protest against a competitive mode of life. This suggestive essay insists on the complexity of the novel, its maturity, and its richness.

The new school of sophisticated Trollope criticism is further enriched by Murray Krieger's study of *Barchester Towers* in *The Classic Vision: The Retreat from Extremity in Modern Literature* (1971). *Barchester Towers* is in the "naïvely classic" category with *Pride and Prejudice*, but the form is more open, and there is more of a challenge to values than Austen permits. Krieger sees *Barchester Towers* in the tradition of Elizabethan comedy: the "comic villain who would gull the others is himself gulled and hooted off the stage." Slope is unmasked as fraudulent moralism. Krieger has a keen sense of Trollope's deft touch and of his scope. He quotes Trollope on Mr Quiverful: "Till we can become divine we must be content to be human, lest in our hurry for a change we sink to something lower." This, says Krieger, is the spirit of Swift.

As for the other Barsetshire novels, *Doctor Thorne* has elicited only two very specialized studies. Michael G. Anthony and Sharon Sanders in "Trollope's Mysterious Periporollida'" (*AN&Q*, 1974) investigate linguistics and medicine in a light and cheerful manner to find that "periporollida" is the medical gobbledegook by which Dr. Rerechild refers to Sir Roger Scatcherd' toes in order to impress Dr. Thorne, much the better doctor, who himself pointedly avoids jargon. The distinguished and learned lawyer Sir Owen Dixon considers "Sir Roger Scatcherd's Will" (*Jesting Pilate and Other Papers and Addresses*, 1965). Trollope took pride in the trial in *Orley Farm* but Sir Owen is obliged to fault it. In *The Warden* and *Doctor Thorne* the portrayal of legal matters is generally accurate. Sir Abraham Haphazard i perfectly correct. But, it is shown in careful detail, Scatcherd's will is impossible, and Sir Owen thanks Trollope for providing an interesting and difficult question, the occasion of an address to his learned colleagues.

Mary Hamer draws insight from manuscript study to illuminate *Framley Parsonage* ("*Framley Parsonage*: Trollope's First Serial," *RES*, 1975). In engaging to write for the *Cornhill* in 1859, Trollope was to reach a much larger audience and "embrace the serialist's commitment to the discipline of his form." Hamer takes a fresh view of *Framley Parsonage* as variations on the theme of pride and reveals Trollope's technique for building on parallels and manipulating multiple plots. This technique, she says, is refined by the new discipline of serial writing. Sonia Bićanić, using evidence from letters and memoranda, corrects some minor errors of memory both in Trollope's account of the genesis of this novel and also in that of *Cornhill* editor George Smith ("Some New Facts about the Beginning of Trollope's *Framley Parsonage*," *SRAZ*, 1960). John J. Glavin in "Trollope's 'Most Natural English Girl'" (*NCF*, 1974) sees in the love story of *Framley Parsonage* a rather steamy enactment of vegetation myth. Some of Glavin's argument is less than responsible, but this short study nevertheless seems surprisingly valid, perhaps just because Trollope does understand and celebrate sexuality. What if Trollope were the "most natural" English novelist!

Juliet McMaster takes up "'The Unfortunate Moth': Unifying Theme in *The Small House at Allington*" (*NCF*, 1971). The image of the moth and the candle—self-destructive behavior—applied in the novel to a subsidiary plot (Cradell's pursuit of Mrs. Lupex) is a theme that draws all parts of the novel together. Many of the characters are similarly perverse: Palliser, Johnny Eames, Crosbie, both Bell and Lily Dale. Lily is somewhat like James's Isabel Archer. The theme of perversity is not uncommon in Trollope, and McMaster makes a strong case for its centrality in this novel.

The Last Chronicle of Barset is acknowledged as one of the best of the whole canon. Some of its art is demonstrated in two short studies by R. Anthony Arthur. In "Authorial Intrusion as Art in *The Last Chronicle*" (*JNT*, 1971) Arthur takes up Henry Grantly's case. Henry would be a dull dog in speech and action, but in fact he is not a dull dog because Trollope intrudes and comments and tells us the interesting psychological processes behind his behavior. This "intrusion" is really "augmenting narration." In "The Death of Mrs. Proudie: Frivolous Slaughter or Calculated Dispatch?" (*NCF*, 1972) Arthur observes how Trollope's self-deprecation often interferes with criticism: his defenders are still apologizing for him "as though to be disciplined and productive are cardinal sins." The case of Mrs. Proudie is classic. Trollope tells us he killed her in response to public taste. But he says elsewhere that the good artist "submits" to his characters; and actually plot and characters, according to Trollope's sophisticated comic method, demanded her death, and the death is part of calculated art.

William A. West makes this novel the occasion for a fruitful analysis, very broad in implication ("*The Last Chronicle*: Trollope's Comic Techniques," *The Classic British Novel*, ed. Howard M. Harper and Charles

Edge, 1972). His defense against the intrusive-author charge and the loose
plot charge is that they represent principles invalid for the genre of comedy.
Trollope's comedy fits the pattern of the Northrop Frye Mythos of Spring:
the novels end, if not in conspicuous procreation, certainly in marriage bells
and "the continuation of life." Trollope is the practitioner of the eighteenth-century comic novel; after him, in Hardy and James, tragedy is the
prestigious form, and its standards become overriding.

G. M. Harvey takes up "Heroes in Barsetshire" (*DR*, 1972) in *The Last
Chronicle*. Crawley, Eames, Henry Grantly, and Conway Dalrymple are all
flawed, but Mr. Harding is the true moral hero. After him, says Harvey,
"there are no heroes in Trollope." Few scholars would agree.

If any fictional character is susceptible of psychoanalysis it is Josiah Crawley, and it is Helen Storm Corsa who puts him on the couch (" 'The Cross
Grainedness of Men': The Rev. Josiah Crawley—Trollope's Study of a
Paranoid Personality," *HSL*, 1973). She puts the new labels on the old
processes responsibly and accurately, one suspects. What is most admirable
is that she deepens our understanding of the novel, and she is modest in her
claims for the science: Trollope himself knew, she observes, all about "the
cross-grainedness."

William H. Marshall in "Stepping Stones of Their Dead Selves" (*The
World of the Victorian Novel*, 1967) has for his center of interest the
withdrawal-of-God theme and sees *The Warden* as focal, with the Archdeacon based in *order* and Harding in *morality*, the one being social and
the other personal. Finally, Mr. Harding is "a modern Adam" who in
passing from his Eden takes the good rather than the evil with him. This is
all rather hard to understand. Marshall does not say where this leaves Eden.
Hugh L. Hennedy in *Unity in Barsetshire* (1971) claims "unity" for each
Barsetshire novel, and for the whole series as well. The unifying theme is
spied out as "clerical vocation." "If it is agreed that the Barsetshire novels
form together what is essentially a series of clerical novels, the question
naturally arises, How do *Doctor Thorne* and *The Small House at Allington*
. . . fit into the series?" How, indeed? "A Note on the Fluctuation of
Fortune in Trollope's Barsetshire" (*VN*, 1967) by Mary D. Smith is more
sound. She computes that Mary Thorne, Miss Dunstable, and Lady Glencora are each described at some point as the richest heiress in England.
From a very un-English address (*CairoSE*, 1966) comes a very English
question, posed by William Gillis: "An Original for Bertie?" E. Wortley
Montagu is the candidate. Barsetshire lives.

The Palliser, or Political, Novels

Arthur Mizener's fine essay "Anthony Trollope: The Palliser Novels"
(*From Jane Austen to Joseph Conrad*, ed. R. C. Rathburn and Martin
Steinmann, Jr., 1958), which opened a new kind of analysis of Trollope,
reprinted in *The Sense of Life in the Modern Novel* (1962) under the title
"The Realistic Novel in the Nineteenth Century." A small but important

event was the publication of a 1928 letter of Max Beerbohm's on the political novels (B. R. McElderry, "Beerbohm on Trollope," *TLS*, 12 Oct. 1967). Beerbohm's breast rebelled hotly against Henry James's condescension to the "lovely trilogy" *Phineas Finn, Phineas Redux*, and *The Prime Minister*. Beerbohm knew which London house was Madame Max Goesler's.

The Palliser novels are now more generally appreciated than they were a decade ago. Some new biographical material, including the delightful campaign poster: "Electors! Vote for Maxwell and Trollope, who won't deceive you," was provided by Arthur Pollard in a lecture at the University of Hull on the centenary of Trollope's own stand for election in Beverly (*Trollope's Political Novels*, 1968). Presenting evidence that Trollope was a better orator than he admits in the *Autobiography*, Pollard shows new analogues between Trollope's own political experience and the elections in *Ralph the Heir* and *Phineas Redux*. But, most interesting of all, he claims that Trollope's own political engagement is at the root of the power of these novels. Critics may have complained that these are political novels with the politics left out, but "that in itself constitutes a positive value, and a criticism of life. What seem to be the big issues are not the real concern of politicians; Palliser's decimal coinage may be the novelist's at once realistic and ironic comment on the whole matter."

Some critiques maintain an older mode. Ramesh Mohan ("Trollope's Political Novels," *IJES*, 1961) can still say that the novels are superficial and repetitive, yet readable and entertaining. Blair G. Kenney in a note on "Trollope's Ideal Statesman: Plantagenet Palliser and Lord John Russell" *NCF*, 1965) notes the parallels, but the interpretation is naïve and vulnerable. Palliser did not, like Russell, "accept a peerage" but was heir to the old Duke, as all the world knows. John Halperin makes a different connection in "Politics, Palmerston and Trollope's Prime Minister" (*ClioW*, 1974) but ignores Bagehot and Briggs. J. R. Dinwiddy's "Who's Who in Trollope's Political Novels" (*NCF*, 1967) pursues the roman à clef line but reflects a great deal of historical knowledge, to modify the identifications made by Chapman and Cockshut. The important characters, like Palliser and Finn, Dinwiddy concludes, can hardly correspond to real people, but the peripheral ones do indeed. He later surveys "Elections in Victorian Fiction" (*VN*, 1974), noting their remarkable frequency. In the 1850s the most notable ones are Thackeray's in *The Newcomes* and Trollope's in *Doctor Thorne*. But the one in *Ralph the Heir* (1871) is "the fullest and most realistic account of any election that any English novelist has written." This novel, as is generally known, reflects elements of Trollope's own experience, which is continued, says Dinwiddy, in *Phineas Redux*. Richard Crossman in "The Politics of Anthony Trollope" (*NS*, 1971) seems to have read only *The Prime Minister* and Pope Hennessy's biography and concludes that Trollope is inferior to Disraeli and has no political vision. John C. Kleis has a larger view ("Passion vs. Prudence: Theme and Technique in Trollope's Palliser Novels," *TSLL*, 1970) and proposes that many of the characters go through a crisis involving at least temporary alienation: Alice

Vavasor, Glencora, Phineas, Madame Max, Violet, Laura Kennedy, and Mabel Grex all face an agonizing choice between passion and prudence, and in each case, recognition of one's own irrational self-destructiveness precedes integration into moral responsibility.

George Watson in his chapter on "The Parliamentary Novel" (*The English Ideology: Studies in the Language of Victorian Politics,* 1973) acclaims the six Palliser novels, along with *Ralph the Heir* and *The Way We Live Now,* as "the summit of English political fiction." In the 1860s and 1870s politics and literature are a two-way affair; men of letters became politicians and life copies art. Disraeli creates the fictional world, and Trollope exploits it. "It is consciously grand. Its fascination lay in its pecking order, which is forever in flux. To watch it was as intriguing as a tournament; and for some men, more concerned with party management than with legislation, the tournament was everything. It was life itself." Trollope's knowledge of the system is "immense"; his prose, as befits a Post Office official, "reveals the subtle nuance of the experienced framer of committee documents." He is "the master of revealing the art of administration as it is." His note of caution is part of "the intelligent mood of the 1860's and 1870's."

Of the series, *Can You Forgive Her?* has called forth three studies. David S. Chamberlain's "Unity and Irony in Trollope's *Can You Forgive Her?*" (*SEL,* 1968) claims that the three plots, about a maiden, a wife, and a widow, are closely integrated around the theme that marriage exacts compromises, for the woman, between romance and prudence and, for the man between public and private life. The Widow Greenow plot, generally judged inferior, is taken here as focal. And the maiden—Alice Vavasor—is the most foolish, risking most by her "modern independence." Juliet McMaster ("'The Meaning of Words and the Nature of Things': Trollope's *Can You Forgive Her?*" *SEL,* 1974) makes a more subtle analysis of the three women, each hesitating between two men. She rescues Alice Vavasor from the many charges against her. Alice is seen as central in a successful problem novel concerned with women's rights, but concerned even more with the relation of language to social understanding. McMaster indicates very clearly the nature of Alice's sexual relationships with Grey, the jilted one, and with George, the brutal cousin, and demonstrates the counterpoint of the Glencora-Burgo plot. This is not altogether new, but her emphasis on Trollope's understanding of language is new and, I believe, important. Trollope may not be, as McMaster says, "hovering on the edge of producing a theory of the unconscious," but she enlarges our sense of him as a psychological novelist. George Levine is less content than McMaster with the novel, in "Can You Forgive Him? Trollope's *Can You Forgive Her?* and the Myth of Realism" (*VS,* 1974). He finds "impressive elements of moral subversion" in these three parallel plots, very complicated in their interrelationships—unusual for a Trollope novel, he says. Trollope imposes on his women "the myth of realism," the myth that "wisdom resides in learning the rules of society and acquiescing in them." Levine chafes at this, calling it an "impossible accommodation"; he is not at all sure he can forgive

Trollope, and he talks about the "ideal." Meantime, he has given us some sensitive readings of the "elements of moral subversion." And, if there are discrepancies in his argument, they are the kind that can lead to further discovery.

Once more, a lawyer has taken up Trollope: Francis Lyman Windolph in *Reflections of the Law in Literature* (1956) includes a discussion of *Phineas Redux*. He tells the story of the murder trial with some observations on the legal principles involved, finds Trollope sound and accurate, and incidentally bets that Trollope will outlast Dickens and Thackeray.

Helmut Klinger makes a convincing analysis in "Varieties of Failure: The Significance of Trollope's *The Prime Minister*" (*EM*, 1974), finding it one of Trollope's most distinguished achievements, successful in its parts as in its general design. He sees the two plots well linked in theme: Lopez puts himself in an impossible position as Emily's husband and as politician, and Palliser too puts himself in an impossible position as Prime Minister. Lopez is doomed, but Palliser by his superior morality emerges victorious over his failures.

Blair Gates Kenney broaches the rich subject of the Trollope-James influence in "The Two Isabels: A Study in Distortion" (*VN*, 1974)—Isabel Boncassen of *The Duke's Children* and Isabel Archer of *The Portrait of a Lady*. He notes some likenesses and makes some contrasts between Trollope's concerns and James's, but the treatment is disappointing. John H. Hagan does a beautifully sensitive analysis in "*The Duke's Children*: Trollope's Psychological Masterpiece" (*NCF*, 1958), which I mention because it was inadvertently omitted from the Stevenson *Guide*.

The work of Ludwig Borinski on Trollope adds up to something almost of book size, and—to my mind—of book importance ("Trollopes Barsetshire Novels" and "Trollopes Palliser Novels," *NS*, 1962 and 1963; "Anthony Trollope: *Phineas Finn, The Irish Member*," *Der englische Roman im 19. Jahrhundert: Interpretationen*, ed. Paul Goetsch et al., 1973). The art of the Palliser novels, he explains, does not differ essentially from the art of the earlier novels: the novelist has already shown himself writing as intimate witness of and participant in English society, classical in his style and moral purpose, preeminent among Victorians in conversation (*Repartee, Salondialog*), and deeply aware of the questionable moral phenomena that are still our concerns now. Borinski's foreign perspective presents Trollope's Englishness in particularly sharp relief: his "characters" are in a line that goes from Chaucer's down to Low's Colonel Blimp; the wit encounters belong to the tradition of Shakespeare and Jane Austen; and English faction and party work by the same processes as cricket and rugby. Trollope is the master of the elements of maneuvering and of *Protokol* in private life as well as in political life. And, as in Lady Laura's conflict between love and honor, Trollope goes further than the comic. You, says Violet to Laura, will be in "real *tragedy*. I shall never go beyond genteel comedy." Phineas, though outwardly rather colorless, is highly developed psychologically, even to the unmasking of his half-known motives and self-deceptions. Trollope's great scenes anticipate James and have never been excelled. Borinski is particularly valuable for setting the Palliser novels in a wide perspective: this series that captures the political life of a nation in its prime is unique in world literature. Chiltern typifies Arnold's "Barbarians": such disaffected English sons and heirs, to be seen all about Europe at the time, suggest the failure of the system of primogeniture in somewhat Arnoldian terms. Students of Trollope will have much to do to sound the many suggestive ideas Borinski takes up: connections with Bagehot's classic *English Constitution* with Dilke's *Greater Britain*, with the American Civil War, with Canadian Federation, with the Arnoldian approach to the Irish Question.

The BBC Television "The Pallisers" increased general interest in Trollope and elicited considerable ephemera, some of it good—such as a *Radio Times* Special issue on "The Pallisers" (1974), which has plenty of stills, a guide, some commentary, and background material, such as an article on "garrotting," with pictures of the implements and incidents, which help to illustrate *Phineas Finn*. For the quality of the television adaptation by Simon Raven, the most authoritative assessment would seem to be Shirley Letwin's "Trollope, the Pallisers and the Way We View Now" (*TLS*, 5 July 1974), and those who have missed the show may take comfort. Letwin finds that the adaptation betrays Trollope and imposes the clichés of contemporary liberal thought. Phineas Finn, for instance, as the liberal hero "comes from the 'wrong' class and therefore does the right things—fornicates and agitates." This article is more than a review; it is an essay that makes Raven's misreading the occasion of fresh critical definition, with a fine sense of Trollope's place in history and in literary tradition. The unfortunate Simon Raven himself writes in understandable distress about the problems of adapting the novels to television ("The Writing of 'The Pallisers,'" *Listener*, 1974). One may note a French view, René Elvin's "Anthony Trollope à la BBC TV" (*NRDM*, 1974), useful because Elvin mediates the "intarissable" Trollope to the outsider. Among the ephemera are some short, bright remarks about Trollope, Dickens, and Disraeli a parliamentary novelists by Benny Green in "Politicians in Print," "Trollope at Westminster," and "Goodbye to the Hustings" (*Spectator*, 1973–74)

The Way We Live Now

Of novels outside the series, *The Way We Live Now* may be the most read and admired. Sabine Nathan takes it as Trollope's recognition that the old bourgeois way is outworn and that the new finance is taking over ("Anthony Trollope's Perception of the Way We Live Now," *ZAA*, 1962) Tony Tanner sees Melmotte as a modern Alchemist, around whom all the vast crowd of the novel revolve, clashing, getting in one another's way abandoning those who need them, cheating at cards or the stock market ("Trollope's *The Way We Live Now*: Its Modern Significance," *CQ*, 1968) Trollope does not go so far "inward" as George Eliot or Henry James but excels at the "panorama of isolated figures," the loneliness in the crowd. P D. Edwards explores, through working with the manuscript plan for the novel, how "Trollope Changes His Mind: The Death of Melmotte in *The Way We Live Now*" (*NCF*, 1963). Trollope originally planned to have him tried for forgery but decided on the quicker death of suicide, at a moment well chosen to preserve effective ambiguity. Roger L. Slakey proposes as one reason for the change of mind that Trollope had just "done" several trials, but he also suggests a thematic reason for the change ("Melmotte's Death: A Prism of Meaning in *The Way We Live Now*," *ELH*, 1967). The theme, he proposes, is a disjunction between words and meaning. "Anyone who traffics in words" with less than honesty comes to nothing. Lady Carbury is not quite honest in her word mongering, but love for her son saves her. Melmotte, however, is left speechless in Parliament, and it is therefore seemly for him to commit suicide soon after. He is "literally Melmotte, a *nal mot*." The argument should not be judged altogether by this bad French or the misuse of "literally"; it has some cogency. Bert G. Hornback in "Anthony Trollope and the Calendar of 1872: The Chronology of *The Way We Live Now*" (*N&Q*, 1963) claims that Trollope writing in 1873 did indeed use the 1872 calendar. The editor of *Notes and Queries* notes some discrepancies, and later P. D. Edwards finds a manuscript in the Bodleian that shows that Trollope used several irreconcilable chronologies ("The Chronology of *The Way We Live Now*," *N&Q*, 1969).

Douglas Hewitt considers the novel at some length in *The Approach to Fiction: Good and Bad Readings of Novels* (1972). *The Way We Live Now* is his test case for the realistic novel, *Little Dorrit* for the symbolic, and *Crotchet Castle* for the novel of ideas, all sharing a concern with the Condition-of-England Question. The realistic mode is as much a convention as the others; with Trollope, the narrator and implied reader constitute a "partnership in honest mediocrity." The narrator is "a man of decent, worthy, conventional but limited standards who is obliged by his honesty and openmindedness to recount events which do not altogether tally with his expectations." Hewitt is somewhat puzzled about whether Trollope knew what he was doing, and he confesses too often to surprise. Another comparative study, on Trollope and Meredith this time, is offered by Daniel Becquemont: "Politics in Literature, 1874–1875: *The Way We Live Now* and *Beauchamp's Career*" (*Politics in Literature in the Nineteenth Century*, ed. Pierre Coustillas). The essay is good in conception but thin in substance.

In "The Way Things Were: The Hundredth Anniversary of a Classic: Anthony Trollope's *The Way We Live Now*" (*HM*, 1975), Robert Lee Wolff continues the tradition of the graceful literary appreciation of Trollope, but scholars must not be misled by the readableness. For Wolff notes the "new breed" of Trollope criticism and uses it, and he brings the insight of a historian to nineteenth-century fiction. He adds to our knowledge of the novel's historical background, correlates it to the contemporary work of Zola and Mark Twain (*La Curée* and *The Gilded Age*), corrects some persistent misreadings (such as the alleged anti-Semitism), and dismisses all cavils about its greatness. The article reproduces the original "parts" cover design and some illustrations.

Other Novels

Avrom Fleishman in *The English Historical Novel: Walter Scott t*
Virginia Woolf (1971) takes notice of the early and weak *La Vendée*. It is
he says, "disfigured by a crude hostility to the Revolution—probably the
result of trying too hard to appeal to the prejudices of the British reading
public." I think, however, that the novel does reflect Trollope's own views
His parents knew Lafayette. And, bad as the novel is, he does show some
understanding for the architects of the Revolution.

J. C. Maxwell in "Cockshut on *Dr. Wortle's School*" (*NCF*, 1958) say
that Trollope is not the rigorist Cockshut makes him out to be but that he
weighs mitigating circumstances, in this case of bigamy.

William Cadbury writes on "The Uses of the Village: Form and Them
in Trollope's *The Vicar of Bullhampton*" (*NCF*, 1963). His categories o
"shape," "form," and "theme" do not seem very helpful, but the essay i
useful for exploratory speculation. Cadbury calls this Trollope's "most reli
gious novel" for the way in which Frank Fenwick exercises Christian charity

Robert M. Polhemus notes the Dostoevskian elements of self-destruction
in "*Cousin Henry*: Trollope's Note from Underground" (*NCF*, 1966). The
point is well taken; it is another example of that "cross-grainedness of men."
Ruth apRoberts believes, however, that she has found the donnée of th
book in Cicero's *De Officiis* ("*Cousin Henry*: Trollope's Note from An
tiquity," *NCF*, 1969) and that the main point of the book is a Ciceronia
moral.

Clement Greenberg's essay "A Victorian Novel," on *The American Sena*
tor, first published in 1944, has been reprinted in *Art and Culture: Critica*
Essays (1961). Edgar F. Harden and Ruth apRoberts ("The Alien Voice
Trollope's Western Senator," *TSLL*, 1966; "Trollope's One World," *SAQ*
1969) both see the novel in the tradition of social criticism by means of th
foreign observer. Hence the Senator, who figures little in the plot, is impor
tant enough for the title of a novel about English society. Harden an
apRoberts should take comfort from the fact that they arrived in thei
different ways at a similar conclusion. Lawrence Twentyman, of this nove
became rather famous. Anthony Wagner discovered a real Lawrenc
Twentyman of Walthamstow (*TLS*, 29 Dec. 1966). Neil Little wrote to sa
that there is another character by the same name in *Ayala's Angel* (*TLS*,
Feb. 1967), and Ursula Bridge wrote to say that it is the same character. A
most of us know, he married Mary Masters' horsey younger sister Kate, an
it worked out very well (*TLS*, 2 Mar. 1967).

Mr. Scarborough's Family, though crying out for critical notice, receive
only a correction of a misprint in the text, from Morchard Bishop: the boo
that Mountjoy takes from the shelf is not Wittier's *Hallelujah* but Wither
(*TLS*, 21 Nov. 1968). George H. Healey supports Morchard Bishop (*TLS*,
May 1969).

David Skilton takes a look at Trollope's science fiction in "*The Fixe*
Period: Anthony Trollope's Novel of 1980" (*SLitI*, 1973). He classifies it a

one of Trollope's studies of idée fixe, except that this time the monomaniac is the narrator. He notes a relationship with Bulwer's *The Coming Race* and compares it at various points with its source, the Jacobean play *The Old Law*. It is good to have this odd and interesting book back in the light and to have Skilton note the conflict—in the words of the old play—as between conscience and the law.

The canny student will have observed in all the foregoing a striking discrepancy: for a novelist now so authoritatively acclaimed, so varied, and so productive on such a consistently high level, remarkably few novels have received critical attention. There is indeed a sort of natural limit to Trollope scholars: not many will have read all the novels. Well—let them read! Let that be a requisite to discourse on the subject. It is hardly painful (pace Marvin Mudrick) to appropriate the ever widening riches of this humane world of Anthony Trollope.

Lines of investigation open invitingly all around. Trollope's studies of Latin classics and their influence have been barely broached. His extensive reading and annotation of Elizabethan and Jacobean drama will assuredly cast new light on the novels. Lawyers read him lovingly and study his cases but have left it to the critic to consider how his philosophy of law is related to his art. Literate politicians seem to be devoted to him, and thereby hangs a—dissertation, at least. The interesting ethics of business may be studied in such novels as *The Three Clerks* and *The Way We Live Now*. Where does Trollope stand in relation to Balzac and the roman-fleuve? What other Continental influences and analogues are there? How do his mother's novels contribute to his own? Does he contribute to the art of P. G. Wodehouse? Why is it that so many Jane Austen scholars are drawn to Trollope, and what precisely is the relationship? What is his relationship to Howells? The striking change in James's criticism of Trollope needs to be traced with care, and the possible debts James owes him. Frank O'Connor's perspicacious Trollope chapter in his *The Mirror in the Roadway* (1956) needs to be meditated on and absorbed. That psychological streaming Snow comments on needs exploration. The casuist theory of apRoberts needs testing. The structures of the novels, the contrapuntal techniques that Gordon Ray speaks of, demand investigation. Publishers need to be persuaded to bring out the rare novels, in good editions. Trollope's illustrators could make a pretty book, with illustrations. And how is it, after all, that Trollope keeps our attention even when he's told us how it's going to turn out? Phenomenologists, welcome! How does it all work?

Trollope rode hard, hunted, lived, read, and wrote hard, a great mass of human energy, beside whom, Leon Edel has said, even Hemingway looks anemic (review of Pope Hennessy's *Trollope* in *SR*, 1972). The oeuvre is big, varied, rich, and full of rewards for the scholar.

THE BRONTËS

❀

Herbert J. Rosengarten

Writings about the Brontës in the period covered by Mildred G. Christian's survey in the Stevenson *Guide* were heavily weighted toward biographical concerns; as she shows clearly, criticism of the novels often took second place to the theories of amateur psychologists or to debates about such matters as the authorship of *Wuthering Heights*. More recently, Brontë studies have been dominated by professional academics—the number of American doctoral dissertations on the Brontës has trebled since 1964—and the result has been a generally healthy swing toward a consideration of the works themselves, with particular emphasis on structure and language. In his critical study of Charlotte Brontë's novels (noted below), Robert Bernard Martin set the tone for much subsequent discussion by rejecting "the Purple Heather School of Criticism and Biography" in favor of greater concentration upon themes and techniques. The recognition that linguistic study can make a significant contribution to literary criticism has produced some important work on Charlotte's use of language and drawn attention to the innovative aspects of her style. At the same time, a greater effort has been made to see the Brontës in relation to their contemporaries, and the current interest in feminism has led to a reassessment of their significance in the history of the women's movement in the nineteenth century. Their reading, too, has been combed for fresh clues concerning the influences on their thought and writing; and a number of recent studies that set their work in a broad social and cultural perspective are valuable reminders that, however isolated they might have been physically, the Brontës were certainly not cut off from the intellectual currents of their age.

Bibliography and Manuscripts

The difficulties facing the student of the Brontës, including the paucity of available aids to manuscript research, are summarized by Mildred G. Chris ian in the Stevenson *Guide* (pp. 215–19), and the situation has changed little since her account. There is still no complete bibliography of the Brontës' writings, an omission made glaringly obvious by the unrevised reprint in 1965 of T. J. Wise's *A Bibliography of the Writings in Prose and Verse of the Members of the Brontë Family* (first published in 1917). That this should still be considered useful is a pointed commentary on the deficiencies of Brontë scholarship. The chaos created by Wise's fragmentation and dispersion of the manuscripts has not been remedied; a reviewer of the Wise reprint comments gloomily on the publisher's failure to provide "what is badly needed, an appendix documenting the Shorter-Wise acquisition and exploitation of the cache of Brontë manuscripts deriving from the Nicholls family" ("More Wise Reprints," *TLS*, 27 Jan. 1966). There is a brief general account of that exploitation in the introduction to Mildred G. Christian's "A Census of Brontë Manuscripts in the United States" (*The Trollopian* [now *NCF*], 1947–48); but her discussion is more guarded than that of T. J. Winnifrith, who raises the possibility that Wise's dishonesty may even have extended to forgery; though having voiced his suspicions, Winnifrith sensibly does not press the case (*The Brontës and Their Background: Romance and Reality*, 1973). Further evidence (if it were needed) of the editorial malpractice of Wise and Shorter is provided in the letters that their collaborator C. W. Hatfield wrote to T. Davidson Cook between 1925 and 1928 (recently acquired by the University of British Columbia); Hatfield speaks bitterly of the sacrilegious treatment of the manuscripts and of the poor transcriptions made by Wise and Shorter, upon which he often had to depend.

Mildred G. Christian's "Census" is still an indispensable guide to American manuscript collections, and she provides a general account of the main British collections in "A Guide to Research Materials on the Major Victorians (Part II): The Brontës" (*VN*, 1958). A few details may be added here. The Robert H. Taylor Collection is now housed at Princeton; it includes the manuscript of "John Henry" (referred to in the "Census" as *The Moores*), from which excerpts are provided by Joseph R. Geer in "An Unpublished Manuscript by Charlotte Brontë" (*BST*, 1966). The manuscript of Charlotte's juvenile tales "The Secret" and "Lily Hart," untraceable when Christian's "Census" was prepared, was discovered among the papers of the Symington family (see the London *Times*, 12 Sept. 1973) and is now held by the University of Missouri at Columbia. Full details of the George Smith Memorial Bequest to the British Museum (including the autograph fair copies of *Jane Eyre, Shirley*, and *Villette*) are printed in *The British Museum Catalogue of Additions to the Manuscripts 1931–1935* (1967).

The Brontë Society continues to publish details of its accessions, often with accompanying text and photographs, in the annual issue of its *Transactions* (*BST*). Of particular interest is the Society's recent acquisition of materials presented by a descendant of George Smith; in addition to over a hundred letters (some unpublished), the gift includes the rejected preface to *Shirley*, "A Word to the Quarterly," the text of which is given in full in *BST* (1975) and in the forthcoming Clarendon edition of the novel. A number of Charlotte's letters to George Smith and his mother were used by Mrs. Humphry Ward when she was preparing her introductions to the Haworth Edition of the Brontë novels (1899–1900); typescript copies of over fifty such letters are included among Mrs. Ward's papers at Columbia University.

Bibliographies of printed materials include the useful survey of primary and secondary works in the *NCBEL* volume for 1800–1900 (1969) and the more selective listings by Ian Watt in his compilation *The British Novel: Scott through Hardy* (1973). Miriam Allott's treatment of "The Brontës" in *The English Novel: Select Bibliographical Guides*, ed. A. E. Dyson (1974), though overlapping Mildred G. Christian's survey in the Stevenson *Guide*, is different in emphasis, examining fewer critical works but in greater detail. Allott gives pride of place to studies of *Wuthering Heights*, especially the seminal interpretation by Lord David Cecil; Charlotte's work is given less attention here because critical studies of her novels are fewer and (in Allott's view) less interesting, "largely because Charlotte, although capable of a comparable intensity of feeling, possesses a less arrestingly original, and therefore intellectually less stimulating, quality of mind and vision."

Since 1970, B. Gilbert Cross has supplied an annual Brontë checklist for *Brontë Society Transactions*, with annotations of critical works. The Brontë Society has also printed an *Analytical Index of the Contents of the Brontë Society Transactions 1895–1967*, compiled by the Society's archivist Amy G. Foster (1968). Individual author bibliographies include Janet M. Barclay's *Emily Brontë Criticism, 1900–1968: An Annotated Check List* (1974), which has almost six hundred items and a brief introduction sketching the major critical trends, and David M. Byers' "An Annotated Bibliography of the Criticism on Emily Brontë's *Wuthering Heights*, 1847–1947" (Diss. Univ. of Minnesota 1973). Anne Passel's "Charlotte Brontë: A Bibliography of the Criticism of Her Novels" (*BB*, 1969, 1970) is helpfully divided into sections on primary sources, criticism, biography, bibliography, and related materials. Among critical books with useful bibliographical materials are John Hewish's *Emily Brontë: A Critical and Biographical Study* (1969), which includes a list of manuscripts and their locations as well as a lengthy list of printed works; and Charles Burkhart's *Charlotte Brontë: A Psychosexual Study of Her Novels* (1973), which has a sound and partially annotated list of modern critical studies.

Editions and Letters

Under the general editorship of Ian Jack, the Clarendon editions of the Brontë novels have begun to make their appearance. The first to be published was *Jane Eyre*, edited by Jane Jack and Margaret Smith (1969; rpt with corrections, 1975). This volume established the pattern to be followed in the rest: a handsomely printed text with significant textual variants at the foot of each page; an introductory account of the novel's composition and publication; a descriptive bibliography of the principal editions; full explanatory notes, and appendixes on background materials. Because the editors of the Clarendon *Jane Eyre* chose to follow the text of the first edition, they came under fire from Bruce Harkness in a review article (*NCF*, 1970); Harkness maintains that the manuscript should have been used as copy-text. He is answered by Ian Jack and Margaret Smith ("The Clarendon *Jane Eyre*: A Rejoinder," *NCF*, 1971), who point out that Charlotte Brontë herself corrected the proofs and that she expressed a preference for the mode of punctuation adopted by the publisher. The Clarendon text is also used in the Oxford English Novels edition of *Jane Eyre*, edited by Margaret Smith (1973); though the textual apparatus of the earlier volume is here omitted, the editor provides an excellent note on the text, which lucidly summarizes the important features of the manuscript. The next volumes in the Clarendon series are *Wuthering Heights*, edited by Hilda Marsden and Ian Jack (1976), and *Shirley*, edited by Margaret Smith and Herbert Rosengarten, to be published shortly.

Good working editions of *Jane Eyre* have been published by Norton and Penguin. The Norton Critical Edition, edited by Richard J. Dunn (1971), acknowledges the value of the Clarendon *Jane Eyre* but follows general practice in choosing the text of the third edition (1848). Appended materials include relevant extracts from Charlotte's letters and the juvenilia and a selection of contemporary and modern critiques. The Penguin *Jane Eyre*, edited by Q. D. Leavis (1966), has a sound introduction, stressing the originality of Charlotte's techniques and the importance of her work as a shaping influence on subsequent developments in the novel. Leavis' note on the text (which is that of the third edition) may raise some eyebrows by its observation that "There is no manuscript of *Jane Eyre*, although there is a holograph in the British Museum."

Shirley is soundly edited for Penguin by Andrew and Judith Hook (1974), who provide sensible explanatory notes and a perceptive introduction commenting on the value of the novel's historical insights. The text is that of the novel's second edition, published in 1852, which includes some changes and corrections made by Charlotte. (The editors of the forthcoming Clarendon *Shirley* have chosen to base their text on the first edition, 1849, incorporating those changes in the second that are most clearly the author's.) The Houghton Mifflin edition of *Villette*, edited by Geoffrey Tillotson and Donald Hawes (1971), follows the text of the first edition (1853) but silently emends some of the irregularities in accidentals. Tillotson's introduction stresses the poetic qualities of Charlotte Brontë's style. The Pan Books edition of *Villette*, edited by Gilbert Phelps (1973), has the advantage of cheapness, but its notes are rather elementary.

Students of *Wuthering Heights* have been well served by a number of recent editions. Thomas C. Moser's *Wuthering Heights: Text, Sources, Criticism* (1962), intended primarily for the undergraduate reader, includes a broad selection of Emily Brontë's poems, as does the Pan Books edition, with an introduction by Elizabeth Jennings and notes by Phyllis Bentley (1967). The Norton Critical Edition of *Wuthering Heights* (1963; rev. 1972) is edited by William M. Sale, Jr., who provides a useful textual commentary outlining the difficulties facing a modern editor. The selection of critical essays in the revised edition includes extracts from Q. D. Leavis' "A Fresh Approach to *Wuthering Heights*" (noted below) and a summary by the editor of those aspects of the Gondal story that may be relevant to a study of the novel's origins. David Daiches has edited the Penguin *Wuthering Heights* (1965) with a helpful critical introduction and brief explanatory notes. Moser, Sale, and Daiches follow the text of the first edition of 1847, in preference to the 1850 text revised by Charlotte Brontë, but they emend some textual irregularities and details of punctuation. Frederick T. Flahiff goes further than this: in his edition for Macmillan's College Classics in English series (1968), he boldly reproduces Newby's original text with "even its most obvious misprints" and inconsistencies of punctuation, as "a gesture towards rehabilitating the novel as it was originally written." In an appendix Flahiff excerpts a passage from the 1850 edition to demonstrate the extensive changes Charlotte made in punctuation and paragraphing. An important contribution to the textual study of *Wuthering Heights* is Ian Jack's exposition of the peculiarities of Newby's text, given in some detail in the introduction to the Clarendon edition (1976). Rejecting the argument that eccentricities of punctuation might conceivably be the author's and should therefore be retained, the editors have sensibly chosen to follow Newby in all essentials, while correcting obvious errors in the accidentals. Selected textual variants from the second edition are listed in an appendix; other appended materials include essays on Gondal and on the novel's chronology by I.-S. Ewbank and an account of Emily Brontë's use of dialect by K. M. Petyt.

Though Anne Brontë has not yet caught the attention of textual editors, her novels have enjoyed a modest revival. Fielden Hughes provides a short biographical preface to the Cassell First Novel Library edition of *Agnes Grey*, edited by Herbert Van Thal (1966); and in 1969, prompted by a BBC television dramatization, Panther Books issued an edition of *The Tenant of Wildfell Hall*, with an introduction by Phyllis Bentley, who praises Anne's depiction of gradual change in the characters of Markham and Huntingdon. Students of the latter novel should be aware that most British editions of the work from 1854 onward lack the novel's opening section, as well as the original chapter headings; the omissions are detailed by G. D. Hargreaves in "Incomplete Texts of *The Tenant of Wildfell Hall*" (*BST*, 1972). Even the 1974 reprint of the World's Classics edition, which for the first time includes the Author's Preface to the Second Edition, suffers from these omissions.

Finally, there are the Folio Society editions of all seven Brontë novels (1964–70) with brief and uneven introductions by "J. H." Though of little critical interest, the volumes are well printed and handsomely illustrated.

Students of the Brontë correspondence must still rely on the works listed in the Stevenson *Guide* (p. 223), chiefly the four volumes in the Shakespeare Head Brontë, edited by T. J. Wise and J. A. Symington (1932), though the deficiencies of that edition are well known to anyone who has compared the printed texts with their manuscript originals. Further doubt is cast on the reliability of the Shakespeare Head versions by T. J. Winnifrith's study of the "Needham copies" (transcriptions of Charlotte's letters made by Ellen Nussey) in "Charlotte Brontë's Letters to Ellen Nussey" (*DUJ*, 1970). Joan Stevens' "Woozles in Brontëland: A Cautionary Tale" (*SB*, 1971) reveals significant errors in the printed version of Charlotte's long letter to Mary Taylor in September 1848. A new edition of the letters, prepared by Mildred G. Christian, is approaching completion, and this should clear up much of the confusion. Christian is also preparing for publication a study of the "Birstall letters," a correspondence recording the controversy surrounding the publication and subsequent disposition of Brontë letters once belonging to Ellen Nussey. A lengthy discussion concerning these letters and their presumed contents occupied the columns of *TLS* between January and March 1970.

Of undoubted interest to scholars is the discovery of three letters in the Coleridge collection at the University of Texas, which are printed with a commentary by Fran Carlock Stephens in "Hartley Coleridge and the Brontës" (*TLS*, 14 May 1970). They include the draft of a letter from Hartley Coleridge to Branwell, praising the latter's translation of Horace's *Odes*, and a letter of Charlotte's to Hartley Coleridge formerly thought to have been sent to Wordsworth (No. 100 in the Shakespeare Head edition of the letters).

Juvenilia

Fannie E. Ratchford's pioneer work on the Brontës' early writings (see the Stevenson *Guide*, pp. 220, 232) has been supplemented, and to some extent corrected, by Winifred Gérin's edition of *Five Novelettes* by Charlotte Brontë (1971). The volume contains transcriptions of tales composed between 1836 and 1839—"Passing Events," "Julia," "Mina Laury," "Captain Henry Hastings," and "Caroline Vernon"—taken from the manuscripts in various American collections. In her general introduction, the editor notes the transition evident in these stories "from writing as an addiction to creative writing impelled by an awakened critical faculty." Gérin's text follows the originals much more faithfully than does Ratchford and DeVane's *Legends of Angria* (1933; rpt. 1973); but her decision to emend Charlotte's erratic punctuation in some places, on the grounds that the reader's enjoyment might otherwise be impaired, may cause more problems than it solves. Also questionable is the unacknowledged omission of manuscript deletions and insertions. A transcription of an excerpt from "Julia" appears in the appendix to Valentine Cunningham's study *Everywhere*

Spoken Against: Dissent in the Victorian Novel (1975); his version retains all the peculiarities of the original, including changes of wording.

The Search after Hapiness: A Tale, first printed by Shorter and Hatfield in *The Twelve Adventurers and Other Stories* (1925), has been newly edited for Harvill Press with an introduction by T. A. J. Burnett (1969). Prior to book publication, the text of this edition appeared in the *Daily Telegraph Magazine* (7 Nov. 1969), and prompted a mild controversy between Burnett and L. R. Chambers in *TLS* (22 Jan., 5 Feb., 5 Mar. 1970). Judith Chernaik gives a full transcription of "An Interesting Passage in the Lives of Some Eminent Men of the Present Time," written by Charlotte in 1830, in "An Unpublished Tale by Charlotte Brontë" (*TLS,* 23 Nov. 1973). In her introductory comment, Chernaik draws attention to the skill with which Charlotte uses the device of the tale within a tale.

The influence of the *Arabian Nights* and James Ridley's *Tales of the Genii* is discussed by Jane W. Stedman in "The Genesis of the Genii" (*BST,* 1965). Raymond and Hélène Bellour, after some rather disparaging remarks about earlier critical failures to deal adequately with the juvenilia, laboriously compare the different accounts by Charlotte and Branwell of Angria's beginnings ("Le Jeu des jeunes hommes: Introduction à l'analyse comparée des écrits de jeunesse de Charlotte et Branwell Brontë," *RE,* 1969). Margaret Blom offers a persuasive analysis of the "psychological puzzle" presented by Angria, tracing the gradual shift from physical to psychological violence in Charlotte's portrayal of the destructive power of sexual passion ("Apprenticeship in 'The World Below': Charlotte Brontë's *Juvenilia,*" *ESIC,* 1975). Blom gives a longer account of the juvenilia in her introductory study *Charlotte Brontë* in the Twayne English Authors Series (1977).

Biography

The reservations often expressed by academic critics concerning the literary relevance of biographical study have neither dispelled the romantic appeal of the Brontës' story nor discouraged enthusiasts from going over old ground. Charlotte Maurat's *The Brontës' Secret* (1967; trans. Margaret Meldrum, 1969) depends heavily on a small number of secondary sources and gives little attention to the adult writings. The "secret," of course, is the world of Angrian and Gondalan fantasy in which the Brontës were immersed for so long. Other works in which the Brontës' literary achievement is subordinated to the romance of their lives include N. Bryson Morrison's *Haworth Harvest: The Lives of the Brontës* (1969) and Maureen Peters' *An Enigma of Brontës* (1974). Of greater value to students are two pictorial biographies with well-chosen illustrations and informative commentaries: *The Brontës and Their World,* by Phyllis Bentley (1969), and *The Brontës,* by Brian Wilks (1974); both are good examples of popularizations that do not vulgarize their subject. Of some interest to the literary historian is the appearance in recent years of fictionalized biographies of the Brontës. Though most of these are intended for younger readers, they make good use of current scholarship. A reliable account combining respect for the facts with strong narrative interest is Phyllis Bentley's *The Young Brontës* (1960). In striking contrast, Jane Amster attempts to convey the fears and fantasies of the Brontë children in a "psycho-biographical novella," *Dream Keepers: The Young Brontës* (1973), a misleading mixture of fact and fiction that paints a bizarre picture of life in the parsonage. In *Girl with a Pen: Charlotte Brontë* (1964), Elisabeth Kyle permits herself greater latitude than would be acceptable in a formal biography; Elfrida Vipont's *Weaver of Dreams: The Girlhood of Charlotte Brontë* (1966) stays more closely to the facts without sacrificing narrative appeal. Margaret J. Miller's *Emily: The Story of Emily Brontë* (1969) manages to convey the pathos of the Brontës' lives without striking any notes of false sentiment.

Standing well above other works of biography is Winifred Gérin's *Charlotte Brontë: The Evolution of Genius* (1967; rpt. with corrections, 1968). The book has been justly charged with an unscholarly inattention to sources and documentation and with superficiality in its critical observations (see, for example, reviews by Barbara Hardy in *NCF*, 1968, and Jane Millgate in *VS*, 1968); nevertheless, its virtues outweigh its faults, and, in bringing together so much detailed information about the circumstances of Charlotte's life, it is a valuable supplement to Mrs. Gaskell's great biography. Gérin gives much consideration to the early influences on Charlotte's imagination, particularly the poems of Byron and the paintings of John Martin, and she presents a coherent account of Angria's growth and development. Also of great interest is her discussion of Charlotte's experiences in Brussels, and she provides much useful information on the Heger family and its background. Margot Peters' *Unquiet Soul: A Biography of Charlotte Brontë* (1975) puts more emphasis on Charlotte's attitudes toward the Woman Question and examines her work in the context of Victorian feminism; but otherwise Peters' book, though readable and informative, offers nothing new in the way of research or interpretation and sometimes presents a distorted picture by using the novels as biographical evidence.

Mrs. Gaskell's *The Life of Charlotte Brontë* (1857) remains the most important source of biographical information, despite its errors and omissions. It has been newly edited by Winifred Gérin for the Folio Society (1971) and by Alan Shelston for Penguin (1975). Gérin incorporates the text of the controversial first edition with the revised text of the third edition; Shelston follows the first edition throughout and gives the revised passages in an appendix and in the notes, which is perhaps less convenient but also less likely to cause confusion. In their respective introductions, both editors stress the effect on the work of Mrs. Gaskell's desire to present Charlotte in the most sympathetic light. Arthur Pollard's study "Mrs. Gaskell's *Life of Charlotte Brontë*" (*BJRL*, 1964–65) examines the biographer's problems in assembling and organizing her material and discusses the revisions forced upon her for the third edition. Pollard collaborated with J.

A. V. Chapple on *The Letters of Mrs. Gaskell* (1966), an invaluable edition, which provides vivid accounts of Mrs. Gaskell's meetings with Charlotte and her father, as well as of the composition and reception of the *Life*.

Also of great biographical interest is *Mary Taylor, Friend of Charlotte Brontë: Letters from New Zealand and Elsewhere,* edited with an introduction by Joan Stevens (1972), which includes some hitherto unpublished letters by Mary Taylor and gives much useful information about the Yorkshire families drawn on by Charlotte for some of her characters. A footnote on Charlotte's relationship with Ellen Nussey is offered by T. J. Winnifrith in "Charlotte Brontë's Calvinism" (*N&Q*, 1970), in which it is suggested that Ellen or her brother Henry may have been the source of Charlotte's early views on eternal damnation.

Impressions by contemporaries, though sometimes colored by the writer's own motives or distorted by the passage of time, are useful aids in reconstructing the circumstances of the Brontës' life in Haworth. One such account, first published anonymously in 1868, is reprinted with a commentary by Kathleen Tillotson in "A Day with Charlotte Brontë in 1850" (*BST*, 1971); the writer, John Stores Smith, was particularly struck by the power of Charlotte's gaze but noted the absence of any wit or brilliance in her conversation. Tillotson describes another brief encounter, one that had important literary consequences: the meeting in 1850 of Charlotte Brontë and Matthew Arnold (" 'Haworth Churchyard': The Making of Arnold's Elegy," *BST*, 1967). Arnold's celebrated condemnation of *Villette* is examined in the light of his own preoccupations in 1853, and Tillotson shows that his attitude was consistent with his rejection at that time of anything "morbid" in literature. But, despite his criticism, Arnold's poem is a sincere tribute by one who felt "essential sympathy with Charlotte Brontë's kind of imaginative creation."

Though there remain some blanks in our knowledge of Charlotte, her life has always been much more accessible to biographers than that of Emily, who left so few documentary clues and whose character remains as elusive as ever. John Hewish's *Emily Brontë: A Critical and Biographical Study* (1969) is to be commended for its judicious sifting of the available materials and its awareness of the problems they raise. Hewish avoids the dangers of Gondal ("The Gondal frontier is best crossed at mapped points, when they exist, and only when there is good reason to do so"); but he makes free use of the poetry as a reflection of Emily's feelings and ideas and also as a key to the understanding of *Wuthering Heights*. Given the paucity of other materials, this is a reasonable approach, though Hewish's assertion that "The Philosopher" is "an embryo or codified statement of what [*Wuthering Heights*] is about" seems something of an oversimplification. The emphasis in Hewish's book is on Emily's thought; readers who want a straightforward account of events may find more to satisfy them in Winifred Gérin's *Emily Brontë: A Biography* (1971). Gérin's intimate knowledge of the Brontë family and their Haworth environment enables her to give more substance to our rather hazy notions about Emily, but the lack of concrete evidence sometimes leads her into the kinds of speculation (about Branwell's influence on Emily, for example) that have always been a weakness in Brontë studies. Gérin's discussion of *Wuthering Heights* skirts literary interpretation, concentrating on sources and influences but throwing little new light on this tangled subject. In an appendix she helpfully provides the texts of Emily's French devoirs, some of which bear the corrections made by M. Heger. A good account of the strengths and weaknesses of Gérin's approach is provided by Robert Bernard Martin in his review of both biographies of Emily noted here (*VS*, 1972).

Biographical studies of other members of the Brontë family have understandably been few. A major contribution in this field is *A Man of Sorrow: The Life, Letters and Times of the Rev. Patrick Brontë, 1777–1861*, by John Lock and Canon W. T. Dixon (1965), an extremely full reconstruction of Patrick Brontë's life, making much use of his correspondence and providing the background missing from Annette Hopkins' biography (see the Stevenson *Guide*, p. 227). Although its value to scholars is limited by the surprising exclusion of footnotes, the tendency to treat traditions as established facts, and the rather novelistic style, this study humanizes the portrait of Patrick Brontë, correcting the persistent impression (deriving from Gaskell's *Life*) that he was selfish or tyrannical and emphasizing his modesty, piety, and courage. Lock and Dixon's review of his career in the Church is heavily drawn on by Valentine Cunningham in *Everywhere Spoken Against: Dissent in the Victorian Novel* (1975). Cunningham's account of the impact of Methodism on the Brontës moves from biography to criticism in order to show how Methodism served Charlotte and Emily as "a referent for passion" and provided them with a rhetoric of feeling. Cunningham also acknowledges a large debt to the work of G. Elsie Harrison (see the Stevenson *Guide*, p. 227), but his approach is more restrained than hers, and his discussion of Methodism is presented with a keener sense of its literary significance.

An interesting challenge to a well-established Brontë tradition comes from Eanne Oram, who defends the Brontës' aunt from the almost universally held view that she exerted a harsh Calvinist influence over the children in the parsonage ("Brief for Miss Branwell," *BST*, 1964). That tradition is upheld, however, by Catherine Curry in "Maria Brontë and the Brontës' Views of Death" (*DM*, 1972–73); Curry asserts that the conflict between Maria's Arminianism and Aunt Branwell's Calvinism created guilt and tension in the minds of Charlotte and Branwell. Such speculative pieces as this may have little or no scholarly significance; but their persistence is a tribute to the enduring power of the Brontë myth, and their value lies in generating fresh interest in the works themselves.

Criticism

Norman Sherry's unpretentious *Charlotte and Emily Brontë* (1969) is a good general introduction to the writers' lives and their works, aimed at the interested student rather than the scholar. Of a similar kind are two volumes in the Profiles in Literature series, W. H. Stevenson's *Emily and Anne Brontë* and Arthur Pollard's *Charlotte Brontë*, both published in 1968; the emphasis here is on an appreciation of the writers' works through a selection of extracts illustrating different aspects of style and structure. Winifred Gérin's two-part introductory survey *The Brontës* (1973, 1974) in the Writers and Their Work series includes a useful discussion of the juvenilia and their relation to the adult writings.

Criticism of the Brontë novels over the past decade has given greater prominence to their social and cultural contexts. In *Their Proper Sphere: A Study of the Brontë Sisters as Early-Victorian Female Novelists* (1966), Inga-Stina Ewbank examines the problems of female authorship in the first half of the nineteenth century and the degree to which the Brontës rebelled against convention. She shows how their concern for truth led them to offend against canons of good taste and propriety; though they were "dutiful Victorian daughters," they wrote "some of the most unwomanly novels of the Victorian period. Custodians of the standard, they yet also helped to undermine that standard." T. J. Winnifrith examines the critical reaction to the Brontës' outspokenness and their frank treatment of difficult subjects (*The Brontës and Their Background: Romance and Reality*, 1973) and finds a surprising degree of prudish hostility to their "coarseness." In its consideration of such matters as the reliability of texts, the differences between the Brontës' religious views, and the novels they are likely to have read, Winnifrith's book is useful as a reference work and as a starting point for further study. Winnifrith also considers the sisters' social attitudes, detecting "a strong strain of wishful thinking and romantic fantasy in the Brontës' writing about aristocrats" and an ambivalence in matters of class and snobbery.

A more theoretical approach to the question of class is taken by Terry Eagleton, who surveys the Brontë novels through an ideological lens in *Myths of Power: A Marxist Study of the Brontës* (1975). Eagleton is doubtless right in believing that sociology can offer new insights into literature; but some readers may find his emphasis on historical forces and class conflict too heavy-handed. He discerns an "inner ideological structure" in the Brontë novels that embodies a fictional version of the contemporary struggle between the industrial bourgeoisie and the landed gentry or aristocracy. Charlotte's novels are seen to attempt a reconciliation between these contending forces, whereas *Wuthering Heights* pursues a more rigorous dialectic, confronting "the tragic truth that the passion and society it presents are not fundamentally reconcilable." Eagleton's reading is suggestive, though suffering at times from the excesses and distortions of a doctrinaire approach.

W. A. Craik provides a more conventional literary assessment in *The Brontë Novels* (1968), in which the focus is wholly on theme, structure, and narrative technique. Craik stresses the originality of Charlotte's ideas, even where her materials are inadequate to her vision (as in *The Professor*); and Anne's novels are given detailed and sympathetic attention, earning praise for their uncompromising moral stance and their clarity of expression. In her account of *Wuthering Heights,* Craik makes the rather surprising assertion that, despite Heathcliff's violence, his actions "on inspection are no more violent than those of other characters, and possibly less cruel"; Craik considerably modifies this view, however, in a subsequent survey article on "The Brontës" in *The Victorians* (ed. Arthur Pollard, 1969), where Heathcliff is described simply as "the most brutal character" in the novel.

Other studies of the Brontës as a group include Winifred Gérin's article on "Byron's Influence on the Brontës" (*KSMB,* 1966), which distinguishes the pictorial, the dramatic, and the philosophic stages of the poet's influence. A revised and shortened version of the essay appears under the same title in *Essays by Divers Hands,* 1972. Gérin's discussion of "The Effects of Environment on the Brontë Writings" (*EDH,* 1970) includes some good insights but relies too much on sentimental evocations of the moors. A more detailed and scholarly study of the Brontës' physical environment and its impact on their work is given by Hilda Marsden in "The North of England in the Novels of the Brontës" (Diss. Univ. of London 1967). Peter Quennell's pleasantly readable but unoriginal essay on the Brontës in *Casanova in London and Other Essays* (1971) praises the skill with which Emily "marries the human and superhuman, and weaves fantastic excesses of feeling into the prosaic familiar pattern of everyday existence." Elizabeth Hardwick's chapter on the Brontës in *Seduction and Betrayal: Women in Literature* (1974) breaks no new ground in its survey of the hardships endured by three well-educated and penniless young women but gives a feeling account of their heroic attempt to find independence through their writing. A rather brief and general survey of feminist issues in the Brontës' work is provided by Hazel Mews in *Frail Vessels: Woman's Role in Women's Novels from Fanny Burney to George Eliot* (1969). Raymond Williams believes that Charlotte's strength lies in her ability to convey "the particular immediate experience," while Emily moves beyond the personal to "the identity of relationship out of which all life comes" (*The English Novel from Dickens to Lawrence,* 1970). A Jungian reading is described in Barbara Hannah's *Striving towards Wholeness* (1971), where the Brontës' novels are treated as psychic revelations, reflections of their struggles with the unconscious in the process of individuation rather than as works of literature. Lord David Cecil, offering "Fresh Thoughts on the Brontës" (*BST,* 1973), recants his previous criticism (in *Early Victorian Novelists,* 1934) that Charlotte's novels lack structural unity, now recognizing "a more fundamental coherence, the coherence of a continuous theme"; but he abides by his interpretation of *Wuthering Heights* as a religious novel dramatizing the eternal principles of storm and calm. Echoes of Cecil may be heard in Frederick Karl's useful chapter on "The Brontës: The Outsider as Protagonist" (*An Age of Fiction: The Nineteenth Century British Novel,* 1964), which treats *Wuthering Heights* as a dramatic poem and compares Emily Brontë's characters to Hardy's in their defiance of the universe. Karl's study of *Jane Eyre* notes its relationship to other apprenticeship novels, an issue also discussed by Harro H. Kühnelt in "Charlotte Brontë: *Jane Eyre*" (*Der englische Roman im 19. Jahrhundert: Interpretationen,* ed. Paul Goetsch, Heinz Kosok, and Kurt Otten, 1973).

Ancillary aids to criticism include Phyllis Whitehead's *The Brontës Came Here* (1963), which is in effect a guidebook identifying the places described or referred to in the novels. Ruth H. Blackburn's compilation *The Brontë Sisters: Selected Source Materials for College Research Papers* (1964) reproduces letters and documents of biographical interest, together with excerpts from contemporary reviews and reminiscences, and extracts relating to the Cowan Bridge controversy. Of limited value as a reference work is Glenda Leeming's *Who's Who in Jane Austen and the Brontës* (1974), a brief and superficial enumeration of the characters, both human and animal, in the printed works. Much more useful is F. B. Pinion's *A Brontë Companion: Literary Assessment, Background, and Reference* (1975), an attractively illustrated handbook that includes a survey of "People and Places in the Novels," a restrained account of the importance of Angria and Gondal, and an appendix on the literary allusions in Charlotte's novels.

Charlotte Brontë

Though the modern critical preference for *Wuthering Heights*, which Mildred G. Christian noted in the first *Guide,* has continued, the solidity and scope of Charlotte's achievement have won much praise from her recent critics. W. A. Craik, Robert Bernard Martin, and Earl A. Knies are among her most sympathetic readers, and all three are firm opponents of the biographical emphasis that used to pervade Brontë studies. Craik's treatment of Charlotte in *The Brontë Novels* is noted above. In *The Accents of Persuasion: Charlotte Brontë's Novels* (1966), Martin approaches the novels through theme and structure; their primary subject is always "the study of the adjustment between the reason and the passions." Torn herself between rational and nonrational impulses, Charlotte achieved her best work when she struck a balance between them, as in *Jane Eyre* or *Villette*; but *The Professor* and *Shirley* suffer from Charlotte's failure to reconcile the claims of imagination with her formal allegiance to realism and objectivity. Martin's coherent and thoughtful discussion, the first full-length study of Charlotte's novels, has influenced later criticism, such as John Halperin's interpretation of *Jane Eyre* in *Egoism and Self-Discovery in the Victorian Novel* (1974). Martin's own treatment of *Jane Eyre* includes restrained comparisons with the biblical and Miltonic treatments of the Samson story, but he rejects the psychological approach that would read in Rochester's fate a symbolic emasculation. (Such views are still popular, however; see, for example, Paula Sullivan's "Rochester Reconsidered: *Jane Eyre* in the Light of the Samson Story," *BST,* 1973).

A recurring criticism of Charlotte's work is that she was unable to distance herself sufficiently from her fictional creations: a view advanced, for example, by Henry James in the course of a friendly debate with Mrs.

Humphry Ward (see William S. Peterson, "Henry James on *Jane Eyre*," *TLS*, 30 July 1971). A different opinion is expressed by Earl A. Knies in *The Art of Charlotte Brontë* (1969); concentrating on Charlotte's handling of narrative point of view and her particular success with the personal narrator, Knies shows that, although she drew much from her own experience, Charlotte consciously reshaped that experience in her fiction. Knies's book incorporates his earlier studies on "The Artistry of Charlotte Brontë: A Reassessment" (*OUR*, 1965) and "The 'I' of *Jane Eyre*" (*CE*, 1966). His attempt to give shape to Charlotte's literary theories is not altogether convincing, since her comments about her craft are relatively few and insubstantial; but his account does give us a sense of the artist trying to impose order on experience. Jack C. Wills makes this the focus of his dissertation, "Charlotte Brontë's Literary Theories" (Univ. of Delaware 1966), and presents some of his findings more briefly in "The Shrine of Truth: An Approach to the Works of Charlotte Brontë" (*BST*, 1970). That Charlotte's formal notions of her art were unclear or inconsistent is suggested by the pull in her fiction between different modes, the realistic and the Gothic, the didactic and the sensational; in *The Homely Web of Truth: A Study of Charlotte Brontë's Novels* (1975) Lawrence Jay Dessner attributes these aesthetic and moral oppositions partly to the influence of her reading and partly to the unresolved conflict between her passionate nature and the claims of orthodox morality. Dessner examines the tension between the romantic and the realistic elements of her novels, concluding that "the nearer she came to realism the more potently did she reproduce the charms of Angria." Dessner perhaps overstates his case in the interests of paradox; but it is clear that Charlotte never succeeded in assimilating her romantic impulses into a form belonging to the tradition of antiromance, a point well made by George Levine in "Realism, or, In Praise of Lying: Some Nineteenth Century Novels" (*CE*, 1970).

In tune with the movement away from biographical interpretation, criticism has been increasingly concerned with the social or political implications of Charlotte's work. Taking an approach he was to develop more fully in *Myths of Power* (noted above), Terry Eagleton examines Charlotte's ambiguous attitude to power and concludes that her novels try to occupy "a middle-ground between reverence and rebellion, land and trade, gentry and bourgeoisie, the patiently deferential and the actively affirmative" ("Class, Power and Charlotte Brontë," *CritQ*, 1972). Despite the sociological overlay, this is not very different from the view presented in more conventional terms by Philip Momberger in "Self and World in the Works of Charlotte Brontë" (*ELH*, 1965): the Brontë hero seeks a middle way, "a pragmatic solution which will satisfy his need for security . . . while allowing him to retain the advantages of freedom and independent identity." Momberger surely strikes the truer note here; Charlotte was not blind to the social conflict of her day, but that conflict was meaningful to her only in relation to the individual's struggle for recognition and acceptance, so that the attempt to politicize her work tends to distort her aims and her achievement.

This is true even of discussions of the feminist aspects of her writing, where Charlotte's social views are more explicitly stated. Determined to present Charlotte Brontë as a guerrilla fighter in the war against male supremacy, Kate Millett offers an intelligent but perverse reading of *Villette*, in which Lucy is seen as merely using Paul to obtain her own freedom, "playing tame" until he liberates her from servitude (*Sexual Politics*, 1970). More balanced estimates of Charlotte's feminist views are provided by Françoise Basch in *Relative Creatures: Victorian Women in Society and the Novel* (trans. Anthony Rudolf, 1974) and Patricia Beer in *Reader, I Married Him: A Study of the Women Characters of Jane Austen, Charlotte Brontë, Elizabeth Gaskell and George Eliot* (1974). Both critics note the inconsistencies and contradictions in Charlotte's handling of the Woman Question; Basch attributes these in part to her emotional immaturity, while Patricia Beer believes that Charlotte was "too soft-centred to found any cause on justice and equity. For her, sentiment was more important than rights."

A lengthier treatment of the subject is provided by Harriet Björk in *The Language of Truth: Charlotte Brontë, the Woman Question, and the Novel* (1974). Björk's study is valuable for its survey of the social and literary contexts of Charlotte's ideas about the role of women and for its comments on the antiromantic element in her writing, but the author tends to list examples and to amass illustrative evidence in the manner of a thesis, with little regard to readability. An error-ridden account of the basic sexual motifs in Charlotte's novels is presented by Annette Schreiber in "The Myth in Charlotte Brontë" (*L&P*, 1968). More sensible is Margaret Blom's "Charlotte Brontë, Feminist *Manquée*" (*BuR*, 1973), a study of Charlotte's ambivalent attitudes toward the submissive roles women were expected to play in Victorian society, particularly in sexual relationships. F. A. C. Wilson interprets this ambivalence as a belief in the flexibility of sexual roles, reflected in her androgynous heroes and heroines; Charlotte "evolves an ideal of love and union by which both partners freely alternate between 'masculine,' or controlling, and 'feminine,' or responsive roles" ("The Primrose Wreath: The Heroes of the Brontë Novels," *NCF*, 1974). Wilson goes on to suggest that in *Wuthering Heights* Emily presents a modified pattern of the androgyne in the relationship between Hareton and Catherine.

Charles Burkhart's *Charlotte Brontë: A Psychosexual Study of Her Novels* (1973) charts some of the unconsciously autobiographical elements in Charlotte's work and would thus seem to revert to an older critical approach; but the title is misleading, for the book is not so much a psychological study as an account of themes and technique, at its best in a discussion of sun and moon imagery in *Villette*. That Charlotte was herself interested in psychological theories, especially phrenology, has long been known; and her application of contemporary notions on this subject is examined by Ian Jack in "Physiognomy, Phrenology and Characterisation in the Novels of Charlotte Brontë" (*BST*, 1970), which helpfully outlines the ideas of Lavater and Gall.

In an important study uniting linguistic analysis with literary interpretation, Margot Peters examines Charlotte's use of adverbs, syntactic inversions, and antithetical structures (*Charlotte Brontë: Style in the Novel*, 1973), showing how these stylistic devices give intensity and dramatic power to Charlotte's depiction of emotional conflict. Peters' attempt to relate such characteristics of language to Charlotte's own psychological state is of questionable validity; and some of her conclusions about punctuation are also rendered doubtful by her failure to compare printed text with manuscript, since the punctuation of the former is as much the work of Charlotte's publisher as of the author herself. Despite this, Peters' book is more systematic and thus more useful to the student of the Brontës than the comparative analyses by Karl Kroeber in *Styles in Fictional Structure: The Art of Jane Austen, Charlotte Brontë, George Eliot* (1971). Kroeber's study is exploratory and somewhat diffuse, with a daunting series of statistical tables; but there are some good observations concerning image patterns in *Jane Eyre* and *Villette*. Another study of Charlotte's use of language is Enid L. Duthie's *The Foreign Vision of Charlotte Brontë* (1975), which is in part an account of Charlotte's experiences in Brussels and her transformation of them into fiction. The biographical elements of the book, however, add little to the findings of Winifred Gérin; its chief value lies in its discussion of Charlotte's exposure to the great masters of French Romanticism and their impact on her style. Duthie argues persuasively that Charlotte developed the rhythm, expressiveness, and syntactic inversions that characterize her mature prose from her reading and writing of French under Heger's guidance. Heger's influence is also examined by Lawrence Jay Dessner in "Charlotte Brontë's 'Le Nid,' an Unpublished Manuscript" (*BST*, 1973) and in *The Homely Web of Truth* (noted above).

Among Charlotte's novels that have been studied individually, *Jane Eyre* continues to draw most critical attention, though not always of a complimentary kind. Sylvère Monod condemns Charlotte's errors and inconsistencies in her use of literary and biblical quotations and even accuses her of intellectual dishonesty ("L'Imprécision dans *Jane Eyre*," *EA*, 1964). Monod's charges are perhaps just, yet somehow seem irrelevant in any consideration of the novel's meaning or impact. In "Charlotte Brontë and the Thirty 'Readers' of *Jane Eyre*" (*Jane Eyre*, Norton Critical Edition, ed. R. J. Dunn, 1971), Monod also complains of Charlotte's bullying attitude toward her readers, whom she imagines as male and treats as "conventional, silly, cowardly, ignorant, and vain"—a characterization that Monod concludes (rather illogically) is drawn from the Brontë sisters' ignorance of men. Q. D. Leavis takes Charlotte to task for "the general confusion of dates, eras, fashions and facts in *Jane Eyre*," though allowing that the novel's power makes us ignore such anomalies ("Dating *Jane Eyre*," *TLS*, 27 May 1965).

A more serious criticism is voiced by Barbara Hardy in her discussion of "Dogmatic Form: Defoe, Charlotte Brontë, Thomas Hardy, and E. M. Forster" (*The Appropriate Form: An Essay on the Novel*, 1964). She detects an inconsistency in the moral pattern of *Jane Eyre*, caused by Charlotte

Brontë's failure to dramatize the growth of Jane's religious feeling while giving close attention to other aspects of her moral development. Jane's conduct seems to be predicated largely upon her inner resources; but at moments of crisis her actions are determined from without, by the workings of a Providence she accepts unquestioningly. Richard Benvenuto also identifies divergent and unharmonized impulses in Jane's moral nature, which he ascribes to Charlotte's own inner division ("The Child of Nature, the Child of Grace, and the Unresolved Conflict of *Jane Eyre*," ELH, 1972). Jane's motivation comes under critical scrutiny by Margaret Blom in "*Jane Eyre*: Mind as Law unto Itself" (*Criticism*, 1973); defending the *Quarterly*'s view of the novel as anti-Christian, Blom sees Jane as being driven by "ruthless egoism" and judges her appeals to Christian morality at moments of crisis to be merely expedient. The assumption underlying such readings, that Charlotte Brontë was inconsistent or even contradictory in her moral outlook as it is dramatized through Jane's experience, is challenged by Arnold Shapiro, who sees consistency in Charlotte's "call for openness and freedom between individuals" and in her protest "against the inhuman treatment of human beings" ("In Defense of *Jane Eyre*," SEL, 1968). Charlotte finds another defender in Jennifer Gribble, who attempts to refute the view that the novelist is guilty of subjective romanticism and an uncritical identification with her heroine, asserting instead that there is a distinction between Jane's imaginative apprehension of reality and the author's controlling insight ("Jane Eyre's Imagination," NCF, 1968). Ruth Yeazell, in "More True than Real: Jane Eyre's 'Mysterious Summons'" (*NCF*, 1974), answers charges that the novel suffers from melodramatic improbabilities, particularly in the final chapters; Yeazell maintains that "the outward pattern of the plot metaphorically enacts the inner drama of Jane's psyche."

Jane's internal conflicts, both conscious and unconscious, have long provided critics with a fruitful source of material. R. E. Hughes examines her struggles in Nietzschean terms in "*Jane Eyre*: The Unbaptized Dionysos" (*NCF*, 1964); defining Jane's conflicting states as Dionysian and Apollonian, Hughes sees the novel as involving "a pre-rational insight into human personality," its Christian elements merely overlaying an intuitive apprehension of deeper mythic patterns. The sexual element in Jane's unconscious is discussed by David Smith in "Incest Patterns in Two Victorian Novels; 1. Her Master's Voice: *Jane Eyre* and the Incest Taboo" (*L&P*, 1965). In this reading, Rochester becomes a father figure, and Bertha is "a perfect projection of the incestuous daughter's archetypal unconscious perception of the evil mother." Not all critics relegate Jane's sexual feelings to the unconscious level; in "Thematic Structure in *Jane Eyre*" (PLL, 1968) Dale Kramer rejects the notion that Jane possesses "inchoate and inexpressible psychosexual motivations" or that she desires to castrate her menfolk; in Kramer's view, she generally shows "an honest, self-aware acceptance of the physical side of life." Geoffrey Wagner, arguing that the novel is a feminist tract "of extraordinary psycho-sexual sophistication," describes it as "profoundly and healthily" sadomasochistic in its treatment of Jane's ambivalent desires and their fulfillment (*Five for Freedom: A Study of Feminism in Fiction*, 1972).

The novel's patterns of imagery and symbol continue to stimulate critical ingenuity. Barbara Hardy's introductory study of *Jane Eyre* in Blackwell's Notes on English Literature series (1964) includes a straightforward account of the novel's principal symbols. David Lodge examines Charlotte's use of elemental images, especially fire, as external correlatives of Jane's inner states that help to bind the literal and the visionary aspects of her experience (*Language of Fiction*, 1966). Donald Ericksen's "Imagery as Structure in *Jane Eyre*" (*VN*, 1966) focuses on the recurrent moon and arboreal images. In "Charlotte Brontë and Bewick's 'British Birds'" (*BST*, 1966) Jane W. Stedman examines the pervasive influence of Bewick's work on *Jane Eyre*; both the drawings and their accompanying text convey images of gloom, waste, and storm that provide Jane with suggestions for the pictures she shows to Rochester at Thornfield. The symbolism of Jane's three paintings has aroused particular interest. To Lawrence E. Moser, S.J., they not only reflect aspects of Jane's nature but reveal elements of "the jagged psychic life" of the author herself ("From Portrait to Person: A Note on the Surrealistic in *Jane Eyre*," *NCF*, 1965). Thomas Langford's "The Three Pictures in *Jane Eyre*" (*VN*, 1967) argues that the paintings are prophetic images of the major sections of Jane's experience, a view Langford repeats and extends in "Prophetic Imagination and the Unity of *Jane Eyre*" (*SNNTS*, 1974). A similar approach is taken by John Hagan in his lengthy study of the novel's themes of imprisonment and liberation as projected through imagery and structural patterns ("Enemies of Freedom in *Jane Eyre*," *Criticism*, 1971). Hagan treats the first and third pictures as "a groundplan of the latter two-thirds of the novel"; the second painting is somewhat unconvincingly set aside as belonging to a different context. In contrast, M. B. McLaughlin interprets all three as "imaginative representations of real and traumatic *past* experiences" ("Past or Future Mindscapes: Pictures in *Jane Eyre*," *VN*, 1972). Jane Millgate's "Narrative Distance in *Jane Eyre*: The Relevance of the Pictures" (*MLR*, 1968) is concerned with their significance as reflections of Jane's immaturity and emotional need at one stage of her development. The same author traces the symbolism of the journey and the quest in *Jane Eyre* and finds much of it drawn from *Pilgrim's Progress* ("Jane Eyre's Progress," *ES*, Anglo-American Supp., 1969).

Shirley has never aroused critical interest to the same extent as *Jane Eyre* or *Villette*, primarily because of its flaws in tone and structure and its depiction of Louis Moore, surely the dullest hero in the Brontë gallery. Earl A. Knies examines some of the theories accounting for the novel's weaknesses, rejecting the biographical approaches of Spens (*E&S*, 1929) and Tompkins (*BST*, 1961) and concluding that Charlotte's main error was in trying to write a typical Victorian novel ("Art, Death, and the Composition of *Shirley*," *VN*, 1965). Other critics, following the example of Jacob Korg (Stevenson *Guide*, p. 238), have attempted to establish the novel's unity. Arnold Shapiro in "Public Themes and Private Lives: Social Criticism in *Shirley*"

(*PLL*, 1968) maintains that the historical and the personal elements of the plot are connected by the theme of selfishness at every level of society. Anne W. Passel describes the novel's structure as contrapuntal, its various themes being interwoven ("The Three Voices in Charlotte Brontë's *Shirley*," *BST*, 1969).

Earlier studies of *Shirley*'s account of Luddism praised Charlotte's sense of history and her evocation of the period (see the article by Asa Briggs noted in the Stevenson *Guide*, pp. 238–39, or Herbert Heaton's "The Economic Background of *Shirley*," *BST*, 1932). A less favorable judgment is passed by the historian E. P. Thompson in *The Making of the English Working Class* (1963; rev. 1968), where *Shirley* is seen as "a true expression of the middle-class myth"; Thompson's view influences subsequent discussions of the novel's use of history by Terry Eagleton in *Myths of Power* (noted above) and Nicholas Rance in *The Historical Novel and Popular Politics in Nineteenth-Century England* (1975). "Charlotte Brontë's *Shirley* and the *Leeds Mercury*" by Herbert Rosengarten (*SEL*, 1976) examines the newspaper reports from which Charlotte took details for her historical setting. In a more general discussion of the novel's themes, A. Norman Jeffares focuses on Charlotte's treatment of the plight of single women ("*Shirley*—A Yorkshire Novel," *BST*, 1969). Background studies include Joan Stevens' "Sidelights on *Shirley*: Brontëana in New Zealand" (*BST*, 1969) and K. W. Ankenbrandt's "Charlotte Brontë's *Shirley* and John Leyden's 'The Cout of Keeldar' " (*VN*, 1968). Ivy Holgate's study "The Structure of *Shirley*" (*BST*, 1962) includes the dubious proposition that Charlotte had first intended to write about Chartism and contemporary industrial unrest; but there is little evidence to support this, and her account is challenged by Laura Grayson in "*Shirley*: Charlotte Brontë's Own Evidence" (*BST*, 1963).

Villette, which is now generally accepted as Charlotte Brontë's maturest work, derives its power largely from the gradual unfolding of Lucy Snowe's complex character. Much critical interest has centered on Charlotte's control of point of view and on the ambiguities of Lucy's perceptions. Martin and Knies are agreed that Lucy is a successful version of the "unreliable narrator"; but Thomas Moser, reviewing Martin's book, accuses Charlotte of failing to maintain consistent control over narrative point of view (*NCF*, 1967). The case for the book's unity and effectiveness is strengthened by E. D. H. Johnson's study of the thematic and structural uses of the ghostly nun as a device marking the stages of Lucy's growth toward self-knowledge (" 'Daring the Dread Glance': Charlotte Brontë's Treatment of the Supernatural in *Villette*," *NCF*, 1966). Charles Burkhart goes further, seeing the nun as the "operative device" in Lucy's psychological development, by means of which she attains fortitude and understanding ("The Nuns of *Villette*," *VN*, 1973). The image patterns reflecting the divisions in Lucy's nature are traced by Herbert R. Coursen, Jr., who draws comparisons with *King Lear* and *Moby Dick* ("Storm and Calm in *Villette*," *Discourse*, 1962). Russel M. Goldfarb attempts a Freudian study of Lucy's "repressed libidinal energies" in *Sexual Repression and Victorian Literature* (1970). A more restrained use of psychology marks Nina Auerbach's comparison of *Jane Eyre* and *Villette* in "Charlotte Brontë: The Two Countries" (*UTQ*, 1973), in which Charlotte is shown to progress from a heroine whose conflicts are externalized in terms of setting to one who is locked within her own divided nature, a movement "from mythopoeic romance to abnormal psychology." This process of internalizing the warring passions is seen by Andrew Hook as the means by which Charlotte Brontë could assimilate the world of romance into a realistic study of moral conflict ("Charlotte Brontë, the Imagination, and *Villette*," in *The Brontës: A Collection of Critical Essays*, ed. Ian Gregor, 1970); romance is here linked with delusion, and Lucy must learn that "there is no salvation to be found either in repression and self-denial or in visionary, romantic yearnings." The greater realism of this novel is also discussed by Robert A. Colby, in "*Villette*: Lucy Snowe and the Good Governess" (*Fiction with a Purpose: Major and Minor Nineteenth-Century Novels*, 1967). Colby regards *Villette* as "the culmination of Charlotte Brontë's campaign to free herself from Angria"; examining its treatment of contemporary ideas about society, religion, and education, he concludes that the novel "assimilates the social and intellectual history of its time to the burning consciousness of Lucy Snowe."

Although *The Professor* has received attention in comprehensive studies of Charlotte's work—in Martin's and Craik's, for example—it remains the least popular of the Brontë novels and has rarely been treated in a scholarly article. J. A. Falconer's "*The Professor* and *Villette*: A Study of Development" (*ES*, 1927) examines the parallels between the two novels; and M. M. Brammer's "The Manuscript of *The Professor*" (*RES*, 1960) is a valuable description of the manuscript alterations made by Charlotte and (after her death) by her husband, A. B. Nicholls. The crudities of *The Professor* are only too apparent; but the novel deserves further critical consideration, not only as a precursor of *Villette* but also as a reworking of some of the materials Charlotte had used in her juvenile tales. The novel has broader significance, too, in its relationship to later developments in psychological realism.

Emily Brontë

Recent criticism of *Wuthering Heights* has refined, though not substantially revised, such influential readings as those by Sanger, Cecil, and Van Ghent. The dividing point in critical debate lies between those who interpret the novel along "metaphysical" or mystical lines and those who find it rooted in social, moral, or psychological concerns. The most persuasive exponent of the metaphysical approach is J. Hillis Miller in *The Disappearance of God: Five Nineteenth-Century Writers* (1963). Miller stresses the transcendental qualities of Emily Brontë's vision, using her poems and the essays she wrote in Brussels to illuminate her portrayal in *Wuthering Heights* of the suffering and isolation attendant on the human condition. In

the love of Heathcliff and Catherine, Miller sees "a process of union, separation, and reunion on a higher level which appears often in writings in the
romantic tradition, and is like the dialectic of Hegel or like Novalis' vision
of human life and history." Though Miller sometimes works at a level of
abstraction rather remote from the gritty specifics of plot and setting, his
reading is coherent and articulate, and its influence has been extensive.
William H. Marshall acknowledges its effect upon his own somewhat
abstruse analysis of the ontology of *Wuthering Heights* in *The World of the
Victorian Novel* (1967). Echoes of Miller may also be heard in two articles
by Irving H. Buchen, "Emily Brontë and the Metaphysics of Childhood and
Love" (*NCF*, 1967) and "Metaphysical and Social Evolution in *Wuthering
Heights*" (*VN*, 1967). Miller and Buchen attach great importance to Emily's
philosophizing in her Brussels essay "Le Papillon," and conclusions similar
to theirs are drawn by Jo Anne A. Willson in " 'The Butterfly' and *Wuthering Heights*: A Mystic's Eschatology" (*VN*, 1968). Denis Donoghue recognizes the novel's realism of detail in treatment of time and place but
maintains that "there are forces in the novel which strain to be released
from empirical allegiance"; and he describes a transcendental pattern in
Emily's imagination similar to that perceived by Miller ("Emily Brontë:
On the Latitude of Interpretation," *The Interpretation of Narrative:
Theory and Practice,* ed. Morton W. Bloomfield, HES, 1970).

Much of the debate concerning the novel's mysticism focuses on the
bond between Heathcliff and Catherine, which Elizabeth Drew describes as
the novel's central mystery (*The Novel: A Modern Guide to Fifteen English Masterpieces*, 1963). The influence of David Cecil and Dorothy Van
Ghent is still evident in the work of critics like Charles I. Patterson, Jr., who
interprets the novel's treatment of love in terms of cosmic forces rather than
human emotion ("Empathy and the Daemonic in *Wuthering Heights*,"
*The English Novel in the Nineteenth Century: Essays on the Literary
Mediation of Human Values,* ed. George Goodin, 1972). Peter D. Grudin's
discussion of the supernatural element shuns mythic generalities in favor of
a careful reading of the text: his object is to demonstrate that the lovers are
reunited in an afterlife whose existence is objectified by means of structural
parallels and interlocking references ("*Wuthering Heights*: The Question
of Unquiet Slumbers," *SNNTS*, 1974). Wayne Burns, arguing against his
own "Panzaic" convictions, believes that the lovers transcend human sexuality and morality in an "immaculate passion" consummated in death ("On
Wuthering Heights," *RecL*, 1972; revised as "In Death They Were Not
Divided: The Moral Magnificence of Unmoral Passion in *Wuthering
Heights*," *HSL*, 1973); and Geoffrey Wagner in *Five for Freedom: A Study
of Feminism in Fiction* (1972) maintains that the novel breaks down the
antinomies of sex and presents a vision of life "beyond biology." In contrast, Robin Grove finds the cause of the lovers' tragedy in their inescapable
involvement in the sexual world; they seek a harmony that exists only in
childhood and that is shattered by the demands of sexual maturity
("*Wuthering Heights*," *CR*, 1965). Others argue for an accommodation

between the sexual and the spiritual; Francis Fike's "Bitter Herbs and Wholesome Medicines: Love as Theological Affirmation in *Wuthering Heights*" (*NCF*, 1968) identifies a movement from *agape* to *eros* and ultimately to a harmony embracing both through the love of Hareton and Cathy. Cecil W. Davies rejects attempts to excuse the conduct of Heathcliff and Catherine or to deny their sexuality but finds their love to be "the book's great positive" and sees in their total identification with each other an embodiment of Emily Brontë's apprehension of mystical experience ("A Reading of *Wuthering Heights*," *EIC*, 1969). Much recent criticism has moved away from mythic or transcendental interpretation to an assertion of the essential humanity of the novel's central experience, as in the reading by Philippa Moody in "The Challenge to Maturity in *Wuthering Heights*" (*CR*, 1962). F. H. Langman expresses impatience with approaches that ignore the moral issues of cruelty and violence and that dissolve the novel's outlines "in a universal solvent of mythopoeic criticism" (*EIC*, 1965); and John Hagan in "Control of Sympathy in *Wuthering Heights*" (*NCF*, 1967) dismisses the "metaphysical-supernaturalist" line in his argument that the cruelty displayed by Heathcliff and Catherine has human causes. The "gut" school of criticism is represented by John Doheny's vigorous assertion of the central characters' human sexuality in "From *PMLA* to *Wuthering Heights*" (*Paunch*, 1964); his attack on what he regards as the overintellectual approach of modern critics prompted a sometimes angry debate with Wade Thompson, William Empson, and Arthur Efron in *Paunch* for 1965 and 1966. Another challenge to the notion that Heathcliff and Catherine embody natural or supernatural forces comes from Herbert Dingle; in "The Origin of Heathcliff" (*BST*, 1972) and again in *The Mind of Emily Brontë* (1974), Dingle explores the subject of incest, earlier proposed by Rebecca West and Eric Solomon (see the Stevenson *Guide*, p. 240). H. P. Sucksmith sees the novel as anticipating Freud's account of the incompatibility of social progress and full sexual freedom; it protests the repression of instinctive life by Victorian society and, through the love of Heathcliff and Catherine, affirms "man and woman's more primitive needs" ("The Theme of *Wuthering Heights* Reconsidered," *DR*, 1974). In this multitude of variations on a single theme one may find ample support for Mildred G. Christian's conclusion that the "contradictory judgments on *Wuthering Heights* are the most striking fact in its critical history" (Stevenson *Guide*, p. 244).

Of those readings that attempt to discuss *Wuthering Heights* in the light of a realistic tradition, Q. D. Leavis' "A Fresh Approach to *Wuthering Heights*" (from *Lectures in America*, by F. R. Leavis and Q. D. Leavis, 1969) is the most forceful and provocative. Unlike the metaphysical critics, Leavis sets no store by the evidence of the poems; she rejects as "preposterous" the notion that the novel could have grown out of the Gondal saga and asks reasonably "whether, the novel being lost, we could have deduced anything even remotely resembling it from the poems." For her, the novel's greatness lies in its study of human love and its depiction of Catherine's irrational and self-destructive impulses, which Leavis examines in an in-

structive (though overlong) parallel with Roché's novel *Jules et Jim*. Persuasive as she is, however, the brusqueness with which she rejects alternative
readings prompts Frank Kermode to take issue with her and defend the
work's inherent plurality of meanings ("A Modern Way with the Classic,"
NLH, 1974; the essay was originally the last of a series of lectures by Kermode, gathered as *The Classic: Literary Images of Permanence and Change*,
1975).

Perhaps the most startling element of Leavis' essay is her rejection of
Heathcliff as a significant creation; she simply dismisses him as being inadequately developed: he is "an enigmatic figure only by reason of his creator's
indecision." Such a view is consistent with her attempt to examine the
novel's realistic treatment of love, since Heathcliff hardly fits our notions of
the ordinary human lover; but it surely does violence to the response of
generations of readers who have found him far from inadequate. Peter
Widdowson speaks for such readers in "Emily Brontë: The Romantic Novelist" (*MSpr*, 1972), asserting that "Heathcliff is the centre and *raison d'être*
of *Wuthering Heights*," "the supreme Romantic individual, manifesting
absolute integrity to Self, expressed in terms of his single-minded passion for
Catherine." Charlotte Brontë, though condemning Heathcliff's evil, acknowledged his centrality and power in her preface to the edition of 1850,
and her view finds a modern supporter in Philip Drew: "Emily Brontë's
achievement is to arouse our sympathy for a lost soul while making it quite
clear that his actions are damnable" ("Charlotte Brontë as a Critic of
Wuthering Heights," *NCF*, 1964). Other critics, while agreeing that Heathcliff wins our sympathy, are less convinced of his depravity. Larry Champion
maintains that, despite his cruelty, Heathcliff is morally superior to those
around him "in a world in which Christianity is both hypocritical and
inept" ("Heathcliff: A Study in Authorial Technique," *BSUF*, 1968).
Thomas Vargish perceives a tragic quality in Heathcliff's obsession with
revenge and draws comparisons with *King Lear* ("Revenge and *Wuthering
Heights*," *SNNTS*, 1971); and Norman Lavers treats Heathcliff as the hero
of a drama whose governing action is "to restore to power the Earnshaw
family" ("The Action of *Wuthering Heights*," *SAQ*, 1973). Walter Reed's
eloquent account of Heathcliff starts with the premise that the Romantic
hero is a figure not defined by clear moral categories, that he is beyond
conventional good or evil; in *Meditations on the Hero: A Study of the
Romantic Hero in Nineteenth-Century Fiction* (1974), Heathcliff is viewed
as "a hero of romantic love," "a hero of timelessness trying to enter a world
of time." Reed treats works by Brontë, Lermontov, Kierkegaard, and Melville that have in common the complex presentation of a heroic figure whose
origins lie beyond the novel tradition, in drama, epic, or poetic romance;
and in this context Heathcliff emerges as "a figure from the heroic past."

The novel's suggestions of mythic patterns and psychic forces are explored
by Jungian critics like Elliott B. Gose, Jr., who regards the fairy-tale elements of the novel (seen by Leavis as immature excrescences) as important
clues to the theme of psychic integration ("*Wuthering Heights*: The Heath

and the Hearth," *NCF*, 1966). He develops his ideas further in *Imagination Indulged: The Irrational in the Nineteenth-Century Novel* (1972). Helene Moglen's "The Double Vision of *Wuthering Heights*: A Clarifying View of Female Development" (*CentR*, 1971) argues that the novel explores the definition of personality "by externalizing and symbolically dramatizing the conflicting elements of the divided self" as these function within the female mind. Other psychological interpretations include Ronald E. Fine's essay on "Lockwood's Dreams and the Key to *Wuthering Heights*" (*NCF*, 1969), which examines the dreams both as expressions of sexual disturbance and as symbolic projections of the novel's themes. In *"Wuthering Heights*: The Binding of Passion" (*NCF*, 1972), William A. Madden uses the Freudian concept of the repetition compulsion to illuminate theme and structure; the novel "presents Emily Brontë's intuition regarding the psychic need to return to, confront, and transcend the origins of a trauma in order to become humanly free and functional." A similar pattern is discerned by Giles Mitchell in "Incest, Demonism and Death in *Wuthering Heights*" *L&P*, 1973), though the force of his argument is weakened by his overemphasis on elements of vampirism and Satanism.

One reaction to psychological or mythic explanations is the attempt to place *Wuthering Heights* within more conventional ethical limits, though here as elsewhere the novel resists easy classification. Inga-Stina Ewbank's restrained and perceptive discussion in *Their Proper Sphere* (noted above), while rejecting the view that the novel embodies a systematic philosophy, finds that its theme of rebellion is placed within a moral framework that "affirms the domesticated virtues of man as a kind and social creature." Ewbank allows for a certain ambivalence in the book's moral judgments; Arnold Shapiro does not, placing it squarely "in the same ethical and moral tradition as the other great Victorian novels" (*"Wuthering Heights* as a Victorian Novel," *SNNTS*, 1969). Another critic to perceive a Victorian moral conscience at work in Emily's writing is Victor A. Neufeldt, who traces a development, first evident in her later poems and culminating in *Wuthering Heights*, "away from escapism and toward an attempt to come to terms with a detestable world" ("Emily Brontë and the Responsible Imagination," *VN*, 1973). In Neufeldt's view the action of the novel demonstrates how personal desires "must be made to operate within a framework of responsibility that recognizes one's duty to love his fellow man." Buford Scrivner believes that Emily Brontë's ethical concern is conveyed in her dramatization of the clash between man's essential being and the claims of the empirical world ("The Ethos of *Wuthering Heights*," *DR*, 1974). A. J. Tough's *"Wuthering Heights* and *King Lear*" (*English*, 1972) identifies a moral theme common to both works, the tremendous force of evil and the eventual triumph of good.

The novel's complexities of structure and the difficulty of establishing the author's attitudes continue to tax critical ingenuity. John Jordan finds the novel to be governed by "a fabric of ironies," asserting that irony is the principal means whereby Brontë conveys her moral judgment ("The

Ironic Vision of Emily Brontë," *NCF*, 1965). The interplay between the mundane, material existence of Lockwood and Nelly Dean and the lyrical, timeless quality of the central action is examined by Ingeborg Nixon in "A Note on the Pattern of *Wuthering Heights*" (*ES*, Supp., 1964) and by Thomas A. Vogler in "Story and History in *Wuthering Heights*" (*Twentieth-Century Interpretations of* Wuthering Heights: *A Collection of Critical Essays*, ed. Thomas A. Vogler, 1968). C. P. Sanger's 1926 essay on the novel's structure is still the best study of Emily Brontë's detailed time scheme and is reprinted in almost all the recent anthologies of criticism noted below; but supplementary work has been done by S. A. Power in "The Chronology of *Wuthering Heights*" (*BST*, 1972) and A. Stuart Daley in "The Moons and Almanacs of *Wuthering Heights*" (*HLQ*, 1974). Daley's article demonstrates convincingly that "Emily Brontë founded the time schemes of the major narrative sequences . . . on the almanacs of two years of her own childhood, namely 1826 and 1827." For Robert Kiely, however, Emily's attention to such realistic details is less important than the novel's essentially romantic quality. Its power resides in its mingling of dream and reality: "*Wuthering Heights* is like dream *and* like life *and* like history *and* like other works of literature precisely because Brontë rejects the exclusiveness of these categories. They continually inform and define one another" (*The Romantic Novel in England*, 1972).

The role of the narrators is still the subject of lively critical debate, particularly since James Hafley's mischievous identification of Nelly Dean as "The Villain of *Wuthering Heights*" (*NCF*, 1958). Blair G. Kenney examines the relationship between sexual frustration and sorcery in "Nelly Dean's Witchcraft" (*L&P*, 1968) and concludes that "sexual jealousies are the bases of Nelly's most puzzling acts." Nelly finds a strong defender in John Fraser, who attacks the sentimental disposition of those who would forgive the cruelty of Heathcliff and Catherine while condemning Nelly for her well-meant interventions ("The Name of Action: Nelly Dean and *Wuthering Heights*," *NCF*, 1965). Gideon Shunami follows Hafley in seeing Nelly as a manipulator but concludes that her unreliability as a narrator stems from a desire to vindicate herself rather than from any evil or malicious motives ("The Unreliable Narrator in *Wuthering Heights*," *NCF*, 1973). In "*Wuthering Heights* and the Limits of Vision" (*PMLA*, 1971), David Sonstroem finds that all the narrators are unreliable; the novel "presents the spectacle of several limited and inadequate points of view— genteel, Christian, pragmatic, animistic—at indecisive war with one another," deliberately creating ambiguity and confusion. A similar conclusion is reached by Malcolm Pittock, who thinks that, through her manipulation of structure, Brontë attempts to convey "the way we apprehend people in real life" ("*Wuthering Heights* and Its Critics," *CS*, 1971). Helmut Viebrock's study of Brontë's narrative method takes as its starting point Virginia Woolf's assertion in *The Common Reader* (1925) that "there is no 'I' in *Wuthering Heights*" and examines the different functions performed by the narrators as "epische Erzähler" and as participants in the action

("Emily Brontë: *Wuthering Heights,*" *Der englische Roman im 19. Jahrhundert: Interpretationen,* ed. Paul Goetsch, Heinz Kosok, and Kurt Otten, 1973).

The novel's paradoxes and contradictions, the mixture of social comedy and mythic truths, of satire and sentiment, are seen by U. C. Knoepflmacher to move to a comic resolution with the restoration of order, and he describes the work as a tragicomic romance (*Laughter & Despair: Readings in Ten Novels of the Victorian Era,* 1971). For Mark Kinkead-Weekes, the conflicting points of view and the different worlds of Heights and Grange represent no contradiction; in "The Place of Love in *Jane Eyre* and *Wuthering Heights*" (*The Brontës: A Collection of Critical Essays,* ed. I. Gregor, 1970), he argues that, in presenting her dualistic vision, Emily Brontë asks us, not to choose one set of values over another, but rather to accept both worlds. Mark Roberts sees this dualism as a dilemma to which Emily Brontë finds no solution; she is drawn to the romantic "energy of the soul" displayed by Heathcliff and Catherine, yet recognizes the force and validity of moral principle as embodied in Edgar Linton (*The Tradition of Romantic Morality,* 1973).

A number of critics have sought to interpret the novel through a study of its style and language. Vincent Buckley notes how the book "fuses qualities of the conventional novel with those of poetic drama"; the formality and restraint of much of its language create a realistic context that helps to guarantee the authenticity of the passions at the novel's center ("Passion and Control in *Wuthering Heights,*" *SoR,* 1964). An interesting contrast to this view is provided by Arnold Krupat in "The Strangeness of *Wuthering Heights*" (*NCF,* 1970); he finds a disparity between matter and manner and thinks that the narrative style of Lockwood and Nelly Dean is made deliberately inadequate to the action to heighten our sense of its remoteness from ordinary experience. Robert B. Pearsall's study of poetic diction, "The Presiding Tropes of Emily Brontë" (*CE,* 1966), includes a suggestive discussion of metaphors reflecting the novel's violent themes and emotions but declines into flimsy biographical assertions about Emily's troubled personality. Zdeněk Vančura examines the correspondences between Heathcliff's character and the harsh irregularities of his dwelling, noting the imagery of enclosure and imprisonment ("The Stones of Wuthering Heights," *PP,* 1970). Elizabeth van de Laar's exhaustive account of imagery, *The Inner Structure of* Wuthering Heights: *A Study of an Imaginative Field* (1969), considers each character as defined by various groups of images in order to determine 'the degree of spiritualization of that character." Though the book is not without interest, its findings could have been presented much more succinctly.

More specialized work on Emily Brontë's language has been done by Keith M. Petyt in *Emily Brontë and the Haworth Dialect: A Study of the Dialect Speech in* Wuthering Heights (1970). Petyt maintains that the dialect forms in the 1847 edition of the novel correspond quite closely to the language of Haworth and its area, and he examines some of the inconsistent

and arbitrary changes in the dialect passages made by Charlotte for the 185c
edition. Emily's "intimate knowledge of the speech of the people around
her" is further demonstrated by Petyt in his article " 'Thou' and 'You' in
Wuthering Heights" (*BST*, 1974). Linguistic analysis is given a more liter
ary application by Jeremy Cott in "Structures of Sound: The Last Sentence
of *Wuthering Heights*" (*TSLL*, 1964–65), which examines the semantic and
phonetic implications of Emily Brontë's diction and syntax at the novel's
conclusion, emphasizing their poetic qualities.

For discussions of the possible sources of *Wuthering Heights*, the reader
may turn to the books on Emily Brontë by Gérin and Hewish, mentioned
above, and to the essay by Q. D. Leavis, who draws a suggestive comparison
with Scott's *The Bride of Lammermoor*. Ruth M. MacKay is convinced that
the *Blackwood's* story "The Bridegroom of Barna" and Hoffmann's "Da
Majorat" were Emily's primary sources for both plot and narrative struc
ture ("Irish Heaths and German Cliffs: A Study of the Foreign Sources of
Wuthering Heights," *BYUS*, 1965); MacKay speaks of "finding the two
tales," apparently unaware that others had already done so (Romer Wilson
in *All Alone*, 1928, and Leicester Bradner in "The Growth of *Wuthering
Heights*," *PMLA*, 1933). B. Gilbert Cross and Peggy L. Cross reject "Da
Majorat" as a direct source, in "Farewell to Hoffmann?" (*BST*, 1970)
Johan van der Woude's short study *Het Mysterie van de Brontës* (1967
returns to the long-discredited theories of William Wright (*The Brontës in
Ireland*, 1893) and maintains that Emily got much of her material for
Wuthering Heights from family tales about Mr. Brontë's Irish forebears. A
useful account of the novel's musical references, particularly to ballads, is
provided by Katherine Ankenbrandt in "Songs in *Wuthering Heights*'
(*SFQ*, 1969). In this connection one might expect to find helpful material in
Jacqueline Simpson's study "The Function of Folklore in *Jane Eyre* and
Wuthering Heights" (*Folklore*, 1974), but the essay disappointingly limits
itself to an enumeration of the folkloric allusions in the two novels, together
with a few comments about their relationship to theme or character. Articles
by J. V. Arnold (*RLC*, 1972) and Patricia Thomson (*RES*, 1973) explore
the relationships between *Wuthering Heights* and George Sand's *Mauprat*
Ralf R. Nicolai considers the possible influence of Kleist's novella *Der
Findling* in "*Wuthering Heights*: Emily Brontë's Kleistian Novel" (*SAB*
1973). On the rather distant chance that Emily may have known something
of Schopenhauer's work, even if only at second hand, Ronald B. Hatch
suggests parallels between Schopenhauerian renunciation and Heathcliff's
passive state at the end of *Wuthering Heights* ("Heathcliff's 'Queer End'
and Schopenhauer's Denial of the Will," *CRCL*, 1974).

Finally, mention should be made of several short introductory studies of
Wuthering Heights, each of which offers lucid and succinct accounts of
major aspects of plot, theme, and technique. Barbara Hardy's *Wuthering
Heights* in Blackwell's Notes on English Literature series (1963), though
intended for high school or undergraduate readers, includes some illuminat
ing disagreement with the popular interpretation by David Cecil. J. F

Goodridge's more comprehensive *Emily Brontë: Wuthering Heights* (1964) provides a useful map of the novel's terrain. Goodridge describes Heathcliff as gradually attaining the stature of a tragic hero, in contrast to the view presented by Margaret Willy in *A Critical Commentary on Emily Brontë's Wuthering Heights* (1966), where Heathcliff is seen as declining into "the conventional 'villain' of melodrama."

Anne Brontë

It was perhaps inevitable that Anne Brontë's novels should seem slight beside those of her sisters and that she should suffer from comparative critical neglect. Lewis K. Tiffany lays the largest portion of blame for this on Charlotte Brontë, who in his view belittled Anne's work by speaking of it (in the Biographical Notice of 1850) in a "condescending and apologetic" manner ("Charlotte and Anne's Literary Reputation," *BST*, 1974). Twentieth-century criticism has been generally more favorable, though sometimes erring in the opposite direction, as when George Moore maintained that *Agnes Grey* is "the most perfect prose narrative in English literature" (*Conversations in Ebury Street*, 1930).

Among Anne Brontë's most ardent advocates in recent years is A. Craig Bell, for whom *The Tenant of Wildfell Hall* is "a story which, in its exposure of human baseness, its sounding of the very depth of human nature, its unflinching portrayal of the struggle between good and evil, has no peer in English fiction" ("Anne Brontë: A Re-Appraisal," *QR*, 1966). The argument is vitiated by its aggressive tone and its contemptuous dismissal of other critics, but Bell is right to draw attention to the novel's unsentimental realism and its powerful portrayal of sexual passion. A less strident claim on Anne Brontë's behalf is entered by T. K. Meier, who considers the themes of conjugal love and conjugal duty in *Wildfell Hall* and the structural use of contrast and comparison ("*The Tenant of Wildfell Hall*: Morality as Art," *RLV*, 1973). Meier asks us to look at Helen more critically and suggests that her self-righteousness and preoccupation with duty "may give some clue as to why Huntington [sic] sought such excesses." Inga-Stina Ekeblad comments on structural features in the novel that may be derived from drama, noting the possible influence of a play by Thomas Middleton ("*The Tenant of Wildfell Hall* and *Women Beware Women*," *N&Q*, 1963).

Anthologies and Surveys of Criticism

There are too many critical anthologies on the Brontës to be described in detail here. *Wuthering Heights* alone has inspired four collections, edited by R. Lettis and W. E. Morris (1961), Alastair Everitt (1967), Thomas A. Vogler (1968), and Miriam Allott (1970). Criticism of *Wuthering Heights* also occupies most of Jean-Pierre Petit's compilation, *Emily Brontë: A Critical Anthology* (1973). Critical writings on both Charlotte and Emily are gathered by Judith O'Neill (1968) and Ian Gregor (1970).

Miriam Allott has edited a casebook on *Jane Eyre* and *Villette* (1973); lik
her volume on *Wuthering Heights*, this offers a broad sampling of Victoria
opinion, as well as modern criticism.

An indispensable aid to the literary historian is Allott's volume on *Th
Brontës: The Critical Heritage* (1974). Beginning with the sparse bu
friendly reviews of the 1846 *Poems*, the volume includes all the significar
notices of the Brontë novels on first publication; a section on general crit
cal opinion in the 1850s and the impact of Mrs. Gaskell's *Life*; and final
"Judgements and Opinions, 1858–99," the latter date being that of tl
publication of the Haworth Edition of the Brontës' works (1899–190
with prefaces by Mrs. Humphry Ward. In her detailed introduction, th
editor notes that, despite charges of coarseness, the early critical reception
Wuthering Heights was by no means as harsh or inimical as Charlott
suggests in her Biographical Notice of 1850. The volume is an importar
record of Victorian taste and critical attitudes; of particular interest
Swinburne's review of Mary Robinson's *Emily Brontë* (1883), which,
Allott says in her excellent introduction, "finally set the seal on the conce
tion of *Wuthering Heights* as an outstanding work of the poetic imagin
tion."

The early critical reception of the Brontës in America is the subject
articles by Jane Gray Nelson ("First American Reviews of the Works
Charlotte, Emily, and Anne Brontë," *BST*, 1964) and Albert J. von Fran
("An American Defence of *Wuthering Heights*—1848," *BST*, 1974). Burtc
R. Pollin provides a useful checklist of criticism in "The Brontës in tl
American Periodical Press of Their Day: One Hundred and Ninety-Thr
Reviews and Comments Annotated" (*BST*, 1975); the list includes Amer
can reprints of articles from British journals.

Translations

The Brontës' novels have been widely translated, and the account give
here must necessarily take the form of an impression rather than a compr
hensive survey. Editions of *Wuthering Heights* and *Jane Eyre* have bee
published in Chinese, Japanese, Hebrew, and Arabic, as well as in virtual
all the languages of Europe. *Shirley* and *Villette* are also available in mar
translations, including Finnish, Croatian, and Czech; and there was a Swe
ish translation of *Shirley* as early as 1854. Anne Brontë's two novels, thoug
less extensively translated, have also enjoyed a surprising degree of succes
since 1967, *The Tenant of Wildfell Hall* has been published in Yugoslavi
Turkey, Finland, and Czechoslovakia, and in the same period there ha
been French, Italian, Turkish, and Finnish versions of *Agnes Grey*. Tl
annual listings in the *Index Translationum* reflect a notable growth
interest in Eastern Europe and the Far East. In the Soviet Union, f
example, *Jane Eyre* is available not only in Russian but also in a Georgi
version (1964) and a Ukrainian translation (1971). *Wuthering Heights* h

ately been translated as *Uruma Laddō* (Sri Lanka, 1970) and *Pogpung eui ondeog* (South Korea, 1972). Only *The Professor* is relatively poorly represented in translation, though in recent years new versions have been published in both French and Italian.

French translations are especially numerous; for the period 1960–1969 alone, the catalogue of the Bibliothèque Nationale records the publication of eleven translations and "adaptations françaises" of *Jane Eyre* and eight translations of *Wuthering Heights*. Though these figures include the reissue of several older translations, they bear witness to an impressive degree of interest. Recent translations include Sylvère Monod's edition of *Wuthering Heights*, entitled *Hurlemont* (1963), and the same translator's *Jane Eyre* (1966), both with critical materials. In 1972 Pierre Leyris published his translation of *Wuthering Heights* with additional material selected by Raymond Bellour; and in the same year Bellour collaborated with four translators to produce an impressive volume of French translations of selected juvenilia (*Charlotte Brontë; Patrick Branwell Brontë*, Choix établi et présenté par Raymond Bellour). Several of the stories or fragments included here, notably Charlotte's "Four Years Ago" ("Quatre ans plus tôt"), have not hitherto appeared in printed transcriptions or among the Shakespeare Head facsimiles. Critical interest in the Brontës has been strong in France from the first, as is evident from David Newton-De Molina's "A Note on an Early French View of Charlotte Brontë" (*BST*, 1970) and Emile Langlois's study "Early Critics and Translators of *Jane Eyre* in France" (*BST*, 1971). Scholarly enthusiasm for the work of Emily Brontë led in 1969 to a seminar held jointly by the Instituts d'Anglais of Lyon and Clermont-Ferrand and the subsequent publication of papers on *Wuthering Heights* by J. P. Petit, N. Lecarme, and J. Rancy in *Études Brontëennes* (1970).

A short selection of books and articles in foreign languages (mainly French) is included by Janet M. Barclay in her checklist of *Emily Brontë Criticism, 1900–1968*, noted above.

Dramatic Adaptations

The melodramatic qualities of the Brontë novels readily lend themselves to stage conventions, and the history of theatrical productions begins in 1848 with John Brougham's version of *Jane Eyre* (see Allardyce Nicoll's *A History of English Drama 1660–1900*, IV, 1955). Dramatic and musical adaptations of *Jane Eyre* and *Wuthering Heights*, as well as the numerous plays about the Brontë family, are catalogued and discussed by Heidemarie Rauth in her dissertation "Dramatisierungen von Leben und Werk der Brontë-Schwestern" (Univ. of Innsbruck 1971), which is summarized in "A Survey of Brontë Plays" (*BST*, 1974). Rauth has also published a separate study of the dramatizations of *Wuthering Heights* (*Emily Brontës Roman Wuthering Heights als Quelle für Bühnen und Film Versionen*, Veröffentlichungen der Univ. Innsbruck, 84, 1974). A convenient list of film and

television productions is given in an appendix to F. B. Pinion's *A Bront*
Companion (1975).

Film adaptations of *Jane Eyre* and *Wuthering Heights* abound. *Jan*
Eyre has received at least ten screen treatments since 1910; the best-know
version is that directed by Robert Stevenson in 1943, with screenplay b
Stevenson and Aldous Huxley, starring Orson Welles and Joan Fontaine
with Elizabeth Taylor as a prim and pretty Helen Burns. Geoffrey Wagne
examines the shortcomings of this production in an interesting compariso
of film and novel, in *The Novel and the Cinema* (1975). The most recen
film of *Jane Eyre*, a rather bland version directed by Delbert Mann in 197c
led Fontana Books to issue a "Special Film Edition" of the novel in th
same year, with a biographically inaccurate introduction and comments o
the making of the film by George Curry. *Wuthering Heights* has bee
adapted for the cinema four times since 1920. William Wyler's productio
in 1939 included a dashing Laurence Olivier as Heathcliff and a gente
Merle Oberon as Catherine Earnshaw, neither very convincing. The screen
play, written by Ben Hecht and Charles MacArthur, takes drastic libertie
with the plot, dispensing with the second half of the novel altogether an
concluding with Heathcliff's demise on the moors, "smiling in death, wit
his arms thrown wide as if in an embrace" (Ben Hecht and Charles Mac
Arthur, *"Wuthering Heights": Synopsis of the Film*, 1939). John Gassne
and Dudley Nichols included this version in their *Twenty Best Film Play*
(1943) in the belief that "for once passion—from adolescence to adulthoo
—has been presented without adulteration" and that by concentrating o
the central relationship of the possessed lovers the film play improves upo
the novel. More recent critics have not been so enthusiastic. George Blue
stone, in *Novels into Film* (1957), is sympathetic to the filmmakers' problen
of translating a complex work into terms comprehensible to a twentieth
century mass audience but notes that Wyler's film bears little relation to it
original, becoming "the story of the stable boy and the lady." Geoffre
Wagner (see above) is much harsher in his condemnation of the novel'
transposition into a vulgar Hollywood love story. Another film of *Wuther*
ing Heights was made in 1970, directed by Robert Fuest; this too excises th
latter part of the novel. Reviews of the four films discussed here may b
found in issues of *BST* for 1939, 1943, and 1971.

Despite the growing mountain of books and articles on the Brontë
considerable scholarly work remains to be done. There are, for example
many omissions or uncertainties in textual and bibliographical matters tha
require attention, such as the lack of a comprehensive scholarly bibliogra
phy of the Brontës' published writings and the fragmentary nature of in
formation concerning manuscripts and their locations. Renewed critica
interest in the juvenilia makes the preparation of complete and accurat
texts doubly important, and it is noteworthy that editorial work of this kinc
is presently being undertaken by doctoral candidates in both the Unitec

tates and Great Britain. The Brontës' critical reception and their place in iterary history are other areas that warrant further study, to supplement he work of scholars like Miriam Allott and Tom Winnifrith; Carol)hmann's "Emily Brontë in the Hands of Male Critics" (*CE*, 1971) is one example of such an approach. Investigation of the Brontës' sources is by no means exhausted; the notes to the Clarendon editions show a greater variety of literary and historical reference than might have been expected, and the nfluence of the Bible awaits fuller examination. So too does the influence of the periodicals and annuals that the Brontës devoured so voraciously as children; writers like Scott, Hogg, and Mary Shelley were frequent contributors to such publications, which abound in stories about orphans, ghosts, and governesses. Brontë studies will never be free of the aura of myth and romance surrounding that most unusual of families; but one hopes that modern textual scholarship and source study will make it easier for the literary critic to arrive at a just and objective estimate of the Brontës' achievement and its significance.

ELIZABETH CLEGHORN GASKELL

James D. Barry

Critics of Elizabeth Gaskell fall into three camps. Fading somewhat in influence are the admirers of *Cranford*, that idyllic and graceful tale (i should perhaps not even be called a novel) which preserves a nostalgia for a bygone era. Recent arrivals in this camp are those who prefer to read *Cranford* as an ironic portrayal of an unsatisfactory society. A second camp —composed of solid, assertive, no-nonsense citizens—champions Mrs. Gaskell's early work, *Mary Barton* and/or *North and South*, as examples o social novels that must be read not only as history or sociology but also a literature. Finally, an increasingly influential group of thoughtful and balanced readers sees Mrs. Gaskell as a maturing artist and considers each o her works in relationship to the others and to her general views, preferring the later fiction but giving all her writings respectful, and perhaps ever admiring, attention.

The reevaluation of Mrs. Gaskell, which might be said to have begun with Annette B. Hopkins' 1952 biography, has perhaps reached fruition with the appearance in the last decade of the *Letters*, seven books about her numerous editions of her works, and a score of critical articles.

Bibliography, Editions, Letters

Both the critical works on Mrs. Gaskell and the editions of her novels published during the last decade provide bibliographies, particularly o writings about her. The Penguin and the Oxford editions of individua novels (noted below) have especially serviceable listings. Three recen bibliographies stand out, however. John Geoffrey Sharps's list in *Mrs. Gaskell's Observation and Invention* (1970) is the most valuable and compre hensive publication to date, though Sharps does not claim completeness. In addition to his "List of Printed Works and Typescripts Cited" (approxi mately five hundred items), he provides a list of "Holders of Gaskell

Ianuscripts." Marjorie Taylor Davis' "An Annotated Bibliography of riticism on Elizabeth Cleghorn Gaskell, 1848–1973" (Diss. Univ. of Mississippi 1974) contains almost five hundred entries. And Miriam Allott's ntry in *NCBEL* provides what everyone except the most intense student ould need—including a statement on manuscript locations.

John Geoffrey Sharps has also writetn a bibliographical essay (*N&Q*, 965) identifying some columns in the *Pall Mall Gazette* (1865) as the work f Mrs. Gaskell. They are made up of bits of Paris news and five humorous tters.

Several editions of Mrs. Gaskell's novels have appeared in recent years. he Penguin and the Oxford English Novels series are, in general, more aluable than the Everyman editions (though the latter provide introducions and bibliographies). This section treats the novels in the order of their riginal publication and the editions of each novel in the order of their apearance.

The Everyman *Mary Barton* (1967) has a brief and informative introducion by Margaret Lane, who stresses the newness of the book's social theme nd the understanding of the Industrial Revolution we gain through John Barton. There is a select bibliography. The 1970 Penguin edition of the ovel, based on the first edition of 1848, was prepared by Stephen Gill. In ddition to a lengthy introduction, this admirably useful edition includes a ibliography particularly strong on Manchester life, a note on Chartism, eprints of Mrs. Gaskell's outline plan for *Mary Barton* and of "Sketches mong the Poor" (a poem by Mr. and Mrs. Gaskell that she referred to as he "germ of Alice"),* and an extensive set of explanatory notes especially seful in identifying chapter mottoes. Gill endorses the notion that fiction hould portray imaginatively what "was demonstrated in blue-books, reoorts, and documentation of all kinds throughout the century, namely, that he gulf between Dives and Lazarus was there, systematized at the very oundation of Victorian prosperity" and praises Mrs. Gaskell for rising bove the novel as document of social history to a successful evocation of ociety through scene and character. While admitting that Mrs. Gaskell's middle-class values clashed with her sympathy for the suffering poor, he nsists that she did not retreat from the world of Victorian unrest but, instead, widened the perimeters of the novel so that it "does not merely reflect but . . . also seeks to interpret and to change" society .

In his chapter in the Stevenson *Guide* James D. Barry called for a study of *Cranford* from germ to fulfillment. Elizabeth Porges Watson's *Cranford* in the Oxford English Novels series (1972) is a response to that call. Her text is based on a collation of the first volume edition of 1853 with the earlier *Household Words* serialization and with the two subsequent editions published before Mrs. Gaskell's death, those of 1855 and 1864. The fifteen pages of explanatory notes comment on variations in these editions, explain refer-

---

* In *EA* (1964), John-Paul Hulin argues that Mrs. Gaskell had written a similar poem, "Rich and Poor," in 1842.

ences to little-known historical personages and local customs, and clarif
allusions. There is also a brief appreciative introduction and a classificatio
of the most important textual changes made by Mrs. Gaskell in 1853. Watso
also reprints, for the first time since its original July 1849 appearance i
Sartain's Union Magazine, the essay "The Last Generation in England
(initial sketches for *Cranford*) and the November 1863 *All the Year Roun*
"sequel," "The Cage at Cranford." The relationship between these tw
items and *Cranford* as a whole is not developed; the bibliography could b
fuller; and the notes could profitably be expanded (to include, for example
biblical passages). Yet Watson provides here the best edition of *Cranford* t
date.

Margaret Lane's brief introduction to the Everyman *Ruth* (1967) focuse
on Elizabeth Gaskell's liberal view of the fallen woman, who retains th
potentiality for a virtuous life and can be stimulated to full and nobl
development by her illegitimate child. Mrs. Gaskell bowed to Victoria
mores, it is true, by requiring Ruth's death, but she nonetheless pioneere
in advancing her readers' understanding of the plight of the fallen woma
Lane provides a serviceable select bibliography.

Martin Dodsworth's stimulating and argumentative introduction to th
Penguin *North and South* (ed. Dorothy Collin, 1970) insists that this nove
be viewed as an account of Margaret Hale's growing up. Although th
critical opinion that the book is essentially an industrial novel is perhap
not so strong as to require Dodsworth's attack, his main points are neverthe
less noteworthy: that *North and South* should be considered alongside *Jan*
Eyre and *Villette*, all three novels concentrating on the integrity, depth
and strength of feeling of their respective heroines—Margaret, Jane, an
Lucy Snowe; that the violence of the riot scene has sexual overtones; an
that the success with which Mrs. Gaskell portrays the passions aroused b
industrial unrest is traceable to their relationship to sexual passion. Doroth
Collin provides a comment on the text, several pages of notes, and a helpfu
glossary of dialect words.

The best edition of *North and South* is in the Oxford English Novel
series (1973). Angus Easson provides an introduction, a note on the text (he
bases his edition on the 1855 first volume edition, collated with the secon
edition, whereas Collin uses the second, also of 1855), a select bibliography
a chronology of Mrs. Gaskell's life, and a full series of explanatory notes
His introduction, not so thought-provoking as Dodsworth's, gives a brie
account of the problems of serial publication, compares *North and South*
favorably to *Hard Times*, and argues the centrality of the relationship
between Margaret and John Thornton.

In a brief and informative introduction to the Everyman edition of *Syl*
via's Lovers (1964), Arthur Pollard pauses over the tragic character of the
story, the irony of the plot, and the account of Sylvia's maturing. There is a
select bibliography. A better edition of *Sylvia's Lovers* is desirable. Its edito
will wish to consult a note on the first two editions in John Geoffre
Sharps's *Mrs. Gaskell's Observation and Invention* (1970).

In an introduction to the Everyman *Wives and Daughters* (1966), Margaret Lane sees the appeal of the book today as resting in Mrs. Gaskell's ability to portray a "vanished world" with a humorous and ironic sophistication that is "curiously modern." The select bibliography is adequate, but there is no statement on the text. Frank Glover Smith bases his 1969 Penguin edition of *Wives and Daughters* on the original 1864–66 serial publication in *Cornhill Magazine* and accompanies the text with a few pages of notes and a stimulating introduction by Laurence Lerner. Not confining his discussion to the novel at hand, Lerner places *Wives and Daughters* in the context of Mrs. Gaskell's other writings and also draws parallels with the social comedy of Jane Austen and the psychological insight of George Eliot, stressing particularly Mrs. Gaskell's skill in portraying marriage. In a letter to *TLS* (14 June 1974) Angus Easson asserts that the Penguin text is misleadingly described as based on the *Cornhill* serialization and that it cannot be viewed as adequate. Having provided examples to illustrate his point, he pleads the necessity of a more definitive text. He has recently reported that his edition is nearing completion.

Mrs. Gaskell's *Cousin Phillis* and her rather extensive and varied output of short fiction are worthy of a modern edition.

Mrs. Gaskell's daughter Meta burned a large collection of family papers—including, presumably, letters from Mrs. Gaskell to her husband—and many other letters were destroyed in World War II bombings. Yet the patient and painstaking effort of J. A. V. Chapple and Arthur Pollard was crowned in 1966 by their admirable edition of *The Letters of Mrs. Gaskell*. It contains approximately six hundred and fifty letters, an enormous number of them written to her daughters and concerned with familial matters. From these and from a large number to a few friends we gain a picture of a vital, thoughtful, and—the word is still appropriate—charming writer. The most captivating letters for most readers are no doubt those that refer to the novels or to other famous Victorians, concerning, for example, Mrs. Gaskell's pain over the response to *Ruth*, her difficulties with Dickens over the serialization of *North and South*, her characterization of Florence Nightingale, her admiration for George Eliot (coupled with her wish that the author of *Adam Bede* was Mrs. Lewes), and her developing friendship with Charlotte Brontë. A most striking aspect of the *Letters* is Mrs. Gaskell's dedicated and passionate involvement in writing *The Life of Charlotte Brontë* (on which there is probably more than on the composition of any of her novels).

Chapple and Pollard might have included some of the more important letters written to Mrs. Gaskell. For example, when we encounter references in three separate letters to Carlyle's valued remarks on *Mary Barton*, we wish for a footnote in which Carlyle's letter (or salient parts of it) might be read. The editors ought to have considered omitting the chops-and-tomato-sauce notes that provide little more information than who is coming to tea

and when and including instead an occasional explanatory footnote (e.g.
on the 1857 events in India that Mrs. Gaskell alludes to).

The letters are arranged chronologically and numbered in such a way
that we can tell whether a particular letter is one in a sequence and, if so,
can refer to its predecessor and/or to its successor. The indexes are superb,
the first to the Gaskell family, the second to literary works, and the third a
general biographical index. Altogether an admirable edition.

John Geoffrey Sharps, who received special thanks from Chapple and
Pollard in their introduction, includes comments on the *Letters* in his *Mrs.
Gaskell's Observation and Invention* (1970). He argues for approximately a
hundred and fifty corrections, suggesting changes of dates, noting misprints
or possible misreadings, and supplying additional information. Albert H.
Preston discusses and reprints nine letters from Mrs. Gaskell to John Greenwood concerned with Haworth and the Brontës (*BJRL*, 1965).

General Biographical and Critical Studies

Both the variety of approaches and the perceptive enthusiasm of recent
writers on Mrs. Gaskell's life and fiction testify to the healthy state of
Gaskell criticism today. The centennial publications of 1965 did not turn
out to be pro forma observances; rather, they launched a series of fruitful
explorations. Several books, of course, have biographical chapters, but the
overall orientation is critical. Annette B. Hopkins' *Elizabeth Gaskell* (1952)
remains the best biography to date, but the publication of the *Letters* and
the richness of the critical studies examined here suggest that a new biography would be appropriate.

In *Mrs. Gaskell: Novelist and Biographer* (1965) Arthur Pollard judiciously guides us through Mrs. Gaskell's life and writings and successfully
carries out his purpose of illustrating "her practice in such matters as the
pattern and function of plot, the types and relationship of characters, the
place of atmosphere and environment, the use of sheer information . . . , and
her application of moral judgment." This paradigm governs Pollard's consideration of Mrs. Gaskell's works. The result, though sometimes mechanical, is a balanced account of her development; it yields a particular
encomium for *Sylvia's Lovers* and a sensitive portrait of Elizabeth Gaskell
that reveals her perceptive and sympathetic vision of life. Early in his book
Pollard reports on Mrs. Gaskell's conviction that she could not have written
fiction when her children were young because their real lives would have
suffered as a result of her immersion in fictitious lives. Pollard's next remark
might well stimulate a future student of Mrs. Gaskell: "The tension between the demands of her fictitious people and her real ones remained with
Mrs. Gaskell to the end of her life."

Edgar Wright's *Mrs. Gaskell: The Basis for Reassessment* (1965) declares
that the traditional view of the unity of her writing as traceable to her
personality is inadequate and in need of revision—as are the views that she
was a talented amateur who took time for fiction away from her duties as

wife and mother, that early Knutsford was her true and best inspiration, and that her art does not develop. Wright supports his argument first by a number of chapters examining her themes and interests (e.g., "Religion and Purpose," "Family and Stability," and "Tradition and Transformation"), then by a discussion of how these themes help us to see her development as a novelist, and finally by a discussion of technique. The fiction is explicitly attended to in all three sections.

Wright stresses Mrs. Gaskell's preoccupation with a society and a set of standards that vary between stability and tradition on the one hand and flexibility and flux on the other: "a ranging between these extremes as she develops her central interest in observing and analyzing the various aspects of individual emotion and behaviour, as controlled by social custom and belief, that combine to form a unified or disorganized society." The individual lives that she writes about mirror the movement between instability and stability in the larger society. And as her writing career advanced she put aside the larger social issues of *Mary Barton* and *North and South* to concentrate on individual lives in small communities. In Wright's view the decision to let modified Cranford values dominate enabled Mrs. Gaskell "to find a stable basis for facing a changing world, and expression for a humorous and sensitive appreciation of human feeling and social behaviour."

Wright provides a perceptive and well-illustrated analysis of Mrs. Gaskell's journey from intrusive moralizer, though sympathetic and ironic observer, to the author who moves the story along and who enters the consciousness of a central character and speaks from that vantage point. Although Wright's discussion of technique is often thought-provoking, it is probably his account of Mrs. Gaskell's evolving attitude toward the individual and society that gives his book its chief value.

Margaret Ganz's *Elizabeth Gaskell: The Artist in Conflict* (1969) interprets Mrs. Gaskell's fiction, including the short stories, as a product of inner tension, a tension between a steadily developing artistic sensibility, which manifested itself chiefly in more sensitive and complex characterizations, and a traditional adherence to religious principles of justice and righteousness. These religious considerations interfere, in Ganz's judgment, with Mrs. Gaskell's artistic development. John Barton, for example, does not quite succeed as a tragic figure because Mrs. Gaskell can neither identify with him completely (though she does understand his bitterness) nor attack the status quo that has allowed such suffering to be. She has decided in this novel "not to establish the responsibility for social deprivation but to warn against the dangers of its moral and psychological repercussions"; she has decided to counsel resignation rather than reform, following what has been a major strain in the Christian tradition. Similarly, P. J. Keating points out in *The Working Classes in Victorian Fiction* (1971) that Mrs. Gaskell fails in *Mary Barton* because she chooses to deal in individual relationships, because she does not face up to problems in the social structure. Keating's book focuses on the last two decades of the century.

Ganz concludes her study with an analysis of *Sylvia's Lovers*. Here Mrs. Gaskell comes closest to portraying life's tragic dimensions, for here she was able to present more subtly the complex motives that bring about misfortune. Although Ganz admires Mrs. Gaskell's skill in *Sylvia's Lovers*, she is more comfortable with her in the novels set in Cranford and Hollingford, with her comic rather than her tragic vision.

John McVeagh's *Elizabeth Gaskell* (1970), a slim volume in the Profile in Literature series, is made up of forty-one extracts selected to illustrate various of Mrs. Gaskell's interests and qualities. McVeagh establishes a number of generalizations—for example, that calamity is a necessary experience if one is to comprehend life—and chooses passages to exemplify them.

Readers interested in an encyclopedic guide to Mrs. Gaskell need look no further than John Geoffrey Sharps's *Mrs. Gaskell's Observation and Invention: A Study of Her Non-Biographic Works* (1970). In his industrious and painstaking effort to define Mrs. Gaskell's observation and invention, Sharps attends explicitly to every one of her known nonbiographic works. Her observation is considered in terms of the real places she uses in her fiction, of the originals of her characters, of the real happenings on which she bases fictional episodes, of her analysis of the structure of society, of her descriptions of scenery, and of her "eye for the telling and significant detail." Invention, a broader area, includes imagination, technique, themes, characterization, and—above all—the great variety of her writing.

Readers may initially feel that Sharps's book is telling them more about Mrs. Gaskell, especially about the connections between fact and fiction, than they care to know. They are likely to be put off by the excessive detail and documentation (475 footnotes in the 56-page chapter on *Wives and Daughters*), and they may become impatient over the relative absence of formal critical analysis in a book of almost seven hundred pages. But they may ultimately be won over by Sharps's methodical and thorough approach —for example, by the emphasis on parallels among various of Mrs. Gaskell's writings or by the analysis of love and courtship in the chapter on *Sylvia's Lovers* or by the evaluation of her ability to portray in *Wives and Daughters* characters who are simultaneously highly individualized and admirably representative of their social classes. The most obvious merits of Sharps's study are the attention to all the minor works; the full bibliography, the most extensive to date (76 pp.); and the eight interesting appendixes—most notably those on "The Genesis of *Mary Barton*" and "The Plot of *North and South*." We have here, in short, a handbook to Mrs. Gaskell's work, one that suggests the need for a critical study of her short fiction.

W. A. Craik ably places Mrs. Gaskell in the tradition of the provincial, or nonmetropolitan, novel and at the same time provides a long and perceptive analysis of each of the five major novels (*Elizabeth Gaskell and the English Provincial Novel*, 1975). One way of characterizing Craik's book as a whole would be to take a close look at her study of a single novel. A better way to show the richness of her approach might be to recount several points she makes about Mrs. Gaskell's originality, about her place in the development of the novel. In *Mary Barton*, for example, Mrs. Gaskell removes death from "an aura of sentiment and sanctity" and promotes its being treated in fiction as an inevitable event. Again, John Barton is the first occurrence in fiction of a character who is both "the victim of economic necessity and also a man and a soul at strife." In *Ruth* we find an enormously complex endeavor to combine a realistic portrayal of a social problem with the examination of moral values and the application of religious belief; it broadens the scope of the novel. Similarly, Mrs. Gaskell's portrayal of John Thornton in *North and South* breaks new ground because she seriously analyzes a mature (over-thirty) lover. Another first is Philip Hepburn of *Sylvia's Lovers*, the first appearance in fiction of a long series of men 'helplessly ruined by the combination of events and the foibles—not venal in themselves—of their own natures," men who appear later in George Eliot, Hardy, and Forster. It is in *Wives and Daughters* that Elizabeth Gaskell admirably balances her three fictional interests: social concerns, the development of individuals within social groups, and the private struggles of individual characters.

Perhaps two final points can further illustrate the interest and the insights of Craik's book. She is particularly taken with Mrs. Gaskell's narrative stance. Unlike Thackeray, George Eliot, and Trollope—all of whom are more directive and obtrusive in their relationships with their readers—Mrs. Gaskell makes her characters' speech carry a heavy burden and prompts her readers to form their own judgments. Lastly, she is remarkable and admirable for not going over ground twice, for always turning to "pastures new." *Sylvia's Lovers*, for example, "stands alone and apart, in the solitude of greatness."

John Gross's 1965 BBC talk on Mrs. Gaskell (in *The Victorian Novel: Modern Essays in Criticism*, ed. Ian Watt, 1971) is a relatively successful effort to characterize the two conventional and unsatisfactory views of Mrs. Gaskell and to propose a synthesis of them. It is not proper to consider her merely a charming recorder of genteel society, nor is it correct to emphasize the original achievements of the industrial novels. Rather her work must be viewed as a whole: both as an effort to be aware of and to balance the traditional Cranford with the new Drumble and as a product of an artist who never allows us "to forget that human beings remain human beings under the most harsh or harrowing circumstances."

Barbara Hardy's 1970 essay in *The Victorians* (ed. Arthur Pollard) is characteristically urbane and thought-provoking. Mrs. Gaskell's individuality as a novelist, Hardy observes, reflects a powerful and wide-ranging sensibility that allows her to write many varieties of fiction well, notably the emphatically sociological, as in *North and South*, and the more psychological, as in *Sylvia's Lovers*. Hardy is particularly admiring of the analysis of feeling in *Sylvia's Lovers*.

Studies Related to Feminism

In *Petticoat Rebels: A Study of the Novels of Social Protest of George Eliot, Elizabeth Gaskell and Charlotte Brontë* (1968), Hazel T. Martin presents what she terms "a paean of admiration to a group of nineteenth-century women." These rebellious women were upset by the conditions of the working class, the religious and moral values of their time, and the Woman Question, that is, "woman's right to think, work, vote, write, etc." In *Mary Barton* Mrs. Gaskell portrays accurately the condition of the poor; in *Ruth* she attacks the double standard and sympathetically characterizes the fallen woman; in *Cranford*, by satirizing the "trivialities of female conduct," she implies that Cranford women could well occupy their minds more usefully. Martin's slim volume is unanalytical and even superficial, but it is an example of a response to women writers that is becoming increasingly prevalent among critics oriented to modern women's concerns.

A superior study is Hazel Mews's *Frail Vessels: Woman's Role in Women's Novels from Fanny Burney to George Eliot* (1969). Focusing on the period between Mary Wollstonecraft's 1792 *Vindication of the Rights of Woman* and John Stuart Mill's 1869 *The Subjection of Women*, Mews studies the ways in which women novelists, minor as well as major, saw "women in relationships," chiefly as women awaiting marriage but also as wives, as mothers, and as individuals standing alone.* Although Mrs. Gaskell wrote privately to Eliza Fox in 1850 that she was "sometimes coward enough to wish that we were back in the darkness where obedience was the only seen duty of women" and although her fictional wives exemplify the conservative contemporary view of wife as submissive helpmate, she broke with tradition in her analysis of the role of the Victorian woman. Two brief quotations from Mews sum up Mrs. Gaskell's contribution: she was able "to extend the sympathy of her readers to the problems of working-class women and of 'fallen' women, and to interpret the challenge of the industrial development in the north, pointing out the significance it held for the women whose lives were affected by it, closely or remotely"; and she accepted "woman's new dual role, the role of the woman of intelligence who also had ties of family, who would bury a God-given talent at her peril, but who would also be called to give final account for any neglect of family obligations." In her analysis of the ways in which such women novelists as Maria Edgeworth, Jane Austen, the Brontës, Elizabeth Gaskell, and George Eliot expanded the roles of women, Mews gives Mrs. Gaskell very high marks—as indeed she should.

In "Taking Care: Some Women Novelists" (*Novel*, 1972), Patricia Meyer Spacks notes Mrs. Gaskell's awareness, particularly in *Wives and Daughters*, of the limited options available to women, of how marriages are undertaken to solve economic problems, to escape moral demands, to find fulfillment. Mrs. Gaskell is seen as ahead of her time in portraying the dilemmas, although she does not provide solutions.

Objecting to the way in which some feminist criticism has treated literature as "a collection of tracts into which you dip for illustrations of your own polemic," Patricia Beer sets out to show how women were portrayed in

---

* Juanita M. Mantovani's 1974 dissertation "The Feminine World View of Elizabeth Cleghorn Gaskell" (Univ. of Southern California) also analyzes Mrs. Gaskell's women characters in their roles as daughters, wives, and mothers.

najor nineteenth-century fiction (*Reader, I Married Him: A Study of the Women Characters of Jane Austen, Charlotte Brontë, Elizabeth Gaskell nd George Eliot*, 1974). Viewing Mrs. Gaskell from this perspective, Beer provides an already worked-over analysis of Mrs. Gaskell's advanced views on prostitution (in *Mary Barton* and *Ruth*) and several fresh insights. Among the latter are: that the Lady Glenmire–Mr. Hoggins romance in *Cranford* emphasizes a woman's sexual needs; that Mrs. Gaskell's women seldom have the opportunity for heroic action but are characteristically condemned to helpless waiting for the turn of events governed by men; that Mrs. Gaskell explores in her fiction what constituted honesty for a woman in a society that demanded at least some hypocrisy.

Françoise Basch's *Relative Creatures: Victorian Women in Society and the Novel* (1974) analyzes the position of women in Victorian England and their portrayal in fiction between 1837 and 1867. Reviews of historical and fictional wives and mothers, single and working women, and fallen women make up the book. Margaret Hale and Molly Gibson exemplify the virtues of the ideal wife-mother: self-sacrifice and empathy for others. Mrs. Gaskell's successful portrayal of narrow-minded and selfish wives is best illustrated by Margaret Hale's mother and Mrs. Gibson. Mrs. Gaskell deserves credit for widening the scope of female occupations, though she clearly does not detail realistically the horrors of working women's lives. With regard to the fallen woman, Mrs. Gaskell emphasizes those circumstances mitigating guilt and attacks as excessive and illustrative of the double standard the world's characteristic chastisement of the fallen woman.

Annoyed that the popularity of *Cranford* has obscured Mrs. Gaskell's "novels of social and psychological realism and her studies of social change," Coral Lansbury argues in *Elizabeth Gaskell: The Novel of Social Crisis* (1975) that Mrs. Gaskell's merits have been insufficiently noted or analyzed and that she deserves to be numbered with Jane Austen, Dickens, Thackeray, and George Eliot. Three of Lansbury's major points can be noted here.

Largely as a result of her Unitarian heritage, Mrs. Gaskell emphasized the uniqueness and complexity of every person, all of us combinations of so-called masculine and feminine characteristics. In this regard, Mrs. Gaskell was impatient with the emphasis on the spiritual qualities of women. From Margaret Hale (in *North and South*) and others we learn Mrs. Gaskell's position, phrased this way by Lansbury: "Women who were made objects of worship, or who sought this role, were confining themselves to the altar or the hearth." Also, we have not only masculine women like Margaret Hale and Faith Benson (*Ruth*) but feminine men like Margaret's father and Faith's brother. Again, Mrs. Gaskell invented a narrative voice that did not necessarily reflect her own views but more likely reflected the views of the average middle-class reader. Lastly, in considering Mrs. Gaskell's view of England's changing society, Lansbury provides a new and stimulating reading of *Wives and Daughters* as a work dealing with "the major social problem of Victorian England. In the most industrialised country of the world, it was still felt necessary to observe and to demand the rights and privilege of a feudal age." The last paragraph of Lansbury's study is worth quoting in full:

> Elizabeth Gaskell possessed the gift that Anatole France discerned in Balzac: she had seen the shape of the future in contemporary events. The Cumnors [*Wives and Daughters*] are with us still, but Nicholas Higgins [*North and South*] cannot be silenced and must be heard. The oligarchy will yield, but it will never wholly relinquish power, for in England, power has always been indirect and wielded obliquely. The aristocracy has long learned not to be offensive in public. To read Engels is to read a theoretical exposition of the working class of Manchester; to read Elizabeth Gaskell is to see a social historian of unusual prescience using fiction as her analytical method. Time has proved her accurate.

Studies of Individual Novels

Graham Handley's "Mrs. Gaskell's Reading: Some Notes on Echoes and Epigraphs in 'Mary Barton'" (*DUJ*, 1967) is a stimulating essay on how Mrs. Gaskell made use of her reading of Keats, Coleridge (strikingly *The Ancient Mariner*), and Ebenezer Eliott, both in the epigraphs themselves and in the resonances of those epigraphs in the narrative itself. It is likely that novelists' use of epigraphs would repay further study.

C. A. Johnson's "Russian Gaskelliana" (*REL*, 1966) summarizes Mrs. Gaskell's impact in Russia, especially important because of her influence on Dostoevsky. The Tauchnitz editions of Mrs. Gaskell's novels apparently had some circulation in Russia, and the magazine *Vremya* [*Time*], edited by the Dostoevsky brothers, published a translation of *Mary Barton* in 1861. Johnson sees various parallels between *Mary Barton* and *Crime and Punishment* —for example, the use of similar biblical imagery and the resemblances between John Barton and Raskolnikov. A fuller development of this influence may be desirable. Johnson also notes the fifty-thousand-copy edition in 1963 of a new translation of *Mary Barton* by T. Kudryavtsera.

David Smith's comparison, "*Mary Barton* and *Hard Times*: Their Social Insights" (*Mosaic*, 1971–72), gives the nod to Dickens. Yes, Mrs. Gaskell did present a most memorable character in John Barton, but her solution to the problems of the Industrial Revolution was either an evasion (emigration to rural Canada) or resignation (acceptance of one's lot, sometimes accompanied by reconciliation between individual members of opposing classes). Dickens, on the other hand, refrained from individualizing characters as he passionately and powerfully portrayed the dehumanization of Coketown, a place made up not of individuals but of the masses assembled to serve the Industrial Revolution. A thought-provoking essay.

Michael D. Wheeler's "The Writer as Reader in *Mary Barton*" (*DUJ*, 1974) challenges the prevailing view that the source of *Mary Barton* was

Mrs. Gaskell's experience with the Manchester poor. Beside this observation and her involvement with Manchester life, we must put her reading. Wheeler details here interesting, if not always completely convincing, parallels between *Mary Barton* and the writings of Caroline Bowles (*Tales of the Factories*) and of Caroline Norton (notably *A Voice from the Factories* and *The Child of the Islands*). He also asserts that comparing Mrs. Gaskell with other contemporary writers, notably Carlyle, will show other literary sources for *Mary Barton*. Rodger L. Tarr's 1969 dissertation on "Carlyle's Influence upon the Mid-Victorian Social Novels of Gaskell, Kingsley, and Dickens" (Univ. of South Carolina) explores this point.

Geoffrey Carnall's "Dickens, Mrs. Gaskell, and the Preston Strike" (*VS,* 1964) finds *North and South* superior to *Hard Times* in its portrayal of the working class. Not concerned with evaluating the novels, Carnall instead studies the difficulties that the novelists encountered in grasping an unfamiliar idea, "the idea that working people could be both radical and responsible, subversive but not violent."

In John Lucas' "Mrs. Gaskell and Brotherhood" (in *Tradition and Tolerance in Nineteenth-Century Fiction,* ed. David Howard et al., 1967) Mrs. Gaskell's social-problem novels get high marks as they are compared with parallel work by Disraeli, Kingsley, and even Dickens. The most fascinating aspect of Lucas' stimulating essay is probably his working out of how flaws that belong to the genre of the social-problem novel come about because of the novelists' failures to carry out their imaginative visions, failures usually brought about by too pat solutions. When an author's recommendations become prominent, they usually get in the way of imaginative exploration; for, after all, "novels, notoriously, have nothing to do with ends, or solutions—not so far as they are works of art, anyway." Mrs. Gaskell fails because she is unable to follow to its logical extremes the consequences of class conflict, because she wants ultimately to depend upon her "gray dream of reconciliation," though part of her knows that this is not enough. In *Mary Barton*, for example, she turns away from the thought 'that the happy *may* be the selfish; that her religion *may* be for the masters only." Yet Mrs. Gaskell succeeds where other social-problem novelists fail because she takes the masses out of the novel and replaces them with realistically human characters. Her industrial world is in sharp contrast to "the world of cliché in which Disraeli and Kingsley's workmen move."

Patrick Brantlinger (*VS,* 1969) consults early Victorian novels—including *Mary Barton* and *North and South*—to determine how novelists viewed trade unionism. Mrs. Gaskell (and Dickens) sympathized with such movements as Chartism and the agitation for shorter workdays and viewed trade unionism as an understandable response by the working class to the callousness of the powerful masters. On the other hand, they did not believe that strikes helped the workingman, and their portrayals of union activity were not therefore particularly supportive or optimistic.

J. A. V. Chapple (*EIC,* 1967) salutes *North and South* as Mrs. Gaskell's "finest work of art." He views it as not primarily about the union of the industrial north and the rural south, as not about conflict between master and workmen, but as about Margaret's "acceptance of the full complexity of living in the real and changing world," an acceptance portrayed with narrative and poetic intensity. J. McVeagh (*EIC*, 1968) objects to Chapple's high evaluation of *North and South* as a wrongheaded disservice to Mrs. Gaskell's artistry. This artistry is essentially leisurely; the fiction is basically structureless; her virtues are found in her vivid and memorable episodes. Because she was not good at directing and controlling a story, her pastoral novels (notably *Cranford, Cousin Phillis*, and *Wives and Daughters*) are our best sources for her best art, for here we can find the use of episode to dramatize her constant theme: that life is composed of suffering and our response to it. Readers of Chapple and McVeagh might well wonder why critics find it so necessary first to settle on a writer's best work and then to trace her artistry to a single quality.

Dorothy W. Collin gives a fascinating account of "The Composition of Mrs. Gaskell's *North and South*" (*BJRL*, 1971). Her effective use of letters, particularly those of Mrs. Gaskell and Dickens, dramatizes the tension that developed over serial publication: Dickens' indignation over how much space was needed in *Household Words* and Mrs. Gaskell's response to what she called "the cruel necessity of compressing." Collin also provides interesting, though not detailed, comparisons between the serial version and the first edition (the manuscript is lost).

In "Mendacity in Mrs. Gaskell" (*Encounter*, 1973), P. N. Furbank finds that Mrs. Gaskell identifies excessively with Margaret Hale in *North and South* when she is supposedly being a detached observer: "Mrs. Gaskell is the poet of deceit; she knows the country of shams better than anyone. Only the trouble is, Miss Matty seems to have taken a hand in writing *North and South*."

Charles Shapiro in "Mrs. Gaskell and 'The Severe Truth'" (*Minor British Novelists*, ed. Charles Alva Hoyt, 1967) delights in not being an authority on Mrs. Gaskell ("so much of her work is so bad"), dismisses James D. Barry's call for a reassessment of her place in English fiction, and proposes that we "love *Cranford* and forgive her for the rest." Shapiro attends to only two novels, *Mary Barton* and *Cranford*. In the first, he pronounces, "all the characters . . . are frightful caricatures, grotesques unredeemed by either artistry or wit" and the plot is "unbelievably forced and foolish." It is *Cranford* that "*is* Mrs. Gaskell, because it is honest, observant, compassionate." Mrs. Gaskell's strength is her knowledge of and love for her characters; these rest on "her femininity, her own qualities as a good woman."

Admitting that what he presents "may seem a very cumbersome exegesis of a simple fiction," Martin Dodsworth ("Women without Men at Cranford," *EIC*, 1963) reads *Cranford* as concerned with "adjustment to the reality-principle," as a novel unified by actions resulting from attempts "to repress sexual needs under the cover of feminism." This stimulating, if fiercely analytical, essay rejects the view that *Cranford* is a charming, structureless series of character sketches; it focuses on the details of the plot and

sserts the unity of these details as residing in Mrs. Gaskell's unconscious
ostility toward the male and in her simultaneous awareness of the inade-
uacy of a society that attempts to structure itself on feminism—note, for
xample, Miss Matty's financial ruin and the final stewardship of Peter
enkyns.

Margaret Tarratt ("*Cranford* and 'the Strict Code of Gentility,'" *EIC*,
968) agrees with Dodsworth that *Cranford* deserves serious treatment but
rgues that its unity is more appropriately traced to Mrs. Gaskell's conscious
urpose: presenting a realistic account of how destructive the strict code of
entility can be and of how Miss Matty comes to realize, in the course of the
ovel, the importance of asserting oneself in opposition to the conventions
f society.

Not precisely so, says Patricia A. Wolfe ("Structure and Movement in
Cranford," *NCF*, 1968). Dodsworth is right in noting the unity and progres-
ion of the novel and in emphasizing the change from rejection to accep-
ance of the male. He is wrong, however, in stressing plot, for *Cranford* is
ssentially the story of Miss Matty's turning away from her sister's abnormal
eminism to her own sensitive and influential femininity. Mrs. Gaskell por-
rays woman as the teacher of society: "she it is who must teach others how
o love and, hence, how to live."

Cranford receives notice of a distinctive kind from Susan R. Gorsky in
'Old Maids and New Women: Alternatives to Marriage in Englishwomen's
Novels, 1847–1915" (*JPC*, 1973). Here Miss Matty becomes an archetypal
ld maid, contrasted with Marion Vincent of Mrs. Ward's 1908 *Testing of
Diana Mallory.*

All admirers of *Cranford* owe themselves the treat of mulling over the
xpression from *Cranford* "How naturally one falls back into the phraseol-
gy of Cranford!" as they read Philip Murray's poem "Fantasia on a Theme
y Mrs. Gaskell" (*Poetry*, 1972). And those who have the opportunity
hould see—and hear—Joan Littlewood and John Well's musical adapta-
ion reported on in *TLS* (21 Nov. 1975). It underlines the need for love to
vercome Cranfordian gentility, and it sounds—yes—charming.

Norman Page's "'Ruth' and 'Hard Times': A Dickens Source" (*N&Q*,
971) develops briefly the influence of Mrs. Gaskell's *Ruth* on Dickens'
Hard Times, particularly the similarities between Bradshaw and Gradgrind.

Graham Handley points out some errors in the dating of events in *Sylvia's
Lovers* (*N&Q*, 1965), though by and large Mrs. Gaskell exercises great care
in historical detail. In any event, the errors "in no way diminish the power-
ul validity of the characters' experiences."

John McVeagh's "The Making of 'Sylvia's Lovers'" (*MLR*, 1970) makes
use of Chapple and Pollard's *Letters* to account for the shortcomings of
Sylvia's Lovers. The "sudden lapse into melodrama" that mars the end of
the novel is explained by the knowledge gained from the *Letters* about the
circumstances of composition. The contrasts between the joyful spirit of the
first volume (Kinraid and Sylvia's) and the misfortunes of the second
volume (Hepburn and Sylvia's)—written a year and a half apart—are so

great that only dedicated and sustained writing could have harmonized th
two in the third volume. But Mrs. Gaskell was so distracted by uncertaintie
as to how to pull the two parts together, by personal problems, and b
importunities from Dickens to finish *A Dark Night's Work* for *All the Yea
Round* that she succumbed to sensational incidents to solve—unsatis
factorily—the problems created earlier.

Marilyn Butler in "The Uniqueness of Cynthia Kirkpatrick: Elizabet.
Gaskell's *Wives and Daughters* and Maria Edgeworth's *Helen*" (*RES*, 1972
champions Edgeworth at the expense of Mrs. Gaskell. Her thesis is that Mr
Gaskell's dependence on Fredrika Bremer's *A Diary* for the plot of *Wive
and Daughters* is insignificant compared to her debt to Maria Edgeworth'
Cecilia for the basic characterization of Cynthia. Mrs. Gaskell is, overall, th
better novelist without a doubt, and *Wives and Daughters* is superior t
Helen, but Maria Edgeworth's portrayal of the interaction among her cen
tral characters and their interaction with the larger society is more able an
sophisticated than Mrs. Gaskell's. And, "however successful," Mrs. Gaskell'
creation of Cynthia is "substantially derivative."

To sum up this review, it can be said that the attention paid to Mrs
Gaskell during the last decade demonstrates that her reputation is probabl
improving. Those readers fond of rankings can be assured that she is n
longer—if indeed she ever was—a merely charming portrayer of a bygon
era, that she occupies a secure position in the development of the socia
novel, that she is surely among the best of the second rank of Victoria
novelists and perhaps has joined the first.

CHARLES KINGSLEY

James D. Barry

Perhaps the most telling single observation to be made about the recent state of Kingsley studies is that W. J. Harvey (*NCBEL*, 1969) lists only one item on Kingsley since the appearance of the Stevenson *Guide* in 1964. Similarly, the *Victorian Studies* annual bibliography for 1974 has not a single entry for Kingsley (though Susan Chitty's *The Beast and the Monk* did appear that year). And what might be called the only significant publication on Kingsley in 1973—*The Kingsleys: A Biographical Anthology*, compiled by Elspeth Huxley—opens with this observation: "Now and again a hitherto obscure family, for no apparent reason, erupts into fame, only to subside within a generation or two into its normal mediocrity. Such a one was the family of Charles Kingsley." The scholarly fame of Charles Kingsley the novelist has no doubt passed; indeed, his appearance in this volume may be an exaggeration of his importance today. This essay discusses the two books just mentioned and about a dozen articles. (There have also been a dozen dissertations in the last decade, several on the influence of Carlyle and Maurice.) It concludes with a note on recent interest in Kingsley (1975).

Susan Chitty's *The Beast and the Monk* (1974) is an adequate, informative, and pleasant (if slow-moving) biography. Two important and recent discoveries prompted its composition: a collection of about three hundred letters from Charles to his wife Fanny released by Kingsley's literary executor, Angela Covey-Crump, and Fanny's 1843 diary. Chitty sets out to provide a new portrait of Kingsley the man, but she never really succeeds in making him come fully alive—except (and this is a significant qualification) in the revelation of his preoccupation with sex. Commenting on the newly available letters and some recently discovered drawings reproduced here, Chitty makes this point: "Kingsley combined an extremely sensuous nature with strict inhibitions instilled by a formidable upbringing. He could only accept the idea of carnal relations with his wife once he had convinced himself that the body was holy and the act of sex a kind of

sacrament in which he was the priest and his partner the victim. Before the
marriage could be consummated the bodies of the lovers must be purified by
mortification, but their rewards would be great, for heaven, he declared
would consist of one perpetual copulation in a literal, physical sense."

The new letters give rise again to the question of the possible need for
collection of Kingsley's letters. James D. Barry reported in the Stevenson
Guide that Robert B. Martin deemed the correspondence unworthy of publication in its entirety. Martin had, of course, made use of his findings in
Charles Kingsley's American Notes (1958) and in the biography The Dust
of Combat (1959). Possibly the letters should be examined once more in
light of the three hundred new love letters. (Fred L. Standley, N&Q, 1969;
William J. Baker, N&Q, 1971; and Alan Jutzi, HLQ, 1971, report on fifty-
five additional letters that would require looking into if this examination
were launched. In fifty-one of these Kingsley wrote to James Hunt about his
lifelong speech difficulty, stammering [see Jutzi].) Despite the extensive use
made of these letters by Chitty, Martin's book remains the best single source
on Kingsley's life.

The Kingsleys: A Biographical Anthology (1973) is a compilation by
Elspeth Huxley of writings by the three Kingsley brothers: Charles, Henry
and George. About half the book is devoted to Charles, Huxley providing a
series of excerpts—or rather snippets—from his works, chronologically arranged and briefly introduced.

In his 1972 The Temper of Victorian Belief: Studies in the Religious
Novels of Pater, Kingsley, and Newman David Anthony Downes examines
Kingsley's religious convictions in general, including the important emphasis on the material world as divinized by the Incarnation, and his fictional
presentation of varieties of religious assent in Hypatia. By analyzing the
actions of several characters in the novel, Downes makes his point that
Hypatia chiefly "represents Kingsley's search for a way of expressing how
religious faith in Christianity happens, and what it means in the most
concrete personalist terms his imagination could conjure. However philo-
sophically vague, there is an attempt at a kind of phenomenology of faith,
what Newman called 'a grammar of assent.' The tenability of Christianity
as believable by people encountering their worlds on the most basic human
levels is what Kingsley was striving to examine."

The result of A. L. Rowse's pilgrimage to Kingsley's home in Eversley was
a three-part appreciative essay in the Contemporary Review (1972–73), an
essay that touches upon many aspects of Kingsley's life—for example, as
rector, naturalist, poet, and novelist. Raymond Chapman (N&Q, 1971)
speculates that Kingsley's use of the Lavington curse in Yeast may have been
traceable to the village of Lavington in Sussex and to Kingsley's acquaintance with Samuel Wilberforce, who had written about it.

In her examination of the use of Blue Books by Victorian novelists as the
basis for their fictional portrayal of contemporary life, Sheila M. Smith
(RES, 1970) discusses Kingsley's use in Yeast of the 1843 Report on the Employment of Women and Children in Agriculture. She finds Kingsley's

ctional re-creation inferior to Disraeli's more imaginative and less diagrammatic use of the same Blue Book in *Sybil*.

Gillian Beer's "Charles Kingsley and the Literary Image of the Country-ide" (*VS*, 1965) admires Kingsley's ability to combine sensitive and moving lescriptions of nature's beauties with an impatience toward that "exclu-ively aesthetic appreciation of the countryside which ignores the plight of he people who live there." The poor and the hungry cannot be expected to espond to nature's beauties; they "require help if their life is to become nything better than a mockery of pastoralism." In *Alton Locke* Kingsley lramatizes "the terrible contrast between the promise of the landscape and he pauper conditions of the labourers" by having the narrator, Alton, liscover this contrast for himself.

Phillipe Daumas (*LanM*, 1969) examines style in *Alton Locke* to demon-strate that Kingsley's attempt in this novel, only partly conscious, was not to lefend Chartism and socialism but to validate his own view of Christianity. His indignation over the suffering of the working classes arises from Chris-ian (charitable), not from revolutionary, motives. The article is too short for Daumas to be more than mildly successful in his demonstration. A more thorough study, Françoise Dottin's essay in *Politics in Literature in the Nineteenth Century* (1974), analyzes the presence of "Chartism and Chris-ian Socialism in *Alton Locke*," a novel in which Kingsley set out "to prove that Radicalism and Chartism had failed because they had rejected God and neglected morals; to give his readers a glimpse of the great things that might be achieved if Christianity and Chartism ever united." Jonathan Raban's 1971 *New Statesman* essay belittles Kingsley's unsuccessful attempt in *Alton Locke* to enter into the lives of the industrial proletariat. Raban likens the middle-class novelist trying to portray the lives of the urban poor to a middle-class intellectual deserting his class—more precisely, ad-venturing sexually among the poor. Finally, two recent editions of *Alton Locke* have been published—a 1967 Collins, introduced by David Lodge, and a 1969 Everyman, introduced by Thomas Byrom. There is also a critical and annotated edition, prepared by Conway K. Pellow as a dissertation (Univ. of Nebraska 1970).

William J. Baker (*SHR*, 1970) presents Kingsley, in his response to the Crimean War, as a figure of Victorian chauvinism. Baker illustrates Kings-ley's uncritical and even enthusiastic bellicosity by references to *Westward Ho!*, to his pamphlet *Brave Words to Brave Soldiers and Sailors*, and to various letters. John O. Waller (*SP*, 1963) examines Kingsley's inconsistent positions on the American Civil War. By temperament and background Kingsley was undoubtedly sympathetic to the Confederate cause and he was identified with that cause in England. Yet he did not support the South vigorously, and *Two Years Ago* reveals encouragement of the antislavery movement. On balance, however, he must be seen as pro-Southern.

Harold R. Gillespie, Jr. (*N&Q*, 1964), gives Kingsley credit for a specific achievement that had been overlooked. Gillespie points out that Gordon S. Haight is mistaken in asserting that Tertius Lydgate of *Middlemarch* is an

innovative character in being both physician as hero and physician ahead o
his time. Fourteen years before *Middlemarch*, in 1857, Kingsley had pre
sented a similar character, Tom Thurnall, in *Two Years Ago*.

In the period covered by this guide (1962 through 1974), it would seem
that scholarly interest in Charles Kingsley has waned, that the winnowing
process has done its work, and that Kingsley has been one of its victims. Yet
the 1975 centenary of his death, though it caused only a ripple in America
was marked in England by several events that suggest a revival. Such a
revival would, if it came to pass, pay little attention to Kingsley the novel
ist. A glance at the centenary publications in England is instructive. Owen
Chadwick (*HJ*) stresses the importance of viewing Kingsley as a whole: a
novelist, poet, historian, theologian, and writer of children's books. Gillian
Beer (*Listener*) discusses the relationship of *The Water Babies* to evolu
tionary theory. Brenda Colloms characterizes her *Charles Kingsley: The
Lion of Eversley* as "an account of Kingsley's life from a social point o
view." And the January number of *Theology*, a celebration of the Kingsley
centenary, includes articles on his fiction, his attitude toward science, hi
Regius professorship of history, and his racial philosophy. Kingsley the
novelist, recent evidence suggests, is clearly fading in significance; Kingsley
as notable and representative Victorian continues, particularly in England
to fascinate.

WILKIE COLLINS

Robert Ashley

Bibliography, Editions, Manuscripts and Letters

The bibliographical listing for Wilkie Collins in W. J. Harvey's "Minor Fiction 1830–1875" in *NCBEL*, which expands and updates the 1941 *CBEL* and its 1957 Supplement, is not complete and has several errors, inaccuracies, and omissions. In addition, one may question the continued classification of Collins as "minor" if George Borrow and Charles Reade are considered "major." Both Norman Page's *Wilkie Collins: The Critical Heritage* (1974) and William H. Marshall's *Wilkie Collins* (1970) contain short but helpful annotated bibliographies. "A Wilkie Collins Check List" (*ESA*, 1960) by R. V. Andrew (not "A. W." Andrew as appears in both Stevenson's 1964 *Guide* and *NCBEL*) still contains the most exhaustive list of Collins' writings, but Andrew's discussion of Collins' contributions to Dickens' Christmas Numbers cannot be trusted. For example, he credits Collins with five of the seven stories in *The Seven Poor Travellers*, but the *Household Words* Office Book indicates that Collins wrote only one story, "The Fourth" (see Anne Lohrli, *Household Words*, Toronto, 1973). In short, no one has yet compiled an authoritative bibliography.

The American reprint industry continues to do well by Collins. The 1974 *Books in Print: Authors* contains twenty-three entries. *The Moonstone* appears nine times (once as an adaptation for "Grade 2 Reading Level") and *The Woman in White* six. *Poor Miss Finch* is also available, as are five collections of Collins' short stories and novelettes. In addition, the AMS Press has reprinted the thirty-volume 1900 Collier edition of Collins' works. *British Books in Print* (1974) lists fifteen editions of *The Moonstone*, four of *The Woman in White*, and one each of *Armadale, The Black Robe, The Dead Secret, My Miscellanies*, and *Tales of Terror and the Supernatural* (a collection of Collins' stories). These statistics, when compared with those of

ten years ago, indicate that Collins is holding his own in both the Unite
States and Great Britain.

On the Continent as well, as the *Index Translationum* for 1971 indicate
he continues to be widely read, although the apparent popularity of *Poc
Miss Finch* and *The Moonstone*'s lack of it are odd. Also odd is the fact tha
the *Index* lists no French translations for the past few years. Collins' Ge:
man reputation receives considerable attention from Siegfried Mews i
"Sensationalism and Sentimentality: Minor Victorian Prose Writers i
Germany" (*MLN*, 1969).

Collins has always been fortunate in his editors. T. S. Eliot, Doroth
Sayers, and Alexander Woolcott have been followed by Kathleen Tillotso
in the Riverside *Woman in White*; Julian Symons, both a writer and hist«
rian of detective fiction, in the Penguin *Woman in White*; Harvey Pet«
Sucksmith in the Oxford English Novels edition of *The Woman in Whit*
(probably the most scholarly of all editions of Collins' novels); noveli:
Anthony Burgess in the Pan Paperback *Moonstone*; and J. I. M. Stewar
scholar and author of detective novels (under the pseudonym Micha«
Innes), in the Penguin *Moonstone*. The latter edition occasioned a perce]
tive review by Patrick Anderson in *The Spectator* (1966).

Collins' plays and letters remain uncollected and unpublished.* B«
twenty-seven letters from Collins to Reade and to Reade's longtime frien
and mistress, the actress Laura Seymour (written 1861–83), are owned b
Michael Reade (Scots Gate, Checkendon, Reading; see Thomas D. Clar«
son, "Wilkie Collins to Charles Reade: Some Unpublished Letters," *Vict«
rian Essays: A Symposium*, ed. Clareson and Warren D. Anderson, 1967
Together with a few isolated letters in other collections, such as the on
owned by Rex Sercombe-Smith of Bournemouth, they are all that remain «
an apparently extensive correspondence. At the conclusion of his essa
Clareson offers the interesting conjecture that Reade's brother Edward, wh
served in the Indian Civil Service, brought back from India a moonston
that Reade showed Collins and that could have provided Collins with th
title of his most famous novel, a possibility that Walter de la Mare ha
suggested earlier. This particular moonstone is still in the possession «
Michael Reade's sister Winwood.

Most of Dorothy Sayers' material on Collins was purchased after h«
death by the Humanities Research Center of the University of Texas. Th
outstanding item in the collection is the completed portion (five chapter.
of a projected full-length biography. In addition there are tables of cor
tents, bibliographies, considerable raw material in notebooks and on not
cards, 152 letters by Collins (these are analyzed in William R. Coleman:
dissertation "The University of Texas Collection of the Letters of Wilki
Collins, Victorian Novelist," Univ. of Texas 1975), and the manuscrip
of the novels *Heart and Science* and *The Law and the Lady*, the play *Th*

* The possibility of a collection of letters is being explored by Peter Carrociolo, togeth«
with John Bradley, of the University of Durham.

ed Vial, the short novel *The Guilty River,* the autobiographical "Remini-
ences of a Story-Teller," an unpublished and unacted play, "The Bird
octor," and many fragments. Professor E. R. Gregory of the University of
oledo is editing the biographical fragment and making a comparison of
e manuscript and published versions of the "Reminiscences." The Sayers
ction of the Marion E. Wade Collection at Wheaton College, Wheaton,
linois, contains some handwritten notes, a bibliography for a study of
ollins, and a list of Collins letters, with prices.

In the early seventies the Pierpont Morgan Library purchased over two
undred letters from Collins to his mother and brother and to his friend
harles Ward, together with other letters of the Collins family and their
rcle, most notably a large number written by Wilkie's father to Mrs.
ollins. The Morgan Library also has the manuscripts of *Hide and Seek,*
he Moonstone, and *The Woman in White*; a portion of Collins' contribu-
on to *No Thoroughfare,* a joint Dickens-Collins Christmas extra for
ickens' magazine *All the Year Round*; and three drafts of the play *The*
rozen Deep, the final manuscript, and a prompt copy partly in Dickens'
and. The Berg Collection in the New York Public Library contains the
anuscripts of *The Black Robe* and *I Say No,* as well as several fragments;
e British Library owns the manuscript of the early novelette *Mr. Wray's*
ash-Box and an early version of *Basil* (in which Basil is called Philip)
gether with a list of alternative titles. Other Collins materials can be
und at the university libraries of Boston, Durham, Harvard, Illinois,
rinceton, University of California, Los Angeles, and Yale, and also at the
olger and Huntington libraries. For further information on the location
f letters and manuscripts, researchers should consult Stevenson's *Guide*
d the Ashley, Davis, and Robinson biographies.

Criticism

nce the appearance of Stevenson's *Guide* in 1964, no biography has been
ublished; no new biographical data have been unearthed, nor does it
pear likely that any will be. However, critical and scholarly interest in
ollins continues undiminished. Not surprisingly, much of this centers on
is relationship and interaction with Dickens. The extreme anti-Collinsian
ttitude was expressed by J. W. T. Ley in the 1924 *Dickensian,* where he
ments Collins' influence on Dickens as "the most unfortunate happening
 Dickens's life" and fails to find "the remotest suggestion" of Dickens'
fluence on Collins; the latter statement seems close to absurd. In a later
ickensian article (1952), T. W. Hill categorically denies Collins' influence.
elson S. Harland reaches a similar, though somewhat muted, conclusion in
Dickens' Plots: 'The Ways of Providence' or the Influence of Wilkie Col-
ns?" (*VN,* 1961), arguing that Dickens' way of developing a plot owed
ore to evangelical Christianity's belief in an "all-pervading design in
uman affairs" than to Collins' influence.

But everyone agrees that the relationship between the two novelists was

close and intimate, especially in their collaboration on the Christm
Numbers of *Household Words* and *All the Year Round* and their particip
tion in amateur theatricals. The latter is the subject of Robert Louis Bra
nan's exhaustive study *Under the Management of Mr. Charles Dickens: H
Production of the Frozen Deep* (1966). Brannan's work reproduces "Th
Prompt-Book" rather than the later version that Collins prepared for pr
fessional production and shows conclusively the strict control exercised b
Dickens in the joint productions of the two novelists. Collins later wrote
fictional version of the play. Although he similarly made a novel (*Jezebel
Daughter*) of the play *The Red Vial*, he usually did the reverse. The dram
tization of his novels is analyzed in Barbara Ann Brashear's dissertatio
"Wilkie Collins: From Novel to Play" (Case Western Reserve 1972).

Despite holding a tight rein, Dickens accorded Collins a status allowed n
other contributor to the two magazines. This point is made by Debora
Thomas in her two articles "Contributors to the Christmas Numbers c
Household Words and *All the Year Round*, 1850–1867" (*Dkn*, 197
and 1974) and by Anne Lohrli in "Household Words and Its 'Office Book'
(*PULC*, 1964).

Following the example of T. S. Eliot and Dorothy Sayers, many schola
and critics have chosen to emphasize *The Moonstone* and Collins' role i
the development of detective fiction. Both Thomas J. Hardy in "The R
mance of Crime," *Books on the Shelf* (1934) and V. S. Pritchett in "Th
Roots of Detection," *Books in General* (1953) offer explanations for th
popularity of the genre and congratulate Collins for his prescience in hi
ting on the source of this popularity. The book-length histories of detectiv
fiction—Howard Haycraft's *Murder for Pleasure* (rev. ed., 1968), A.
Murch's *The Development of the Detective Novel* (rev. ed., 1968), an
Julian Symons' *Mortal Consequences* (British title *Bloody Murder*, 197
Penguin rev. ed., 1974)—analyze not only *The Moonstone* but other Collir
stories and novels with prominent elements of detection. Symons, howeve
denies *The Moonstone*'s claim to being the first English detective nove
This honor belongs, he says, to *The Notting Hill Mystery*, serialize
anonymously in 1862 and published three years later in book form as th
work of Charles Felix, presumably a pseudonym. In 1945 Maurice Richar
son had included this whodunit, together with *The Woman in White, D
Jekyll and Mr. Hyde*, and Le Fanu's *Carmilla*, in an anthology entitle
Novels of Mystery from the Victorian Age, but he neglected to point ou
that "Felix" anticipated Collins by six years.

In many ways the most fascinating recent study of Collins appears in *Th
Dangerous Edge* (1975), in which Gavin Lambert advances the thesis tha
crime specialists (he discusses Collins, Doyle, Buchan, Amber, Chandle
Simenon, and Hitchcock) are driven to the dangerous edge by some trau
matic childhood experience that they exorcise in their fiction (or film in th
case of Hitchcock). Lambert emphasizes that Collins was an "outsider
whose attitude toward crime, criminals, and detectives was ambivalen
hence the relatively minor role played by the world-weary Sergeant Cuff an
his admiration for villains like Count Fosco. Essentially the same point

ade by John Reed in his provocative article "English Imperialism and the nacknowledged Crime of *The Moonstone*" (*ClioW*, 1973), the unac-owledged crime being the original theft of the diamond from its rightful indu owners, a fact that the insensitive, respectable, imperialist-minded, iddle-class characters fail to realize (see also Reed's discussions of Collins his *Victorian Conventions*, 1975). A hint of this anti-imperialism of Col-as was earlier given in Peter Wolfe's "Point of View and Characterization Wilkie Collins' *The Moonstone*" (*ForumH*, 1965). Lambert's trauma eory was to some extent anticipated in psychologist Charles Rycroft's he Analysis of a Detective Story" in *Imagination and Reality: Psycho-alytical Essays* (1968). Rycroft uses *The Moonstone* to demonstrate that e popularity of detective stories "arises from their ability to reawaken the terest and curiosity aroused by the primal scene," a theory first enunciated Geraldine Pederson-Krag in "Detective Stories and the Primal Scene" syQ, 1949). By far the best psychological analysis of *The Moonstone* is bert D. Hutter's "Dreams, Transformations, and Literature: The Impli-tions of Detective Fiction" (*VS*, 1975); unlike many other psychological terpreters, Hutter is well read in Collins criticism and does not wrench e entire novel to fit a preconceived theory.

Conan Doyle's indebtedness to Collins has always been considered some-hat conjectural. In the opinion of the Swedish scholar S. B. Liljegren The Parentage of Sherlock Holmes," *Irish Essays and Studies*, Stockholm, 71), there is no doubt of the debt. Doyle wrote detective stories "because e success of Wilkie Collins had showed him the way to fame and money," e plot of *The Sign of the Four* was "partly copied" from *The Moonstone*, d Sherlock Holmes was obviously an imitation of Sergeant Cuff.

Far more has been written about *The Moonstone* than about any other ollins novel. Yet Collins himself preferred *The Woman in White*, as do th Maurice Richardson and U. C. Knoepflmacher. Richardson's discus-on of *The Woman in White* in the introduction to *Novels of Mystery from e Victorian Age* is notable for its analysis of Sir Percival Glyde as a "by no eans unsubtle, pantomime demon of a character . . . full of sociological gnificance." In words that recall both Lambert and Reed, Knoepflmacher scribes *The Woman in White* "as a unique instance of a mid-Victorian vel in which the author openly acknowledges an anarchic and asocial unterworld as a powerfully attractive alternative to the ordered, civilized orld of conventional beliefs" ("The Counterworld of Victorian Fiction and he Woman in White," *The Worlds of Victorian Fiction*, ed. Jerome H. uckley, 1975). Another intriguing theory is Peter Caracciolo's that Dante's ic is the main source for the novel's symbolism, both explicit and implicit Wilkie Collins' 'Divine Comedy': The Use of Dante in *The Woman in hite*," *NCF*, 1971). In fact, there are distinct signs of an increasing interest *The Woman in White*; it is, for instance, the only Collins novel to be the bject of an entire dissertation (William L. Brightman, "A Study of *The oman in White*," Diss. Univ. of Washington 1974; see also C. H. Muller, ncident and Characterization in *The Woman in White*," *UES*, 1973).

Aside from his two masterpieces, Collins' individual novels have received scant attention. Worth mentioning, however, is Dougald MacEachen "Wilkie Collins' *Heart and Science* and the Vivisection Controversy" (*V* 1966), a controversy that MacEachen shows attracted the attention not on of Collins but also of Lewis Carroll, Hardy, Shaw, and Browning. The sho stories are discussed in Muller's "Victorian Sensationalism: The Sho Stories of Wilkie Collins" (*UES*, 1973).

Critics like T. S. Eliot who sparked the renewal of interest in Colli treated him primarily as a highly skilled writer of melodrama and escap literature. But there has been an increasing tendency, noticeable in some of the writers already mentioned, to evaluate Collins on his own terms, that to consider him the serious novelist he always claimed to be. This trend w certainly evident as early as 1948, when MacEachen wrote his "Wilk Collins: Victorian Crusader" (Diss. Univ. of Cincinnati). But it reached i height in William H. Marshall's *Wilkie Collins* (TEAS, 1970). Marsha rightly calls his book the first "to deal exclusively with the literary art of Wilkie Collins." Marshall's conclusion is that Collins, while recognizing th conflicting claims of the ordinary reading public and the intelligentsia, wa unlike Dickens, rarely able to reconcile them. Two recent unpublishe dissertations present Collins as somewhat more successful. In "Wilkie Co lins and the Sensation Novel" (Univ. of North Carolina 1967), James M Daniel Heldman, Jr., states that though Collins "thought of himself as story teller, he refused to divorce character from action and insisted that successful novel of incident must be a novel of character as well." Roger V Dennis in "Wilkie Collins and the Conventions of the Thesis Nove (Univ. of Alabama 1973) asserts that Collins used these conventions mor skillfully than his contemporaries because he did not sacrifice plot an character to propaganda.

The most recent major addition to Collins scholarship is, of course, No man Page's *Wilkie Collins: The Critical Heritage* (1974). The preface an the introduction, both worth reading by all Collinsians, discuss many of th topics mentioned above. Page's statement in the preface that Collins wa "widely read and widely reviewed during a longer period than almost ar other novelist of his time" should put to rest forever the legend that th Collins of the 1870s and 1880s was a pitiful but heroic figure laborious. and painfully grinding out wretched novels that nobody bothered to rea Page's introduction also warns against making "inflated claims" for Collin Since Collins made inflated claims for himself, they have to be considere but such consideration often makes him seem dull. And, as T. S. Elio pointed out, the one fault Collins rarely possesses is dullness.

Film Versions

Since his novels are more readily adaptable to film than to stage, it is no surprising that several motion pictures and television dramas owe their origin to Collins. In concluding the introduction to his *Critical Heritag*

Jorman Page remarks that in "the art of the cinema—for example, in the ork of Alfred Hitchcock and other masters of the 'psychological thriller' . . Collinsian plot-situations and character-types have a habit of recurring. Enthusiasts of the genre will, for instance, recognize in the Mr. Gutman of ohn Huston's *The Maltese Falcon* a latter-day Count Fosco.)" As a matter f fact, the same actor, Sidney Greenstreet, played both Gutman in *The Maltese Falcon* and Fosco in Warner Brothers' 1948 version of *The Woman i White*. Beginning with a 1912 production by Gem-Universal, *The Woman in White* has been far and away the film adapter's favorite. Even ith such titles as *The Dream Woman, Tangled Lives, The Twin Pawns,* nd *Crimes at the Dark House,* and with credit given to "Wilkie Cooper," ie plot summaries indicate clearly that these adaptations are based on *The Woman in White*. Undoubtedly the finest adaptation of a Collins novel was ie BBC's four-part Masterpiece Theatre production of *The Moonstone,* nown during the winter of 1972 by the Public Broadcasting System in the nited States. Of Collins' lesser-known novels *The New Magdalen* has in- ired three films, one with the title *Mercy Merrick* (the name of the eroine); a 1910 version starred Pearl White.

The past decade has been fruitful for Collins scholarship, most notably in ie work of Reed, Lambert, and Knoepflmacher in examining Collins as an lien rebel who rather subtly attacked the most cheerful foundations of ictorian respectability. There is still need for a complete and accurate ollins bibliography, an anthology of his plays, and a collection of his tters.

CHARLES READE

Wayne Burns

At present, Charles Reade is the most neglected of the major nineteenth
century novelists. Although Thomas D. Clareson has completed his full
scale biography of Reade, no major studies of any kind have appeared in
print during the period under review. Indeed, only a few books and articles
have dealt with either Reade or his work, and of these, only two, perhaps
three, contribute significantly to scholarship and criticism on Reade.

Thomas D. Clareson's "Wilkie Collins to Charles Reade: Some Unpublished Letters" (*Victorian Essays: A Symposium*, ed. Warren D. Anderson
and Thomas D. Clareson, 1967) discusses "twenty-seven letters written by
Wilkie Collins to Reade or Laura Seymour and dating between June 2,
1861 and July 17, 1883." These letters, which range all the way from social
invitations to the extended criticism of Reade's *Free Labour* (the dramatic
adaptation of *Put Yourself in His Place*) that Collins includes in his letter of
29 May 1871, "have their ultimate value," as Clareson himself explains, "in
confirming without doubt the intimacy of Reade and Collins."

Avrom Fleishman's brief study of *The Cloister and the Hearth* (in his
The English Historical Novel, 1971) provides a new and incisive analysis of
Reade's best-known novel. After discussing Reade's Baconian and anti-
Carlylean ideas in some detail, Fleishman goes on to show how Reade
embodied his ideas and theories of history in the novel "to tell of the
unsung heroes of common life and to debunk the myth of the Middle Ages."
But even though Reade achieves "an unquestionably powerful evocation of
history," the novel is still, according to Fleishman, "shackled by his
[Reade's] Protestant, Whiggish perspective":

> In the portrait of his unsung hero, the father of Erasmus, Reade paints a
> stereotype of the Victorian virtues, common both to Reade's creed and to his
> arch-enemy Carlyle's. The honest, grave, reverential, mildly sadistic, sex-ob-
> sessed but self-repressive Gerard may have existed in the fifteenth century but
> he is a hero of the nineteenth. By setting him up to contrast with his age and

to draw our sympathy towards him, Reade turns the historical setting itself into the hero's antagonist. The novel becomes the story of the hero *against* his age. Gerard's quest, vocation, and rebellion are drawn not as responses to the special qualities of the medieval-Renaissance transition but as the inevitable chafings of a free man against the bit of society. Not only does such a structure imply a return to the Carlylian heroics against which Reade rebelled: it is a fundamentally unhistorical attitude which sees cultural forms exclusively as a set of impediments to the individual's free expression. Reade is not only a Whig but a liberal: society is merely an epiphenomenon, and only the individual has reality and worth.

In trying to show the limitations of Reade's historical "perspective" Fleishman has perhaps revealed the limitations of his own critical perspective. And there are other difficulties too, deriving primarily from Fleishman's misunderstanding of Reade's anti-Carlylean heroics. Nevertheless, in its own terms, Fleishman's criticism is intelligent and well argued and should stimulate further discussion of *The Cloister and the Hearth.*

In "The Case against Trade Unions in Early Victorian Fiction" (*VS,* 1969) Patrick Brantlinger also finds Reade shackled by his individualist ideas and attitudes. Brantlinger insists that Reade's *Put Yourself in His Place* (1867) has "nothing in common with the stories of Dickens and Mrs. Gaskell. Whereas they, as well as Carlyle, Disraeli, Charlotte Brontë, and Kingsley, argue for forgiveness and a rapprochement between the classes, Reade argues for invading 'the Manchester district with a hundred thousand special constables.' . . . That is the notion of a writer who equates sensational news clippings with reality." While this may seem like harsh criticism, there is no denying that much of it is justified. But there is also no denying that Reade's motives in attacking the unions were quite different from those that Brantlinger attributes to him. Reade saw the unions as oligarchies—violent and inhumane and dirty oligarchies that would deny the freedom of the individual workman, much as the oligarchies that he believed he himself had encountered (among his publishers and critics and detractors) had tried to deny his personal and artistic freedom.

Coral Lansbury is still another critic who attributes Reade's limitations to his intellectual commitments. In the chapter she devotes primarily to Reade's play *Gold* ("Charles Reade Strikes Gold," *Arcady in Australia,* 1970) Lansbury argues that Reade's treatment of Australia (both in *Gold,* 1853, and later in his novel *It Is Never Too Late to Mend,* 1856) follows the conventions established by Samuel Sidney and made popular by Dickens and Bulwer-Lytton—conventions based on Sidney's misguided attempts to present Australia as Arcady. That Reade adhered to these conventions, presuming that they were as all-pervasive as Lansbury contends, is doubtless true, but that his adherence contributes to the inadequacy and unfairness of his treatment of Australia in the ways that she contends is open to serious question. In contending, for example, that Reade failed to understand the colonial gentry when he dismissed them as the "Hairy-stocracy," Lansbury seems to be writing, not as a scholar or critic, but as a patriot defending th[e] traditions and culture of her native land. This is also true in her criticism o[f] many other passages, and the impression is deepened by the fact that she ha[s] apparently made no effort to acquaint herself with previous scholarship tha[t] relates to Reade and Australia.

W. J. B. Owen's "A Byronic Shipwreck in the Pacific" (*N&Q*, 1963) dea[ls] with a long passage from another of Reade's lesser novels (Chs. x–xxv o[f] *Foul Play*). Owen argues, unconvincingly, that Reade drew the passag[e] having to do with a shipwreck and the "subsequent voyage of the survivor[s] in an open boat to a Pacific island" from "the well known account of th[e] shipwreck in Byron's *Don Juan*, Canto II." Yet even if the parallels Owe[n] cites were actual borrowings they would still be of little consequence. Afte[r] all, Reade was a notorious borrower, and there is nothing particularly sig nificant in these parallels or borrowings.

C. H. Muller's "Charles Reade and *The Cloister and the Hearth: A* Survey of the Novel's Literary Reception and Its Historic Fidelity" and hi[s] "Charles Reade's *Hard Cash*: False Art and Pure Fiction" (*UES*, 1971) ar[e] apparently intended to provide "a two-part study of Reade's documentar[y] methods." But the two articles, "based on extracts from a doctoral disserta tion submitted to the University of London," do little more than repea[t] with added illustrations, what previous scholars have said about Reade['s] documentary techniques.

Critical interest in Reade has been steadily waning for over a hundre[d] years now. And while there are good reasons for this decline—reasons tha[t] have, perhaps, been too much stressed—there are equally good reasons wh[y] his fiction should still merit scholarly and critical attention. *Griffith Gaun[t]*, for all its sensationalism, will bear comparison with even the great Victoria[n] novels; and *Christie Johnstone, It Is Never Too Late to Mend, Hard Cash*, and *The Cloister and the Hearth* will certainly bear closer critical scrutin[y] than they have yet been given. Then there are all the as yet unexplore[d] questions having to do with Reade's influence on other writers. To cite onl[y] one example: Henry James in his review of Hardy's *Far from the Maddin[g] Crowd* notes that Bathsheba is "a young lady of the inconsequential, wilfu[l] mettlesome type which has lately become so much the fashion for heroine[s] and of which Mr. Charles Reade is in a manner the inventor—the typ[e] which aims at giving one a very intimate sense of a young lady's womanish ness." And in these remarks James has only begun to suggest the extent o[f] Reade's influence on *Far from the Madding Crowd*. For, if Bathsheba is a[ ] type of heroine of which Reade "is in a manner the inventor," then Gabrie[l] Oak is an even more clear-cut example of a type of hero, more specifically a[ ] type of Resourceful Hero, of which Reade is also "in a manner the in ventor."

But Reade himself did not think of his Resourceful Hero as a literar[y] type. He conceived of him as nothing less than the answer to Carlyle and al[l] the Carlyleans, in everything from philosophy to politics to social reform[.] And he conceived of himself as the ultimate embodiment, in real life, of hi[s]

wn heroic type, in everything from his efforts to free lunatics to his activ-
ies in behalf of free labor and women's rights. For these and other reasons
hat have yet to be fully explored, Reade still remains almost as much of an
nigma as he was in his own time, when he was alternately hailed as a
enius (or at least as a man of enormous talent and energy) and dismissed
s a crank or even as a madman. And yet the Princeton and the London
ibrary collections of his notebooks and note cards (see Stevenson *Guide*,
p. 287–89), running to thousands of pages and containing material that
night contribute to a fuller understanding not only of him and his work
ut of every phase of Victorian life and art, remain unedited and seemingly
nexamined.

GEORGE ELIOT

U. C. Knoepflmacher

As recently as 1948, in *A Literary History of England*, Samuel C. Chew could say of George Eliot, "No other Victorian novelist of major rank is so little read today." By now, however, the novelist is more respected than Margaret Oliphant, whose presumed "resemblance" to George Eliot led Chew to group the two together. According to Alan Roper, former editor of *Nineteenth-Century Fiction*, from "the beginning of 1967 to the middle of 1974," George Eliot ranked fifth (after James, Dickens, Hawthorne, and Melville—three Americans and but one other eminent Victorian) as the subject for essays submitted to that journal. The submissions on *Middlemarch*, however, exceeded those on *Portrait of a Lady, Moby-Dick, Great Expectations,* and *The Scarlet Letter* and were outnumbered only by discussions of *Wuthering Heights.* Although this single statistic is admittedly inconclusive, there is no question that the "post-1945 phenomenon" to which the late W. J. Harvey alluded in his chapter on George Eliot in the Stevenson *Guide* has catapulted into an even more impressive "post-1960 phenomenon." More was written on George Eliot from 1960 to 1974 than in the entire century between the appearance of *Adam Bede* in 1859 and the publication of the books by Jerome Thale, Barbara Hardy, and Reva Stump in 1959.

George Eliot's reinstatement as a major writer and seminal thinker can be traced to a variety of causes: among them, the general resurgence of interest in all things Victorian, the new attention given to the female imagination, and the higher respect paid to the mixture of "honest doubt" and religious yearning found in her work. More specifically, her return to preeminence was facilitated by Gordon S. Haight's monumental edition of *The George Eliot Letters* (1954–55), by the weight of F. R. Leavis' pronouncements, and by the acumen of fine critics such as Hardy, Thale, Stump, and W. J. Harvey. Since the latter modestly devoted but one sentence to his own *The Art of George Eliot* (1961) in his 1964 chapter, it seems proper to recall the significance of Harvey's skillful assault on those post-Jamesian critics who

r so long had snubbed George Eliot for the presumably ponderous and
itrusive effect of her authorial interventions. Today, we may still debate
hether to call her narrator a "he" or a "she" or to view her/him as an
androgynous" speaker, but the fact remains that we have learned from
Harvey to regard this narrative voice as integral to the formal aspects of
George Eliot's art. As J. Hillis Miller puts it, "The narrator is an all-
embracing consciousness which surrounds the minds of the characters,
knows them from the inside, but also sees them in terms of their relations to
ne another and in terms of the universal facts of human nature which they
exemplify" (*The Form of Victorian Fiction*, 1968).

Could it be that this unifying "consciousness," straining, like Mr.
Casaubon, "mentally to construct" reality "as it used to be, in spite of ruin
nd confusing changes," yet also able, unlike Mr. Casaubon, to imply what
ught to be, to animate tissues of relations with amazing empathy and
understanding, is at the very core of our current infatuation with George
Eliot? Mary Ann Evans' dislocation, her separation from the settled, traditional order of her youth, was countered by fictions in which the past
became reconstituted, in which lost relations could be replaced by fictive
relations, recast into what Raymond Williams calls "a socially selective
landscape." Williams is rather hard on George Eliot for her "impersona-
ions" and translocations. In "The Knowable Community in George Eliot's
Novels" (*Novel*, 1969) and in *The Country and the City* (1973) he faults
her for withholding a "full response to existing society," for finding value
only as a "general condition" in the past, and for upholding "in the
present" a mere "particular and private sensibility, the individual moral
action." Williams seems closer to the mark than Calvin Bedient, who objects
even more strenuously to George Eliot's novels, but for exactly the opposite
reasons. For Bedient, the chastisement of all antisocial impulses converts
George Eliot into the apologist of a too bland "social self" that "spells the
end of vital coloring, the spontaneous and individual impulse, of human
beings" (*Architects of the Self: George Eliot, D. H. Lawrence, and E. M.
Forster*, 1972).

As Mr. Snell, the landlord in *Silas Marner*, would say, "The truth lies
atween you: you're both right and wrong, as I allays say." Williams is
correct in holding that George Eliot's *Daniel Deronda* is the logical culmination of a disenchantment with Victorian social values already apparent in
the earlier fictions; for his part, Bedient, too, is right in regarding the same
novel as the most pronounced version of George Eliot's "ritual journey to
the social self." Yet, since both men are right, each is also wrong. George
Eliot's art is both self-reflexive and social, as her two most nearly perfect
works, *Silas Marner* and *Middlemarch*, demonstrate. And it is her Victorian
ability to live with inconsistency and paradox that not only defies the one-
eyed standards of judgment brought to bear by Bedient, Williams, and
other critics but also accounts, I think, for her appeal to readers who live in
and react to a reality as contradictory as that to which she responded. It may
well be that George Eliot's reputation will again diminish (or will require

different forms of justification) in a more regulated order of the future. Bu
until the advent of that millennium, I strongly suspect that we will con
tinue to value her own striving for order and relation and be more tha
willing to wink on those occasions when her efforts are, in her own word
about *Romola*, "wanting due proportion." The "phenomenon" noted b
Harvey thus seems destined to last for a long time.

Bibliography, Editions, Letters

William H. Marshall's fairly thorough listings in "A Selective Bibliograph
of Writings about George Eliot, to 1965" (*BB*, 1967) will be updated i
David Leon Higdon's forthcoming "A Bibliography of George Eliot Crit
cism, 1965–1975" in the same journal. Higdon's copious listings, whic
include dissertations and many items not cited in this chapter, will eventu
ally become part of a book-length bibliography. Jerome Beaty's chapter i
A. E. Dyson's *The English Novel: Select Bibliographical Guides* (1974
provides a most helpful overview of major texts, critical commentaries, an
selected background readings. Gordon S. Haight describes the manuscript
private papers, and "association books" at Yale in "The George Eliot an
George Henry Lewes Collection" (*YULG*, 1971). And Hollis L. Cate trace
the early publishing history of six of the novels in America in "The Initia
Publication of George Eliot's Novels in America" (*ForumH*, 1969).

There is still no complete critical edition of the works, although th
Clarendon Press now intends to publish all the novels under the editorshi
of Gordon S. Haight. Haight's own Riverside edition of *The Mill on th
Floss* (1961) is still the best, since it reproduces all important textua
variants. The Penguin English Library now provides the best editions o
five other novels: W. J. Harvey's edition of *Middlemarch* (1965) is not quit
as "fully annotated" as it might have been (there are, moreover, a few
minor mistakes: J. F. Oberlin was born in 1740 and not in 1770; when
Ladislaw suggests that Casaubon should have read German scholars, he i
obviously referring to mythographers such as Creuzer and not to Strauss'
Das Leben Jesu); Barbara Hardy's edition of *Daniel Deronda* (1967
collates the text of the 1878 Cabinet Edition with the 1876 text but record
only "one or two particularly interesting changes" in the otherwise helpfu
notes; Q. D. Leavis' edition of *Silas Marner* (1967), well annotated, thoug
somewhat idiosyncratically, appends "A Note on Dialect"; Peter Coveney'
edition of *Felix Holt* (1972) contains some elaborate notes that are distract
ing in their special pleading but wisely reproduces the "Address to Workin
Men, by Felix Holt" and a note on the complicated law of entail used in th
plot; finally, David Lodge's edition of *Scenes of Clerical Life* (1973), muc
needed, reproduces important variants and emendations and reprints "How
I Came to Write Fiction." The introductions to these five editions ar

iscussed in the section on criticism of individual works, below, as are the
ntroductions to John Paterson's edition of *Adam Bede* (1968) and to
eorge Levine's edition of *Felix Holt* (1970).

There is no new edition of *Romola*; the Everyman edition of that novel
eems to be out of print. The long-announced Norton Critical Edition of
Middlemarch had yet to appear at the time this survey was written. George
Eliot's translation of Strauss's *The Life of Jesus Critically Examined*, long
ut of print, has been reprinted with an introduction and annotations by
eter C. Hodgson (1972), who notes "a few omissions and errors."

Thomas Pinney's edition of *Essays of George Eliot* (1963) contains twenty-
nine selections, from the early "Poetry and Prose: From the Notebook of an
Eccentric" (1846) to the posthumously published "Leaves from a Notebook" (1883). The judicious selections well display the ranges and riches of
George Eliot's interests. Particularly welcome is the hitherto unpublished
Notes on Art," which, if taken as relevant to her theory of the novel,
contains important modifications of her earlier conceptions of realism in
iction." Pinney's headnotes and annotations are excellent, and his appendixes on "George Eliot's Periodical Essays and Reviews" (he lists over
eventy items) and "Articles Wrongfully or Doubtfully Attributed to
George Eliot" establish the canon with authority. His interesting point that
he anonymity of the essay allowed George Eliot to speak out on the ques-
ion of woman's place in society far more freely than in the novels ought to
be marked by the novelist's new feminist critics.

Of interest, too, to feminists might be the mini essay on "Conformity"
hat Pinney reprints, together with other entries omitted by Charles Lee
Lewes, in "More Leaves from George Eliot's Notebook" (*HLQ*, 1966). As
Pinney explains, Lewes' contention that he had selected from the notebook
all essays not already published in *Theophrastus Such* was untrue, since he
'silently passed over" almost a third of the manuscript pages. The longest
and most interesting of the notebook entries is an essay on "Historic Guidance," in which George Eliot denies, among other things, Comte's notion
that historical continuity invariably can act as a positive principle and
guide.

In "George Eliot's Periodical Contributions" (Diss. Yale 1966) James
Darius Rust devotes much space to attributions already settled by Pinney,
yet has interesting remarks about George Eliot's place among Victorian
reviewers. The essays also occupy Michael Wolff in "Marian Evans to
George Eliot: The Moral and Intellectual Foundations of Her Career"
(Diss. Princeton 1958), a careful study in the history of ideas.

John C. Pratt and Victor A. Neufeldt have prepared a critical edition of
two *Middlemarch* notebooks, one in the Folger Library, the other in the
Berg Collection of the New York Public Library, to be printed on micro-
fiche by the University of California Press. Promised for the Salzburg Romantic Reassessment series is an edition by William Baker of notebooks at
the Carl H. Pforzheimer Library. And in her preface to a 1974 edition of the
1847 *Ranthorpe* Barbara Smalley holds that George Henry Lewes' melo-

dramatic potboiler deserves to be reread because it presumably contain
similarities to "the Rosamond-Lydgate part of *Middlemarch* and th
Gwendolen-Grandcourt part of *Daniel Deronda*."

An eighth volume of Haight's *The George Eliot Letters,* not yet in prin
when this essay was written, is to contain letters that have surfaced in th
last twenty years, as well as errata. One such letter, an exuberant burlesqu
of a Teufelsdröckhian "Professor Bücherwurm, Moderig University," is re
printed by Haight in "A New George Eliot Letter" (*TLS,* 12 Feb. 1971
YULG, 1971). Haight also reproduces eight even more significant letters i
"New George Eliot Letters to John Blackwood" (*TLS,* 10 Mar. 1972). I
one of these, George Eliot tells her publisher that, though able to rerea
Adam Bede and *The Mill,* she could not bring herself to correct the *Scene*
and *Silas* because the reading excited her and carried her "away from th
present." In a plea for "bound-in manuscripts" for his supplementar
volume (*TLS,* 15 Mar. 1974) Haight explains that some letters, as well a
leaves from a notebook with readings for *The Spanish Gypsy,* were boun
into a "Large-Paper Edition" published by Houghton Mifflin in 1908. I
"Unpublished George Eliot Letters" (*TLS,* 16 May 1968) Joan Bennet
reproduces a series of letters written by Lewes, George Eliot, and John Cros
to Jane Maria Strachey, the mother of James and Lytton Strachey, "a warn
and welcome friend."

Biography

In reading Elfrida Vipont's *Towards a High Attic: The Early Life o
George Eliot* (1970) and Rosemary Sprague's *George Eliot: A Biography*
(1968) one is reminded of the narrator's sly remark in *Middlemarch* that, i
"Mrs. Lemon had undertaken to describe Juliet or Imogen, these heroine:
would not have seemed poetical." Whereas Mrs. Lemon made the poetica
seem prosaic, both Vipont (Elfrida Foulds, also the author of *The Girlhoo
of Charlotte Brontë*) and Sprague (the author of many a historical romance
for "young readers") eagerly try to reverse the process. In Vipont's book the
result is charming because unabashedly fictional (" 'Oh, Mary Ann, you *are*
a silly,' scolded her older brother"). When Sprague applies the same poetic
license, however, the pretensions of a "careful study" are quickly shattered:
here, too, Isaac Evans invariably calls Mary Ann a "silly," while Robert
Evans just as invariably calls her his "little wench." And Mary Ann hersel
—considered by all, according to Sprague's kind embellishment, to be "an
extremely elegant and beautiful young woman"—soon transmutes her first
abortive romance into "the poignant delineation of Maggie Tulliver's hope-
less love for Philip Wakem [?]." Life, it would appear, always imitates *The
Mill on the Floss.*

Sprague and Vipont, as well as Frank Wilson Kenyon in *The Consuming
Flame: The Story of George Eliot* (1970), draw heavily on Haight's edition
of the *Letters.* (Sprague also borrows extensively from his *George Eliot and*

John Chapman, 1940, and from Kitchel's *George Lewes and George Eliot*, 1933.) The letters are also used, but in infinitely more fruitful fashion, in the two major biographies we have by Haight himself and by Ruby Redinger, which nicely complement each other.

Haight's *George Eliot: A Biography* (1968) scrupulously gathers all known facts; he allows that "one might be tempted to look for psychological explanations" of such developments as the asceticism that Mary Ann indulged in after her mother's death, yet always concludes that "such speculations are futile; one can tell only the facts." Although one may not agree with U. C. Knoepflmacher's irreverent criticism of these "self-imposed limitations" ("Mr. Haight's George Eliot: 'Wahrheit und Dichtung,' " *VS*, 1969), it is true that Haight's biography is better read as a careful reference work than as an interpretation of the woman behind the novels. Read in that fashion, the book's chief thesis—that George Eliot, in Bray's words, "was not fitted to stand alone"—and the occasional search for the "originals" of some of her fictional characters are less important than its authoritative and exhaustive compilation of all the details of George Eliot's life history. Carefully correcting many factual errors or false attributions, Haight also reprints for the first time Marianne's (she was not yet Mary Ann or Marian at the time) 1834 school notebook, which contains a somewhat priggish essay on "Affectation and Conceit" and the story "Edward Neville." The latter, which seems to owe much to Scott's *Redgauntlet*, interestingly has for its protagonist "an outcast from society, an alien from my family, a deserter, and a regicide." Since the fifteen-year-old created this alienated hero before her own acute alienations from father, religion, brother, and society, Haight's caution about a too ready identification of creations with creator may after all be justified.

Ruby Redinger's *George Eliot: The Emergent Self* (1975) is as massive as Haight's book and ought to be regarded as its companion volume (or "pendant," as the Victorians would have said). This is so not only because she so often refers to Haight's biography but also because, with only minimal disagreements about basic facts, she boldly tries to isolate the psychological dynamic he eschews. Redinger's subtitle signals her appropriation of Lewes' notion of "emergence" (his term for "an unpredictable result arising from known sources"): by tracing the confluence of internal causes and external events, she tries to chart the course that led the multiple selves of Mary Ann Evans to become consolidated in the more secure creative intelligence called "George Eliot." Although Redinger's psychological determinism is seldom reductive or falsifying, some of the strands in the personality "modulation" she examines remain less believable than others. She also overvalues, I think, the benefits of the "dual solitude" enjoyed by Lewes and George Eliot and is far less effective when, in the last third of the book, she gives a hurried account of all the fiction. A little distracting, too, are the repeated references to "psychosomatic" illnesses and accidents (Sara Hennell catches a cold because rejected by Mary Ann, Robert Evans breaks a leg because he wants his daughter back) and to the pathological enmities of rivals (though correct on Harriet Martineau, Redinger fails to allow some justice to Eliza Lynn Linton's malice and rather exaggerates Carlyle's presumed resentment of the "strong-minded woman"). Still, the book's considerable merits by far outweigh such occasional imbalances. Especially effective is Redinger's running analysis of Cross's biographical cover-ups; the revelations she manages to extract from the "Brother and Sister" sonnets, the poem "Self and Life," the essay on "Women in France," and other minor writings by George Eliot, as well as by Lewes, are impressive.

Even if its 116 illustrations are good to have for their own sake, Marghanita Laski's *George Eliot and Her World* (1973) is more than a picture book with a slim text, for it contains a skillful condensation of salient events as well as original surmises. Unlike Haight, who is harsh on Herbert Spencer ("an egoist who could love nothing but his 'image' "), and unlike Redinger, who deeply resents the psychic damage done by Robert and Isaac Evans, Laski proposes a new villain of sorts: George Henry Lewes himself. More willing than either Haight or Redinger to give some credence to Eliza Lynn Linton's innuendos, she contends that Lewes' managerial manipulations considerably "coarsened" George Eliot as a public figure; she also supports, though cautiously, the inference that, after Lewes' death, on rummaging through his papers, a shocked George Eliot found proofs of his infidelity. If plausible, such a "post-mortem discovery" would certainly help account for the sudden dearth of reverential laments and the "astonishingly quick" involvement with "nephew" Johnny Cross.

Cross figures prominently in the second half of Richard Ellmann's dazzling "Dorothea's Husbands," a chapter in *Golden Codgers: Biographical Speculations* (1973) first published in *TLS* (16 Feb. 1973). Ellmann first considers two "originals" usually proposed for the character of Casaubon: like Haight, he dismisses Mark Pattison and entertains Brabant (though, unlike Haight, he somehow forgets that George Eliot ironically applied her own 1843 epithet for Brabant, "archangel," to the scholar Dorothea sees as Milton's Raphael). After adding two more prototypes, he decides that the intensity of Casaubon's portrait could stem only from the novelist's need to exorcise her own "casaubonism," the "fruitless fantasies, of which she too felt victim." Yet, suggests Ellmann, if the "search for Casaubon begins with others and ends with George Eliot" herself, "the search for Ladislaw spreads out from her to her husband and beyond." Heeding, like Laski, the hints of the sharp-tongued Eliza Lynn Linton, Ellmann regards Ladislaw's impact on Dorothea as "an idealized registration of the effect on George Eliot of her meeting" with the vivacious young Cross in Rome just three and a half months before she began her masterpiece. Dodo's marriage to Will, "George Eliot's only adulterous act," was a fantasy destined to become "legalized" by Lewes' widow.

As her poem "Stradivarius" suggests, George Eliot deeply distrusted all art that relies on sudden inspiration. For herself, she preferred the Wordsworthian reexcitation of earlier emotions as a safer creative process. Ellmann's essay thus helps explain why the consummately controlled portrait of Casaubon should be so superior to the blurred delineation of Ladislaw: present emotions or current fantasies were always more difficult to incarnate for George Eliot than for a Keats or Dickens. This insight, however, seems to have been slighted by most of the distinguished scholars who preferred to engage Ellmann in debates over particulars—debates often conducted with something like the "melancholy embitterment" that marked Casaubon's disputations with his rivals Carp, Pike, and Tench.

Readers who want a full-scale re-creation of the Great Debate over George Eliot's Husbands that took place in *TLS*, will have to be content with a brief historical account of its highlights. The debate opened when John Sparrow attacked Ellmann for dismissing the plausibility of his own "conjectural account" of Mark Pattison as a model for Casaubon (16 Mar.); deeming Ellmann's reply (30 Mar.) to be unsatisfactory, Sparrow tried to marshal new material to support his hypothesis (4 May). The dispute was broadened with the entry of two new letter writers: Leon Edel sided with Sparrow (11 May) and Gordon S. Haight with Ellmann (1 June). An exchange of opponents ensued, with Sparrow engaging Haight (15 June) and Ellmann responding to Edel (22 June). Other scholars welcomed the opportunity of voicing their own views. Barbara and Emrys Jones politely questioned the validity of linking George Eliot's "alleged guilt" over her youthful fantasies to Casaubon's dry labors (9 Mar.); Barbara Hardy, on the other hand, agreed that "the troubled intensities of sexual feeling" in *Middlemarch* must have had their origins in "personal experience" (25 May). Surmises about literary influences and analogues, rather than about biographical determinants, were advanced by Margaret Maison (16 Mar.), Miriam Allott (23 Mar.), and Philip Collins (18 May).

Less speculative, yet the fruit of diligent research, is A. C. Wood's "George Eliot's Maternal Ancestry" (*N&Q*, 1972), which, though providing little new information about Christiana Pearson, carefully documents her genealogy (there was an Isaac Pearson in four successive generations!). Also anchored in solid fact are the publications of the George Eliot Fellowship in Warwickshire: the prime virtue of the mimeographed volumes issued annually by the Fellowship and of illustrated pamphlets such as Dorothy Dodds's *George Eliot Country* (2nd ed., 1965) lies in the substantial sense they offer of the physical aspects of localities so dear to George Eliot's memory and imagination. To know that the stone tower of Chilvers Coton Church, described in the opening sentences of "Amos Barton," still retains "the friendly expression of former days" despite the nave's obliteration in a 1941 Nazi air raid somehow seems highly reassuring. Most scholarly among these publications is Alyce Lynes's *George Eliot's Coventry: A Provincial Town in the 1830's and 1840's* (1970), which draws on the 1845 Health of Towns Report, the 1850 Coventry Directory and Gazetteer, and other sources in order to re-create the surroundings of two important phases of George Eliot's "provincial life."

Lynes's pamphlet was written for the 150th anniversary of George Eliot's birth (no postage stamp was issued on that occasion) and so was Gordon S.

Haight's "George Eliot and John Blackwood" (*Blackwood's*, 1969), which distills the high points of that significant interaction. No memorable insights into that other significant interaction are provided in Edgar W. Hirshberg's "George Eliot and Her Husband" (*EJ*, 1967), although the remark that Daniel Deronda is "a sort of Jewish Adam Bede" will briefly linger in my remembrances. Helen Barolini's "George Eliot as Mary Ann Cross" (*SAQ*, 1972) is more engaging in its witty, slightly acid, account of the George Eliot Fellowship's "anticipatory celebrations" for the 150th anniversary than in its attempted explanations of the sources of George Eliot's "penchant for respectability." In his chapter on George Eliot in *The Victorian Debate: English Literature and Society, 1832–1901* (1968), Raymond Chapman relies on biographical details to support the proposition that George Eliot never really shed "the categories and attitudes of Evangelical Christianity."

Lastly, the outstanding BBC television playlet on George Eliot's life shown on "NET Biography" in the United States in 1971 deserves a yearly revival: warm, humorous, brilliantly acted, the play is deeply moving. There was a hush in our living room when Mary Ann's and Lewes' stretched fingertips groped and grasped each other with the same "spasmodic movement" that precedes Dorothea's and Will's handclasp.

General Criticism

Gordon S. Haight's edition of *A Century of George Eliot Criticism* (1965) is a valuable compilation of over fifty assessments, from Samuel Lucas' admiring 1858 review of *Scenes of Clerical Life* to George Levine's 1962 essay on "Determinism and Responsibility"; George R. Creeger's edition of *George Eliot: A Collection of Critical Essays* (1970) supplies nine pieces of a more recent vintage (except for Barbara Hardy's "The Moment of Disenchantment" and Creeger's own "An Interpretation of *Adam Bede*," all were published in the 1960s). Both collections also include Henry James's "*Daniel Deronda*: A Conversation," also found, of course, in F. R. Leavis' *The Great Tradition* (1948). The essays by various hands expressly written for Barbara Hardy's *Critical Essays on George Eliot* (1970) are discussed individually in this section and the next.

George Eliot and Her Readers: A Selection of Contemporary Reviews (ed. John Holmstrom and Laurence Lerner, 1966) concentrates on the Victorian responses to *The Mill on the Floss*, *Middlemarch*, and *Daniel Deronda*, the three novels still most frequently discussed today; at least one notice of each of the other novels is also included, although there are no commentaries on the poetry or on *Theophrastus*. The "linking paragraphs" the editors furnish are helpful, yet hardly equal in value to the apparatus provided by David R. Carroll in his fuller selection in *George Eliot: The Critical Heritage* (1971). Carroll reprints over fifty items published in George Eliot's lifetime, some posthumous appreciations (though none after

1885, the year of Cross's *Life*), and several of George Eliot's reactions to critics; again, no estimates of *The Spanish Gypsy* and *The Legend of Jubal* are reproduced. A thoughtful forty-page introduction charts the "graph of her reputation" with extreme skill. Carroll's opinion that the novelist over-reacted to criticism is shared by James D. Benson in " 'Sympathetic' Criticism: George Eliot's Response to Contemporary Reviewing" (*NCF*, 1975). Benson deduces that George Eliot was more pleased by reviews showing an emotional receptivity to her work than by appraisals of her technical skill. In "An Annotated Bibliography of British Criticism of George Eliot" (Diss. Ohio State Univ. 1974) James W. Geibel charts George Eliot's reputation among the Victorians, while Anna Katona assesses her more recent reputation in "The Changing Image of George Eliot" (*HSE*, 1965).

Intended for the novice rather than for specialists are three introductory works entitled *George Eliot*, written, respectively, by Walter Allen (1964), R. T. Jones (1970), and A. E. S. Viner (1971). Whereas Allen devotes the first third of his book to the life and Viner interweaves biography throughout his account of the novels, Jones adopts a New Critical stance when he regards the texts as "self-explanatory." Perhaps it is this freedom from the background material that Viner and Allen feel obligated to offer that makes Jones's discussion of six novels (he omits *Scenes* and *Romola*) seem fresher and more appealing. The difference can be illustrated by a look at each man's discussion of *Daniel Deronda*. Viner opens incongruously by informing us that George Eliot "suffered her first attack of kidney stone" while starting to work on the novel, and Allen, for his part, begins almost as incongruously with a lengthy rehearsal of Henry James's and Leavis' opinions of *Deronda* and of George Eliot's early anti-Semitism and later philo-Semitism; Jones, on the other hand, starts off by saying, with delightful directness: "Most of George Eliot's novels begin by creating the place in which the action is to pass. . . . This novel, on the other hand, opens with a chance encounter in a place remote from the scenes of the action that follows." Although the three books are all useful, students would prefer Jones's. A different type of introduction to the works is available in the volume of extracts edited by Ian Adam in the Profiles in Literature series (1969). The extracts grouped under "Milieu" and "Character" are intended to emphasize the "original side" to George Eliot's genius, while those bunched under "Dialogue" and "Narrative" supposedly illustrate her "more traditional (and somewhat neglected) novelistic strengths."

The international recognition that George Eliot again enjoys is well demonstrated by three serviceable foreign-language books: Senzo Furuya's *George Eliot* (Tokyo, 1966), Pietro de Logu's *La narrativa di George Eliot* (Bari, 1969), and Anna Katona's *A Valóságábrázolás Problémái George Eliot Regényeiben* [*The Representation of Reality in George Eliot's Fiction*] (Budapest, 1969). A sixty-page discussion of George Eliot's realism as seen through Soviet eyes can be found in Y. M. Kondrat'ev's "Glavnye asobennosti esteticheski pozitsii Dzhordzh Eliot [Chief Characteristics of George Eliot's Aesthetic Values]" (*UZMGPIL*, 1967).

Studies of Special Aspects

Place in Literary Tradition

Three authors who, in emulation of F. R. Leavis, place George Eliot within a common tradition shared with other novelists are C. B. Cox in *The Free Spirit: A Study of Liberal Humanism in the Novels of George Eliot, Henry James, E. M. Forster, Virginia Woolf, and Angus Wilson* (1963), U. C. Knoepflmacher in *Religious Humanism and the Victorian Novel: George Eliot, Walter Pater, and Samuel Butler* (1965), and Laurence Lerner in *The Truthtellers: Jane Austen, George Eliot, D. H. Lawrence* (1967). All three of these critics locate George Eliot among seekers who relied on fiction to order moral chaos in a godless world; yet the company each devises for her suggests his own distinct emphasis. For Cox, who is the least sympathetic toward George Eliot, she becomes a straw person; like Bedient, whose *Architects of the Self*, discussed earlier, includes two of Cox's five authors and two of Lerner's trio, Cox deplores George Eliot's unwillingness to endorse wholeheartedly those defiant "free spirits" who, like Maggie or Dorothea, clash with "established routines." For all her insights into the dilemma of such characters, Cox concludes, George Eliot has "nothing practical to offer except simple Christian truisms." Knoepflmacher, whose study is more historically circumscribed, takes an opposite view. For him, it is precisely George Eliot's inability to accept Christian dogma that led her to seek alternatives and made possible both the "masterful balancing of science and religion in *Middlemarch*" and the imbalance of her attempted "Hebraist synthesis in *Daniel Deronda*." For Lerner, in a less patterned discussion than Cox's and a more wide-ranging context than Knoepflmacher's, George Eliot provides a via media between the rationalism of Jane Austen and the irrationalism of Lawrence: whereas Austen rewards those characters who resist impulse and Lawrence exalts those who surrender to it, George Eliot tries to find ways to equate impulse with reason. Although her attempts to do so may not always succeed and even though in *The Mill* she approaches the "more radical immorality of Lawrence," she is neither a pre-Romantic moralist like Austen nor a "Romantic subversive" like Lawrence but, rather, a "positive" Romantic.

Lerner's concluding typology—"made historical," as he says, "with delicious and dangerous ease"—also seems to underlie Knoepflmacher's *George Eliot's Early Novels: The Limits of Realism* (1968), a study that attempts to document George Eliot's retreat from the severely limited empirical realism defined in her essays on fiction toward a more "romantic" conception of the relation between art and reality. Finding that "the imperfections of her philosophy led to the perfection of her art," Knoepflmacher clearly prefers her incursions into romance to her more direct confrontations with the harsh evolutionary world she represented as Shepperton, Milby, St. Ogg's, and Grimsworth; as a result, his lengthy discussion of "The Lifted Veil" and of the momentary reconciliation achieved in *Silas Marner* are among the best portions of his book. He is least satisfactory in a chapter on *The Mill on the Floss* that brings out his overfondness for distracting comparisons and juxtapositions, also evident elsewhere; also unfortunate, perhaps, are his too ready acceptance of George Eliot's own terminology and epistemology and his failure to provide a more theoretical framework for the discussion of formal realism. Still, his close reading of each fiction as a "mental phase" that reacts on its immediate predecessor does contribute to an important elucidation of George Eliot's artistic growth.

George Levine, too, asserts that "George Eliot was moving to a new mode" at a time in which "the myth of realism had ceased being satisfying" to writers. In "Realism, or, in Praise of Lying: Some Nineteenth Century Novels" (*CE*, 1970), perhaps the best of the essays concerned with questions of form, Levine equates realism with "the tradition of comedy" and shows how conventions used by Austen are adopted "with a difference not altogether satisfying" by George Eliot when she insists that the real and the moral are identical. In "Ruskin and George Eliot's 'Realism' " (*Criticism*, 1965), Darrel Mansell, Jr., goes to *Modern Painters*, III, and to George Eliot's notebooks and essays, to prove that she, like Ruskin, never meant to be a copyist of outward nature but, rather, hoped to anchor subjective impressions in a "truthfulness" based on precise observation. Good in his choice of touchstones, right in bias and emphasis, Mansell nonetheless gives the erroneous impression that George Eliot's ideas were fixed and self-sufficient: to consider the credo of Chapter xix of *Adam Bede* as coequal with the later "Notes on Form in Art" is to ignore the gradual fashion in which George Eliot's aesthetic evolved. Mansell avoids this trap in "George Eliot's Conception of 'Form' " (*SEL*, 1965) when he rightly relates "Notes on Form in Art" to *Middlemarch*. In an essay that relies on Sandor Ferenczi's "Stages in the Development of the Sense of Reality" (*First Contributions to Psycho-Analysis*, 1952), Bernard J. Paris creates a value-laden hierarchy from the base "secret" cravings of the fairy tale, to the more reality-oriented but still "self-indulgent" science fiction, to the "truly mature" fiction of George Eliot ("George Eliot, Science Fiction, and Fantasy," *Extrapolations*, 1964).

Style and Technique

Although there are no new book-length studies that can be placed beside W. J. Harvey's or Reva Stump's, considerable attention is still being paid to George Eliot's narrative methods, to her imagery, and to her prose style. K. M. Newton's "The Role of the Narrator in George Eliot's Novels" (*JNT*, 1973) mounts an able defense of the authorial comments that critics like Walter Allen still deride as "intrusive, indeed obtrusive"; Newton is good on the calculated "anti-dramatic" effects such comments can produce and, though more remains to be said on the subject, also makes important distinctions among the different kinds of narrators George Eliot employs.

Elizabeth Ermarth stresses the "human limitation" of the narrators in "Method and Moral in George Eliot's Narrative" (*VN*, 1975), while J. R. Tye studies the novelist's "epigraphic personae" in "George Eliot's Unascribed Mottoes" (*NCF*, 1967), a topic advantageously enlarged by David Leon Higdon in "George Eliot and the Art of the Epigraph" (*NCF*, 1970). Higdon complements his discussion with useful appendixes that list the sources of all borrowed epigraphs in *Felix Holt, Middlemarch*, and *Daniel Deronda*. In "Contrasting Pairs of Heroines in George Eliot's Fiction" (*SNNTS*, 1974), Constance Marie Fulmer adds little to Barbara Hardy's discussion of such pairings except to point out that the device goes as far back as the 1847 essay "A Little Fable with a Great Moral." Sheldon Liebman in "The Counterpoint of Characters in George Eliot's Early Novels" (*RLV*, 1968) looks at contrasts between what he calls the "man-of-duty" and the "man-of-love," but veers off into a digression on river imagery.

Two studies devoted to such "thoughts entangled in metaphor" (to quote *Middlemarch* again) are Daniel P. Deneau's "The River and the Web in the Works of George Eliot" (*RS*, 1967) and Dianella Savoia's "Le imagini dell'acqua nel linguaggio di George Eliot [Water Imagery in George Eliot's Language]" (*Aevum*, 1973). If Deneau maintains that George Eliot's reliance on words such as "threads," "fibers," and "strands" demonstrates that "web imagery" is far more dominant in her work than river images, Savoia insists that, to the contrary, it is the use of water imagery that is the hallmark of her style. To prove her point, she not only combs through the novels as Deneau does but also looks at the earlier prose.

Only a computer could settle Savoia's and Deneau's conflicting claims, and it is exactly to that keypunched oracle to which Karl Kroeber turns in *Styles in Fictional Structure: The Art of Jane Austen, Charlotte Brontë, George Eliot* (1971), an experiment in quantification already briefly assessed by Richard D. Altick in his chapter on "General Materials" in this volume. Kroeber has some lucid remarks about George Eliot's "pictorializing language." He rightly feels that it would be rewarding to study how "the handling of the same images changes" from novel to novel: he points out that in *Adam Bede*, for example, "words and phrases referring to water are predominantly 'literal,' " whereas in *The Mill*, despite the actual presence of the river, and more fully in *Middlemarch* the figurative connotations are more copious. It is true, perhaps, that most of Kroeber's generalizations could have been made without the aid of his tabulations of nouns, verbals, adjectives, and ratios of subordinating conjunctions to connecting conjunctions. Indeed, some of his remarks—he notes that George Eliot "works at a deeper level than Brontë and represents a more complex vision of society than does Austen"—sound suspiciously subjective and also quite familiar. But, even when they confirm existing critical opinions or remain, as he readily admits, "dubious, their implications not fully clear," his findings deserve to be consulted.

Also concerned with stylistic matters are Roland Hall in "Some Antedatings from George Eliot and Other Nineteenth-Century Authors" (*N&Q*,

8) and Wallace Hildick in *Word for Word: A Study of Authors' Altera-
ns with Exercises* (1965). Hall finds that George Eliot's translations of
auss and Feuerbach contain many words that "antedate their earliest
urrence recorded in the *O.E.D.*"; even though he makes no effort to
erpret his findings, it is obvious that the prominence of hyphenated or
npounded words ("counter-question," "self-affirmation," "standpoint,"
termediateness," "unassailableness") stem from her efforts to render the
rman original as faithfully as possible. Hildick starts his study of au-
rial alterations with George Eliot because he finds that her emendations
er a wide variety and "a similarly wide range of complexity" not found in
revisions of other authors. Since he confines himself to *Middlemarch*, his
esentation of fifteen extracts ought to be read in conjunction with Jerome
aty's fine study of that novel's proofs, mentioned in the next section.
stly, in *Prose Styles: Five Primary Types* (1966), Huntingdon Brown
otes passages from Thucydides' *History* and from *Middlemarch* as joint
istrations of what he calls the "deliberative style."

Ideas

Reacting against what he feels is the dominant concern with formal
ocedures is Ian Milner, both in "George Eliot's Realist Art" (*ZAA*, 1964)
d in *The Structure of Values in George Eliot's Art* (1968). Milner's book,
iich treats all the fictions except the *Scenes* and "The Lifted Veil" (which
has examined in a separate article), is also designed as an antidote to the
:ent critical emphasis on George Eliot's evasions and negations. Arguing
at she is best understood as a positive or constructive moralist who be-
ved in "the worth and the potential of the human personality," he de-
nds her "idealized figures" as "primary and inseparable elements of her
eated world." If Milner never quite glosses over the inconsistencies in
:orge Eliot's art perhaps too greedily seized upon by other critics, he
netheless tends to uphold intention above execution: thus, Romola,
lix, Ladislaw, Mordecai, and Deronda, though unconvincing to twentieth-
ntury readers, must be respected because they illustrate the nineteenth-
ntury belief that ideal people "do exist, no matter how mercenary the
ciety in which they live." Unarguable as such a thesis may be, it tells us
ore about aspirations than about the incarnation of ideology into com-
lling art.

In "The Otherness of George Eliot" (*JML*, 1970), a review essay, Bernard
Paris faults Milner for always judging George Eliot according to Marxist
standards of social realism." Paris' strictures, however, stem from his own
70 conversion to Horneyan psychology—a conversion that leads him not
nly to censure Milner for accepting George Eliot's values but also to reject
:orge Eliot herself for creating a mere "defense system" that "contains no
iteria by which to distinguish healthy from unhealthy values" (a view
iat also informs a 1974 essay on *The Mill*, discussed below). As Paris
imself seems to imply, his reproof of Milner is a covert act of self-criticism,

a reproof directed at his own earlier stance in *Experiments in Life: Geo Eliot's Quest for Values* (1965). In that book, Paris so completely identi with George Eliot's humanist ethic that he regards all her fictions as selfsame record of a "quest for values" he enthusiastically endorses as tot satisfying the "needs of the heart" and mind. This single-mindedness the unfortunate effect of preventing him from bringing strikingly new terpretations to novels flattened into a uniform presentation of a creed, it also permits him to offer the fullest and most careful account we have George Eliot's interaction with the "cosmology of science," as we see it Mill's *Logic* and the positivistic philosophies of Comte, Spencer, Lewes, a Feuerbach.

Neil Roberts in *George Eliot: Her Beliefs and Art* (1975) sees himself providing a corrective to Paris' insufficient attention to the relation betwe ideology and achieved art. Yet his book is primarily "a critical study" th belies the prominence given to her "beliefs" in its title and dust jacket. contains old-fashioned readings, some quite astute, that have little dir relation to the intellectual background of Positivism and Evangelicalism sketchily rehearsed in its introduction and opening chapter.

A more exclusive identification of George Eliot with the philosophy Positivism is undertaken in Thakur Guru Prasad's *Comtism in the Nov of George Eliot* (1968), a book that chooses to disregard the novelist's press misgivings about the codified assumptions of Comte and of his Engl disciples. George Eliot and Lewes "were Positivists without being Comtist says N. N. Feltes, and they likewise drew a sharp distinction "between t essential materialist hypothesis of Phrenology and the religion of Cra oscopy" ("Phrenology: From Lewes to George Eliot," *SLitI*, 1968). In more wide-ranging essay, "George Eliot and the Unified Sensibilit (*PMLA*, 1964), Feltes discusses the importance of emotion or intuition the notion of "wholeness," valued as much by George Eliot as by Lewes a Newman. Arguing that the novels deliberately set out "to oppose the ki of calculating and amoral individualism" that Victorian intellectuals dr from Darwin's notion of competitive and pitiless struggles in a fortuito world, K. M. Newton claims to detect Darwinian features in the portraits egotists such as Christian in *Felix Holt* and Lapidoth in *Daniel Deron* ("George Eliot, George Henry Lewes, and Darwinism," *DUJ*, 1974). Mo productive affinities between the "particularizing" tendencies of P Raphaelite painters and George Eliot's artistic ideals are taken up by Jo Murdock in an interesting, if somewhat diffuse, interdisciplinary stud ("English Realism: George Eliot and the Pre-Raphaelites," *JWCI*, 1974).

In "Ideas in George Eliot" (*MLQ*, 1966) and in "Idea and Image in th Novels of George Eliot," a posthumous essay in Barbara Hardy's edition Critical Essays on George Eliot (1970), W. J. Harvey voices his disconte with those critics who "attempt to decompose her mind into an intellectu spectrum with individual colours labelled Comte, Feuerbach, Spence Lewes, Darwin, Huxley, etc." Instead, he argues, in his fine last essay o George Eliot, that a whole "nexus of ideas" can be found in her adheren

the formula that "ontogeny recapitulates phylogeny": adults contain
ir childhoods; individuals contain their cultural past and, as biological
ducts, likewise contain "the whole of the evolutionary past." After ex-
ining in some detail the manifestations of this "three-ply thread" in the
vels, Harvey connects it to other strands, particularly to her belief "that
gedy is to be found not merely in high-life romance or in extreme situa-
ns, but in homely and monotonous existence, in the great, ordinary
rse of everyday life."

n *Will and Destiny: Morality and Tragedy in George Eliot's Novels*
75) Felicia Bonaparte grapples with similar concerns, even though she is
t as interested as Harvey is in the actual incarnation of ideas into
ieved art and, in fact, seems to have written without knowledge of his
portant 1970 essay (her bibliography lists only two works of scholarship
lished after 1967). Instead of moving from novel to novel, she arranges
r material according to conceptual categories ("Destiny," "Character in
tion," "Knowledge and Morality," and "Morality and Tragedy"), which,
turn, are broken up into smaller abstract units. The method has obvious
vantages and disadvantages, the latter probably outweighing the former,
ce, as in Paris' handling, George Eliot emerges as a philosopher-artist
ose stable and uniform beliefs can be flatly extracted from any work, any
erance. Yet the book codifies much that is useful and fresh. Particularly
od are the steady links to Greek tragedy: "the destiny that Aeschylus
led Zeus, Sophocles Apollo, and Euripides Dionysus has become the force
necessity."

Like Bonaparte, Dorothee Supp in *Die Tragik bei George Eliot* (1969)
shes to understand "George Eliot's tragedy as a context of ideas as well as
artistic form"; at times belaboring the self-evident, she meticulously
scriminates between the tragedy visited on characters who fail to live up
accepted moral standards (Arthur Donnithorne and Tito) and the
gedy experienced through conflict with an "outward situation" (Maggie
ulliver and Savonarola). H. S. Kakar in "George Eliot's Treatment of
in and Suffering" (*LHY*, 1965) comments on the "tragic process" in-
lved when the novelist has her characters confront suffering and recognize
n inexorable moral law whose operation justifies and consecrates it."
arrel Mansell, Jr., in "George Eliot's Conception of Tragedy" (*NCF*,
67) and "A Note on Hegel and George Eliot" (*VN*, 1967) also writes
out the fates visited both on those who deny "consequences" and on those
hose heroic temper clashes with the "commonplace, or Hegelian, general."
eacting against the tendency to describe such laws as "inexorable" or
leterministic," Elizabeth Ermarth shows how George Eliot manages to
eserve "a realm of human freedom apart from natural necessity" ("In-
rnations: George Eliot's Conception of 'Undeviating Law,'" *NCF*, 1974).
n Adam in "Character and Destiny in George Eliot's Fiction" (*NCF*,
65) and William E. Buckler in "Memory, Morality, and the Tragic Vision
the Early Novels of George Eliot" (in *The English Novel in the Nine-
enth Century*, ed. George Goodin, 1972) address themselves to the vexing

question of how a belief in the causality of all events, including mer
events, can be reconciled with a manifest belief in human responsibil
Adam finds that George Eliot resolves this problem only when she sidest
it at the end of her career when Deronda "does not choose, but is chose
Buckler, in turn, believes that she solves it in the earlier, pastoral nov
particularly *Silas Marner*, where memory becomes a "means for making
moralist relevant to the psychologist and for mediating between the classi
concept of tragedy of character and the incipient naturalistic idea of
tragedy of circumstances."

The different emphases of Adam and Buckler lead into a consideration
two other kinds of studies—those that treat George Eliot as a moralist a
those that treat her as a pastoralist. In the first of these categories are Er
Hester's "George Eliot's Messengers" (*SEL*, 1967), William M. Sal
"George Eliot's Moral Dilemma" (*CorLQ*, 1968), Ted R. Spivey's "Geo
Eliot: Victorian Romantic and Modern Realist" (*SLitI*, 1968), Edward
Hurley's "Death and Immortality: George Eliot's Solution" (*NCF*, 196
and Bert G. Hornback's "The Moral Imagination of George Eliot" (*PL
1972). Of these, perhaps the only truly original contribution is Hester's lo
at those secondary figures who, like the Rev. Tryan or Mordecai, act "
modern secular angels who lead the protagonists" to a moral baptism (
equation of Eppie and Savonarola as fellow messengers casts some dout
however, on the value of his grouping). But the most sensitive of the
discussions surely is Sale's sympathetic account of "the poignant, sometin
almost insupportable, sense of the sadness of human life we find in h
fiction."

The attempts to come to terms with the "roots of piety" that led Geor
Eliot to re-create a solid rural past take various shapes, though all disc
sions make the obligatory bow to William Wordsworth and include t
obligatory allusion to her 1856 essay on Riehl, "The Natural History
German Life." Most successful in uniting Wordsworth with Riehl
Thomas Pinney in "The Authority of the Past in George Eliot's Novel
(*NCF*, 1966), an essay with wide implications: "her essay on Riehl, with
analogy between man's relation to his past and the plant rooted in
sustaining soil, places George Eliot in the tradition of 'emotional natur
ism,' stemming from Burke, and passing through Wordsworth and Scott
Still, the asocial Wordsworth and the sociologically minded Riehl are di
cult to press together: the fusion suggested in the title of Deborah Hell
Rozen's "George Eliot and Wordsworth: 'The Natural History of Germa
Life' and Peasant Psychology" (*RS*, 1973) belies the essay's final contentio
that it is Wordsworth's "own self-explanation" that George Eliot follows.
J. Sambrook, on the other hand, stresses the Riehl-like and un-Word
worthian concern with "social setting" ("The Natural Historian of O
Social Classes," *English*, 1963).

John Bayley in "The Pastoral of Intellect" (in Hardy's *Critical Essa*
1970) also tries to bridge commitment and retreat by speaking of the "h
toric pastoral" that George Eliot presumably devised in *Romola* and *Dan*

ronda, but not *Middlemarch.* Michael Squires, however, contends that
h Polonian categories as "rural novel, regional novel, provincial novel,
colic novel, georgic novel, or lyrical novel" are either too broad or too
gue to describe earlier novels such as *Adam Bede* and *Silas Marner;* he
erefore treads back to Theocritus to vindicate his own version of the
storal in *The Pastoral Novel: Studies in George Eliot, Thomas Hardy,*
d *D. H. Lawrence* (1974). For his part, Henry Auster in *Local Habita-*
ns: Regionalism in the Early Novels of George Eliot (1970) finds that
gionalism, "flexibly understood," is the term that best explains the "unify-
g concern" of *Scenes of Clerical Life, Adam Bede, The Mill,* and *Silas*
arner. If Squires is more precise in his definition of pastoralism than
uster in his indefinite use of regionalism—a term that comes to stand for
ealism," memory, scientific objectivity, the subjectivity of "autobio-
aphic" recollection, topography, "background," Scott, Wordsworth, and
uch more—neither author's conceptualizations greatly aid us in under-
anding the novels. Though too rigidly clinging to these conceptualizations
d far too deferential to all previous critical utterances, both authors have
telligent insights, especially on the setting of *Silas Marner,* which Squires
scribes as an antiurban retreat that "offers the possibility of fulfillment"
d Auster regards as a more harshly treated world of "crudeness" that shows
"dreary side" despite the softening "potential for genuine sociability."
Auster's survey of George Eliot's later novels in "George Eliot and the
odern Temper" (in *The Worlds of Victorian Fiction,* ed. Jerome Buck-
y, 1975) relies on still another rubric, "modernism"; Thomas Deegan,
owever, finds that the later works are shaped by "her concept of the his-
rical imagination" ("George Eliot's Novels of the Historical Imagina-
on," *ClioW,* 1972). Neither context proves particularly rewarding in
fferentiating these novels from the earlier, rural fictions. William Myers in
George Eliot: Politics and Personality" (in *Literature and Politics in the*
ineteenth Century, ed. John Lucas, 1971) finds the thinking on history
d politics in the later novels both "original and magnificently precise"
it also "remarkably ill-disciplined." Carlyle's doctrine that "every man has
eroic possibilities" is applied to the "potential" heroes and heroines in the
ovels by Darrel Mansell, Jr., in " 'Possibilities' in George Eliot's Novels"
S, 1968).
Three studies that depart from these rather well-beaten paths are Rudolf
illgradter's *Die Darstellung des Bösen in den Romanen George Eliots*
970), Langdon Elsbree's "The Purest and Most Perfect Form of Play:
me Novelists and the Dance" (*Criticism,* 1972), and Barbara Hardy's
ituals and Feeling in the Novels of George Eliot (1973). Villgradter's
osthumous study is theological in emphasis: he applies to her first four
ctions the notions of evil that George Eliot inherited yet altered (her later
eatment of Tito and Grandcourt might have been a better choice). Hardy
nd Elsbree, on the other hand, deal with social, rather than religious, rites.
While Hardy provides an overview of George Eliot's general "reverence" for
tual and concludes that, for her, the very act of storytelling was ritualistic,

Elsbree more specifically shows "how in George Eliot the dance is sy_
tomatic of the corruption of the play element" in a "culture in which
distinctions between work and play are becoming obscured."

The Woman Question

Despite the attention paid to George Eliot in current courses on Wo_
en's Studies, there is still no book-length discussion from a feminist persp_
tive (though one promising study prepared by Eleanor O'Neal will str_
the "matriarchal" symbology and attitudes that George Eliot increasin_
used to oppose patriarchal values). This neglect seems intentional, for c_
discovers in feminist writings the repeated accusation that George El_
insufficiently questioned the male-centered and male-dominated attitudes_
Victorian culture. Thus, for instance, in the annotated bibliography _
pended to Susan Koppelman Cornillon's edition of essays, *Images _
Women in Fiction: Feminist Perspectives* (1972), we are told that it_
"difficult to avoid feeling some resentment of George Eliot for making _
heroines so much less venturesome than she was in her own life." Similar_
in "Would We Have Heard of Marian Evans?" (*Ms. Magazine*, 1973), G_
Godwin demands what George Eliot clearly never will provide: "We ne_
more patterns of desire. We need models of women—and men—who exp_
everything, and set out to get it."

The complaint (underlying, too, Lee R. Edwards' treatment of *Mid_
march* in an essay discussed in the next section) obviously resembles that_
socialist critics who deplore George Eliot's innate conservatism (Willia_
Cox, and others) of Lawrentians like Bedient who find her too dispassic_
ate, of lapsed believers like Paris who see her neuroticism as "unhealthy."_
only she were to proclaim our own cherished beliefs, fully, loudly, witho_
reservations, these critics seem to say. Irritated at her refusal to do so, th_
chide her for her "timidity." To stereotype George Eliot as a conform_
who blinks at the inequities in the Victorian treatment of women is da_
gerously reductive, however, as Mary Ellmann shrewdly recognizes when s_
speaks of the strong "sexual hostility" that permeates the handling _
Lydgate's male arrogance (*Thinking about Women*, 1968). George Eli_
may be unduly hard on Hetty Sorrel's "obtuse hope, her trembling e_
lashes, her rushing surrender," as Elizabeth Hardwick notes (*Seduction a_
Betrayal*, 1974), but she also severely censures "the double standar_
through Adam's condemnation of Hetty's seducer ("Let 'em put *him* on _
trial"), as Françoise Basch is quick to apprehend in *Relative Creature_
Victorian Women in Society and the Novel* (1974). Likewise, thoug_
Donald Stone correctly observes that "George Eliot provided little in t_
way of encouragement for the New Woman" ("Victorian Feminism and t_
Nineteenth-Century Novel," *WS*, 1972), it is also true that George Eliot is_
her "most outspoken" when she indicts "the inadequate education, bo_
intellectual, moral, and emotional, given to young women in Englan_
(Hazel Mews, *Frail Vessels: Woman's Role in Women's Novels from Fan_

rney to George Eliot, 1969). Indeed, as Robert A. Colby convincingly
ws by placing The Mill against contemporary "school novels" and
ddlemarch in apposition to "novels of female emancipation" (in Fiction
h a Purpose: Major and Minor Nineteenth-Century Novels, 1968), the
vings of Maggie and Dorothea dramatize the repressiveness of a male-
ninated society. Patricia Meyer Spacks goes even further when she per-
tively analyzes George Eliot's "complicated pessimism" and notes that
 women "grow more surely than men" because the men are constricted
 "fantasized" notions of prowess but that society also cuts women off
om full expression of the meaning of their growth" (The Female Imagi-
tion, 1975). Given George Eliot's firm insistence on sharp sexual distinc-
ns in her letters and in her works, it may be mistaken to superimpose
rginia Woolf on her in order to find "the possibility of androgyny" in a
iddle" march between "masculine and feminine," as Carolyn G. Heil-
n tries to do in her interesting Toward a Recognition of Androgyny
73); but to dismiss both writers for being insufficiently revolutionary, as
te Millett does in Sexual Politics (1970), surely is a perverse denial of
ir profound contribution to the female tradition in the English novel.

Criticism of Individual Works

quick check of the manuscript of David Leon Higdon's bibliography
eals that from 1965 to 1975 the number of essays and dissertations on
ddlemarch (over 100) by far outdistances the discussions of Daniel
ronda (36), The Mill on the Floss (31), Adam Bede (27), Romola (15),
as Marner (13), Felix Holt (10), and Scenes of Clerical Life (8). There is
t a handful of critical assessments of "The Lifted Veil," "Brother Jacob,"
e poetry, and the essays.

Scenes of Clerical Life

The well-intentioned attempts to come to terms with Scenes of Clerical
fe are good to have (there was no available criticism at the time of the
evenson Guide), but more serious work remains to be done on George
iot's first formal venture into fiction. Lamentably, the critical portions of
e one book-length study we have, Thomas Noble's George Eliot's 'Scenes
 Clerical Life' (1965), are extremely disappointing. Oblivious to the acute
fferences among the three novellas, Noble judges them as good or bad
otographic replicas of a known world (even Milly Barton's melodramatic
athbed scene is, for him, a "realistic picture of what was going on").
ountering Noble's dismissal of the second of the Scenes, U. C. Knoep-
macher tries to show that it differs from "Amos Barton" in that its
mance elements are subversively deployed to tease us into an awareness of
e "ordinary life" lurking beneath the melodramatic surface ("George
iot's Anti-Romantic Romance: 'Mr. Gilfil's Love-Story,'" VN, 1967).

Primarily concerned with "Janet's Repentance," Daniel P. Deneau ¿
detects a marked progression "from nearly imageless prose to a prose t
contains a moderately complex and moderately successful system of imag
("Imagery in the *Scenes of Clerical Life*," *VN*, 1965). And, in a two-p
complement to Deneau, David Leon Higdon dwells on the metaph
treatment of the characters as plants ("*Scenes of Clerical Life*: Idea thro
Image," *VN*, 1968). In his attractive introduction to the Penguin edition
the *Scenes* (1973), David Lodge reverses the usual judgments by somew
hyperbolically hailing "Amos Barton" as perhaps "the most original" w
of fiction George Eliot ever wrote; he finds "a naturalness, a clean econo
of line, a confidence in the significance of the quotidian." Derek and S
Oldfield examine "the scaffolding of a coherent humanistic philosop
(also examined more extensively by Noble, who goes unmentioned),
"vitiating flaw of sentimentality," and the "penetrating social coverage"
" 'Scenes of Clerical Life': The Diagram and the Picture" (in Barb
Hardy's *Critical Essays*, 1970). The links between George Eliot's and G
worthy's use of Gluck's aria "Che farò senza Euridice" that Freimut Fre
tries to establish are minimal (" 'Che farò' bei George Eliot und Jo
Galsworthy: Der englische Gentleman und die Musik im 19. Jahrhunder
LWU, 1971).

Adam Bede

As might be expected, the quality of discussions of *Adam Bede* is g
erally much higher than that of the essays on the *Scenes*, with profita
attention being given to the novel's literary conventions and religic
archetypes, its symbolic pictorialism, its definition of "Nature." Respondi
directly or indirectly to Ian Gregor's important "The Two Worlds of *Ad*
Bede" (in his and Brian Nichols' *The Moral and the Story*, 1962), crit
seem to agree with him that *Adam Bede* is a watershed that lies betwe
Austen's fusion of communal and individual interests and Hardy's la
separation of the two; yet they also try to find ways to assert against h
that George Eliot did manage to blend commitment and alienation, fal
and social analysis, into successful wholes. Thus, pictorialism, Wordswor
mythology, religion, and literary tradition are repeatedly invoked to con
both an ancestry and a cohesion on the novel's dialectical tensions.

This common aim informs essays as disparate as Murray Krieger's "*Ada*
Bede and the Cushioned Fall: The Extenuation of Extremity," in *T*
Classic Vision (1971); Joseph Wiesenfarth's "*Adam Bede* and Myth" (*PL*
1972); David Leon Higdon's "The Iconographic Backgrounds of *Ada*
Bede, Chapter 15" (*NCF*, 1972) and "*Sortes Biblicae* in *Adam Bede*" (*PL*
1973); and Christopher Herbert's "Preachers and the Schemes of Nature
Adam Bede" (*NCF*, 1975). By far the most comprehensive of these discu
sions, Krieger's essay (like the interpretations of *Adam Bede* by Knoe
flmacher and Squires in books assessed in the previous section) looks at t
broad literary antecedents that permit George Eliot to stop short of trage

rieger also is good on the clash between "secrecy" and "openness" in the
vel). The essays by Wiesenfarth and Higdon concentrate on more limited
dels and analogues (Prometheus, Jacob and Rachel, St. Paul), whereas
erbert, more effectively, contrasts the theologies of Dinah and Rector
vine and likens the "mixed judgments" passed on both to the novel's
ually ambivalent treatment of nature. He concludes that George Eliot's
nultaneous tendency to attack and to affirm was her one way of reconcil-
g "unsolvable paradoxes." (Is *Adam Bede* thus closer to the "negative
pability" of *Middlemarch*? A question future critics might tackle.)

For John Paterson, the "two worlds" of *Adam Bede* are really one and the
ne: he hails its author as a "conscientiously naïve and ingenuous" writer.
though Paterson's well-intentioned defense seems to be more of a covert
tack against the formalism of Flaubert and James than a response to
orge Eliot's craft, his delicately written introduction to the Riverside
ition of the novel (1968) is far superior to F. R. Leavis' strangely per-
nctory preface to the Signet edition (rpt. in *Anna Karenina and Other
says*, 1969). Sensitive, too, yet quite different in its defense of the novel, is
n Adam's "The Structure of Realisms in *Adam Bede*" (*NCF*, 1975), not
be confused by unwary readers with "The Structure of Values in *Adam
de*" (*PP*, 1966) by Ian Milner (Ch. ii of *The Structure of Values in
orge Eliot's Novels*, discussed in the previous section). Carefully distin-
ishing among "pictorial," dramatic, and analytic modes of "realism,"
dam disputes Gregor's thesis about the novel's failure to integrate incom-
tible realities by arguing that they are "mediated by the mind of the
thor."

John Goode's sophisticated " 'Adam Bede' " (in Hardy's *Critical Essays*)
eats, among other topics, the "Spencerian formulas" of adaptability and
nadaptation that George Eliot tests through Dinah and Hetty. Also con-
rned with characterization are D. R. Beeton in "Aspects of *Adam Bede*"
SA, 1971), Michael Edwards in "A Reading of *Adam Bede*" (*CritQ*,
72), and Bruce K. Martin in "Rescue and Marriage in *Adam Bede*" (*SEL*,
72). Edwards and Martin partly address themselves to the question of
inah's authenticity, a task Kathleen Watson undertakes in more interest-
g fashion in "Dinah Morris and Mrs. Evans: A Comparative Study of
ethodist Diction" (*RES*, 1971). Watson and Valentine Cunningham in a
ief but helpful addendum (*RES*, 1972) look at the retailoring of Wes-
yan terms, while in "Hymns in George Eliot's Fiction" (*NCF*, 1974)
muel J. Rogal comments on attitudes toward psalmody and hymnody.

In "Miss Evans, Miss Mulock, and Hetty Sorrel" (*ELN*, 1965) Robert A.
olby convincingly aligns *Adam Bede* with Dinah Mulock Craik's *A Wom-
n's Thoughts about Women* (1858) without even once succumbing to the
mptation of suggesting that Dinah Morris might owe her first name to the
uthor whose lack of "high culture" George Eliot derogated. In "Nathaniel
awthorne and George Eliot," another good comparative essay, Nicolaus
ills relates the treatment of community and "religious struggle" in *Adam
ede* and *The Scarlet Letter* (*American and English Fiction in the Nine-*

teenth Century, 1973). More incidental links between Hetty Sorrel a
Mary Hamilton, the forlorn maiden of the ballads, and between Arth
Donnithorne and John Moore's Zeluco are made by Thomas G. Burton
"Hetty Sorrel, the Forlorn Maiden" (VN, 1966) and Irving H. Buchen
"Arthur Donnithorne and Zeluco" (VN, 1963). Roland F. Anderso
lengthy rehearsal of the correspondence with Blackwood is undertak
because of the unlikely conjecture that it was her publisher whom Geo
Eliot had in mind when she chose to address "one of my readers" in Chap
xvii ("George Eliot Provoked: John Blackwood and Chapter Seventeen
Adam Bede," MP, 1973).

The Mill on the Floss

Criticism of The Mill on the Floss continues to concern itself with t
ending, which Barbara Hardy in " 'The Mill on the Floss' " (in her o
edition of Critical Essays) goes so far as to call "a false catharsis" and an a
of "bad faith." Noting that the foreshadowings of the flood "are uninvolv
with action," Hardy finds the entire novel to be "the least progressive of
of George Eliot's studies in character and morality," a fiction "whose mer
and flaws show how art can tell difficult truths and consoling lies." A simil
view, but arrived at in different fashion, emerges in George Levine's "Int
ligence as Deception: The Mill on the Floss" (PMLA, 1965), an importa
essay. By looking at the novel's Comtean and Feuerbachian underpinnin
Levine tries to show that the elaborate application of such "intellectu
systems" allowed George Eliot to evade the experiential dilemmas she h
raised. Turning to Hegel rather than to Comte and Feuerbach, Sara 2
Putzell sees the drowning as the only possible synthesis: "Just as she ar
Tom together transcend their previous antithetical relationship, Magg
herself transcends the antithesis within herself" (" 'An Antagonism of Val
Claims': The Dynamics of The Mill on the Floss," SEL, 1975). Thou
Putzell's reliance on still another intellectual system does not necessari
blunt Levine's charges, many of her insights are excellent. Good, too, in
dialectical approach is David Molstad's "The Mill on the Floss and A
tigone" (PMLA, 1970), which meaningfully links the novel to Geor
Eliot's essay on "The Antigone and Its Moral." John Hagan spends far to
much firepower on Levine and other critics and delivers considerably le
than the "reinterpretation" he promises; yet he does make the worthwhi
point that Maggie's last renunciation is designed, not to illustrate à Kemp
or Feuerbach, but to point up Tom's culminating "insensitivity" ("A Rei
terpretation of The Mill on the Floss," PMLA, 1972). Going one ste
further is David Leon Higdon in "Failure of Design in The Mill on t
Floss" (JNT, 1973). Like Putzell and Hagan, Higdon notes the parall
endings of each of the novel's three volumes, yet asserts that "the actio
idea, and structure organic to the work" were violated when George Eli
followed "Tom's recognition" with the drowning. Also concerned with t
drowning, Keith Brown chides George Eliot for ignoring the elementa

s of physics when he notes that the large pieces of wreckage could never
ve overtaken Tom and Maggie's boat ("The Ending of 'The Mill on the
oss,'" *N&Q*, 1964). More tolerant is Jerome H. Buckley when he con-
des his chapter on the novel in *Season of Youth: The Bildungsroman
m Dickens to Golding* (1974) by sensibly reminding us that the book's
nterest and power lie in the unfolding of [an incomplete] life rather than
the end imposed upon it."

Instead of relying on ideological or structural scaffoldings, several critics
ve turned to Maggie's internal psychic dynamics. This approach, however
teresting, often tends to blur the distinctions between art and life. Thus,
en Bernard J. Paris (in "The Inner Conflicts of Maggie Tulliver: A
orneyian Analysis," *CentR*, 1969; rpt. in *A Psychological Approach to
ction*, 1974) finds in Maggie an "unhealthy" death wish that represents
he extreme form of her self-effacing solution" or when Elizabeth Ermarth
milarly decides that the final chapters accurately reflect the outcome of
aggie's sexist upbringing and her consequent "confusion and ambiva-
nce" ("Maggie Tulliver's Long Suicide," *SEL*, 1974), the discussion badly
eds to be rounded out with a more probing consideration of her creator's
vn conflicts and their transmutations. Paris' charge that George Eliot
oses sight between inward and outward" might be justly leveled at his and
marth's character case studies, as well as at David Smith's "'In Their
eath They Were Not Divided': The Form of Illicit Passion in *The Mill on
e Floss*" (*L&P*, 1965), a one-sided treatment of the "passionate death" of
other and sister as an incestuous orgasmic fulfillment. More balanced is
ichael Steig's unfortunately titled "Anality in *The Mill on the Floss*"
Novel, 1974), which relies on Freud's concept of the anal phase, as modi-
d by Erikson, to discuss George Eliot's "intuitive" grasp of the "deter-
inants of character and their cultural ramifications." The best of these
itics, Steig is also the only one to pay some attention to the subject of
gression, a subject worth considering more fully by future practitioners of
e psychoanalytical approach.

In "Perfect Pyramids: *The Mill on the Floss*" (*TSLL*, 1971), Lynne
idaback Roberts looks at the novel's time schemes and "temporal
nbiguity." She sees the image of the river as an intended refutation of our
rational sense of time" and the flood as a deliberate pressure on the reader
) "take apart our world." The novel itself thus "forces us to see the limita-
ons of every rational structure we have created to order our experience."
omething similar, I think, is what John Freeman fitfully tries to articulate
1 "George Eliot's Great Poetry" (*CQ*, 1970) when he holds that *The Mill*,
ke great poetry (but somehow unlike *Middlemarch*), dissolves "historic
ime" and "reawakens our past emotions and arranges them in new rela-
onships." In her provocative "Demonism and Maggie Tulliver" (*NCF*,
975), Nina Auerbach detects and defends against F. R. Leavis the "conven-
onal 'feminine' subterranean language" of Gothic romances and vampire
ories. More stolid than Roberts, Freeman, or Auerbach is R. H. Lee's
The Unity of *The Mill on the Floss*" (*ESA*, 1964), which contends against

"Lesley" Stephen that the vitality of the first five books stems, not fro
nostalgia for childhood, but from the need to provide a careful documen
tion of family and society. N. N. Feltes relies on precisely such documen
tion to trace the permutation of "the social and economic relations of 183
to the fifties and *Little Dorrit* ("Community and the Limits of Liability
Two Mid-Victorian Novels," *VS*, 1974). And in "Education in 'The Mill
the Floss' " (*REL*, 1966) A. W. Bellringer links the novel to contempora
critiques of educational theory.

In "Music and Musical Allusion in 'The Mill on the Floss' " (*Criticis*
1974), William J. Sullivan carefully looks at George Eliot's "selection a
arrangement of musical details" from works such as Handel's *Acis a*
Galatea and D. F. E. Auber's *Masaniello* in order to show that such sy
bolic details "broaden and deepen our comprehension of the main cha
acters." Symbolism also occupies U. C. Knoepflmacher in "On Time, Rive
and Tragedy: George Eliot and Matthew Arnold" (*VN*, 1968), the be
portion of his chapter on *The Mill on the Floss* in *George Eliot's Ear*
Novels, and Paul A. Makurath, Jr., in "The Symbolism of the Flood
Eliot's *The Mill on the Floss*" (*SNNTS*, 1975). Knoepflmacher's "The I
trusion of Tragedy: *The Ordeal of Richard Feverel* and *The Mill on t.*
Floss" (in *Laughter & Despair*, 1971) is notable only for the contrasts
Meredith's novel.

Essays on borrowings by later writers from *The Mill* are discussed in tl
next section. It is worth pointing out here, however, that the novel th
attracted Proust and Clarín continues to appeal to intelligent readers on tl
Continent such as Liana Stănculescu ("Mit si leitmotif la George Elio
The Mill on the Floss [Myth and Theme in George Eliot: *The Mill on tl*
Floss]," *BLU*, 1969), F. Bolton ("Le Manuscrit du *Mill on the Floss*," *E*.
1965), and Jacques Blondel ("Morale, psychologie, destinée dans 'Le Moul
sur la Floss,' " *LanM*, 1965).

Silas Marner

No longer undervalued as an uncomplicated book for tenth grader
Silas Marner is being recognized as a major work that, in its balancing o
separate stories and its testing of the myths by which human beings try o
order experience, points ahead to the more intricate form of *Middlemarc*
If Fred C. Thomson in "The Theme of Alienation in *Silas Marner*
(*NCF*, 1965) still feels compelled to look for a "tragic vision" in the novel o
compensate for its presumed didacticism and "slickly" executed efforts "o
pass for objective reality," no such apologies are needed by subsequen
critics. In one of the subtlest treatments of the novel, "*Silas Marner*: R
versing the Oracles of Religion" (*Literary Monographs*, 1967), David F
Carroll examines its dual process of decomposition and reconstitution
whereas George Eliot first demands that "we perform a kind of demyth
ologizing, removing the myths, the superstitions, and the miracles," sh
later allows that "valid myths of order are a direct expression of love

ile invalid myths of chance result from an absence of love." The impact
Carroll's fine essay is evident in Joseph Wiesenfarth's "Demythologizing
as Marner" (*ELH*, 1970), less valuable for the reassertion of the "myth of
demythologized world" than for rich cross-references to archetypes in
imm's fairy tales and the work of German mythographers. Bruce K. Mar-
in "Similarity within Dissimilarity: The Dual Structure of *Silas Marner*"
SLL, 1972) takes issue with Carroll, Thale, and Knoepflmacher for the
ess they place on the differences between Silas' and Godfrey's stories and
phasizes, instead, the "shared trait of sympathy" that binds them.
Although Martin does not say so, "similitude within dissimilitude" is
ordsworth's phrase, of course, and important affinities between *Silas* and
poetry of Wordsworth are well examined by both Q. D. Leavis in her
roduction to the Penguin edition (1967) and Lilian Haddakin in her
apter on the novel in Hardy's *Critical Essays* (1970). A trans-Atlantic
del and analogue is convincingly proposed by Jonathan R. Quick in
las Marner as Romance: The Example of Hawthorne" (*NCF*, 1974). Ian
ilner's "Structure and Quality in *Silas Marner*" (*SEL*, 1966; rpt. in *The
ucture of Values*) stresses the communal values that bring about Silas' "re-
manization." Lastly, David Leon Higdon in "Sortilege in *Silas Marner*"
LL, 1974) discusses the drawing of lots, while Robert I. Simon, M.D., in
Narcolepsy and the Strange Malady of Silas Marner" (*AJP*, 1968) approves
the "refreshingly nonclinical description" of a "state of catatonia en-
untered in a variety of clinical syndromes, especially in schizophrenia."

Romola

Robert Browning considered *Romola* the "noblest and most heroic
ose poem" when it first appeared, but in recent years only Virgil A.
terson in "*Romola*: A Victorian Quest for Values" (*PhilP*, 1967) and
licia Bonaparte in a still unpublished assessment of the book's epic struc-
re seem to concur with this view. Peterson is helpful in tracing *Romola*'s
urfold "moral growth" (from "humanism" to "hedonism" to "theology"
"compassion unsupported by authority or ideology") yet fails to convince
en he asserts that this growth is itself evidence of the "artistic unity" that
hers feel the novel lacks. One such critic is George Levine in " 'Romola' as
ble" (In Hardy's *Critical Essays*, 1970); looking at the "unresolved tension
tween novel and romance," he concludes that "romance, while appearing
resolve the problems which the book raised, resolved, in fact, nothing."
vrom Fleishman, too, considers the novel to be an experiment that failed
The English Historical Novel: Walter Scott to Virginia Woolf (1971). He
aises the "severely conscientious portrait of a total society" and favorably
kens Romola's rejection of Florentine politics to the earlier rejection of
political structures by Scott's or Thackeray's heroes"; yet, unlike Lawrence
ston, III, who maintains in "Setting and Theme in *Romola*" (*NCF*, 1966)
at "public and private action" are meaningfully connected, Fleishman
ncludes that George Eliot "failed to find a historical community for her

heroine." In "Piero di Cosimo: An Alternate Analogy for George Elio
Realism" (*VN*, 1967), Edward T. Hurley pruposes that George Eliot
holds the painter as an exemplar of an art that is both mimetic and sy
bolic, an insight intelligently expanded by William J. Sullivan in "T
Sketch of The Three Masks in *Romola*" (*VN*, 1972) and "Piero di Cosi
and the Higher Primitivism in *Romola*" (*NCF*, 1972). Sources occu
Gennaro A. Santangelo in "Villari's *Life and Times of Savonarola*:
Source for George Eliot's *Romola*" (*Anglia*, 1972) and Lawrence Poston
in "*Romola* and Thomas Trollope's *Filippo Strozzi*" (*VN*, 1964), wh
Curtis Dahl checks off the likenesses and differences between two Protesta
incursions into Catholic Italy in "When the Deity Returns: *The Marl
Faun* and *Romola*" (*PLL*, 1969). In " 'Esse Viditur' in 'Romola' " (*N&
1970), Jill Perry contends that George Eliot's misuse of a Latin phrase v
intentional and ironic.

Felix Holt

Some of the disappointment over *Romola* spills into discussions of *Fe.
Holt, the Radical*, a novel more respectfully treated perhaps, yet with t
same disturbed sense that here, too, George Eliot fails to develop or fu
realize the organic interaction she promises between personal fortunes and
wider public life. Arnold Kettle's " 'Felix Holt, the Radical' " (in Hard
Critical Essays, 1970) asks all the right questions: "Is this to be a novel abo
Radicalism or about Mrs. Transome?" Is there any irony directed towa
Felix? Why does the "excessively tortuous" plot rely on such a "formidal
paraphernalia of legal detail"? Why is there "almost no resolution"? Ket
proposes two chief reasons for the novel's failure: George Eliot's simi
taneous middle-class "support and fear of democracy" and her "inability
see herself as a character in history." The second of these reasons w
necessitate more pondering in the future, but the first has been extensive
taken up by Michael Wolff in "The Uses of Context: Aspects of the 1860'
(*VS*, Suppl., 1965), W. F. T. Myers in "Politics and Personality in *Fe*
Holt" (*RMS*, 1966), George Levine in his introduction to the Norton ec
tion (1970), Fred C. Thomson in "Politics and Society in *Felix Holt*" (
The Classic British Novel, ed. Harper and Edge, 1972), David Craig
"Fiction and the 'Rising Industrial Classes' " (*EIC*, 1967; rpt. in *The Re
Foundation: Literature and Social Change*, 1973), Peter Coveney in f
introduction to the Penguin edition of the novel (1975), Linda Bamber
"Self-Defeating Politics in George Eliot's *Felix Holt*" (*VS*, 1975), ar
Lenore Wisney Horowitz in "George Eliot's Vision of Society in *Felix Hol
(*TSLL*, 1975). Even though all these writers ultimately agree that Geor
Eliot offers, through Felix, a mere "high-mindedness" that is unrooted
any particular activity or historical movement, each has distinct insights
offer. Wolff (who, after his article appeared, was engaged in a debate
Harold J. Harris, *VS*, 1965), Myers, and Coveney place the novel's conserv
tive outlook into the context of Carlyle's and Arnold's own reactions to tl

ond Reform Bill, of Comte's political theory, and of Marx's critique of
uerbach; Thomson, whose earlier essay on "The Legal Plot in *Felix
olt*" (*SEL*, 1967) is valuable, prefers to seek the origins of her Tory Posi-
ism in George Eliot herself. Bamber, who is especially good in assessing
w the novelist's "political moralism triumphs over her reformist sym-
thies," astutely contrasts *Felix Holt* to *Middlemarch*. Standing apart from
these critics is Michael Edwards, who advances the interesting thesis that
e "disappointment" all of them voice forms "part of the novel's desired
ect": the book produces "a formal alienation designed to alienate one
m the world as the work perceives it" ("George Eliot and Negative
rm," *CritQ*, 1974).

Middlemarch

The plethora of discussions of *Middlemarch* underscores the novel's
mingly inexhaustible appeal, yet also necessitates my having to set aside
ne items. In addition to Patrick Swinden's useful *Casebook* on *Middle-
arch* (1972), there are two collections of original essays: Middlemarch: *N G 157*
itical Approaches to the Novel (1967), edited by Barbara Hardy, and *g. II*
is Particular Web: Essays on Middlemarch (1975), edited by Ian Adam.
th are high in quality and provide a wide spectrum of ways of reading
d thinking about the novel.
The Hardy volume, dedicated to the memory of W. J. Harvey (who
ntributed two of the eight essays), is the better planned and more con-
ned with questions of methodology. It ranges profitably from Jerome
aty's fascinating detective work on the proof corrections and Harvey's
rvey of the novel's initial reception to the more formal aspects that fruit-
lly occupy Mark Schorer (structure), Derek Oldfield (characterization),
d Hilda M. Hulme (imagery). Harvey also looks at the "intellectual
ckground" for Casaubon's mythography and Lydgate's biology, but,
ooring without information he could have obtained from the Folger note-
ok, he is unduly apologetic about "tedious and irrelevant" details and
es away from the insight that Casaubon's and Lydgate's researches act as
oil for George Eliot's creation of a more fluid system of meaning that goes
yond their fixities. Harvey's hesitance may owe something to the impress
Barbara Hardy's own skeptical stance on the volume. Her worry about
e common critical tendency of "reducing particulars to generalization and
aracter to concept," however, leads her to conduct a successful experiment
"surface" reading of a single chapter. In the book's final essay, J. M. S.
ompkins supports Hardy by urging in stout Johnsonian fashion that the
ard particularities" of *Middlemarch* be not forsaken by symbol hunters.
The Adam volume collects five papers given at *Middlemarch* centenary
eetings in 1971 and 1972 (a clever report on one meeting is furnished by
liet McMaster in *VS*, 1972). Gordon S. Haight's spirited counterattack on
ose who regard Will Ladislaw as an "eminent failure" dovetails nicely
th Barbara Hardy's contention that more emphasis should be given to the

passional life of the characters; similarly, a joint interest in the "visions
unity" entertained by the main figures links Gillian Beer's study of the wa
in which *Middlemarch* goes beyond the solipsistic consciousness of "T
Lifted Veil" to U. C. Knoepflmacher's look at the wide-spreading assoc
tional ripples created by some seemingly inconsequential allusions. Ontolo
cal questions underlie David Carroll's brilliant discrimination between t
very different orders of reality in the novel: "one in which monsters purs
their devilish creators" and "the other in which the fragmented world of fa
is vivified, redeemed."

As this overview of two collections suggests, there is no single, domina
issue that attracts critics of *Middlemarch*. Still, in a good many of the
discussions and in others as well, there seems to be considerable division
to whether the novel is governed by historical fidelity or by the ever prese
mid-Victorian narrator's subjective projection "into the past of her chi
hood the issues facing her as an adult." In his introduction to the Pengt
edition (1965) W. J. Harvey adopts a middle position by calling the no
"a historical document not only of the 1830's, but also of the 1860's a
1870's," a stand also taken by Michael York Mason in "*Middlemarch* a
History" (*NCF*, 1971). Going beyond Harvey and Mason, however, a
Brian Swann in "*Middlemarch*: Realism and Symbolic Form" (*ELH*, 19
and in "*Middlemarch* and Myth" (*NCF*, 1973) and J. Hillis Miller
"Narrative and History" (*ELH*, 1974) and in "Optic and Semiotic
Middlemarch" (in *The Worlds of Victorian Fiction*, ed. Jerome Buckl
1975). Written in partial response to Calvin Bedient's contention th
Middlemarch is "in effect, all vehicle, all medium, all transparency: dead
itself" in "*Middlemarch*: Touching Down," *HudR*, 1969), Swann's *EL*
essay tries to show that even the most "literal plot pattern" always acts a
symbolic representation of "some ideal George Eliot has in mind." Pressi
even further in his own *ELH* essay, Miller argues that *Middlemarch* on
seems to assert "the metaphysical system of history it in fact so elaborate
deconstructs," a thesis that also underlies his interesting discussion of t
novel's optical metaphors and their epistemological implications.

Among the many discussions of imagery and language, Hilda M. Hulm
"*Middlemarch* as Science-Fiction: Notes on Language and Imager
(*Novel*, 1968), Norbert Kohl's "George Eliot, 'Middlemarch': 'Prelude'
eine Interpretation" (*DVLG*, 1968), Isobel Armstrong's " 'Middlemarch':
Note on George Eliot's 'Wisdom' " (in Hardy's *Critical Essays*, 1970), a
Robert Kiely's "The Limits of Dialogue in *Middlemarch*" (in Buckle
The Worlds of Victorian Fiction, 1975) are all superior. By way of contra
Robert P. Griffin's "Image and Intent: Some Observations on Style
Middlemarch" (*ForumH*, 1969) is disappointing, while P. Di Pasqual
"The Imagery and Structure of *Middlemarch*" (*ES*, 1971) is better read a
survey of existing criticism than as the intended "consideration of the im
ery as it fuses plot, character, and setting." Peter K. Garrett's remarks on t
novel's merely "auxiliary" and "quasi-symbolic devices" are suspect beca
they are primarily made to fit a far too tidy curve from the suppos

mplicity of *Middlemarch* to the increasing "complexity" of James, Conrad, awrence, and Joyce (*Scene and Symbol from George Eliot to James Joyce,* 969).

Concerned with aspects of structure are Neil D. Isaacs in "*Middlemarch*: rescendo of Obligatory Drama" (*NCF*, 1963), Suzanne Ferguson in "Mme. aure and Operative Irony in *Middlemarch*: A Structural Analogy" (*SIE*, 963), and Bert G. Hornback in "The Organization of *Middlemarch*" *PLL*, 1966). In "The Method of *Middlemarch*" (*NCF*, 1966), Richard S. yons draws some valuable conclusions from an intensive study of a single hapter.

If character is subordinated to symbol or structure in such responses, it is central concern in studies such as "Ladislaw and the *Middlemarch* Vi-on," by Jane Marie Luecke (*NCF*, 1964), and "The Concept of 'Crisis' in *Middlemarch*," by Eugene Hollahan (*NCF*, 1974), two good defenses of Vill that precede the fuller apologia by Haight in the Adam collection. ometimes such studies become animated chiefly by the critic's affection for he figure thus lifted out of the novel. This is true, certainly, in Russell M. ioldfarb's "Caleb Garth of *Middlemarch*" (*VN*, 1964). Kindly insisting hat Caleb is "impossible to overlook," Goldfarb points out dubious links etween "the rhetoric of Thomas Carlyle" and Caleb's speeches and thus at east makes the carpenter harder to overlook. Showing little commiseration, n the other hand, is Gordon S. Haight in "Poor Mr. Casaubon" (in *Nineteenth-Century Perspectives: Essays in Honor of Lionel Stevenson,* ed. Clyde de L. Ryals, 1974), an essay that also provides his last word on Spar-ow's "absurd" identification of the character with Mark Pattison (see the ection on Biography, above). Most character studies understandably prefer o focus on the "foundress of nothing," Dorothea Brooke. These include Robert Hasting's "Dorothea Brooke: The Struggle for Existence in *Middle-narch*" (*Thoth*, 1963), Lloyd Fernando's "George Eliot, Feminism, and Dorothea Brooke" (*RES*, 1963), A. P. Riemer's "Ariadne and Cleopatra: The Treatment of Dorothea in *Middlemarch*" (*SoRA*, 1966), T. J. Collits' *Middlemarch* and Moral Sympathy" (*CR*, 1967), and Robert F. Damm's Sainthood and Dorothea Brooke" (*VN*, 1969). Fernando's essay, as well as is "Special Pleading and Art in *Middlemarch*: The Relations between the exes" (*MLR*, 1972), complement Lee R. Edwards' hardly atypical response o "the text's attitudes towards women" in "Women, Energy, and *Middle-narch*" (*MR*, 1972; rpt. in *Woman: An Issue,* 1972). For feminists who do not want to be as "angered, puzzled, and finally depressed" by the novel's urface concessions to a male hegemony as Edwards professes to be, U. C. Knoepflmacher's "*Middlemarch*: An Avuncular View" (*NCF*, 1975) might e a welcome antidote in its insistence that George Eliot carries on a sus-ained critique of patriarchal values through her presentation of uncles and athers. Interesting, too, is Barbara Hardy's discussion of the "restricted reatment of sex" in "Implication and Incompleteness: George Eliot's *Middlemarch*" in *The Appropriate Form* (1971).

The novel's intellectual and cultural underpinnings are examined in still another cluster of essays. James F. Scott reads *Middlemarch* as a dramatize appraisal of "the Comtean view of social change" ("George Eliot, Pos tivism, and the Social Vision of *Middlemarch*," *VS*, 1972), while Larry M Robbins detects the impact of John Stuart Mill in the novel's handling of public opinion ("Mill and *Middlemarch*: The Progress of Public Opinion, *VN*, 1967). In an effective note on "George Eliot's 'Pier Glass': The Deve opment of a Metaphor" (*MP*, 1969), N. N. Feltes spots Herbert Spencer a the "eminent philosopher among my friends" mentioned in the famou opening of Chapter xxvii; Ian Adam, looking at another well-known pa sage in Chapter xx, is equally convincing in tracing it to "The Physica Basis of Life" ("A Huxley Echo in 'Middlemarch,'" *N&Q*, 1964). Conside able attention has been paid to the novel's incorporation of scientifi medical, and mythographic knowledge. Michael York Mason's "*Middl march* and Science: Problems of Life and Mind" (*RES*, 1971) and Rober A. Greenberg's "Plexuses and Ganglia: Scientific Allusion in *Middlemarch* (*NCF*, 1975) are excellent; but Patrick J. McCarthy's "Lydgate, 'The New Young Surgeon' of *Middlemarch*" (*SEL*, 1970) and C. L. Cline's "Qualifica tions of the Medical Practitioners of *Middlemarch*" (in Ryals's *Nineteenth Century Perspectives*, 1974) might have profited from some of the medica information distilled from the Folger notebooks by John Clark Pratt in h introduction to "A *Middlemarch* Miscellany" (Diss. Princeton 1965 Daniel P. Deneau's good "Eliot's Casaubon and Mythology" (*AN&Q*, 1968 has since been superseded by the work on mythography done by Harvey Swann, and Knoepflmacher, but Hugh Witemeyer in "George Eliot, Nau mann, and the Nazarenes" (*VS*, 1974) opens new avenues when he suggest that Naumann's "neo-typological theory of history painting," modeled afte Overbeck and Führich, "has significant affinities with Casaubon's reductive Christian mythography."

The relation of *Middlemarch* to earlier classics and earlier writers sti needs more careful attention (its impact on later writers is covered in th next section). Christopher Heywood's "A Source for *Middlemarch*: Mi Braddon's *The Doctor's Wife* and *Madame Bovary*" (*RLC*, 1970) promise more than it delivers, while Roland A. Duerksen's "Shelley in *Middle march*" (*KSJ*, 1965) is better on Lewes' Shelleyan connections than on th actual references in the novel. E. E. Duncan-Jones identifies Hazlitt as th man whom George Eliot calls "the most brilliant English critic of his day and whose misunderstanding of Catholic iconography she corrects in Chap ter xix ("Hazlitt's Mistake," *TLS*, 27 Jan. 1966). Seiji Fujita's chapter o "*Middlemarch* and *Vanity Fair*" is perhaps the most original portion of h sensitive but modest *Structure and Motif in* Middlemarch (1969); som further links between the two novels are made by U. C. Knoepflmacher i "*Middlemarch*: Affirmation through Compromise" (*Laughter & Despai* 1971). J. S. Szirotny discusses Dickens' and George Eliot's allusion t *Agamemnon* in "A Classical Reference in 'Hard Times' and 'Middl march'" (*N&Q*, 1968), and S. P. Meyer (*TLS*, 25 Jan. 1968) corrects Bert C Hornback's allegation that the narrator's comment on George Borrow

hronologically "inappropriate" (*TLS*, 21 Dec. 1967) by recalling that both
,avengro and *The Romany Rye* deal "with the period of *Middlemarch*."

Finally, a few noteworthy studies that do not fall into any of the above
ategories are Hollis L. Cate's "George Eliot's *Middlemarch*: Its Initial
\merican Publication and Reception, 1871–1874" (*XUS*, 1965); Frederick
Villey's "Appearance and Reality in *Middlemarch*" (*SoR*, 1969); A. L.
rench's "A Note on *Middlemarch*" (*NCF*, 1971), a perversely unfriendly
eading; June Skye's "George Eliot and St. Peter's" (*N&Q*, 1972); D. M.
lill's "Why Did Mr. Keck Edit the 'Trumpet'?" (*NM*, 1973); and Robin
.ee's " 'Middlemarch'—A Hundred Years Later" (*Standpunte*, 1973).

Daniel Deronda

Critics of *Daniel Deronda* hardly bristle anymore at F. R. Leavis' long-
.oftened blast against the "astonishing badness" of the Mordecai-Mirah-
Daniel business, although Harold Fisch in "*Daniel Deronda* or *Gwendolen
Harleth*?" (*NCF*, 1965) still takes up the anti-Leavis gauntlet, while, in the
)pposite camp and in a better essay than Fisch's, Carole Robinson confirms
ind complicates the old prejudices by carefully wading through "the dreary
:errain through which the reader must pass after the marriage of Gwendolen
ind Grandcourt" ("The Severe Angel: A Study of *Daniel Deronda*," *ELH*,
₁964). Most other critics, however, seem to find enough that interests them
in the novel's radical departures from the earlier fictions, such as its dislocation of social identity or its experimental disruptions of time. In a rewarding fresh analysis, Jean Sudrann declares that the novel is concerned with
'the harsh exigencies of how 'to be' in exile" and hence peoples its world
with a greater "variety of 'aliens' " than those found before ("*Daniel
Deronda* and the Landscape of Exile," *ELH*, 1970). Like Barbara Hardy,
who praises the decision to leave Daniel "poised on the edge of a future
which is deliberately left 'vague and grand' " (introduction to Penguin
edition, 1967), Sudrann stresses the importance of the book's deliberate
avoidance of a "sentimental return" to the past, an emphasis confirmed by
John P. Kearney in "Time and Beauty in *Daniel Deronda*" (*NCF*, 1971).

Three essays by Brian Swann—"Eyes in the Mirror: Symbolism in *Daniel
Deronda*" (*NCF*, 1969), "George Eliot and the Play: Symbol and Metaphor
of the Drama in *Daniel Deronda*" (*DR*, 1972), and "George Eliot's
Ecumenical Jew, or, The Novel as Outdoor Temple" (*Novel*, 1974)—are
marred by persistent diffuseness and the failure to adhere to a central
theme, yet deserve to be read for good incidental insights. Without focus,
too, as well as innocent of existing criticism, is Anne Sedgley's "*Daniel
Deronda*" (*CR*, 1970), again worth perusing for occasional insights. Oblivi-
ous to previous criticism also are Leon Gottfried in "Structure and Genre in
Daniel Deronda" (in *The English Novel in the Nineteenth Century*, ed.
George Goodin, 1972), a rather thin essay, and George Wing in "The
Motto to Chapter xxi of *Daniel Deronda*: A Key to All George Eliot's
Mythologies?" (*DR*, 1974), a more interesting, though overstated, discussion

in which the earlier combats with "the power of Ignorance" are brought t
bear on Gwendolen's story.

In "*Mansfield Park, Daniel Deronda,* and Ordination" (*MP,* 1965
David R. Carroll notes similarities in tone and situation only to stress th
differences that led George Eliot "to contrive an elaborate system of cros
references" that Austen did not need. Both David Leon Higdon in "Eliot'
Daniel Deronda, Chapter 36" (*Explicator,* 1972) and Joseph Wiesenfarth i
"The Medea in 'Daniel Deronda' " (*NS,* 1973) dwell on Euripedean echoe
in the characterization of Lydia Glasher. D. R. Beeton's "George Eliot'
Greatest and Poorest Novel: An Appraisal of *Daniel Deronda*" (*ESA,* 1966
offers little more than enthusiastically endorsed excerpts from some nove
called "*Gwendolen Harleth*"; nor do the rapid-fire generalizations in Be
Euwema's "Denial and Affirmation in Victorian Thought" (*JGE,* 1969
leave a deep impression, despite the Profuse Use of Capital Letters at th
End.

Laurence Lerner's judicious look at the stages of Gwendolen's "conver
sion" in "The Education of Gwendolen Harleth" (*CritQ,* 1965; rpt. in *Th
Truthtellers,* 1967) makes Albert R. Cirillo's more minute documentation o
each and every phase of Gwendolen's relation to Daniel seem overlong and
almost tedious by comparison, were it not for the shrewd remarks about th
role of music in the novel ("Salvation in *Daniel Deronda*: The Fortunat
Overthrow of Gwendolen Harleth," *Literary Monographs,* 1967). Also con
cerned with music are Shirley Frank Levenson in "The Use of Music ii
Daniel Deronda" (*NCF,* 1969), a rather derivative essay, and William J
Sullivan in an interesting note on "The Allusion to Jenny Lind in *Danie
Deronda*" (*NCF,* 1974). In a search for the "original" of the musicia
Klesmer, Ian Milner cautiously proposes the names of Felix Mendelssohr
and Dr. Antonin Springer, the Czech historian ("Herr Klesmer: George
Eliot's Portrait of the Artist," *PP,* 1964), while Gordon S. Haight, more
persuasively, favors Anton Rubinstein ("George Eliot's Klesmer" in *Imag
ined Worlds: Essays on Some English Novels,* ed. Maynard Mack and Iar
Gregor, 1968). Douglas C. Fricke's "Art and Artists in *Daniel Deronda*'
(*SNNTS,* 1973) also dwells on Klesmer, viewing him as the "ideal" artist.

Pointing out, long ago, that George Eliot would have known that "in
pure Hebrew" the word "Klesmer" means "instruments of music," Edward
N. Calisch speculated that her preparation in Hebraic studies must have
been extraordinarily thorough (*The Jew in English Literature,* 1909). This
speculation is borne out by William Baker's *George Eliot and Judaism*
(1975), which adopts the title of the book by David Kaufmann that appeared in George Eliot's lifetime and that has recently been reprinted by
Haskell House (1970). Although Baker incorporates much peripheral material that could have been greatly condensed (Rahel Levin, the Palestine
Exploration Society, Spinoza, Sephardo in *The Spanish Gypsy*), his compre-
hensiveness remains helpful. Two portions of his book have appeared as
articles—"George Eliot's Readings in Nineteenth Century Jewish Historians" (*VS,* 1972) and "The Kabbalah, Mordecai, and George Eliot's

Religion of Humanity" (*YES*, 1973)—and he intends to edit some of the *Deronda* notebooks in the future. In " 'Daniel Deronda': George Eliot and the Political Scene" (in Hardy's *Critical Essays*), Graham Martin pours Karl Marx's scorn of Feuerbach's "dirty-judaical" impracticality on *Daniel Deronda*, but to fault George Eliot for "removing the ideal aspirations associated with Deronda from any effective engagement with the English scene" is rather willfully to deny that it is precisely her sad sense that such "effective engagements" are no longer possible or meaningful in Victorian society that is the starting point of her novel. Nor is the novel really evasive; Erwin Hester shows how its allusions to the American Civil War, the Jamaica uprising, and the Austro-Prussian War acquire "a metaphorical significance" ("George Eliot's Use of Historical Events in *Daniel Deronda*," *ELN*, 1966). Of little value to the specialist is Mary Graham Lund's "George Eliot and the Jewish Question" (*Discourse*, 1970), a stitchwork of quotations from letters and *Theophrastus Such*.

Lesser Works

Though often mentioned in the discussions of the novels, the lesser works have received little attention in their own right. There is not a single study of *Theophrastus* since Mallock's 1879 essay. Thomas Pinney and Michael Wolff (whose works on the essays were discussed in the first section of this survey) are the only writers with genuine insights into the prose; Stuart Hampshire's "George Eliot's Essays" (in *Modern Writers and Other Essays*, 1969) is far too brief, and Rosalind Russell's "George Eliot—Journalist" (*ContempR*, 1969) is even more superficial than her "George Eliot and Her Poetry" (*ContempR*, 1963). Cynthia A. Secor's "The Poems of George Eliot: A Critical Edition" (Diss. Cornell 1970) certainly deserves to be published: a careful edition, it also boasts what is unquestionably the best introduction to the poetry. In "The German Original of a George Eliot Poem" (*N&Q*, 1974), Maurice Stang locates a poem by Siegfried August Mahlmann that Mary Ann Evans translated for Miss Lewis in 1840. Two essays on the only first-person narrative George Eliot ever published are Edward Hurley's " 'The Lifted Veil: George Eliot as Anti-Intellectual" (*SSF*, 1968) and Ian Milner's "George Eliot's Prague Story" (*PSE*, 1973). And, in "George Eliot's Projected Napoleonic War Novel: An Unnoted Reading List" (*NCF*, 1975), William Baker dwells on the interests that were "simmering" toward the "masterpiece" that remained unwritten.

Relations to Other Writers

The renewed sense of the importance of George Eliot's manifold connections to other novelists and thinkers, already evident in the triangular structure of books such as Lerner's *The Truthtellers* and Knoepflmacher's *Religious Humanism* and in the abundant cross-references that always mark even the most formalistic discussions of her work, has led to a considerabl body of comparative studies. These fall into four distinct categories. Ther is first the kind of study that stresses the direct impact of a given author o work on a single novel by George Eliot: such essays are included in th previous section; there is secondly the study of the more general influenc of, say, Comte or Hegel, on George Eliot's theories and practice: such essay are covered in the section on general criticism. There remain, however, tw further types of comparative studies: those that examine her impact o contemporary or later writers and those that set her in apposition to othe novelists, without claiming actual influence or interdependence. Both type are considered in this section, which I have arranged in national pigeon holes in full awareness of Mr. Brooke's own unsatisfactory experience witl this method: "Ah, pigeon-holes will not do. I have tried pigeon-holes, bu everything gets mixed in pigeon-holes."

John Philip Couch's *George Eliot in France: A French Appraisal o George Eliot's Writings, 1858–1960* (1967) is extremely valuable ir documenting the unbroken prestige the novelist enjoyed in France. Begin ning with the opinions of reviewers from 1858 to 1880, Couch examines the criticism of Emile Montégut and Edmond Scherer, two warm admirers; he then shows how Brunetière's defense of her work was enlisted in a polemic against Zola's naturalism and ends by examining her reputation in the early twentieth century, when, though her audience shrank somewhat, her new advocates "included for the first time writers and critics who would soon achieve international prominence," such as Bergson, Brémond, Proust Gide, and academics like Madeleine Cazamian. Also looking at the enlist ment of George Eliot in the attack on the naturalists is R. J. Sealy in "Brunetière, Montégut—and George Eliot" (*MLR*, 1971). In a chapter that owes much to Franklin Gary's pioneering essay, "In Search of George Eliot: An Approach through Marcel Proust" (*Symposium*, 1933), Margaret Mein discusses the "features that Proust admired in George Eliot" (*A Foretaste of Proust: A Study of Proust and His Precursors*, 1974). Both Brunetière and Henry James hoped for an eventual union of George Eliot's "sympathie" and Flaubert's "composition," but Barbara Smalley's interesting attempt to bring the two great novelists together in *George Eliot and Flaubert: Pi oneers of the Modern Novel* (1974) remains more laudable in its intentions than in its execution: only a guarded introductory chapter contains mean ingful juxtapositions. Using George Sand primarily "as a convenient symbol of the emotional, idealistic side of George Eliot's writing," Patricia Thom son also notes concrete similarities between Jacques and Silas Marner in "The Three Georges" (*NCF*, 1963). Finally, in "Isolation and Integrity: Madame de Lafayette's Princesse de Clèves and George Eliot's Dorothea Brooke" (*RLC*, 1970) Mildred S. Greene notes the common "Pascalian espousal of other-worldliness" of two differently treated heroines.

More serious work remains to be done on George Eliot's relations to German writers other than Strauss and Feuerbach. Although the value of Mary Teresa J. Engel's "The Literary Reputation of George Eliot in Germany, 1857–1970" approaches that of Couch's *George Eliot in France*, it may remain unpublished (Diss. Univ. of Detroit 1974). And the publications we do have are all disappointingly brief: the single page that L. H. C. Thomas devotes to George Eliot's essays on Germany in "Germany, German Literature, and Mid-Nineteenth Century British Novelists" (in *Affinities: Essays in German and English Literature*, ed. R. W. Last, 1971) offers a bare checklist; Valentine Cunningham's account of the "opportunistic use" George Eliot made of an article on Heine in her own essay on the poet at least provides a starting point for a much needed comparative study ("George Eliot, Julian Fane, and Heine," *N&Q*, 1971). Similarly, George Eliot and Gottfried Keller need to be more thoroughly compared; Allan Casson's two-page discussion of minor analogues ("*The Mill on the Floss* and Keller's *Romeo und Julia auf dem Dorfe*," *MLN*, 1960) overlooks the larger parallels: both writers were born in 1819, both were influenced by Strauss and Feuerbach, both turned from journalism to fiction, both validated their agnosticism by going back to a known agrarian past.

Strangely enough, the relations to Russian, Polish, and Spanish writers have received far more extended attention. In "Turgenev and George Eliot: A Literary Friendship" (*MLR*, 1971), Patrick Waddington pieces together several unpublished letters for a fascinating story (in 1880 Turgenev invited George Eliot to come to Moscow for the unveiling of Pushkin's statue). In "George Eliot's *Adam Bede* and Tolstoy's Conception of *Anna Karenina*" (*MLR*, 1966), W. Gareth Jones relies on superficial similarities in hair style and gesture to pronounce that the "prototype for Anna Karenina is Hetty Sorrel"; more guarded in her claims and hence more convincing is Edwina Jannie Blumberg in "Tolstoy and the English Novel: A Note on *Middlemarch* and *Anna Karenina*" (*SlavR*, 1971). David J. Welsh's attempt to bring together George Eliot and the Polish novelist Eliza Orzeszkowa (1846–1910) in "Two Talkative Authors: Orzeszkowa and George Eliot" (*PolR*, 1965) goes little beyond the assertion that both display stylistic qualities "regarded nowadays as 'old-fashioned.'" Matters of style and "structural consequence" also occupy D. Ridley Beeton in "Joseph Conrad and George Eliot: An Indication of the Possibilities" (*PolR*, 1975), a too inconclusive essay. Much richer is Barry W. Ife's discussion in the first half of "Idealism and Materialism in Clarín's *La Regenta*: Two Comparative Studies" (*RLC*, 1970) of significant affinities between *The Mill on the Floss* and an 1884 novel by the Spanish critic Leopoldo Alas.

Also considerable is the number of studies of George Eliot's impact on American writers. Biancamaria Pisapia's documentation of Henry James's conflicting estimates of George Eliot in "George Eliot e Henry James" (*SA*, 1967) is perhaps more valuable than her search for "elementi eliottiani" in his fictions (although the links between *Romola* and *Roderick Hudson* are persuasive). If Pisapia stresses James's borrowings, George Levine prefers to emphasize his dissociations: he finds that James "does not flinch at the inescapable insight—an insight which George Eliot consistently dodges from *The Mill on the Floss* to *Daniel Deronda*, despite her protestations to the contrary—that the mistake once made is irrevocable" ("Isabel, Gwendolen and Dorothea," *ELH*, 1963). In "The Fractured Crystal in *Middlemarch* and *The Golden Bowl*" (*MFS*, 1973), Scott Byrd insists that James converted a "vivid image from *Middlemarch* into a central symbol." Important connections between George Eliot and William Dean Howells are drawn by Jack H. Wilson in "Howells' Use of George Eliot's *Romola* in *April Hopes*" (*PMLA*, 1969) and by William Alexander in "Howells, Eliot, and the Humanized Reader" (in *The Interpretation of Narrative: Theory and Practice*, ed. Morton W. Bloomfield, 1970). Wilson also examines George Eliot's "contribution," via *Romola* and *Middlemarch*, to Edward Eggleston's fiction in "Eggleston's Indebtedness to George Eliot in *Roxy*" (*AL*, 1970). In a two-part essay, "Robert P. Warren's Tollivers and George Eliot Tullivers" (*UR*, 1970), Russell M. Goldfarb considers the "important pointed allusions to one of the classics of English literature" made evident through the "Tolliver signature, the importance of the flood, and the theme of incest" in the novel *Flood*.

A book that engagingly connects George Eliot to one American and one British author is Robert Coles's *Irony in the Mind's Life: Essay on Novels by James Agee, Elizabeth Bowen, and George Eliot* (1974). Discussing *A Death in the Family, The Death of the Heart,* and *Middlemarch* as ironic constructs that tell us much, respectively, about childhood, youth, and the grown-up years, Coles pays homage to the novelist's ability to encompass a psychological "complexity of feeling" that the psychiatrist may prefer to type or codify. His warm tribute to George Eliot's "canny psychological and sociological appraisals" is always carefully documented; he is particularly illuminating when he discusses the portrait of Bulstrode as "perhaps the one from whom we learn the most": through Bulstrode's conflicts, Coles maintains, George Eliot is able to "show us how even under the most compelling and extraordinary of *psychological* circumstances, we are all agents of one another, members of one or another Middlemarch."

Finally, back to England herself. In an extremely suggestive essay, "D. H. Lawrence and the Apocalyptic Types" (*CritQ*, 1968; rpt. in *Continuities* 1968), Frank Kermode relates George Eliot to that other Midlands fabulist: despite Lawrence's discontent with her fictions, the Brangwen sisters and the "very concept of the big double novel earlier called *The Sisters*" show the depth of her influence. Kermode nicely rearranges "familiar elements in *Middlemarch*" to show how much it shares with Lawrence, but he is always aware of the acute differences: whereas George Eliot "was powerfully under the influences of demythologizing Germans," Lawrence "was, though uneasily, a remythologizer." Compared to Kermode's important essay (as well as his "Novel, History, and Type," *Novel*, 1968, which connects the novelists more sketchily) and to Lerner's distinctions in *The Truthtellers*, Robin Lee's "Irony and Attitude in George Eliot and D. H. Lawrence" (*ESA*, 1973) seems more tangential.

Another gap in our understanding of "continuities" is filled by two studies of George Eliot's impact on Walter Pater, David J. DeLaura's "*Romola*

nd the Origin of the Paterian View of Life" (*NCF*, 1966) and Donald L.
Hill's "Pater's Debt to *Romola*" (*NCF*, 1968). Noting that as late as 1890
Pater remembered a phrase "incidentally given" to Piero di Cosimo in
Romola, DeLaura speculates that it might have been his reading of that
novel "that set Pater on the road to the essays which were gathered in 1873
as *Studies in the History of the Renaissance*." The repeated references to
Savonarola in those essays also corroborate this speculation, according to
DeLaura. Hill disagrees. He notes that Savonarola's asceticism would have
been less appealing to Pater than "the artists whose 'humanistic' spirit was
the object of his absorbing quest." Since George Eliot herself, however, is
ambiguous about Savonarola and, very much like Pater, contrasts his "visions" with the secular humanism of artists like di Cosimo, DeLaura's case is
hardly weakened by Hill's objections.

George Eliot's deep impression on the writer who cast her as Theresa in
The Autobiography of Mark Rutherford is examined briefly by Stephen
Merton in "George Eliot and William Hale White" (*VN*, 1964) and far
more carefully by Wilfred H. Stone in "Hale White and George Eliot"
(*UTQ*, 1956). Stone concludes from the strange remarks about "Mrs. A." in
"Confessions of a Self-Tormentor" that White saw George Eliot "not only as
a potent intellect and moral force but, in a curiously English and Puritan
way, as a *femme fatale*." Hopkins, who cruelly derided "the overdone reputation of the Evans-Eliot-Lewis[sic]-Cross woman," nonetheless also came
under her spell, according to Grover Smith in "A Source for Hopkins'
Spring and Fall' in *The Mill on the Floss*" (*ELN*, 1963), a somewhat
unconvincing note. More thorough and persuasive is Raymond S. Nelson's
account of Bernard Shaw's "ironic adaptation" of *The Mill on the Floss* in a
1910 work ("*Fanny's First Play* and *The Mill on the Floss*," *ShawR*, 1969).

Not much has been written to connect the Brontës to George Eliot,
besides Kroeber's book. Barbara Hardy's "Mrs. Gaskell and George Eliot"
(in Arthur Pollard's *The Victorians*, 1970), really two separate essays, includes a few worthwhile contrasts. Lastly, since this survey began a little
derisively with Samuel Chew's likening of George Eliot to Mrs. Oliphant, it
seems only proper to make amends by according the prominence that comes
with the last entry to Kathleen Watson's "George Eliot and Mrs. Oliphant:
A Comparison in Social Attitudes" (*EIC*, 1969), an intelligent vindication
of those reviewers who supposed *Salem Chapel* to have sprung from no
"other pen than that to which we owe *Adam Bede* and *Scenes of Clerical
Life*."

It may be proper to end this lengthy survey with some suggestions as well
as with a self-chastising reminder of its inadequacies. First, however, a remark provoked by the discovery of so much redundant criticism: Is it really
necessary even in a fallen, publish-or-perish world to commit to print all
those readings and interpretations that merely swerve a few degrees from
existing discussions? And is there not also a similar superfluity in all those

essays, on all sides of the Atlantic, in which the writer assumes that no one
else could have noticed that Hetty Sorrel "disturbs the settled life of the
entire community" or that Daniel Deronda seems "excessively idealized".
The perusal of so much that overlaps or merely rephrases earlier formula-
tions makes one almost share George Eliot's own distrust of criticism: "
think there is more than enough literature of the criticising sort urged upon
people's attention by the periodicals. To read too much of it seems to me
seriously injurious: it accustoms men and women to formulate opinion
instead of receiving deep impressions." Her shrewd remark painfully applies
not only to a good many of the items I have discussed but also, just as
painfully, to my own easy formulation of opinions in this criticism of criticisms (a modern refinement that not even George Eliot could have anticipated!).

In a more constructive and accepting vein, however, let me simply list a
few topics that might be explored in the future by "literature of the criticising sort." Redinger's biography suggests that the time is ripe for a psychological approach to the novels done with tact and skill (indeed, one such
study is already being promised by Laura Comer Emery for 1976). Given the
scattered discussions of musical echoes and musical analogies in George
Eliot's fiction, a much fuller study of the theoretical and practical implications of her extensive knowledge of music might not seem amiss; her interest
in painting also merits continued attention. We need to understand more
thoroughly why George Eliot chose to return to her earliest authorial voice
in *Theophrastus Such*; indeed, a study that would carefully distinguish her
various "voices" could yield interesting results. The copious references in
existing criticism to connections between George Eliot and Wordsworth
suggest we could use a good book-length consideration of affinities and
differences. Likewise, though her love of Scott is often mentioned, the exact
results of her indebtedness remain to be investigated more carefully; we also
need essays on her relations to Austen, Bachofen, Balzac, Browning, Fielding, Goethe, Lamb, the Shelleys, Thackeray, Trollope, the anthropologists
of the 1870s, and many more. A dual, contrasting study of George Eliot and
Dickens along the lines of George Steiner's *Tolstoy or Dostoevski?* can perhaps be attempted someday (with a chapter on brothers and sisters in *The
Mill* and *Hard Times?*). Feminist criticism needs to confront George Eliot
with greater open-mindedness: What is the "female" quality of her art?
How does she differ from other woman novelists? From male novelists with
similar fables? Even though the attention to George Eliot's pessimism and
sense of tragedy is unavoidable, we also need to look more closely at her
humor, her comic sense. A monograph on the uniqueness of her naming of
characters and places might prove interesting. George Eliot's translation of
Spinoza should at last be edited, assessed, and published; her accomplishments as a translator, indeed, her quite Arnoldian notions about translation
itself, deserve to be separately examined. And, as Redinger has shown, the
poetry *can* be taken seriously. Finally, though biography is not likely to
progress soon beyond Haight and Redinger, more remains to be done, es-

ɔecially on the later career of the always self-analytical and doubting ɔelebrity, as well as on the relation to Herbert Spencer, which may need reevaluation when the letters he sealed are opened in 1985.

Secure in that Choir Invisible, George Eliot undoubtedly looks with a mixture of revulsion, melancholy, and amusement at our busy and overly eager intrusions into her heart and her intelligence. She would most certainly also smile at the untrustworthiness of this account of critical writings as they have mirrored themselves on my mind. I can do no better than to go to one of her earlier pronouncements and, in expiation, ask the reader to apply her wise and wary reservations to my words in this chapter: "Examine your words well, and you will find that even when you have no motive to be false, it is a very hard thing to say the exact truth, even about your own immediate feelings—much harder than to say something fine about them which is *not* the exact truth."

GEORGE MEREDITH

Gillian Beer

C. L. Cline concludes his chapter on Meredith in the Stevenson *Guide* by asking:

> Where do all of these riches in scholarship and criticism leave us? Biographers and historical scholars would seem to have done most of their work with Meredith. Though new facts will surely continue to be discovered, they will be predictably minor in importance. What has not been done extensively is to re-examine Meredith's novels in the light of contemporary standards of criticism. Only when this has been done can Meredith take his rightful place in the literary canon.

Meredith has not yet become fully integrated into the canon of major nineteenth-century fiction as it is discussed within the universities, and perhaps he never will be. One problem that modern readers have with the novels is that, intellectually at least, Meredith was of the conquering party. Many of the ideas he asserts aggressively and demonstrates at length have become our starting points. We now acknowledge, perhaps too easily, the claims of the unconscious, the need for a fiction that registers those shifting processes of the inner life that can scarcely be recorded in action:

> An audience will come to whom it will be given to see the elementary machinery at work: who, as it were, from some slight hint of the straws, will feel the winds of March when they do not blow. To them will nothing be trivial, seeing that they will have in their eyes the invisible conflict going on around us, whose features a nod, a smile, a laugh of ours perpetually changes.
>
> (*The Ordeal of Richard Feverel*, Ch. xxv)

On the other hand, we have not yet been surfeited with a fiction that debates its own autocratic nature. Nabokov has reminded us of the scintilating insights that a style permeated with metaphor and with self-distrust can create. Meredith still exhausts and exhilarates his readers. The spasmodic and provisional nature of his fiction—his preoccupation with the problematical—makes him particularly fruitful reading for anyone interested in the imaginative debates of his time. Issues such as the prowess of the unconscious, the interpenetration of sexual passion and politics, the "providential" organization of fiction, and the balked potentiality of women are not only reflected in his plots but explicitly articulated, sometimes in discussions, sometimes in metaphors. Meredith has been the subject of so many revivals and enthusiasms, so much abjuring and irritability, that what he needs now is neither the critical "indulgence" that Barbara Hardy in *Meredith Now* (ed. Ian Fletcher, 1971) finds too common nor the "defensiveness" about taking him seriously that Judith Wilt comments on in her review of the same volume (*VS*, 1974). Margaret Conrow offers a long essay on "Coming to Terms with Meredith" in *The English Novel in the Nineteenth Century* (ed. George Goodin, 1972). It is from this attitude that we must now go forward.

Bibliography and Manuscripts

The Meredith section in *NCBEL* (1969) provides a useful, though not exhaustive, list of studies in chronological order down to the 1960s.

Michael Collie's *George Meredith: A Bibliography* (Toronto, 1974) is an invaluable tool for the scholar or critic. Collie sets forth clearly the ways in which his bibliography is wider in scope than that prepared by Buxton Forman in 1922:

> . . . it attempts authoritative statements on the development of Meredith as a writer; on the circumstances in which individual books were written; on the relationship of the manuscripts where they exist to first editions; on the evolution of a text through various editions during Meredith's lifetime; on the significance of publications in the United States; and on the central place in Meredith's writing life of the collected editions.

Collie's work can encompass these ambitious aims partly because of the wry fact that there are few editions of Meredith's books between the first and the collected editions. The collected editions therefore have a particular literary-historical importance. Their appearance from the mid-1880s onward consolidated Meredith's reputation and helped create the widespread surge of interest in him that allowed Eliot, in the first version of *The Waste Land*, to represent literary aspirations in the figure of the tailor who reads Meredith. Collie excludes the collected editions from his discussion of the earlier publishing history of each book and gives them a section of their own toward the end of his bibliography. This allows him to concentrate on the revisions of individual novels and poems, which led "in every case to the establishment of the definitive text in a volume in one of the collected editions," for which Meredith revised the whole of his work at least twice.

The Altschul Collection in the Beinecke Library, Yale University, is the most extensive and important of all Meredith collections. In addition to printed books, there are manuscripts of letters, novels, and poems, including the manuscript of *Modern Love*. Meredith's ten working notebooks and two collections of loose leaves include preliminary material—usually very brief (a line or two, a jotted aphorism), but occasionally more extensive —for *Richard Feverel, Sandra Belloni, Vittoria, The Adventures of Harry Richmond, Beauchamp's Career, Celt and Saxon, Diana of the Crossways,* and *One of Our Conquerors*. An edition of the notebooks and portfolio notes is in preparation by Gillian Beer and Margaret Harris. The collection also includes holographs of versions—some fragmentary—of the following novels: (1) *The Adventures of Harry Richmond*; an edition based on this manuscript is being prepared by Sven-Johan Spånberg. (2) *The Egoist*. (3) *The Tragic Comedians*; for details of his changes in proof and of compositors' misreadings of Meredith's always difficult hand see Gillian Beer's "Meredith's Revisions of *The Tragic Comedians*" (*N&Q*, 1964). (4) *Celt and Saxon*. (5) *Diana of the Crossways* (fragment); see Joyce Elaine Measure's "Meredith's *Diana of the Crossways*: Revisions and Reconsiderations" (Diss. Univ. of Wisconsin 1966). (6) *One of Our Conquerors*; two manuscripts, of which one is an earlier version entitled "A Conqueror in Our Time": see F. C. Thomson's "Stylistic Revisions in *One of Our Conquerors*" (*YULG*, 1961) and his "The Design of *One of Our Conquerors*" (*SEL*, 1962). (7) *Lord Ormont and His Aminta*. (8) *The Amazing Marriage*; three manuscripts: see Judith Ann Sage's "The Making of Meredith's *The Amazing Marriage*" (Diss. Ohio State Univ. 1966) and also her "George Meredith and T. L. Peacock: A Note on Literary Influence" (*ELN*, 1967), comparing a scene in the early version with *Crochet Castle*. M. Y. Shaheen writes "On the Manuscripts of *The Amazing Marriage*" (in *N&Q*, 1975).

The Pierpont Morgan Library has the typescript of *The Amazing Marriage* and also the complete holograph of *Diana of the Crossways*. The Huntington Library has a ninety-five-page fragment of *Diana*, and the Fales Collection at New York University has still another fragment of *Diana*. The Widener Library of Harvard University has the holograph of "The Tale of Chloe." A fuller account of manuscript holdings can be found in Michael Collie's *George Meredith: A Bibliography* (Toronto, 1974).

Mention should be made of a recurrent conundrum in Meredith criticism to which the manuscripts and letters provide an answer. Meredith referred to *The Adventures of Harry Richmond* as an "autobiographic" tale. A number of unwary critics have assumed that this means, not simply a first-person narrative, as it pretty clearly does, but a tale based on his own life. The situation has been further bedeviled by a joking letter from Meredith to Maxse, written at Christmas 1866 but dated Christmas 1870, in which Meredith imagines the comic apocalypse of Maxse's thinking and actions.

He ends the letter: "I have just finished the History of the inextinguishable Sir Harry Firebrand of the Beacon, Knight Errant of the 19th century, in which mirror you may look and see—My dear Fred and his loving friend George Meredith" (Cline, I, 352).

This "History" is a fictive work for which from time to time Meredith jotted down ideas in the notebooks (continuing to do so until the end of his life). It is *not* a lost work; nor is it either *Harry Richmond* or *Beauchamp's Career*. These matters have been fully dealt with by Cline and Stevenson. Moreover, R. B. Hudson set out the relationship between the early draft notes on Richmond Roy in the Altschul Collection, Beinecke Library, and *The Adventures of Harry Richmond* in "Meredith's Autobiography and *The Adventures of Harry Richmond*" (*NCF*, 1954). John W. Morris gives a thoroughly documented analysis of "Meredith's Unintentional Literary Hoax" (*TSL*, 1965). As Morris remarks, "These rather easy-to-discover facts, together with the preposterous letter itself, should have precluded any possibility of misunderstanding." Yet six years later a contributor to *Meredith Now* falls into the trap and builds a theory based on all these old errors. Dare one hope that scholars and critics may be alerted by this summary?

Editions: Letters, Poems, Novels

During the past twelve years Meredith has been well served by scholars and critics. Phyllis Bartlett's edition of the poems, which includes much previously unpublished material, is about to appear. C. L. Cline's *The Letters of George Meredith*, 3 vols. (1970) contributes about two thousand new letters to our information about Meredith and supplants W. M. Meredith's 1912 edition. Showing the extent to which William Meredith edited and conflated his father's letters, Cline adds immensely to our knowledge of Meredith's friendships and of the circumstances surrounding his second marriage. His edition brings out vividly the fierce and merry style with which Meredith characteristically grappled his correspondents to him, but it also shows the variety of his writing: the elliptical double entendres of his letters to Hardman, the high-spirited and resilient arguments with Maxse, the haggard and yet distanced nobility of the letters at the time of his second wife's death. Certainly the involuted gaiety of the letters disproves the old idea that Meredith first wrote simply and then sat down to complicate his perceptions. Language as a way both of fending off experience and of engaging it deeply is registered in the mannered and yet spontaneous resourcefulness of the letters. Something of the same quality can be seen in the articles Meredith wrote for *The Pall Mall Gazette* in the 1860s, identified by Gillian Beer (*MLR*, 1965). Material for the study of Meredith's life with Mary in the 1850s remains tantalizingly sparse, although new material is beginning to surface. Manuscript Notebook 9 in the Beinecke Library at Yale, with its throng of poems from that period, creates a poignant image of the breakup of the marriage as it came home to Meredith.

L. T. Hergenhan's edition of *The Adventures of Harry Richmond* (1970) includes useful appendixes on Meredith's revisions of the published texts and incorporates data from Hergenhan's "Meredith's Revisions of *Harry Richmond*" (*RES*, 1963). Margaret Harris' edition of *One of Our Conquerors* (Univ. of Queensland Press, 1975) offers helpful textual notes, and Harris is also preparing an edition of *Beauchamp's Career*. A Norton Critical Edition of *The Egoist* is forthcoming. At present the most reliable edition is that edited by George Woodcock for the Penguin English Library (1968). No film versions of Meredith's novels have been attempted, and no recent translations of the novels have appeared.

Biography and Reputation

Diane Johnson's *The True History of the First Mrs. Meredith and Other Lesser Lives* (1973) is a biography of Mary Meredith that also tells what happened to her three children: Edith, child of her first marriage to Edward Nicoll; Arthur, child of her marriage to Meredith; and Harold Felix, child of her love for Henry Wallis. The book, written in sympathetic mimicry of a Victorian novel of a very un-Meredithian kind, is full of winning insights into the condition of persons with whom Meredith was deeply involved, and it reports some fascinating research into the lives of Edith and Felix. Unfortunately, however, Johnson uses Meredith as Victorian bogeyman in such a way as to belie her claim that she is allowing her persons full historical and psychological reality. The vitiating condescension toward him has an effect demeaning to Mary as well; there was more to this marriage on both sides than disaffection, oppression, and coldness. "Fulness of love sleeps in us like a sea / After night's tempest, O thou lovely thing." The manuscript poems of the 1850s, among which that fragment appears, make their passionate and abrasive relationship clear—and so, of course, do the novels, which Johnson uses only very selectively and partially.

In *George Meredith: The Critical Heritage* (1971), a collection of reviews of Meredith's publications, Ioan Williams provides a "selection of articles and comments about [Meredith's] work which were made during his time." T. H. Hutton's trenchant opening to a review of *The Egoist* expresses a typical contemporary reaction: "We have been amused, impressed, bored, and filled with admiration and disappointment by Mr. George Meredith's new story." The whereabouts of much of the basic material used by Williams is indicated by L. T. Hergenhan (Hergenham in Williams' volume) in an unpublished London University dissertation of 1960. Hergenhan's work has now fortunately found wider circulation through a number of articles he published on the reception of Meredith's novels: "The Reception of George Meredith's Early Novels" (*NCF*, 1964); "Meredith's Use of Revision: A Consideration of the Revisions of *Richard Feverel* and *Evan Harrington*" (*MLR*, 1964); "Meredith Attempts to Win Popularity: Con-

mporary Reactions" (*SEL*, 1964); "A Note on Some of Meredith's
ontemporary Reviewers" (*N&Q*, 1964); "George Meredith and 'The
nuffling Moralist': Moral Disapproval of His Early Works and Its Effects"
Balcony, 1966); "Meredith Achieves Recognition: The Reception of
eauchamp's Career and *The Egoist*" (*TSLL*, 1969). Kenneth Graham's
nglish Criticism of the Novel 1865–1900 (1965) includes some intelligent
nd useful discussion of Meredith. A vivid sense of Meredith's reputation
oward the end of his life can often be gathered from the incidental com-
nents about him made by other writers. Yeats, for example, once remarked
nat Maude Gonne was a "Diana of the Crossways," and Meredith's *Harry
Richmond* and *The Egoist*, along with George Eliot's *Middlemarch*, are the
nly English novels to appear on a list of "favorite books" that Edith
Wharton compiled in 1898 (reported by R. W. B. Lewis in his 1975 biogra-
hy of Wharton). C. W. Field's "Herman Hesse as Critic of English and
American Literature" (*Monatshefte*, 1961) includes extensive quotations
rom Hesse's review of *The Egoist*, and M. Y. Shaheen describes and quotes
rom an unpublished lecture by E. M. Forster that offers a fuller account of
orster's reactions to Meredith than does *Aspects of the Novel* ("Forster on
Meredith," *RES*, 1973). An appraisal of "Meredith's Reputation" from his
ime to the present has been most recently attempted by John Lucas in
Meredith Now (ed. Ian Fletcher, 1971).

General Criticism

The full-length critical studies of Meredith's fiction published during the
period covered by this review are V. S. Pritchett, *George Meredith and
English Comedy* (1969); Gillian Beer, *Meredith: A Change of Masks. A
Study of the Novels* (1970); *Meredith Now: Some Critical Essays*, ed. Ian
Fletcher (1971); Donald David Stone, *Novelists in a Changing World:
Meredith, James, and the Transformation of English Fiction in the 1880's*
1972); and Judith Wilt, *The Readable People of George Meredith* (1975).
Material from these studies is cited in the discussion of individual novels
below. The value of all such critical studies can be enriched if they are
supplemented by a reading of Cline's edition of the letters. Pritchett's short
book, which was prepared as the Clark Lectures at Cambridge, sees Meredith essentially as a performer, a wit who inveterately moves into the center
of attention in his fiction. Pritchett emphasizes that Meredith's foreign
upbringing allowed him to appraise the sicknesses of English society with
unusual disengagement. He sees Meredith's special comic subject as being
the analysis of romantic egoism. Pritchett's general evaluation of Meredith
follows traditional lines and sometimes dismisses him too easily, but his
succinct and witty book is full of exact insights: "the important characters
in Meredith are always extremists because they have to carry this thing he
called Idea."

Gillian Beer in *Meredith: A Change of Masks* sees Meredith as a consciously experimental novelist, extending the techniques of fiction in order

to register the discontinuities among the inner lives of individuals, the
actions, and the activities of the society in which they live. She organizes th
book in terms of the novelistic problems explored by Meredith in *Th
Ordeal of Richard Feverel, The Adventures of Harry Richmond, The Egoi*
Diana of the Crossways, and *The Amazing Marriage*. One of the princip
themes emerging from this study is Meredith's distrustful attraction to th
romance versions of experience proffered by characters and narrators withi
the novels and often created through metaphor. Meredith's attempt to co
trol the creative libertinism of the imagination gives his fiction much of i
energy. A useful element in the discussion is the analysis of unpublishe
notebooks, drafts of the novels, and other manuscript fragments.

Donald David Stone in *Novelists in a Changing World* sees Meredith a
essentially Victorian, opposed to the modernism—or at the least the ope
ing toward modernism—of Henry James. He comments: "The rejection c
Meredith, which began during the First World War, accompanied th
increasing disbelief among intellectuals in the durability of civilized value
in the transforming capabilities of the individual will, or in the intrinsical
rational construction of society—three of Meredith's key ideas." Th
polarizing of the two writers implicit in the organization of his book lea
Stone to surprising judgments, such as that the ending of *Diana of th
Crossways* is "facile" and that the novel "exhausted the possibility tha
fiction could still be written for Victorian readers." "Victorian" in th
book, as in Diane Johnson's, is sometimes less a historical than a pejorativ
term. But Stone's analysis of *One of Our Conquerors* is illuminated by h
sense of James's different achievement in the same period of the 1880s. H
suggests a way of looking at the 1880s that has its own coherence, though i
the process Meredith is made to appear too monolithic and James to
volatile.

Judith Wilt's *The Readable People of George Meredith* explores th
reader's role in Meredith's fiction, analyzing the contrarieties of narratio
in his novels and the extent to which the reader is obliged to make the tex
In contrast to Stone, she interprets Meredith as a novelist creating an
requiring a modern phenomenology of reading if he is to be understood
"Two voices, one the true tone of philosophy, the other its flaw, its vice, i
shadow of cynicism, sentimentalism, egoism, fatalism, struggle for control c
the narrative." She sees this struggle as paradigmatic of the ordering c
narrative in Meredith's novels, and she reads Adrian Harley's role in *Ric*
ard Feverel in this light.

Studies of Individual Novels

Richard Feverel

Discussion of *Richard Feverel* in the 1960s was bedeviled by problem
of form derived from New Criticism and from Jamesian demands for "tota

levance." A number of articles argue for and against the artistic unity of
the novel, often by emphasizing one element in its complex interweaving.
The debate was initiated by John W. Morris, who argues in "Inherent
Principles of Order in *Richard Feverel*" (*PMLA*, 1963) that, since *Richard
Feverel* follows the form of New Comedy, not only implicitly but by actual
reference within the text, the tragic ending perversely disrupts the expectations Meredith has induced. The death of Lucy is artistically without
justification. Henri A. Talon in "Le comique, le tragique, et le romanesque
dans *The Ordeal of Richard Feverel*" (*EA*, 1964) argues that the novel fails
because it incorporates elements so disparate as to be impossible to fuse
satisfyingly. Lawrence Poston III's "Dramatic Reference and Structure in
The Ordeal of Richard Feverel" (*SEL*, 1966) responds by arguing that
despite the element of New Comedy the dramatic form of the novel can be
seen in a different way, so that the "dramatic references, in conjunction
with the rising and falling action, can be analyzed into a five-act structure
giving coherence to the novel's tragic pattern." Ioan Williams emphasizes
"The Organic Structure of *The Ordeal of Richard Feverel*" (*RES*, 1967),
and John R. Reed develops a related argument in "Systematic Irregularity:
Meredith's Ordeal" (*PLL*, 1971). The debate moves to the area of rhetoric in
David E. Foster's "Rhetorical Strategy in *Richard Feverel*" (*NCF*, 1971):
the 'dark' side of the narrative voice allows a shift from the comic to a
tragic mode," while Jacob Korg in "Expressive Styles in *The Ordeal of
Richard Feverel*" (*NCF*, 1972) suggests that by parodying generic styles
Meredith exposes the folly of those characters who suffer from fixed literary
ideas.

   Another approach to *Richard Feverel*, one that has become increasingly
fruitful, is to set it in its context of controversy about education and science
and to track its intellectual history. P. D. Edwards shows some of the connections between the attitudes toward "Education and Nature in *Tom
Jones* and *The Ordeal of Richard Feverel*" (*MLR*, 1968): "both novels
assume that the closer man is to his natural state the better person he will
be—but Meredith believes that education can nullify even the strongest
natural impulses." This method of commentary works particularly well
when a writer can also show the devious means by which *Feverel* acts as a
critique of the ideas it embodies. In this respect Terry H. Grabar's " 'Scientific' Education and Richard Feverel" (*VS*, 1970) is outstanding, as is Sven-
Johan Spånberg's "The Theme of Sexuality in *The Ordeal of Richard
Feverel*" (*SN*, 1974). Grabar discusses the origin of "the System" and sees Sir
Austin as a caricature of the advanced educational theorists of the day,
offering "a mishmash of the most bruited ideas of the time." He inevitably
tracks the sources of much educational theory to Rousseau (as does Juliet
Mitchell with rather ostentatious caution in "*The Ordeal of Richard
Feverel*: A Sentimental Education" in *Meredith Now*). But Grabar goes
further. He discriminates between the views of associationist-utilitarian and
pessimistic thinkers and shows their points of agreement: "education must
be based on scientific observation of the evolutionary stages of human de-

velopment, but what those phases were, nobody knew." Recalling th
Meredith was educated for two years at the Moravian school in Neuwied, I
shows the influence of Moravian ideas of sequestration and example in "tl
System." And he demonstrates the apparent irony but basic sympathy wi
which Meredith used Spencer's 1858 essay on "Moral Education." Followi
much the same method as Grabar, Spånberg points to Acton's *Prostitutic*
and *The Functions and Disorders of the Reproductive Organs* in an a
tempt to clarify what the *Spectator* reviewer meant by claiming that S
Austin has "sound physiological views."

Using evidence of a more literary nature, Spånberg also sets *Richa*
Feverel in relation to *Sir Charles Grandison,* to *Emile,* and to Stendha
novels in his monograph *The Ordeal of Richard Feverel and the Traditio*
of Realism (Upsala, 1974). In a lively essay in *Nineteenth-Century Perspe*
tives: Essays in Honor of Lionel Stevenson (ed. C. de L. Ryals et al., 1974
B. F. Fisher places the novel in the category of "sensation fiction" ("Sens
tion Fiction in a Minor Key: *The Ordeal of Richard Feverel*"). He sets it i
the tradition of the mock Gothic exemplified by *Northanger Abbey* an
Nightmare Abbey, but he also demonstrates that Meredith uses Goth
elements for his own purposes: "And so the old familiar haunted castl
peopled with madness and rife with horrors, is domesticated into a mor
realistic fiction in that the madness and death are here made psychologicall
plausible."

Another aspect of the book that continues to fascinate critics is the crea
tive ordering of personal and deeply painful experience that Meredit
attempts in the novel. In *Hiding the Skeleton* (1966), John Henry Smit
offers a thorough comparison of the imagery of *The Ordeal of Richa*
Feverel and *Modern Love.* Phyllis Bartlett had already pointed out th
extent to which Meredith mockingly incorporates his own juvenilia int
Richard Feverel, assigning his love poems of the early 1850s to the poetaste
Diaper Sandoe and the young Richard ("Richard Feverel, Knight-Errant,
BNYPL, 1959). In *Meredith: A Change of Masks* (1970) Gillian Beer show
the close affinities between Meredith's early notebooks and Sir Austin
"Pilgrim's Scrip," an avenue of inquiry which is further explored by Caro
lyn I. Holt in "Sir Austin and His Scrip" (*JNT,* 1974). Beer sees Sir Austin a
the reader's guide, as well as his prey, while Judith Wilt in *The Readab*
People (1975) brings out the extent to which Adrian Harley shares tha
double function, serving as a kind of shadow narrator.

Monica Mannheimer in *The Generations in Meredith's Novels* (Stoc
holm, 1972) discusses the father-son paradigm. In *Laughter & Despai*
(1971), U. C. Knoepflmacher tellingly compares the autobiographic impuls
in *Richard Feverel* and *The Mill on the Floss.* He discusses the ways i
which the tragic endings of these two novels derive from the symbolic need
of the writers and depend upon the authors' own experience as expressed i
the fiction. He concludes that Meredith validates the tragedy in a way tha
George Eliot did not succeed in doing: "Lucy's death, capricious as it is, i
integral to Meredith's purpose. Its swiftness and unexpectedness are neces

ry. . . . By exposing the deficiencies of Richard and Sir Austin, Meredith
.n rid himself and his readers from the debilitating sense of despair he
tributes to these two characters." In *Season of Youth: The Bildungsroman
om Dickens to Golding* (1974) Jerome Buckley groups together *Richard
everel*, *Evan Harrington*, and *Harry Richmond* in a chapter entitled "His-
.ories of Father and Son." He sees Richard's development as permanently
rested by the death of Lucy, in contrast to Harry's complete initiation
.to adult life, and prefers the later novel for its "unity of tone and point of
ew."

Beauchamp's Career and Other Novels of Mid-Career

The novels immediately after *Richard Feverel* have not been widely
iscussed, but they have given rise to several of the most interesting pieces of
Meredith criticism of the past few years: David Howard's essay "Meredith in
.he Margin" in *Meredith Now* discusses *Rhoda Fleming* in terms of
peripheralism." This novel is often read as Meredith's simplest, but How-
rd remarks that it is "a pattern of flight, pursuit, and abortive contact." It
.atches "the desperation and exasperation of a lower class, and the appre-
.ension and condescension of an upper class. The fundamental tactic in this
.lass conflict is to avoid contact." Jean Sudrann sensitively registers this
.eliberate "blurring," this "fabric of visions obscurely realised by each of
.he chief characters" in "The Linked Eye and Mind: A Concept of Action
n the Novels of Meredith" (*SEL*, 1964).
C. L. Cline offers some manuscript evidence about "Emilia in England"
.om "Sir William Hardman's Journal" (*BC*, 1966). In *Literature and Poli-
ics in the Nineteenth Century* (ed. John Lucas, 1971) Howard discusses
.andra Belloni*, *Vittoria*, and *Beauchamp's Career* in "George Meredith:
Delicate' and 'Epical' Fiction." This excellent essay shows the ways in
vhich political issues are explored through novelistic means; he comments,
or example, "The political attitude of *Beauchamp's Career* enforced by the
vhole weight of its incidents and imagery is that of the postponed moment." His description of *Sandra Belloni* includes an appraisal of the lan-
uage that Meredith creates for Emilia—the way in which she is not just
life-joy" but both simple and unpredictable. Howard and Wilt both
rovide full, dextrous readings, alive to Meredith's poignant schemes for
nmeshing the reader in the turmoil of his characters and in the emotional,
ocial, political, and intellectual issues raised by that turmoil.
Evan Harrington is not so subtle a book, and the most useful articles have
analyzed its comic freedoms: Richard Stevenson's "Innovations of Comic
Method in George Meredith's *Evan Harrington*" (*TSLL*, 1973) and J. M. S.
Tompkins "On Re-Reading Evan Harrington" (*Meredith Now*, 1971).
Tompkins gives us a salutary reminder: "Readers were not embarrassed, as
they sometimes are now, by seeming to discern, under the brilliant surface,
old sores, open wounds and remembered bruises. It is probable that Meredith was tougher minded about social prejudice than we are, as the

eighteenth-century was tougher minded about lunacy and the sixteen
about taming shrews. . . . We need not assume that the purgation was fin
and complete; a book is not a man." Margaret Tarratt in " 'Snips,' 'Sno
and the 'True Gentleman' in *Evan Harrington*" (*Meredith Now*) points
the literary associations with Carlyle's *Sartor Resartus* and Thackera'
Book of Snobs.

The comparison with Carlyle has been fruitful for a good many rece
critics of Meredith, and it comes out particularly strongly in *Meredith No*
the collection in which Tarratt's essay appears. It is brilliantly explored
Ian Fletcher's essay in this collection, "*The Shaving of Shagpat*: Meredit
Comic Apocalypse," which tracks the urgent and sometimes mocking det
within that work to Shelley, to Romantic and Christian transcendence, to tl
Spasmodics (Bailey, Horne, and Alexander Smith), to Carlyle, and
Ariosto: it is "the *Orlando's* world of painful metamorphosis, of peripe
and the obsessive quest to reduce the intense pointless play of plural life
unity that remains most relevant." One of the fullest treatments of the
lationship between Meredith and Carlyle is J. W. Morris' "*Beauchamp
Career*: Meredith's Acknowledgment of His Debt to Carlyle" in *Studies*
Honor of John C. Hodges and Alwin Thaler (1961). Morris tends to flatte
the contradictory impulses in Meredith's feelings toward Carlyle, impuls
that are forcefully expressed in the figure of Dr. Sharpnel. Kurt Otten
"George Meredith: *Beauchamp's Career*" in *Der englische Roman in*
Jahrhundert: Interpretationen (ed. Paul Goetsch et al., 1973) needs to e
plain to German readers how it is possible for Carlyle, despite his fasci
heritage, to be an inspiration to a radical novelist. He reminds them of th
other Carlyle who was read as a forerunner of Marx's early writings. Otte
sees *Beauchamp's Career* as radical in intent even though its hero is d
picted as helpless between the contraries of, on the one side, "Radikalism
und Sozialismus" and, on the other, "Imperialismus und Nationalismus.
He indicates the extent to which the novel is conceived in terms of patrio
ism—a point made also by Arnold Kettle in *Meredith Now*, who emphasiz
the way in which Meredith "uncompromisingly breaks through the bou
geois convention that the private and the public life are separable." Kett
demonstrates Meredith's approach in his excellent analysis of the "rightness
of the horsewhip episode, which works as a historical metaphor. The prol
lem that Otten touches on, that "like Plato's philosopher-kings" Meredit
expresses ideas whose significance "is spiritual and utopian rather tha
political and concrete," is at the center of Gillian Beer's examination of tl
novel, which she reads as a radical work beset by problems about the meta
phoric nature of action and preoccupied with the nature and possibility c
heroism when the ideal for which the hero is struggling goes beyond ind
vidualism. Another aspect of the struggle between metaphor and fact i
Meredith is discussed in Thornton Y. Booth's *Mastering the Event: Con
mitment to Fact in George Meredith's Fiction* (1967).

David Howard's essay " 'Delicate' and 'Epical' Fiction," mentione
above, is useful on the political implications of *Beauchamp's Career*. Mer
dith's mounting interest in political and social transformation in the late

art of his career is touched on in Maurice McCullen's "A Matter of 'Prin-
ple': Treatment of the Poor in George Meredith's Fiction 1879–1895"
LN, 1970) and Richard L. Newby's "Meredith as Social Reformer"
McNR, 1971–72). Daniel Becquemont discusses Trollope's *The Way We
ive Now* alongside *Beauchamp's Career* in "Politics in Literature 1874–
5" (*Politics and Literature in the Nineteenth Century*, Lille: Centre
Etudes Victoriennes, 1974).

Harry Richmond, *The Egoist*, and the Last Novels

The two novels written on either side of *Beauchamp's Career—The
Adventures of Harry Richmond* and *The Egoist*—are more indirect in their
critique of society. *Harry Richmond* in particular has been studied from the
point of view of style and genre more than for its comparative critique of
German and English society or for Richmond Roy's Merdle-like attack on
English assumptions at a banquet in his honor. Barbara Hardy's shrewd and
imaginative essay on the uses of imagery in her "A Way to Your Hearts
through Fire or Water" is collected in her *The Appropriate Form: An Essay
on the Novel* (1964). Margaret Tarratt in "*The Adventures of Harry
Richmond*: Bildungsroman and Historical Novel" (*Meredith Now*) helpfully tracks the associations between *Wilhelm Meister* and *Harry Richmond*.

With *The Egoist* we reach the traditional focus of Meredith's reputation,
but there has been a comparative dearth of articles of real interest on this
novel over the past few years, though there has been more vitality in the
critical books already mentioned and in Donald R. Swanson's *Three Conquerors* (The Hague, 1969), which also discusses "General Ople and Lady
Camper" and *One of Our Conquerors* as part of an extended argument
about authority and egoism. There have been a few thoughtful articles on
the functions of "egoism" in the book: for example, I. H. Buchen's "Science,
Society and Individuality: *The Egoist*" (*UKCR*, 1964), his "The Egoists in
The Egoist: The Sensualists and the Ascetics" (*NCF*, 1964), and John
Goode's "The Egoist: Anatomy or Striptease" (*Meredith Now*). Goode relates Comte's and Spencer's ideas about the ego to the activity of *The Egoist*
and ends with a revealing comparison with *A Portrait of a Lady*: "James,
we feel, spares Isabel with an admiration of her suicidal embrace of duty
because he has postulated only death as the alternative. Meredith postulates
life, not as a realized complexity, but as an undeniable but unaccom-
modated determination." The imagery of the book is discussed in R. B.
Wilkenfeld's "Hands Around: Image and Theme in *The Egoist*" (*ELH*,
1967).

One of the most incisive interpretations of the novel is Kate Millett's in
her *Sexual Politics* (1970). She praises "the rare wonder of [Meredith's]
comprehension of the women in the book—a feat of astounding empathy"
and "his superb background information on the powers of environment and
conditioning that have made these people what they are," but she dislikes
Clara's marriage: "Meredith knows how to save her from the egoist, but he
can think of nothing else to do with her." He "mistakes the liberating

turmoil of the sexual revolution for the mundane activities of a matc
making bureau." I wish Kate Millett had also discussed *Diana of the Cro
ways*, which raises the problem of marriage in a far more recalcitrant for
James Gindin in *Harvest of a Quiet Eye* (1972) comments on Meredith
consistent defense of the New Woman in contrast to "the rigid, restricte
shallow woman promoted by the stereotype." But Pritchett in *Meredith an
English Comedy* points out with characteristic shrewdness that the equali
of the sexes for Meredith meant the conflict of the sexes. Lois J. Fowle
tackles this subject in "*Diana of the Crossways*: A Prophecy for Feminism
in *In Honor of Austin Wright* (ed. J. Baim et al., 1972), and demonstrate
Meredith's sober treatment of the problematical relationship between se
ual freedom and full emancipation. The difficulties that beset a woman i
achieving emancipated selfhood are studied in a strikingly persuasive an
devious argument by Jan B. Gordon in "*Diana of the Crossways*: Interna
History and the Brainstuff of Fiction" (*Meredith Now*). Bringing to be
anthropological and psychological categories, the essay explores the functio
of gossip in this novel and its role in Diana's perception of herself. This is
challenging pursuit of a theme that is crucial to Meredith—the extent t
which the fictive simplifications of gossip stabilize as well as disrupt th
sense of self. Dame Gossip becomes one of the two narrators of Meredith
last novel, *The Amazing Marriage*.

The Tragic Comedians, drawing upon the history of Ferdinand Lassalle
the German Socialist leader, is a ferocious and overwrought book. Leoné
Ormond in *Meredith Now* discusses the image patterns that Meredith too
over and transformed from his German source. There is room for furthe
exploration of Meredith's unusually strong German creative affiliation:
Bernice Williams discusses his skill as a translator in "George Meredith
Translator" (*ErasmusR*, 1970).

Of the three last novels *Lord Ormont and His Aminta* has understand
ably received scant attention, though Barbara Hardy makes good use of i
in her essay in *Meredith Now*, "*Lord Ormont and His Aminta* and *Th
Amazing Marriage*." *Lord Ormont*, she observes, "shows Meredith at hi
most sentimental, and where the famous artificiality serves the interests o
the sentimentality." Joseph Kruppa was among the first to suggest a co
herent way of approaching "Meredith's Late Novels" (*NCF*, 1964).

One of Our Conquerors, in contrast, has been grappled with enthusiasti
cally by a number of critics. This difficult, ambitious, deeply moving book i
at last back in print. Perhaps this will make it a more frequent part o
studies of late nineteenth-century fiction, where its knotty and unwieldy
presence is vital. Donald R. Swanson makes it the apex of his subtle study o
"conquerors" in Meredith's work. Bernard A. Richards explores the issue o
its obscurity in "*One of Our Conquerors* and the Country of the Blue'
(*Meredith Now*). He sees it as an attempt to do in a novel what Blake
would only attempt in "Prophetic Books." Gillian Beer in "*One of Our
Conquerors*: Language and Music," in the same collection, analyzes it as "a
novel about language and the limits of language": "Morally, the novel

veals the responsibilities imposed by language and by the articulated
•nsciousness. Decoratively, it allows Meredith to try out stylistic effects
hich ignore his readers. In his late novels Meredith often seems to have
st faith in language as communication. In *One of Our Conquerors*, this
ss of faith is both a theme and a temptation. Beyond language lies silence,
usic, and death. Each of these in turn dominates the novel." The novel
ises many issues, concerned as it is with the perils in English society at all
vels of consciousness and the unconscious. *One of Our Conquerors*, natu-
lly enough, has attracted work on style—a field curiously little penetrated
. Meredith studies over the last few years, except as part of an analytical
gument, such as that developed by John Halperin in *The Language of
editation: Four Studies in Nineteenth Century Fiction* (1973) and *Egoism
d Self-Discovery in the Victorian Novel: Studies in the Ordeal of Knowl-
dge in the Nineteenth Century* (1974). Margaret Harris writes on " 'The
raternity of Old Lamps': Some Observations on George Meredith's Prose
yle," emphasizing the need to express the intangible and subjective
rough figurative language (*Style*, 1973). Serge Cottereau offers a detailed
udy of one technique in Meredith's late novels—the apparently omniscient
arrators' use of "we": "Resources et ambiguïtés d'un procédé stylistique: La
remière Personne du pluriel dans les derniers romans de George Meredith"
A, 1965) and he extends his range of psychological and linguistic argument
 "Répression, censure, et justification dans les romans de George Mere-
ith" (*EA*, 1974).
  The reader, Dame Gossip, and the novelist as narrator constitute the
ve" of *The Amazing Marriage*, and the relations among the three have
en studied by Hardy, Beer, and Wilt. The "we" of romance formulas is
tted against the "I" of individual insight. These critics have also seen the
ook as Meredith's final attempt to probe the problematical nature of mar-
age, with its other, uneasy, yet according "we."

  Criticism over the past few years has tended, perhaps naturally enough, to
oncentrate on the two novels most often taught in university courses: *The
rdeal of Richard Feverel* and *The Egoist*. Surprisingly few writers in the
holarly journals have thought it worthwhile to range further in their
eading, despite offering concentrated and highly appreciative analyses of
eir chosen novels. Moreover, little use has yet been made of the new
esources offered by Cline's edition of the letters. Meredith should now be
ecognized as crucial—and no longer simply a "crux"—in the creativity of
e later nineteenth and earlier twentieth centuries. In an elliptical writer
words on the page" may lose considerable import if we ignore the way they
int at the shared preoccupations of a society. There is room for much work
n the intellectual and social issues registered in Meredith's fiction. We
eed good texts of the novels. We need, too, criticism that will demonstrate
ot only "the elementary machinery at work" but, as Meredith says later in
e same passage, the way that "in real life all hangs together."

SAMUEL BUTLER

Daniel F. Howard

At least by his own assertion, Butler wrote not for his contemporaries b⊔
for posterity. Obviously, however, there was a good deal of defensiveness ⊔
this assertion, for like most authors he was an avid and sensitive follower ⊔
his reviews. His letters show that he certainly never minded when his co⊔
temporaries took favorable notice of him, but for the most part they c⊔
operated with his expressed desire for the favor of posterity by not readi⊔
anything he wrote except *Erewhon* (and only four thousand copies of th⊔
were sold in the first twenty-seven years following its publication in 187⊔
Thus, unlike all the other novelists discussed in this volume, Butler is ⊔
phenomenon of the twentieth century, not the nineteenth, and the mater⊔
als available for studying him are best seen in the context of their eme⊔
gence after his death. As his most comprehensive bibliographer remark⊔
"Butler's career culminated not in 1902 with his death but rather in t⊔
years following 1919 [the date of his friend Jones's massive biography⊔
(Stanley B. Harkness, *The Career of Samuel Butler*, 1955).

Bibliography, Manuscripts, Editions

The standard bibliography through 1953 is Stanley B. Harkness' *The C⊔
reer of Samuel Butler* (1955). There are enough minor errors, omission⊔
and inconsistent citations* to encourage one to check out individual item⊔
but Harkness' is an indispensable guide not only to Butler's own public⊔
tions but also to nineteenth-century and later reviews and criticism. Har⊔
ness has a section listing "Casual Comment" on Butler, compiled from

---

* J. B. Fort cites some of these (including the embarrassing omission of his ow⊔
Samuel Butler l'écrivain: Étude d'un style, 1935) in a nevertheless favorable review ⊔
Études Anglais (1956). An American, Harkness is not scrupulous about citing variation⊔
among the English, Continental, and American publications of Butler material. Mu⊔
geridge's book, for example, is listed by Harkness as having been published in 193⊔
though the English date is 1936.

etime's reading with a dedication to his subject—an extremely useful list
 items that ordinarily are not indexed under Butler's name. Another
rangement that students of Butler's reputation will welcome is a listing of
views by magazine, as well as by author (when known) and by the book
viewed.

An excellent, earlier, more descriptive bibliography, on which Harkness
aws, is A. J. Hoppé's (1925). Hoppé has the precision of a professional
bliophile, and he has the interest of would-be collectors at heart, whereas
arkness serves as a vade mecum for the Butler enthusiast who would like
 know where to turn next. Butler is well served by having both as bib-
graphers.

Two catalogues of library holdings of Butler material complement the
bliographies: *The Samuel Butler Collection at St. John's College, Cam-
idge: A Catalogue and a Summary* (1921), by Henry Festing Jones and A.
 Bartholomew; and *A Catalogue of a Collection of Samuel Butler in the
apin Library, Williams College, Williamstown, Mass.* (1945), by Carroll
 Wilson. In 1957 Helmut E. Gerber published, in the first number of his
nglish Fiction in Transition,* an annotated secondary bibliography of work
at had appeared since 1953 (Harkness' cutoff date). Trends in Butler
iticism through 1958 are analyzed in Lee Elbert Holt's "Samuel Butler Up
 Date" (*EFT*, 1960). Gerber and others continued to furnish an an-
tated bibliography in the first number of each year of *English Fiction in
ransition* (since 1963 retitled *English Literature in Transition*) through
75. They no longer do so annually but promise occasional reviews of the
erature at longer intervals. Roger Parsell and Hans-Peter Breuer are pre-
ring a volume on Butler for the Northern Illinois University Press's series
 Annotated Secondary Bibliographies.

Butler carefully preserved nearly everything he wrote. He made copies,*
metimes even of routine letters to tradesmen, and he stored copies of his
ore important manuscripts (including one of *The Way of All Flesh* and
e Notebooks) in Jones's flat in case of fire. The Notebooks are actually all
cond, rather than first, drafts, for Butler regularly went over notes he had
tted on scraps of paper, culled out those he liked, touched them up,
pied them over, indexed them, and bound them in hard covers with his
wn press. The original scraps were discarded, but the date of the original
try was recorded in the final version. The original copy of the Notebooks
 in the Chapin Library at Williams College (which also has many tissue
pies); a second copy, very difficult to read, is in the British Library. The
otebooks contain not only the notes that Butler's various executors have
lected from and published but the autobiographical accounts of his rela-
ns with his father, Pauli, Jones, Miss Savage, etc., first published in

---

* Butler called them "pressed copies," sheets of tissue, probably chemically impregnated,
t in a press on top of a page written in black ink. See Charles C. Nickerson, "Samuel
tler's Copying Process" (*VPN*, 1971).

Butleriana, ed. A. T. Bartholomew (1932). A detailed description of t
manuscript Notebooks and the differences between them and the publish
selections is in Lee Elbert Holt's "The Note Books of Samuel Butle
(*PMLA,* 1945). A complete scholarly edition of the Notebooks has long be
needed and is now in preparation by Hans-Peter Breuer and Roger Parse

Butler's General Correspondence, chronologically arranged, is bound
sixteen large volumes in the British Library. Though heavily drawn up
by Jones for his *Memoir,* it still contains a great many letters that have n
been used. One of the revelations in this manuscript correspondence is th
Butler made great use of his own letters. Incredibly, many of the letters th
are so well incorporated in *The Way of All Flesh,* including Christin
famous "death-bed" letter to her sons, are almost word-for-word copies
letters from Butler's own parents.

In addition to the General Correspondence, a few letters have been p
served by Butler's correspondents themselves (tissue copies of these oft
exist in the General Correspondence). The Chapin Library holds forty-ni
letters and postcards to and from his sister May, edited with others from t
General Correspondence by Daniel F. Howard (1962), and thirty-seven, st
unpublished, to and from his artist friend Charles Gogin. An interesti
correspondence with Robert Bridges, the Poet Laureate, in which both m
discuss their work, is privately held by the Bridges family; those abo
Butler's work on Shakespeare's sonnets are printed in an article by Dona
E. Stanford in *Shakespeare Quarterly* (1971); the article also contains
sound evaluation of Butler's contribution to Shakespeare studies.

The manuscripts of *The Way of All Flesh, Erewhon* (the first and revis
versions), and *Erewhon Revisited* are in the British Library, along wi
some curiosities, like the papers of his grandfather that he did *not* use in I
two-volume *Life and Letters of Dr. Samuel Butler* and a translation fro
Martin Chuzzlewit into Homeric Greek. Most other manuscripts are
Cambridge, at St. John's College and the Fitzwilliam Museum, but that
Life and Habit is at Shrewsbury School; of *Luck or Cunning?,* for son
reason, at the Bodleian; of *The Fair Haven* at Christchurch, New Zealan
and of the Italian and Homeric studies at the towns in Italy that Butl
associated most closely with their genesis.

Although there have been many reprints of Butler's individual nove
(which, because of their valuable introductions, are discussed below und
Later Criticism), the twenty-volume Shrewsbury Edition (1923–26) is t
only complete collection, containing, in addition to the major works, tv
volumes of collected essays and one volume of selections from the Not
books. Although most of the texts are unexceptionable, those of the follo
ing three volumes are grossly distorted:

1. *Erewhon.* The text is Butler's 1901 revision—revised some thirty yea
after he first wrote the book. An author's revisions so much later are alwa
interesting and may significantly improve the work, as in Henry James

w York Edition, but Butler's revisions cripple his work and should be
d quite separately. For an analysis of the effects of his changes and
ditions, see Ellen Douglass Leyburn's *Satiric Allegory: Mirror of Man*
56; rpt. 1969) and also Lee Elbert Holt's "Samuel Butler's Revisions of
ewhon" (*PBSA*, 1944). A new scholarly edition, using the basic text reed by Butler in July 1872 (after the first publication in March 1872) and
ving variants from the 1901 edition and the manuscript separately, is
ing prepared by Hans-Peter Breuer and Daniel F. Howard for publica-
n in 1978.

2. *The Way of All Flesh.* The text is not Butler's but that of his executor,
eatfeild, who made hundreds of minor and some major changes in a
nuscript that almost always reads better in the original version. Though
ny might agree with Streatfeild's apparent distaste for Overton's last-
nute revelation that Ernest has an irregular liaison and an illegitimate
n named Ted, the paragraphs in which all this is disclosed cannot be
ently excised. Streatfeild also changed Butler's title, *Ernest Pontifex*, pre-
ring the more generic subtitle *The Way of All Flesh.* Thus the world will
vays know the novel as *The Way of All Flesh*, but it is rather as if we
ew *Middlemarch* as *A Study of Provincial Life, Vanity Fair* as *A Novel
thout a Hero*, and *Moby Dick* as *The Whale.* The only edition that prints
e text from the manuscript, on which Butler wrote "Revised, finally cor-
cted and ready for the press without being further looked at," is the
verside (ed. Daniel F. Howard, 1964). A paperback edition using How-
d's text but with an introduction and notes by Roger Robinson is to be
blished in 1976 in London and Sydney by Pan Books.

3. The Notebooks. The Shrewsbury Edition prints only selections, and
aders should know that Jones often conflates two or more notes, makes
gnificant ellipses, and puts in his own transitions—all without acknowl-
gment. See the Holt article cited above under Bibliography, Manuscripts,
litions. The separate volumes of selections edited by Bartholomew (1931/
) and Keynes and Hill (1951) are preferable. The definitive edition,
w in preparation by Breuer and Parsell, promises to be the most important
cument in Butler scholarship since the *Memoir*.

Life and Letters

tler's biography and letters are inextricably intertwined. When Henry
sting Jones wrote his two-volume *Memoir* he had virtually all the papers
ailable today. He let Butler speak for himself as fully as possible, and so
e *Memoir* is a chronological stringing together of a generous selection
om the General Correspondence and the Notebooks, the transitions being
pplied by Jones. Since 1919 further biographical information has been
tained by viewing the same materials in contexts other than chronologi-
l. Thus, for example, while Jones used parts of the Butler-Savage cor-
spondence to further his day-by-day narrative, a different understanding

of Butler's life results from reading the complete correspondence, as a u
in itself, in Keynes and Hill's edition (1935). So too Butler's accounts of
relation with the persons important in his life mean something differe
when read together in their entirety, as autobiography, in *Butleriana* (19
than when excerpted for the facts they supply about a period in Butle
life.

Jones's *Memoir* is by far the fullest biography, though minor and ma
works parade by at the same stately pace. A lively, somewhat journalis
biography is Philip Henderson's *The Incarnate Bachelor* (1953). Henders
makes good use of Butler's manuscripts, though, in keeping with the hi
premium he puts on readability, his citations are vague or nonexistent. St
Henderson's is the biography to be recommended to someone just getti
interested in Butler. Clara Stillman's *Samuel Butler: A Mid-Victori
Modern* (1932) is a thoughtful review of the career, more than of the li
and C. E. M. Joad's *Samuel Butler* (1924) is an excellent presentation
Butler's ideas in the context of intellectual history. A charming defense
the Butler family, who seem like ogres to some readers of *The Way of*
Flesh, Mrs. R. S. Garnett's *Samuel Butler and His Family Relations* (19
offers some family letters in full (Jones's excerpts always makes them se
more brusque than they are), and a sympathetic understanding of h
things probably were. Together with Daniel F. Howard's edition of t
complete Butler-May letters (1962), Arnold Silver's edition of *The Fam
Letters of Samuel Butler* (1962) offers the best insight into the life th
formed the basis of *The Way of All Flesh*. Butler's father (the chief c
respondent in Silver's edition) was a remarkably good letter writer, and
scores many points off a son who characteristically thrusts and parries with
debater's skill, catching his father in a hidden attitude here, an ungenero
implication there. But the old man is never beaten on the narrow, reaso
able ground on which they both insist on standing, nor on issues that are
the real ones between them. There is conclusive evidence that when Butl
felt most thwarted by his father he turned to a more satisfying kind
writing: *The Way of All Flesh*. The ebbing and flowing of his inspirati
for this novel in relation to his irritation with Canon Butler are charted
Daniel F. Howard in "The Critical Significance of Autobiography in *T
Way of All Flesh*" (*VN*, 1960). Without being aware of this article, t
psychoanalyst Phyllis Greenacre wrote a fascinating "psycho-biography"
Butler and Darwin, *The Quest for the Father* (1963). Never straining t
biographical details she uses, she demonstrates an uncanny similarity l
tween the intense reactions that Darwin and Butler had to their fathers a
offers a psychiatric explanation for the bitterness of Butler's attack
Darwin. Readers of Butler's fiction will find the patterns of personal re
tionships she observes in Butler's life suggestive, though of course n
determinative.

Butler's liveliest correspondence is with Eliza Mary Ann Savage (e
Geoffrey Keynes and Brian Hill, 1935), a fellow student at Heatherley's A
School in London. Miss Savage admired Butler's writing and became bo

s severest and most encouraging critic, notably of *The Way of All
esh*, on which he was working off and on from 1873 to 1883. Miss Savage
ved naughtiness in Butler, and their letters have the tone of two pals
nusing each other with irreverent references to parents, priests, Dar-
nians—and all Butler's other enemies. In assembling this correspondence
the last years of his life, long after Miss Savage's death, Butler was
pecially moved. He annotated her letters with replies to questions she had
ked twenty-five years before and wrote explanations of his motives and
nduct at the time. He brooded on his inability to achieve the intimacy
ncluding sexual intimacy) that she had sought with him. His regret and
s disappointment with himself are expressed in "Miss Savage" and in
ree Shakespearean sonnets, first published in full in *Butleriana* (1932).
he third sonnet, with the final couplet, "And here, alas! at any rate to
e / She was an all too, too impossible she," obviously embarrassed Jones.
hile printing the first two sonnets, he suppressed the third, both in the
emoir and in the selections from the Notebooks that constitutes Volume
x of the Shrewsbury Edition. Acknowledging that he had also found a
ird sonnet, he says it is "too unfinished for publication"—though it is
ot.

Another fellow student at Heatherley's, John Butler Yeats, remembers
utler as the prototypal English gentleman, "the politest, the most cere-
onious of men" but with the public school sneer that compels respect.
eats, acting very much the Irishman abroad, notes the "melting kindness"
ehind the sneer and sketches a charming portrait of his distant friend, the
assion of whose life was to be a painter after the manner of Giovanni
ellini. "It was vain; he had no talent," Yeats decided (*Essays Irish and
merican*, 1919; rpt. 1969).

In *The Cradle of "Erewhon": Samuel Butler in New Zealand* (1959)
oseph Jones fills out the details of Butler's life in New Zealand, many of
hich are available in Butler's own *A First Year in Canterbury Settlement*
863). Jones gives an interesting account of the conditions and the per-
onalities in the colony at that time, but his critical theorizing about the
ays in which New Zealand was a "cradle" for *Erewhon* is as weak as the
etaphor itself. Of greater literary value is P. B. Maling's *Samuel Butler at
Mesopotamia* (Wellington, N.Z., 1960), which contains evidence of Butler's
eveloping style in the "Forest Creek Manuscript." Roger Robinson's im-
ortant paper examining Butler's relation to the literature of exploration is
orthcoming in the New Zealand journal *Landfall*.

A new biography of Butler would not be likely to provide any revelations.
He loved to share his secrets with posterity and rather wished he had more.
ertainly he didn't want to bury any. The unused manuscript letters and
he unpublished parts of the Notebooks will fill out the record (which is
lready, thanks to Butler himself, pretty full) but do not, I think, call for a
ew full-scale biography.

Reputation and Early Criticism

Butler loved to be on the attack, and the impulse to prove someone or oth
an old humbug was never far beneath his motive for writing. Certainly
wanted, in his phrase, "to advance the claims" of Handel, Erasmus Darwi
Holbein, the authoress of the *Odyssey*, the "real" Shakespeare, and ma
others whom he "championed," but what almost invariably spurred him
action was the work of someone he saw as a fool, a fraud, or a cheat. F
most famous quarrel was with Charles Darwin, a pupil of Butler's gran
father at Shrewsbury School, a friend of Butler's father (they once spent
holiday together gathering insects), and a man who showed a kindly aff
tion for young Butler—even occasionally having him as a weekend visit
Like most others whom Butler chose as his "opponents," Darwin was und
standably mystified by the stream of vilification that his former frie
poured upon him as Butler developed his own theories of evolution. B
ler's sprightly "bourgeois" prose translation of the *Odyssey* sprang from
indignation at the ornate translation of Butcher and Lang. (A good clas
cist himself, twelfth in his year at Cambridge, Butler had little use f
academic classical scholars.) His two-volume *Life and Letters of Dr. Sam*
Butler, a biography of his grandfather, the headmaster of Shrewsbu
School, was written largely to put down the Arnoldians, who, it seemed
Butler, exaggerated the contribution to education made by Dr. Thom
Arnold, headmaster of Rugby and, in Butler's view, his grandfather's riv
The genesis of *Shakespeare's Sonnets Reconsidered* was Butler's convictic
that Sidney Lee and William Archer had falsely identified Mr. W. H.

Having sought, even invented, enemies all his life, Butler would ha
been pleased to know that they persisted after his death. At first the esta
lishments he had attacked—the Church, the universities, men of science ar
art—showed their contempt by silence; but, as V. S. Pritchett commen
Butler at his death left behind the manuscript of *The Way of All Fles*
"one of the time-bombs of literature . . . waiting to blow up the Victori
family and with it the whole great pillared and balustraded edifice of t
Victorian novel" (*The Living Novel*, 1947).

Butler's friend and first literary executor, R. A. Streatfeild, publishe
The Way of All Flesh a year after Butler's death, to an initial reactic
suggested by the title of the *TLS* review, "A Bitter Legacy" (22 May 190
At first there was little public response (it was not even reprinted un
1908), but by World War 1 the novel was swept forward by a growi
disillusionment with "Victorianism," an "ism" that few could define but
despised. George Bernard Shaw, the champion of the New, admired Butle
iconoclasm and touted him as a genius (in the same firmament as Wagne
who had been and continued to be neglected by the Establishment. In t
1880s it had been Butler's ingenious theories of evolution that attract
Shaw, but within weeks of the publication of the posthumous novel he w
ecstatically proclaiming that it superseded *all* nineteenth-century literatu

etter to Henry Salt, 2 Aug. 1903). Shaw continued to adulate Butler for
.e next fifty years—notably in his preface to *Major Barbara* (1907) and in
long brilliant review article in the *Manchester Guardian* (7 Nov. 1919,
v. and rpt. in *Pen Portraits and Reviews*, 1932)—thereby commanding
tention for Butler's writings. Claude T. Bissell assesses Butler's influence
ı Shaw, his greatest proselytizer (*DR*, 1961).

At the same time, a quieter group of disciples was lovingly assembling the
·cord. *Erewhon*, rather than *The Way of All Flesh*, was their rallying
ɔint, and they sought to solidify Butler's reputation as polymath—satirist,
ientist, classicist, painter, composer, etc.—not as the revolutionary seer
tat Shaw perceived. This group, led by Butler's friend Henry Festing
ɔnes, arranged performances of Butler's Handel-like oratorios; donated his
ıintings, and even his furniture, to institutions chosen to immortalize him;
ɪd began to release selections from an extensive collection of papers and
otebooks. Selections from the Notebooks began to appear regularly in the
ew Quarterly Review in 1907 and, when they proved popular, were col-
·cted, added to, and published as a volume. The volume was greeted with a
ɪvorable front-page review in *TLS* (5 Dec. 1912), and Butler's fame began
ɔ spread. In 1908 a group of thirty-two disciples had organized an *Erewhon*
ʾinner, with quotations from his work on the menu, speeches about him,
ɪd miscellaneous reminiscences. Soon the Dinner became an annual
vent, and the guest list became increasingly distinguished; the fact that 160
ttended in 1914, just before World War I put a stop to the yearly
ɪtual, indicates Butler's popularity.

Robert Graves remembers that, as a schoolboy in 1913, he spent his
·ocket money to buy all the books of Butler's that he could and was point-
ɪly told by a member of the school staff that *The Way of All Flesh* was "a
·ook that no gentleman would read" (*Spectator*, 15 Dec. 1923). A reputa-
ion so based on the young was bound to spread rapidly. The first biography
·f Butler, by Gilbert Cannan, appeared in 1915—an admiring tribute to an
·ld friend—and, public interest continuing to grow, John F. Harris fol-
ɔwed with a more balanced biography the next year.

By the end of World War I Butler's friends had been successful in making
he *Erewhon* Butler known—the man who had ingeniously stood Victorian
ustoms on their heads and who had seen things differently and kept a lively
ɪotebook, but not one who fundamentally threatened the social structure
hat had come to an end in World War I. Shaw's emphasis on the Butler of
The Way of All Flesh, the prophet out of his time, was still a minority
ɔosition—though it was not to remain so. In 1919 Jones completed his
ɪassive two-volume *Memoir*, significantly entitled *Samuel Butler, Author of
'Erewhon."* The tag was appropriate to the subject's fame: *Erewhon* had
ɪdeed been the best known of Butler's books, the only one that had made
ɪoney, and Jones did need to distinguish his subject from the like-named
ɪuthor of *Hudibras*, as well as from Butler's grandfather; but identifying
Butler as the author of *Erewhon* also unwittingly marked the *Memoir* as the
chief document in the hagiography of Butler. It is a week-by-week account

of his life—Jones even prints Butler's packing lists for various outings. .
the end of his long labor, worried that he may have produced an "omniu
gatherum," Jones consoled himself by remembering that Butler once d
missed such worries: "Yes," Butler is said to have rejoined, "but *life* is :
omnium gatherum." Fortunately, the enormous amount of information
the *Memoir*'s handsomely printed volumes is available through a supe
index by A. T. Bartholomew, who was to succeed Jones as Butler's litera
executor (Streatfeild had bequeathed the executorship to Jones, as B:
tholomew was to do to Geoffrey Keynes and Brian Hill, the curre
executors).

The publication of the *Memoir* brought the two images of Butler, icon
clast and universal genius, into direct conflict. It was extensively reviewe
with most reviewers pleased to discover that Butler was a Victorian wl
shared some of their revulsion against the era (the anti-Victorian clima
may perhaps be judged by the popularity of Strachey's *Eminent Victorian*
which appeared the year before). Shaw, however (in the review in tl
Manchester Guardian cited above), was a little disappointed to find that h
idol had feet of clay, that Butler's later life particularly seemed petty an
self-satisfied; and the "vanity" implied in the details of Butler's life elicite
a vitriolic reaction from Maurice Hewlett in a review in *Fortnightly Revie*
(1919). Nevertheless, Shaw continued to assess *The Way of All Flesh* as
work of genius, and the novel became a central document in the intellectu:
life between the wars. Virginia Woolf, in her essay "Mr. Bennett and Mr
Brown" (1924), makes the famous claim that "on or about December, 191
human nature changed," and she notes that "the first signs of it [th
change] are recorded in the books of Samuel Butler, in *The Way of A*
Flesh in particular." Joyce read the novel in 1903–04, just as he was fo
mulating the autobiographical subject that became *Stephen Dedalu*
(Richard Ellmann, *James Joyce*, 1959), and the influence of *The Way of A*
Flesh on that book and on *A Portrait of the Artist as a Young Man* i
pervasive.* E. M. Forster and D. H. Lawrence testify to Butler's impact o
them (John Henry Raleigh defines the "Butler-Forster-Lawrence tradition
in "Victorian Morals and the Modern Novel," *Time, Place, and Idea*, 1968
Lee Elbert Holt demonstrates the pervasive influence of Butler on Forster i
PMLA, 1946, and P. N. Furbank's forthcoming *E. M. Forster: A Life* show
the marked indebtedness of Forster to Butler as early as 1907. A good com
parison of Butler and Lawrence can be found in U. C. Knoepflmacher'
"The Rival Ladies: Mrs. Ward's *Lady Connie* and Lawrence's *Lady Chat*
terley's Lover," *VS*, 1960). Somerset Maugham in *Of Human Bondag*
(1915) reveals his debt very obviously, and Arnold Bennett was an earl'

---

* The evidence that Joyce read *The Way of All Flesh* is circumstantial but over
whelming. For an account of the facts see E. L. Epstein, "James Joyce and *The Way o*
All Flesh" (*JJQ*, 1969). Ilse Dusoir Lind makes a critical connection between the *Por*
trait and *The Way of All Flesh* (*VN*, 1956). Hugh Kenner argues persuasively tha
Butler may have inspired Joyce's *Ulysses* as well: *The Authoress of the Odyssey* was i
Joyce's library; in that book Butler maintained that the authoress entered her poem ir
the character of Nausicaa, and the Nausicaa section of *Ulysses* is narrated in the styl
of a lady novelist (*The Pound Era*, 1971).

904), ardent enthusiast (see Bennett's *Journals*). Ford Madox Ford, who akes the odd statement that he didn't like Butler personally because he is rude to old ladies and young persons (Ford was still in his teens when utler died), nevertheless admits that "*The Way of All Flesh* and *The ayboy of the Western World* are the two great milestones on the road of rely English letters between *Gulliver's Travels* and Joyce's *Ulysses*" *Return to Yesterday*, 1932). By 1924 C. E. M. Joad could testify to the per- siveness of Butler's influence on the popular imagination as well: "Com- ete editions of his works, cheap editions of his works, biographies and ommentaries have carried his name into the remotest suburbs, where, since e modern disrespect for anything over thirty years old has preceded him, e is welcomed with open arms, as one who knows all about one's parents, id can take them down with an effectiveness that even the advantages onferred by one's own inside information will never enable one to equal."

Perhaps the most moving tribute to Butler's importance in the twentieth entury was the series of Third Programme talks organized by the BBC in 952 in honor of the fiftieth anniversary of Butler's death. The distinction f the speakers—E. M. Forster, Graham Hough, Philip Toynbee, and J. W. avidson—and especially the Establishment auspices fully justified Butler's ith in the judgment of posterity. (The talks are printed in the June and uly 1952 issues of the *Listener*.)

In America, where *The Way of All Flesh* was first published in 1910, utler's reputation burgeoned with the help of well-known men of letters ke William Lyon Phelps (*The Advance of the English Novel*, 1916; intro- uction to *The Way of All Flesh*, Dutton, 1916; Everyman, 1927); Henry eidel Canby (*YR*, 1920; *Definitions*, 1920; *Definitions: Second Series*, 924); and Robert Morss Lovett (*Nation*, 28 Feb. 1920; *Preface to Fiction*, 931). By 1923 *The Way of All Flesh* had gone through twelve printings in he United States. His popularity was later enhanced by critics like Edmund Vilson (1933; rpt. in *The Triple Thinkers*, 1938) and R. P. Blackmur (1932; pt. in *The Double Agent*, 1935).

In France, Jean Blum was the first to recognize Butler's stature as a umanist rather like Bergson (*Mercure de France*, 1910). Later, Valery arbaud, at the time the most influential critic of foreign literature, was ntroduced to Butler's work by Gide and took to it with great enthusiasm— "since Goethe no man has come closer to realizing the ideal of the universal rtist" (*Revue de Paris*, 15 Aug. 1923). In 1920 Larbaud began translating elections from *Erewhon*, the Notebooks, and *The Way of All Flesh* in the restigious *Nouvelle Revue Français*. A study of Larbaud's "masterpiece of ranslation" by Allison Connell appears in the first volume of *Canadian Review of Comparative Literature* (1974). Also in 1920, Larbaud organized a very successful *conférence* on Butler at Adrienne Monnier's bookshop— like the one he was to hold in the same place the following year to launch Joyce's *Ulysses*. Abel Chevalley was one of the first critics to recognize the seminal influence that Butler had on modernist literature (*Le Roman anglais de notre temps*, 1921; trans., 1925).

At the same time that Butler's fame as a "modern" Victorian spread

rapidly, his more conservative admirers continued their efforts to memo
alize him. A beautiful, expensive edition of his collected works, t
Shrewsbury Edition, was printed in twenty volumes (1923–26); more e
cerpts from the Notebooks were brought out, as well as Butler's detaile
accounts of his long, morbid fascination with Charles Paine Pauli (tl
model for Towneley) and of his relations with his father and Miss Savag
Hugh Kingsmill contributed a balanced account of Butler's role in cham
ing Victorian attitudes in a long chapter in his *After Puritanism* (192g
Clara Stillman's good critical-biographical account of his career, *Samu
Butler: A Mid-Victorian Modern* (1932), though too much the victim of tl
prejudice for modernism implied in its subtitle, is marked by a keen unde
standing of Butler's emotional responses—in his life as well as in his wri
ings.

By 1936 the disparity between the rather fussy bachelor dilettante wh
was being enshrined in all this fine paper and the image of Butler as
prophet was too much for a young Butler-like journalist, Malcolm Mug
geridge. In a book entitled *The Earnest Atheist*, Muggeridge announces h
determination to explode the myth of this so-called "pioneer rebel an
inveigher against cant" and proceeds to demonstrate that Butler's muc
praised prophecies are in fact juvenile perceptions of Butler's own narrov
experience. Muggeridge's most telling exposé is of Butler's silliest book, o:
Shakespeare's sonnets (1899), which maintains, among other doggedly li
eral readings, that the sonnets tell the story of a single homosexual episod
into which Mr. W. H. entrapped Shakespeare and for which Shakespear
was forever tortured. Butler's reconstruction of Shakespeare's life from th
sonnets is preposterous and, as Muggeridge shows, is really a projection o
his own experience with Pauli.

It was Butler himself who set the tone of partisanship that will probabl
always surround him. Butler himself didn't really believe that a bad or sill
book could be written by a good person; the book was the man, and a
temperate view that works like *Erewhon* and *The Way of All Flesh* have
marks of greatness on them while others, like *Shakespeare's Sonnets Recon
sidered*, are less than curiosities would have been as foreign to him as to
Muggeridge. Muggeridge's book is a great striving after what has become
critical commonplace: that Butler's writing is *always* about the persona
details of his life. Shakespeare's sonnets just do not happen to be a good
"peg" (Butler's term) on which to hang them.

Muggeridge smashed the idol of Butler the hero that Jones and others
had lovingly created. His reading of Butler's private papers, published to
deify, revealed a stodgy human being. While there was some clucking in the
reviews about Muggeridge's bad temper (a "crosspatch of a book" E. M.
Forster called it, and Howard Mumford Jones condescendingly entitled his
review "Earnest Biographer," *SatR*, 13 Mar. 1937), at least Muggeridge's
book set all readers on the same track to an understanding of Butler, not as
Higgs, dropped godlike into a caricatured society, but as a complicated, not
always admirable participant in a complicated society.

The intellectual climate in the thirties was favorable to the reexamina-
on of the stereotype of Victorianism that had dominated the twenties—as
ie appearance of G. M. Young's two-volume *Early Victorian England* in
ı34 testifies. It was no longer necessary to use Butler as a cudgel, and G. D.
. Cole, the distinguished professor of political theory who came to admire
utler's writing, sums up the acceptance of Butler as a man of his age that
nderlies all the best work of the last three decades:

> Acute critic as he was of many Victorian values, he was very much a Victorian
> himself. His perception seldom travelled far from the Victorian middle-class
> home and family; and when it did his view of things became superficial at
> once. . . . No one ever insisted more firmly than Butler on the Victorian
> virtue of having enough money to live on securely in a comfortable *bourgeois*
> way; and no one ever upheld more strongly the importance of prudence—
> surely the most *bourgeois* of all the virtues.
>
> (Preface to *The Essential Samuel Butler*, 1949)

Later Criticism

The keenest overall critic of Butler is P. N. Furbank, whose little book
Samuel Butler (1948; rpt. 1972) is all the more remarkable for being an
undergraduate prize essay, or rather a group of loosely linked essays. No one
ıas ever better defined Butler's habits of mind and distinguished the intel-
ectual consistency in all his books. There is a youthful, Leavis-like cockiness
n Furbank's claim that in his first three essays he has "treated topics which
ire indispensable to any study of Butler," but he is quite right, and, while
,ome of his insights into Butler's personality are prefigured in Clara Still-
nan's study (cited above), his understanding is both fresh and brilliant.
The last four essays in Furbank's book are more miscellaneous and uneven,
hough with some acute observations—for example, about Butler and Wilde
ıs contrasting examples of the Victorian eccentric.

Lee Elbert Holt contributes what he accurately describes as "a critical
summary of Butler's work and an attempt to reevaluate its worth" in
Twayne's English Authors Series (1964). Holt is a sound and knowledgeable
(though partisan) commentator on the works, and his book is a complement
to Henderson's biography.

The Way of All Flesh

As Butler came to be understood apart from the partisanship that
brought him fame but distorted his real significance, a flood of reprints—
especially of *The Way of All Flesh*—introduced him to new audiences in
schools and colleges and at the newsstand. Some of the best criticism of *The
Way of All Flesh* appears in introductions written for these new readers;
unfortunately, however, those interested today may have difficulty finding

the editions, many of them long out of print and haphazardly stocked
libraries. Shaw's introduction to the World's Classics edition (1936), esse
tially a judicious reworking of his review of the *Memoir* in the *Guardian*
Nov. 1919), is still one of the most persuasive statements about the nov
William Lyon Phelps's introduction to the Dutton edition (1916; rpt.
Everyman, 1927) is significant as an early enthusiastic American reactio
Also interesting because it contains the opinions of a major literary figure
the Limited Editions Club reprint of 1936, with an introduction by Th
odore Dreiser, who tries ingenuously to reconcile his love of the novel wi
the lack of any tragic dimension in Butler the man. The most searchin
criticism is by F. W. Dupee (Fawcett World Library, 1967; also publishe
in *NYRB*, 24 Aug. 1967), Morton Dauwen Zabel (Modern Library, 195
rev. in *Craft and Character in Modern Fiction*, 1957), and Richard Hogga
(Penguin, 1966). This last edition contains useful annotation by Jam
Cochrane. The introduction to Daniel F. Howard's Riverside edition (cite
above) traces the influences on Butler during the eleven years that I
worked sporadically on *The Way of All Flesh* and analyzes the structure o
the novel. Roger Robinson, in the Pan edition cited above, comments pe
ceptively on the ambiguity of the comedy and satire in *The Way of A
Flesh*.

Claude T. Bissell's "A Study of *The Way of All Flesh*" (in *Nineteent
Century Studies*, ed. Herbert Davis et al., 1940) remains a fine defense of th
cohesiveness of the novel against charges that it was a mere outpouring o
spite. Bissell is one of the first to assert the artistic validity of Butler
evolutionary theory as a part of the fiction.

The theme of William H. Marshall's *The World of the Victorian Nove
(1967)—that Victorian writers struggle to express the problems of living i
a relativistic world but that absolutist assumptions dominate their ways o
thinking about that experience—is well illustrated by *The Way of All Flesh*
much better illustrated in fact than by some of the other novels he discusse
He shows that the rectory in which Ernest grows up is dominated by a
reactionary concept of experience, one assumed to be derived from divin
law but actually based on the desire to protect parents from their natura
enemies, children. Children grow in two ways: by encountering experienc
that modifies them, somewhat the way the introduction of a new strain
changes a hybrid plant, *and* by discovering a true self, their inheritanc
from their forebears. Therefore, the way for parents to control their childre
is to prepackage experience to emphasize the values of duty, self-control
and submission to a quasi-ecclesiastical ritual, while stereotyping their fore
bears in order to hide the dynamism of their true ancestry. If parents are
able to so manipulate their children, creating personalities for them, thei
own domain is thereby buttressed by dependent beings who are unequippec
to live in the real, relativist world and who consequently can be manipu
lated by "will-shaking," the threat of taking away the money needed to
insulate children from the relativist world. His acute reading of the novel in
terms of Butler's evolutionary theory leads one to appreciate the imagina

ve power of the theory as myth rather than as science. In "The Use of
mbols in *The Way of All Flesh*" (*TSL*, 1965), Marshall expands some of
ese points.

Certainly the history of Butler's emergence in the twentieth century in-
ines commentators to take *The Way of All Flesh* more as a document in
e struggle for children's liberation than as a novel, whereas, like many
her seminal books in the history of literature, *The Way of All Flesh*
aches beyond its immediate predecessors, to root sources, and outward to
nlikely realms of language, in this case to scientific and theological argu-
ent. The yoking of sources in this book is naïve—in comparison, say, to
oyce's *Ulysses*—but Butler didn't need to study the Bible as Joyce did the
dyssey (in Butler's translation, as a matter of fact); it was part of him.
unyan too was part of him—as George Eliot, Meredith, Thackeray, and
ickens were not—and it is doubtful that he consciously knew that he was
riting an ironic *Pilgrim's Progress* (even though *The Way of All Flesh* is
ull of echoes of Bunyan, and originally the protagonist was named Chris-
an). But Overton *is* Evangelist, and Ernest is guided by little scraps of
pside-down Scripture and do-it-yourself evolutionary theory. Further study
f the structure and the materials of both *The Way of All Flesh* and *Ere-
hon* might well follow the lead of Marshall, and also of U. C. Knoepfl-
acher in "Ishmael or Anti-Hero? The Division of Self in *The Way of All
'lesh*" (*EFT*, 1961). Knoepflmacher incorporates some of his excellent
nalysis in this essay in a much more broadly based study of Butler's crea-
ion, in books written in the 1870s and early 1880s, of a faith apart from
evealed religion. Knoepflmacher's *Religious Humanism and the Victorian
Novel: George Eliot, Walter Pater, and Samuel Butler* (1965) is a splendid
elineation of the pervasive nineteenth-century artistic problem of incor-
orating evolutionary concepts into sensibilities yearning for a lost faith.
The book is historically well grounded, but its greatest achievement is in
efining these writers' trial of the imagination. Since Butler read little of,
nd cared less about, George Eliot and Walter Pater, the connection among
hem does not float readily to mind, but in Knoepflmacher's book students
f Butler are offered a whole new perspective on him as an artist *in* his time
rather than as a "mid-Victorian modern."

Butler himself would have been even more surprised to find himself
linked to Thomas Hardy in the ingenious Knoepflmacher's next book,
Laughter & Despair: Readings in Ten Novels of the Victorian Era (1971).
Butler seems to have been totally unaware of Hardy's existence, but that
hardly matters: Knoepflmacher is not tracing influences but establishing,
brilliantly, patterns in Victorian fiction. He compares *Jude the Obscure*
with *The Way of All Flesh* in terms of their use of tragic and comic formulas that are inadequate to present the experience that each novel tries to
convey. The relevance of "despair" to *Jude* is clear, but it takes more doing
to apply "laughter" to *The Way of All Flesh*. Knoepflmacher's point is that
there is no Celestial City to reach, and therefore Butler turns to a comic plot
of wish fulfillment in which Overton (who is said to be a writer of stage

comedies, including a burlesque of *Pilgrim's Progress*) converts his godson a life of ironic detachment—the opposite of earnestness—and then produc the money to pay for it. Even Butler knew there was something tinny abou this part of the novel (see the Butler-Savage letters, 1883–84), but he was the frontier of the modern novel and trying, in the last section of *The Wo of All Flesh*, to use a fairy-tale plot resolution more appropriate to th conclusion of *David Copperfield*, a novel a generation removed.

Peter Coveney's classic *The Image of Childhood: The Individual an Society: A Study of the Theme in English Literature* (1967; first publishe as *Poor Monkey*, 1957) reveals the historical breadth of *The Way of A Flesh*. Butler asserts the active existence in Ernest of the eighteenth-centur craftsman, the nineteenth-century entrepreneur, the Anglican Puritan, an the disengaged capitalist. Inevitably the poor child must struggle hopelessl with the social, religious, and emotional turmoil of a whole century, and is hardly any wonder that if he is saved at all it is by the secular "grace" c his aunt's bequest. Butler's place in the theme of Coveney's study is ind cated by the title of the chapter on Butler: "The End of the Victoria Child."

F. R. Leavis has no use for Butler—I suspect largely because the Blooms bury Group liked him so much—and, in an otherwise admiring introductio to Peter Coveney's *The Image of Childhood* (1967), finds it necessary t chide Coveney for paying so much attention to *The Way of All Flesh*, "tha morbidly egotistic, self-ignorant and Pharisaical performance . . . , smal minded, blind and odiously complacent."

Donald David Stone comments provocatively (*Novelists in a Changin World*, 1972) on the contrast between Ruskin and Butler as autobiogra phers. Ruskin's wistful desire for a lost or perishing past leads him t emphasize those moments in his life at which a delicate personal synthesis i overwhelmed by chaos, whereas Butler constantly seeks moments that ar confluences of hitherto unrecognized selves. But the best "placing" of *Th Way of All Flesh* in literary history is Jerome Hamilton Buckley's *Season o Youth: The Bildungsroman from Dickens to Golding* (1974). Buckle gracefully brings a great deal of information to bear on the novel, which h accepts as a major work without for a moment blinking at its faults. Lik every other critic from Miss Savage onward, he finds the ending a terribl falling off, Ernest being left "the most self-satisfied hero in the history of th English Bildungsroman," but in examining the novel against the bildungs roman, one of the genres to which it belongs, he demonstrates its strikin originality. His discussion of Gosse's often compared *Father and Son* i especially revealing of the difference between a trivial and a serious work Though Buckley acknowledges that Ernest's quest is not merely for present self but for selves buried in time, he is not so sensitive as Marshal and Knoepflmacher to the mythic disruptions of the realistic surface that ar thereby introduced. Butler's evolutionary theory is indeed "quirkish," a Buckley says, but Marshall is right in insisting that the theory is the inform ing myth of the novel; it forces Butler to present attempted rape, prison marriage, and parenthood—all of which were light-years away from his personal experience—because they are allegorically necessary. Ernest is not just a person; he is what his name Pontifex announces, a "bridge builder." Unfortunately, as Buckley comments, Butler never could write about what he hadn't lived; so these necessary episodes stick out for what they are— rocky outcroppings on the book's basic structure. When John the coachman arrives to dissolve Ernest's marriage, we are in a Victorian melodrama—and Butler is artistically faulty in so casting it—but the necessity to undo Ernest's marriage proceeds from a genre other than realistic fiction, one that needs to be recognized.

Erewhon

Erewhon has needed less introducing than *The Way of All Flesh*. Having been seen quite clearly in 1872 for what it was—its targets being the institutions that are traditionally targets of satire—*Erewhon* did not interact so violently with the zeitgeist of the twentieth century. It is interesting, however, that *Erewhon* attracted Aldous Huxley, who introduced the Limited Editions Club (with illustrations by Rockwell Kent, 1934); and it clearly influenced a line of twentieth-century utopian fiction, including H. G. Wells's *A Modern Utopia* (1905), Huxley's *Brave New World* (1932), and Orwell's *Nineteen Eighty-Four* (1949). It is an irony of history that Butler should have been taken up by Aldous Huxley, the grandson of Thomas Huxley, the Darwinian biologist whom Butler regarded as one of his chief enemies. In the Signet edition (1961) Kingsley Amis also offers acute admiration of *Erewhon*'s wit and fancy, though the satire of evolutionary theory bores him. Another response that reveals as much about the critic himself as about *Erewhon* is Lewis Mumford's: in the 1927 Modern Library edition he is attracted to Butler's joyous application of enlightened amateurism, "the chief glory of [England's] intellectual life"—one of the desiderata of Mumford's own writing.

Because *Erewhon* belongs to a very mixed genre indeed—Polonius might have tried to define it as autobiographical-parodiacal-inverse-utopian-satirical-treatisical-fictional—it has long intrigued those interested in genre criticism. It surfaces often in Northrop Frye's *Anatomy of Criticism* (1957), displaying, variously, characteristics of the low mimetic and satire, particularly Menippean satire, which typically produces "violent dislocations in the customary logic of narrative" and sometimes tends to overwhelm pedantic targets "with an avalanche of their own jargon."

From the very beginning, readers of *Erewhon* have been uncertain about Butler's "message" in the book. For example, at first glance it would seem that the Colleges of Unreason, with their total impracticality, hypothetical language, and Professors of Evasion, represent a condemnation of Oxford and Cambridge. But the case is not so simple: the Colleges turn out to be quite delightful places that serve to counterbalance the dangerous tendency of the practical world to make decisions by pure reason alone—always, in Butler's view, a mistake. So too the Musical Banks, with their worthless currency and pietism. They seem to expose the essential hypocrisy of the

English Church; but, though silly, they prove to be not only harmless but useful repositories for idealism that might otherwise disturb The Way Things Are, and they offer convenient places for people to meet and share a harmless pretense. Actually, *Erewhon* is not, as many literal-minded readers have supposed, an indictment of middle-class English life but a representation of a complex of attitudes toward it, articulated in styles ranging from burlesque to straightforward didacticism. The book's intellectual targets have also seemed unclear. The Book of Machines particularly has often been seen to satirize Darwin's *Origin of Species*—much to Butler's horror because at this time in his life he was a great admirer of Darwin and considered the *Origin* superb. He had intended, he quickly added in the preface to a reissue of *Erewhon*, to parody not the *Origin* but the argument of the standard eighteenth-century theological work *The Analogy of Religion* by Bishop Joseph Butler (no relation). What in fact had happened was that Butler was finding his own distinctive way of arguing: by imitating—in order to reject—*The Analogy*, the single most important rhetorical influence on him when he was a student at Cambridge. At the same time he was employing the rhetoric of Darwin, which for the last ten years had fascinated him. The simple view is that he had rejected a theist master for a scientific one; but actually *Erewhon* demonstrated a synthesis of the two, yet also reflects a deep-rooted skepticism about the validity of each, however ingeniously executed. Thus *Erewhon* confronts Butler's doubts about the central intellectual influences in his life—indeed in Victorian life. The philosophies and rhetorics involved are well analyzed by Hans-Peter Breuer (*MP*, 1975). Breuer cites other examples of the intersection of eighteenth-century and modern philosophies in "The Source of Morality in Butler's *Erewhon*" (*VS*, 1973).

A. Dwight Culler writes brilliantly about *Erewhon* in "The Darwinian Revolution and Literary Form" (*The Art of Victorian Prose*, ed. George Levine and William Madden, 1968). He sees Darwin himself as standing traditional theological argument on its head and Butler as carrying the process further, into fiction: "I do not know any other work of English literature which illustrates quite so clearly as does *Erewhon* the influence of the Darwinian explanation upon literary form," Culler says. His article is remarkable for its breadth of association of Butler's literary enterprise with philosophers from Hume to Malthus, Godwin, Bentham, and Mill and with writers including Wilde, Shaw, Lewis Carroll, and Pater. Culler's demonstration of the rich adaptability of the "Darwinian technique" to literature makes his final conclusion—that it is probably not available for any profound literary exploitation—rather puzzling, but his essay is essential for students of *Erewhon*.

The best discussion of the problem of ascertaining positive values in *Erewhon* is a chapter in A. E. Dyson's *The Crazy Fabric: Essays in Irony* (1965). In "The Problem of Spiritual Authority in the Nineteenth Century," in *Essays in English Literature from the Renaissance to the Victorian Age Presented to A. S. P. Woodhouse* (ed. Millar MacClure and F. W.

Watt, 1964), Northrop Frye locates the "spiritual authority" of *Erewhon* in the high Ydgrunites. They have no need to run reason as hard as Butler himself did (thereby exposing its absurdity), for they have an instinctive sense of true proportion and an ability to live content within themselves, the absurdity of others swirling around outside.

Studies of Special Aspects

The question inevitably arises, How good was Butler as an evolutionist? It does not lead one very far, and readers of this guide may wish to approach it indirectly. His ideas have no scientific currency now, and scientists tend to look on them as the ingenious constructions of a literary man—which they are. It is fair to say that in 1860, when Butler read *The Origin of Species* in New Zealand (the book had not yet become a cause célèbre), he needed two things: a rhetoric for the writing career he was about to begin and, more generally, a substitute for the prayers that he reports having stopped saying on the night his ship sailed from England. He studied and restudied Darwin's remarkably literary book, absorbed its subject matter and its procedure, and practiced its application in the articles he wrote in New Zealand. By the time he realized that it offered no substitute for faith, he could turn to eighteenth-century evolutionists and so make his own combination, one indicated (in a different spirit) in the title of one of his books, *Evolution Old and New.*

For a view of Butler's place in scientific and intellectual history, C. E. M. Joad's 1924 book is still a model of clarity. An understanding, lucid modern assessment of Butler as a theorist in relation to Lamarck and Darwin can be found in George Gaylord Simpson's *This View of Life: The World of an Evolutionist* (1964). In *Apes, Angels, and Victorians* (1955) William Irvine assesses Darwin's place in the history of evolutionary thought and comments on Butler's role. Butler's contribution to evolutionary theory is treated sympathetically by Basil Willey in *Darwin and Butler: Two Versions of Evolution* (1960). In *Into the Unknown: The Evolution of Science and Fiction from Francis Godwin to H. G. Wells* (1970), Robert Philmus comments perceptively on the significance of Butler's intellectual habit of literalizing scientific theory, creating his own myth out of it and foreshadowing some of the concerns of science fiction. For a discussion of other fictional uses of Darwinism in the nineteenth and twentieth centuries, see Leo J. Henkin, *Darwinism in the English Novel, 1860–1910* (1963). The book is not critically acute, but it does provide a perspective for evaluating Butler's achievement in this genre.

A book notable for its sensitivity to the literary effect of evolution on nineteenth-century writers is Georg Roppen's *Evolution and Poetic Belief* (Oslo, 1956). While Roppen identifies the tenets of Butler's position and relates them to those of other theorists, he is refreshingly aware that they are most significant not as articles of faith but as imaginative structures. Butler has an "imaginative preoccupation with the evolutionary idea: despite comedy and caricature, it is to Butler a new and fascinating instrument of thought."

Butler's overwhelming, unvarying artistic dedication was to Handel. It is difficult to define the significance that a writer's taste in another art has for his fiction, but a remarkable study is Hans-Peter Breuer's "Samuel Butler and George Frederick Handel" (*DR*, 1975/76). Breuer shows how Butler participated in the peculiarly English and middle-class idolatry of Handel in the nineteenth century, admiring the comfortably controlled ecstasy of the oratorios as opposed to the tragic turbulence of Beethoven and other Romantic composers. The connections among Handel, changing modes of popular worship, and styles of orchestral performance reveal characteristics of Butler's aesthetic principles.

With Breuer's article as a model, a study of Butler's art criticism and his work as a translator of the *Odyssey* and the *Iliad* could provide further insights into his relation to his time. An appreciation of the significance of Butler as the enlightened amateur that Mumford so admires is yet to come.

David Grene's introduction to the University of Chicago Press edition of Butler's *The Authoress of the Odyssey* (1967) is an excellent evaluation of the significance of Butler's extraordinary theory for an understanding of the Homeric poem. He points out that Butler's straightforward reading led him to conclusions denied by the scholars of his time but generally accepted by classical experts today. As for his insistence that the *Odyssey* was written by a woman who lived in Trapani, Sicily, and who put herself into the poem as Nausicaa—it is best taken as a metaphor that draws attention to the details of the *Odyssey*. Butler would have despised such condescension, and argued further for the literal truthfulness of his theory, but it is exactly his determination to push metaphors to a bedrock of literal accuracy that gives his imagination such vitality. Hugh Kenner catches the essence of the imagination that inheres in all of Butler's work and that proved so important for modern fiction. "Theirs [Butler's and Joyce's] were the first and second creative minds to take the post-Schliemann Homer seriously: to imagine what it might mean to believe that the *Odyssey* was composed by a real person in touch with the living details of real cities, real harbors, real bowls and cups and pins and spoons, real kings, real warriors, real houses. Horace had believed in a real Homer, making things up; there were slips because he sometimes nodded. Wolf had believed in a number of bards, making things up; there were inconsistencies because they didn't check one another's work. Butler, in the age of the novel, worked from a different psychology of creation: the poet using knowledge of an immediate and experienced world, and making errors when he [she] got beyond that knowledge and had to guess" (*The Pound Era*, 1971).

In his review of Butler studies up to 1959 (*EFT*, 1960), Lee Elbert Holt comments on the need to reassess Butler's relation to his time and to ours.

Marshall, Knoepflmacher, and Buckley offer splendid models for connecting him with Victorian fiction, without insisting upon particular indebtedness and influences—which, because of Butler's narrow but deep classical learning and almost total lack of reading in contemporary literature, are hardly ever there. Both *Erewhon* and *The Way of All Flesh*, as well as the too often neglected "Memoir" section of *The Fair Haven*, are what Butler might have called "reversions" to classic models (had he been interested in literary as well as evolutionary history) and "crossings" with the current languages of theology and science. They all can be profitably studied as the mixed genres they are, with attention both to the theological argumentation read by nineteenth-century undergraduates at Cambridge, like Bishop Butler's *Analogy* (1736) and Paley's *View of the Evidences of Christianity* (1794), and to Darwin's *The Origin of Species*—competing and intertwined influences.

More remains to be done in response to Holt's call, in 1960, for further study of Butler's relation to *our* time. William Van O'Connor's "Samuel Butler and Bloomsbury" (in *From Jane Austen to Joseph Conrad*, ed. Robert C. Rathburn and Martin Steinmann, 1958) is a useful, largely factual account of Butler's fame in Virginia Woolf's circle; and off and on Buckley compares *The Way of All Flesh* as a bildungsroman with the novels of Wells, Lawrence, Joyce, and later writers. Without making specific comparisons, Dyson's *The Crazy Fabric* puts Butler in a generalized context of twentieth-century ironists: Strachey, Huxley, Waugh, and Orwell. But a study directed to twentieth-century novels comparable to Knoepflmacher's on Victorian fiction would be most valuable, and both *Erewhon* and *The Way of All Flesh* could illumine and be illuminated by the elements of scientific and technological fantasy that mark the fiction of Huxley, Orwell, Barth, Vonnegut, and Pynchon.

THOMAS HARDY

Michael Millgate

That Hardy tells a good, if gloomy, tale has always been widely acknowledged, and his reputation with the general reader has never seriously declined since the days when he was universally revered as the Grand Old Man of English letters: an analysis of the National Portrait Gallery's sales of postcards during 1966–67 showed that Hardy portraits were outsold only by those of (in descending order) T. E. Lawrence, George Bernard Shaw, Shakespeare, Queen Elizabeth I, Emily Brontë, and Charlotte Brontë. During the last several years his work has apparently become more popular than ever, perhaps because of sharpened appreciation of the Wessex setting —as reflected, for example, in John Schlesinger's film of *Far from the Madding Crowd* and the BBC television productions of some of the short stories —and increased recognition of the major novels as classic evocations of that rural way of life which has become the more highly valued the further it has receded into an irrecoverable past. Scholars, of course, are nostalgic by profession, but the spectacular increase in the specifically academic study of Hardy during the twelve years (1963–74) covered by this survey must also be seen in terms of the general interest in the Victorian period and the ongoing revaluation of the "modern" and of the extent to which the formal characteristics of both Hardy's fiction and his verse seem especially accessible to current critical approaches. The result, in any case, has been an astonishing explosion of Hardiana, one that shows no signs of dying away before 1978, the fiftieth anniversary of Hardy's death, and perhaps not even then.

Bibliography

Two of the most important events during the period covered by this survey were the publication of a corrected reissue of Richard L. Purdy's indispensable *Thomas Hardy: A Bibliographical Study* (1954, 1968) and the

nclusion, in the Stevenson *Guide* (1964), of George S. Fayen, Jr.'s discriminating survey of Hardy scholarship to the end of 1962 (with a few subsequent items). Also of major significance were the appearance of Fayen's
Hardy section in the third volume of *NCBEL* (1969) and the publication of
the massive compilation of Helmut E. Gerber and W. Eugene Davis,
Thomas Hardy: An Annotated Bibliography of Writings about Him (1973),
The very ambitiousness of the latter attempt—to list and describe all writings about Hardy published between 1871 and 1969—virtually guaranteed
a certain incidence of omission and error, much of which will no doubt be
rectified in a planned supplementary volume. But the unevenness of the
annotations seems less readily justifiable, and room still exists for a more
efficiently and consistently presented annotated checklist, especially of the
criticism and scholarship of the last twenty or thirty years. A useful gesture
in that direction is made by B. J. Alexander's "Criticism of Thomas Hardy's
Novels: A Selected Checklist" (*SNNTS*, 1972), which brings up-to-date the
list published by Maurice Beebe and others (*MFS*, 1960). Of considerably
lesser scope are the surveys by Michael Millgate (*ELT*, 1971) and F. B.
Pinion (in *The English Novel: Selected Bibliographical Guides*, ed. A. E.
Dyson, 1974), while H. A. T. Johnson's *Thomas Hardy 1874-1974: An
Annotated Reading List* (Manchester, 1974) is engagingly enthusiastic
but insufficiently methodical. Useful for its inclusion of out-of-the-way items
is the *Thomas Hardy Catalogue: A List of the Books by and about Thomas
Hardy, O.M. (1840-1928) in Dorset County Library*, compiled by Kenneth
Carter and June M. Whetherly (2nd ed., Dorchester, 1973).

Perhaps this is the place to mention the Thomas Hardy Society (Secretary: Rev. John Yates, The Vicarage, Haselbury Plucknett, Crewkerne,
Somerset, TA18 7PB). Many Hardy scholars and Hardy enthusiasts have
been associated with its activities during recent years, and its publications—
including a *Newsletter* and the recently instituted *Thomas Hardy Society
Review* (an annual, ed. F. B. Pinion and Harold Orel)—provide members
with a convenient method of keeping informed about conferences, publications, etc., in various parts of the world.

Editions and Texts

Of the numerous North American paperback editions of individual Hardy
novels over the last few years, several have good critical introductions—for
example, those by John Paterson (*The Return of the Native*), Arnold Kettle (*Tess of the d'Urbervilles*), and Robert B. Heilman (*Jude the Obscure*)
for the never completed "Standard Edition" (1966)—and some, including
the Norton Critical Editions of *The Return of the Native*, by James Gindin
(1969), and *Tess*, by Scott Elledge (1965), provide useful supplementary
materials. Few, however, show much concern with textual matters. One
notable exception is the 1967 edition of *Jude* by Robert C. Slack, whose
introduction describes the significant differences between the first edition

text of 1895 and the revision of 1903, while F. R. Southerington's 1972 edition of the same novel—though marred by an unhelpful introduction—ventures to incorporate the 1895 text of the scene in which the throwing of the pig's "pizzle" brings about Jude's first meeting with Arabella.

Apart from Southerington's, these editions all follow, some a little shakily, the Wessex Edition of 1912, obviously a defensible copy-text for what Fredson Bowers has called "practical editions"; on the other hand, none of them represents any refinement of the Wessex text. The London house of Macmillan, publishers of the original Wessex Edition, brought out simultaneously in 1974 eight volumes of the so-called New Wessex Edition; six more titles were promised for 1975, with the eventual prospect of a nearly complete Hardy, prose and verse, in the same format. The first eight are attractively produced volumes, all with useful notes, some with excellent introductory essays (e.g., David Lodge on *The Woodlanders*, John Bayley on *Far from the Madding Crowd*), a few incorporating a certain amount of textual investigation (e.g., Lodge on *The Woodlanders* again and Barbara Hardy on *The Trumpet-Major*). The texts themselves, however, are simply resettings of the original Wessex texts, modified by house-styling and the inevitable compositorial errors. Moreover, the hardcover and paperback versions represent, rather confusingly, different impositions of the text, with quite discrepant pagination, so that the edition is unusable even as a point of general reference. The Clarendon Press is said to be planning scholarly editions of some of the novels, though not of all, and of the collected poems. In the meantime—and conceivably in the very long run—scholars and critics must continue to depend upon the original Wessex Edition (regrettably, the very useful Library, or Greenwood, "Edition," consisting of late issues of the Wessex volumes, has now been allowed to go out of print), and it would mark a great improvement in the general standard of scholarly living if the Wessex Edition could be adopted as a standard source for all quotations and references.

As Robert C. Schweik observes in "Current Problems in Textual Scholarship on the Works of Thomas Hardy" (*ELT*, 1971), little advantage has as yet been taken of the solid groundwork provided by Purdy's descriptive bibliography. Dieter Riesner's "Zur Textgeschichte von Hardys Romanen" (*Archiv*, 1963) surveys and evaluates textual scholarship in the Hardy field, but valuable contributions since then have been relatively few in comparison to the multiplication of purely critical writings and to the range and importance of the work to be done. Riesner is himself the author of "Kunstprosa in der Werkstatt: Hardys *The Mayor of Casterbridge* 1884–1912," in Dieter Riesner and Helmut Gneuss, eds., *Festschrift für Walter Hübۀ* (1964), a fine study of the textual history of the novel from the manuscript to the Wessex text of 1912 and of the critical implications of Hardy's revisions. (Christine Winfield's "The Manuscript of Hardy's *The Mayor of Casterbridge*," *PBSA*, 1973, is largely a duplication of Riesner's work.) *The Woodlanders* has been extensively dealt with by Dale Kramer in his Western Reserve dissertation of 1963 and in subsequent articles, most

mprehensively in the two-part study "Revision and Vision: Thomas
ardy's *The Woodlanders*" (*BNYPL*, 1971). Marilyn A. S. Hubbart's
ssertation, "Thomas Hardy's *The Woodlanders*: A Critical and An-
otated Edition" (Univ. of Nebraska 1971), is not without interest but adds
ttle to Kramer's work. The latter, however, in "A Query concerning the
Handwriting in Hardy's Manuscripts" (*PBSA*, 1963), perhaps makes too
uch of two changes made by Emma Hardy in *The Woodlanders* manu-
ript, neither of them incompatible with either dictation or copying from
n unclear original.

Two Oxford dissertations have made valuable contributions in recent
ears: Simon Gatrell's "A Critical Edition of Thomas Hardy's Novel *Under
he Greenwood Tree*" (1973) supports its choice of the manuscript as copy-
ext by a fascinating analysis of the vagaries of the first edition compositors,
hile Juliet Grindle's "A Critical Edition of Thomas Hardy's *Tess of the
'Urbervilles*" (1974)—a forerunner to her forthcoming Clarendon Press
dition of the novel—also makes a solid case for its adoption of the manu-
ript "accidentals."

John Laird's important essay "The Manuscript of Hardy's *Tess of the
'Urbervilles* and What It Tells Us" (*AUMLA*, 1966) provides an astute
olution to the problems posed by the multiple layers of the *Tess* manu-
cript, although it goes on to offer a rather exaggerated account of the effect
f Hardy's revisions upon the characterization of Tess herself. (Laird's
xpanded study, *The Shaping of* Tess of the d'Urbervilles, was published
n 1975.) The need for caution in interpreting revisions is emphasized by
Dieter Riesner's "Über die Genesis von Thomas Hardys *The Return of the
Native*" (1963), which insists that Hardy's original conception of that novel
liffered from published versions less dramatically than suggested by John
Paterson's *The Making of* The Return of the Native (1960). Riesner also
points out that Paterson overlooked some stages in the transmission of
Hardy's text. Additional information about the prepublication history of
he novel is supplied by F. B. Pinion's "The Composition of *The Return
of the Native*" (*TLS*, 21 Aug. 1970).

Other novels have received serious, if less comprehensive, treatment.
Though primarily critical in emphasis, Dieter Riesner's "Thomas Hardy:
Far from the Madding Crowd" (in Paul Goetsch et al., eds., *Der englische
Roman im 19. Jahrhundert: Interpretationen*, 1973) is a detailed study that
draws upon knowledge of the novel's textual history and of the revisions
made at various stages. In "The Early Development of Hardy's *Far from the
Madding Crowd*" (*TSLL*, 1967) Robert C. Schweik probes the manuscript
for evidence of Hardy's initial conception and points to the probability that
the roles of Fanny Robin and Boldwood were largely or even wholly the
result of late revision. Schweik's "A First Draft Chapter of Hardy's *Far from
the Madding Crowd*" (*ES*, 1972) was slightly anticipated by Clarice Short's
"A Rejected Fragment of *Far from the Madding Crowd*" (*BRMMLA*,
1971), but it offers much the more detailed and useful description of the
"sheep-rot" episode, which was deleted from the first draft of the novel but

for some reason not destroyed. Schweik's "The 'Duplicate' Manuscript of Hardy's *Two on a Tower*: A Correction and a Comment" (*PBSA*, 1966) usefully modifies statements about the manuscript made by Carl J. Weber (*PBSA*, 1946), while Alistair Macleod's dissertation, "A Textual Study of Thomas Hardy's *A Group of Noble Dames*" (Notre Dame 1969), though otherwise disappointing, does bear interestingly upon Hardy's response to editorial pressures. Also worth mentioning here, though neither in fact progresses much beyond the information already available in Purdy's bibliography, are Norman Page's "Thomas Hardy's Forgotten Illustrators" (*BNYPL*, 1974) and Robert F. Kaufman's dissertation, "The Relationship between Illustration and Text in the Novels of Dickens, Thackeray, Trollope, and Hardy" (New York Univ. 1974).

Hardy's nonfiction prose has been collected and sensibly annotated by Harold Orel in *Thomas Hardy's Personal Writings: Prefaces, Literary Opinions, Reminiscences* (1966). Grateful as all Hardy scholars must be for this convenient gathering together of such widely scattered material, the volume's usefulness is limited in that it contains textual errors, records only the Wessex Edition versions of the prefaces to the novels (although the earlier versions arguably possess greater historical interest and are certainly harder to find), and merely summarizes, as Purdy had already done, many minor items—so that anyone wishing to read the full text of, say, Hardy's charming obituary of Lucy Baxter must still seek it out in the files of *The Times* (London) or the *Dorset County Chronicle*. A major event of 1974 was the appearance of Volume I of a projected two-volume edition by Lennart A. Björk of *The Literary Notes of Thomas Hardy* (GothSE, 29). This first stage—containing the greater part of the notebook known as "Literary Notes I" and the whole of the so-called "1867" notebook—consists of two parts, a carefully presented text and a corresponding set of identifications and annotations. Though the annotations occasionally seem overextended, this is a minor flaw in a most valuable piece of scholarship, involving prodigies of sheer hard detective labor. G. Stevens Cox's rather less satisfactory transcription of "*The Trumpet-Major* Notebook" appeared serially in the *Thomas Hardy Year Book* for 1971, 1972–73, and 1973–74; this notebook is to be published—along with others, including the "Facts" notebook and the two "Memoranda" books incompletely transcribed by Evelyn Hardy in *Thomas Hardy's Notebooks* (1955)—in an edition of Hardy's "personal" notebooks being prepared by Richard H. Taylor.

Work on Richard L. Purdy and Michael Millgate's Clarendon Press edition of Hardy's collected letters is well advanced, with publication of the first volume expected early in 1978. In the meantime Hardy's extensive and important correspondence with Mrs. Henniker (for which publication permission was granted by the Hardy trustees prior to the agreement with the Clarendon Press) has appeared in *One Rare Fair Woman: Thomas Hardy's Letters to Florence Henniker, 1893–1922* (1972), edited and extensively annotated by Evelyn Hardy and F. B. Pinion. Other Hardy letters have also appeared, individually or in small groups: Simon Nowell-Smith, for ex-

nple, prints a few items from the Macmillan Hardy archive in *Letters to
Macmillan* (1967); the letters to Baron d'Erlanger, composer of the opera
ased on *Tess of the d'Urbervilles*, are woven into an attractive article,
"Tess in the Opera House," by Desmond Hawkins (*ContempR*, 1974); and
the correspondence with Sir George Douglas in the National Library of
Scotland has been skimmed, often inaccurately, by W. M. Parker (*English*,
1963). Richard Cary (*CLQ*, 1971) has usefully calendared the letters from
and about Hardy in the library of Colby College, while Carl J. and Clara
Carter Weber performed a similar service for the several thousand extant
letters *to* Hardy in *Thomas Hardy's Correspondence at Max Gate: A Descriptive Check List* (1968). Despite its curiously inappropriate title (the
letters in question have long been in the Dorset County Museum), this is a
useful, though by no means infallible, reference work for anyone with a
special interest in Hardy's literary career. Letters received by Hardy are
printed in Pierre Coustillas's "Some Unpublished Letters from Gissing to
Hardy" (*ELT*, 1966), a valuable reminder and documentation of an intriguing (if largely abortive) literary friendship; in Carl Ziegler's "Thomas
Hardy's Correspondence with German Translators" (*ELT*, 1968), derived
from Ziegler's modest but useful dissertation on Hardy's reception in Germany (Vanderbilt 1966); and in two articles by Patricia Hutchins, "Ezra
Pound and Thomas Hardy" (*SoR*, 1968) and the interesting but inaccurate
"Thomas Hardy and Some Younger Writers" (*JML*, 1973).

Biography

The publication in 1966 of Lois Deacon and Terry Coleman's *Providence
and Mr. Hardy*—a skillful elaboration of earlier pamphlets by Lois Deacon
alone (*Tryphena and Thomas Hardy*, 1962; *Hardy's Sweetest Image*, 1964)
—ensured that Hardy biography should for several years be reduced almost
exclusively to arid debate over the role played by Hardy's cousin Tryphena
Sparks in his life and work. The debate was arid because there was so little
to sustain it. Although *Providence and Mr. Hardy* ranges suggestively, not
to say sensationally, over many aspects of Hardy's career, it completely fails,
by any standards of scholarship or even of probability, to establish its central thesis that Tryphena was born Hardy's niece, became his mistress, bore
his child, and haunted his imagination. Because it seemed impossible to
dispose absolutely of the protean "facts" and self-generating "hypotheses" so
bewilderingly advanced by Deacon and Coleman, their theories at first
gained a good deal of popular acceptance and even induced some hedging
of academic bets: Tryphena figured prominently in John Fowles's best-
selling novel, *The French Lieutenant's Woman*, and in 1971 F. R. Southerington, who had early emerged as a strong supporter of Lois Deacon,
included as appendixes to his *Hardy's Vision of Man* some highly tenuous
biographical arguments, which added little to *Providence and Mr. Hardy* or
to his own earlier pamphlets (notably *Hardy's Child: Fact or Fiction?*,

1968). Since then the tide has run very much the other way. Hostile criticism of *Providence and Mr. Hardy*, initiated by D. J. Enright's fine review in the *New Statesman* for 10 June 1966 and most persistently sustained by F. B. Pinion (see, e.g., his "The Hardy Fable: A Popular Misconception" in *D* 1971–72, and his review of Southerington's edition of *Jude the Obscure* in *N&Q*, 1972), received effective reinforcement in 1973 from Robert Gittings' "Thomas Hardy and Tryphena Sparks" (*TLS*, 27 Apr.) and in 1974 from Walter F. Wright's "A Hardy Perennial" (*PrS*). Southerington defended his position in (among others) *Agenda*, 1972; *Dorset Year Book, 1972–73*; and *Notes and Queries*, 1973, and it is true that *Providence and Mr. Hardy* did supply some interesting information about Tryphena Sparks herself (see also Anna Winchcombe, "Four Letters from Tryphena Sparks," in *Dorse* 1972; rpt. in *THY*, 1972–73) and about Hardy's friendship with Horace Moule (see also Evelyn Hardy, "Thomas Hardy and Horace Moule: Vindication of a Suicide" [editor's title], *TLS*, 23 Jan. 1969, and subsequent correspondence to 13 Mar.). But no serious credence is now given to theories that were never based on anything other than two unidentified photographs such as we all have in our family albums and the repeated direction of leading questions at an old lady fast declining into blindness, senility, and death.

Several of the pamphlets in the Tryphena controversy first appeared in the series of "monographs" published by the Toucan Press and subsequently collected in J. Stevens Cox, ed., *Thomas Hardy: Materials for a Study of His Life, Times and Works* (1968) and *Thomas Hardy: More Materials for a Study of His Life, Times and Works* (1971). These two volumes represent an extraordinary body of miscellaneous information, often inaccurate and tendentious but occasionally of real if limited biographical significance. Of particular interest in the first volume are the reminiscences of Gertrude Bugler, Norman Atkins, and May O'Rourke, the reprinting of Emma Hardy's religious writings, the account of Hermann Lea's relationship with Hardy as photographer and topographer, and Lois Deacon's essay on Hardy's maternal grandmother—the second printing incorporating the essential photographs omitted from the first. Though generally less useful, the later volume is worth turning to for Richard Brinkley's comments on Hardy as a regional novelist, for the texts of the Hardy wills, and for the reprintings of the sale catalogues for Max Gate and for that part of Hardy's library dispersed at Florence Hardy's death. The *Thomas Hardy Year Book*, edited by J. Stevens Cox and G. Stevens Cox, was introduced as a successor to the Toucan Press pamphlets and has displayed precisely the same miscellaneity—although M. E. Bath's "Thomas Hardy and Evangeline F. Smith" (1973–74) may be cited as an instance of the items of genuine interest that have appeared.

Minor items published elsewhere include H. O. Lock's "Max Gate" (*DY*, 1962–63), Michael Millgate's "Thomas Hardy and Rosamund Tomson" (*N&Q*, 1973), and Norman Page's "Hardy, Mrs. Oliphant, and *Jude the Obscure*" (*VN*, 1974). Three partly overlapping items by Carl J. Weber—

Hardy's Debut—How a Literary 'Career Was Determined' One Hundred Years Ago" (*PBSA*, 1965), "Hardy's Debt to Sir Frederick Macmillan" (*LN*, 1967), and "Two Fires at Max Gate," in Max F. Schulz et al., eds., *Essays in American and English Literature Presented to Bruce Robert Mc-Derry, Jr.* (1968)—are essentially reworkings of already familiar materials; or is there anything very substantial in J. O. Bailey's "Ancestral Voices in *Jude the Obscure*" (in Howard M. Harper, Jr., and Charles Edge, eds., *The Classic British Novel*, 1972) or in "Thomas Hardy" (*CLQ*, 1971), a posthumously published article by Irene Cooper Willis—of whom it is perhaps worth remarking that, although she became in effect Hardy's literary executor, she never met him and, indeed, knew the second Mrs. Hardy less intimately than is often supposed.

Florence Hardy is pleasantly, if briefly, evoked in the pages of Basil Willey's *Cambridge and Other Memories 1920–1953* (1966) but somewhat brusquely treated by Wilfred Blunt in a one-sided account (in *Cockerell*, 1965) of Sydney Cockerell's relationship with her and with her husband. Hardy's first wife, on the other hand, receives fuller justice than usual in "Thomas Hardy and Emma" (*E&S*, 1966) by Henry Gifford—who, as a relative, is able to supply a good deal of useful information about Emma's family—and in "Emma Hardy and the Giffords," an essay by Robert Gittings included in F. B. Pinion, ed., *Thomas Hardy and the Modern World* (1974). Gittings brings fresh research to bear upon Gifford family history and can argue with some cogency that Emma's personality and mental condition have been much misunderstood; altogether less persuasive is his attempt to thrust upon Florence Hardy the responsibility for such misrepresentation. There are also interesting biographical reflections, especially upon Emma Hardy, in the notes to T. R. M. Creighton, ed., *Poems of Thomas Hardy: A New Selection* (1974).

Our knowledge of Hardy as architect has been greatly extended by C. J. P. Beatty in his dissertation, "The Part Played by Architecture in the Life and Work of Thomas Hardy, with Particular Reference to the Novels" (London Univ. 1963), and in his invaluable edition of *The Architectural Notebook of Thomas Hardy* (1966), a photographic reproduction of Hardy's surviving architectural notebook supplemented by a richly informative introduction. Beatty's briefer contributions include "A Church Design by Thomas Hardy" (*THY*, 1973–74) and "Thomas Hardy's St. Juliot Drawings" (*ArchR*, 1962). Apart from some suggestive comments by D. Drew Cox in "The Poet and the Architect" (*Agenda*, 1972), little use has yet been made of the material Beatty has made available, and it is much to be hoped that he will himself exploit it further.

There were no other major advances in Hardy biography during the period between 1963 and 1974. *Concerning Thomas Hardy: A Composite Portrait from Memory* (1968), edited by D. F. Barber, offers little more than a loosely linked series of extracts from the Toucan Press pamphlets and may safely be ignored. F. E. Halliday's *Thomas Hardy: His Life and Work* (1972) is lively, appreciative, and well illustrated, but without scholarly

significance, while perhaps all that need be said of the revised and e
panded edition (1965) of Carl J. Weber's *Hardy of Wessex: His Life an
Literary Career* is that it preserves most of the strengths and weaknesses (
the original version of 1940 but omits some useful material previously su
plied in the appendixes. J. I. M. Stewart's *Thomas Hardy: A Critic
Biography* (1971) is remarkable from a biographical standpoint chiefly fc
its refreshingly down-to-earth treatment of Hardy's relationships wit
Tryphena and Emma and for an excellent chapter on the "Life"—which
also provocatively discussed by Paul Zietlow in *Moments of Vision: Th
Poetry of Thomas Hardy* (1974). Clearly there is room and need for muc
more work in this area, though two studies did appear in 1975, too late fo
evaluation here: *Young Thomas Hardy* by Robert Gittings, and *Thom
Hardy: An Illustrated Biography* by Timothy O'Sullivan. There is also th
prospect, still at some distance, of a full-scale biography by Michael Mil
gate, whose *Thomas Hardy: His Career as a Novelist* (1971) intersperses it
specifically critical chapters with essays on various aspects of Hardy's lif
and background.

General Criticism: Books

It is somewhat alarming to register the rising incidence of books on Hard
since the early 1970s. Apart from the 1964 reprintings of the already well
known volumes by Albert Guerard and Harvey Curtis Webster—the forme
with a new chapter on the poetry, the latter with a brief additional prefac
—only a handful of critical volumes appeared in the years between 196
and 1969. Roy Morrell's *Thomas Hardy: The Will and the Way* (1965) i
an engagingly personal, idiosyncratically organized study that takes seri
ously, even overseriously, Hardy's claims to be considered "an evolutionary
meliorist" rather than a deterministic pessimist. Benjamin Sankey's *Th
Major Novels of Thomas Hardy* (1965), incorporating a number of sepa
rately published articles, touches briefly but appreciatively upon Hardy'
style and upon various aspects of his narrative technique and his characteri
zation, especially of minor and intermediate figures. Arnold Kettle's 1966
lecture, *Hardy the Novelist: A Reconsideration*, is briefer still, but it ranges
widely and shrewdly over the more positive features of Hardy's provincial
ism and determinism; it also modifies Kettle's earlier pronouncements (in
his *Introduction to the English Novel*) on *Tess of the d'Urbervilles* and is
especially good on *Jude the Obscure*, calling Jude himself "a true hero of
our time." Both *Tess* and *Jude* receive full and deeply sympathetic analyses
in Irving Howe's *Thomas Hardy* (1967), which draws upon his admirable
introduction to *Jude* (1965) and upon other previously published pieces.
Much the most influential of the critical books published during the 1960s,
it is cast in the form of a critical biography and aimed largely at the general
reader; for the Hardy specialist its value lies in its many particular insights,
including its emphasis upon Hardy's "openness to the feminine principle,"

pon the sheer power of the presentation of Tess herself as "a natural
rl."

The many books published during the period 1970–74 are difficult to
1aracterize in general terms. Numerous as they are, they tend to represent
corresponding number of critical approaches and to show few consistent
atterns—apart from a widespread tendency to concentrate on familiar
:xts and ignore the less familiar. Early in the 1970s, for example, appeared
1ree books, widely divergent in almost every respect, which nonetheless
roved capable, each in its own way, of breaking fresh critical ground. J.
Iillis Miller's *Thomas Hardy: Distance and Desire* (1970), the first
1henomenological approach to Hardy, remains the most consistently
rovocative of recent studies. Miller, viewing all of Hardy's work as "woven
ogether in a single fabric," seeks to identify persistent underlying structures
nd pervasive themes—especially "distance as the source of desire and desire
s the energy behind attempts to turn distance into closeness"—and even
hose unsympathetic to his basic approach must find themselves challenged
y his analyses of Hardy's habits of withdrawal and of the Hardian narra-
ive voice as not merely a "fictional invention" but "the most important
nvention of all, the one which generates the rest and without which the rest
ould not come into existence." Less sophisticated but, at its best, equally
uggestive, Jean R. Brooks's *Thomas Hardy: The Poetic Structure* (1971) is
n attractively energetic and enthusiastic approach to the fiction by way of
he verse. Though its readings are occasionally forced, the book succeeds in
lrawing attention to many previously unremarked details of imagery, motif,
nd structural pattern. Michael Millgate's *Thomas Hardy: His Career as a
Novelist* (1971), on the other hand, takes a largely contextual approach,
eeking in its extended analyses of each of the novels "to bring the results of
cholarly research directly to bear upon the processes of analysis and eval-
1ation—to consider Hardy's fiction in the context of available biographical
ind bibliographical knowledge and in relation to the social and intellectual
nilieux within which he lived and worked at various periods."

The specifically biographical aspects of Millgate's book have already been
ouched upon, as have those of J. I. M. Stewart's *Thomas Hardy: A Critical
Biography* (1971). Although Stewart's analyses cover a good deal of already
amiliar ground and tend at times to sidestep the central problems, his
riticism achieves at its best a fine appreciative "rightness" few other Hardy
ritics can match. Readers who steer clear of the appendixes to F. R.
Southerington's *Hardy's Vision of Man* (1971) will find it an intelligent and
sustained attempt to come to terms with the development of Hardy's ideas
ind with the nature and implications of his attitudes toward human existence; though Hardy sometimes despairs, Southerington concludes, his
works irrepressibly express "a sense of man's worth and the essential
seriousness of his values."

Four other studies published during the early 1970s offer insights of a
useful but more limited kind. Those in Bert G. Hornback's *The Metaphor
of Chance: Vision and Technique in the Works of Thomas Hardy* (1971)

derive from an emphasis upon the intensification of dramatic crises th
Hardy achieves by associating them with ancient and prehistoric settin
eloquent of the long, pathetic history of human mischancing; those
Detlef von Ziegesar's *Romananfänge und Romanschlüsse bei Thom.
Hardy: Versuch einer formorientierten Interpretation* (1971) depend up
a systematic study of the beginnings and endings of all of Hardy's nove
There are interesting comments on Hardy's manipulation of convention
nineteenth-century structural patterns toward more "open" and hence mo
"modern" conclusions and on his "displacement" of his narrator by the u
of passive and impersonal forms and shifts of perspective to characte
within the novel or to implied onlookers. Perry Meisel's *Thomas Hard
The Return of the Repressed. A Study of the Major Fiction* (1971) argue
not altogether persuasively, that Hardy's later fiction, and especially *Jud*
exhibits the reassertion of instinctive impulses that had been deliberate
repressed in the early works. Despite the promise of its title, Merryn Wi
liams' *Thomas Hardy and Rural England* (1972) proves to be disappoin
ingly sketchy in its treatment of the historical background and of the nove
themselves; even the more innovative discussion of other rural literatur
fictional and nonfictional, from the Victorian period* invokes few exampl
and rarely adventures beyond description and quotation, so that the book
entirely acceptable conclusion—that Hardy's realistic penetration of "co
ventional stereotypes" enabled him to see the contemporary rural situatio
in its full complexity—carries less weight than it should.

Foremost among the several books on Hardy published in 1974 is *Th
Great Web: The Form of Hardy's Major Fiction* by Ian Gregor, whos
approach to fiction as "an unfolding process" seems especially appropriat
to Hardy's novels, with their formal dependence upon revelation and stor
and the pervasive presence of a controlling yet brooding narrative voic
Although he does not consistently follow through his own approach in th
treatment of individual novels, Gregor is a wonderfully alert *reader* o
Hardy, and his book assumes major importance as a series of fresh and ofte
exciting analyses, especially of *The Mayor of Casterbridge* and *Jude*. Th
other books of the year are of lesser interest. Penelope Vigar's *The Novels o
Thomas Hardy: Illusion and Reality* maintains that Hardy's method i
"essentially that of a painter," more specifically an impressionist painte
but while the approach works well for particular novels (notably *Th
Woodlanders*) it scarcely amounts to an adequate account of the fiction as
whole. R. J. White's *Thomas Hardy and History*, left unfinished at th
author's death, has been edited by James Gibson. As a distinguished his
torian, White was interested in Hardy chiefly as the author of *The Dynasts
his comments on *The Trumpet-Major* and other novels are insubstantial a
literary criticism, but there are some lively, commonsensical observations o
Hardy's ideas and attitudes in general and on aspects of his early life—th

---

* Though it has only occasional references to Hardy, W. J. Keith's *The Rural Tradition
A Study of the Non-Fiction Prose Writers of the English Countryside* (1974) offers an ad
mirable treatment of this topic.

atter approached by analogy with the more fully documented instance of
D. H. Lawrence. *Thomas Hardy and the Modern World*, edited by F. B.
Pinion (1974), makes available the lectures given at a summer school organized by the Thomas Hardy Society in 1973. Robert Gittings' contribution on Emma Hardy has already been mentioned, and the volume as a
whole—though unequal in quality—is well worth looking at. General
studies published in 1975, too late for consideration here, include Dale
Kramer's *Thomas Hardy: The Forms of Tragedy* and Virginia R. Hyman's
Ethical Perspective in the Novels of Thomas Hardy.

Albert J. Guerard, ed., *Hardy: A Collection of Critical Essays* (1963)
remains a convenient anthology of previously published criticism, while of
the three introductory studies to appear during the period under review
Richard C. Carpenter's *Thomas Hardy* (1964) is the most substantial,
George Wing's *Hardy* (1963) the most readable, and Trevor Johnson's
Thomas Hardy (1968) the most enthusiastic. F. B. Pinion's *A Hardy
Companion: A Guide to the Works of Thomas Hardy and Their Back-
ground* (1968) is a useful work of general reference, notable for its extensive
"Dictionary of People and Places." Denys Kay-Robinson's *Hardy's Wessex
Reappraised* (1971), an enterprising survey of the "originals" of the build-
ings and locations of Hardy's fictional Wessex, might also have been called a
Hardy "companion"; its appeal is less to the Hardy scholar than to the
Hardy pilgrim—though the latter may, of course, be a scholar too!

Two collections of contemporary reviews have appeared. The earlier,
Thomas Hardy and His Readers (1968), put together by Laurence Lerner
and John Holmstrom, is rendered unsatisfactory by its inaccuracies, its
unindicated elisions, and its limited scope. *Thomas Hardy: The Critical
Heritage* (1970), edited by R. G. Cox, is altogether fuller and better informed and much more given to printing items in their entirety, but it is
nonetheless disappointing in its coverage and in its failure to identify more
of the anonymous reviewers. The initial reception of Hardy's fiction is
rather inconclusively discussed in at least two dissertations—by Hildegard
Schill (London Univ. 1963) and by Arthur F. Minerof (New York Univ.
1965)—and in a few articles, of which Joan B. Pinck's "The Reception of
Thomas Hardy's *The Return of the Native*" (*HLB*, 1969) is much the most
substantial. Clearly, more work might usefully be done in this area, even if
there is unlikely to be, in the near future, a market for another collection
of reviews.

There are, of course, several books devoted to Hardy's verse, of which any
serious student of the novels will need to be aware, among them Harold
Orel's *Thomas Hardy's Epic-Drama: A Study of "The Dynasts"* (1963),
Walter F. Wright's *The Shaping of "The Dynasts": A Study in Thomas
Hardy* (1967), Kenneth Marsden's *The Poems of Thomas Hardy: A Critical
Introduction* (1969), and J. O. Bailey's *The Poetry of Thomas Hardy: A
Handbook and Commentary* (1970). Of particular interest are Paul Ziet-
low's *Moments of Vision*, already mentioned, and Donald Davie's splen-
didly provocative *Thomas Hardy and British Poetry* (1972). Davie was the

editor of the Thomas Hardy Special Issue of *Agenda* (1972), which was also concerned almost exclusively with the verse.

General Criticism: Articles and Parts of Books

"What Kind of Fiction Did Hardy Write?" asks Ian Gregor in the title of his 1966 article in *Essays in Criticism*. Though the question remains without a wholly satisfactory answer, many critics have attempted in the last few years to advance the discussion or at least to clarify its terms. Gregor himself, in the article cited, borrows a phrase from D. H. Lawrence to celebrate the "sensuous understanding" of Hardy's novels and traces a movement, in *Tess* and *Jude*, toward a richer individual psychology and a progressive domestication of such cosmic concepts as Necessity. In a later article "Hardy's World" (*ELH*, 1971), Gregor sees the novels and the world of Wessex itself as constituting, in Hardy's own phrase, a "series of seemings"; focused on *The Woodlanders*, this essay represents a preliminary investigation of themes and perceptions more fully developed in *The Great Web*. Some of the ideas in J. Hillis Miller's *Thomas Hardy: Distance and Desire* are similarly adumbrated by the brief Hardy references in his *The Form of Victorian Fiction* (1968), where a passage from *A Pair of Blue Eyes* is used to demonstrate the possibilities of the coexistence in fiction of "many different related temporal rhythms," each eloquent of "a present which lives and moves in the yearnings of its incompletions." For Barbara Hardy in *The Appropriate Form* (1964), on the other hand, Hardy's novels, and especially *Jude*, provide examples of the distorting effects of "dogmatic form," while David Lodge in "Thomas Hardy and Cinematographic Form" (*Novel*, 1974) seizes upon *The Return of the Native* as "a 'cinematic novel' *avant la lettre*." Though some of Lodge's perceptions are less innovative than he seems to suppose, his discussion is suggestive in itself and in its relationship to the ongoing critical debate about Hardy's narrative perspectives.

As John Paterson points out in *The Novel as Faith: The Gospel According to James, Hardy, Conrad, Joyce, Lawrence and Virginia Woolf* (1973), Hardy did not "keep the faith" in the Jamesian sense insofar as he failed to accept the realist premise that the reader must submit absolutely to the illusion of the fiction. Yet—as Lodge perceives—Hardy shows an extraordinary concern with the precise physical location from which any particular fictional action is viewed, and his readiness to transfer responsibility from one identified or merely postulated viewer to another in order to accommodate such shifting perspectives has fascinating implications for his narrative methods generally. These matters are touched upon in the books by Millgate, Detlef von Ziegesar, and, especially, Hillis Miller. Daniel R. Schwarz, though at odds with Miller's critical approach, is stimulated by his arguments to offer a series of commentaries on the role and implicit characterization of Hardy's principal narrators ("The Narrator as Character in Hardy's Major Fiction," *MFS*, 1972), while Paul Goetsch in *Die Romankon-*

ption in England 1880–1910 (1967) touches upon Hardy's use of observer gures in the course of a broader analysis of the opposition in the novels etween objective and subjective reality. Hardy's obsession with visualiza-ion is approached from quite another angle in an excellent article by Lloyd ernando, "Thomas Hardy's Rhetoric of Painting" (*REL*, 1965). Fernando rgues—as Penelope Vigar has done more recently—that Hardy was deeply fluenced by the visual arts, to the extent that he often "imagined the ssentials of a picture to lend vividness to his writing even when no actual ainting or model existed": in *The Return of the Native*, unfortunately, he creation of "what is virtually a series of tableaux," not so much pictures f reality as "pictures of pictures," results in a weak plot, static characteriza-ion, and a substitution of self-consciously "fine" writing for genuine in-ights.

Although the question of Hardy's "philosophy" has happily receded omewhat from the forefront of critical debate, there have been several ignificant contributions to our understanding of the intellectual contexts ithin which Hardy wrote. Much the most influential of these has been David DeLaura's densely argued analysis, in " 'The Ache of Modernism' in Hardy's Later Novels" (*ELH*, 1967), of the "contemporary matrix" of Hardy's "modern" novels—*The Return of the Native, Jude,* and especially *ess.* DeLaura concerns himself particularly with Hardy's response to Mat-hew Arnold's religious ideas as dramatized in terms of such Arnoldian gures as Clym Yeobright and Angel Clare, arguing that despite Hardy's ympathetic reading of "advanced" nineteenth-century thinkers he re-nained (as shown by his ambiguous presentation of Sue Bridehead) dis-rustful and even fearful of "the optimistic ideal of a modern secular and ational culture." David Daiches has some sensible observations on Hardy's undamental pessimism in *Some Late Victorian Attitudes* (1969), but in The Coming Universal Wish Not to Live in Hardy's 'Modern' Novels" *NCF*, 1972) Lawrence J. Starzyk makes insufficient allowance for the com-lexities and contradictions of Hardy's work when he argues that the lead-ng "modern" characters—especially Clym, Tess, and Jude—are seekers of leath in life, here defined as "a radical dissociation from life consistent with ontinued existence." In *The Turn of the Novel: The Transition to Mod-rn Fiction* (1966) Alan Friedman offers—despite occasional extravagances —a splendidly perceptive and refreshingly independent consideration of the ronies and reversals implicit in the structures, and especially the conclu-ions, of *Far from the Madding Crowd, Tess,* and *Jude*: the "modernity" of *ude*, for example, consists for Friedman in the ending's outrageous chal-enge to the long-established ritualistic functions, in fiction, of marriages nd deaths. Lewis B. Horne, on the other hand, argues in " 'The Art of Renunciation' in Hardy's Novels" (*SNNTS*, 1972) that *Jude* is the culmina-ion of a shift in Hardy's handling of the theme of renunciation from a ositive, and characteristically nineteenth-century, valuation in the early novels to an eventual negative, and characteristically twentieth-century, valuation.

Hardy's achievement is viewed in longer perspectives by Dieter Riesner i
" 'Veteris Vestigia Flammae': Thomas Hardy und die klassische Humanitä
(in Horst Meller and Hans-Joachim Zimmermann, eds., *Lebende Antik*
Symposion für Rudolf Sühnel, 1967), a valuable survey of Hardy's ear
classical reading and of the pervasive influence of the classics on his wor
Riesner sees Hardy as having close affinities with the great Greek traged
ans; Dale Kramer in "Hardy's Prospects as a Tragic Novelist" (*DR*, 197
invokes classical and other precedents in an attempt to define the trag
qualities of Hardy's novels, suggesting that the best of them exempli
Richard B. Sewall's dictum that the universals in conflict within the trag
work must remain in ambiguous tension. The emphasis on traditional pa
toral, both classical and Renaissance, in Michael Squires's *The Pastor*
Novel: Studies in George Eliot, Thomas Hardy, and D. H. Lawrence (197
proves in the end somewhat limiting: though Squires deals thoroughly wit
the specific pastoral motifs he identifies in *Under the Greenwood Tree, Fa*
from the Madding Crowd, and *The Woodlanders*, he has little to say c
their implications for Hardy's attitude toward his audience or his stance as
regionalist. The Hardy chapter in Harold E. Toliver's *Pastoral Forms an*
Attitudes (1971) examines the varying "reciprocal responses between natur
and society" in the major novels from *The Return of the Native* onwar
and while the discussion as a whole remains inconclusive some individua
perceptions stand out—for example, the suggestion that at the end of *Tes*
the elegiac and "documentary" impulses at first conflict but finally combin
Charles E. May sounds a dissenting note in "*Far from the Madding Crow*
and *The Woodlanders*: Hardy's Grotesque Pastorals" (*ELT*, 1974) an
somewhat overstates his contention that the customary categorization o
these particular novels as pastorals takes no account of their emphasis o
"the totally estranged world of the absurd and the grotesque."

In "Thomas Hardy's Use of the Gothic: An Examination of Five Repre
sentative Works" (*NCF*, 1963) James F. Scott describes the methods used i
Desperate Remedies and four short stories to supply "the groundless fancie
of Gothic romance with a credible basis in regional custom and belief"; i
"Spectacle and Symbol in Thomas Hardy's Fiction" (*PQ*, 1965) Scott argue
that Hardy's occasional weakness for "pseudo-symbolic" Gothic effects mus
be set against those moments when he achieves genuine symbolic power an
complexity, often by using architecture or landscape to supply focal point
for his images. The symbolic and associative potentialities of regional land
scape, considered at length in Bert Hornback's book, are also touched upo
by Avrom Fleishman in the Hardy section of *The English Historical Novel*
Walter Scott to Virginia Woolf (1971). Hardy's use of the prehistoric fea
tures of the Wessex landscape as points of human and moral reference is, fo
Fleishman, one of the ways in which *Tess of the d'Urbervilles* becomes "
symbolic model of the pattern of British historical experience," even whil
the more specifically historical *The Trumpet-Major* remains, at best,
record of local manners, an example of *Kulturgeschichte*. Wessex, as fictio
and fact, has been well discussed by W. J. Keith in a number of articles: i

Critical Approaches to Hardy's Wessex" (*RACUTE*, 1963) he stresses the importance, to Hardy's regional conception, of the centrality of Casterbridge and the eloquent "pastness" of the whole Dorset landscape, while in "Thomas Hardy and the Literary Pilgrims" (*NCF*, 1969) he evokes in lively fashion the early enthusiasts who went in search of the "originals" of Hardy's fictional settings and discusses their possible influence upon Hardy's own elaboration of Wessex as a self-consistent world. Keith's "Thomas Hardy and the Name 'Wessex' " (*ELN*, 1968) establishes that Hardy's use of the name in a contemporary sense was anticipated by William Barnes and Charles Kingsley, though *not* by George Eliot; and L. MacKenzie Osborne's "The 'Chronological Frontier' in Thomas Hardy's Novels" (*SNNTS*, 1972) points to a deliberate opposition in Hardy's work between time as destroyer ("clock-time") and time as sustainer of the rhythms and continuities of the past ("Wessex time").

Hardy's relationship to his time and place receives an especially rich and authoritative discussion from Raymond Williams in a chapter of *The Country and the City* (1973) that absorbs and supersedes his earlier treatment of Hardy in *Critical Quarterly* (1964) and *The English Novel: From Dickens to Lawrence* (1970). Hardy's fictional world, so responsive to social and economic actualities as he had himself experienced them, is seen by Williams as resistant to analysis in terms of such broad abstract patterns as rural versus urban, or stability versus intrusion; its strength and importance lie in the very density and sensitivity with which it dramatizes the full complexity of the contemporary processes of change and mobility and stresses the centrality of work, the pervasiveness of class divisions, and the crucial nature of the marriage choice. In "Thomas Hardy and Social Change" (*SoRA*, 1969), Philip Bull argues with a good deal of cogency that Hardy's approval of the traditional agricultural society was strongly qualified by his awareness of improvements in the changing social conditions and moral outlook of his time. There is an implicit challenge here to Douglas Brown's thesis—first advanced in his *Thomas Hardy* (1954; rev. ed., 1961) and reasserted in his fine reading of *The Mayor of Casterbridge* in the Studies in English Literature series (1962)—that Hardy's central concern was agricultural decline; Brown's thesis is directly challenged, again with considerable effectiveness, in J. C. Maxwell's essay, "The 'Sociological' Approach to *The Mayor of Casterbridge*," in Maynard Mack and Ian Gregor, eds., *Imagined Worlds: Essays on Some English Novels and Novelists in Honour of John Butt* (1968).

Numerous articles enlarge upon perceived influences and points of comparison between Hardy and a wide variety of other writers. G. Singh, for example, considers Hardy's possible indebtedness to the pessimism of Leopardi (*RLMC*, 1964), James Hazen writes on "*Tess of the d'Urbervilles* and *Antigone*" (*ELT*, 1971), and C. Heywood, in two overlapping articles (*NCF*, 1963; *RLC*, 1964), establishes some broad resemblances between *The Return of the Native* and Miss Braddon's *The Doctor's Wife*. Hardy's influence on D. H. Lawrence is explored in some detail by Richard Swigg in

Lawrence, Hardy, and American Literature (1972) and more briefly b
Richard D. Beards (*DHLR*, 1969), K. W. Salter (*English*, 1973), and Ros
Marie Burwell (*WHR*, 1974). More purely comparative are such articles a
those on Hardy in relation to Faulkner (Peter L. Irvine, *ArQ*, 1966, and
David W. Jarrett, *Novel*, 1973), Hauptman (Charles R. Bachman, *RLV*
1969), and Melville (Nicolaus C. Mills, *TSLL*, 1970; rev. in his *America*
and English Fiction in the Nineteenth Century, 1973).

The language and style of Hardy's novels have received relatively littl
attention: even the excellent chapter on *Tess of the d'Urbervilles* in Davi
Lodge's *Language of Fiction: Essays in Criticism and Verbal Analysis of th*
English Novel (1966) focuses only intermittently—though always sugges
tively—on stylistic issues. There are worthwhile comments, however, i
Benjamin Sankey's "Hardy's Prose Style" (*TCL*, 1965), one of the article
absorbed into *The Major Novels of Thomas Hardy* (see preceding section)
and in Terry Eagleton's "Thomas Hardy: Nature as Language" (*CritQ*
1971), which explores in *The Return of the Native* and other novels pa
terns of imagery in which material realities become articulate symbols
Hardy's use of dialect, somewhat inconclusively discussed by Patrici
Ingham in *Literary English since Shakespeare*, ed. George Watson (1970), i
massively documented by Ulla Baugner in a published Stockholm Univer
sity dissertation, *A Study on the Use of Dialect in Thomas Hardy's Novel*
and Short Stories with Special Reference to Phonology and Vocabular
(1972). Baugner probably exaggerates the direct influence of William
Barnes, but her research has important implications for any consideration o
Hardy as regionalist and "historian" of local folkways. C. H. Salter argue
(somewhat obliquely) in "Hardy's 'Pedantry' " (*NCF*, 1973) that Hardy'
use of self-consciously literary or recondite phraseology is essentially func
tional, especially as a means of contrasting the "small" world of Wesse
with the "large" world beyond its boundaries. General and particula
aspects of Hardy's literary allusions are considered in William F. Hall'
"Hawthorne, Shakespeare and Tess: Hardy's Use of Allusion and Refer
ence" (*ES*, 1971) and in a very useful dissertation, "Allusion in Thoma
Hardy's Early Novels: A Stylistic Study" (Indiana Univ. 1969), b
Marlene A. Springer. Modest in itself, Patrick M. Hartwell's "A Quantita
tive Approach to Thomas Hardy's Prose Style" (*CCC*, 1970)—an offshoot o
his dissertation (Univ. of California, Los Angeles, 1970)—is useful as a
indication of what might be achieved by quantitative analyses of a mor
extensive and systematic kind. Computers have their uses, and it is to b
hoped that they will eventually be employed not only in specific stylisti
exercises but also in the preparation of a comprehensive concordance o
Hardy's work in prose and verse. Ideally, of course, such a concordanc
should be based upon a scholarly text, but—as an alternative to infinit
postponement—the Wessex Edition will serve.

Studies of Individual Works

Early Novels

Apart from discussions incorporated in books on Hardy already mentioned—and therefore excluded from this section—little significant criticism has been focused on Hardy's first published novel, *Desperate Remedies*. Lawrence O. Jones (*NCF*, 1965) writes well on the distinctive and even "idiosyncratic" qualities that Hardy brought to the sensation-novel convention (a topic also touched upon by George Wing, *SEL*, 1973), C. J. P. Beatty (*THY*, 1971) discusses the influence upon the novel of Hardy's early architectural experiences, and Curtis C. Smith (*Thoth*, 1967) argues that Hardy, in *Desperate Remedies* and *A Pair of Blue Eyes*, was already using setting to establish, for example, Cytherea's normality and health.

Under the Greenwood Tree, praised for its pastoral qualities in several recent books, has received no substantial discussion elsewhere, although Samuel Hynes, introducing *Great Short Works of Thomas Hardy* (1967), has some good brief observations on the novel and on Hardy's role as "parish historian." Robert A. Draffan's article in *English* (1973) makes the sound but not especially original point that the novel shows signs of authorial condescension toward the characters and seems altogether less idyllic than is sometimes assumed.

There are mildly interesting comments on *A Pair of Blue Eyes* in the Curtis C. Smith article just mentioned, in a 1972 article by Arthur K. Amos (*CLT*), and in Michael Steig's "The Problem of Literary Value in Two Early Hardy Novels" (*TSLL*, 1970), which concludes that *A Pair of Blue Eyes* is superior to *Far from the Madding Crowd* in that "it offers no reassurance to reconcile us to the claims of the super-ego, of society and convention."

Far from the Madding Crowd

Far from the Madding Crowd itself is given a disappointingly conventional reading by Elizabeth Drew in *The Novel: A Modern Guide to Fifteen English Masterpieces* (1963) and an excessively gloomy one by Roselee Robison in "Desolation in *Far from the Madding Crowd*" (*DR*, 1971). Howard Babb (*ELH*, 1963) expatiates on the use of natural settings as a source of moral criteria in the novel, while in "The Mirror and the Sword: Imagery in *Far from the Madding Crowd*" (*NCF*, 1964) Richard C. Carpenter sees evidence of a "strong Freudian thread" in those scenes, such as Oak's shearing of the sheep and Troy's dazzling swordplay, in which Hardy portrays "the quintessence of the passional life in symbolic terms." The article by Michael Squires (*NCF*, 1970) is incorporated in his book (cited in preceding section).

The Return of the Native

Though rarely innovative, Robert Fricker's essay on *The Return of th*
Native in *Der englische Roman: Vom Mittelalter zur Moderne,* ed. Franz I
Stanzel (1969) is thorough and discriminating, especially in its treatment o
the patterns of relationships between the characters as individuals and a
groups. Exploring themes also well discussed by David DeLaura (see pr
ceding section), Lennart Björk's "'Visible Essences' as Thematic Structui
in Hardy's *The Return of the Native*" (*ES*, 1972) posits the Eustacia-Clyi
relationship as a deliberate, irreconcilable antithesis, in both aesthetic an
philosophical terms, between Antiquity and the Nineteenth Century,
demonstration "that the light, optimism, and luxuriance of the Hellen
view of life have had to yield to the philosophical resignation and em
tional restraint of the nineteenth century." In "*The Return of the Native* a
a Tragedy in Six Books" (*NCF*, 1971) Richard Benvenuto speculates, n
altogether persuasively, that Hardy changed the ending of the novel und
pressure but "kept his original conception with a vengeance" by using th
sixth book to show Clym's "high aspirations corrupting themselves"; a
opposing case, for the integrity of Book VI, is well argued by F. G. Atkinso
THY, 1972–73). Robert Evans ("The Other Eustacia," *Novel*, 1968) se
Eustacia's role as tragic heroine undercut by the reader's developing awar
ness of her as adolescent, self-pitying, and foolishly romantic; Richa
Benvenuto ("Another Look at the Other Eustacia," *Novel*, 1970), howeve
refers ambiguities associated with Eustacia to Hardy's ambivalence towai
the individualistic values she embodies, leaving David Eggenschwiler (*NC*
1971) to bridge the gap by arguing that the presentation of Eustacia, fa
from being confused, is precisely designed to provide "a double perspecti\
on the romantic heroine." Ken Zellefrow in "*The Return of the Nativ*
Hardy's Map and Eustacia's Suicide" (*NCF*, 1973) neatly observes that sin
Eustacia had to cross a road to reach Shadwell Weir she must have know
where she was and what she was doing, while Dale Kramer (*N&Q*, 1965) h
a brief but useful comment on the novel's time scheme.

Minor Novels of the Middle Period

The articles on *The Hand of Ethelberta* by George Wing (*SNNT.*
1972) and Paul Ward (*THY*, 1971) warrant mention chiefly because th
run counter to the prevailing neglect of an exasperating but deeply intere
ing novel.

Few essays have been devoted to the three minor novels that follow
The Return of the Native. An M.A. thesis on *The Trumpet-Major* I
Michael Edwards (Univ. of Birmingham 1967) contains useful informatio
about the manuscript and about Hardy's historical researches, while Dav
W. Jarrett develops in "Hawthorne and Hardy as Modern Romancer
(*NCF*, 1974) the interesting idea that Hardy in *A Laodicean* was drawii
directly upon Hawthorne's *The House of the Seven Gables* but with th

m of absorbing romance conventions within the novel form rather than of
serting, as Hawthorne had done, the independence of romance.

The Mayor of Casterbridge

Frederick R. Karl's article on *The Mayor of Casterbridge* in *An Age of
iction* (1964; rpt. in 1965 as *A Reader's Guide to the Nineteenth Century
ritish Novel*) revises and slightly expands his 1960 article in *Modern Fiction
udies*. Robert B. Heilman, taking up topics explored more briefly in his
xcellent introduction to the Riverside edition of 1962, argues in "Hardy's
Mayor: Notes on Style" (*NCF*, 1964) that Hardy's stylistic ineptitudes are
ltimately absorbed within an overall imaginative strength, while in "Har-
y's *Mayor* and the Problem of Intention" (*Criticism*, 1963) he contends
lat the narrative commentary on the characters often conflicts with their
ramatized presentation. Duane D. Edwards in "*The Mayor of Casterbridge*
Aeschylean Tragedy" (*SNNTS*, 1972) sees the narrator as not omniscient
ut subjectively choric, and Robert Kiely in "Vision and Viewpoint in *The
Mayor of Casterbridge*" (*NCF*, 1968) stresses the importance of "seeing" in
le novel—the way in which characters view themselves and the perspective
ften dependent upon an actual physical viewpoint) they have on others.
lorman Page touches upon similar points during his discussion of "literary
icture-making" in "Hardy's Pictorial Art in *The Mayor of Casterbridge*"
A, 1972). While Robert C. Schweik ("Character and Fate in Hardy's *The
Mayor of Casterbridge*," *NCF*, 1966) sees the presentation of Henchard as
ecoming increasingly deterministic, Dale Kramer ("Character and the
ycle of Change in *The Mayor of Casterbridge*," *TSL*, 1971) stresses the
ovel's enactment of an essentially cyclical view of human history, and
eymour Migdal ("History and Archetype in *The Mayor of Casterbridge*,"
NNTS, 1971) points out that the ending constitutes not a restoration of
le traditional order but the establishment of a new commercial order in
hich the tragic sensibility itself no longer has a place. Though its docu-
lentation is not always accurate, Christine Winfield's "Factual Sources of
wo Episodes in *The Mayor of Casterbridge*" (*NCF*, 1970) shows convinc-
1gly that the incidents of the wife-selling and of Henchard's bankruptcy
earing were drawn from material Hardy turned up during a systematic
ading of early volumes of the *Dorset County Chronicle*.

The Woodlanders

In the most illuminating of recent articles on *The Woodlanders*, "The
thical Structure of Hardy's *The Woodlanders*" (*Archiv*, 1974), Robert C.
chweik effectively demonstrates that Hardy was deliberately reflecting
ontemporary debates over the proper adjustment of egoism and altruism
nd dramatizing, especially through Marty South, his sense of the severe
uman costs likely to be extorted by the exigencies of moral choice. Michael
teig, on the other hand, in "Art versus Philosophy in Hardy: *The Wood-

landers" (*Mosaic*, 1971) finds philosophical inconsistencies in the novel and speculates that these may be the consequence of Hardy's deliberate creation of a narrator "nearly as fumbling and unreliable in his search for the meaning of human existence as are the novel's characters." In his interesting article "The Shifted 'Centre of Altruism' in *The Woodlanders*: Thomas Hardy's Third 'Return of a Native'" (*ELH*, 1971), Peter J. Casagrand notes Hardy's statement that *The Woodlanders* was conceived in the 1870s compares that work, *Under the Greenwood Tree*, and *The Return of the Native* as "return fables," and suggests that Hardy's several return novels (among them *The Mayor of Casterbridge, Tess*, and *Jude*) "embody in their very structures the central experience of his life and art—the relationship of the old and the new, of the past and the present." F. B. Pinion's "The Country and Period of *The Woodlanders*" (*THY*, 1971) examines the topographical and historical contexts of the novel and makes a good case for dating its action circa 1878.

Tess of the d'Urbervilles

Bruce Hugman's slim volume on *Tess of the d'Urbervilles* (1970) in the Studies in English Literature series fails to reflect the structure or sequence of the novel but contains individual insights of some value. More consistently rewarding are Franz K. Stanzel's "Thomas Hardy: *Tess of the d'Urbervilles*" (in Horst Oppel, ed., *Der moderne englische Roman: Interpretationen*, 1965), a close analysis of the manipulative role of the narrator and of the almost imperceptible shifts between the narrator's point of view and that of Tess herself, and Lucille Herbert's "Hardy's Views in *Tess of the d'Urbervilles*" (*ELH*, 1970), a rich discussion of the ways in which the narrator's position as both generalizing historian and Tess's advocate is set off against the specifically immediate and "local" views associated with Tess herself and with a Wessex world that is itself a *paysage moralisé*, probably derived from eighteenth-century topographical poetry and capable in any case of yielding abstract meanings. Of wider relevance for Hardy studies than its title suggests, Peter R. Morton's "*Tess of the d'Urbervilles*: A Neo-Darwinian Reading" (*SoRA*, 1974) interprets the novel as incorporating a wholly pessimistic and deterministic vision derived largely from August Weissman's *Essay on Heredity*. Morton argues that access to neo-Darwinist ideas enabled Hardy to reinvigorate the pathetic fallacy: Tess's fate is as determined as that of the birds and animals, products of selective evolution with which she is so often compared; what her human consciousness gives her is chiefly a far greater potential for pain.

The recurrent imagery of Tess as trapped or hunted animal is usefully picked out by Philip Mahone Griffith (*TSE*, 1963), while Joseph J. Egan (*TSL*, 1970) stresses the prefigurative imagery in the novel, Lewis B. Horne (*TSLL*, 1971) the use of the sun and land as symbols, and Terence Wright (*DUJ*, 1972) the pervasive visual imagery, especially of figures in landscapes. Acknowledging Hardy's penchant for "graphic crudities of effect," Tony

Tanner ("Colour and Movement in Hardy's *Tess of the d'Urbervilles*," *CritQ*, 1968) splendidly illuminates the color patterning in the novel, the cumulative impact of "visible omens," the importance of movement, and the way in which the full weight of the merging images and tragic ironies of the novel are brought consistently to bear on the figure of Tess herself. Several critics, including W. Eugene Davis (*NCF*, 1968), Laurence Lerner *The Truthtellers: Jane Austen, George Eliot, D. H. Lawrence*, 1967), and Bernard J. Paris (*NCF*, 1969), have been exercised over the question of Tess's "purity," but readings of the novel in feminist terms by Geoffrey Wagner (*Five for Freedom: A Study of Feminism in Fiction*, 1972) and—more perceptively, though still rather casually—by Elizabeth Hardwick *Seduction and Betrayal: Women in Literature*, 1974) have broken little fresh ground, perhaps because Hardy was himself Tess's most passionate advocate. Arthur Efron, in an excessively leisurely article (*Paunch*, 1967), has some useful comments on the wider sexual themes of the novel, while James Hazen in "The Tragedy of Tess Durbeyfield" (*TSLL*, 1969) sees Tess as acting out the martyrdom of the natural self under the pressures of Victorian social and moral attitudes as embodied in Angel Clare. Angel himself, Hazen believes, is to some extent redeemed by his suffering and enhanced self-knowledge; Robert B. Heilman ("*Gulliver* and Hardy's *Tess*: Houyhnhnms, Yahoos, and Ambiguities," *SoR*, 1970) goes further and finds both Angel and Alec to be more attractive and complex figures than most critics have been willing to allow. It is, however, T. B. Tomlinson's contention in "Hardy's Universe: *Tess of the d'Urbervilles*" (*CR*, 1973) that the weakness of Hardy's presentation of Angel "leaves Alec, and the side of Tess that answers instinctively to Alec's flesh and blood qualities, the dominant impulse in the book." Among several other articles of minor interest are Henry Kozicki's "Myths of Redemption in Hardy's *Tess of the d'Urbervilles*" (*PLL*, 1974), which identifies Tess as a "ritual scapegoat," and H. L. Weatherby's "Atheological Symbolism in Modern Fiction: An Interpretation of Hardy's *Tess of the d'Urbervilles*" (*SHR*, 1970), which seeks to show that Hardy deliberately emptied the novel of Christian hope. A useful anthology is *Twentieth Century Interpretations of "Tess of the d'Urbervilles": A Collection of Critical Essays* (1969), edited, and well introduced, by Albert J. LaValley.

Jude the Obscure

Jude the Obscure, though by no means one of the most visually suggestive of Hardy's works, has been filmed for BBC television and presented in North America on Masterpiece Theatre. Of the many essays the novel has provoked the most remarkable is Fernand Lagarde's "A propos de la construction de *Jude the Obscure*" (*Caliban*, 1966), an astonishing—though ultimately resistible—analytical tour de force that sees Hardy as aspiring in *Jude* to the architectural tightness of the contemporary "well-made" play, takes at face value his statements about its geometrical patterning, and minutely traces the possible ramifications of such patterning throughout the novel's structure. Ian Gregor's treatment of *Jude* in *The Great Web* (see General Criticism: Books) absorbs his contribution to Ian Gregor and Walter Stein, eds., *The Prose for God: Religious and Anti-Religious Aspects of Imaginative Literature* (1973) and draws upon an earlier piece in Maynard Mack and Ian Gregor, eds., *Imagined Worlds* (1968); the *Imagined World* essay, however, has independent value, especially for its emphasis on the novel's concern with "an internal quest for the reality of the self." For Barry N. Schwartz that quest is doomed to failure: "Jude asks meaning and purpose from a world that denies him both" ("*Jude the Obscure* in the Age of Anxiety," *SEL*, 1970). For Janet Burstein in "The Journey beyond Myth in *Jude the Obscure*" (*TSLL*, 1973) Jude is isolated in "a fictional world scarred by its enforced separation from the age of myth," its loss of traditional "harmony and coherence."

William H. Marshall in *The World of the Victorian Novel* (1967) suggests that because Jude never realizes that the war between flesh and spirit is inherent in the universe, not just in himself, he fails to appreciate the role of Father Time as prophet and teacher, "revealing to modern man the sole course that is meaningfully his in the face of universal disorder." Lewis B. Horne (*SAQ*, 1974) sees Father Time in somewhat similar terms, as representing modern times and values and as initiating Jude and Sue, through his act of sacrifice, into the negations of "the satanic new religion of Modernism." For U. C. Knoepflmacher (in the course of a perceptive essay in *Laughter & Despair: Readings in Ten Novels of the Victorian Era*, 1971) Father Time is the personification of Hardy's own despairing vision, a vision so overwhelming that it seems best to think of the novel not as a tragedy but as "an elegy lamenting the death of nineteenth-century idealism"; Richard Benvenuto, on the other hand, sees Father Time as embodying an objective, abstract perception of human existence that is shared by the narrator and accepted by Jude in his final despair but implicitly challenged throughout the novel by the love and idealism of Jude's own individualistic perception—one which "personalizes the world . . . makes what he sees an extension of himself and endows it with human values" ("Modes of Perception: The Will to Live in *Jude the Obscure*," *SNNTS*, 1970).

John Sutherland's "A Note on the Teasing Narrator in *Jude the Obscure*" (*ELT*, 1974) nicely argues that Hardy wanted to divorce the narrator from the hero in order to make clear that the novel was *not* his own personal testament. The well-informed essay on *Jude* in Jerome Hamilton Buckley's *Season of Youth: The Bildungsroman from Dickens to Golding* (1974) touches judiciously upon biographical issues in developing its argument that by the end of the novel "Hardy for the first time in English fiction has successfully adapted the form of the Bildungsroman to the true and proper ends of tragedy"—a view not shared by Frank M. Giordano, Jr. (*SNNTS*, 1972), who finds Jude's final rejection of society so absolute as to make the novel almost a satire or inversion of the bildungsroman.

William J. Hyde in "Theoretic and Practical Unconventionality in *Jude he Obscure"* (*NCF*, 1965) sees Hardy as working deliberately with Mill's ideas of freedom and Arnold's opposition between Hellenism and Hebraism. Related observations have since been made by David DeLaura (see preceding section), H. L. Weatherby (*SHR*, 1967), Barbara Fass (*CLQ*, 1974), and especially Ward Hellstrom (in George Goodin, ed., *The English Novel in the Nineteenth Century: Essays on the Literary Mediation of Human Values,* 1972), who explores Hardy's use of Arnoldian ideas and illusions with persuasive thoroughness. Michael Hassett's "Compromised Romanticism in *Jude the Obscure"* (*NCF*, 1971) is interesting for the way in which it takes Hardy's literary allusions seriously (especially those to Shelley's *Epipsychidion*) and considers their relevance to the novel's themes and values, while Masao Miyoshi's *The Divided Self: A Perspective on the Literature of the Victorians* (1969) comments breezily on Sue's Shelleyan role as Jude's "intellectual beauty, epipsyche, and double." Robert B. Heilman's "Hardy's Sue Bridehead" (*NCF*, 1966; rev. as intro. to the 1966 "Standard Edition") offers an excellent analysis of Sue and of the failure of Sue and Jude to find "philosophical bases of life that are emotionally satisfactory"; Michael Steig's "Sue Bridehead" (*Novel,* 1968) maintains that Sue's bewildering sexual advances and retreats fit precisely Wilhelm Reich's specification for the "hysterical character." Elizabeth Hardwick's "Sue and Arabella" (*NYRB,* 14 Nov. 1974) is more exclusively sympathetic to the former and hostile to the latter than most other recent criticism; but Arabella is defended by Frederick P. W. McDowell (*ELN*, 1964), and A. O. Cockshut, discussing *Jude* briefly in *The Unbelievers: English Agnostic Thought 1840–1890* (1964), points out that if Arabella represents animality she also represents marriage and convention.

Other Fiction

Hardy's other fictional prose has received far too little attention. On *The Well-Beloved*, for example, there are only the articles, sensible but slight, by Helmut E. Gerber (*ELN*, 1963) and Paul Ward (*THY*, 1972–73) and the introduction to the New Wessex Edition by J. Hillis Miller. Irving Howe's book includes some good brief comments on the short stories, and popular interest in them has to some extent been revived by the BBC television dramatizations of six so-called "Wessex Tales," among them "A Tragedy of Two Ambitions" and "The Melancholy Hussar." But neither of the standard short-story surveys—Wendell V. Harris' "English Short Fiction in the 19th Century" (*SSF*, 1968) and T. O. Beachcroft's *The Modest Art: A Survey of the Short Story in English* (1968)—has anything substantial to say about Hardy, and John Wain's introduction to *Selected Short Stories of Thomas Hardy* (1966) is disappointingly sketchy. Norman Page, however, in "Hardy's Short Stories: A Reconsideration" (*SSF*, 1974) ventures to arrange the stories into discussable categories, while Hans G. Hönig in *Studien zur englischen Short Story am Ende des 19. Jahrhunderts: Stevenson, Hardy, Kipling und Wells* (1971) points out that writing stories was very much a professional business for Hardy and suggests that the stories are better read together, as grouped in volumes, than separately, as originally published. Charles E. May in "Hardy's Diabolical *Dames*: A Generic Consideration" (*Genre*, 1974) helpfully presents the stories in *A Group of Noble Dames* as a series of romantic treatments of extreme psychological types—in the tradition of Poe and Hawthorne but with the difference that Hardy's grotesque and often horrific episodes are firmly located in the real world rather than in the supernatural. Also valuable is Alexander Fischler's "Theatrical Techniques in Thomas Hardy's Short Stories" (*SSF*, 1966): its suggestive discussion of Hardy's fondness for "staging" opening tableaux and other scenic effects has an interest extending beyond the short stories themselves to wider issues of Hardy's handling of narrative distance and point of view.

These are, indeed, the issues on which much of the best Hardy criticism has been focused in recent years, but from a range of viewpoints so broad and various as to seem almost irreconcilable. At the moment, the Hardy field seems to lack any very distinctive character: there is immense, perhaps excessive, activity, but little sense of direction and cumulation. There exists a clear need for critics capable of absorbing what is most fruitful in such newer approaches as stylistics, structuralism, and hermeneutics and of pursuing the resulting insights without sacrificing the older virtues of close reading and persistent fidelity to the text of the individual work. In any case, comprehension of Hardy is likely to remain partial and fragmentary until the proper study of his fiction is understood as comprehending the minor as well as the major works, as demanding an adequate familiarity with the verse, and as ideally dependent upon a far richer knowledge of Hardy's life and times, his text and creative methods, than we have at present.

ROBERT LOUIS STEVENSON

Robert Kiely

Personal and literary charm has almost been the undoing of Robert Louis Stevenson. Most readers admit that he had it, but few can agree on a definition of what it is and whether or not it can be an advantage for a serious writer. To some, Stevenson's charm was a moral, almost heroic quality, bravery and good cheer in the face of pain and failure; to others, it was primarily an intellectual trait, a sign of an agile wit; to some it was a spiritual gift, an inner grace responsible for a charitable sensitivity to all mankind; to still others, it was a psychological problem, a neurotic defense for an extreme preoccupation with the self; and to many, Stevenson's charm was merely a trivial substitute for talent, a surface beneath which lay nothing much.

In an anthology of poetic tributes entitled *In Praise of Stevenson*, edited by Vincent Starrett in 1919, admirers like J. M. Barrie, Edmund Gosse, Andrew Lang, John Masefield, A. E. Housman, and Richard Burton refer to a mythical, magical, almost sacred Stevenson: "Prospero in Samoa"; "We hear you speak, like Moses"; "Scotland laments, 'Louis was my Benjamin' "; "Louis, our priest and our knight"; "that intimate and magic name." Even allowing for the fact that many of these tributes were written by grieving friends soon after Stevenson's death in 1894, the stress on intimacy and otherworldliness is significant. In his art as in his life, Stevenson seemed to offer something highly personal but at the same time elusive, precious but evanescent.

For the first half century after his death, the major efforts at understanding Stevenson were biographical. Scores of memoirs, recollections, tributes, small- and large-scale life studies appeared. Even the criticism of this period and earlier—by Henry James (1887), Frank Swinnerton (1914), G. K. Chesterton (1927)—consists of portraits of the artist drawn from his works. Only in the last fifteen to twenty years have critics tried—while acknowledging the power of Stevenson's personality—to assess rigorously and

systematically the aesthetic, moral, intellectual, and psychological quality o
his writing, particularly his prose fiction.

Part of the appeal as well as part of the problem in dealing with Steven
son studies is, then, that until quite recently they have tended to paralle
the direct and frequently emotional response to the man and to his sup
porters and detractors. The secondary literature about Stevenson and hi
work has a kind of melodrama and flair all its own. It is full of extremes—
saccharine eulogies and outrageous assaults, moving testimonials and
sentimental jingles, extravagant claims and condescending dismissals. From
the beginning, there were voices calling for balance and judicious calm
predicting a quick end to the furor and a settled "place" for Stevenson
among British writers. In his 1919 book of praises, Starrett observes that
"the proverbial pendulum still oscillates gently." Looking back on the fifty
ungentle years of criticism and biography following that statement, one
recognizes the degree of wishful thinking mixed with that modest admission
of discord and hesitates—even in this period of apparent critical objectivity
—to make complacent predictions for the future.

Bibliography

While no complete bibliography of Stevenson exists, there are two early
bibliographies and a number of quite recent catalogues of particular collections that are useful to the scholar. The oldest standard bibliographies are
W. F. Prideaux's *A Bibliography of the Works of Robert Louis Stevenson*
(1903; rev. F. V. Livingston, 1917) and J. H. Slater's *Robert Louis Stevenson: A Bibliography of His Complete Works* (1914). A later review of
Stevenson material is contained in T. G. Ehrsam and R. H. Deily's *Bibliographies of Twelve Victorian Authors* (1936). Though it makes no claim
to completeness, the most thorough general compilation of titles by and
about Stevenson is in J. C. Furnas' biography of Stevenson, *Voyage to
Windward* (1951). All of Stevenson's works through the serial publication
of *Treasure Island* in 1881 are listed in R. G. Swearingen's "Stevenson's
Prose Writings 1850–1881: An Index and Finding-List" (*SSL*, 1974).

The most important collections of Stevenson's surviving book-length
manuscripts are at Yale (the notebook version of *An Inland Voyage, the
Amateur Emigrant*, the intermediate version of *Dr. Jekyll and Mr. Hyde,
The Wrong Box, The Ebb-Tide*, and the intermediate versions of *Catriona*
and *St. Ives*), the Pierpont Morgan Library (*Dr. Jekyll and Mr. Hyde* and
Weir of Hermiston), the Huntington Library (notebook version of *Travels
with a Donkey, Kidnapped*, "The Beach of Falesá"), and the Widener
Collection at Harvard ("Memoirs of Himself" and the final version of
Catriona). Letters and other notebooks and fragments may be found by
consulting Stevenson catalogues, among the most important of which are
*Stevenson: 1850–1894, Catalogue of the Stevenson Collection, Edinburgh
Public Library* (1950); the six-volume compilation by George McKay of the
extraordinary holdings of the Beinecke Library at Yale, *A Stevenson Li-*

rary: Catalogue of a Collection of Writings by and about Robert Louis Stevenson Formed by Edward J. Beinecke (1951–64); and, most recently, Alexander Wainwright's *Robert Louis Stevenson: A Catalogue of the Henry E. Gerstley Stevenson Collection, the Stevenson Section of the Morris L. Parrish Collection of Victorian Novelists, and Items from Other Collections in the Department of Rare Books and Special Collections of the Princeton University Library* (1971).

Editions

There are several collected editions of Stevenson. Most are decent; two or three are particularly handsome; none is textually much more authoritative than another. The later editions include larger numbers of poems, essays, and letters, but all contain the major novels and short stories. The earliest collection, the first volumes of which were reviewed by Stevenson, is the Edinburgh edition (1894–98), which Sidney Colvin, Stevenson's friend and literary executor, began working on before the author's death. The Thistle (1902), Pentland (1906–07), and Swanston (1911–12) editions are alike in essentials except that the Pentland has an introductory essay by Edmund Gosse and the Swanston a long personal reminiscence and literary evaluation by Andrew Lang. Stevenson's widow and stepson edited the most beautiful collection in 1922–23, the Vailima, which includes "The Hanging Judge," new poems, and other material not in earlier editions. Unfortunately, parts of the previously unpublished material were inaccurately transcribed by Lloyd Osbourne and cannot be regarded as reliable. The most recent edition, the South Seas, published in thirty-two volumes in 1925, contains the largest collection of letters.

Two of the best selections of Stevenson's writings are *Novels and Stories by Robert Louis Stevenson* (1945), a compact volume with a perceptive introduction by V. S. Pritchett, and the comprehensive *Robert Louis Stevenson: Collected Poems* (1950; 2nd ed., 1971) edited by one of the major contributors to Stevenson scholarship and criticism in the past three decades, Janet Adam Smith. The most significant scholarly publication of particular works is James D. Hart's *From Scotland to Silverado* (1966), comprising "The Amateur Emigrant," "The Silverado Squatters," and four essays on California, that is, all Stevenson's previously published and unpublished writings about his trip to California in 1879–80. *The Amateur Emigrant* manuscript, Stevenson's essays on San Francisco and Monterey, and his contributions to the *Monterey Californian*, all edited by R. G. Swearingen, are scheduled to be published in limited editions by Lewis Osborne, Ashland, Oregon. A number of Stevenson's plays were privately printed during the 1920s. More recently, an unpublished play, "Antolycus in Service," has been edited from the Folger Library manuscript by N. B. Schiffman (Diss. Univ. of South Carolina 1973).

Recent translation activity in France includes publication of Pierre Leyris' version of several of the short stories (*Olalla des Montagnes et autres contes noirs*, 1975) and the launching of a projected series of translation under the editorship of Francis Lacassin, that will total twenty-two volume (Five of the volumes in this series have never been previously published i French.)

The paperback editions of Stevenson's works reflect his continuing pop larity among young readers and the growing interest in his work on the pa of scholars and critics. At this writing, there were twelve paperback edition of *Treasure Island* in print, eight of *Kidnapped*, and five of *Dr. Jekyll an Mr. Hyde*. Of particular note for students of Stevenson is the Dutton *Maste of Ballantrae*; the Riverside *Poetry and Prose of Robert Louis Stevenson* with a useful introduction by Bradford Booth; Hart's *From Scotland t Silverado* in Harvard paperback, and *In the South Seas* and *Island Night Entertainments*, both published in paper by the University of Hawaii Pres

Stevenson was a prolific, entertaining, and often spontaneous lette writer. After his death, Sidney Colvin, under the supervision of Mrs. Steve son, edited and published selected letters first in *Vailima Letters* (1895 then in the two-volume *Letters to His Family and Friends* (1899), an ultimately in an expanded four-volume edition entitled *The Letters o Robert Louis Stevenson* (1911). In an effort to protect Stevenson's literar and personal reputation as a cross between Peter Pan and St. Anthony o the Desert, Colvin not only omitted from publication but literally paste over references to sex, religion, money, and family that he thought migl put Stevenson in even the palest light of controversy. Whether or not thes deletions have had much effect on Stevenson's literary reputation is difficu to say, but they have undoubtedly contributed to the unjust caricature o Stevenson as a simpering moralist and thereby to the difficulty some reader have in trying to return to his work with an unprejudiced mind.

Two special collections of letters to particular friends have done much t show dimensions of Stevenson's mind and character that were diffused slighted, or distorted in the Colvin collection. Janet Adam Smith's *Henr James and Robert Louis Stevenson: A Record of Friendship and Criticis* (1948) contains all the known correspondence between the two author including five previously unpublished letters of Stevenson's, as well a James's "The Art of Fiction"; Stevenson's response, "A Humble Remon strance"; James's important 1887 essay "Robert Louis Stevenson"; and h 1899 review of *The Letters of Robert Louis Stevenson*, in which he refers t the "singular beauty" of the later correspondence and suggests that Steve son ranks with "the very first" of "our best letter-writers." In an exceller introduction, Smith explains why she wanted this material published in on place: "In the houses where James's novels are a long row in the study, mos of the Stevensons are up in the nursery or schoolroom. . . . Yet in the lifetime the two men were linked, not only by the closest ties of person affection, but by a common concern for the craft of the novelist and for th whole art of literature."

If Smith's collection shows Stevenson as a more serious, self-conscious, an mature craftsman than some readers have given him credit for, *R. L. S*

evenson's *Letters to Charles Baxter* (1956), compiled by DeLancey
rguson and Marshall Waingrow, reveals him as a loyal flesh-and-blood
iend unafraid to betray doubt, anger, distress, and confusion, as well as
it and moral strength. Stevenson's association with Baxter, dating back to
udent days in Edinburgh, was one of his closest and longest friendships. Of
e 250 letters that Stevenson is known to have written Baxter, Colvin used
out one fifth, and, as the editors of the 1956 compilation point out, "the
ajority of [Colvin's] texts are incomplete, frequently without marks of
mission." The Ferguson-Waingrow book therefore "is the first time that
e complete correspondence [to Baxter] has been published."

Clearly, one of the great needs in Stevenson scholarship is an authorita-
ve edition of the complete letters. At the time of his death, Bradford
ooth had undertaken this project and had published an account of his
ork in progress in *The Harvard Library Bulletin* of April 1967 under the
tle "The Vailima Letters of Robert Louis Stevenson." Among other find-
gs, Booth noted the extreme financial pressure brought to bear on Steven-
n by his wife and her family. Ernest J. Mayhew is completing the edition
f the letters left unfinished by Booth, and it is expected that the first
olumes will be published by Yale University Press within a year or two.
n the meantime, apart from the James and Baxter collections and quota-
ons in the Balfour and Furnas biographies, Colvin remains the scholar's
nly source for the correspondence. And, as Janet Adam Smith observes,
Sooner or later, the student of Stevenson finds that his gratitude to Sidney
olvin for preserving and collecting Stevenson's letters is swallowed up in
xasperation at his handling of them."

Biography

he biographical warfare over Stevenson began in 1901 soon after the pub-
cation of the official family-approved *The Life of Robert Louis Stevenson*
y Graham Balfour, a cousin who had spent two and a half years with the
riter in Vailima. Relying heavily on family documents, Balfour stresses
tevenson's personal attractiveness and moral virtue. He praises his energy,
ersatility, and generosity, dwells on his courage in the midst of suffering,
nd even excuses slips into banality by saying, "Whenever he uttered a com-
on-place, it will usually be found that he had discovered the truth of it for
imself." Through his rare combination of sympathy and charm, Stevenson,
n Balfour's view, was inspiration personified: "Besides admiration and
ope, he has raised within the hearts of his readers a personal feeling
owards himself which is nothing less deep than love."

W. E. Henley, who had been a friend and collaborator in Stevenson's
arly days and who had written a famous and affectionate jingle entitled
Apparition" in the series *In Hospital* (1873–75), attributed considerably
ore spice to Stevenson's character:

A deal of Ariel, just a streak of Puck,
Much of Antony, of Hamlet most of all,
And something of the Shorter-Catechist.

Even in the early days Henley did not think of his friend in the same wa
Balfour did, and by 1901 he looked back on a bitter break with Stevenso
and the many years in which Stevenson's literary and personal reputatio
had far outshone his own. In response to Balfour's biography, Henley pul
lished an essay in the December 1901 issue of *Pall Mall Magazine* entitle
"R. L. S.," which coined some new phrases and established the battle line
over Stevenson for years to come. "I take a view of Stevenson which is m
own, and which declines to be concerned with this Seraph in Chocolate, th
barley-sugar effigy of a real man." For Henley there were two Stevensons, h
vivacious young friend and the famous and pious moralizer who "is not m
old, riotous, intrepid, scornful Stevenson at all." Henley dismisses Stever
son's books and his much acclaimed style as "so perfectly achieved that th
achievement gets obvious." In a final outburst of resentment and candor, h
says that he prefers to remember Stevenson "before his books began to se
and his personality was a marketable thing."

Alexander H. Japp in *Robert Louis Stevenson: A Record, an Estimate
and a Memorial* (1905) acknowledges the charm of the "scornful" Stevenso
but does not agree that he had become too moralistic: "Owing to some kin
or twist, due, perhaps, mainly to his earlier sufferings, and the teachings h
then received, he could not help giving it always a turn to what he himsel
called 'tailforemost' or inverted morality." The most insistent theme i
Japp's book and one that informed Stevenson studies for the following thre
decades is summed up in one short sentence: "It is impossible to separat
Stevenson from his work."

Few biographers took Japp's view more literally than E. Blantyre Simp
son, who in *The Robert Louis Stevenson Originals* (1913) searches throug
Stevenson's writings for real-life prototypes on the ground that "all hi
works are legible signposts which point to his routes through life." Anothe
more picturesque version of the same approach is Clayton Hamilton's *O
the Trail of Stevenson* (1915), which has Walter Hale's handsome illustra
tions of the places where Stevenson lived and visited and commentaries o
their importance in his writing.

Though there had been poems, reviews, short recollections, and the Bal
four *Life* earlier, the 1920s witnessed the largest outpouring of book-length
biographies and reminiscences by Stevenson's family and friends. Despit
sentimental rhetoric, most contain enough that is genuine to be of continu
ing interest to the student of Stevenson's life. The works of particular not
in this category are *Robert Louis Stevenson*, by Isobel Osbourne Strong
Field (1920); *I Can Remember Robert Louis Stevenson*, edited by Rosalin
Masson (1922); *An Intimate Portrait of Robert Louis Stevenson*, by Lloy
Osbourne (1924); *Cummy's Diary*, by Alison Cunningham (1926); and *R. L
S. and His Sine Qua Non*, by Adelaide Boodle (1926).

The two most important biographical studies of Stevenson in the 1920s give new life to the controversy over his personality and moral character by introducing the subject of sex and, more specifically, an alleged liaison in his Edinburgh days with a girl named Claire. In *Robert Louis Stevenson: Man and Writer* (1924), J. A. Steuart promises to be more objective than Balfour and to avoid further sweetening of "the barley-sugar effigy." Although Steuart introduces Claire and refuses to accord Stevenson major status as a writer, his terms are euphemistic and his tone protective, so that the effect is still largely hagiographic: "If Robert Louis Stevenson in his youth sowed wild oats with a somewhat lavish hand, did not Augustine and certain other eminent saints do the same?" For Steuart, Claire, like the consumption, was something Stevenson got over, and that is what counts: "It is his valour, tried as by fire at many a turn, more than ought else that enchants, inspires, and endears him to the people of two hemispheres." George S. Hellman in *The True Stevenson: A Study in Clarification* (1925) protests that "the desire to discuss the remissness of others happens to be alien to my temperament" and then proceeds with the relish of a Hercule Poirot to uncover the evidence for Stevenson's sexual relationship with Claire and with Fanny before their marriage and to disclose various expressions of religious skepticism that had been suppressed by the family. For Steuart, Stevenson was still a saint; for Hellman, he became a hypocrite, a fraud, and a failure: "a frustrated protagonist in the fight to free literature from the manacles of narrow morality . . . an oversexed man who has for generations been held up for the emulation of youth; a devoted artist who yet relinquished themes that seemed to him of preponderant significance for art and life; a delightful egoist who remains an examplar of abnegation and self-denial."

No new biographical information was brought out in the following two decades, and the flow of reminiscences began quite naturally to subside. Jean-Marie Carré's *The Frail Warrior* (1930), translated from the French by Eleanor Hard, continued the popular tradition of the heroic invalid. Janet Adam Smith's *R. L. Stevenson* (1937) is a straightforward, compact contribution to the Great Lives series. Though essentially a summary of previously published facts, it has the freshness and good sense characteristic of all Smith's work on Stevenson. Her prose is direct and lucid, neither clouded by worshipful mists nor edgy with an appetite for character assassination. Moreover, without going into literary criticism, she concludes the book by taking issue with the doctrine that Stevenson's works cannot be separated from his life: "All that made him different was largely irrelevant to his life as a writer. His story was full of romantic accidents; but he has other claims to be remembered."

The best-informed, most balanced, and still the most nearly authoritative biography of Stevenson is *Voyage to Windward: The Life of Robert Louis Stevenson*, by J. C. Furnas (1951). Access to unpublished letters and other material, as well as the passage of years, provided Furnas with the ideal opportunity to write a new life. As he himself puts it: "With the centenary

of his birth, much fresh evidence, clearing up important passages in his li
that were hitherto obscure, has come available. This novel of actuality, th
case history with the values of fiction, demands full retelling." Furnas' sty
is novelistic, but the substance of the book is the fruit of diligent resear<
and judicious reflection. In addition to an extensive bibliography of wor
about Stevenson, there are excellent appendixes on the history of Steve
son's reputation and on the controversy surrounding Claire. No furth
work on the life of Stevenson can proceed without reference to Furnas.

Two other biographies of Stevenson that appeared in the 1950s are M<
colm Elwin's *The Strange Case of Robert Louis Stevenson* (1950), in whic
most of Stevenson's troubles are blamed on his marriage to Fanny, ar
Richard Aldington's more moderate *Portrait of a Rebel* (1957).

More recent biographical studies have not replaced Furnas, but have on
added individual touches to the portrait. *Last Witness for Robert Lou
Stevenson* (1960) was written by Elsie Noble Caldwell, a close friend <
Stevenson's stepdaughter, Isobel. Based on personal accounts by Isobel an
on family documents relating to the final years in Samoa, it is a defense <
Stevenson's private and public life among the islanders. Of particular inte
est to students of Stevenson's marriage, Margaret Mackay's *The Violer
Friend: The Story of Mrs. Robert Louis Stevenson* (1968) presents a mor
sympathetic view than Elwin's of Fanny's influence on Stevenson's reput
tion before and after his death. David Daiches' *Robert Louis Stevenson an
His World* (1973) is a short, generously illustrated sketch of Stevenson's li
and times.

The latest biography of Stevenson is James Pope Hennessy's *Robert Lou
Stevenson* (1974), a balanced, cultivated, gentlemanly reassembling of th
familiar material. What is of note about Hennessy's biography, other tha
its elegance and good sense, is that it returns Stevenson to the realm <
polite and literate popular culture. Hennessy does not assume that his read
ers will be shocked by the "revelations" of the 1920s, nor does he wish 1
claim too much, morally or aesthetically, for Stevenson. He calls him "th
great exhilarator," drawing attention to an achievement less easy to take fc
granted in the 1970s than in the 1920s. He also says that Stevenson "ha
style" as a writer and as a man, leaving it to the critics to work out th
details but allowing no doubt that he himself thinks it was an extremel
good thing to have had.

It should be noted that a hardy subspecies of Stevenson biography is th
"regional life," a category of books that treat his artistic and other activitie
in the various parts of the world-where he lived or visited. Although th
important regional details have been incorporated into the major biogra
phies, these specialized studies abound, and even a partial listing gives som
idea of their range and of Stevenson's importance as a traveler and loc<
colorist: Arthur Johnstone's *Recollections of Robert Louis Stevenson in th
Pacific* (1905); Katharine Q. Osbourne's *Robert Louis Stevenson in Cal
fornia* (1911); E. Blantyre Simpson's *Robert Louis Stevenson's Edinburg
Days* (1913); Stephen Chalmer's *The Penny Piper of Saranac* (1916); W. C
Lockett's *Robert Louis Stevenson at Davos* (n.d.); David B. Morris' *Rober

Louis Stevenson and the Scottish Highlanders (1929); Richard A. Bermann's *Home from the Sea: Robert Louis Stevenson in Samoa* (1939); Anne Roller Issler's *Stevenson at Silverado* (1939); *Happier for His Presence: San Francisco and Robert Louis Stevenson* (1949); *Our Mountain Hermitage* 1950); Martha Mary McGaw's *Stevenson in Hawaii* (1950); Moray McLaren's *Stevenson and Edinburgh* (1950); and Edward Rice's *Journey to Upolu: Robert Louis Stevenson, Victorian Rebel* (1974).

Despite all this activity by the biographers there still remains a gap to fill. While the Furnas biography has been of great value, it is not sufficiently detailed or comprehensive to qualify as a definitive life of Stevenson. A scholarly biography with extensive critical evaluation of the literary achievement as it relates to the life, as planned by R. G. Swearingen, is still very much needed.

Criticism

Early Commentaries

The extraordinary interest in Stevenson the man colored criticism of his writing so much that the tone, if not the explicit subject, of early commentaries is nearly always personal. Even the most judicious essays seem either affectionate or hostile rather than merely positive or negative, as though the man behind the sentences were always somehow clearly in view. The earliest, most extended, and most important piece of criticism in this vein is Henry James's "Robert Louis Stevenson" (1888), first published in the *Century Magazine* and later reprinted in *Partial Portraits*. James, of course, knew and liked Stevenson, and there is mention of his charm and boyishness in the essay, but the main portion of the piece deals with Stevenson's essays, stories, and novels. James singles out two aspects of Stevenson's craft that later critics would come back to again and again: his elegant prose style and his growing power as a serious narrative artist.

James's description of Stevenson's style is itself a stylistic tour de force. He wonders, metaphorically, whether Stevenson would pose in the nude, quickly concludes that he would not, and then likens his style to "a complexity of curious and picturesque garments." He distinguishes between those who consider literary form "a code of signals" or "words as numbers" and Stevenson, for whom language is "as the keyboard of a piano." He praises Stevenson for having a "manner" and for being "gallant" with words "as if language were a pretty woman and a person who proposes to handle it had, of necessity, to be something of a Don Juan." The grace, precision, and musical beauty of Stevenson's style deserve to be admired in themselves, according to James, but his later fiction (meaning especially *Kidnapped*, since this essay was written in 1887) reveals a psychological depth and dramatic force, an ability to represent "the very logic and rhythm of life" of the sort associated with novel writing at its best.

In the years immediately preceding and following Stevenson's death, before the book-length assessments began to appear, a large number of shorter critical pieces—periodical essays, reviews, and lectures—were published. In the *Atlantic Monthly* of April 1895, C. T. Copeland, Lecturer in English at Harvard, wrote a detailed and laudatory critique, indicative of the high esteem in which Stevenson was held in America. Copeland stresses the quality of Stevenson's style, calls him "the most impeccable of artists," a writer whose work sustains "the classic note of the best English prose."

The debate over Stevenson's future place among men of letters also began in the periodicals. In the *Bookman* of February 1895, Ian Maclaren declares that "our master," Stevenson, "will go to the high table and sit down with Virgil and Shakespeare and Goethe and Scott." Not many years later, Clement K. Shorter asserts in *Sphere* (7 Dec. 1901) that "Robert Louis Stevenson is not an epoch-making writer; he has no place with the very greatest masters in fiction or in thoughtful essay-writing." Though most critical attention was paid to Stevenson's prose, some notice was taken of his poetry and drama. Edmund Gosse in *Questions at Issue* (1893) published a revised version of an earlier essay claiming brilliance for Stevenson's poetry, though of a less sustained and developed kind than one finds in the prose. In a lecture on "Robert Louis Stevenson: The Dramatist," delivered in 1903, Arthur Wing Pinero argues that Stevenson had the talent to be a great playwright but that he did not take the theater seriously enough or work hard enough on his dramatic pieces to achieve his potential. Portions of this lecture and other occasional and periodical commentaries, primarily from the last two decades of the nineteenth century, were collected and edited by J. A. Hammerton in *Stevensoniana* (1903).

The difficulty of separating personal from literary considerations persisted even in those early full-length studies that claimed criticism as their only aim. In the first critical book about Stevenson, *Robert Louis Stevenson: A Critical Study* (1914), Frank Swinnerton insists that he is not writing a biography or an appreciation, but, as his subtitle says, a critical study. Yet, though he moves title by title through Stevenson's works, Swinnerton's method is neither detached nor analytical. His book is a series of opinions, purportedly about the writings, but really about the man. He speaks of Stevenson's nervous, vain, and superficial charm, his "Puritanical obtuseness," his tendency "to love uncritically." In a judgment typical of his confused focus, Swinnerton observes that all Stevenson's works "are seen nowadays to be consumptive." His conclusion is not a literary one at all but an unsubstantiated attack on Stevenson's honesty: "If it spring not from a personal vision of life, but is only a tedious virtuosity, a pretence, a conscious toy, romance as an art is dead. . . . And if it is dead, Stevenson killed it."

In the next major critical study of Stevenson, *Robert Louis Stevenson* (1927), G. K. Chesterton also feels the need to declare at the outset that "this is not a biography." But he at least admits being fascinated by Stevenson's personality and acknowledges the difficulty the critic faces in trying to avoid talking about it. Chesterton's solution is to review Stevenson's books

'with illustrations from his life; rather than to write his life with illustrations from his books." The result is impressionistic, digressive, epigrammatic
—what one expects from Chesterton—not more analytical than Swinnerton,
but a great deal more self-aware, intelligent, and entertaining. When he
does, from time to time, circle in on the books, Chesterton shows himself
sensitive to language and literary convention. He dissociates himself from
the "Victorian whitewashers and the post-Victorian mud-slingers" and, true
to his word, does not claim too much for Stevenson. His book is finally a
defense, not so much of the personality, but of the mood and style of the
books. He argues, for example, that the originality of *Treasure Island* derives from its appearing "in an age shadowed by Schopenhauer and Wells.
. . . 'Yo ho ho' was precisely what Stevenson, with his exact choice of words,
particularly desired to say just then."

The period from the late 1920s until the late 1940s was the low point in
Stevenson's reputation as a serious writer—though he was still considered
entertaining for the young—and a time when little sustained critical attention was paid to his writings in England and America. In fact, in America,
where acclaim for his work had once been second only to that of his native
Scotland, Thomas Beer in *The Mauve Decade* (1926) could refer to a
fourteen-year period, as if to a closed episode, when "a moving syrup of
appreciation supported the gay invalid on its sweetness." The most serious
investigation of Stevenson in these decades was a moral and literary evaluation published in France, *La Vocation de Robert Louis Stevenson* (1930),
by L. E. Chrétien.

Later Studies

After the twenty-year lull in Stevenson criticism, the first effort at a
general reassessment was David Daiches' remarkable contribution to The
Makers of Modern Literature series entitled *Robert Louis Stevenson: A
Revaluation* (1947). Compact and unpretentious, Daiches' book is nonetheless an excellent general introduction to Stevenson's writing and the first
since James that is neither defensive nor hostile. Daiches notes the lack of
interest in Stevenson since the passing of the "cult" and yet argues that his
'writings are worth serious examination. They possess qualities of craftsmanship which make many a contemporary novelist look silly, and, further,
his literary ideals and his attitude to art represent an important development in modern literature." Daiches stresses the importance of Stevenson's
romanticism, his Scottish background, and, most interestingly—given the
problems Stevenson's personality seems to have created for other critics—his
ability to transform his own impulses and experiences into literature.
Daiches sees Stevenson as a prototype of the modern literary exile: "His
greatest achievement was to use nostalgia dramatically, to suppress all personal emotion while utilizing that emotion in serious (sometimes tragic)
fiction. This transmuting of autobiographical into aesthetic impulses is an
impressive achievement, and . . . one which only Joyce has surpassed." In a

lecture, later published as *Stevenson and the Art of Fiction* (1951), Daiches extends his discussion of Stevenson's aesthetics and the moral patterns of his work.

Daiches, while acknowledging Stevenson's talents as a poet and essayist stresses the art of narrative as his primary gift. In *Robert Louis Stevenson and the Fiction of Adventure* (1964), Robert Kiely undertakes the first extensive and detailed textual analysis of Stevenson's major novels and short fiction. By assembling and interpreting critical statements in essays reviews, and correspondence, Kiely reconstructs Stevenson's aesthetic theory the evolution of which can be traced in the novels and short stories Through close readings of the boy's adventure books, comic satires, island fables, and epic novels, Kiely follows the transition in Stevenson's fiction "from sleight of hand to artistry, from adventure as an entertaining counterfeit to adventure as a symbolic chart of the formidable risks in which life involves all men." Edwin M. Eigner in *Robert Louis Stevenson and Romantic Tradition* (1966) takes Stevenson's fiction with equal seriousness but lays his emphasis on Stevenson's place in the tradition of the nineteenth century romance, dwelling on literary parallels, influences, and conventions particularly that of the doppelgänger. A more specialized attempt to place Stevenson in a literary tradition is Harold Francis Watson's *Coasts of Treasure Island: A Study of Backgrounds and Sources for Robert Louis Stevenson's Romance of the Sea* (1969). A history of the "nautical novel' from 1800 until 1881 and a discussion of possible sources for *Treasure Island*, the book treats Stevenson's most famous adventure novel as "an example, and in some sort the culmination, of the nineteenth century tale of the sea."

The most recent book-length critical study of Stevenson is Irving S. Saposnik's *Robert Louis Stevenson* (1974). Composed of a short outline of Stevenson's life and a commentary on the plays, poems, essays, and fiction, the study is in line with recent efforts to take Stevenson as a mature writer whose romances have deep roots in real human experience. The discussions of the psychological patterns in "Markheim" and *Dr. Jekyll and Mr. Hyde* are particularly refreshing, but the book's format is too much that of the short survey to allow for fully developed analyses of most of Stevenson's writing. Nearly everything is touched on, but very little is dwelt upon at sufficient length.

References to Stevenson's style occupy paragraphs and pages in a large number of general critical studies and collections of belles lettres in England and America by writers as diverse as John Jay Chapman and Virginia Woolf. H. W. Garrod's two essays on "The Poetry of R. L. Stevenson" in *The Profession of Poetry* (1929) and *Essays Mainly on the Nineteenth Century Presented to Sir Humphrey Milford* (1948) are among the most appreciative and extensive analyses of Stevenson's verse. Some of the more recent and noteworthy chapters on Stevenson's fiction appear in Leslie Fiedler's *No! In Thunder* (1960), which claims, among other things, that "pre-sexual" flirtations take place among the male characters of *Treasure*

Island and *Kidnapped*; Paul Goetsch's *Die Romankonzeption in England 1880–1910* (1967); W. W. Robson's "The Sea Cook: A Study in the Art of Robert Louis Stevenson," in *On the Novel: A Present for Walter Allen from His Friends and Colleagues*, ed. B. S. Benedikz (1971); Barbara Hannah's *Striving towards Wholeness* (1971), a muddled Jungian study of Stevenson, Mary Welch, and the Brontës; and Hans G. Hönig's somewhat mechanical *Studien zur englischen Short Story am Ende des 19 Jahrhunderts: Stevenson, Hardy, Kipling und Wells* (1971).

The pattern of periodical articles about Stevenson has roughly paralleled that of the book-length studies, though at the beginning the articles preceded and often influenced the writing of the books and more recently the books have tended to reawaken interest in Stevenson and stimulate the writing of articles. As has been shown, the periodical criticism of Stevenson's works from the 1880s through the 1920s was largely impressionistic and personal. From the 1930s on into the 1950s reference to Stevenson in critical periodicals is casual and sporadic. Since the publication, between the late 1940s and the early 1960s, of the works of restoration by Smith, Daiches, Furnas, Hart, and Kiely, the periodical literature on Stevenson has once again begun to flow.

Two short studies of Stevenson's moral essays are particularly worth mentioning, Merle M. Bevington's "Locke and Stevenson on Comparative Morality" (*N&Q*, 1960) and F. C. Riedel's "A Classical Rhetorical Analysis of Some Elements of Stevenson's Essay Style" (*Style*, 1969). Two valuable articles on the Scottish connection are Nathaniel Elliott's "Robert Louis Stevenson and Scottish Literature" (*ELT*, 1969) and Fred B. Warner, Jr.'s "Stevenson's First Scottish Story" (*NCF*, 1969). By far the greater number of recent critical essays has focused on individual works of fiction, reflecting an increased interest in Stevenson's narrative art and its moral and psychological implications. Joseph J. Egan has published several provocative articles showing symbolic and thematic patterns in particular works: " 'Markheim': A Drama of Moral Psychology" (*NCF*, 1966); "From History to Myth: A Symbolic Reading of *The Master of Ballantrae*" (*SEL*, 1968); "Dark in the Poet's Corner: Stevenson's 'A Lodging for the Night' " (*SSF*, 1970); and "Grave Sites and Moral Death: A Reexamination of Stevenson's 'The Body Snatcher' " (*ELT*, 1970). Other worthwhile studies tracing narrative patterns of particular works include Robert E. Bonds's "The Mystery of *The Master of Ballantrae*" (*ELT*, 1964); Irving S. Saposnik's "Stevenson's 'Markheim': A Fictional Christmas Sermon" (*NCF*, 1966); and F. B. Warner's "The Significance of Stevenson's 'Providence and the Guitar' " (*ELT*, 1971).

Contemporary commentaries on Stevenson's language pay relatively little attention to the celebrated musicality of his style but a good deal to the structural and stylistic techniques that contribute to the total effect of a particular work. As earlier critics had once praised or condemned Stevenson for a style that seemed splendid (or superficial) enough to be considered separately from substance or meaning, modern critics have explored what they regard as the necessary relationship between Stevenson's craft and the total significance of his literary work. Among the best articles in this vein have been James F. Kilroy's "Narrative Techniques in *The Master of Ballantrae*" (*SSL*, 1967); James Walt's comparison of "Stevenson's 'Will o' the Mill' and James's 'The Beast in the Jungle' " (*UES*, 1970); Anne M. Scott's "The Images of Light in Stevenson's *Weir of Hermiston*" (*English*, 1970); and Hayden W. Ward's " 'The Pleasure of Your Heart': *Treasure Island* and the Appeal of Boys' Adventure Fiction" (*SNNTS*, 1974).

No other works of Stevenson have received so much attention as *Treasure Island* and *The Strange Case of Dr. Jekyll and Mr. Hyde*. Both have appeared in hundreds of separate editions, collections, and translations. And both have been made more than once into popular, even sensational, films. Spencer Tracy's Dr. Jekyll had moments of genuine power amid the otherwise melodramatic rendering of the story. (One wishes that some talented director would stumble on Dylan Thomas' script of *The Beach of Falesá*, published by Stein and Day in 1963.) But, though both *Treasure Island* and *Jekyll and Hyde* have continued to inspire the most popular interest in Stevenson, *Jekyll and Hyde* has monopolized the attention of critics. From the beginning, critics have debated over the story, some arguing that it is a grotesque melodrama with little serious significance, others that it is a moral allegory with stern Scottish Puritan overtones, and still others that, beneath the melodramatic and allegorical surface, lie profound psychological insights. Recent critics have tended to take the last position, as can be seen in Masao Miyoshi's "Dr. Jekyll and the Emergence of Mr. Hyde" (*CE*, 1966), Joseph J. Egan's "The Relationship of Theme and Art in *The Strange Case of Dr. Jekyll and Mr. Hyde*" (*ELT*, 1966), Irving S. Saposnik's "The Anatomy of *Dr. Jekyll and Mr. Hyde*" (*SEL*, 1971; rpt. as Ch. vi in his *Robert Louis Stevenson*, 1974), and Frank Zaic's "Robert Louis Stevenson: *The Strange Case of Dr. Jekyll and Mr. Hyde*," in *Der englische Roman im 19 Jahrhundert: Interpretationen* (ed. P. Goetsch, H. Kosok, and K. Otten, 1973).

It is clear that following the uproar and the lull critics have, with persisting rigor, taken up Stevenson's texts, especially the fiction, examined them, and found them mature and rich in themselves as well as indicative of important literary changes that brought about the great modernist experiments of the twentieth century. For a long time it seemed that Stevenson's art depended so much on the presence or at least the memory of the man that it could last only so long as there were those who remembered or could conjure up the author. It appeared, in other words, as if Stevenson's writing were an extended form of conversation, with the charms but also the limitations that implies. Stevenson once wrote that "it is the mark of genuine conversation that the sayings can scarce be quoted with their full effect beyond the circle of common friends. To have their proper weight they should appear in a biography, and with the portrait of the speaker." Perhaps the most important achievement of modern Stevenson criticism is that it has shown that his best work has survived the portraits and the "circle of common friends" and is therefore not merely better than good conversation but altogether different.

In addition to the publication of the complete letters and of a comprehensive and scholarly biography, one looks forward to continued efforts to examine his fiction within the tradition of the serious novel and to critical works that will explore, not Stevenson's sentimental ties with family and friends, but his literary and intellectual associations with contemporaries other than James and his relationship to the late Victorian period as a whole.

GEORGE MOORE

Jacob Korg

George Moore continues to be regarded as a novelist who is insufficiently appreciated, and studies devoted to him are often offered as "revivals" or "revaluations." The main collections of his books and manuscripts are outside England, and research on him has been largely the domain of French and American scholars. It is striking, in particular, that his leading critic is a French graduate of the Sorbonne. But the situation appears to be changing: there are clear signs that English critics are beginning to take a renewed interest in Moore.

Primary Materials and Major Studies

There is no unified listing of the abundant Moore research material in various collections, and information about it is hard to find. Most of it is in the United States, but widely scattered; the manuscript of *Esther Waters*, for example, is divided among at least four libraries. Of the libraries listed in *NCBEL* as possessing Moore materials, the New York Public Library (Berg Collection) has a large number of significant editions and proof sheets, miscellaneous manuscript materials, and many letters, including 209 to T. Fisher Unwin, which have been published in *George Moore in Transition* (see below); and the Humanities Research Center at the University of Texas has miscellaneous proofs, typed manuscripts, and numerous letters, including 540 to W. K. Magee and 63 to David Garnett. In addition to those listed in *NCBEL* the following libraries have significant Moore collections: Cornell University Library (Frank Fayant Collection), Arizona State University, the Huntington Library, the Fountain Lawn Library of Bucknell University, and New York University Library (Fales Collection).

If Moore's case is an example, literary revivals move very slowly. Malcolm Brown's study of 1955, the first book-length work on Moore in many years, was called *George Moore: A Reconsideration*, but, as late as 1970, Martin Seymour-Smith in an article titled "Rediscovering George Moore" observed:

"Far from having left Moore behind, we are only just beginning to catch up with him now." Moore criticism has increased and become somewhat more specialized in recent years, and about half a dozen of his best-known titles have been reprinted. The most significant of these is the variorum edition of *Confessions of a Young Man* edited by Susan Dick (1972), which reproduces the text of the first edition with variant readings from the nine other versions Moore published, together with an introduction, critical notes, and an index.

The most substantial recent contributions to Moore studies have been *George Moore: L'Homme et l'œuvre (1852–1933)*, by Jean C. Noël (1966), a Sorbonne thesis of seven hundred pages that ranks as the most massive and informative work on Moore ever published; *A Bibliography of George Moore*, by Edwin Gilcher (1970), a thorough and specialized descriptive bibliography of Moore's publications; and *George Moore in Transition: Letters to T. Fisher Unwin and Lena Milman, 1894–1910*, edited by Helmut E. Gerber (1968). In addition, two useful collections of criticism have appeared: *George Moore's Mind and Art*, edited by Graham Owens (1968), which contains both reprinted and original material on Moore's style, development, and Wagnerian interests; and *The Man of Wax: Critical Essays on George Moore*, edited by Douglas A. Hughes (1971), which consists entirely of reprinted essays and excerpts, together with a chronology and a bibliography.

Noël's *George Moore: L'Homme et l'œuvre* examines all of Moore's writing within the framework of his life, personality, and times, on an appropriately elaborate scale. It is Noël's general view that Moore's energies were essentially egocentric but that he made intellectual and artistic progress by assimilating those qualities of the men he met and the books he read that had affinities with latent aspects of his own character. Noël is particularly successful in arguing that the apparent inconsistencies of Moore's career were simply varied efforts to achieve absolute honesty and sincerity. He sees Moore's first, or "impressionist," period as one in which he adopted different ways of resolving the conflict between his own feelings and the facts of life he encountered, sometimes yielding to sensuousness or sentimentality, sometimes acknowledging the claims of realism. After achieving a certain equilibrium in *Esther Waters*, Moore turned to a quest for forms and styles capable of expressing his personal philosophy. The search for a medium was accompanied by a growing awareness of the general problems of humanity, which, according to Noël, became the dominant concern of Moore's work after *The Brook Kerith*. Noël feels that, in this last stage of his development, Moore achieved enough self-knowledge to overcome his egotism and to write altruistic novels embodying his ideal of pure narrative form.

George Moore: L'Homme et l'œuvre contains an enormous amount of biographical, critical, and bibliographical information and is well qualified to serve as a Moore encyclopedia (though its proofreading, at least in the English passages, is quite undependable). Each of its four main sections is preceded by a year-by-year chronology of Moore's publications, readings, travels, and miscellaneous activities, and the footnotes are generously informative. There are some interesting illustrations, a bibliography of secondary sources, and an extensive descriptive bibliography (in French) which occupies about a fifth of the volume.

The bibliographical section of Noël's book has been superseded, at least for English readers, by Edwin Gilcher's more complete and more thoroughly detailed *Bibliography of George Moore*. In his introduction Gilcher states that his aim is "not only to describe fully all of Moore's works in first editions, both English and American . . . but also all subsequent editions containing substantial revisions, briefly noting the extent of the rewriting and listing subsequent editions of a particular text. In addition, for the benefit of collectors detailed descriptions are given of all illustrated, signed and limited editions." Gilcher's bibliography is a definitive record of Moore's publications and is likely to remain the best source of information about them for some time. Listings of recent and current publications on Moore appear among the annotated bibliographies published periodically in *English Literature in Transition*.

Two of Moore's books have recently been translated. *Esther Waters* has appeared in an Italian translation by Mario Praz (Milan, 1970), and *Celibate Lives* has been translated into French by Pierre Leyris as *Albert Nobbs et autres vies sans hymen* (1971).

In *George Moore in Transition: Letters to T. Fisher Unwin and Lena Milman, 1894–1910* Helmut E. Gerber has constructed a solidly informative volume around some three hundred letters by providing extensive connective comments, which make up more than half the text. The letters are of interest mainly as sources of information about the composition and publication of Moore's books. The volume approaches the status of a life and letters for the sixteen-year period covered, focusing principally on Moore's work and the publishing scene. (Gerber reports that he is editing a second annotated collection of Moore's correspondence; larger and more significant than the first, it will contain about thirteen hundred letters to and by Moore, most of them previously unpublished.)

Two of Moore's traits emerge sharply from this mass of material. First, he regarded the publisher as a subordinate who must obey the author's orders about such questions as typefaces, pressruns, royalties, and, above all, revisions and reissues. Second, he had a mania for revision, a practice whose results continue to provide scholars with tasks of collation and analysis. Moore could not see his work in print without embarking on more or less extensive revision, and he could apparently rework the same material indefinitely. Gerber seems justified in concluding that this shows, not perfectionism, but a chronic indecisiveness, a view supported by the studies Jay Jernigan has made of the texts of two of the novels. In "The Forgotten Serial Version of George Moore's *Esther Waters*" (*NCF*, 1968) Jernigan describes the hitherto unrecorded appearance of ten chapters of the novel in the *Pall Mall Gazette* of October 1893, in a version that was revised before its publication in book form the following year. And in "The Bibliographical and Textual Complexities of George Moore's *A Mummer's Wife*"

BNYPL, 1970) he compares four separate versions, showing that while the
first revision was limited to stylistic improvements, the last, published in
1917, thirty-two years after the first edition, amounted to a thorough rewriting, with one quarter of the original text omitted and changes on nearly
every page. Noël, who devotes a long section of his book to a study of
Moore's revisions, identifies a number of motives for them: economy,
euphony, the substitution of concrete language for abstractions, the improvement of narrative structure, the introduction of new ideas, and, as
Jernigan also finds, the sharpening and even radical alteration of character
delineation.

Biography and Topical Criticism

The volumes by Noël and Gerber have made substantial contributions to
what is known of Moore's life and thoughts, and a number of recent books
and articles add information about specific topics, especially the relations
between Moore and other literary figures.

Influences

His relations with Yeats are discussed by Ann Saddlemyer in " 'All Art
Is a Collaboration'? George Moore and Edward Martyn" (*The World of W.
B. Yeats*, ed. Robin Skelton and Ann Saddlemyer, 1965); by Jack Wayne
Weaver in "An Exile Returned: Moore and Yeats in Ireland" (*Éire*, 1968);
and by Meredith Cary in "Yeats and Moore: An Autobiographical Conflict"
(*Éire*, 1969). Sara Ruth Watson in "George Moore and the Dolmetsches"
(*ELT*, 1963) describes Moore's participation in the circle of artists and
writers who attended the concerts given by Arnold Dolmetsch in his Dulwich home beginning in 1894. Moore's interest in aestheticism and in the
renewal of lost cultures, especially the Irish, led him to support Dolmetsch's
revival of ancient instruments and music. Watson shows that he drew on his
visits to Dulwich for *Evelyn Innes*, using Dolmetsch as a model for Mr.
Innes and incorporating into the novel some of his lore about ancient
music. Vineta Colby in her study of nineteenth-century female writers, *The
Singular Anomaly* (1970), reviews the relationship between Moore and Mrs.
Pearl Richards Craigie, the novelist who wrote under the pseudonym John
Oliver Hobbes. Moore collaborated with Mrs. Craigie in writing plays, and
she figures in his writing both as the subject of some damaging comments in
his autobiographies and as the original of a number of his heroines, including Evelyn Innes and Mildred Lawson.

Lending Libraries

Moore's attack on the moral restrictions imposed by lending libraries, a
significant event in the history of Victorian public morality, is covered by an

excellent account in *Mudie's Circulating Library and the Victorian Novel,* by Guinevere L. Griest (1970). Griest denies Moore's claim that he and his publisher, Henry Vizetelly, overturned the three-volume novel, showing that its sudden collapse in 1895 was due partly to pressure that had been maintained for a long time by publishers and authors but mainly to inherent economic causes. She also offers much information about the fate of Moore's work in the circulating libraries and about his view of their influence on literature.

Artistic and Intellectual Development

Surveys of Moore's career as a whole generally choose between emphasizing its conspicuous shifts and renewals and seeking some continuity among them. Herbert Howarth follows the first course in his chapter on Moore in *The Irish Writers 1880–1940* (1958), sensitively formulating the roles of aesthete, rebel, social critic, folk hero, cosmopolite, and savior that Moore adopted throughout his life. Acknowledging that Moore often reversed himself, Howarth nevertheless tries to resolve the contradictions by identifying recurrent themes in Moore's work. *Esther Waters,* he finds, reflects Moore's interest in the subject of procreation, manifested in his writing on "Celibates," his opposition to bringing children into an unjust world, and his determination to make sex a topic of open discussion. Howarth describes Moore's aesthetic use of Wagner's operas in his novels and relates the heroic element in Wagner to another of Moore's preoccupations, the messianism that he thought embedded in the Irish consciousness and that encouraged him for a time to see himself as an Irish Siegfried capable of exposing and remedying his country's ills.

Returning to this subject in "Dublin 1899–1911: The Enthusiasms of a Prodigal" (*George Moore's Mind and Art,* ed. Graham Owens, 1968), Howarth finds that the plays and stories about Irish life that Moore wrote after his return to Ireland show that he had established a congenial relation with Irish subjects. In this essay Howarth assesses *Hail and Farewell* as a unique work, autobiographical only in form, which was really intended to rectify the Irish state of mind by attacking some of its basic convictions through a self-critical, mock-heroic, liberating performance that would serve as both a message and an example.

In another essay in *George Moore's Mind and Art,* "George Moore's Early Fiction," Milton Chaikin traces Moore's development through *Celibates,* identifying in some detail the numerous influences he responded to and the differing directions in which he moved in novel after novel. Chaikin observes that, after beginning as a writer of limited stylistic competence who imitated French models, Moore turned from the naturalist emphasis on sensation and the physical world to an interest in psychological processes and to methods marked by selection and restraint, ultimately achieving an independent manner through a process of trial and error.

George Moore: The Artist's Vision, the Storyteller's Art, by Janet Eagleson Dunleavy (1973), is an introductory study that emphasizes the early novels and their sources. It follows Moore's progress from a linear mode of narration to more complex constructions, placing the point of change at the revision of *Vain Fortunes* in 1895. The new methods that Moore used after this are rather sketchily described as structures dependent on associations, thoughts, and feelings rather than on objective reportage. Much better is Dunleavy's account of Moore's conscious effort to impart rhythm, pattern, and continuity to the prose of *The Brook Kerith*. This book is especially strong on the effect Moore's study of art had on his novels, showing that his stylistic devices, descriptions, and methods of establishing mood and atmosphere often stemmed from his knowledge of contemporary painting.

A. Norman Jeffares' *George Moore* (1965), a brief introductory account of Moore's life and major works, concludes that, though undervalued today, Moore was a serious artist who influenced the development of English literature. In "Rediscovering George Moore" (*Encounter*, 1970) Martin Seymour-Smith makes even stronger claims for Moore's importance. Observing that reprints of his work are beginning to appear after a period of comparative neglect, Seymour-Smith says that he expects Moore to attract more attention because his work acquires fuller meaning when it is read in "the modern context." His strengths, according to Seymour-Smith, are his insight into character, his grasp of the artist's moral problems, his understanding of the psychology of women, and his proto-Freudian awareness of sexual feelings.

Noël's view that Moore's career represents, not a series of frivolous flirtations with novelty, but the search of a complex mind for an adequate medium of expression, is a theme that appears in much of the recent criticism. According to Graham Hough in "George Moore and the Novel" (*REL*, 1960; rpt. in his *Image and Experience*, 1960; and in *George Moore's Mind and Art*, 1968), Moore came on the scene at a time when English fiction was divided between the realistic novel and the novel of sensibility, and the vacillation of his early period reflects his effort to find his way through these currents. The influence of Yeats and his return to Ireland enabled him to find his own voice and to form his concept of the novel as an independent, integrated aesthetic creation. Hough observes that Moore displayed great moral virtue, a trait he is seldom given credit for, both in working devotedly to achieve his mature style and in portraying sympathetically characters whose attitudes were totally unlike his own.

Giving a more detailed statement of a similar view, Raffaella Maiguashca Uslenghi in a lengthy and important article, "Una prospettiva di unità nell'arte di George Moore" (*EM*, 1964), argues that Moore never deviated from the artistic aims expressed in *Confessions of a Young Man*. She shows that he opened himself to such influences as naturalism and aestheticism because they were forms of rebellion but that he soon left these loyalties behind because they forced him to suppress elements of his temperament, inhibiting his search for artistic freedom. Only when he came back to Ireland, says Uslenghi, did Moore succeed in liberating himself from external influences and in finding themes that corresponded with his talents and suited his aesthetic interests. Ireland deepened his feeling for history and fostered the development of the lyrical and satiric modes whose incongruous alternation with each other Uslenghi regards as a distinctively Moorean characteristic. She feels that Moore's true originality manifests itself in his autobiographies, where he simply narrates at will, without didactic or speculative intentions, constructing rhythmical sequences of events resembling medieval and oriental tales rather than the well-made plots of the English tradition. Uslenghi argues that Moore's career was a sustained effort to obey the moral imperative presented by his ideal of art.

Helmut E. Gerber in "George Moore: From Pure Poetry to Pure Criticism" (*JAAC*, 1967) develops a similar argument, approaching the question of Moore's artistic intentions through his critical views rather than his fiction. Protesting that Moore's facetious moods have been allowed to obscure the dedicated, self-disciplined artist in him, Gerber asserts that he was consistently motivated by the conviction that "All art is autonomous and the perfection of form is virtue." He describes his borrowings as inessential, demonstrating that, although Moore employed a wide range of sources, he selected elements that corresponded to his own principles and used them in original ways. His critical attitudes were ultimately formulated as a doctrine of "pure poetry," which opposed conventional morality and didacticism, emphasizing concreteness and formal perfection. Gerber usefully surveys the evaluations of Moore's critical views offered by several critics (Susanne K. Langer, Herbert Read, John Crowe Ransom, and Ruth Z. Temple) and concludes that Moore's ideas anticipated those of the New Criticism and linked Romantic and modern doctrines of the independence of the artist.

Relations to Other Artists

Recent studies of Moore's work in relation to that of other writers and artists usually attempt to define his originality instead of emphasizing influences, as earlier criticism did. Accordingly, Lilian R. Furst in "George Moore et Zola: Une Réévaluation" (*Les Cahiers naturalistes*, 1971) minimizes the influence of Zola, arguing that Moore's naturalism was derived from "Le Roman expérimental" rather than from Zola's novels, which he did not know well. She points out that neither *L'Assommoir*, which is generally considered to be the source of *A Mummer's Wife*, nor *Nana*, which is supposed to have suggested some of the elements of *Esther Waters*, corresponds to naturalist doctrines and that these novels could not have provided models for Moore. Observing that Zola's poetic power has little to do with Moore's realism, Furst offers the tentative conclusion that Moore's realistic novels tend to follow the traditions of such English examples as *Adam Bede* and *Tess of the D'Urbervilles*.

On the other hand, William F. Blissett in "George Moore and Literary Wagnerism" (*CL*, 1961; rpt. in *George Moore's Mind and Art*, 1968, and in

The Man of Wax, 1971) maintains that another influence conventionally associated with Moore, that of Wagner, was a vital element of his literary imagination. He points out that Wagnerian operas appear in *Hail and Farewell* not only as subjects but as models of narrative form and sources of metaphor and contends that Moore's style became an effort to blend the various resources offered by his medium into a single continuity, following the analogy of the music drama. Noël agrees that the example of music, especially Wagner's, exerted an important influence on Moore's concept of style and observes that Wagner's techniques were not incompatible with naturalism, for Zola's methods of composition were reminiscent of music generally and of Wagner particularly.

Noël feels, however, that Moore's allusions to Schopenhauer simply reflect a current fashion and that neither the author nor any of his characters can really be called an advocate of Schopenhauer's philosophy. But Michael W. Brooks in "George Moore, Schopenhauer and the Origins of *The Brook Kerith*" (*ELT*, 1969) suggests that Schopenhauer's ideas provided Moore with the idea of renunciation to which many of his early characters turn. The theme reappears in *The Brook Kerith*, where it no longer appears as a resolution to individual problems but becomes, through Jesus' experiences, an aspect of man's intuitive knowledge of the conditions of his existence.

Prose Style

Noël devotes a great deal of attention to Moore's extraordinary ventures in prose style. He discusses in detail the stylistic qualities of each of Moore's works, describing the use of musical forms, the adoption of a biblical manner, the *griserie verbale* of his efforts at restraint, the oral quality of his later stories, and many other facets of this eventful subject. A long study of Moore's revisions reveals a great deal about his notions of style, and one chapter, "Prose Naissante," an analysis of the changes made in a single passage, shows Moore bringing his prose into line with his stylistic standards. Graham Owens' "The Melodic Line in Narrative" (*George Moore's Mind and Art*, 1968) deals with the style Moore began cultivating with *The Untilled Field* in 1903, providing an admirably specific analysis of its components and giving convincing examples. This valuable essay enables us to see how Moore's prose anticipated the work of later experimentalists like Joyce and Gertrude Stein by borrowing its formal principles from the flow of the mind and from the thematic, recurrent constructions found in music.

Among the eleven authors chosen by Paul Goetsch in *Die Romankonzeption in England, 1880–1910* (Heidelberg, 1967) to illustrate the opinions novelists held about the relationship between art and life, Moore and Gissing are identified as those most responsive to the influence of naturalism, though neither was a thoroughgoing naturalist. On the basis of evidence from Moore's critical statements and the novels themselves, Goetsch finds that in the middle of his career Moore thought of the novel as a personal expression embodying formal aesthetic properties that nevertheless gave the illusion of actuality and reflected the mystery and spiritual problems of life. The later style emerged when his interest in mental processes led to a subjective emphasis and a prose manner that imitated the flow of consciousness. Bonamy Dobrée's "George Moore's Final Works" (*George Moore's Mind and Art*, 1968; rpt. in *The Man of Wax*, 1971) pays considerable attention to the later style, contending that it creates an appropriate air of remoteness and effortlessly adapts itself to the various requirements of narration, while braiding the elements of the story together through its consistency of tone.

Studies of Individual Works

Esther Waters

Criticism of *Esther Waters*, which has always attracted more attention than any of Moore's other novels, usually focuses on the question of its debt to naturalism. Noël describes the circumstances of the novel's publication and its critical reception and deals with the issue of naturalism by maintaining that, while it admittedly reflects many of the naturalist principles, it also served as a point of departure for Moore's later manner. It is unlike a naturalist novel in paying considerable attention to the thoughts of its characters and in adopting a placidly resigned, rather than a pessimistic, attitude toward the evils of life. Further, it exhibits some techniques that are original with Moore, such as his painterly approach to description and his way of endowing words and phrases with symbolic qualities by repeating them, so that they have the effect of defining a psychological space: "le cercle étroit à l'intérieur duquel l'individu peut ou croit pouvoir exercer sa volonté. . . ."

Some critics consider the naturalist element of *Esther Waters* a serious liability. Carol Ohmann in "George Moore's *Esther Waters*" (*NCF*, 1970) finds that Moore's use of naturalist themes and methods entailed an adherence to the ordinary that drains the novel of imaginative vitality. Brian Nicholas in "The Case of 'Esther Waters' " (*The Moral and the Story*, ed. Ian Gregor and Brian Nicholas, London, 1962; rpt. in *The Man of Wax*, 1971) observes that Moore can be seen trying to fulfill the aims of three incompatible kinds of fiction in *Esther Waters*: the traditional English novel, the social novel associated with Zola, and the aesthetically oriented narration characteristic of the 1890s. It does not articulate a definitive moral statement because it places an independent character in a socially determined milieu, inconsistently presenting Esther both as a victim of social forces and as a patient and enduring heroine who succeeds in resisting them. In an essay that examines the conflicts between convention and the sense of personal responsibility experienced by three of Moore's heroines, "George Moore as Historian of Consciences" (*Imagined Worlds*, ed. Maynard Mack and Ian Gregor, 1968), Peter Ure differs with Nicholas, arguing that Esther is a consistent character who is guided, after the confusion of her youth, by concern with the welfare of her family. He describes the fate of Kate Ede, in *A Mummer's Wife*, as the result of her attempt to shift from conventional standards to those of Bohemian theater people; however, he sees Alice Barton's repudiation of Irish country life, in *A Drama in Muslin*, as a triumphant growth of conscience.

Other critics deny that naturalism plays any part of consequence in *Esther Waters*. Uslenghi takes the novel as an illustration of Moore's pure aestheticism, on the ground that it is free of doctrine, detached in tone, and concerned primarily with developing the artistic potentialities of its story. Dunleavy observes that its materials are drawn from memory, not from investigation, as Zola's were; for its people and settings are composites assembled from scattered sources in Moore's Irish background. (Her contention here is mistaken in at least one particular, for Paul Sporn in "*Esther Waters*: The Sources of the Baby-Farm Episode," *ELT*, 1968, has shown that Moore borrowed some of the language and details for one of the most effective sections of the novel from an article in *ContempR*, 1890.) Dunleavy concludes that *Esther Waters* is not naturalistic, except in certain derivative passages, but is rather an anticipation of the original methods Moore was to develop in later narratives. And Donald E. Morton in "Lyrical Form and the World of *Esther Waters*" (*SEL*, 1973), which might well have been written as a reply to Ohmann, finds in the novel a "lyrical objectivity" achieved by merging external events and the heroine's feelings into a single narrative progression, so that the novel as a whole amounts to a respectful acceptance of Esther's vision of the world.

A Drama in Muslin and The Lake

Two novels seldom singled out by Moore's critics, *A Drama in Muslin* and *The Lake*, have been the subjects of separate short studies. A. Norman Jeffares in his article on the former in *Essays Presented to Amy G. Stock*, edited by R. K. Kaul (Rajasthan, 1965; rpt. in *George Moore's Mind and Art*, 1968) classifies it as a regional novel because it deals with the theme traditionally associated with fiction of the Irish countryside, the contrast between landlords and peasants. But it also addresses other subjects, such as the condition of women, events connected with revolutionary politics, and the psychological dimensions of social life among the gentry. In "Marriage and Class Conflict: The Subversive Link in George Moore's *A Drama in Muslin*" (*ClioW*, 1973) Paul Sporn argues that two of these themes, the degradation of young women seeking marriage and the suffering of tenant farmers, are attacks upon the social system itself. Max E. Cordonnier in "Siegfried in Ireland: A Study of Moore's *The Lake*" (*DM*, 1967) praises the novel for its subtle tracing of the psychological conflict that leads Father Gogarty to reject the impersonal dictates of institutional morality. In "Design in George Moore's *The Lake*" (*Modern Irish Literature*, ed. Raymond

J. Porter and James D. Brophy, 1972) Eileen Kennedy shows how the details of the novel function as symbols reflecting this development.

Short Stories and Influence on Joyce

Discussions of Moore's short stories generally assert or imply some relationship between Moore and Joyce, but Charles Burkhart in "The Short Stories of George Moore" (*SSF*, 1968; rpt. in *The Man of Wax*, 1971) points out that most of Moore's stories are tales, employing the primitive storytelling resources of oral narrative and based on premises quite different from those of the single-episode, epiphanic modern short story. They reflect the influence of Turgenev and embody two of Moore's principles: that literature should project the author's personality and yet remain objective and that fiction should consist of a rhythmic flow of narrative. In "The 'Artist' Stories in *The Untilled Field*" (*ELT*, 1971), Kenneth B. Newell points out that having the first edition of the volume begin and end with a story about an artist who tries unsuccessfully to use Irish materials creates a bracketing effect, which suggests that artists were cut off from the simple country life depicted in the other stories, and contributes to the pathos of the collection as a whole. In a second article, "The 'Wedding Gown' Group in George Moore's *The Untilled Field*" (*Éire*, 1973), Newell argues that the four stories in question are not allegorical but simply exhibit the mystery and pathos of Moore's vision of life.

Although Newell sees little advantage in viewing these stories as forerunners of Joyce's, most discussions of the tenuous relationship between Moore and Joyce rely heavily on the similarities between *The Untilled Field*, Moore's volume of stories about the countryside, and *Dubliners*, Joyce's stories about city life; however, even those critics who feel that Joyce made use of Moore's example hasten to acknowledge that Joyce's book is far superior. Brendan Kennelly in "George Moore's Lonely Voices: A Study of His Short Stories" (*George Moore's Mind and Art*, 1968) shows that Moore achieved some varied and effective treatments of loneliness, the characteristic subject of the Irish short story, and anticipated Joyce in portraying people as the passive victims of their lives and dreams. Eileen Kennedy in "Moore's *Untilled Field* and Joyce's *Dubliners*" (*Éire*, 1970) recalls that, while Joyce never succeeded in meeting Moore, he did read his short stories and called them "damned stupid." Nevertheless, he may have drawn some inspiration for his far better book from Moore's, for the two have in common similar characters, such as clerks and artists, the themes of repression and exile, and an emphasis on the narrowness of Irish life.

The possibility that Joyce responded to other parts of Moore's work is raised by Eileen MacCarvill, who devotes the last chapter of *Les Années de formation de James Joyce à Dublin* (1958) to Moore's influence, observing that Moore's interest in the revival of Gaelic and the artistic theories and discussions of language in *Confessions of a Young Man* were parts of the Dublin milieu in which Joyce grew up and may have stimulated the younger man's thoughts on these subjects. Phillip L. Marcus in "George Moore's Dublin 'Epiphanies' and Joyce" (*JJQ*, 1967–68) suggests that the Dublin impressions found in *Parnell and His Island* and *A Drama in Muslin* may have played a part in the formation of Joyce's descriptive techniques. Albert J. Solomon's "A Moore in *Ulysses*" (*JJQ*, 1973) entertainingly reviews Moore's role as an offstage character in Joyce's novel; a part of Stephen Dedalus' consciousness is occupied by his not having been invited to a party planned by Moore for the evening of Bloomsday. In "Joyce's Schooling in the Field of George Moore" (*Éire*, 1974) B. K. Scott reviews the whole question of Joyce's indebtedness to the older writer and shows that, in spite of Joyce's contemptuous remarks about Moore's books, he knew them intimately, respected them, and learned much from them.

A reversal in the critical estimate of Moore appears to be under way. He is now regarded less as an irresponsible "man of wax," open to every passing trend, than as a purposeful artist of considerable stature. Recent studies have therefore turned from external influences to the scrutiny of his intentions and accomplishments. There appear to be three promising avenues for continuing this exploration of Moore's full dimensions. The unpublished manuscripts, letters, drafts, and corrected proofs held by a number of libraries ought to reveal further details about his working methods. The novels written after 1894 and the autobiographies deserve serious attention as contributions to the art of prose narrative. And Moore's life should be reexamined: the biographical facts are well known by now, but we need to penetrate his poses and ironies and locate the true centers of his sensibility.

GEORGE GISSING*

Jacob Korg

Substantial new areas of biographical and bibliographical information about Gissing, long neglected as a novelist, have been opened in recent years. This development is due mainly to the work of a single scholar, Pierre Coustillas of the University of Lille, who has done the major share of research on Gissing, making contributions in nearly every form, ranging from the publication of new letters to specialized bibliographical investigation. The most recent books on Gissing, however, have come from England.

Manuscripts, Editions, Bibliography, Translations

Nearly all of Gissing's manuscripts have found their way into collections in the United States. Locations of the manuscripts of his novels are given in *NCBEL* and in Michael Collie's 1975 bibliography (see below). The principal collections of letters, notebooks, and similar materials, some of them still unpublished, are in the New York Public Library (Berg Collection), the Beinecke Library at Yale University, and the Pforzheimer Library.

Pierre Coustillas, among his other activities, has enlarged the canon by discovering and publishing a number of works found in manuscript. These include two short stories, "My First Rehearsal" and "My Clerical Rival," published together as a volume (1970), and *George Gissing: Essays and Fiction* (1970), a collection of hitherto unpublished writings consisting of six short stories and a novelette, "All for Love"; "The Hope of Pessimism," an important expression of Gissing's state of mind in 1882; and the short descriptive sketch "Along Shore." Coustillas has supplied an introduction

* Parts of this survey appeared in somewhat different form in "George Gissing: A Survey of Research and Criticism," *The British Studies Monitor* (Sept. 1973) and are included here by kind permission of the editor, Roger Howell, Jr.

describing Gissing's activities and opinions at the time most of these pieces were written and notes discussing each of them in detail and relating them to Gissing's other works. The recent emergence of four groups of continuing publications indicates an increased interest in Gissing and his work. There have been two sets of offset reprints of his novels, neither aiming at completeness. Between 1968 and 1971 the AMS Press of New York published reprints of all but three of the novels, many of them facsimiles of the first editions. The similar series published by the Harvester Press of Brighton, which is now in progress, offers the advantage of useful introductions and notes. Since 1968 the Enitharmon Press of London has been issuing a Gissing series of limited editions containing uncollected writings, critical essays, biographical studies, and similar materials. *The Gissing Newsletter*, a quarterly edited by Coustillas, is now in its twelfth year.

Michael Collie's *George Gissing: A Bibliography* (1975), the first descriptive bibliography devoted to Gissing, covers only books, excluding periodical publications, and limits itself to editions published in Gissing's lifetime and the first editions of posthumous works. While it gives a great deal of information drawn from manuscripts of the works, as well as from published sources, it is so badly marred by misprints and factual errors that it lacks the authority necessary for a useful bibliography. Additional sources of bibliographical information are *The Rediscovery of George Gissing: A Reader's Guide* (the catalogue prepared by Coustillas and John Spiers for the Gissing exhibition held at the National Book League in the summer of 1971) and the notes Coustillas has supplied for the Harvester Press editions of the novels. A bibliography of secondary materials, *George Gissing: An Annotated Bibliography of Writings about Him* by Joseph J. Wolff (1974), has been developed from listings that originally appeared in *English Literature in Transition*. Wolff's bibliography contains nearly twelve hundred entries, beginning with the first review of *Workers in the Dawn*, and lists allusions to Gissing in books on other subjects as well as publications expressly devoted to him.

Among the translations of Gissing's work that have appeared in recent years are *Un'ispirazione ed altre novelle* (Como, 1970; rpt. 1975), an Italian translation by Francesco Badolato of eight short stories with a short biographical and critical introduction; a Chinese translation by Yang Fu Kuang of *The Private Papers of Henry Ryecroft*, called *Szu Chi Sui Pi (An Essay on the Four Seasons*, Tainan, 1969); and a Swedish translation by Fanny Ekenstierna of the same book, *Ur Henry Ryecrofts Privata Papper* (Stockholm, 1929; reissued 1963). Coustillas has published a French translation of the Ryecroft papers, *Les Carnets d'Henry Ryecroft* (1966), in a bilingual edition with an introduction that gives an informative sketch of

Gissing's life and work and discusses the composition, sources, and critical reception of the book. The notes are exceptionally valuable; besides identifying references and allusions, they relate each of the sections into which *Ryecroft* is divided to sources and analogues in Gissing's works, letters, and journals, enabling the reader to see them in depth against the background of his experiences.

Many of Gissing's short stories have appeared in Japanese translation, as well as in English texts edited for Japanese students. Gissing enjoys a rather special position among Japanese students of English, a situation described in "Gissing in Japan" by Shigeru Koike (*Gissing East and West*, 1970). Koike makes it clear that the Japanese interest in Gissing centers on the Ryecroft papers and has not, until recently, been extended to his novels, though translations and reprintings of the short stories appear consistently. He reports that a translation of *The House of Cobwebs* in its entirety appeared in 1951 and a translation of *New Grub Street* in 1969.

Biography and Letters

Gillian Tindall's *The Born Exile* (1972) is a full-length portrait of Gissing that shrewdly and realistically probes the recesses of a complex personality, depicting it as fairly unpleasant and profoundly vulnerable. Drawing on biographical sources, both published and unpublished, as well as on the novels, Tindall sets out to illuminate Gissing's attitudes about a wide range of subjects. She deals with his thoughts about sex, marriage, altruism, suicide, class, female equality, food, writing, and reading, as well as with his consciousness of his identity as a writer, and develops interesting revisionist views of his relations with the women he loved. The facts are ably assembled, and the discussion often moves expansively beyond them into entertaining speculations that are both suggestive and debatable. Tindall acknowledges, as a general principle, that the best novels are those that escape the dominance of the author's private concerns, and she believes that at least two of Gissing's achieve this level. But, because she is intent mainly on projecting a clear impression of an elusive and troubled personality, she concentrates on examining Gissing's books for the sake of what they reveal about the man and tends to bypass their literary qualities.

Class and class differences are among the most persistent themes in Gissing's novels. His private views on these subjects are examined in "George Gissing, Bohème Bourgeois," by Pierre Coustillas (*AdUM*, 1968). Gissing was opposed to many of the ordinary social rules, such as the moral limits imposed on literature, and was never able to conform to conventional expectations, but he was also attracted by the social grace of the well-to-do and by the opportunities for culture and study offered by middle-class life. Connecting Gissing's conflict about social relationships with his view that the artist, though independent in his work, remains subject to the limitations of ordinary life, Coustillas concludes that Gissing admired those who could overcome this ambiguity by resisting the corruption of material rewards and maintaining the visible dignity of the artist.

Since education was one of Gissing's central interests and one of the themes of his novels, it is appropriate for Shigeru Koike to ask, in "The Education of George Gissing" (*English Criticism in Japan*, ed. Earl Miner, Tokyo, 1972), why his passion for education paradoxically led to failure and alienation rather than social acceptance. Koike shows that Gissing originally thought of education as a way of escaping the limitations of his provincial, lower-middle-class origin but that he found it neither intellectually liberating nor socially advantageous when pursued with this motive. Gissing claimed that he eventually learned to value intuitive intelligence over mere intellect, but Koike observes that he never embodied this conviction in a novel. His conclusion that Gissing's lifelong program of self-improvement came to nothing is possibly too pessimistic, for Gissing often reported that he took pleasure in sheer intellectual activity, and his classical studies, together with his travels in Greece and Italy, were a vital spiritual resource. A sense of the education that played a part in forming Gissing's love of study is conveyed in Coustillas' *George Gissing at Alderley Edge* (1969), an account of the school where Gissing was a student and boarder from 1872 to 1875, of its colorful headmaster, and of some of the friends Gissing made there. It contains memoirs about Gissing by men who had been his schoolmates and a reminiscence of the school by Gissing himself.

Coustillas has published a number of memoirs and groups of letters that add much to what is known about Gissing's life and thoughts. The most startling of these appear in "George Gissing à Manchester" (*EA*, 1963), which quotes the full text of some letters written to Gissing in 1876 by a friend at Owens College and an extract from the college records; these documents reveal some crucial facts about Gissing's friendship with the girl who became his first wife and about his dismissal from the college. But the largest and most important group of letters recently published is a correspondence written in 1898 and 1899 to the woman who was to live with him during the last four years of his life: *The Letters of George Gissing to Gabrielle Fleury*, edited by Coustillas (1964). Coustillas' introduction gives an account of Gabrielle Fleury and of the part she played in Gissing's life and provides informative annotations for the letters. In *The Born Exile* (1962), Gillian Tindall makes use of these letters, as well as those written to Gissing's friends by Gabrielle Fleury, to examine the relationship between the two in some detail. Coustillas has also edited two Enitharmon Press volumes containing sequences of letters written by Gissing, *Henry Hick's Recollections of George Gissing* (1973) and *George Gissing's Letters to Edward Clodd* (1973), supplying introductory material and prefatory notes to each of the letters that set them against the background of Gissing's domestic life, writing activities, and travels.

One of Gissing's closest friends in later life was H. G. Wells, who is a significant figure in Gissing studies, not only because of the well-known description of the circumstances surrounding Gissing's death in *Experiment in Autobiography,* but also because he wrote some controversial reviews and essays about his friend's work and became involved in a dispute with Gabrielle Fleury. In "George Gissing et H. G. Wells" (*EA,* 1962) Coustillas shows that the areas of agreement between the two were limited, that Gissing did not consider Wells a good critic of his work, and that Wells interfered unnecessarily in Gabrielle's affairs after Gissing's death. Coustillas illuminates Wells's villainy further, in "The Stormy Publication of Gissing's *Veranilda*" (*BNYPL,* 1968), by tracing the complicated dissensions connected with Gissing's posthumous novel through some unpublished letters and a series of little-known statements and reviews in periodicals.

General Criticism

Adrian Poole's *Gissing in Context* (1975), the first general critical survey since Frank Swinnerton's book of 1912, is the most significant recent contribution to Gissing studies; it succeeds in showing that he was a far better novelist than has hitherto been supposed and makes it impossible to treat his work with the condescension usually accorded it in the past. Poole, who is surely one of the best-equipped critics ever to be attracted to Gissing, treats him unapologetically as a full participant in the Victorian consciousness rather than as a subject for reclamation and refreshingly focuses on the art of his fiction and the sensibility that produced it rather than on the puzzle of his personality. Without altering the general impression that Gissing's sincere effort to record social realities accurately was circumscribed by subjective limitations, Poole brings a new depth and precision to the task of defining the nature of Gissing's fictional world. There are informative separate chapters on the backgrounds of Gissing's main themes, as well as excellent comparisons between Gissing and his contemporaries, but Poole's main interest is the analysis of Gissing's style, imagery, narrative patterns, characterization, and other expressive resources. Although Poole makes only moderate claims, he nevertheless exposes dimensions of Gissing's work that put the writer on an entirely new footing within the ranks of the Victorian novelists.

Comments on the general range of Gissing's work have been brought together in two collections of criticism: *George Gissing: The Critical Heritage,* edited by Coustillas and Colin Partridge (1972), contains contemporary criticism and reviews of the novels, and *Collected Articles on George Gissing,* edited by Coustillas (1968), reprints more recent assessments. George Orwell anticipated the postwar growth of interest in a writer whose interests and temperament strikingly resemble his own; while he was unable either to undertake the biography he was once asked to do or write the long essay on Gissing that he apparently intended, he did produce two pieces on him: "Not Enough Money" (*Tribune,* 2 Apr. 1943) and a general evaluation, "George Gissing" (*LonM,* June 1960; rpt. in his *Collected Essays,* Vol. IV, and in *Collected Articles*). Although he never read all of Gissing's work,

Orwell said that, "merely on the strength of *New Grub Street, Demos,* and *The Odd Women,* I am ready to maintain that England has produced very few better novelists." He does not treat Gissing's views as ideas but is content to accept them as attitudes or even prejudices that Gissing had a perfect right to express. He feels, however, that Gissing could take an impartial approach to many of the issues in his novels because he was not deeply interested in social justice and had no strong moral motivations. In his analysis of Gissing's approach to fiction in *Die Romankonzeption in England, 1880–1910* Paul Goetsch maintains that there is no real contradiction between Gissing's insistence that his novels are personal statements and the fact that nearly all of them are devoted to social criticism. But Goetsch finds Gissing indecisive about whether fiction should deal with actuality or with a reality of its own, whether it should be objective or self-expressive, and examines the biographical and philosophical bases of this indecision.

George Gissing: A Study in Literary Leanings, by Oswald Davis (1966; rpt. 1974), is an affectionate general discussion, touching on the essays and short stories as well as on the novels and modestly aiming to do no more than communicate one reader's appreciation of Gissing. Davis is especially responsive to Gissing's intimate details of London life and people, to his descriptions of urban settings, to the delicate but firm tensions of his plots, which are best displayed in the shorter and slighter narratives, and to elements of proportion and design. He dwells on the irony of the classical scholar's preoccupation with the slums and the tragedy of Gissing's love for aesthetic values in the face of a public indifferent to them and convincingly demonstrates Gissing's talent for defining characters of some spiritual complexity. A shorter general study is "Gissing's Characterization," by C. J. Francis (*LHY,* 1962; rpt. in *GN,* 1967), an examination of the way in which heredity and environment, along with temperament, operate in the novels as determinants of character.

A useful overview of the numerous short stories Gissing wrote is offered in "An Approach to Gissing's Short Stories" by Wendell V. Harris (*SSF,* 1965). Harris shows that Gissing produced successful and original stories when he gave up sensational plots and wrote uneventful sketches about humble or eccentric people displaying a will to survive in the face of misfortune.

Criticism of Individual Works

New Grub Street

Turning to the criticism of individual novels, we find that *New Grub Street,* universally considered Gissing's best novel, has had most of the attention. It has been reprinted frequently in recent years, and three of these editions have introductions by critics who agree that its main strength lies in its balance between the accurate depiction of the external realities reflecting the commercialization of literature and the personal resentments that Gissing channeled into such features as the dramatization of emotional conflicts, an informed sympathy for his characters, and a sound fictional structure. Irving Howe's introduction to the Riverside edition (1962; rpt. in Howe's *A World More Attractive*, 1963) interprets the artistic detachment Gissing sometimes claimed to possess as a flight from the painful emotions aroused by unpleasant realities and finds that these emotions, rather than considered judgment, determined his attitudes. Both Howe and John Gross, in his introduction to the Bodley Head edition (1967), comment on the atmosphere of gloom that dominates London in the novel, making it a prototype of the inhuman modern city. Gross believes that *New Grub Street* is stronger than Gissing's other novels because it is based on firsthand knowledge. But it was also written out of an obsessional preoccupation with the problems it treats, and Gross finds evidence of related emotional disturbances in Gissing's behavior at key points in his life. Gross, like Bernard Bergonzi in his introduction to the Penguin English Library edition (1968), warns that the value of the book as social history is limited by the personal feelings Gissing poured into it. Bergonzi observes that while Gissing was successful in establishing the oppressive reality of a writer's life in a commercial age—symbolized by the Reading Room of the British Museum—he was probably mistaken in thinking that literature was more commercialized than it had been before; Gissing, according to Bergonzi, expected no improvement in the system that he shows causing so much harm, but seemed resigned to it.

P. J. Keating's *George Gissing: New Grub Street* (1968) defines the novel's theme by examining the attitudes the numerous writers in the book adopt toward their craft. In his summarizing paragraph, Keating observes:

> In *New Grub Street* Gissing set out to analyse a whole society's response to literary culture. He found no genuine response at all and could see no hope for the future. The forces of commercialism, symbolised by the triumphant careers of Milvain and Whelpdale, sweep all before them: destroying the craftsman, ignoring the artist and blinding the man of letters. Standing silently in the background is the reading public—a vast, inert, helpless and hopeless mass. Totally unaware that a struggle is taking place the great majority of readers surrender their minds to the tradesmen, adopting the second rate as the norm and rejecting as worthless that which they are incapable of understanding. Every attempt to actively oppose, or establish a compromise with the forces of commercialism, is doomed to failure; for such an attempt can lead only to an undermining of one's own integrity, foreshortening of one's own vision. All the artist can do is turn his back on society.

Gissing portrays this essentially sociological development by incorporating a wide spectrum of opinions about literature and society into his story, using the Reading Room as a symbolic center to which all his writers must come to replenish their stores of knowledge. Keating is critical of the other symbols, however, because, like some of Gissing's observations about the events, they emphasize the obvious unnecessarily. He feels that the heavy stress on

Reardon's consciousness of his misfortunes expresses Gissing's own resentment and weakens the novel's value as a controlled response to the spectacle
of the decline of literature. In "Gissing's *New Grub Street*" (*The Worlds of
Victorian Fiction*, HES, No. 6, 1975) Jerome H. Buckley also recognizes
that the novel is divided between social criticism and the expression of
personal feelings. But he observes that Gissing's analyses of a mind much
like his own are often coldly objective and that the autobiographical elements he introduced are usually well assimilated.

Gissing's critics rarely notice his symbols, or approve of them when they
do, but Robert L. Selig in " 'The Valley of the Shadow of Books': Alienation in Gissing's *New Grub Street*" (*NCF*, 1970) shows that the novel is
organized into a system of symbols that is as effective an expressive resource
as its realism. Employing the insights of theoreticians of the communication
media, Selig interprets Reardon's (and Gissing's) love of the classics as a
preference for an oral literary tradition that brought author and audience
together and the Reading Room and all the activities connected with it as
agencies of the separation and impersonality implied by print. The two
obsessions that dominate most of the characters, printed literature and
money, are inhuman abstractions that are surprisingly analogous; between
them they define the alienation that is the subject of *New Grub Street*.

Although Gissing never revised *New Grub Street* for republication,
Michael Collie in "Gissing's Revision of *New Grub Street*" (*YES*, 1974)
convincingly argues that the version he prepared for Gabrielle Fleury to
translate into French, which is about a third shorter than the original, is the
equivalent of a revision. Minor episodes, some characterization, and much
authorial comment were eliminated, but the most striking change was the
reduction of attention given the influence of social forces on the lives of the
characters. This has the effect of making Reardon's matrimonial problems
more prominent and of shifting the novel's emphasis from realism to psychological study.

Demos

The political theme of *Demos*, which divided contemporary reviewers,
became a subject of controversy again in 1968–69, when two critics published articles on it in consecutive numbers of *Victorian Studies*. In "Gissing,
Morris, and English Socialism" (*VS*, 1968) John Goode uses *Demos* to
illustrate the general problem of defining relationships between novels and
the "contemporary consciousness." Acknowledging that the novel is "generally accurate" both in rendering social conditions and in reflecting specific
situations in the current socialist movement, Goode nevertheless maintains
that, though "very near to the truth," it is "far enough from it to be totally
misleading." The ideology of its socialism belongs to the period of the
Owenite cooperatives and would not have been supported by socialists in
the 1880s; moreover, it casts the aristocracy, rather than the middle class, as
the antagonists of working people. The socialist enterprises in it destroy the
beauty of the countryside, in contradiction to Morris' theories, and the

character who represents Morris expresses a vague aesthetic idealism rather than the policy of violent revolution Morris himself sometimes advocated. The novel's inconsistent political amalgam, compounded of the Positivism of Comte, the moral evolutionism of Herbert Spencer, and the pessimism of Schopenhauer, reflects the confusion of contemporary ideologies. Goode concludes that the socialism of *Demos* existed only in the imagination of socialists and is significant for that reason.

In an article, apparently written independently, that appeared in the next number of *Victorian Studies*, " '*Demos*': The Ordeal of the Two Gissings" (1969), Alan Lelchuk argues that, in spite of the hostility to socialism found in *Demos* and in Gissing's correspondence, the vital and well-rounded portrayal of the novel's socialist leader and his ideas amounts to an advocacy of socialist principles. Lelchuk feels that Gissing wrote both as a novelist and as an antisocialist zealot in *Demos* and that the former involuntarily made so strong a case for socialism that it survives the attacks of the latter. The survival of this radical spirit, Lelchuk believes, is confirmed by the later novels, which deal with the evils that socialism sought to correct. *Victorian Studies* gave Goode and Lelchuk space to comment on each other's essays in its next issue (*VS*, 1969), and in their observations the two critics offer each other some interesting, if rather severe, lessons in critical method. John Lucas in "Conservatism and Revolution in the 1880s" (*Literature and Politics in the Nineteenth Century*, ed. John Lucas, 1971) shows that the opinions expressed in *Demos* correspond with those found in two antisocialist novels published in the same year, W. H. Mallock's *The Old Order Changes* and Henry James's *The Princess Casamassima*. Coustillas' "Political Responses to *Demos*" (*Politics and Literature in the Nineteenth Century*, 1974) surveys the political interpretations of *Demos*, giving a careful critical analysis of the views of Goode, Lelchuk, and Lucas.

Among the sources for assessing Gissing's views on socialism are some short articles he wrote in 1880 for the *Pall Mall Gazette*, which have been reprinted as *Notes on Social Democracy*, edited by Jacob Korg (1968). In these articles, Gissing gives some facts about the Social Democratic party especially in Germany, describes the provisions and disastrous effects of Bismarck's antisocialist law of 1878, and speculates on the future of socialism. Some of Gissing's political views are also perceptible in another of his rare journalistic ventures, the articles he wrote as English correspondent for a Russian periodical in 1881 and 1882. Harry E. Preble in "Gissing's Article for *Vyestnik Europy*" (*VN*, 1963) gives an idea of their contents. Though devoted mainly to reporting political events, they also reflect Gissing' youthful opposition to war and imperialism, sympathy for the poor, anti-clericalism, confidence in the power of the workers to govern themselves and distrust of government institutions, particularly Parliament.

There have been two facsimile reprints of *Demos*: the one published by the AMS Press (1971) has an introduction by Korg that describes Gissing' disillusionment with socialism and takes the view that the novel's real subject is the fate of individual characters rather than the influence of ideology

he Harvester Press reprint (1972) contains explanatory notes and an intro-
luction by Coustillas that places the attitudes expressed in the novel within
he framework of Gissing's political opinions, sketches the socialist activities
;oing on in London during the time it was being written, and gives an
.ccount of its publication and a survey of the reviewers' responses to it.
Observing that Gissing intended to give a general impression of the socialist
cene rather than a factual report, Coustillas attributes much of the novel's
·itality to Gissing's ambivalence toward the movement. He concludes with
he interesting suggestion that Gissing might have been more sympathetic
·vith modern socialism because it is less violent than the Victorian variety.
The nonpolitical aspects of *Demos* have attracted some critical attention.
Tindall, who notes that many of Gissing's novels reflect a suspicion that
.ltruism is often based on secret self-esteem, feels that *Demos* is a variation
»n this theme, for it traces the moral degeneration the Mutimer family
indergoes as a result of Richard Mutimer's philanthropic enterprise, an
:ffort that is really egotistic in its origins. C. J. Francis, in *"Demos" (GN,*
974), agrees that the novel's subject is Mutimer's moral bankruptcy rather
han the exposure of socialism and points out that its dramatic structure is
.ppropriate to the development of character. He feels that the theme
3issing undertook, the effort of a man without moral resources to accom-
»lish something worthwhile, is excellent but that its treatment is spoiled by
3issing's bias.

Isabel Clarendon

Isabel Clarendon, published in 1886, was until recently the only one of
3issing's novels that had never been reprinted; Gissing had been asked to
evise it for a second edition but had declined. It is an interesting novel for
everal reasons: it is his first attempt to write about a social setting free of
»overty; it contains the first instance of the self-defeating, idealistic young
nan who is the typical Gissing protagonist; it achieves some success in
lepicting psychological development; and it shows Gissing responding to
he influences of other writers. The Harvester Press reprinting of *Isabel
Clarendon* (ed. Coustillas, 1969) is a facsimile of the two-volume first edi-
ion. Coustillas' introduction gives valuable information about the circum-
tances in which the novel was written and, after surveying the unfavorable
:omments of contemporary reviewers, defends it in a careful critical analy-
.is. He notes the improvement in characterization, the well-planned
.tructure, and the tactful, economical development of plot and character as
trong points in its favor and reviews in detail the aspects of the novel that
:xhibit the influences of Meredith, Turgenev, and Schopenhauer.

The Nether World

In "George Gissing's *The Nether World"* (*Tradition and Tolerance in
Vineteenth-Century Fiction*, ed. David Howard, John Lucas, and John

Goode, 1967), John Goode introduces his study of the novel he consider.
"pivotal" in Gissing's career by explaining Gissing's rejection of the Comtis
philosophy that had attracted him in his early twenties. Like his characte
Eldon in *Demos*, Gissing came to feel that the social processes embodied a
kind of fate, a view that did not harmonize with Comte's rationalism bu
belonged, rather, to the class of "theological" beliefs Comte's philosophy
repudiated. Goode shows, in some detail, that *The Nether World* treat
poverty as a metaphysical force that cannot be assigned to any human
motive but that arises spontaneously from the conditions prevailing in ar
industrial society and imposes a powerful determinism on the lives of the
characters. In *The Nether World* it destroys such values as philanthropy
love, talent, and the desire for improvement, creating a spiritual wasteland
where the usual standards of civilized life lose their meaning. In his intro
duction to the Harvester Press edition of *The Nether World* (1974), Goode
elaborates on his view that the novel's poetic dimension transcends its
reportorial qualities. While it is notably accurate in rendering life ir
Clerkenwell and showing that the problems found there cannot be rem
edied by benevolence, it also articulates a self-contained world that operate
as a metaphor for actuality rather than as a representation of it.

Gissing is the most prominent figure in P. J. Keating's *The Working
Classes in Victorian Fiction* (1971), a study of the novelists of the latter par
of the century who paid sympathetic attention to the lives of the poor
instead of using them for shock value or social criticism. He was the firs
novelist to make a sustained effort to write about the poor in a way that wa
both accurate and artistically responsible. Determined to be brutally objec
tive, he nevertheless merged aesthetic motives and social protest in writing
his five novels of poverty. Keating makes an excellent contribution in differ
entiating Gissing from earlier social novelists on the ground that he re
placed their sentimentality and idealism with realism and sympathy
However, he made only a limited advance. His understanding of the poor
was usually superficial, for his working-class protagonists are really ladie
and gentlemen in disguise, reflecting middle-class tastes and values and
having little in common with their fellows. Only in *The Nether World*
Keating points out, did Gissing treat slum life as a distinct culture, instead
of as a degenerate form of other life-styles, and survey the motives and
destinies available to the poor in some depth and with great tolerance
Gissing does not avoid the sensational entirely but does balance it with quie
realism, and his hero is a genuine workingman with feelings and idea
appropriate to his station.

Thyrza

Thyrza, Gissing's most subdued novel of poverty, has usually beer
overshadowed by his more vigorous treatments of the subject, but Gilliar
Tindall, in her discussion of it in *The Born Exile* (1972), evaluates it as a
well-controlled performance that presents the daily life of the poor in a

balanced, objective manner. Its heroine is an idealization of Gissing's first wife, and there are other autobiographical elements in it, but Gissing's handling of them demonstrates that he had overcome some of his early illusions and could now make effective use of material drawn from his own life. In an introduction to the Harvester Press reprint of *Thyrza* (1974), Jacob Korg shows that its critical treatment of education as a means of training character is augmented by a subtle use of landscape and setting to suggest that nonintellectual physical experience is a stronger influence. Korg notes that Gissing intended the book to embody a contest between high ideals and practical purposes, reflecting the contrast between the spirit of ancient Greek civilization and that of modern life. Herbert Rosengarten, in "The Theme of Alienation in *Thyrza*" (*GN*, 1966), interprets this division as a demonstration of society's inability to do justice to the imaginativeness and idealism of the novel's heroine.

The Odd Women

Gissing devoted one of his best novels, *The Odd Women*, to the problems presented by the position of women in Victorian society, but the subject was a lifelong preoccupation and appears in nearly all his books. In a general discussion of his women characters, "Gissing's Feminine Portraiture" (*ELT*, 1963), Coustillas briefly sketches the female relatives who influenced the novelist's ideas about women and shows that Gissing oscillated between idealistic and realistic portrayals of women, sometimes attempting close readings of character, sometimes withdrawing to the treatment of externals. While he had no reform theories and felt that women belonged in the home, he was nevertheless distrustful of marriage and analyzed its failings in a number of his most perceptive novels. Some of them, especially *The Odd Women*, take up such social problems as employment, education, and marital rights, showing the need for greater freedom but also demonstrating a reluctance to sacrifice the Victorian notion of femininity. Lloyd Fernando in "Gissing's Studies in 'Vulgarism': Aspects of His Antifeminism" (*SoRA*, 1970) goes further, arguing that Gissing was not only skeptical of female equality but hostile to it. Fernando finds that Gissing's view of the status of women hinged upon his hatred of "vulgarity"; he favored better education for women because he thought it would promote refinement, but opposed it when a measure of emancipation produced vulgar and offensive women.

In her chapter on this subject in *The Born Exile* (1972), Gillian Tindall, who feels that many of the marriages in the novels reflect Gissing's speculations and fantasies about his own situation, examines his marital experiences in detail, relating them to his fictional treatment of the Woman Question. Two preconceptions colored his attitude toward women: a romantic idealism that made him especially vulnerable to disillusionment and a conviction that it was impossible for a poor man like himself to marry an intellectual equal. Yet, Tindall points out, *The Odd Women* dramatizes the

plight of educated women who cannot find husbands, and many of it:
characters are based on women Gissing knew. The importance he attributec
to the intellectual component of love is brought forward in "Love anc
Culture in 'Workers in the Dawn' " by Michel Ballard (*GN*, 1974), whicl
describes the appearance in Gissing's first novel of a characteristic linkage
between sexual love and the love of art and learning. Its plot, in which the
hero rejects mere physical attractiveness and turns to a woman of cultivatec
mind, expresses Gissing's feeling that the two impulses are "emotional anc
intellectual sides of a complex unity. . . ."

In "*The Odd Women* di George Gissing e Il Movimento Femminista"
(*AION-SG*, 1967), Maria Teresa Chialant observes that, while the novel car
be considered a feminist document, it virtually ignores the problems o:
working-class women, confining itself to two major themes: the freedom t(
work and the rights and duties of marriage, both middle-class concerns
Chialant points out that industrialization tended to divide the interests o
working-class and middle-class women, for the primary need of the firs
group was protection from exploitation by factory owners while the seconc
demanded legal and social equality with men. *The Odd Women*, Chialan
concludes, shows that Gissing was skeptical about some aspects of the femi
nist movement, particularly its economic and political demands, but that he
was attracted by its vitality and took a prophetic view of the need for
change in the social position of women. As a critique of marriage, however
it was somewhat behind its time, according to Joyce Evans' "Some Notes on
The Odd Women and the Woman's Movement" (*GN*, 1966). Noting tha
many couples were already living on the egalitarian basis Gissing recom
mended, Evans devotes a part of her article to a comparison between the
women's bureau in the novel and the organization that suggested it, the
Society for Promoting the Employment of Women. Gissing's study o
women's problems is interestingly exploited in a recent novel by Gai
Godwin, *The Odd Woman* (1973), whose heroine, an unmarried woman
professor, assigns Gissing's novel to her class in women's literature, on the
ground that it is pertinent enough to temper her students' optimism abou
relations between the sexes, and uses it to examine her personal problems
comparing the possibilities of her own situation with the fates of Gissing'
women.

Topical Studies

Gissing's awareness of women's problems manifests itself in the sensitive
treatment of female characters throughout his novels. Paul Sporn, ir
"Gissing's *Demos*: Late-Victorian Values and the Displacement of Conjuga
Love" (*SNNTS*, 1969), shows that *Demos* singles out marriage as a source o
disturbance to three women of different situations and social classes. The
story most fully presented is that of the protagonist's wife, whose forcec
marriage Sporn holds responsible for driving her into a relationship witl

strong homosexual overtones, a view Gillian Tindall corroborates in her discussion of *Demos* in *The Born Exile* (1972).

Two interesting recent studies evaluate Gissing's criticism of the popular culture that was a notable phenomenon of his time. In "A Sad Heart at the Late-Victorian Culture Market: George Gissing's *In the Year of Jubilee*" (*SEL*, 1969), Robert L. Selig examines one of the later novels as an exposure of the way in which mass media debase public tastes and attitudes. Gissing must have been one of the first acute observers of mass culture, showing, in *In the Year of Jubilee*, that modern education fails to serve the needs of women, that popular songs suggest sentimental and inadequate attitudes toward love, and that advertising cynically manipulates mass behavior for mercenary aims. Chialant's "L'intellettuale tardo-vittoriano di fronte alle sviluppo dell'industria culturale [The Late-Victorian Intellectual in Relation to the Development of the Culture Industry]" (*AION-SG*, 1974) takes Gissing's reaction to the publishing scene in *New Grub Street* as a paradigm of the uneasiness late Victorian intellectuals felt about the cultural effects of industrialism. After tracing the rise of George Newnes and the "new journalism" he sponsored, she acknowledges that Gissing was an able observer of these developments, in spite of his antidemocratic prejudices. He was aware that, as Christopher Caudwell would later show, art in a bourgeois setting leads either to vulgarization or to private fantasy, for *New Grub Street* shows its writers choosing between these alternatives. But Gissing's conservative notions about art led him to focus on the degenerate elements of popular culture and to miss its positive qualities, such as the enlargement of the public for art and the potentiality for social change it created. Chialant's view that Gissing overlooked the dangerous power the media have for manipulating opinion probably stems from her concentration on *New Grub Street*, where the subject hardly arises; as Selig points out, this issue is heavily stressed in *In the Year of Jubilee*.

Gissing was influenced by Dickens, and his *Charles Dickens: A Critical Study* (1898) occupies a permanent place in Dickens criticism; both Edmund Wilson and George Orwell were indebted to it for basic insights into Dickens' frame of mind. Pierre Coustillas' volume *Gissing's Writings on Dickens* (1969) reveals the full extent of Gissing's concern with Dickens during the last years of his life; it reprints two reviews he published anonymously in *TLS* (1902) and contains an essay by Coustillas (expanded from "Gissing's Writings on Dickens: A Bio-Bibliographical Survey," *Dkn*, 1965) that gives a detailed account of the work Gissing did after the appearance of his critical study had earned him a reputation as an authority on Dickens. In "Dickens, Gissing e Orwell" (*AION-SG*, 1969), Chialant makes use of Gissing's and Orwell's criticisms of Dickens to establish an affinity among the social views of all three. She shows that Gissing and Orwell shared Dickens' ambiguous feelings about the poor and, like him, suffered from a conflict between a desire for social justice and an attachment to middle-class privileges. Both advocated socialism for a time but feared losing their individuality to a political system; both sympathized with the poor but felt separated from them by cultural differences; and both ultimately understood that their youthful radicalism had been an expression of unconscious guilt. Their mutual interest in Dickens is further evidence that they had much in common.

As this survey shows, Gissing studies have focused primarily on the biographical record and the assessment of his social insights, and changing perceptions about the relations of literature and society are bound to encourage continuing reinterpretations of both areas. But the success of Adrian Poole's study has demonstrated the value of reading the novels as imaginative works. It has suggested that our understanding of them would be greatly improved if the resources of modern criticism were employed to interpret their imagery, language, and structure and the interrelationships among such components as characters, events, and settings.

Contributors

Richard D. Altick	Ohio State University
Ruth apRoberts	University of California, Riverside
Robert Ashley	Ripon College
James D. Barry	Loyola University of Chicago
Gillian Beer	Girton College, Cambridge
Wayne Burns	University of Washington
Robert A. Colby	Queens College, City University of New York
Philip Collins	University of Leicester
Curtis Dahl	Wheaton College (Massachusetts)
George H. Ford	University of Rochester
Daniel F. Howard	Rutgers University
Robert Kiely	Harvard University
U. C. Knoepflmacher	University of California, Berkeley
Jacob Korg	University of Washington
Michael Millgate	University of Toronto
Herbert J. Rosengarten	University of British Columbia

Index